DNS and BIND

Other resources from O'Reilly

Related titles   DNS and BIND Cookbook™   DNS on Windows Server
                                                  2003

oreilly.com   *oreilly.com* is more than a complete catalog of O'Reilly books. You'll also find links to news, events, articles, weblogs, sample chapters, and code examples.

oreillynet.com is the essential portal for developers interested in open and emerging technologies, including new platforms, programming languages, and operating systems.

Conferences   O'Reilly brings diverse innovators together to nurture the ideas that spark revolutionary industries. We specialize in documenting the latest tools and systems, translating the innovator's knowledge into useful skills for those in the trenches. Visit *conferences.oreilly.com* for our upcoming events.

Safari Bookshelf (*safari.oreilly.com*) is the premier online reference library for programmers and IT professionals. Conduct searches across more than 1,000 books. Subscribers can zero in on answers to time-critical questions in a matter of seconds. Read the books on your Bookshelf from cover to cover or simply flip to the page you need. Try it today for free.

FIFTH EDITION

DNS and BIND

Cricket Liu and Paul Albitz

Beijing · Cambridge · Farnham · Köln · Paris · Sebastopol · Taipei · Tokyo

DNS and BIND, Fifth Edition
by Cricket Liu and Paul Albitz

Published by O'Reilly Media, Inc., 1005 Gravenstein Highway North, Sebastopol, CA 95472.

O'Reilly books may be purchased for educational, business, or sales promotional use. Online editions are also available for most titles (*safari.oreilly.com*). For more information, contact our corporate/institutional sales department: (800) 998-9938 or *corporate@oreilly.com*.

Editor: Mike Loukides	**Cover Designer:** Edie Freedman
Production Editor: Matt Hutchinson	**Interior Designer:** David Futato
Copyeditor: Mary Anne Weeks Mayo	**Cover Illustrator:** Karen Montgomery
Proofreader: Matt Hutchinson	**Illustrators:** Robert Romano and Jessamyn Read
Indexer: Ellen Troutman-Zaig	

Printing History:

October 1992:	First Edition.
January 1997:	Second Edition.
September 1998:	Third Edition.
April 2001:	Fourth Edition.
May 2006:	Fifth Edition.

 This book uses RepKover™, a durable and flexible lay-flat binding.

ISBN: 0-596-10057-4

[M]

Table of Contents

Preface

You may not know much about the Domain Name System—yet—but whenever you use the Internet, you use DNS. Every time you send electronic mail or surf the World Wide Web, you rely on the Domain Name System.

You see, while you, as a human being, prefer to remember the *names* of computers, computers like to address each other by number. On an internet, that number is 32 bits long, or between 0 and 4 billion or so.* That's easy for a computer to remember because computers have lots of memory ideal for storing numbers, but it isn't nearly as easy for us humans. Pick 10 phone numbers out of the phone book at random and then try to remember them. Not easy? Now flip to the front of the phone book and attach random area codes to the phone numbers. That's about how difficult it would be to remember 10 arbitrary internet addresses.

This is part of the reason we need the Domain Name System. DNS handles mapping between hostnames, which we humans find convenient, and internet addresses, which computers deal with. In fact, DNS is the standard mechanism on the Internet for advertising and accessing all kinds of information about hosts, not just addresses. And DNS is used by virtually all internetworking software, including electronic mail, remote terminal programs such as *ssh*, file transfer programs such as *ftp*, and web browsers such as Microsoft's Internet Explorer.

Another important feature of DNS is that it makes host information available all over the Internet. Keeping information about hosts in a formatted file on a single computer only helps users on that computer. DNS provides a means of retrieving information remotely from anywhere on the network.

More than that, DNS lets you distribute the management of host information among many sites and organizations. You don't need to submit your data to some central site or periodically retrieve copies of the "master" database. You simply make sure

---

* And, with IP version 6, it's a whopping 128 bits long, or between 0 and a 39-digit decimal number.

your section, called a *zone*, is up to date on your *nameservers*. Your nameservers make your zone's data available to all the other nameservers on the network.

Because the database is distributed, the system also needs to be able to locate the data you're looking for by searching a number of possible locations. The Domain Name System gives nameservers the intelligence to navigate through the database and find data in any zone.

Of course, DNS does have a few problems. For example, the system allows more than one nameserver to store data about a zone, for redundancy's sake, but inconsistencies can crop up between copies of the zone data.

But the *worst* problem with DNS is that despite its widespread use on the Internet, there's really very little documentation about managing and maintaining it. Most administrators on the Internet make do with the documentation their vendors see fit to provide and with whatever they can glean from following the Internet mailing lists and Usenet newsgroups on the subject.

This lack of documentation means that the understanding of an enormously important internet service—one of the linchpins of today's Internet—is either handed down from administrator to administrator like a closely guarded family recipe, or relearned repeatedly by isolated programmers and engineers. New zone administrators suffer through the same mistakes made by countless others.

Our aim with this book is to help remedy this situation. We realize that not all of you have the time or the desire to become DNS experts. Most of you, after all, have plenty to do besides managing your zones and nameservers: system administration, network engineering, or software development. It takes an awfully big institution to devote a whole person to DNS. We'll try to give you enough information to allow you to do what you need to do, whether that's running a small zone or managing a multinational monstrosity, tending a single nameserver or shepherding a hundred of them. Read as much as you need to know now, and come back later if you need to learn more.

DNS is a big topic—big enough to require two authors, anyway—but we've tried to present it as sensibly and understandably as possible. The first two chapters give you a good theoretical overview and enough practical information to get by, and later chapters fill in the nitty-gritty details. We provide a roadmap up front to suggest a path through the book appropriate for your job or interest.

When we talk about actual DNS software, we'll concentrate almost exclusively on BIND, the Berkeley Internet Name Domain software, which is the most popular implementation of the DNS specs (and the one we know best). We've tried to distill our experience in managing and maintaining zones with BIND into this book. (One of our zones, incidentally, was once one of the largest on the Internet, but that was a long time ago.) Where possible, we've included the real programs we use in administration, many of them rewritten into Perl for speed and efficiency.

We hope that this book will help you get acquainted with DNS and BIND if you're just starting out, refine your understanding if you're already familiar with them, and provide valuable insight and experience even if you know 'em like the back of your hand.

Versions

The fifth edition of this book deals with the new 9.3.2 and 8.4.7 versions of BIND as well as older versions of BIND 8 and 9. While 9.3.2 and 8.4.7 are the most recent versions as of this writing, they haven't made their way into many vendors' versions of Unix yet, partly because both versions have only recently been released and many vendors are wary of using such new software. We also occasionally mention other versions of BIND because many vendors continue to ship code based on this older software as part of their Unix products. Whenever a feature is available only in the 8.4.7, or 9.3.2 version, or when there is a difference in the behavior of the versions, we try to point out which version does what.

We use *nslookup*, a nameserver utility program, very frequently in our examples. The version we use is the one shipped with the 9.3.2 BIND code. Older versions of *nslookup* provide much, but not quite all, of the functionality in the 9.3.2 *nslookup*. We've used commands common to most *nslookup*s in most of our examples; when this was not possible, we tried to note it.

What's New in the Fifth Edition?

Besides updating the book to cover the most recent versions of BIND, we've added a fair amount of new material to the fifth edition:

- Coverage of SPF, the Sender Policy Framework, in Chapter 6
- More extensive coverage of dynamic update and NOTIFY, including signed dynamic updates and BIND 9's new *update-policy* mechanism, in Chapter 10
- Incremental zone transfer, also in Chapter 10
- Forward zones, which support conditional forwarding, in Chapter 10
- IPv6 forward and reverse mapping using AAAA records and *ip6.arpa*, respectively, at the end of Chapter 10
- Transaction signatures, also known as TSIG, a new mechanism for authenticating transactions, in Chapter 11
- An expanded section on securing nameservers, in Chapter 11
- An expanded section on dealing with Internet firewalls, in Chapter 11
- Coverage of the revised DNS Security Extensions, or DNSSECbis, a mechanism for digitally signing zone data, also in Chapter 11

- A new chapter (Chapter 16) on the design of a complete DNS architecture for an organization
- ENUM, which maps E.164 telephone numbers to URIs, in Chapter 17
- Internationalized Domain Names, or IDN, a standard for encoding Unicode characters in the labels of domain names, in Chapter 17
- A revised section on accommodating Active Directory with BIND, in Chapter 17

Organization

This book is organized, more or less, to follow the evolution of a zone and its administrator. Chapters 1 and 2 discuss Domain Name System theory. Chapters 3 through 6 help you decide whether or not to set up your own zones, then describe how to go about it, should you choose to. The middle of the book, Chapters 7 through 11, describe how to maintain your zones, configure hosts to use your nameservers, plan for the growth of your zones, create subdomains, and secure your nameservers. Chapters 12 through 16 deal with troubleshooting tools, common problems, and the lost art of programming with the resolver library routines. Chapter 16 puts it all together in an end-to-end architecture.

Here's a more detailed, chapter-by-chapter breakdown:

Chapter 1, *Background*
> Provides a little historical perspective and discusses the problems that motivated the development of DNS, then presents an overview of DNS theory.

Chapter 2, *How Does DNS Work?*
> Goes over DNS theory in more detail, including the organization of the DNS namespace, domains, zones, and nameservers. We also introduce important concepts such as name resolution and caching.

Chapter 3, *Where Do I Start?*
> Covers how to get the BIND software if you don't already have it, what to do with it once you've got it, how to figure out what your domain name should be, and how to contact the organization that can delegate your zone to you.

Chapter 4, *Setting Up BIND*
> Details how to set up your first two BIND nameservers, including creating your nameserver database, starting up your nameservers, and checking their operation.

Chapter 5, *DNS and Electronic Mail*
> Deals with DNS's MX record, which allows administrators to specify alternate hosts to handle a given destination's mail. This chapter covers mail-routing strategies for a variety of networks and hosts, including networks with Internet firewalls and hosts without direct Internet connectivity. The chapter also covers the Sender Policy Framework, which uses DNS to authorize mail servers sending mail from particular email addresses.

Chapter 6, *Configuring Hosts*

Explains how to configure a BIND resolver. We also include notes on the idiosyncrasies of the Windows resolver.

Chapter 7, *Maintaining BIND*

Describes the periodic maintenance administrators must perform to keep their zones running smoothly, such as checking nameserver health and authority.

Chapter 8, *Growing Your Domain*

Covers how to plan for the growth and evolution of your zones, including how to get big and how to plan for moves and outages.

Chapter 9, *Parenting*

Explores the joys of becoming a parent zone. We explain when to become a parent (create subdomains), what to call your children, how to create them (!), and how to watch over them.

Chapter 10, *Advanced Features*

Goes over some less common nameserver configuration options that can help you tune your nameserver's performance and ease administration.

Chapter 11, *Security*

Describes how to secure your nameserver and how to configure your nameservers to deal with Internet firewalls, and describes two new security enhancements to DNS: the DNS Security Extensions and Transaction Signatures.

Chapter 12, *nslookup and dig*

Shows the ins and outs of the most popular tools for doing DNS debugging, including techniques for digging obscure information out of remote nameservers.

Chapter 13, *Reading BIND Debugging Output*

Is the Rosetta stone of BIND's debugging information. This chapter will help you make sense of the cryptic debugging information that BIND emits, which in turn will help you better understand your nameserver.

Chapter 14, *Troubleshooting DNS and BIND*

Covers many common DNS and BIND problems and their solutions, and then describes a number of less common, harder-to-diagnose scenarios.

Chapter 15, *Programming with the Resolver and Nameserver Library Routines*

Demonstrates how to use BIND's resolver routines to query nameservers and retrieve data from within a C program or a Perl script. We include a useful (we hope!) program to check the health and authority of your nameservers.

Chapter 16, *Architecture*

Presents an end-to-end design for DNS infrastructure, including external nameservers, forwarders, and internal nameservers.

Chapter 17, *Miscellaneous*

Ties up all the loose ends. We cover DNS wildcards, hosts and networks with intermittent Internet connectivity via dialup, network name encoding, additional record types, ENUM, IDN, and Active Directory.

Appendix A, *DNS Message Format and Resource Records*

Contains a byte-by-byte breakdown of the formats used in DNS queries and responses, as well as a comprehensive list of the currently defined resource record types.

Appendix B, *BIND Compatibility Matrix*

Contains a matrix showing the most important features of the most popular BIND releases.

Appendix C, *Compiling and Installing BIND on Linux*

Contains step-by-step instructions on how to compile the 9.3.2 version of BIND on Linux.

Appendix D, *Top-Level Domains*

Lists the current top-level domains in the Internet domain namespace.

Appendix E, *BIND Nameserver and Resolver Configuration*

Summarizes the syntax and semantics of each of the parameters available for configuring nameservers and resolvers.

Audience

This book is intended primarily for system and network administrators who manage zones and one or more nameservers, but it also includes material for network engineers, postmasters, and others. Not all of the book's chapters will be equally interesting to a diverse audience, though, and you don't want to wade through 17 chapters to find the information pertinent to your job. We hope the following roadmap will help you plot your way through the book:

System administrators setting up their first zones

Should read Chapters 1 and 2 for DNS theory, Chapter 3 for information on getting started and selecting a good domain name, then Chapters 4 and 5 to learn how to set up a zone for the first time. Chapter 6 explains how to configure hosts to use the new nameservers. Later, they should read Chapter 7, which explains how to "flesh out" their implementation by setting up additional nameservers and adding zone data. Chapters 12 through 14 describe troubleshooting tools and techniques.

Experienced administrators

May benefit from reading Chapter 6 to learn how to configure DNS resolvers on different hosts, and Chapter 7 for information on maintaining their zones. Chapter 8 contains instructions on planning for a zone's growth and evolution, which should be especially valuable to administrators of large zones. Chapter 9 explains parenting—creating subdomains—which is *de rigueur* reading for those considering the big move. Chapter 10 covers many new and advanced features of the BIND 9.3.2 and 8.4.7 nameservers. Chapter 11 goes over securing nameservers, which may be of particular interest to experienced administrators. Chapters 12 through 14 describe tools and techniques for troubleshooting, which even advanced administrators may find worth reading. Chapter 16 may help administrators get a grasp of the big picture.

System administrators on networks without full Internet connectivity
Should read Chapter 5 to learn how to configure mail on such networks, and Chapters 11 and 17 to learn how to set up an independent DNS infrastructure.

Programmers
Can read Chapters 1 and 2 for DNS theory, then Chapter 15 for detailed coverage of how to program with the BIND resolver library routines.

Network administrators not directly responsible for any zones
Should still read Chapters 1 and 2 for DNS theory, Chapter 12 to learn how to use *nslookup* and *dig*, and Chapter 14 for troubleshooting tactics.

Postmasters
Should read Chapters 1 and 2 for DNS theory, then Chapter 5 to find out how DNS and electronic mail coexist. Chapter 12, which describes *nslookup* and *dig*, will also help postmasters dig mail-routing information from the domain namespace.

Interested users
Can read Chapters 1 and 2 for DNS theory, and then whatever else they like!

Note that we assume you're familiar with basic Unix system administration, TCP/IP networking, and programming using simple shell scripts and Perl. We don't assume you have any other specialized knowledge, though. When we introduce a new term or concept, we'll do our best to define or explain it. Whenever possible, we'll use analogies from Unix (and from the real world) to help you understand.

Obtaining the Example Programs

The example programs in this book* are available electronically via FTP from the following URLs:

- *ftp://ftp.uu.net/published/oreilly/nutshell/dnsbind/dns.tar.Z*
- *ftp://ftp.oreilly.com/published/oreilly/nutshell/dnsbind/*

In either case, extract the files from the archive by typing:

```
% zcat dns.tar.Z | tar xf -
```

---

* Examples are also available online at *http://examples.oreilly.com/dns5*.

System V systems require the following *tar* command instead:

```
% zcat dns.tar.Z | tar xof -
```

If *zcat* is not available on your system, use separate *uncompress* and *tar* commands.

If you can't get the examples directly over the Internet but can send and receive email, you can use *ftpmail* to get them. For help using *ftpmail*, send an email to *ftpmail@online.oreilly.com* with no subject and the single word "help" in the body of the message.

How to Contact Us

You can address comments and questions about this book to the publisher:

O'Reilly Media, Inc.
1005 Gravenstein Highway North
Sebastopol, CA 95472
800-998-9938 (in the United States or Canada)
707-829-0515 (international/local)
707-829-0104 (fax)

O'Reilly has a web page for this book, which lists errata and any additional information. You can access this page at:

http://www.oreilly.com/catalog/dns5

To comment or ask technical questions about this book, send email to:

bookquestions@oreilly.com

For more information about books, conferences, software, Resource Centers, and the O'Reilly Network, see the O'Reilly web site at:

http://www.oreilly.com

Conventions Used in This Book

We use the following font and format conventions for Unix commands, utilities, and system calls:

- Excerpts from scripts or configuration files are shown in constant-width font:

  ```
  if test -x /usr/sbin/named -a -f /etc/named.con
  then
          /usr/sbin/named
  fi
  ```

- Sample interactive sessions, showing command-line input and corresponding output, are shown in constant-width font, with user-supplied input in bold:

  ```
  % cat /var/run/named.pid
  78
  ```

- If the command must be typed by the superuser (root), we use the sharp, or pound sign (#):

      # **/usr/sbin/named**

- Replaceable items in code are printed in constant-width italics.

- Domain names, filenames, functions, commands, Unix manpages, Windows features, URLs, and programming elements taken from the code snippets are printed in italics when they appear within a paragraph.

 This icon signifies a tip, suggestion, or general note.

 This icon signifies a warning or caution.

Using Code Examples

This book is here to help you get your job done. In general, you may use the code in this book in your programs and documentation. You do not need to contact us for permission unless you're reproducing a significant portion of the code. For example, writing a program that uses several chunks of code from this book does not require permission. Selling or distributing a CD-ROM of examples from O'Reilly books *does* require permission. Answering a question by citing this book and quoting example code does not require permission. Incorporating a significant amount of example code from this book into your product's documentation *does* require permission.

We appreciate, but do not require, attribution. An attribution usually includes the title, author, publisher, and ISBN. For example: "*DNS and BIND*, Fifth Edition, by Cricket Liu and Paul Albitz. Copyright 2006 O'Reilly Media, Inc., 0-596-10057-4."

If you feel your use of code examples falls outside fair use or the permission given above, feel free to contact us at *permissions@oreilly.com*.

Safari® Enabled

 When you see a Safari® Enabled icon on the cover of your favorite technology book, that means the book is available online through the O'Reilly Network Safari Bookshelf.

Safari offers a solution that's better than e-books. It's a virtual library that lets you easily search thousands of top tech books, cut and paste code samples, download chapters, and find quick answers when you need the most accurate, current information. Try it for free at *http://safari.oreilly.com*.

Quotations

The Lewis Carroll quotations that begin each chapter are from the Millennium Fulcrum Edition 2.9 of the Project Gutenberg electronic text of *Alice's Adventures in Wonderland* and Edition 1.7 of *Through the Looking-Glass*. Quotations in Chapters 1, 2, 5, 6, 8, and 14 come from *Alice's Adventures in Wonderland*, and those in Chapters 3, 4, 7, 9–13, and 15–17 come from *Through the Looking-Glass*.

Acknowledgments

The authors would like to thank Ken Stone, Jerry McCollom, Peter Jeffe, Hal Stern, Christopher Durham, Bill Wisner, Dave Curry, Jeff Okamoto, Brad Knowles, K. Robert Elz, and Paul Vixie for their invaluable contributions to this book. We'd also like to thank our reviewers, Eric Pearce, Jack Repenning, Andrew Cherenson, Dan Trinkle, Bill LeFebvre, and John Sechrest for their criticism and suggestions. Without their help, this book would not be what it is (it'd be much shorter!).

For the second edition, the authors add their thanks to their sterling review team: Dave Barr, Nigel Campbell, Bill LeFebvre, Mike Milligan, and Dan Trinkle.

For the third edition, the authors salute their technical review Dream Team: Bob Halley, Barry Margolin, and Paul Vixie.

For the fourth edition, the authors owe a debt of gratitude to Kevin Dunlap, Edward Lewis, and Brian Wellington, their crack review squad.

For the fifth edition, the authors would like to thank their crack team of technical reviewers, João Damas, Matt Larson, and Paul Vixie, and Silvia Hagen for her last-minute help with IPv6.

Cricket would particularly like to thank his former manager, Rick Nordensten, the very model of a modern HP manager, on whose watch the first version of this book was written; his neighbors, who bore his occasional crabbiness for many months; and of course his wife Paige for her unflagging support and for putting up with his tap-tap-tapping during her nap-nap-napping. For the second edition, Cricket would like to add a thank you to his former managers, Regina Kershner and Paul Klouda, for their support of Cricket's work with the Internet. For the third edition, Cricket acknowledges a debt of gratitude to his partner, Matt Larson, for his co-development of the Acme Razor. For the fourth edition, Cricket thanks his loyal, furry fans, Dakota and Annie, for kisses and companionship, and wonderful Walter B. for popping his head into the office and checking on Dad now and again. For the fifth edition, he must mention the other new addition, the fabulous Baby G. And he sends his thanks to his friends and colleagues at Infoblox for their hard work, their generous support, and their company.

Paul would like to thank his wife, Katherine, for her patience, for many review sessions, and for proving that she could make a quilt in her spare time more quickly than her spouse could write his half of a book.

## CHAPTER 1

Background

The White Rabbit put on his spectacles. "Where shall I begin, please your Majesty?" he asked.
"Begin at the beginning," the King said, very gravely, "and go on till you come to the end: then stop."

It's important to know a little ARPAnet history to understand the Domain Name System (DNS). DNS was developed to address particular problems on the ARPAnet, and the Internet—a descendant of the ARPAnet—is still its main user.

If you've been using the Internet for years, you can probably skip this chapter. If you haven't, we hope it'll give you enough background to understand what motivated the development of DNS.

A (Very) Brief History of the Internet

In the late 1960s, the U.S. Department of Defense's Advanced Research Projects Agency, ARPA (later DARPA), began funding the *ARPAnet*, an experimental wide area computer network that connected important research organizations in the United States. The original goal of the ARPAnet was to allow government contractors to share expensive or scarce computing resources. From the beginning, however, users of the ARPAnet also used the network for collaboration. This collaboration ranged from sharing files and software and exchanging electronic mail—now commonplace—to joint development and research using shared remote computers.

The Transmission Control Protocol/Internet Protocol (TCP/IP) protocol suite was developed in the early 1980s and quickly became the standard host-networking protocol on the ARPAnet. The inclusion of the protocol suite in the University of California at Berkeley's popular BSD Unix operating system was instrumental in democratizing internetworking. BSD Unix was virtually free to universities. This meant that internetworking—and ARPAnet connectivity—were suddenly available cheaply to many more organizations than were previously attached to the ARPAnet.

Many of the computers being connected to the ARPAnet were being connected to local area networks (LANs), too, and very shortly the other computers on the LANs were communicating via the ARPAnet as well.

The network grew from a handful of hosts to tens of thousands of hosts. The original ARPAnet became the backbone of a confederation of local and regional networks based on TCP/IP, called the *Internet*.

In 1988, however, DARPA decided the experiment was over. The Department of Defense began dismantling the ARPAnet. Another network, the NSFNET, funded by the National Science Foundation, replaced the ARPAnet as the backbone of the Internet.

In the spring of 1995, the Internet made a transition from using the publicly funded NSFNET as a backbone to using multiple commercial backbones, run by telecommunications companies such as SBC and Sprint, and long-time commercial internetworking players such as MFS and UUNET.

Today, the Internet connects millions of hosts around the world. In fact, a significant proportion of the non-PC computers in the world are connected to the Internet. Some commercial backbones carry a volume of several gigabits per second, tens of thousands of times the bandwidth of the original ARPAnet. Tens of millions of people use the network for communication and collaboration daily.

On the Internet and Internets

A word on "the Internet," and on "internets" in general, is in order. In print, the difference between the two seems slight: one is always capitalized, one isn't. The distinction between their meanings, however, *is* significant. The Internet, with a capital "I," refers to the network that began its life as the ARPAnet and continues today as, roughly, the confederation of all TCP/IP networks directly or indirectly connected to commercial U.S. backbones. Seen up close, it's actually quite a few different networks—commercial TCP/IP backbones, corporate and U.S. government TCP/IP networks, and TCP/IP networks in other countries—interconnected by high-speed digital circuits. A lowercase internet, on the other hand, is simply any network made up of multiple smaller networks using the same internetworking protocols. An internet (little "i") isn't necessarily connected to the Internet (big "I"), nor does it necessarily use TCP/IP as its internetworking protocol. There are isolated corporate internets, for example.

An *intranet*, with a little i, is really just a TCP/IP-based internet, used to emphasize the use of technologies developed and introduced on the Internet on a company's internal corporate network. An *extranet*, on the other hand, is a TCP/IP-based internet that connects partner companies, or a company to its distributors, suppliers, and customers.

The History of the Domain Name System

Through the 1970s, the ARPAnet was a small, friendly community of a few hundred hosts. A single file, *HOSTS.TXT*, contained a name-to-address mapping for every host connected to the ARPAnet. The familiar Unix host table, */etc/hosts*, was compiled from *HOSTS.TXT* (mostly by deleting fields Unix didn't use).

HOSTS.TXT was maintained by SRI's *Network Information Center* (dubbed "the NIC") and distributed from a single host, SRI-NIC.* ARPAnet administrators typically emailed their changes to the NIC, and periodically FTP'ed to SRI-NIC and grabbed the current *HOSTS.TXT* file. Their changes were compiled into a new *HOSTS.TXT* file once or twice a week. As the ARPAnet grew, however, this scheme became unworkable. The size of *HOSTS.TXT* grew in proportion to the growth in the number of ARPAnet hosts. Moreover, the traffic generated by the update process increased even faster: every additional host meant not only another line in *HOSTS.TXT*, but potentially another host updating from SRI-NIC.

When the ARPAnet moved to TCP/IP, the population of the network exploded. Now there was a host of problems with *HOSTS.TXT* (no pun intended):

Traffic and load
> The toll on SRI-NIC, in terms of the network traffic and processor load involved in distributing the file, was becoming unbearable.

Name collisions
> No two hosts in *HOSTS.TXT* could have the same name. However, while the NIC could assign addresses in a way that guaranteed uniqueness, it had no authority over hostnames. There was nothing to prevent someone from adding a host with a conflicting name and breaking the whole scheme. Adding a host with the same name as a major mail hub, for example, could disrupt mail service to much of the ARPAnet.

Consistency
> Maintaining consistency of the file across an expanding network became harder and harder. By the time a new *HOSTS.TXT* file could reach the farthest shores of the enlarged ARPAnet, a host across the network may have changed addresses or a new host may have sprung up.

The essential problem was that the *HOSTS.TXT* mechanism didn't scale well. Ironically, the success of the ARPAnet as an experiment led to the failure and obsolescence of *HOSTS.TXT*.

The ARPAnet's governing bodies chartered an investigation to develop a successor for *HOSTS.TXT*. Their goal was to create a system that solved the problems inherent in a

---

* SRI is the former Stanford Research Institute in Menlo Park, California. SRI conducts research into many different areas, including computer networking.

unified host-table system. The new system should allow local administration of data yet make that data globally available. The decentralization of administration would eliminate the single-host bottleneck and relieve the traffic problem. And local management would make the task of keeping data up-to-date much easier. The new system should use a hierarchical namespace to name hosts. This would ensure the uniqueness of names.

Paul Mockapetris, then of USC's Information Sciences Institute, was responsible for designing the architecture of the new system. In 1984, he released RFCs 882 and 883, which described the Domain Name System. These RFCs were superseded by RFCs 1034 and 1035, the current specifications of the Domain Name System.* RFCs 1034 and 1035 have since been augmented by many other RFCs, which describe potential DNS security problems, implementation problems, administrative gotchas, mechanisms for dynamically updating nameservers and for securing zone data, and more.

The Domain Name System, in a Nutshell

The Domain Name System is a distributed database. This structure allows local control of the segments of the overall database, yet data in each segment is available across the entire network through a client/server scheme. Robustness and adequate performance are achieved through replication and caching.

Programs called *nameservers* constitute the server half of DNS's client/server mechanism. Nameservers contain information about some segments of the database and make that information available to clients, called *resolvers*. Resolvers are often just library routines that create queries and send them across a network to a nameserver.

The structure of the DNS database, shown in Figure 1-1, is similar to the structure of the Unix filesystem. The whole database (or filesystem) is pictured as an inverted tree, with the root node at the top. Each node in the tree has a text label, which identifies the node relative to its parent. This is roughly analogous to a "relative pathname" in a filesystem, like *bin*. One label—the null label, or " "—is reserved for the root node. In text, the root node is written as a single dot (.). In the Unix filesystem, the root is written as a slash (/).

Each node is also the root of a new subtree of the overall tree. Each of these subtrees represents a partition of the overall database—a *directory* in the Unix filesystem, or a *domain* in the Domain Name System. Each domain or directory can be further divided into additional partitions, called *subdomains* in DNS, like a filesystem's subdirectories. Subdomains, like subdirectories, are drawn as children of their parent domains.

---

* RFCs are Request for Comments documents, part of the relatively informal procedure for introducing new technology on the Internet. RFCs are usually freely distributed and contain fairly technical descriptions of the technology, often intended for implementors.

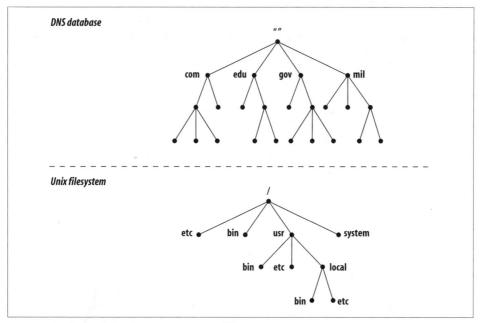

Figure 1-1. The DNS database versus a Unix filesystem

Every domain has a unique name, like every directory. A domain's *domain name* identifies its position in the database, much as a directory's *absolute pathname* specifies its place in the filesystem. In DNS, the domain name is the sequence of labels from the node at the root of the domain to the root of the whole tree, with dots (.) separating the labels. In the Unix filesystem, a directory's absolute pathname is the list of relative names read from root to leaf (the opposite direction from DNS, as shown in Figure 1-2), using a slash to separate the names.

In DNS, each domain can be broken into a number of subdomains, and responsibility for those subdomains can be doled out to different organizations. For example, an organization called EDUCAUSE manages the *edu* (educational) domain but delegates responsibility for the *berkeley.edu* subdomain to U.C. Berkeley (Figure 1-3). This is similar to remotely mounting a filesystem: certain directories in a filesystem may actually be filesystems on other hosts, mounted from remote hosts. The administrator on host *winken*, for example (again, Figure 1-3), is responsible for the filesystem that appears on the local host as the directory */usr/nfs/winken*.

Delegating authority for *berkeley.edu* to U.C. Berkeley creates a new *zone,* an autonomously administered piece of the namespace. The zone *berkeley.edu* is now independent from *edu* and contains all domain names that end in *berkeley.edu*. The zone *edu,* on the other hand, contains only domain names that end in *edu* but aren't in delegated zones such as *berkeley.edu*. *berkeley.edu* may be further divided into subdomains, such as *cs.berkeley.edu,* and some of these subdomains may themselves be

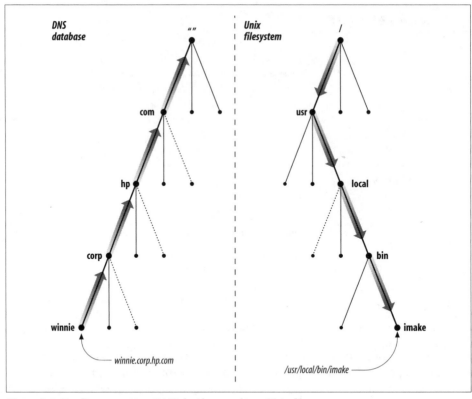

Figure 1-2. Reading names in a DNS database and in a Unix filesystem

separate zones, if the *berkeley.edu* administrators delegate responsibility for them to other organizations. If *cs.berkeley.edu* is a separate zone, the *berkeley.edu* zone doesn't contain domain names that end in *cs.berkeley.edu* (Figure 1-4).

Domain names are used as indexes into the DNS database. You might think of data in DNS as "attached" to a domain name. In a filesystem, directories contain files and subdirectories. Likewise, domains can contain both hosts and subdomains. A domain contains those hosts and subdomains whose domain names are within the domain's subtree of the namespace.

Each host on a network has a domain name, which points to information about the host (see Figure 1-5). This information may include IP addresses, information about mail routing, etc. Hosts may also have one or more *domain name aliases*, which are simply pointers from one domain name (the alias) to another (the official, or *canonical*, domain name). In Figure 1-5, *mailhub.nv*… is an alias for the canonical name *rincon.ba.ca*….

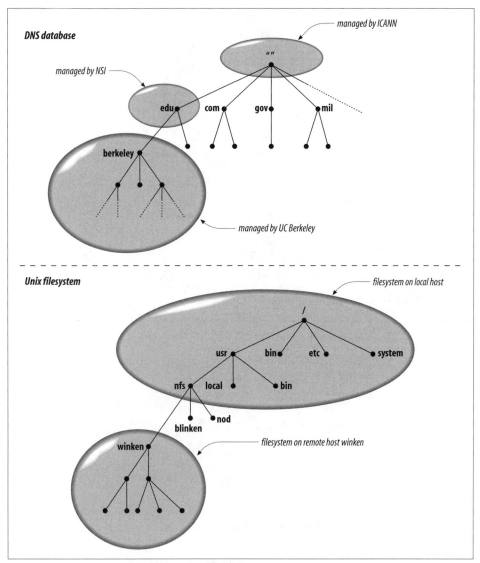

Figure 1-3. Remote management of subdomains and of filesystems

Why all the complicated structure? To solve the problems that *HOSTS.TXT* had. For example, making domain names hierarchical eliminates the pitfall of name collisions. Each domain has a unique domain name, so the organization that runs the domain is free to name hosts and subdomains within its domain. Whatever name they choose for a host or subdomain won't conflict with other organizations' domain names because it will end in their unique domain name. For example, the organization that runs *hic.com* can name a host *puella* (as shown in Figure 1-6) because it knows that the host's domain name will end in *hic.com*, a unique domain name.

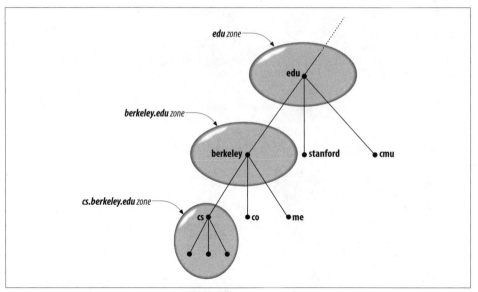

Figure 1-4. The edu, berkeley.edu, and cs.berkeley.edu zones

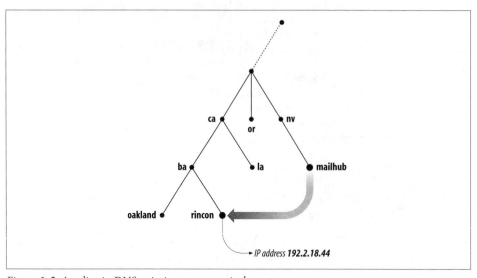

Figure 1-5. An alias in DNS pointing to a canonical name

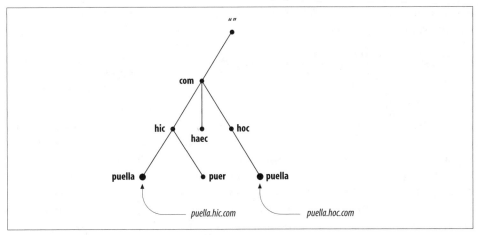

Figure 1-6. Solving the name collision problem

The History of BIND

The first implementation of the Domain Name System was called JEEVES, written by Paul Mockapetris himself. A later implementation was BIND, an acronym for *Berkeley Internet Name Domain*, written by Kevin Dunlap for Berkeley's 4.3 BSD Unix. BIND is now maintained by the Internet Systems Consortium.[*]

BIND is the implementation we'll concentrate on in this book and is by far the most popular implementation of DNS today. It has been ported to most flavors of Unix and is shipped as a standard part of most vendors' Unix offerings. BIND has even been ported to Microsoft's Windows NT, Windows 2000, and Windows Server 2003.

Must I Use DNS?

Despite the usefulness of the Domain Name System, there are some situations in which it doesn't pay to use it. There are other name-resolution mechanisms besides DNS, some of which may be a standard part of your operating system. Sometimes the overhead involved in managing zones and their nameservers outweighs the benefits. On the other hand, there are circumstances in which you have no other choice

---

[*] For more information on the Internet Systems Consortium and its work on BIND, see *http://www.isc.org/sw/bind/*.

but to set up and manage nameservers. Here are some guidelines to help you make that decision:

If you're connected to the Internet…

…DNS is a must. Think of DNS as the *lingua franca* of the Internet: nearly all of the Internet's network services use DNS. That includes the Web, electronic mail, remote terminal access, and file transfer.

On the other hand, this doesn't necessarily mean that you have to set up and run zones *by* yourself *for* yourself. If you've only got a handful of hosts, you may be able to join an existing zone (see Chapter 3) or find someone else to host your zones for you. If you pay an Internet service provider for your Internet connectivity, ask if it'll host your zone for you, too. Even if you aren't already a customer, there are companies that will help out, for a price.

If you have a little more than a handful of hosts, or a lot more, you'll probably want your own zone. And if you want direct control over your zone and your nameservers, you'll want to manage it yourself. Read on!

If you have your own TCP/IP-based internet…

…you probably want DNS. By an internet, we don't mean just a single Ethernet of workstations using TCP/IP (see the next section if you thought that was what we meant); we mean a fairly complex "network of networks." Maybe you have several dozen Ethernet segments connected via routers, for example.

If your internet is basically homogeneous and your hosts don't need DNS (say they don't run TCP/IP at all), you may be able to do without it. But if you've got a variety of hosts, especially if some of those run some variety of Unix, you'll want DNS. It'll simplify the distribution of host information and rid you of any kludgy host-table distribution schemes you may have cooked up.

If you have your own local area network or site network…

…and that network isn't connected to a larger network, you can probably get away without using DNS. You might consider using Microsoft's Windows Internet Name Service (WINS), host tables, or Sun's Network Information Service (NIS) product.

But if you need distributed administration or have trouble maintaining the consistency of data on your network, DNS may be for you. And if your network is likely to soon be connected to another network, such as your corporate internet or the Internet, it'd be wise to set up your zones now.

## CHAPTER 2

How Does DNS Work?

"…and what is the use of a book," thought Alice,
"without pictures or conversations?"

The Domain Name System is basically a database of host information. Admittedly, you get a lot with that: funny dotted names, networked nameservers, a shadowy "namespace." But keep in mind that, in the end, the service DNS provides is information about internet hosts.

We've already covered some important aspects of DNS, including its client/server architecture and the structure of the DNS database. However, we haven't gone into much detail, and we haven't explained the nuts and bolts of DNS's operation.

In this chapter, we'll explain and illustrate the mechanisms that make DNS work. We'll also introduce the terms you'll need to know to read the rest of the book (and to converse intelligently with your fellow zone administrators).

First, though, let's take a more detailed look at the concepts introduced in the previous chapter. We'll try to add enough detail to spice it up a little.

The Domain Namespace

DNS's distributed database is indexed by domain names. Each domain name is essentially just a path in a large inverted tree, called the *domain namespace*. The tree's hierarchical structure, shown in Figure 2-1, is similar to the structure of the Unix filesystem. The tree has a single root at the top.* In the Unix filesystem, this is called the *root directory* and is represented by a slash (/). DNS simply calls it "the root." Like a filesystem, DNS's tree can branch any number of ways at each intersection point, or node. The depth of the tree is limited to 127 levels (a limit you're not likely to reach).

---

* Clearly this is a computer scientist's tree, not a botanist's.

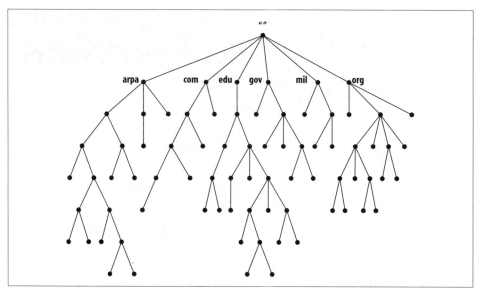

Figure 2-1. The structure of the DNS namespace

Domain Names

Each node in the tree has a text label (without dots) that can be up to 63 characters long. A null (zero-length) label is reserved for the root. The full domain name of any node in the tree is the sequence of labels on the path from that node to the root. Domain names are always read from the node toward the root ("up" the tree), with dots separating the names in the path.

If the root node's label actually appears in a node's domain name, the name looks as though it ends in a dot, as in "www.oreilly.com." (It actually ends with a dot—the separator—and the root's null label.) When the root node's label appears by itself, it is written as a single dot, ".", for convenience. Consequently, some software interprets a trailing dot in a domain name to indicate that the domain name is *absolute*. An absolute domain name is written relative to the root and unambiguously specifies a node's location in the hierarchy. An absolute domain name is also referred to as a *fully qualified domain name*, often abbreviated FQDN. Names without trailing dots are sometimes interpreted as relative to some domain name other than the root, just as directory names without a leading slash are often interpreted as relative to the current directory.

DNS requires that sibling nodes—nodes that are children of the same parent—have different labels. This restriction guarantees that a domain name uniquely identifies a single node in the tree. The restriction really isn't a limitation because the labels need to be unique only among the children, not among all the nodes in the tree. The same restriction applies to the Unix filesystem: you can't give two sibling directories or two files in the same directory the same name. As illustrated in Figure 2-2, just as you can't have two *hobbes.pa.ca.us* nodes in the namespace, you can't have two */usr/bin* directories. You can, however, have both a *hobbes.pa.ca.us* node and a *hobbes.lg.ca.us* node, as you can have both a */bin* directory and a */usr/bin* directory.

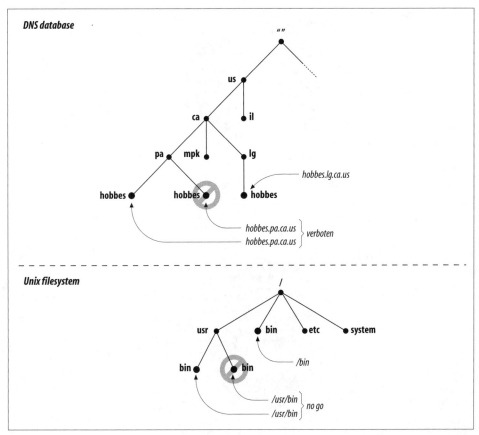

Figure 2-2. Ensuring uniqueness in domain names and in Unix pathnames

Domains

A *domain* is simply a subtree of the domain namespace. The domain name of a domain is the same as the domain name of the node at the very top of the domain. So, for example, the top of the *purdue.edu* domain is a node named *purdue.edu*, as shown in Figure 2-3.

Likewise, in a filesystem, at the top of the */usr* directory, you'd expect to find a node called */usr*, as shown in Figure 2-4.

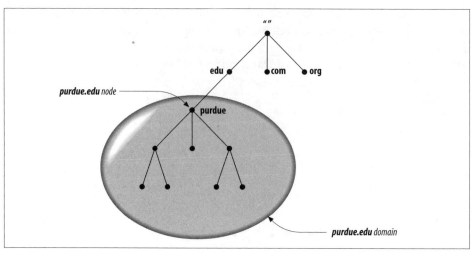

Figure 2-3. The purdue.edu domain

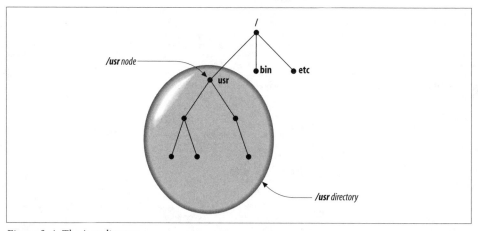

Figure 2-4. The /usr directory

Any domain name in the subtree is considered a part of the domain. Because a domain name can be in many subtrees, a domain name can also be in many domains. For example, the domain name *pa.ca.us* is part of the *ca.us* domain and also part of the *us* domain, as shown in Figure 2-5.

So in the abstract, a domain is just a subtree of the domain namespace. But if a domain is simply made up of domain names and other domains, where are all the hosts? Domains are groups of hosts, right?

The hosts are there, represented by domain names. Remember, domain names are just indexes into the DNS database. The "hosts" are the domain names that point to information about individual hosts, and a domain contains all the hosts whose domain names are within the domain. The hosts are related *logically*, often by geography or

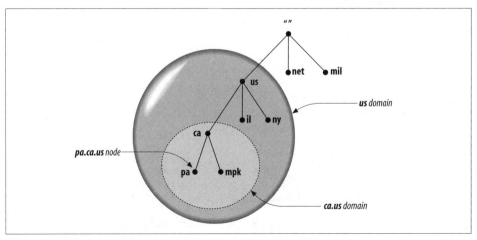

Figure 2-5. A node in multiple domains

organizational affiliation, and not necessarily by network or address or hardware type. You might have 10 different hosts, each of them on a different network and perhaps even in different countries, all in the same domain.

One note of caution: don't confuse domains in DNS with domains in NIS. Though an NIS domain also refers to a group of hosts, and both types of domains have similarly structured names, the concepts are quite different. NIS uses hierarchical names, but the hierarchy ends there: hosts in the same NIS domain share certain data about hosts and users, but they can't navigate the NIS namespace to find data in other NIS domains. NT domains, which provide account-management and security services, also don't have any relationship to DNS domains. Active Directory domains, however, are closely related to DNS domains. We discuss the relationship between DNS and Active Directory domains in Chapter 17.

Domain names at the leaves of the tree generally represent individual hosts, and they may point to network addresses, hardware information, and mail-routing information. Domain names in the interior of the tree can name a host *and* point to information about the domain; they aren't restricted to one or the other. Interior domain names can represent both the domain they correspond to and a particular host on the network. For example, *hp.com* is both the name of the Hewlett-Packard Company's domain and a domain name that refers to the hosts that run HP's main web server.

The type of information retrieved when you use a domain name depends on the context in which you use it. Sending mail to someone at *hp.com* returns mail-routing information, while *ssh*ing to the domain name looks up the host information (in Figure 2-6, for example, *hp.com*'s IP address).

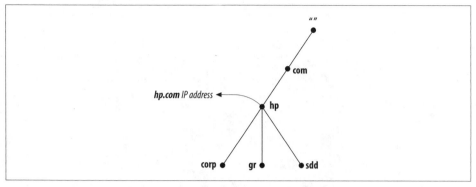

Figure 2-6. An interior node with both host and domain data

A domain may have several subtrees of its own, called *subdomains*.[*]

A simple way of determining if a domain is a subdomain of another domain is to compare their domain names. A subdomain's domain name ends with the domain name of its parent domain. For example, the domain *la.tyrell.com* must be a subdomain of *tyrell.com*, because *la.tyrell.com* ends with *tyrell.com*. It's also a subdomain of *com*, as is *tyrell.com*.

Besides being referred to in relative terms, as subdomains of other domains, domains are often referred to by *level*. On mailing lists and in Usenet newsgroups, you may see the terms *top-level domain* or *second-level domain* bandied about. These terms simply refer to a domain's position in the domain namespace:

- A top-level domain is a child of the root.
- A first-level domain is a child of the root (a top-level domain).
- A second-level domain is a child of a first-level domain, and so on.

Resource Records

The data associated with domain names is contained in *resource records*, or RRs. Records are divided into classes, each of which pertains to a type of network or software. Currently, there are classes for internets (any TCP/IP-based internet), networks based on the Chaosnet protocols, and networks that use Hesiod software. (Chaosnet is an old network of largely historic significance.) The internet class is by far the most popular. (We're not really sure if anyone still uses the Chaosnet class, and use of the Hesiod class is mostly confined to MIT.) In this book, we concentrate on the internet class.

---

[*] The terms "domain" and "subdomain" are often used interchangeably, or nearly so, in DNS documentation. Here, we use subdomain only as a relative term: a domain is a subdomain of another domain if the root of the subdomain is within the domain.

Within a class, records come in several types, which correspond to the different varieties of data that may be stored in the domain namespace. Different classes may define different record types, though some types are common to more than one class. For example, almost every class defines an *address* type. Each record type in a given class defines a particular record syntax to which all resource records of that class and type must adhere.

If this information seems sketchy, don't worry: we'll cover the records in the internet class in more detail later. The common records are described in Chapter 4, and a more comprehensive list is included as part of Appendix A.

The Internet Domain Namespace

So far, we've talked about the theoretical structure of the domain namespace and what sort of data is stored in it, and we've even hinted at the types of names you might find in it with our (sometimes fictional) examples. But this won't help you decode the domain names you see on a daily basis on the Internet.

The Domain Name System doesn't impose many rules on the labels in domain names, and it doesn't attach any *particular* meaning to the labels at a given level of the namespace. When you manage a part of the domain namespace, you can decide on your own semantics for your domain names. Heck, you could name your subdomains A through Z, and no one would stop you (though they might strongly recommend against it).

The existing Internet domain namespace, however, has some self-imposed structure to it. Especially in the upper-level domains, the domain names follow certain traditions (not rules, really, because they can be and have been broken). These traditions help to keep domain names from appearing totally chaotic. Understanding these traditions is an enormous asset if you're trying to decipher a domain name.

Top-Level Domains

The original top-level domains divided the Internet domain namespace organizationally into seven domains:

com
> Commercial organizations, such as Hewlett-Packard (*hp.com*), Sun Microsystems (*sun.com*), and IBM (*ibm.com*).

edu
> Educational organizations, such as U.C. Berkeley (*berkeley.edu*) and Purdue University (*purdue.edu*).

gov
> Government organizations, such as NASA (*nasa.gov*) and the National Science Foundation (*nsf.gov*).

mil

> Military organizations, such as the U.S. Army (*army.mil*) and Navy (*navy.mil*).

net

> Formerly organizations providing network infrastructure, such as NSFNET (*nsf.net*) and UUNET (*uu.net*). Since 1996, however, *net* has been open to any commercial organization, like *com* is.

org

> Formerly noncommercial organizations, such as the Electronic Frontier Foundation (*eff.org*). Like *net,* though, restrictions on *org* were removed in 1996.

int

> International organizations, such as NATO (*nato.int*).

Another top-level domain called *arpa* was originally used during the ARPAnet's transition from host tables to DNS. All ARPAnet hosts originally had hostnames under *arpa*, so they were easy to find. Later, they moved into various subdomains of the organizational top-level domains. However, the *arpa* domain remains in use in a way you'll read about later.

You may notice a certain nationalistic prejudice in our examples: we've used primarily U.S.-based organizations. That's easier to understand—and forgive—when you remember that the Internet began as the ARPAnet, a U.S.-funded research project. No one anticipated the success of the ARPAnet, or that it would eventually become as international as the Internet is today.

Today, these original seven domains are called *generic top-level domains*, or gTLDs. The "generic" contrasts them with the country-code top-level domains, which are specific to a particular country.

Country-code top-level domains

To accommodate the increasing internationalization of the Internet, the implementers of the Internet namespace compromised. Instead of insisting that all top-level domains describe organizational affiliation, they decided to allow geographical designations, too. New top-level domains were reserved (but not necessarily created) to correspond to individual countries. Their domain names followed an existing international standard called ISO 3166.* ISO 3166 establishes official, two-letter abbreviations for every country in the world. We've included the current list of top-level domains as Appendix D.

---

* Except for Great Britain. According to ISO 3166 and Internet tradition, Great Britain's top-level domain name should be *gb*. Instead, most organizations in Great Britain and Northern Ireland (i.e., the United Kingdom) use the top-level domain name *uk*. They drive on the wrong side of the road, too.

New top-level domains

In late 2000, the organization that manages the Domain Name System, the Internet Corporation for Assigned Names and Numbers, or ICANN, created seven new generic top-level domains to accommodate the rapid expansion of the Internet and the need for more domain name "space." A few of these were truly generic top-level domains, like *com*, *net*, and *org*, while others were closer in purpose to *gov* and *mil*: reserved for use by a specific (and sometimes surprisingly small) community. ICANN refers to this latter variety as *sponsored TLDs*, or *sTLDs*, and the former as *unsponsored gTLDs*. Sponsored TLDs have a charter, which defines their function, and a sponsoring organization, which sets policies governing the sTLDs and oversees their operation on ICANN's behalf.

Here are the new gTLDs:

aero
> Sponsored; for the aeronautical industry

biz
> Generic

coop
> Sponsored; for cooperatives

info
> Generic

museum
> Sponsored; for museums

name
> Generic; for individuals

pro
> Generic; for professionals

More recently, in early 2005, ICANN approved two more sponsored TLDs, *jobs*, for the human resources management industry, and *travel*, for the travel industry. Several other sponsored TLDs were also under evaluation, including *cat*, for the Catalan linguistic and cultural community, *mobi*, for mobile devices, and *post*, for the postal community. So far, only *mobi* has been delegated from the root. You can check out ICANN at *http://www.icann.org*.

Further Down

Within these top-level domains, the traditions and the extent to which they are followed vary. Some of the ISO 3166 top-level domains closely follow the United States's original organizational scheme. For example, Australia's top-level domain, *au*, has subdomains such as *edu.au* and *com.au*. Some other ISO 3166 top-level domains follow the *uk* domain's lead and have organizationally oriented subdomains such as *co.uk* for corporations and *ac.uk* for the academic community. In most cases, however, even these geographically oriented top-level domains are divided up organizationally.

That wasn't originally true of the *us* top-level domain, though. In the beginning, the *us* domain had 50 subdomains that corresponded to—guess what?—the 50 U.S. states.* Each was named according to the standard two-letter abbreviation for the state—the same abbreviation standardized by the U.S. Postal Service. Within each state's domain, the organization was still largely geographical: most subdomains corresponded to individual cities. Beneath the cities, the subdomains usually corresponded to individual hosts.

As with so many namespace rules, though, this structure was abandoned when a new company, Neustar, began managing *us* in 2002. Now *us*—like *com* and *net*—is open to all comers.

Reading Domain Names

Now that you know what most top-level domains represent and how their namespaces are structured, you'll probably find it much easier to make sense of most domain names. Let's dissect a few for practice:

lithium.cchem.berkeley.edu
> You've got a head start on this one, as we've already told you that *berkeley.edu* is U.C. Berkeley's domain. (Even if you didn't already know that, though, you could have inferred that the name probably belongs to a U.S. university because it's in the top-level *edu* domain.) *cchem* is the College of Chemistry's subdomain of *berkeley.edu*. Finally, *lithium* is the name of a particular host in the domain— and probably one of about a hundred or so, if they have one for every element.

winnie.corp.hp.com
> This example is a bit harder, but not much. The *hp.com* domain in all likelihood belongs to the Hewlett-Packard Company (in fact, we gave you this earlier, too). Its *corp* subdomain is undoubtedly its corporate headquarters. And *winnie* is probably just some silly name someone thought up for a host.

fernwood.mpk.ca.us
> Here, you'll need to use your understanding of the *us* domain. *ca.us* is obviously California's domain, but *mpk* is anybody's guess. In this case, it would be hard to know that it's Menlo Park's domain unless you know your San Francisco Bay Area geography. (And no, it's not the same Menlo Park that Edison lived in— that one's in New Jersey.)

---

* Actually, there are a few more domains under *us*: one for Washington, D.C., one for Guam, and so on.

---

daphne.ch.apollo.hp.com

We've included this example just so you don't start thinking that all domain names have only four labels. *apollo.hp.com* is the former Apollo Computer subdomain of the *hp.com* domain. (When HP acquired Apollo, it also acquired Apollo's Internet domain, *apollo.com*, which became *apollo.hp.com*.) *ch.apollo.hp.com* is Apollo's Chelmsford, Massachusetts site. *daphne* is a host at Chelmsford.

Delegation

Remember that one of the main goals of the design of the Domain Name System was to decentralize administration? This is achieved through *delegation*. Delegating domains works a lot like delegating tasks at work. A manager may break up a large project into smaller tasks and delegate responsibility for each of these tasks to different employees.

Likewise, an organization administering a domain can divide it into subdomains. Each subdomain can be delegated to other organizations, which means that an organization becomes responsible for maintaining all the data in that subdomain. It can freely change the data and even divide its subdomain into more subdomains and delegate those. The parent domain retains only pointers to sources of the subdomain's data, so that it can refer queriers there. The domain *stanford.edu*, for example, is delegated to the folks at Stanford who run the university's networks (Figure 2-7).

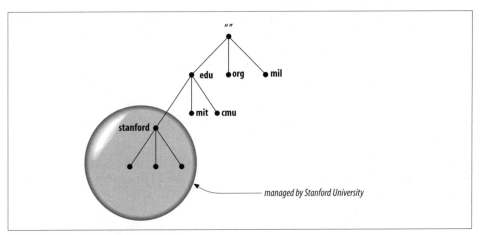

Figure 2-7. stanford.edu is delegated to Stanford University

Not all organizations delegate away their whole domain, just as not all managers delegate all their work. A domain may have several delegated subdomains and contain hosts that don't belong in the subdomains. For example, the Acme Corporation (it supplies a certain coyote with most of his gadgets), which has a division in Rockaway and its headquarters in Kalamazoo, might have a *rockaway.acme.com* subdomain and a *kalamazoo.acme.com* subdomain. However, the few hosts in the Acme sales offices scattered throughout the United States would fit better under *acme.com* than under either subdomain.

We'll explain how to create and delegate subdomains later. For now, it's important only that you understand that the term delegation refers to assigning responsibility for a subdomain to another organization.

Nameservers and Zones

The programs that store information about the domain namespace are called *nameservers*. Nameservers generally have complete information about some part of the domain namespace, called a *zone*, which they load from a file or from another nameserver. The nameserver is then said to have *authority* for that zone. Nameservers can be authoritative for multiple zones, too.

The difference between a zone and a domain is important, but subtle. All top-level domains and many domains at the second level and lower, such as *berkeley.edu* and *hp.com*, are broken into smaller, more manageable units by delegation. These units are called zones. The *edu* domain, shown in Figure 2-8, is divided into many zones, including the *berkeley.edu* zone, the *purdue.edu* zone, and the *nwu.edu* zone. At the top of the domain, there's also an *edu* zone. It's natural that the folks who run *edu* would break up the *edu* domain: otherwise, they'd have to manage the *berkeley.edu* subdomain themselves. It makes much more sense to delegate *berkeley.edu* to Berkeley. What's left for the folks who run *edu*? The *edu* zone, which contains mostly delegation information for the subdomains of *edu*.

The *berkeley.edu* subdomain is, in turn, broken up into multiple zones by delegation, as shown in Figure 2-9. There are delegated subdomains called *cc*, *cs*, *ce*, *me*, and more. Each subdomain is delegated to a set of nameservers, some of which are also authoritative for *berkeley.edu*. However, the zones are still separate and may have totally different groups of authoritative nameservers.

A zone contains all the domain names the domain with the same domain name contains, except for domain names in delegated subdomains. For example, the top-level domain *ca* (for Canada) has subdomains called *ab.ca*, *on.ca*, and *qc.ca*, for the provinces Alberta, Ontario, and Quebec. Authority for the *ab.ca*, *on.ca*, and *qc.ca* domains may be delegated to nameservers in each province. The *domain ca* contains all the data in *ca* plus all the data in *ab.ca*, *on.ca*, and *qc.ca*. However, the *zone ca* contains only the data in *ca* (see Figure 2-10), which is probably mostly pointers to the delegated subdomains. *ab.ca*, *on.ca*, and *qc.ca* are separate zones from the *ca* zone.

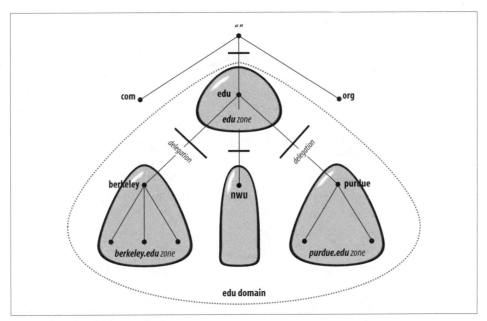

Figure 2-8. The edu domain broken into zones

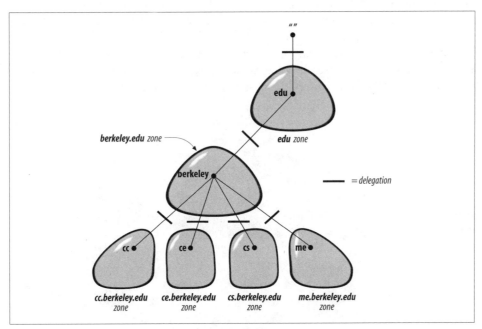

Figure 2-9. The berkeley.edu domain broken into zones

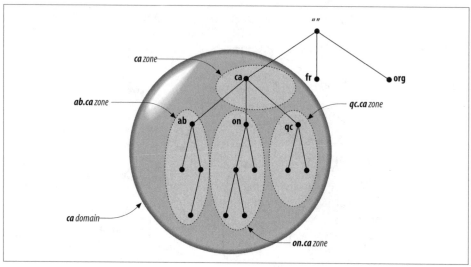

Figure 2-10. The domain ca…

The zone also contains the domain names and data in any subdomains that aren't delegated away. For example, the *bc.ca* and *sk.ca* (British Columbia and Saskatchewan) subdomains of the *ca* domain may exist but not be delegated. (Perhaps the provincial authorities in British Columbia and Saskatchewan aren't yet ready to manage their subdomains, but the authorities running the top-level *ca* domain want to preserve the consistency of the namespace and implement subdomains for all the Canadian provinces right away.) In this case, the zone *ca* has a ragged bottom edge, containing *bc.ca* and *sk.ca* but not the other *ca* subdomains, as shown in Figure 2-11.

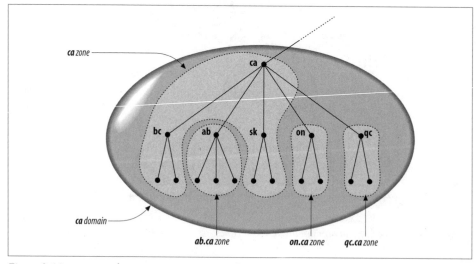

Figure 2-11. …versus the zone ca

Now it's clear why nameservers load zones instead of domains: a domain may contain more information than the nameserver needs because it can contain data delegated to other nameservers.* Since a zone is bounded by delegation, it will never include delegated data.

If you're just starting out, your domain probably won't have any subdomains. In this case, since there's no delegation going on, your domain and your zone will contain the same data.

Delegating Subdomains

Even though you may not need to delegate parts of your domain just yet, it's helpful to understand a little more about how the process of delegating a subdomain works. Delegation, in the abstract, involves assigning responsibility for some part of your domain to another organization. What really happens, however, is the assignment of authority for a subdomain to different nameservers. (Note that we said "nameservers," not just "nameserver.")

Your zone's data, instead of containing information in the subdomain you've delegated, includes pointers to the nameservers that are authoritative for that subdomain. Now if one of your nameservers is asked for data in the subdomain, it can reply with a list of the right nameservers to contact.

Types of Nameservers

The DNS specs define two types of nameservers: primary masters and secondary masters. A *primary master nameserver* for a zone reads the data for the zone from a file on its host. A *secondary master nameserver* for a zone gets the zone data from another nameserver authoritative for the zone, called its *master server*. Quite often, the master server is the zone's primary master, but that's not required: a secondary master can load zone data from another secondary. When a secondary starts up, it contacts its master nameserver and, if necessary, pulls the zone data over. This is referred to as a *zone transfer*. Nowadays, the preferred term for a secondary master nameserver is a *slave*, though many people (and some software, including Microsoft's DNS console) still use the old term.

Both the primary master and slave nameservers for a zone are authoritative for that zone. Despite the somewhat disparaging name, slaves aren't second-class nameservers. DNS provides these two types of nameservers to make administration easier. Once you've created the data for your zone and set up a primary master nameserver, you don't need to copy that data from host to host to create new nameservers for the

---

* Imagine if a root nameserver loaded the root domain instead of the root zone: it would be loading the entire namespace!

zone. You simply set up slave nameservers that load their data from the primary master for the zone. The slaves you set up will transfer new zone data when necessary.

Slave nameservers are important because it's a good idea to set up more than one authoritative nameserver for any given zone. You'll want more than one for redundancy, to spread the load around and to make sure that all the hosts in the zone have a nameserver close by. Using slave nameservers makes this administratively workable.

Calling a *particular* nameserver a primary master nameserver or a slave nameserver is a little imprecise, though. We mentioned earlier that a nameserver can be authoritative for more than one zone. Similarly, a nameserver can be a primary master for one zone and a slave for another. Most nameservers, however, are either primary for most of the zones they load or slave for most of the zones they load. So if we call a particular nameserver a primary or a slave, we mean that it's the primary master or a slave for *most* of the zones for which it's authoritative.

Zone Datafiles

The files from which primary master nameservers load their zone data are called, simply enough, *zone datafiles*. We often refer to them as *datafiles*. Slave nameservers can also load their zone data from datafiles. Slaves are usually configured to back up the zone data they transfer from a master nameserver to datafiles. If the slave is later killed and restarted, it reads the backup datafiles first, then checks to see whether its zone data is current. This both obviates the need to transfer the zone data if it hasn't changed and provides a source of the data if the master is down.

The datafiles contain resource records that describe the zone. The resource records describe all the hosts in the zone and mark any delegation of subdomains. BIND also allows special directives to include the contents of other datafiles in a zone datafile, much like the *#include* statement in C programming.

Resolvers

Resolvers are the clients that access nameservers. Programs running on a host that need information from the domain namespace use the resolver. The resolver handles:

- Querying a nameserver
- Interpreting responses (which may be resource records or an error)
- Returning the information to the programs that requested it

In BIND, the resolver is a set of library routines that is linked to programs such as *ssh* and *ftp*. It's not even a separate process. The resolver relies almost entirely on the nameservers it queries: it has the smarts to put together a query, to send it and wait for an answer, and to resend the query if it isn't answered, but that's about all. Most of the burden of finding an answer to the query is placed on the nameserver. The DNS specs call this kind of resolver a *stub resolver*.

Other implementations of DNS have had smarter resolvers that could do more sophisticated things that had more advanced capabilities, such as following referrals to locate the nameservers authoritative for a particular zone.

Resolution

Nameservers are adept at retrieving data from the domain namespace. They have to be, given the limited intelligence of most resolvers. Not only can they give you data about zones for which they're authoritative, they can also search through the domain namespace to find data for which they're not authoritative. This process is called *name resolution*, or simply *resolution*.

Because the namespace is structured as an inverted tree, a nameserver needs only one piece of information to find its way to any point in the tree: the domain names and addresses of the root nameservers (is that more than one piece?). A nameserver can issue a query to a root nameserver for any domain name in the domain namespace, and the root nameserver will start the nameserver on its way.

Root Nameservers

The root nameservers know where the authoritative nameservers for each of the top-level zones are. (In fact, some of the root nameservers are authoritative for some of the generic top-level zones.) Given a query about any domain name, the root nameservers can at least provide the names and addresses of the nameservers that are authoritative for the top-level zone the domain name ends in. In turn, the top-level nameservers can provide the list of authoritative nameservers for the second-level zone that the domain name ends in. Each nameserver queried either gives the querier information about how to get "closer" to the answer it's seeking or provides the answer itself. The root nameservers are clearly important to resolution. Because they're so important, DNS provides mechanisms—such as caching, which we'll discuss a little later—to help offload the root nameservers. But in the absence of other information, resolution has to start at the root nameservers. This makes the root nameservers crucial to the operation of DNS; if all the Internet root nameservers were unreachable for an extended period, all resolution on the Internet would fail. To protect against this, the Internet has 13 root nameservers (as of this writing) spread across different parts of the network.* One is on PSINet, a commercial Internet backbone; one is on the NASA Science Internet; two are in Europe; and one is in Japan.

---

* In fact, the 13 "logical" root nameservers comprise many more physical nameservers. Most of the root servers are either load-balanced behind a single IP address, a "shared unicast" group of distributed nameservers that use the same IP address, or some combination of the two.

Being the focal point for so many queries keeps the roots busy; even with 13, the traffic to each root nameserver is very high. A recent informal poll of root nameserver administrators showed some roots receiving tens of thousands of queries per second.

Despite the load placed on root nameservers, resolution on the Internet works quite well. Figure 2-12 shows the resolution process for the address of a real host in a real domain, including how the process corresponds to traversing the domain namespace tree.

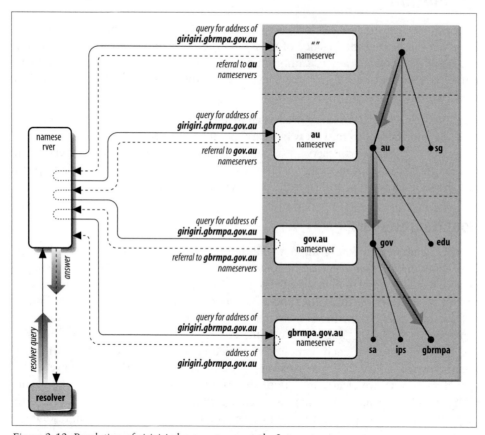

Figure 2-12. Resolution of girigiri.gbrmpa.gov.au on the Internet

The local nameserver queries a root nameserver for the address of *girigiri.gbrmpa.gov.au* and is referred to the *au* nameservers. The local nameserver asks an *au* nameserver the same question, and is referred to the *gov.au* nameservers. The *gov.au* nameserver refers the local nameserver to the *gbrmpa.gov.au* nameservers. Finally, the local nameserver asks a *gbrmpa.gov.au* nameserver for the address and gets the answer.

Recursion

You may have noticed a big difference in the amount of work done by the nameservers in the previous example. Four nameservers simply returned the best answer they already had—mostly referrals to other nameservers—to the queries they received. They didn't have to send their own queries to find the data requested. But one nameserver—the one queried by the resolver—had to follow successive referrals until it received an answer.

Why couldn't the local nameserver simply have referred the resolver to another nameserver? Because a stub resolver wouldn't have had the intelligence to follow a referral. And how did the nameserver know not to answer with a referral? Because the resolver issued a *recursive* query. Queries come in two flavors, *recursive* and *iterative*, also called *nonrecursive*. Recursive queries place most of the burden of resolution on a single nameserver. *Recursion*, or *recursive resolution*, is just a name for the resolution process used by a nameserver when it receives recursive queries. As with recursive algorithms in programming, the nameserver repeats the same basic process (querying a remote nameserver and following any referrals) until it receives an answer.

Iteration, or *iterative resolution*, on the other hand, refers to the resolution process used by a nameserver when it receives iterative queries.

In recursion, a resolver sends a recursive query to a nameserver for information about a particular domain name. The queried nameserver is then obliged to respond with the requested data or with an error stating either that data of the requested type doesn't exist or that the domain name specified doesn't exist.* The nameserver can't just refer the querier to a different nameserver, because the query was recursive.

If the queried nameserver isn't authoritative for the data requested, it will have to query other nameservers to find the answer. It could send recursive queries to those nameservers, thereby obliging them to find the answer and return it (and passing the buck), or it could send iterative queries and possibly be referred to other nameservers "closer" to the domain name it's seeking. Current implementations are polite and by default do the latter, following the referrals until an answer is found.†

A nameserver that receives a recursive query that it can't answer itself will query the "closest known" nameservers. The closest known nameservers are the servers authoritative for the zone closest to the domain name being looked up. For example, if the nameserver receives a recursive query for the address of the domain name *girigiri.gbrmpa.gov.au*, it first checks whether it knows which nameservers are

---

* Most BIND nameservers can be configured to ignore or refuse recursive queries; see Chapter 11 for how to do this and why you'd want to.

† The exception is a nameserver configured to forward all unresolved queries to a designated nameserver, called a forwarder. See Chapter 10 for more information on using forwarders.

authoritative for *girigiri.gbrmpa.gov.au*. If it does, it sends the query to one of them. If not, it checks whether it knows the nameservers for *gbrmpa.gov.au*, and after that *gov.au*, and then *au*. The default, where the check is guaranteed to stop, is the root zone, because every nameserver knows the domain names and addresses of the root nameservers.

Using the closest known nameservers ensures that the resolution process is as short as possible. A *berkeley.edu* nameserver receiving a recursive query for the address of *waxwing.ce.berkeley.edu* shouldn't have to consult the root nameservers; it can simply follow delegation information directly to the *ce.berkeley.edu* nameservers. Likewise, a nameserver that has just looked up a domain name in *ce.berkeley.edu* shouldn't have to start resolution at the root to look up another *ce.berkeley.edu* (or *berkeley.edu*) domain name; we'll show how this works in the "Caching" section.

The nameserver that receives the recursive query always sends the same query that the resolver sent it—for example, for the address of *waxwing.ce.berkeley.edu*. It never sends explicit queries for the nameservers for *ce.berkeley.edu* or *berkeley.edu*, though this information is also stored in the namespace. Sending explicit queries could cause problems—for example, there may be no *ce.berkeley.edu* nameservers (that is, *ce.berkeley.edu* may be part of the *berkeley.edu* zone). Also, it's always possible that an *edu* or *berkeley.edu* nameserver would know *waxwing.ce.berkeley.edu*'s address. An explicit query for the *berkeley.edu* or *ce.berkeley.edu* nameservers would miss this information.

Iteration

Iterative resolution doesn't require nearly as much work on the part of the queried nameserver. In iterative resolution, a nameserver simply gives the best answer *it already knows* back to the querier. No additional querying is required. The queried nameserver consults its local data (including its cache, which we'll talk about shortly), looking for the data requested. If it doesn't find the answer there, it finds the names and addresses of the nameservers closest to the domain name in the query in its local data and returns that as a referral to help the querier continue the resolution process. Note that the referral includes *all* nameservers listed in the local data; it's up to the querier to choose which one to query next.

Choosing Between Authoritative Nameservers

Some of the card-carrying Mensa members in our reading audience may be wondering how the nameserver that receives the recursive query chooses among the nameservers authoritative for the zone. For example, we said that there are 13 root nameservers on the Internet today. Does the nameserver simply query the one that appears first in the referral? Does it choose randomly?

BIND nameservers use a metric called *roundtrip time*, or RTT, to choose among nameservers authoritative for the same zone. Roundtrip time is a measurement of how long a remote nameserver takes to respond to queries. Each time a BIND nameserver sends a query to a remote nameserver, it starts an internal stopwatch. When it receives a response, it stops the stopwatch and makes a note of how long that remote nameserver took to respond. When the nameserver must choose which of a group of authoritative nameservers to query, it simply chooses the one with the lowest roundtrip time.

Before a BIND nameserver has queried a nameserver, it gives it a random roundtrip time value lower than any real-world value. This ensures that the BIND nameserver queries all nameservers authoritative for a given zone in a random order before playing favorites.

On the whole, this simple but elegant algorithm allows BIND nameservers to "lock on" to the closest nameservers quickly and without the overhead of an out-of-band mechanism to measure performance.

The Whole Enchilada

What this amounts to is a resolution process that, taken as a whole, looks like Figure 2-13.

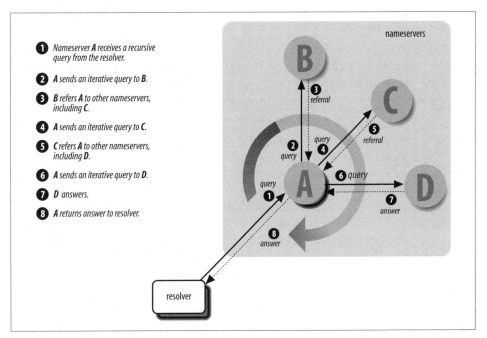

Figure 2-13. The resolution process

A resolver queries a local nameserver, which then sends iterative queries to a number of other nameservers in pursuit of an answer for the resolver. Each nameserver it queries refers it to another nameserver that is authoritative for a zone further down in the namespace and closer to the domain name sought. Finally, the local nameserver queries the authoritative nameserver, which returns an answer. All the while, the local nameserver uses each response it receives—whether a referral or the answer—to update the RTT of the responding nameserver, which will help it decide which nameservers to query to resolve domain names in the future.

Mapping Addresses to Names

One major piece of functionality missing from the resolution process as explained so far is how addresses get mapped back to domain names. Address-to-name mapping produces output that is easier for humans to read and interpret (in logfiles, for instance). It's also used in some authorization checks. Unix hosts map addresses to domain names to compare against entries in *.rhosts* and *hosts.equiv* files, for example. When using host tables, address-to-name mapping is trivial. It requires a straightforward sequential search through the host table for an address. The search returns the official hostname listed. In DNS, however, address-to-name mapping isn't so simple. Data, including addresses, in the domain namespace is indexed by name. Given a domain name, finding an address is relatively easy. But finding the domain name that maps to a given address would seem to require an exhaustive search of the data attached to every domain name in the tree.

Actually, there's a better solution that's both clever and effective. Because it's easy to find data once you're given the domain name that indexes that data, why not create a part of the domain namespace that uses addresses as labels? In the Internet's domain namespace, this portion of the namespace is the *in-addr.arpa* domain.

Nodes in the *in-addr.arpa* domain are labeled with the numbers in the dotted-octet representation of IP addresses. (Dotted-octet representation refers to the common method of expressing 32-bit IP addresses as four numbers in the range 0 to 255, separated by dots.) The *in-addr.arpa* domain, for example, can have up to 256 subdomains, one corresponding to each possible value in the first octet of an IP address. Each subdomain can have up to 256 subdomains of its own, corresponding to the possible values of the second octet. Finally, at the fourth level down, there are resource records attached to the final octet giving the full domain name of the host at that IP address. That makes for an awfully big domain: *in-addr.arpa*, shown in Figure 2-14, is roomy enough for every IP address on the Internet.

Note that when read in a domain name, the IP address appears backward because the name is read from leaf to root. For example, if *winnie.corp.hp.com*'s IP address is 15.16.192.152, the corresponding node in the *in-addr.arpa* domain is *152.192.16.15. in-addr.arpa*, which maps back to the domain name *winnie.corp.hp.com*.

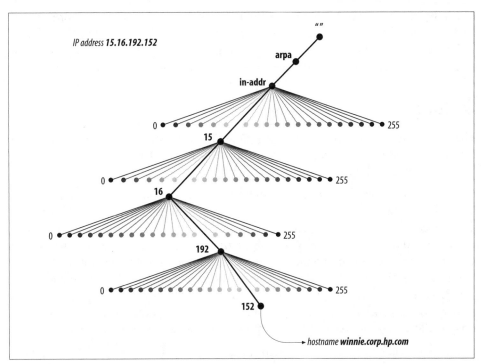

Figure 2-14. The in-addr.arpa domain

IP addresses could have been represented the opposite way in the namespace, with the first octet of the IP address at the bottom of the *in-addr.arpa* domain. That way, the IP address would have read correctly (forward) in the domain name. IP addresses are hierarchical, however, just like domain names. Network numbers are doled out much as domain names are, and administrators can then subnet their address space and further delegate numbering. The difference is that IP addresses get more specific from left to right, while domain names get less specific from left to right. Figure 2-15 shows what we mean.

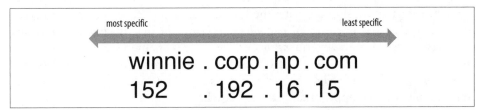

Figure 2-15. Hierarchical names and addresses

Making the first octets in the IP address appear highest in the tree enables administrators to delegate authority for *in-addr.arpa* zones along network lines. For example, the *15.in-addr.arpa* zone, which contains the reverse-mapping information for all hosts whose IP addresses start with 15, can be delegated to the administrators of network 15/8. This would be impossible if the octets appeared in the opposite order. If the IP addresses were represented the other way around, *15.in-addr.arpa* would consist of every host whose IP address *ended* with 15—not a practical zone to try to delegate.

Caching

The whole resolution process may seem awfully convoluted and cumbersome to someone accustomed to simple searches through the host table. Actually, though, it's usually quite fast. One of the features that speeds it up considerably is *caching*.

A nameserver processing a recursive query may have to send out quite a few queries to find an answer. However, it discovers a lot of information about the domain namespace as it does so. Each time it's referred to another list of nameservers, it learns that those nameservers are authoritative for some zone, and it learns the addresses of those servers. At the end of the resolution process, when it finally finds the data the original querier sought, it can store that data for future reference, too. The BIND nameserver even implements *negative caching*: if a nameserver responds to a query with an answer that says the domain name or data type in the query doesn't exist, the local nameserver will also temporarily cache that information.

Nameservers cache all this data to help speed up successive queries. The next time a resolver queries the nameserver for data about a domain name the nameserver knows something about, the process is shortened quite a bit. The nameserver may have cached the answer, positive or negative, in which case it simply returns the answer to the resolver. Even if it doesn't have the answer cached, it may have learned the identities of the nameservers that are authoritative for the zone the domain name is in and be able to query them directly.

For example, say our nameserver has already looked up the address of *eecs.berkeley.edu*. In the process, it cached the names and addresses of the *eecs.berkeley.edu* and *berkeley.edu* nameservers (plus *eecs.berkeley.edu*'s IP address). Now if a resolver were to query our nameserver for the address of *baobab.cs.berkeley.edu*, our nameserver could skip querying the root nameservers. Recognizing that *berkeley.edu* is the closest ancestor of *baobab.cs.berkeley.edu* that it knows about, our nameserver would start by querying a *berkeley.edu* nameserver, as shown in Figure 2-16. On the other hand, if our nameserver discovered that there was no address for *eecs.berkeley.edu*, the next time it received a query for the address, it could simply respond appropriately from its cache.

In addition to speeding up resolution, caching obviates a nameserver's need to query the root nameservers to answer any queries it can't answer locally. This means it's not as dependent on the roots, and the roots won't suffer as much from all its queries.

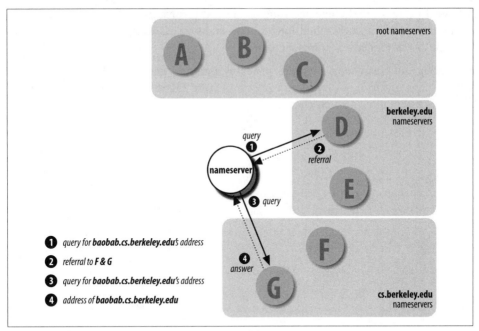

Figure 2-16. Resolving baobab.cs.berkeley.edu

Time to Live

Nameservers can't cache data forever, of course. If they did, changes to that data on the authoritative nameservers would never reach the rest of the network; remote nameservers would just continue to use cached data. Consequently, the administrator of the zone that contains the data decides on a *time to live* (TTL) for the data. The time to live is the amount of time that any nameserver is allowed to cache the data. After the time to live expires, the nameserver must discard the cached data and get new data from the authoritative nameservers. This also applies to negatively cached data: a nameserver must time out a negative answer after a period in case new data has been added on the authoritative nameservers.

Deciding on a time to live for your data is essentially deciding on a trade-off between performance and consistency. A small TTL helps ensure that data in your zones is consistent across the network, because remote nameservers will time it out more quickly and be forced to query your authoritative nameservers more often for new data. On the other hand, this increases the load on your nameservers and lengthens the average resolution time for information in your zones.

A large TTL reduces the average time it takes to resolve information in your zones because the data can be cached longer. The drawback is that your information will be inconsistent longer if you make changes to the data on your nameservers.

But enough of this theory—you're probably antsy to get on with things. There's some homework to do before you can set up your zones and nameservers, though, and we'll assign it in the next chapter.

## CHAPTER 3

Where Do I Start?

> *"What do you call yourself?" the Fawn said at last.*
> *Such a soft sweet voice it had!*
>
> *"I wish I knew!" thought poor Alice. She answered,*
> *rather sadly, "Nothing, just now."*
>
> *"Think again," it said: "that won't do."*
>
> *Alice thought, but nothing came of it. "Please, would*
> *you tell me what you call yourself?" she said timidly.*
> *"I think that might help a little."*
>
> *"I'll tell you, if you come a little further on," the Fawn*
> *said. "I can't remember here."*

Now that you understand the theory behind the Domain Name System, we can attend to more practical matters. Before you set up your zones, you may need to get the BIND software. Usually, it's standard in most Unix-based operating systems. Often, though, you'll want to seek out a more recent version with all the latest functionality and security enhancements.

Once you have BIND, you need to decide on a domain name for your main zone; this may not be quite as easy as it sounds because it entails finding an appropriate place in the Internet namespace. With that decided, you need to contact the administrators of the parent of the zone whose domain name you've chosen.

One thing at a time, though. Let's talk about where to get BIND.

Getting BIND

If you plan to set up your own zones and run nameservers for them, you first need the BIND software. Even if you plan to have someone else run the nameservers for your zones, it's helpful to have the software around. For example, you can use a local nameserver to test your zone datafiles before giving them to your remote nameserver administrator.

Most commercial Unix vendors ship BIND with the rest of their standard TCP/IP networking software. And the networking software is usually included with the operating system, so you get BIND free. Even if the networking software is priced separately, you've probably already bought it, since you clearly do enough networking to need DNS, right?

If you don't have a version of BIND for your flavor of Unix, though, or if you want the latest, greatest version, you can always get the source code. As luck would have it, it's freely distributed. The source code for the most up-to-date versions of BIND as of this writing (the BIND 8.4.7 and 9.3.2 releases) is available via anonymous FTP from the Internet Software Consortium's web site, *ftp.isc.org*, in */isc/bind/src/8.4.7/ bind-src.tar.gz* and */isc/bind9/9.3.2/bind-9.3.2.tar.gz,* respectively. Compiling these releases on most common Unix platforms is relatively straightforward.* The ISC includes a list of Unix-ish operating systems that BIND is known to compile on in the file *src/INSTALL* (for BIND 8) and *README* (for BIND 9), including several versions of Linux, Unix, and even Windows. There's also a list of other Unix-ish and not-so-Unix-ish (MPE, anyone?) operating systems BIND has supported in the past, most recent versions of BIND will probably compile on these systems without much effort. Regardless of which category your operating system falls into, we strongly recommend reading all of the sections of the file that are relevant to your OS. In Appendix C, we also include instructions for compiling BIND 8.4.7 and 9.3.2 on Linux; it's a remarkably short appendix.

Some of you may already have a version of BIND that came with your operating system, but you're wondering whether you need the latest, greatest version of BIND. What does it have to offer that earlier versions of BIND don't? Here's an overview:

Security fixes
> Arguably the most important reason to run the newest BIND is that only the most recent versions are patched against most attacks, some of them widely known. BIND 8.4.7 and BIND 9.3.2 are resistant to all well-known attacks. Earlier versions of BIND have widely known vulnerabilities. Historically, BIND 9 has a much better security track record than BIND 8 (that is, significantly fewer vulnerabilities have been found in BIND 9 nameservers).

> If you're running a nameserver on the Internet, we strongly recommend that you run BIND 9.3.2, or at the very least BIND 8.4.7, or whatever the current released version is as you read this.

Security features
> BIND 8 and BIND 9 support access lists on queries, zone transfers, and dynamic updates. BIND 9 also supports views, which allow you to run multiple, virtual

---

* Compiling early versions of BIND 9 (before 9.1.0) can be a little tricky because these versions require *pthreads* and many OSes sport broken *pthreads* implementations. BIND 9.1.0 and later can be built without *pthreads* by running *configure --disable-threads*.

nameserver configurations on a single nameserver. Certain nameservers, particularly those running on bastion hosts or other security-critical hosts, may require these features.

We cover these features in Chapter 11.

DNS UPDATE

BIND 8 and BIND 9 support the Dynamic Update standard described in RFC 2136. This allows authorized agents to update zone data by sending special update messages to add or delete resource records. (Older versions of BIND don't support Dynamic Update.) BIND 9 supports finer-grained authorization of dynamic updaters than BIND 8 does.

We cover Dynamic Update in Chapter 10.

Incremental zone transfer

Current versions of BIND 8 (such as 8.4.7) and BIND 9 support incremental zone transfer, which allows slave nameservers to request just the changes to a zone from their master servers. This makes zone transfers faster and more efficient, and is particularly important for large, dynamic zones. In our experience, BIND 9's implementation is much more robust than BIND 8's.

If, after reading through this list and checking the appendix, you're convinced you need BIND 8 or BIND 9's features and neither a BIND 8 nor BIND 9 nameserver comes with your operating system, download the source code and build your own.

Handy Mailing Lists and Usenet Newsgroups

Instructions on how to port BIND to every possible version of Unix could consume another book this size, so we'll have to refer you to the BIND users mailing list (*bind-users@isc.org*) or the corresponding Usenet newsgroup (*comp.protocols.dns.bind*) for further help.* The folks who read and contribute to the BIND users mailing lists can be enormously helpful in your porting efforts. Before sending mail to the list asking whether a particular port is available, be sure to check the searchable archive of the mailing list at *http://www.isc.org/index.pl?/ops/lists*. Also, take a look at the ISC's BIND web page at *http://www.isc.org/sw/bind* for notes or links specific to your operating system.

Another mailing list you might be interested in is the *namedroppers* list. Folks on the *namedroppers* mailing list are involved in the IETF working group that develops extensions to the DNS specifications, DNSEXT. For example, the discussion of a

---

* To ask a question on an Internet mailing list, all you need to do is send a message to the mailing list's address. If you'd like to join the list, however, you have to send a message to the list's maintainer first, requesting that your electronic mail address be added to the list. Don't send this request to the list itself; that's considered rude. The Internet convention is that you can reach the maintainer of a mailing list by sending mail to *list-request@domain*, where *list@domain* is the address of the mailing list. So, for example, you can reach the BIND users mailing list's administrator by sending mail to *bind-users-request@isc.org*.

new, proposed DNS record type would probably take place on *namedroppers* instead of the BIND users mailing list. For more information on DNSEXT's charter, see *http://www.ietf.org/html.charters/dnsext-charter.html*.

The address for the *namedroppers* mailing list is *namedroppers@ops.ietf.org*. The list is gatewayed into the Internet newsgroup *comp.protocols.dns.std*. To join the *namedroppers* mailing list, send mail to *namedroppers-request@ops.ietf.org* with the text "subscribe namedroppers" as the body of the message.

Finding IP Addresses

You'll notice that we gave you a number of domain names of hosts that have *ftp*able software, and the mailing lists we mentioned include domain names. This should underscore the importance of DNS: see what valuable software and advice you can get with the help of DNS? Unfortunately, it's also something of a chicken-and-egg problem: you can't send email to an address with a domain name in it unless you've got DNS set up, so how can you ask someone on the list how to set up DNS?

Well, we could give you the IP addresses for all the hosts we mentioned, but since IP addresses change often (in publishing timescales, anyway), we'll show you how you can *temporarily* use someone else's nameserver to find the information instead. As long as your host has Internet connectivity and the *nslookup* program, you can retrieve information from the Internet namespace.

To look up the IP address for *ftp.isc.org*, for example, you could use:

```
% nslookup ftp.isc.org. 207.69.188.185
```

This instructs *nslookup* to query the nameserver running on the host at the IP address 207.69.188.185 to find the IP address for *ftp.isc.org*, and should produce output like:

```
Server:  ns1.mindspring.com
Address:  207.69.188.185

Name:    ftp.isc.org
Address: 204.152.184.110
```

Now you can FTP to *ftp.isc.org*'s IP address, 204.152.184.110.

How did we know that the host at IP address 207.69.188.185 runs a nameserver? Our ISP, Mindspring, told us—it's one of their nameservers. If your ISP provides nameservers for its customers' use (and most do), use one of them. If your ISP doesn't provide nameservers (shame on them!), you can *temporarily* use one of the nameservers listed in this book. As long as you use it only to look up a few IP addresses or other data, the administrators probably won't mind. It's considered very rude, however, to point your resolver or query tool at someone else's nameserver permanently.

Of course, if you already have access to a host with Internet connectivity *and* have DNS configured, you can use it to *ftp* what you need.

Once you have a working version of BIND, you're ready to start thinking about your domain name.

Choosing a Domain Name

Choosing a domain name is more involved than it may sound because it entails both choosing a name *and* finding out who runs the parent zone. In other words, you need to find out where you fit in the Internet domain namespace, then find out who runs that particular corner of the namespace.

The first step in picking a domain name is finding where in the existing domain namespace you belong. It's easiest to start at the top and work your way down: decide which top-level domain you belong in, then which of that top-level domain's subdomains you fit into.

Note that in order to find out what the Internet domain namespace looks like (beyond what we've already told you), you'll need access to the Internet. You don't need access to a host that already has name service configured, but it would help a little. If you don't have access to a host with DNS configured, you'll have to "borrow" name service from other nameservers (as in our previous *ftp.isc.org* example) to get you going.

On Registrars and Registries

Before we go any further, we need to define a few terms: registry, registrar, and registration. These terms aren't defined anywhere in the DNS specs. Instead, they apply to the way the Internet namespace is managed today.

A *registry* is an organization responsible for maintaining a top-level domain's (well, zone's, really) datafiles, which contain the delegation to each subdomain of that top-level domain. Under the current structure of the Internet, a given top-level domain can have no more than one registry. A *registrar* acts as an interface between customers and registries, providing registration and value-added services. Once a customer has chosen a subdomain of a top-level zone, the customer's registrar submits to the appropriate registry the zone data necessary to delegate that subdomain to the nameservers the customer specified. The registries act, more or less, as wholesalers of delegation in their top-level zone. The registrars then act as retailers, usually reselling delegation in more than one registry.

Registration is the process by which a customer tells a registrar which nameservers to delegate a subdomain to and provides the registrar with contact and billing information. To give you some concrete examples of registries and registrars in the real world, Public Interest Registry runs the *org* registry. VeriSign currently acts as the registry for the *com* and *net* top-level domains. There are dozens of registrars for *com*, *net*, and *org*, including GoDaddy.com, Register.com, and Network Solutions. An organization called EDUCAUSE runs the registry and is the only registrar for *edu*. But before we get too off-track, let's get back to our story.

Where in the World Do I Fit?

If your organization is attached to the Internet outside of the United States, you first need to decide whether you'd rather request a subdomain of one of the generic top-level domains, such as *com*, *net*, and *org*, or a subdomain of your country's top-level domain. The generic top-level domains aren't exclusively for U.S. organizations. If your company is a multi- or transnational company that doesn't fit in any one country's top-level domain, or if you'd simply prefer a generic top-level to your country's top-level domain, you're welcome to register in one. If you choose this route, skip to the section "The generic top-level domains" later in this chapter.

If you opt for a subdomain under your country's top level, you should check whether your country's top-level domain is registered and, if it is, what kind of structure it has. Consult our list of the current top-level domains (Appendix D) if you're not sure what the name of your country's top-level domain would be.

Some countries' top-level domains, such as New Zealand's *nz*, Australia's *au*, and the United Kingdom's *uk*, are divided organizationally into second-level domains. The names of their second-level domains, such as *co* or *com* for commercial entities, reflect organizational affiliation. Others, like France's *fr* domain and Denmark's *dk* domain, are divided into a multitude of subdomains managed by individual universities and companies, such as the University of St. Etienne's domain, *univ-st-etienne.fr*, and the Danish Unix Users Group's *dkuug.dk*. Many top-level domains have their own web sites that describe their structures. If you're not sure of the URL for your country's top-level domain's web site, start at *http://www.allwhois.com*, a directory of links to such web sites.

If your country's top-level domain doesn't have a web site explaining how it's organized, but you have some idea of which subdomain you belong in, you can use a DNS query tool such as *nslookup* to find the email address of the technical contact for the subdomain. (If you're uncomfortable with our rushing headlong into *nslookup* without giving it a proper introduction, you might want to skim Chapter 12.)

To find out whom to ask about a particular subdomain, you'll have to look up the corresponding zone's start of authority (SOA) record. In each zone's SOA record, there's a field that contains the electronic mail address of the zone's technical contact.* (The other fields in the SOA record provide general information about the zone—we'll discuss them in more detail later.)

---

* The subdomain and the zone have the same domain name, but the SOA record really belongs to the zone, not the subdomain. The person at the zone's technical contact email address may not manage the whole subdomain (there may be additional delegated subdomains beneath), but he should certainly know the purpose of the subdomain.

For example, if you're curious about the purpose of the *csiro.au* subdomain, you can find out who runs it by looking up *csiro.au*'s SOA record:

```
% nslookup - 207.69.188.185
> set type=soa          Look for start of authority data
> csiro.au.             for csiro.au
Server:  ns1.mindspring.com
Address: 207.69.188.185#53

csiro.au
        origin = zas.csiro.au
        mail addr = hostmaster.csiro.au
        serial = 2005072001
        refresh = 10800
        retry   = 3600
        expire  = 3600000
        minimum ttl = 3600
> exit
```

The *mail addr* field is the Internet address of *csiro.au*'s contact. To convert the address into Internet email address format, change the first "." in the address to an "@". So *hostmaster.csiro.au* becomes *hostmaster@csiro.au*.[*]

whois

The *whois* service can also help you figure out the purpose of a given domain. Unfortunately, there are many *whois* servers—most good administrators of top-level domains run one—and they don't talk to each other like nameservers do. Consequently, the first step to using *whois* is finding the right *whois* server.

One of the easiest places to start your search for the right *whois* server is at *http://www.allwhois.com* (Figure 3-1). We mentioned earlier that this site has a list of the web sites for each country code's top-level domain; it also sports a unified *whois* search facility.

Say you were wondering what a particular subdomain of *jp* was for. You can click on "Japan (jp)" in the list of registries at the bottom of *http://www.allwhois.com/* and jump directly to a web page that lets you query the right *whois* server, as shown in Figure 3-2.

Obviously, this is a useful web site if you're looking for information about a domain outside the United States.

---

[*] This form of Internet mail address is a vestige of two former DNS records, MB and MG. MB (mailbox) and MG (mail group) were supposed to be DNS records specifying Internet mailboxes and mail groups (mailing lists) as subdomains of the appropriate domain. MB and MG never took off, but the address format they would have dictated is used in the SOA record, maybe for sentimental reasons.

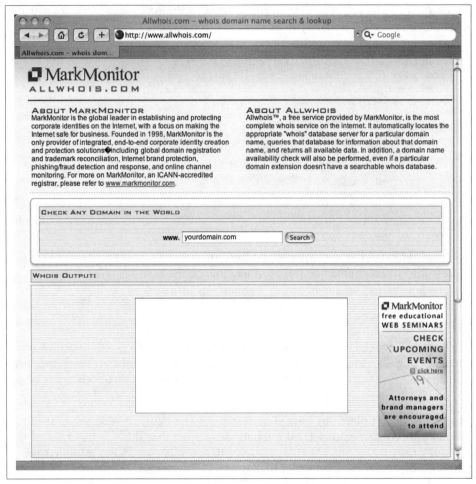

Figure 3-1. The www.allwhois.com web site

Once you've found the right web site or the right contact, you've probably found the registrar. Outside the United States, most domains have a single registrar. A few, though, such as Denmark's *dk* and Great Britain's *co.uk* and *org.uk*, have multiple registrars. However, most registries' web sites contain links to their registrars, so you can use the registry's web site as a starting point.

Back in the U.S.A.

In true cosmopolitan spirit, we covered international domains first. But what if you're from the good ol' U.S. of A.?

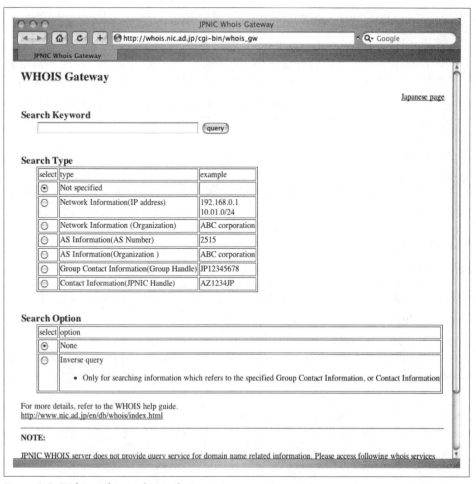

Figure 3-2. Web interface to the jp whois server

If you're in the United States, where you belong depends mainly on what your organization does and how you'd like your domain names to look. If your organization falls into one of the following categories, you may want to consider joining *us*:

- K–12 (kindergarten through 12th grade) schools
- Community colleges and technical vocational schools
- State and local government agencies

That's because these organizations have historically registered under *us*, according to the namespace design documented in RFC 1480. In that design, a high school, for example, would register under *k12.<state>.us*, where *<state>* is the two-letter postal abbreviation for the state in which the school is located. A city government would register under *ci.<state>.us*, and a county government under *co.<state>.us*.

However, even these organizations don't need to follow this rigid structure. Many K–12 schools, community colleges, and government agencies register subdomains of *org* or even *com*. The registry that runs *us* has relaxed the restrictions placed on *us* registrants, too: now you can register in either the *locality space* (*<state>.us*) or the *expanded space*. In the expanded space, you could register (for example) *acme.us* rather than *acme.co.us*.

Many people, however, prefer the better-known generic top-level domains. For information on registering in one of those, read on.

The generic top-level domains

As we said, there are many reasons why you might want to ask for a subdomain of one of the generic top-level domains, such as *com*, *net*, and *org*: you work for a multi- or transnational company, you like the fact that they're better-known, or you just prefer the sound of your domain name with "com" on the end. Let's go through a short example of choosing a domain name under a generic top-level domain.

Imagine you're the network administrator for a think tank in Hopkins, Minnesota. You've just gotten a connection to the Internet through a commercial ISP. Your company has never had so much as a dialup link, so you're not currently registered in the Internet namespace.

Since you're in the United States, you have the choice of joining either *us* or one of the generic top-level domains. Your think tank is world-renowned, though, so you feel *us* wouldn't be a good choice. A subdomain of a generic top-level domain would be best.

But which one? As of this writing, there are five open to anyone:

biz
> A new generic top-level domain

com
> The original generic top-level domain, and the best known

info
> A new generic top-level domain

net
> Originally used by networking organizations, but now open to anyone

org
> Originally used by nonprofit and other noncommercial organizations, but now open to anyone

The think tank is known as The Gizmonic Institute, so you decide *gizmonics.com* might be an appropriate domain name. Now you've got to check whether the name *gizmonics.com* has been taken by anyone, so you use an account you have at UMN:

```
% nslookup
Default Server:  ns.unet.umn.edu
Address:  128.101.101.101

> set type=any           Look for any records
> gizmonics.com.         for gizmonics.com
Server:  ns.unet.umn.edu
Address:  128.101.101.101

gizmonics.com    nameserver = ns1.11l.net
gizmonics.com    nameserver = ns2.11l.net
```

Whoops! Look like *gizmonics.com* is already taken (who would have thought?) Well, *gizmonic-institute.com* is a little longer, but still intuitive:[*]

```
% nslookup
Default Server:  ns.unet.umn.edu
Address:  128.101.101.101

> set type=any               Look for any records
> gizmonic-institute.com.    for gizmonic-institute.com
Server:  ns.unet.umn.edu
Address:  128.101.101.101

*** ns.unet.umn.edu can't find gizmonic-institute.com.: Non-existent host/domain
```

gizmonic-institute.com is free, so you can go on to the next step: picking a registrar.

Choosing a registrar

Choose a registrar? Welcome to the brave new world of competition! Before the spring of 1999, a single company, Network Solutions, Inc., was both the registry and sole registrar for *com*, *net*, and *org*, as well as *edu*. To register a subdomain of any of these generic top-level domains, you had to go to Network Solutions.

In June 1999, ICANN, the organization that manages the domain namespace (we mentioned ICANN in the last chapter) introduced competition to the registrar function of *com*, *net*, and *org*. There are now dozens of *com*, *net*, and *org* registrars from which you can choose. For more information, check out the InterNIC site (operated by ICANN) at *http://www.internic.net/regist.html*.

---

[*] If you're having a hard time figuring out a good domain name, many registrars' web sites provide suggestions for free. For example, *www.nameboy.com* recommends various combinations of "gizmonic" and "institute," even using rhyming words.

What About Non-ASCII Characters?

Some registrars now permit you to register domain names that contain non-ASCII characters, including accented characters from European languages. These are referred to as *internationalized domain names*. This may look like a tempting option, particularly if you work for, say, Nestlé. Is it really worthwhile?

Generally speaking, no. While you can register domain names that include these characters, there's almost no software out there that will actually look them up. If a user types an accented character into a web browser, chances are—today, anyway—that he won't get to the right place.

There's a standard for encoding these characters in domain names, which we'll discuss in Chapter 17. But as of this writing, the most popular web browser, Internet Explorer, and most email software don't support it.[a] The registrars that permit registration of internationalized domain names do, and will gratefully accept your money and register your encoded internationalized domain name, but almost no one will be able to look it up. Until support for internationalized domain names is widespread, about the only purpose of registering such names serves is to protect your tradename.

a. Microsoft has said that IE 7.0 will support internationalized domain names.

We won't presume to tell you how to pick a registrar, but take a look at the price of registration, the registrar's reputation for customer service, and any other services the registrar provides that interest you. See if you can get a nice package deal on registration and aluminum siding, for example.

Checking That Your Network Is Registered

Before proceeding, you should check whether your IP network or networks are registered. Some registrars won't delegate a subdomain to nameservers on unregistered networks, and network registries (we'll talk about them shortly) won't delegate an *in-addr.arpa* zone that corresponds to an unregistered network.

An IP network defines a range of IP addresses. For example, the network 15/8 is made up of all IP addresses in the range 15.0.0.0 to 15.255.255.255. The network 199.10.25/24 starts at 199.10.25.0 and ends at 199.10.25.255.

The InterNIC, now operated by ICANN, was once the official source of all IP networks; they assigned all IP networks to Internet-connected networks and made sure no two address ranges overlapped. Nowadays, the InterNIC's old role has been largely assumed by Internet service providers (ISPs), who allocate space from their own networks for customers to use. If you know your network came from your ISP, the larger network from which your network was carved is probably registered (to

A Sidebar on CIDR

Once upon a time, when we wrote the first edition of this book, the Internet's 32-bit address space was divided into three main classes of networks: Class A, Class B, and Class C. Class A networks were networks in which the first octet (the first eight bits) of the IP address identified the network, and the remaining bits were used by the organization that was assigned the network to differentiate hosts on the network. Most organizations with Class A networks also subdivided their networks into subnetworks, or subnets, adding another level of hierarchy to the addressing scheme. Class B networks devoted two octets to the network identifier and two to the host; Class C networks gave three octets to the network identifier and one to the host.

Unfortunately, this small/medium/large system of networks didn't work well for everyone. Many organizations were large enough to require more than a Class C network, which could accommodate at most 254 hosts, but too small to warrant a full Class B network, which could serve 65,534 hosts. Many of these organizations were allocated Class B networks anyway. Consequently, Class B networks quickly became scarce.

To help solve this problem and create networks that were just the right size for all sorts of organizations, Classless Inter-Domain Routing, or CIDR (pronounced "cider"), was developed. As the name implies, CIDR does away with the old Class A, Class B, and Class C network designations. Instead of allocating one, two, or three octets to the network identifier, the allocator could assign any number of contiguous bits of the IP address to the network identifier. So, for example, if an organization needed an address space roughly four times as large as a Class B network, the powers-that-be could assign it a network identifier of 14 bits, leaving 18 bits (four Class Bs' worth) of space to use.

Naturally, the advent of CIDR made the "classful" terminology outdated—although it's still used a good deal in casual conversation. Now, to designate a particular CIDR network, we specify the particular high-order bit value assigned to an organization, expressed in dotted octet notation, and how many bits identify the network. The two terms are separated by a slash. So 15/8 is the old, Class A-sized network that begins with the eight-bit pattern 00001111. The old, Class B-sized network 128.32.0.0 is now 128.32/16. And the network 192.168.0.128/25 consists of the 128 IP addresses from 192.168.0.128 to 192.168.0.255.

your ISP). You may still want to double-check that your ISP took care of registering its network, but you don't have to (and probably can't) do anything yourself, except nag your ISP if it didn't register their network. Once you've verified its registration, you can skip the rest of this section and move on.

It's not necessary to register RFC 1918 address space (e.g., the networks 10/8, 192.168/16). In fact, you can't because these networks are used by so many different organizations.

If your network was assigned by the InterNIC, way back when, or you are an ISP, you should check to see whether your network is registered. Where do you go to check whether your network is registered? Why, to the same organizations that register networks, of course. Each of these organizations, called *regional Internet registries*, or RIRs, handle network registration in some part of the world. In North America, the American Registry of Internet Numbers (ARIN; *http://www.arin.net*) hands out IP address space and registers networks. In Asia and the Pacific, the Asia Pacific Network Information Center (APNIC; *http://www.apnic.net*) serves the same function. In Europe, it's the RIPE Network Coordination Centre (*http://www.ripe.net*). And Latin America and the Caribbean are served by the Latin America and Caribbean Internet Addresses Registry (LACNIC; *www.lacnic.net*). Each RIR may also delegate registration authority for a region; for example, LACNIC delegates registration authority for Mexico and Brazil to registries in those countries. Be sure to check for a network registry local to your country.

If you're not sure your network is registered, the best way to find out is to use the *whois* services provided by the various network registries to look for your network. Here are the URLs for each registry's *whois* web page:

ARIN
> *http://www.arin.net/whois/index.html*

APNIC
> *http://www.apnic.net/search/index.html*

RIPE
> *http://www.ripe.net/perl/whois/*

LACNIC
> *http://lacnic.net/cgi-bin/lacnic/whois?lg=EN*

If you find your network isn't registered, you need to get it registered before setting up your *in-addr.arpa* zones. Each registry has a different process for registering networks, but most involve money changing hands (from your hands to theirs, unfortunately).

You may find out that your network is already assigned to your ISP. If this is the case, you don't need to register independently with the RIR.

Once all your Internet-connected hosts are on registered networks, you can register your zones.

Registering Your Zones

Different registrars have different registration policies and procedures, but most, at this point, handle registration online, through their web sites. Since you found or chose your registrar earlier in the chapter, we'll assume you know which web site to use.

The registrar will need to know the domain names and addresses of your nameservers and enough information about you to send a bill or charge your credit card. If you're not connected to the Internet, give the registrar the IP addresses of the Internet hosts that will act as your nameservers. Some registrars require that you already have operational nameservers for your zone. (Those that don't may ask for an estimate of when the nameservers will be fully operational.) If that's the case with your registrar, skip ahead to Chapter 4 and set up your nameservers. Then contact your registrar with the requisite information.

Most registrars will also ask for some information about your organization, including an administrative contact and a technical contact for your zone (who can be the same person). If your contacts aren't already registered in the registrar's *whois* database, you'll also need to provide information to register them in *whois*. This includes their names, surface mail addresses, phone numbers, and electronic mail addresses. If they are already registered in *whois*, just specify their *whois handles* (unique alphanumeric IDs) in the registration.

There's one more aspect of registering a new zone that we should mention: cost. Most registrars are commercial enterprises and charge money for registering domain names. Network Solutions, the original registrar for *com*, *net*, and *org*, charges $35 per year to register subdomains under the generic top-level domains. (If you already have a subdomain under *com*, *net*, or *org* and haven't received a bill from Network Solutions recently, it'd be a good idea to check your contact information with *whois* to make sure they have a current address and phone number for you.)

If you're directly connected to the Internet, you should also have the *in-addr.arpa* zones corresponding to your IP networks delegated to you.* For example, if your company was allocated the network 192.201.44/24, you should manage the *44.201.192.in-addr.arpa* zone. This will let you control the IP address-to-name mappings for hosts on your network. Chapter 4 also explains how to set up your *in-addr.arpa* zones.

In the section "Checking That Your Network Is Registered," we asked you to find the answers to several questions: is your network a slice of an ISP's network? Is your network, or the ISP's network that your network is part of, registered? If so, in which RIR? You'll need these answers to get your *in-addr.arpa* zones.

If your network is part of a larger network registered to an ISP, you should contact the ISP to have the appropriate subdomains of its *in-addr.arpa* zone delegated to you. Each ISP uses a different process for setting up *in-addr.arpa* delegation. Your ISP's web page is a good place to research that process. If you can't find the information there, try looking up the SOA record for the *in-addr.arpa* zone that corresponds to your ISP's network. For example, if your network is part of UUNET's 153.35/16 network, you

---

* For information on IPv6 reverse-mapping, see Chapter 11.

could look up the SOA record of *35.153.in-addr.arpa* to find the email address of the technical contact for the zone.

If your network is registered directly with one of the regional Internet registries, contact it to get your *in-addr.arpa* zone registered. Each network registry makes information on its delegation process available on its web site.

Now that you've registered your zones, you'd better take some time to get your house in order. You have some nameservers to set up, and in the next chapter, we'll show you how.

CHAPTER 4
Setting Up BIND

*"It seems very pretty," she said when she had finished
it, "but it's rather hard to understand!" (You see she
didn't like to confess, even to herself, that she couldn't
make it out at all.) "Somehow it seems to fill my head
with ideas—only I don't exactly know what they are!"*

If you have been diligently reading each chapter of this book, you're probably anxious to get a nameserver running. This chapter is for you. Let's set up a couple of nameservers. Others of you may have read the table of contents and skipped directly to this chapter. (Shame on you!) If you are one of those people, be aware that we may use concepts from earlier chapters and expect you to understand them already.

There are several factors that influence how you should set up your nameservers. The biggest is what sort of access you have to the Internet: complete access (e.g., you can FTP to *ftp.rs.internic.net*), limited access (restricted by a security firewall), or no access at all. This chapter assumes you have complete access. We'll discuss the other cases in Chapter 11.

In this chapter, we set up two nameservers for a few fictitious zones as an example for you to follow in setting up your own zones. We cover the topics in this chapter in enough detail to get your first two nameservers running. Subsequent chapters fill in the holes and go into greater depth. If you already have your nameservers running, skim through this chapter to familiarize yourself with the terms we use or just to verify that you didn't miss something when you set up your servers.

Our Zone

Our fictitious zone serves a college. Movie University studies all aspects of the film industry and researches novel ways to (legally) distribute films. One of our most promising projects involves research into using IP as a film distribution medium. After visiting our registrar's web site, we have decided on the domain name *movie.edu*. A recent grant has enabled us to connect to the Internet.

Movie U. currently has two Ethernets, and we have plans to add another network or two. The Ethernets have network numbers 192.249.249/24 and 192.253.253/24. A portion of our host table contains the following entries:

```
127.0.0.1       localhost

# These are our main machines

192.249.249.2  shrek.movie.edu shrek
192.249.249.3  toystory.movie.edu toystory toys
192.249.249.4  monsters-inc.movie.edu monsters-inc mi

# These machines are in horror(ible) shape and will be replaced
# soon.

192.253.253.2  misery.movie.edu misery
192.253.253.3  shining.movie.edu shining
192.253.253.4  carrie.movie.edu carrie

# A wormhole is a fictitious phenomenon that instantly transports
# space travelers over long distances and is not known to be
# stable.  The only difference between wormholes and routers is
# that routers don't transport packets as instantly--especially
# ours.

192.249.249.1  wormhole.movie.edu wormhole wh wh249
192.253.253.1  wormhole.movie.edu wormhole wh wh253
```

And the network is pictured in Figure 4-1.

Setting Up Zone Data

Our first step in setting up the Movie U. nameservers is to translate the host table into equivalent DNS zone data. The DNS version of the data has multiple files. One file maps all the hostnames to addresses. Other files map the addresses back to host-names. The name-to-address lookup is sometimes called *forward mapping*, and the address-to-name lookup, *reverse mapping*. Each network has its own file for reverse-mapping data.

As a convention in this book, a file that maps hostnames to addresses is called *db. DOMAIN*. For *movie.edu*, this file is called *db.movie.edu*. The files mapping addresses to hostnames are called *db.ADDR*, where ADDR is the network number without trailing zeros or the specification of a netmask. In our example, the files are called *db.192.249.249* and *db.192.253.253*; there's one for each network. (The *db* is short for database.) We'll refer to the collection of *db.DOMAIN* and *db.ADDR* files as *zone datafiles*. There are a few other zone datafiles: *db.cache* and *db.127.0.0*. These

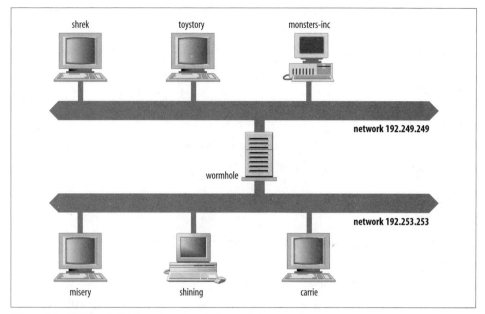

Figure 4-1. The Movie University network

files are overhead. Each nameserver must have them, and they are more or less the same for each server.

To tie all the zone datafiles together, a nameserver needs a configuration file; for BIND versions 8 and 9, it is usually called *named.conf*. The format of the zone data-files is common to all DNS implementations: it's called the *master file format*. The format of the configuration files, on the other hand, is specific to the nameserver implementation—in this case, BIND.

The Zone Datafiles

Most entries in zone datafiles are called *DNS resource records*. DNS lookups are case-insensitive, so you can enter names in your zone datafiles in uppercase, lowercase, or mixed case. We tend to use all lowercase. However, even though lookups are case-insensitive, case is preserved. That way, if you add records for *Titanic.movie.edu* to your zone data, people looking up *titanic.movie.edu* will find the records, but with a capital "T" in the domain name.

Resource records must start in the first column of a line. The resource records in the example files in this book do start in the first column, but they may look indented because of the way the book is formatted. In the DNS RFCs, the examples present the resource records in a certain order. Most people have chosen to follow that order, as we have here, but the order is not a requirement. The order of resource records in the zone datafiles is as follows:

SOA record
> Indicates *authority* for this zone

NS record
> Lists a *nameserver* for this zone

Other records
> Data about hosts in this zone

Of the other records, this chapter covers:

A
> Name-to-address mapping

PTR
> Address-to-name mapping

CNAME
> Canonical name (for aliases)

Those of you who have some experience with the master file format will no doubt look at our data and say to yourselves, "It would have been shorter to specify it this other way…." We're not using abbreviations or shortcuts in our zone data, at least not initially, so that you'll understand the full syntax of each resource record. Once you understand the long version, we'll go back and "tighten up" the files.

Comments

The zone datafiles are easier to read if they contain comments and blank lines. Comments start with a semicolon and finish at the end of the line. As you might guess, the nameserver ignores comments and blank lines.

Setting the Zone's Default TTL

Before we start writing our zone datafile, we have to find out what version of BIND we're running. (To find out your version, use *named –v*. If yours doesn't recognize *–v*, it's probably older than BIND 8.2.) The version makes a difference because how you set the default time to live for a zone changed in BIND 8.2. Prior to BIND 8.2, the last field in the SOA record set the default TTL for a zone. But just before BIND 8.2 came out, RFC 2308 was published, which changed the meaning of the final field in the SOA record to the *negative caching TTL*. This is how long a remote nameserver can cache *negative responses* about the zone, answers that say that a particular domain name or the type of data sought for a particular domain name doesn't exist.

So how do you set a default TTL for a zone in BIND 8.2 and later? With the new $TTL control statement. $TTL specifies the time to live for all records in the file that follow the statement (but precede any other $TTL statements) and don't have an explicit TTL.

The nameserver supplies this TTL in query responses, allowing other servers to cache the data for the TTL interval. If your data doesn't change much, you might consider using a default TTL of several days. One week is about the longest value that makes sense. You can use a value as short as a few minutes, but we don't recommend a TTL of zero because of the amount of DNS traffic it causes.

Since we're running a new version of BIND, we need to set a default TTL for our zones with a $TTL statement. Three hours seems about right to us, so we start our zone datafiles with:

```
$TTL 3h
```

If you're running a nameserver older than BIND 8.2, don't try adding a $TTL statement: the nameserver won't understand it and will treat it as a syntax error.

SOA Records

The next entry in each of these files is the start of authority resource record. The SOA record indicates that this nameserver is the best source of information for the data within this zone. Our nameserver is *authoritative* for the zone *movie.edu* because of the SOA record. An SOA record is required in each *db.DOMAIN* and *db.ADDR* file. There can be one, and only one, SOA record in a zone datafile.

We added the following SOA record to the *db.movie.edu* file:

```
movie.edu. IN SOA toystory.movie.edu. al.movie.edu. (
                        1       ; Serial
                        3h      ; Refresh after 3 hours
                        1h      ; Retry after 1 hour
                        1w      ; Expire after 1 week
                        1h )    ; Negative caching TTL of 1 hour
```

The name *movie.edu.* must start in the first column of the file. Make sure the name ends with a trailing dot, as ours does here, or you'll be surprised at the result! (We'll explain later in this chapter.)

The IN stands for Internet. This is one *class* of data; other classes exist, but none of them is currently in widespread use. Our examples use only the IN class. The class field is optional. If the class is omitted, the nameserver determines the class from the statement in the configuration file that instructs it to read this file. We'll cover this later in the chapter, too.

The first name after SOA (*toystory.movie.edu.*) is the name of the primary nameserver for the *movie.edu* zone. The second name (*al.movie.edu.*) is the mail address of the person in charge of the zone if you replace the first "." with an "@". Often you'll see *root*, *postmaster*, or *hostmaster* as the email address. Nameservers won't use this address; it's meant for human consumption. If you have a problem with a zone, you can send a message to the listed email address. BIND provides another resource record type, RP (responsible person), for this purpose, too. The RP record is discussed in Chapter 7.

The parentheses allow the SOA record to span more than one line. Most of the fields within the parentheses of the SOA record are for use by slave nameservers and are discussed when we introduce slave nameservers later in this chapter. For now, assume these are reasonable values.

We add similar SOA records to the beginning of the *db.192.249.249* and *db.192.253.253* files. In these files, we change the first name in the SOA record from *movie.edu.* to the name of the appropriate *in-addr.arpa* zone: *249.249.192.in-addr.arpa.* and *253.253.192.in-addr.arpa.*, respectively.

NS Records

The next entries we add to each file are NS (nameserver) resource records. We add one NS record for each nameserver authoritative for our zone. Here are the NS records from the *db.movie.edu* file:

```
movie.edu.   IN NS  toystory.movie.edu.
movie.edu.   IN NS  wormhole.movie.edu.
```

These records indicate that there are two nameservers for the zone *movie.edu*. The nameservers are on the hosts *toystory.movie.edu* and *wormhole.movie.edu*. Multihomed hosts, such as *wormhole.movie.edu*, are excellent choices for nameservers because they are *well-connected*; in other words, they are directly accessible by hosts on more than one network and are closely monitored. We'll cover more on where to place your nameservers in Chapter 8.

As with the SOA record, we add NS records to the *db.192.249.249* and *db.192.253.253* files, too.

Address and Alias Records

Next, we create the name-to-address mappings. We add the following resource records to the *db.movie.edu* file:

```
;
; Host addresses
;
localhost.movie.edu.       IN A    127.0.0.1
shrek.movie.edu.           IN A    192.249.249.2
toystory.movie.edu.        IN A    192.249.249.3
monsters-inc.movie.edu.    IN A    192.249.249.4
misery.movie.edu.          IN A    192.253.253.2
shining.movie.edu.         IN A    192.253.253.3
carrie.movie.edu.          IN A    192.253.253.4
;
; Multi-homed hosts
;
```

```
wormhole.movie.edu.       IN A    192.249.249.1
wormhole.movie.edu.       IN A    192.253.253.1
;
; Aliases
;
toys.movie.edu.           IN CNAME toystory.movie.edu.
mi.movie.edu.             IN CNAME monsters-inc.movie.edu.
wh.movie.edu.             IN CNAME wormhole.movie.edu.
wh249.movie.edu.          IN A    192.249.249.1
wh253.movie.edu.          IN A    192.253.253.1
```

The first two blocks are probably not a surprise. The A stands for address, and each resource record maps a name to an address. *wormhole.movie.edu* is a multihomed host. It has two addresses associated with its name and therefore two address records. Unlike host-table lookups, a DNS lookup can return more than one address for a name; a lookup of *wormhole.movie.edu* returns two. If the requestor and nameserver are on the same network, some nameservers place the "closest" address first in the response for better performance. This feature is called *address sorting* and is covered in Chapter 10. If address sorting does not apply, the addresses are *rotated* between queries so subsequent responses list them in a different order. This feature is called *round robin* and is also covered in more detail in Chapter 10.

The third block has the host-table aliases. For the first three aliases, we created CNAME (canonical name) resource records. However, we created address records for the other two aliases (more on this in a moment). A CNAME record maps an alias to its canonical name. The nameserver handles CNAME records differently from the way aliases are handled in the host table. When a nameserver looks up a name and finds a CNAME record, it replaces the name with the canonical name and looks up the new name. For example, when the nameserver looks up *wh.movie.edu*, it finds a CNAME record pointing to *wormhole.movie.edu*. It then looks up *wormhole.movie.edu* and returns both addresses.

There is one thing to remember about aliases like *toys.movie.edu*: they should never appear on the right side of a resource record. Stated differently, you should always use the canonical name (e.g., *toystory.movie.edu*) in the data portion of the resource record. Notice that the NS records we just created use the canonical name.

The final two entries solve a special problem. Suppose you have a multihomed host, such as *wormhole.movie.edu*, and you want to check one of the interfaces. One common troubleshooting technique is to *ping* the interface to verify that it is responding. If you *ping* the name *wormhole.movie.edu*, the nameserver returns both addresses for the name. *ping* uses the first address in the list. But which address is first?

With the host table, we choose the address we want by using either *wh249.movie.edu* or *wh253.movie.edu*; each name refers to *one* of the host's addresses. To provide an equivalent capability with DNS, we don't make *wh249.movie.edu* and *wh253.movie.edu* into aliases (CNAME records). That results in both addresses for *wormhole.movie.edu* being returned when the alias is looked up. Instead, we use address records. Now, to check the operation of the 192.253.253.1 interface on *wormhole.movie.edu*, we *ping wh253. movie.edu* because it refers to only one address. The same applies to *wh249.movie.edu*.

To state this as a general rule: if a host is multihomed (has more than one network interface), create an address (A) record for each alias unique to one address and then create a CNAME record for each alias common to all the addresses.

Now, don't tell your users about names like *wh249.movie.edu* and *wh253.movie.edu*. Those names are meant for system-administration purposes only. If users learn to use names such as *wh249.movie.edu*, they'll be confused when the name doesn't work for them in such places as *.rhosts* files. That's because these places need the name that results from looking up the address: the canonical name, *wormhole.movie.edu*.

Since we use A (address) records for the *wh249.movie.edu* and *wh253.movie.edu* aliases, you might ask, "Is it okay to use address records instead of CNAME records in *all* cases?" Well, using address records instead of CNAME records doesn't cause problems with most applications because most applications care only about finding IP addresses. There is one application—*sendmail*—whose behavior changes, though. *sendmail* usually replaces aliases in mail headers with their canonical names; this *canonicalization* happens only if the names in the mail header have CNAME data associated with them. If you don't use CNAME records for aliases, your *sendmail* will have to understand all the possible aliases your host might be known by, which will require extra *sendmail* configuration on your part.

In addition to the problem with *sendmail*, users might be confused when they try to figure out the canonical name to enter in their *.rhosts* file. Looking up a name that has CNAME data leads them to the canonical name, whereas address data won't. In this case, users should instead be looking up the IP address to get the canonical name, as *rlogind* does, but users like these never seem to be on systems we administer.

PTR Records

Next, we create the address-to-name mappings. The file *db.192.249.249* maps addresses to hostnames for the 192.249.249/24 network. The DNS resource records used for this mapping are PTR (pointer) records. There is one record for each network interface on this network. (Recall that addresses are looked up as names in DNS. The address is reversed and *in-addr.arpa* is appended.)

Here are the PTR records we added for network 192.249.249/24:

```
1.249.249.192.in-addr.arpa.   IN PTR wormhole.movie.edu.
2.249.249.192.in-addr.arpa.   IN PTR shrek.movie.edu.
3.249.249.192.in-addr.arpa.   IN PTR toystory.movie.edu.
4.249.249.192.in-addr.arpa.   IN PTR monsters-inc.movie.edu.
```

There are a couple of things you should notice about this data. First, addresses should point to only a single name: the canonical name. Thus, 192.249.249.1 maps to *wormhole.movie.edu*, not to *wh249.movie.edu*. You can create two PTR records, one for *wormhole.movie.edu* and one for *wh249.movie.edu*, but most software is not prepared to see more than one name for an address. Second, even though *wormhole.movie.edu* has two addresses, you see only one of them here. That's because this file shows only addresses on the network 192.249.249/24, and *wormhole.movie.edu* has only one address on that network.

We created similar data for the 192.253.253/24 network.

The Completed Zone Datafiles

Now that we've explained the various resource records in the zone datafiles, we'll show you what they look like with all the data in one place. Again, the actual order of these resource records does not matter.

Here are the contents of the file *db.movie.edu*:

```
$TTL 3h
movie.edu. IN SOA toystory.movie.edu. al.movie.edu. (
                        1       ; Serial
                        3h      ; Refresh after 3 hours
                        1h      ; Retry after 1 hour
                        1w      ; Expire after 1 week
                        1h )    ; Negative caching TTL of 1 hour

;
; Name servers
;
movie.edu.   IN NS   toystory.movie.edu.
movie.edu.   IN NS   wormhole.movie.edu.


;
; Addresses for the canonical names
;
localhost.movie.edu.        IN A    127.0.0.1
shrek.movie.edu.            IN A    192.249.249.2
toystory.movie.edu.        IN A    192.249.249.3
monsters-inc.movie.edu.    IN A    192.249.249.4
misery.movie.edu.          IN A    192.253.253.2
shining.movie.edu.         IN A    192.253.253.3
carrie.movie.edu.          IN A    192.253.253.4
wormhole.movie.edu.        IN A    192.249.249.1
wormhole.movie.edu.        IN A    192.253.253.1


;
; Aliases
;
toys.movie.edu.        IN CNAME toystory.movie.edu.
mi.movie.edu.          IN CNAME monsters-inc.movie.edu.
wh.movie.edu.          IN CNAME wormhole.movie.edu.


;
; Interface specific names
;
```

```
wh249.movie.edu.        IN A    192.249.249.1
wh253.movie.edu.        IN A    192.253.253.1
```

Here are the contents of the file *db.192.249.249*:

```
$TTL 3h
249.249.192.in-addr.arpa. IN SOA toystory.movie.edu. al.movie.edu.(
                        1       ; Serial
                        3h      ; Refresh after 3 hours
                        1h      ; Retry after 1 hour
                        1w      ; Expire after 1 week
                        1h )    ; Negative caching TTL of 1 hour


;
; Name servers
;
249.249.192.in-addr.arpa.   IN NS  toystory.movie.edu.
249.249.192.in-addr.arpa.   IN NS  wormhole.movie.edu.


;
; Addresses point to canonical name
;
1.249.249.192.in-addr.arpa.  IN PTR wormhole.movie.edu.
2.249.249.192.in-addr.arpa.  IN PTR shrek.movie.edu.
3.249.249.192.in-addr.arpa.  IN PTR toystory.movie.edu.
4.249.249.192.in-addr.arpa.  IN PTR monsters-inc.movie.edu.
```

And here are the contents of the file *db.192.253.253*:

```
$TTL 3h
253.253.192.in-addr.arpa. IN SOA toystory.movie.edu. al.movie.edu. (
                        1       ; Serial
                        3h      ; Refresh after 3 hours
                        1h      ; Retry after 1 hour
                        1w      ; Expire after 1 week
                        1h )    ; Negative caching TTL of 1 hour
;
; Name servers
;
253.253.192.in-addr.arpa.   IN NS  toystory.movie.edu.
253.253.192.in-addr.arpa.   IN NS  wormhole.movie.edu.


;
; Addresses point to canonical name
;
1.253.253.192.in-addr.arpa.  IN PTR wormhole.movie.edu.
2.253.253.192.in-addr.arpa.  IN PTR misery.movie.edu.
3.253.253.192.in-addr.arpa.  IN PTR shining.movie.edu.
4.253.253.192.in-addr.arpa.  IN PTR carrie.movie.edu.
```

The Loopback Address

A nameserver needs one additional *db.ADDR* file to cover the *loopback* network: the special address that hosts use to direct traffic to themselves. This network is (almost) always 127.0.0/24, and the host number is (almost) always 127.0.0.1. Therefore, the name of this file is *db.127.0.0*. No surprise here; it looks like the other *db.ADDR* files.

Here are the contents of the file *db.127.0.0*:

```
$TTL 3h
0.0.127.in-addr.arpa. IN SOA toystory.movie.edu. al.movie.edu. (
                        1       ; Serial
                        3h      ; Refresh after 3 hours
                        1h      ; Retry after 1 hour
                        1w      ; Expire after 1 week
                        1h )    ; Negative caching TTL of 1 hour

0.0.127.in-addr.arpa.   IN NS   toystory.movie.edu.
0.0.127.in-addr.arpa.   IN NS   wormhole.movie.edu.

1.0.0.127.in-addr.arpa.  IN PTR localhost.
```

Why do nameservers need this silly little file? Think about it for a second. No one was given responsibility for network 127.0.0/24, yet systems use it for a loopback address. Since no one has direct responsibility, everyone who uses it is responsible for it individually. You could omit this file, and your nameserver would operate. However, a lookup of 127.0.0.1 might fail because the root nameserver contacted wasn't itself configured to map 127.0.0.1 to a name. To prevent surprises, you should provide the mapping yourself.

The Root Hints Data

Besides your local information, the nameserver also needs to know where the nameservers for the root zone are. You must retrieve this information from the Internet host *ftp.rs.internic.net* (198.41.0.6). Use anonymous FTP to retrieve the file *db.cache* from the *domain* subdirectory.

```
;       This file holds the information on root name servers needed to
;       initialize cache of Internet domain name servers
;       (e.g. reference this file in the "cache  .  <file>"
;       configuration file of BIND domain name servers).
;
;       This file is made available by InterNIC
;       under anonymous FTP as
;           file                /domain/db.cache
;           on server           FTP.INTERNIC.NET
;       -OR-                    RS.INTERNIC.NET
;
;       last update:    Jan 29, 2004
;       related version of root zone:   2004012900
;
;
; formerly NS.INTERNIC.NET
;
```

```
.                              3600000  IN  NS    A.ROOT-SERVERS.NET.
A.ROOT-SERVERS.NET.            3600000      A     198.41.0.4
;
; formerly NS1.ISI.EDU
;
.                              3600000      NS    B.ROOT-SERVERS.NET.
B.ROOT-SERVERS.NET.            3600000      A     192.228.79.201
;
; formerly C.PSI.NET
;
.                              3600000      NS    C.ROOT-SERVERS.NET.
C.ROOT-SERVERS.NET.            3600000      A     192.33.4.12
;
; formerly TERP.UMD.EDU
;
.                              3600000      NS    D.ROOT-SERVERS.NET.
D.ROOT-SERVERS.NET.            3600000      A     128.8.10.90
;
; formerly NS.NASA.GOV
;
.                              3600000      NS    E.ROOT-SERVERS.NET.
E.ROOT-SERVERS.NET.            3600000      A     192.203.230.10
;
; formerly NS.ISC.ORG
;
.                              3600000      NS    F.ROOT-SERVERS.NET.
F.ROOT-SERVERS.NET.            3600000      A     192.5.5.241
;
; formerly NS.NIC.DDN.MIL
;
.                              3600000      NS    G.ROOT-SERVERS.NET.
G.ROOT-SERVERS.NET.            3600000      A     192.112.36.4
;
; formerly AOS.ARL.ARMY.MIL
;
.                              3600000      NS    H.ROOT-SERVERS.NET.
H.ROOT-SERVERS.NET.            3600000      A     128.63.2.53
;
; formerly NIC.NORDU.NET
;
.                              3600000      NS    I.ROOT-SERVERS.NET.
I.ROOT-SERVERS.NET.            3600000      A     192.36.148.17
;
; operated by VeriSign, Inc.
;
.                              3600000      NS    J.ROOT-SERVERS.NET.
J.ROOT-SERVERS.NET.            3600000      A     192.58.128.30
;
; operated by RIPE NCC
;
.                              3600000      NS    K.ROOT-SERVERS.NET.
K.ROOT-SERVERS.NET.            3600000      A     193.0.14.129
;
```

```
; operated by ICANN
;
.                               3600000     NS    L.ROOT-SERVERS.NET.
L.ROOT-SERVERS.NET.             3600000     A     198.32.64.12
;
; operated by WIDE
;
.                               3600000     NS    M.ROOT-SERVERS.NET.
M.ROOT-SERVERS.NET.             3600000     A     202.12.27.33
; End of File
```

The domain name "." refers to the root zone. Since the root zone's nameservers change over time, don't assume this list is current. Download a new version of *db.cache*.

How is this file kept up to date? As the network administrator, that's your responsibility. Some old versions of BIND did update this file periodically. That feature was disabled, though; apparently, it didn't work as well as the authors had hoped. Sometimes the changed *db.cache* file is mailed to the *bind-users* or *namedroppers* mailing list, which we introduced in Chapter 3. If you are on one of these lists, you are likely to hear about changes.

Can you put data other than root nameserver data in this file? You can, but it won't be used. Originally, the nameserver installed this data in its cache. However, the use of the file has changed (subtly) though the name "cache file" stuck. The nameserver stores the data it reads from this file in a special place in memory as the *root hints*. It does not discard the hints if their TTLs drop to zero, as it would with cached data. The nameserver uses the hint data to query the root nameservers for the current list of root nameservers, which it caches. When the cached list of root nameservers times out, the nameserver again uses the hints to get a new list.

Why does the nameserver bother querying a nameserver in the root hints file—probably itself a root nameserver—for a list of root nameservers when it already has a list? Because that nameserver almost certainly knows the *current* list of root nameservers, while the file may be out of date.

What are the 3600000s for? That's an explicit time to live for the records in the file. In older versions of this file, this number was 99999999. Since the contents of this file were originally cached, the nameserver needed to know how long to keep those records active. 99999999 seconds was just a very long time; the root nameserver data was to be kept in cache for as long as the server ran. Since the nameserver now stores this data in a special place and doesn't discard it if it times out, the TTL is unnecessary. But it's not harmful to have the 3600000s, and it makes for interesting BIND folklore when you pass responsibility to the next nameserver administrator.

Setting Up a BIND Configuration File

Now that we've created the zone datafiles, a nameserver must be instructed to read each file. For BIND, the mechanism for pointing the server to its zone datafiles is the configuration file. Up to this point, we've been discussing files whose data and format are described in the DNS specifications. The syntax of the configuration file, though, is specific to BIND and is not defined in the DNS RFCs.

The BIND configuration file syntax changed significantly between version 4 and version 8. Mercifully, it didn't change at all between BIND 8 and BIND 9. BIND 4 came out so long ago that we are not going to cover its configuration here. You'll have to find an earlier edition of our book (you should be able to find a cheap used copy) if you are still running one of those ancient beasts. In the configuration file, you can use any of three styles of comments: C-style, C++-style, or shell-style:

```
/* This is a C-style comment */
// This is a C++-style comment
# This is a shell-style comment
```

Usually, configuration files contain a line indicating the directory in which the zone datafiles are located. The nameserver changes its directory to this location before reading the zone datafiles. This allows the filenames to be specified relative to the current directory instead of as full pathnames. Here's how a directory line looks in an *options* statement:

```
options {
        directory "/var/named";
        // Place additional options here.
};
```

Only one *options* statement is allowed in the configuration file, so any additional options mentioned later in this book must be added along with the *directory* option.

On a primary server, the configuration file contains one *zone* statement for each zone datafile to be read. Each line starts with the keyword *zone* followed by the zone's domain name and the class (*in* stands for Internet). The type *master* indicates this server is a primary nameserver. The last line contains the filename:

```
zone "movie.edu" in {
        type master;
        file "db.movie.edu";
};
```

Earlier in this chapter, we mentioned that if you omit the class field from a resource record, the nameserver determines the right class to use from the configuration file. The *in* in the *zone* statement sets that class to the Internet class. The *in* is the default class for a *zone* statement, so you can leave out the field entirely for Internet class zones.

Here is the configuration file line to read the root hints file:

```
zone "." in {
        type hint;
        file "db.cache";
};
```

As mentioned earlier, this file is not for general cache data. It contains only the root nameserver *hints*.[*]

By default, BIND expects the configuration file to be named */etc/named.conf*. The zone datafiles for our example are in the directory */var/named*. Which directory you use doesn't really matter. Just avoid putting the directory in the root filesystem if the root filesystem is short on space, and make sure that the filesystem the directory is in is mounted before the nameserver starts. Here is the complete */etc/named.conf* file:

```
// BIND configuration file

options {
        directory "/var/named";
        // Place additional options here.
};

zone "movie.edu" in {
        type master;
        file "db.movie.edu";
};

zone "249.249.192.in-addr.arpa" in {
        type master;
        file "db.192.249.249";
};

zone "253.253.192.in-addr.arpa" in {
        type master;
        file "db.192.253.253";
};

zone "0.0.127.in-addr.arpa" in {
        type master;
        file "db.127.0.0";
};

zone "." in {
        type hint;
        file "db.cache";

};
```

[*] Actually, BIND 9 has a built-in *hints* zone, so you don't need to include a *zone* statement for the hints zone in *named.conf*. However, including one doesn't hurt, and it gives us the willies not to see one in the configuration file, so we include one anyway.

Abbreviations

At this point, we have created all the files necessary for a primary nameserver. Let's go back and revisit the zone datafiles; there are shortcuts we didn't use. Unless you see and understand the long form first, though, the short form can look very cryptic. Now that you know the long form and have seen the BIND configuration file, we'll show you the shortcuts.

Appending Domain Names

The second field of a *zone* statement specifies a domain name. This domain name is the key to the most useful shortcut. This domain name is the *origin* of all the data in the zone datafile. The origin is appended to all names in the zone datafile that don't end in a dot and will be different for each zone datafile because each file describes a different zone.

Since the origin is appended to names, instead of entering *shrek.movie.edu*'s address in *db.movie.edu* like this:

```
shrek.movie.edu.   IN A    192.249.249.2
```

we could have entered it like this:

```
shrek   IN A    192.249.249.2
```

In the *db.192.24.249* file, we entered this:

```
2.249.249.192.in-addr.arpa.  IN PTR shrek.movie.edu.
```

Because *249.249.192.in-addr.arpa* is the origin, we could have entered:

```
2  IN PTR shrek.movie.edu.
```

Remember our earlier warning not to omit the trailing dot when using the fully qualified domain names? Suppose you forget the trailing dot. An entry like:

```
shrek.movie.edu   IN A    192.249.249.2
```

turns into an entry for *shrek.movie.edu.movie.edu*, not what you intended at all.

The @ Notation

If a domain name is the *same* as the origin, the name can be specified as "@". This is most often seen in the SOA record in the zone datafiles. The SOA records could have been entered this way:

```
@ IN SOA toystory.movie.edu. al.movie.edu. (
                        1       ; Serial
                        3h      ; Refresh after 3 hours
                        1h      ; Retry after 1 hour
                        1w      ; Expire after 1 week
                        1h )    ; Negative caching TTL of 1 hour
```

Repeat Last Name

If a resource record name (that starts in the first column) is a space or tab, then the name from the last resource record is used. You use this if there are multiple resource records for a name. Here's an example in which there are two address records for one name:

```
wormhole   IN A    192.249.249.1
           IN A    192.253.253.1
```

In the second address record, the name *wormhole* is implied. You can use this shortcut even if the resource records are of different types.

The Shortened Zone Datafiles

Now that we have shown you the abbreviations, we'll repeat the zone datafiles, making use of these shortcuts.

Here are the contents of the file *db.movie.edu*:

```
$TTL 3h
;
; Origin added to names not ending
; in a dot: movie.edu
;

@ IN SOA toystory.movie.edu. al.movie.edu. (
                        1       ; Serial
                        3h      ; Refresh after 3 hours
                        1h      ; Retry after 1 hour
                        1w      ; Expire after 1 week
                        1h )    ; Negative caching TTL of 1 hour


;
; Name servers (The name '@' is implied)
;
           IN NS   toystory.movie.edu.
           IN NS   wormhole.movie.edu.


;
; Addresses for the canonical names
;
localhost      IN A     127.0.0.1
shrek          IN A     192.249.249.2
toystory       IN A     192.249.249.3
monsters-inc   IN A     192.249.249.4
misery         IN A     192.253.253.2
shining        IN A     192.253.253.3
carrie         IN A     192.253.253.4

wormhole       IN A     192.249.249.1
               IN A     192.253.253.1
```

```
;
; Aliases
;
toys        IN CNAME toystory
mi          IN CNAME monsters-inc
wh          IN CNAME wormhole


;
; Interface specific names
;
wh249       IN A     192.249.249.1
wh253       IN A     192.253.253.1
```

Here are the contents of the file *db.192.249.249*:

```
$TTL 3h
;
; Origin added to names not ending
; in a dot: 249.249.192.in-addr.arpa
;

@ IN SOA toystory.movie.edu. al.movie.edu. (
                        1         ; Serial
                        3h        ; Refresh after 3 hours
                        1h        ; Retry after 1 hour
                        1w        ; Expire after 1 week
                        1h )      ; Negative caching TTL of 1 hour


;
; Name servers (The name '@' is implied)
;
    IN NS  toystory.movie.edu.
    IN NS  wormhole.movie.edu.


;
; Addresses point to canonical names
;
1  IN PTR wormhole.movie.edu.
2  IN PTR shrek.movie.edu.
3  IN PTR toystory.movie.edu.
4  IN PTR monsters-inc.movie.edu.
```

Here are the contents of the file *db.192.253.253*:

```
$TTL 3h
;
; Origin added to names not ending
; in a dot: 253.253.192.in-addr.arpa
;

@ IN SOA toystory.movie.edu. al.movie.edu. (
                        1         ; Serial
                        3h        ; Refresh after 3 hours
                        1h        ; Retry after 1 hour
                        1w        ; Expire after 1 week
                        1h )      ; Negative caching TTL of 1 hour
```

```
;
; Name servers (The name '@' is implied)
;
    IN NS  toystory.movie.edu.
    IN NS  wormhole.movie.edu.


;
; Addresses point to canonical names
;
1  IN PTR wormhole.movie.edu.
2  IN PTR misery.movie.edu.
3  IN PTR shining.movie.edu.
4  IN PTR carrie.movie.edu.
```

Here are the contents of the file *db.127.0.0*:

```
$TTL 3h
@ IN SOA toystory.movie.edu. al.movie.edu. (
                    1         ; Serial
                    3h        ; Refresh after 3 hours
                    1h        ; Retry after 1 hour
                    1w        ; Expire after 1 week
                    1h )      ; Negative caching TTL of 1 hour

    IN NS  toystory.movie.edu.
    IN NS  wormhole.movie.edu.

1  IN PTR localhost.
```

While looking at the new *db.movie.edu* file, you may notice that we could have removed *movie.edu* from the hostnames of the SOA and NS records like this:

```
@ IN SOA toystory al (
                    1         ; Serial
                    3h        ; Refresh after 3 hours
                    1h        ; Retry after 1 hour
                    1w        ; Expire after 1 week
                    1h )      ; Negative caching TTL of 1 day

    IN NS  toystory
    IN NS  wormhole
```

You can't do this in the other zone datafiles because their origins are different. In *db.movie.edu*, we leave these names as fully qualified domain names so that the NS and SOA records are exactly the same for all the zone datafiles.

Hostname Checking

If your nameserver is BIND 4.9.4 or newer (and most are), you have to pay extra attention to how your hosts are named. Starting with Version 4.9.4, BIND checks hostnames for conformance to RFC 952. If a hostname does not conform, BIND considers it a syntax error.

Before you panic, you need to know that this checking applies only to names that are considered hostnames. Remember, resource records have a name field and a data field—for example:

```
<name>      <class>  <type>  <data>
toystory    IN       A       192.249.249.3
```

Hostnames are in the name fields of A (address) and MX (covered in Chapter 5) records. Hostnames are also in the data fields of SOA and NS records. CNAMEs do not have to conform to the host-naming rules because they can point to names that are not hostnames.

Let's look at the host-naming rules. Hostnames are allowed to contain alphabetic characters and numeric characters in each label. The following are valid hostnames:

```
ID4            IN A 192.249.249.10
postmanring2x  IN A 192.249.249.11
```

A hyphen is allowed if it is in the middle of a label:

```
fx-gateway     IN A 192.249.249.12
```

 Underscores are not allowed in hostnames.

Names that are not hostnames can consist of any printable ASCII character.

If a resource record data field calls for a *mail address* (as in SOA records), the first label, since it is not a hostname, can contain any printable character, but the rest of the labels must follow the hostname syntax just described. For example, a mail address has the following syntax:

```
<ASCII-characters>.<hostname-characters>
```

For example, if your mail address is *key_grip@movie.edu*, you can use it in an SOA record even with the underscore. Remember, in a mail address you replace the "@" with a ".", like this:

```
movie.edu. IN SOA toystory.movie.edu. key_grip.movie.edu. (
                    1        ; Serial
                    3h       ; Refresh after 3 hours
                    1h       ; Retry after 1 hour
                    1w       ; Expire after 1 week
                    1h )     ; Negative caching TTL of 1 hour
```

This extra level of checking can cause dramatic problems at sites that upgrade from a liberal version of BIND to a conservative one, especially sites that have standardized on hostnames containing an underscore. If you need to postpone changing names until later (you will still change them, right?), this feature can be toned down to produce warning messages instead of errors or to simply ignore that the names are illegal. The following configuration file statement turns the errors into warning messages:

```
options {
        check-names master warn;
};
```

The warning messages are logged with *syslog*, which we'll explain shortly. The following configuration file statement ignores the errors entirely:

```
options {
        check-names master ignore;
};
```

If the nonconforming names came from a zone that you back up (and have no control over), then add a similar statement that specifies *slave* instead of *master*:

```
options {
        check-names slave ignore;
};
```

And if the names come in responses to queries and not in zone transfers, specify *response* instead:

```
options {
        check-names response ignore;
};
```

Here are BIND's defaults:

```
options {
        check-names master fail;
        check-names slave warn;
        check-names response ignore;
};
```

Name checking can also be specified on a per-zone basis, in which case it overrides name-checking behavior specified in the *options* statement for this particular zone:

```
zone "movie.edu" in {
        type master;
        file "db.movie.edu";
        check-names fail;
};
```

> The *options* line contains three fields (*check-names master fail*), whereas the zone line check contains only two fields (*check-names fail*). This is because the *zone* line already specifies the context (the zone named in the *zone* statement).

Tools

Wouldn't it be handy to have a tool to translate your host table into master file format? There is such a beast, written in Perl: *h2n*, a host-table-to-master-file converter.

You can use *h2n* to create your zone datafiles the first time and then maintain your data manually. Or you can use *h2n* over and over again. As you've seen, the host table's format is much simpler to understand and modify correctly than the master file format. So, you could maintain */etc/hosts* and rerun *h2n* to update your zone datafiles after each modification.

If you plan to use *h2n*, you might as well start with it, because it uses */etc/hosts*—not your hand-crafted zone data—to generate the new zone datafiles. We could have saved ourselves a lot of work by generating the sample zone datafiles in this chapter with the following:

```
% h2n -d movie.edu -s toystory -s shrek \
-n 192.249.249 -n 192.253.253 \
-u al.movie.edu
```

(To generate a BIND 4 configuration file, add *–v 4* to the option list.)

The *–d* and *–n* options specify the domain name of your forward-mapping zone and your network numbers. You'll notice that the names of the zone datafiles are derived from these options. The *–s* options list the authoritative nameservers for the zones to use in the NS records. The *–u* (user) is the email address in the SOA record. We cover *h2n* in more detail in Chapter 7, after we've covered how DNS affects email.

BIND 9 Tools

If you are running BIND 9, you have handy new tools to help maintain your nameserver files: *named-checkconf* and *named-checkzone*. These tools reside in */usr/local/sbin*. As you might guess, *named-checkconf* checks the configuration file for syntax errors, and *named-checkzone* checks a zone file for syntax errors.

First, run *named-checkconf*, which checks */etc/named.conf* by default:

```
% named-checkconf
```

If you have an error, *named-checkconf* displays an error message, such as this one:

```
/etc/named.conf:14: zone '.': missing 'file' entry
```

If there are no errors, you won't see any output.

Next, run *named-checkzone* for each of your zone files:

```
% named-checkzone movie.edu db.movie
zone movie.edu/IN: loaded serial 4
OK
```

As you can see, everything is okay, and the current serial number is 4.

Running a Primary Nameserver

Now that you've created your zone datafiles, you are ready to start a couple of nameservers. You'll need to set up two nameservers: a primary nameserver and a

---

slave nameserver. Before you start a nameserver, though, make sure that the *syslog* daemon is running. If the nameserver reads the configuration file and zone datafiles and sees an error, it logs a message to the *syslog* daemon. If the error is bad enough, the nameserver exits. If you've run the BIND 9 *named-checkconf* and *named-checkzone*, you should be all set, but check for syslog errors anyway, just to be safe.

Starting Up the Nameserver

At this point, we assume the machine you are running on has the BIND nameserver and the support tool *nslookup* installed. Check the *named* manual page to find the directory the nameserver executable is in and verify that the executable is on your system. On BSD systems, the nameserver started its life in */etc*, but may have migrated to */usr/sbin*. Other places to look for *named* are */usr/etc/in.named* and */usr/sbin/in.named*. The following descriptions assume that the nameserver is in */usr/sbin*.

To start up the nameserver, you must become root. The nameserver listens for queries on a reserved port, so it requires root privileges. The first time you run it, start the nameserver from the command line to test that it is operating correctly. Later, we'll show you how to start up the nameserver automatically when your system boots.

The following command starts the nameserver. We ran it on the host *toystory.movie.edu*.

```
# /usr/sbin/named
```

This command assumes that your configuration file is called */etc/named.conf*. You can put your configuration file elsewhere, but then you have to tell the nameserver where it is using the *–c* command-line option:

```
# /usr/sbin/named -c conf-file
```

Check for Syslog Errors

The first thing to do after starting your nameserver is to check the *syslog* file for error messages. If you are not familiar with *syslog*, look at the *syslog.conf* manual page for a description of the *syslog* configuration file or the *syslogd* manual page for a description of the *syslog* daemon. The nameserver logs messages with facility *daemon* under the name *named*. You might be able to find where *syslog* messages are logged by looking for the *daemon* facility in */etc/syslog.conf*:

```
% grep daemon /etc/syslog.conf
*.err;kern.debug;daemon,auth.notice /var/adm/messages
```

On this host, the nameserver *syslog* messages are logged to */var/adm/messages*, and *syslog* saves only those that are at severity LOG_NOTICE or higher. Some useful messages are sent at severity LOG_INFO; you might like to see some of these. You can decide if you want to change the log level after reading Chapter 7, where we cover *syslog* messages in more detail.

When the nameserver starts, it logs a *starting* message:

```
% grep named /var/adm/messages
Jan 10 20:48:32 toystory named[3221]: starting BIND 9.3.2 -c named.boot
```

The *starting* message is not an error message, but there might be other messages with it that are error messages. The most common errors are syntax errors in the zone datafiles or configuration file. For example, if you forget the resource record type in an address record:

```
shrek  IN  192.249.249.2
```

you'll see the following *syslog* error message:

```
Jan 10 20:48:32 toystory named[3221]: db.movie.edu:24: Unknown RR type:
              192.249.249.2
```

Or, if you misspell the word "zone" in */etc/named.conf*:

```
zne "movie.edu" in {
```

you'll see the following *syslog* error message:

```
Mar 22 20:14:21 toystory named[1477]: /etc/named.conf:10:
              unknown option 'zne'
```

If BIND finds a name that doesn't conform to RFC 952, you'll see the following *syslog* error message:

```
Jul 24 20:56:26 toystory named[1496]: db.movie.edu:33: a_b.movie.edu: bad
              owner name
```

If you have a syntax error, check the line numbers mentioned in the *syslog* error message to see if you can figure out the problem. You've seen what the zone datafiles are supposed to look like; that should be enough to figure out most simple syntax errors. Otherwise, you'll have to go through Appendix A to see the gory syntactic details of all the resource records. If you can fix the syntax error, do so and then reload the nameserver with *ndc* (BIND 8) or *rndc* (BIND 9), the name daemon controller:

```
# ndc reload
```

so that it rereads the zone datafiles.* You'll see more information in Chapter 7 on using *ndc* and *rndc* to control the nameserver.

Testing Your Setup with nslookup

If you have set up your local zones correctly, and your connection to the Internet is up, you should be able to look up a local and a remote domain name. We'll now step

---

* For a BIND 9 nameserver, you'd need to use *rndc*, but we haven't shown you how to configure that yet. Skip ahead to Chapter 7 if you'd like to see how that's done. *ndc* works without much configuration, though.

---

you through the lookups with *nslookup*. There is a whole chapter in this book on *nslookup* (Chapter 12), but we cover it in enough detail here to do basic nameserver testing.

Set the local domain name

Before running *nslookup*, you need to set the host's local domain name. With this configured, you can look up a name like *carrie* instead of having to spell out *carrie.movie.edu*; the system adds the domain name *movie.edu* for you.

There are two ways to set the local domain name: *hostname(1)* or */etc/resolv.conf*. Some people say that, in practice, more sites set the local domain in */etc/resolv.conf*. You can use either. Throughout the book, we assume the local domain name comes from *hostname(1)*.

Create a file called */etc/resolv.conf* with the following line starting in the first column (substitute your local domain name for *movie.edu*):

```
domain movie.edu
```

Or, set *hostname(1)* to a domain name. On the host *toystory*, we set *hostname(1)* to *toystory.movie.edu*. Don't add a trailing dot to the name.

Look up a local domain name

nslookup can be used to look up any type of resource record, and it can be directed to query any nameserver. By default, it looks up A (address) records using the first nameserver specified in *resolv.conf*. (Without a nameserver specified in *resolv.conf*, the resolver defaults to querying the local nameserver.) To look up a host's address with *nslookup*, run *nslookup* with the host's domain name as the only argument. A lookup of a local domain name should return almost instantly.

We ran *nslookup* to look up *carrie* :

```
% nslookup carrie
Server: toystory.movie.edu
Address: 192.249.249.3

Name:    carrie.movie.edu
Address: 192.253.253.4
```

If looking up a local domain name works, your local nameserver has been configured properly for your forward-mapping zone. If the lookup fails, you'll see something like this:

```
*** toystory.movie.edu can't find carrie: Non-existent domain
```

This means that *carrie* is not in your zone data. Check your zone datafile; you didn't set your local domain name in *hostname(1)*, or some nameserver error occurred (though you should have caught the error when you checked the *syslog* messages).

Look up a local address

When *nslookup* is given an address to look up, it knows to make a PTR query instead of an address query. We ran *nslookup* to look up *carrie*'s address:

```
% nslookup 192.253.253.4
Server: toystory.movie.edu
Address: 192.249.249.3

Name:    carrie.movie.edu
Address: 192.253.253.4
```

If looking up an address works, your local nameserver has been configured properly for your *in-addr.arpa* (reverse-mapping) zones. If the lookup fails, you'll see the same error messages as when you looked up a domain name.

Look up a remote domain name

The next step is to try using the local nameserver to look up a remote domain name, such as *ftp.rs.internic.net* or another system you know of on the Internet. This command may not return as quickly as the last one. If *nslookup* fails to get a response from your nameserver, it waits a little longer than a minute before giving up:

```
% nslookup ftp.rs.internic.net
Server: toystory.movie.edu
Address: 192.249.249.3

Name:     ftp.rs.internic.net
Addresses: 198.41.0.6
```

If this works, your nameserver knows where the root nameservers are and how to contact them to find information about domain names in zones other than your own. If it fails, either you forgot to configure the root hints file (and a *syslog* message will show up), or the network is broken somewhere and you can't reach the nameservers for the remote zone. Try a different remote domain name.

If these first lookups succeeded, congratulations! You have a primary nameserver up and running. At this point, you are ready to start configuring your slave nameserver.

One more test

While you're testing, though, run one more test. Check whether your parent zone's nameservers have properly delegated to your domain. If your parent required you to have your two nameservers running before delegating your zones, skip ahead to the next section.

This test takes two steps. First, you'll need to find the IP address of one of your parent's nameservers. Next, you'll query your parent's nameserver to check the NS records (the delegation information) for one of your zones.

Here's step one: find the IP address of your parent's nameservers. To do this, ask your nameserver to find the NS records for your parent's zone. You will use *nslookup* again, but you will add *–type=ns* to tell *nslookup* to query for nameserver records.

Here's an example. Suppose we are setting up the *hp.com* zone, and we need to find out the nameservers for *com*, our parent.

```
% nslookup -type=ns com.
Server: toystory.movie.edu
Address: 192.249.249.3#53

Non-authoritative answer:
com       nameserver = i.gtld-servers.net
com       nameserver = j.gtld-servers.net
com       nameserver = k.gtld-servers.net
com       nameserver = l.gtld-servers.net
com       nameserver = m.gtld-servers.net
com       nameserver = a.gtld-servers.net
com       nameserver = b.gtld-servers.net
com       nameserver = c.gtld-servers.net
com       nameserver = d.gtld-servers.net
com       nameserver = e.gtld-servers.net
com       nameserver = f.gtld-servers.net
com       nameserver = g.gtld-servers.net
com       nameserver = h.gtld-servers.net

a.gtld-servers.net      internet address = 192.5.6.30
a.gtld-servers.net      AAAA IPv6 address = 2001:503:a83e::2:30
b.gtld-servers.net      internet address = 192.33.14.30
b.gtld-servers.net      AAAA IPv6 address = 2001:503:231d::2:30
c.gtld-servers.net      internet address = 192.26.92.30
d.gtld-servers.net      internet address = 192.31.80.30
e.gtld-servers.net      internet address = 192.12.94.30
f.gtld-servers.net      internet address = 192.35.51.30
g.gtld-servers.net      internet address = 192.42.93.30
h.gtld-servers.net      internet address = 192.54.112.30
i.gtld-servers.net      internet address = 192.43.172.30
j.gtld-servers.net      internet address = 192.48.79.30
k.gtld-servers.net      internet address = 192.52.178.30
l.gtld-servers.net      internet address = 192.41.162.30
m.gtld-servers.net      internet address = 192.55.83.30
```

Next, you need to query one of your parent's nameservers for the NS records for your zone. Again, you'll use *nslookup* with *–type=ns*, but this time you'll also add *–norecurse* to tell *nslookup* not to ask the nameserver to recursively look up the data for you. Also, you need to query your parent's nameserver directly, instead of sending the query to your own nameserver. (Your nameserver has NS records for your zone, but that's not what you need to check.) To query your parent's nameserver instead of your own, add the name of one of your parent's nameservers to the end of the *nslookup* statement. Here's an example where we queried the *com* nameserver *b.gtld-servers.net* for the NS records for *hp.com*:

```
% nslookup -type=ns -norecurse hp.com. b.gtld-servers.net.
Server:  b.gtld-servers.net
Address: 192.33.14.30#53

Non-authoritative answer:
hp.com  nameserver = am1.hp.com
hp.com  nameserver = am3.hp.com
hp.com  nameserver = ap1.hp.com
hp.com  nameserver = eu1.hp.com
hp.com  nameserver = eu2.hp.com
hp.com  nameserver = eu3.hp.com

am1.hp.com      internet address = 15.227.128.
am3.hp.com      internet address = 15.243.160.
ap1.hp.com      internet address = 15.211.128.
eu1.hp.com      internet address = 16.14.64.50
eu2.hp.com      internet address = 16.6.64.50
eu3.hp.com      internet address = 16.8.64.50
```

Everything has been set up correctly for *hp.com*, as you might expect.

If your nameserver successfully looked up *ftp.rs.internic.net*, and it looked up the servers for your parent's domain, your server is set up correctly, and you can contact the rest of the Internet. If your parent zone's nameserver does not contain NS records for your zone, your zone is not registered with your parent nameservers. That's not a problem, at first, because systems within your zones can look up the domain names of other systems both within and outside of your zones. You'll be able to access the Web and FTP to local and remote systems. But not being registered will shortly become a problem. Hosts outside your zones can't look up domain names in your zones; you may not be able to send email to friends in remote zones, and you certainly won't get any responses. To fix this problem, contact the administrators of your parent zones, and have them check the delegation of your zones.

Editing the Startup Files

Once you have confirmed that your nameserver is running properly and can be used from here on, you'll need to configure it to start automatically and set *hostname(1)* to a domain name in your system's startup files (or set up your domain name in */etc/resolv.conf*). Check to see if your vendor has already set up the nameserver to start on bootup. You may have to remove comment characters from the startup lines, or the startup file may test to see if */etc/named.conf* exists. To look for automatic startup lines, use:

```
% grep named /etc/*rc*
```

or, if you have System V–style *rc* files, use:

```
% grep named /etc/rc.d/*/S*
```

If you don't find anything, add lines like the following to the appropriate startup file somewhere after your network interfaces are initialized by *ifconfig*:

```
if test -x /usr/sbin/named -a -f /etc/named.conf
then
        echo "Starting named"
        /usr/sbin/named
fi
```

You may want to wait to start the nameserver until after the default route is installed or your routing daemon (*routed* or *gated*) is started, depending on whether these services need the nameserver or can get by with */etc/hosts*.

Find which startup file initializes the hostname and change *hostname(1)* to a domain name. For example, we changed:

```
hostname toystory
```

to:

```
hostname toystory.movie.edu
```

Running a Slave Nameserver

You need to set up another nameserver for robustness. You can (and probably will eventually) set up more than two authoritative nameservers for your zones. Two nameservers are the minimum; if you have only one nameserver, and it goes down, no one can look up domain names. A second nameserver splits the load with the first server or handles the whole load if the first server is down. You *could* set up another primary nameserver, but we don't recommend it. Instead, set up a slave nameserver. You can always change a slave nameserver to a primary nameserver if you decide to expend the extra effort it takes to run multiple primary nameservers.

How does a server know if it's the primary or a slave for a zone? The *named.conf* file tells the nameserver whether it is the primary or a slave on a per-zone basis. The NS records don't tell us which server is the primary for a zone and which servers are slaves; they only say who the servers are. (Globally, DNS doesn't care; as far as the actual name resolution goes, slave servers are as good as primary servers.)

What's the difference between a primary nameserver and a slave nameserver? The crucial difference is where the server gets its data. A primary nameserver reads its data from zone datafiles. A slave nameserver loads its data over the network from another nameserver. This process is called a *zone transfer*.

A slave nameserver is not limited to loading zones from a primary nameserver; it can also load from another slave server.

The big advantage of slave nameservers is that you maintain only one set of zone datafiles for a zone, the ones on the primary nameserver. You don't have to worry about synchronizing the files among nameservers; the slaves do that for you. The caveat is that a slave does not resynchronize instantly: it polls to see if its zone data is current. The polling interval is one of those numbers in the SOA record that we haven't explained yet. (BIND versions 8 and 9 support mechanisms to speed up the distribution of zone data, which we'll describe later.)

A slave nameserver doesn't need to retrieve all its zone data over the network; the overhead files, *db.cache* and *db.127.0.0*, are the same as on a primary, so keep a local copy on the slave. That means that a slave nameserver is a primary for *0.0.127.in-addr.arpa*. Well, you *could* make it a slave for *0.0.127.in-addr.arpa*, but that zone's data never changes; it may as well be a primary.

Setup

To set up your slave nameserver, create a directory for the zone datafiles on the slave nameserver host (e.g., */var/named*) and copy over the files */etc/named.conf*, *db.cache*, and *db.127.0.0*:

```
# rcp /etc/named.conf host:/etc
# rcp db.cache db.127.0.0 host:db-file-directory
```

You must modify */etc/named.conf* on the slave nameserver. Change every occurrence of *master* to *slave* except for the *0.0.127.in-addr.arpa* zone, and add a *masters* line with the IP address of the primary nameserver, which will act as the slave's master for these zones.

If the original configuration file line was:

```
zone "movie.edu" in {
        type master;
        file "db.movie.edu";
};
```

then the modified line looks like this:

```
zone "movie.edu" in {
        type slave;
        file "bak.movie.edu";
        masters { 192.249.249.3; };
};
```

This tells the nameserver that it is a slave for the zone *movie.edu* and that it should track the version of this zone kept on the nameserver at 192.249.249.3. The slave nameserver keeps a backup copy of this zone in the local file *bak.movie.edu*.

For Movie U., we set up our slave nameserver on *wormhole.movie.edu*. Recall that the configuration file on *toystory.movie.edu* (the primary) looks like this:

```
options {
        directory "/var/named";
};
```

```
zone "movie.edu" in {
        type master;
        file "db.movie.edu";
};

zone "249.249.192.in-addr.arpa" in {
        type master;
        file "db.192.249.249";
};

zone "253.253.192.in-addr.arpa" in {
        type master;
        file "db.192.253.253";
};

zone "0.0.127.in-addr.arpa" in {
        type master;
        file "db.127.0.0";
};

zone "." in {
        type hint;
        file "db.cache";

};
```

We copy *letc/named.conf*, *db.cache*, and *db.127.0.0* to *wormhole.movie.edu*, and edit the configuration file as previously described. The configuration file on *wormhole.movie.edu* now looks like this:

```
options {
        directory "/var/named";
};

zone "movie.edu" in {
        type slave;
        file "bak.movie.edu";
        masters { 192.249.249.3; };
};

zone "249.249.192.in-addr.arpa" in {
        type slave;
        file "bak.192.249.249";
        masters { 192.249.249.3; };
};

zone "253.253.192.in-addr.arpa" in {
        type slave;
        file "bak.192.253.253";
        masters { 192.249.249.3; };
};
```

```
zone "0.0.127.in-addr.arpa" in {
        type master;
        file "db.127.0.0";
};

zone "." in {
        type hint;
        file "db.cache";
};
```

This causes the nameserver on *wormhole.movie.edu* to load *movie.edu, 249.249.192. in-addr.arpa*, and *253.253.192.in-addr.arpa* over the network from the nameserver at 192.249.249.3 (*toystory.movie.edu*). It also saves a backup copy of these files in */var/ named*. You may find it handy to isolate the backup zone datafiles in a subdirectory. We name them with a unique prefix such as *bak*, since, on rare occasions, we may have to delete all the backup files manually. It's also helpful to be able to tell at a glance that they're backup zone datafiles so that we're not tempted to edit them. We'll cover more on backup files later.

Now start up the slave nameserver. Check for error messages in the *syslog* file as you did for the primary server. As on the primary, the command to start up a nameserver is:

```
# /usr/sbin/named
```

One extra check to make on the slave that you didn't have to make on the primary is to see that the nameserver created the backup files. Shortly after we started our slave nameserver on *wormhole.movie.edu*, we saw *bak.movie.edu, bak.192.249.249*, and *bak.192.253.253* appear in the */var/named* directory. This means the slave has successfully loaded these zones from the primary and saved a backup copy.

To complete setting up your slave nameserver, try looking up the same domain names you looked up after you started the primary server. This time, you must run *nslookup* on the host running the slave nameserver so that the slave server is queried. If your slave is working fine, add the proper lines to your system startup files so that the slave nameserver is started when your system boots up, and *hostname(1)* is set to a domain name.

Backup Files

Slave nameservers are not *required* to save a backup copy of the zone data. If there is a backup copy, the slave server reads it on startup and later checks with the master server to see if the master server has a newer copy instead of loading a new copy of the zone immediately. If the master server has a newer copy, the slave pulls it over and saves it in the backup file.

Why save a backup copy? Suppose the master nameserver is down when the slave starts up. The slave will be unable to transfer the zone and therefore won't function as a nameserver for that zone until the master server is up. With a backup copy, the slave has zone data, although it might be slightly out of date. Since the slave does not have to rely on the master server always being up, it's a more robust setup.

To run without a backup copy, remove the *file* line in the configuration file. However, we recommend configuring all your slave nameservers to save backup copies. There is very little extra cost to saving a backup zone datafile, but it will cost you dearly if you get caught without a backup file when you need it most.

SOA Values

Remember this SOA record?

```
movie.edu. IN SOA toystory.movie.edu. al.movie.edu. (
                    1        ; Serial
                    3h       ; Refresh after 3 hours
                    1h       ; Retry after 1 hour
                    1w       ; Expire after 1 week
                    1h )     ; Negative caching TTL of 1 hour
```

We never explained what the values between the parentheses were for.

The serial number applies to all the data within the zone. We chose to start our serial number at 1, a logical place to start. But many people find it more useful to use the date in the serial number instead, like 2005012301. This format is YYYYMMDDNN, where YYYY is the year, MM is the month, DD is the day, and NN is a count of how many times the zone data was modified that day. These fields won't work in any other order because no other order gives a value that always increases as the date changes. This is critical: whatever format you choose, it's important that the serial number always increase when you update your zone data.

When a slave nameserver contacts a master server for zone data, it first asks for the serial number on the data. If the slave's serial number for the zone is lower than the master server's, the slave's zone data is out of date. In this case, the slave pulls a new copy of the zone. If a slave starts up, and there is no backup file to read, it will always load the zone. As you might guess, when you modify the zone datafiles on the primary, you must increment the serial number. Updating your zone datafiles is covered in Chapter 7.

The next four fields specify various time intervals, in seconds by default:

refresh

> The refresh interval tells a slave for the zone how often to check that the data for this zone is up to date. To give you an idea of the system load this feature causes, a slave makes one SOA query per zone per refresh interval. The value we chose, three hours, is reasonably aggressive. Most users will tolerate a delay of half a working day for things like zone data to propagate when they are waiting for their new workstation to become operational. If you provide one-day service for your site, you could consider raising this value to eight hours. If your zone data

doesn't change very often or if all of your slaves are spread over long distances (as the root nameservers are), consider a value that is even longer, say 24 hours.

retry

If the slave fails to reach the master nameserver after the refresh interval (the host could be down), it starts trying to connect every *retry* seconds. Normally, the retry interval is shorter than the refresh interval, but it doesn't have to be.

expire

If the slave fails to contact the master nameserver for *expire* seconds, the slave expires the zone. Expiring the zone means that the slave stops giving out answers about the zone because the zone data is too old to be useful. Essentially, this field says that at some point, the data is so old that giving out no data is better than giving out stale data. Expire times on the order of a week are common— longer (up to a month) if you frequently have problems reaching your updating source. The expiration time should always be much larger than the retry and refresh intervals; if the expire time is smaller than the refresh interval, your slaves will expire the zone before trying to load new data.

negative caching TTL

TTL stands for *time to live*. This value applies to all negative responses from the nameservers authoritative for the zone.

 On versions of BIND before BIND 8.2, the last field in the SOA record is *both* the default time to live and the negative caching time to live for the zone.

Those of you who have read earlier versions of this book may have noticed the change in the format we used for the SOA record's numeric fields. Once upon a time, BIND understood units of seconds only for the four fields we just described. (Consequently, a whole generation of administrators know that there are 608,400 seconds in a week.) Now, with all but the oldest BIND nameservers (4.8.3), you can specify units besides seconds for these fields and as arguments to the TTL control statement, as was shown earlier in this chapter. For example, you can specify a three-hour refresh interval with *3h*, *180m*, or even *2h60m*. You can also use *d* for days and *w* for weeks.

The right values for your SOA record depend on the needs of your site. In general, longer times cause less load on your nameservers and can delay the propagation of changes; shorter times increase the load on your nameservers and speed up the propagation of changes. The values we use in this book should work well for most sites. RFC 1537 recommends the following values for top-level nameservers:

```
Refresh       24 hours
Retry          2 hours
Expire        30 days
Default TTL    4 days
```

There is one implementation feature you should be aware of. Older versions (pre-4.8.3) of BIND slaves stop answering queries during a zone load. As a result, BIND was modified to spread out the zone loads, reducing the periods of unavailability. So, even if you set a low refresh interval, your slaves may not check as often as you request. BIND attempts a certain number of zone loads and then waits 15 minutes before trying another batch.

Now that we've told you all about how slave nameservers poll to keep their data up to date, BIND 8 and 9 change how zone data propagates! The polling feature is still there, but BIND 8 and 9 add a notification when zone data changes. If both your primary server and your slaves run BIND 8 or 9, the primary notifies the slave that a zone has changed within 15 minutes of loading a new copy of that zone. The notification causes the slave server to shorten the refresh interval and attempt to load the zone immediately. We'll discuss this more in Chapter 10.

Multiple Master Servers

Are there other ways to make your slave nameserver's configuration more robust? Yes—you can specify up to 10 IP addresses of master servers. In the configuration file, add them after the first IP address and separate them with semicolons:

```
zone "movie.edu" in {
        type slave;
        file "bak.movie.edu";
        masters { 192.249.249.3; 192.249.249.4; };
};
```

Or with BIND 9.3 and later, you can give a name to the list of IP addresses for your masters, and then refer to the name. This saves repeating the IP addresses for each zone. Here's an example:

```
masters "movie-masters" {
        192.249.249.3; 192.249.249.4;
};

zone "movie.edu" in {
        type slave;
        file "bak.movie.edu";
        masters { movie-masters; };
};
```

The slave queries the master server at each IP address in the order listed until it gets a response. Through BIND 8.1.2, the slave always transferred the zone from the first master nameserver to respond if that master had a higher serial number. The slave tried successive master servers only if the previous master didn't respond. From BIND 8.2 on, however, the slave actually queries all the master nameservers listed and transfers the zone from the one with the highest serial number. If multiple master servers tie for the highest serial number, the slave transfers the zone from the first of those masters in the list.

The original intent of this feature was to allow you to list all the IP addresses of the host running the primary nameserver for the zone if that host were multihomed. However, since there is no check to determine whether the contacted server is a primary or a slave, you can list the IP addresses of hosts running slave servers for the zone if that makes sense for your setup. That way, if the first master server is down or unreachable, your slave can transfer the zone from another master nameserver.

Adding More Zones

Now that you have your nameservers running, you might want to support more zones. What needs to be done? Nothing special, really. All you need to do is add more *zone* statements to your configuration file. You can even make your primary a slave server for some zones and make your slave server primary for some zones. (You may have already noticed that your slave server is primary for *0.0.127.in-addr.arpa*.)

At this point, it's useful to repeat something we said earlier in this book. Calling a *given* nameserver a primary nameserver or a slave nameserver is a little silly. Nameservers can be—and usually are—authoritative for more than one zone. A nameserver can be a primary for one zone and a slave for another. Most nameservers, however, are either primary for most of the zones they load or slave for most of the zones they load. So if we call a particular nameserver a primary or a slave, we mean that it's the primary or a slave for *most* of the zones it loads.

What's Next?

In this chapter, we showed you how to create nameserver zone datafiles by translating */etc/hosts* to equivalent nameserver data, and how to set up a primary and a slave nameserver. There is more work to do to complete setting up your local zones, however: you need to modify your zone data for email and configure the other hosts in your zone to use your nameservers. You may also need to start up more nameservers. These topics are covered in the next few chapters.

## CHAPTER 5

DNS and Electronic Mail

And here Alice began to get rather sleepy, and went on saying to herself, in a dreamy sort of way, "Do cats eat bats? Do cats eat bats?" and sometimes "Do bats eat cats?" for, you see, as she couldn't answer either question, it didn't much matter which way she put it.

I'll bet you're drowsy too, after that looong chapter. Thankfully, this next chapter discusses a topic that will probably be very interesting to you system administrators and postmasters: how DNS affects electronic mail. And even if it isn't interesting to you, at least it's shorter than the last chapter.

One of the advantages of the Domain Name System over host tables is its support of advanced mail routing. When mailers had only the *HOSTS.TXT* file (and its derivative, */etc/hosts*) to work with, the best they could do was to attempt delivery to a host's IP address. If that failed, they could either defer delivery of the message and try again later or bounce the message back to the sender.

DNS offers a mechanism for specifying backup hosts for mail delivery. The mechanism also allows hosts to assume mail-handling responsibilities for other hosts. This lets diskless hosts that don't run mailers, for example, have mail addressed to them processed by their servers.

DNS, unlike host tables, allows arbitrary names to represent electronic mail destinations. You can—and most organizations on the Internet do—use the domain name of your main forward-mapping zone as an email destination. Or you can add domain names to your zone that are purely email destinations and don't represent any particular host. A single logical email destination may also represent several mail servers. With host tables, mail destinations were hosts, period.

Together, these features give administrators much more flexibility in configuring electronic mail on their networks.

MX Records

DNS uses a single type of resource record to implement enhanced mail routing: the MX record. Originally, the MX record's function was split between two records—the MD (mail destination) and MF (mail forwarder) records. MD specified the final destination to which a message addressed to a given domain name should be delivered. MF specified a host that would forward mail on to the eventual destination, should that destination be unreachable.

Early experience with DNS on the ARPAnet showed that separating the functions didn't work very well. A mailer needed both the MD and MF records attached to a domain name (if both existed) to decide where to send mail; one or the other alone wouldn't do. But an explicit lookup of one type or another (either MD or MF) would cause a nameserver to cache just that record type. So mailers either had to do two queries, one for MD and one for MF records, or they could no longer accept cached answers. This meant that the overhead of running mail was higher than that of running other services, which was eventually deemed unacceptable.

The two records were integrated into a single record type, MX, to solve this problem. Now a mailer just needed all the MX records for a particular domain name destination to make a mail-routing decision. Using cached MX records was fine, as long as the TTLs matched.

MX records specify a *mail exchanger* for a domain name: a host that will *either* process *or* forward mail for the domain name (through a firewall, for example). *Processing* the mail means either delivering it to the individual to whom it's addressed or gatewaying it to another mail transport, such as X.400. *Forwarding* means sending it to its final destination or to another mail exchanger closer to the destination via SMTP, the Internet's Simple Mail Transfer Protocol. Sometimes forwarding the mail involves queuing it for some amount of time, too.

In order to prevent mail-routing loops, the MX record has an extra parameter, besides the domain name of the mail exchanger: a *preference value*. The preference value is an unsigned 16-bit number (between 0 and 65535) that indicates the mail exchanger's priority. For example, the MX record:

```
peets.mpk.ca.us.    IN    MX    10 relay.hp.com.
```

specifies that *relay.hp.com* is a mail exchanger for *peets.mpk.ca.us* at preference value 10.

Taken together, the preference values of a destination's mail exchangers determine the order in which a mailer should use them. The preference value itself isn't important, only its relationship to the values of other mail exchangers: is it higher or lower than the values of this destination's other mail exchangers? Unless there are other records involved, this:

```
plange.puntacana.dr.  IN  MX  1 listo.puntacana.dr.
plange.puntacana.dr.  IN  MX  2 hep.puntacana.dr.
```

does exactly the same thing as:

```
plange.puntacana.dr.  IN  MX  50  listo.puntacana.dr.
plange.puntacana.dr.  IN  MX  100 hep.puntacana.dr.
```

Mailers should attempt delivery to the mail exchangers with the *lowest* preference values first. This may seem a little counterintuitive: the *most* preferred mail exchanger has the *lowest* preference value. But since the preference value is an unsigned quantity, this lets you specify a "best" mail exchanger at preference value 0.

If delivery to the most-preferred mail exchanger(s) fails, mailers should attempt delivery to less-preferred mail exchangers (those with *higher* preference values), in order of increasing preference value. That is, mailers should try more-preferred mail exchangers before they try less preferred mail exchangers. More than one mail exchanger may share the same preference value, too. This gives the mailer its choice of which to send to first. However, the mailer must try all the mail exchangers at a given preference value before proceeding to the next higher value.

For example, the MX records for *oreilly.com* might be:

```
oreilly.com.    IN   MX    0 ora.oreilly.com.
oreilly.com.    IN   MX   10 ruby.oreilly.com.
oreilly.com.    IN   MX   10 opal.oreilly.com.
```

Interpreted together, these MX records instruct mailers to attempt delivery to *oreilly.com* by sending in the following order:

1. *ora.oreilly.com*
2. Either *ruby.oreilly.com* or *opal.oreilly.com*
3. The remaining preference 10 mail exchanger (the one not used in Step 2)

Of course, once the mailer successfully delivers the mail to one of *oreilly.com*'s mail exchangers, it can stop. A mailer successfully delivering *oreilly.com* mail to *ora.oreilly.com* doesn't need to try *ruby.oreilly.com* or *opal.oreilly.com*.

Note that *oreilly.com* isn't a particular host; it's the domain name of O'Reilly's main forward-mapping zone. O'Reilly uses the domain name as the email destination for everyone who works there. It's much easier for correspondents to remember the single email destination *oreilly.com* than to remember which host—*ruby.oreilly.com*? *amber.oreilly.com*?—each employee has an email account on.

This requires, of course, that the administrator of the mailer on *ora.oreilly.com* maintain a file of aliases for all email users at O'Reilly, forwarding their mail to the hosts on which they read it, or run a server that offers users remote access to their mail stores, such as a POP or IMAP server. What if a destination doesn't have any MX records, but has one or more A records? Will a mailer simply not deliver mail to that destination? Actually, you can compile recent versions of *sendmail* to do just that. Most vendors, however, have compiled their *sendmail*s to be more forgiving: if no MX records exist but one or more A records do, they'll at least attempt delivery to the address. Version 8 of *sendmail,* compiled "out of the box," will try the address of a mail destination without MX records. Check your vendor's documentation if you're not sure whether your mail server will send mail to destinations with only address records.

Even though nearly all mailers will deliver mail to a destination with just an address record and no MX records, it's still a good idea to have at least one MX record for each legitimate mail destination. Most mailers, including *sendmail,* will always look up the MX records for a destination first when there is mail to deliver. If the destination doesn't have any MX records, a nameserver—usually one of your authoritative nameservers—still must answer that query, and then *sendmail* will go on to look up A records. That takes extra time, slows mail delivery, and adds a little load to your zone's authoritative nameservers. If you simply add an MX record for each mail destination pointing to a domain name that maps to the same address an address lookup would return, the mailer sends only one query, and the mailer's local nameserver caches the MX record for future use.

Finally, note that you can't use an IP address instead of a domain name to identify the mail exchanger (in the field after the preference value). While some mailers are forgiving enough to accept an IP address, some aren't, so your mail will fail unpredictably.

Movie.edu's Mail Server

At *movie.edu,* we have a single mail hub, *postmanrings2x.movie.edu. postmanrings2x* runs both an SMTP server and an IMAP server with accounts for all *movie.edu* mail users.

To direct mail servers on the Internet to send mail addressed to users at *movie.edu* to our mail hub, we add this MX record to *db.movie.edu*:

```
movie.edu.  IN  MX  10 postmanrings2x.movie.edu.
```

Our ISP runs a backup SMTP server as a service for customers; it will queue mail for us if our mail server or our connection to the Internet fails. To tell Internet mailers to try it if *postmanrings2x* isn't available, we add another MX record to the *movie.edu* zone datafile:

```
movie.edu.  IN  MX  20 smtp.isp.net.
```

What's a Mail Exchanger, Again?

The idea of a mail exchanger is probably new to many of you, so let's go over it in a little more detail. A simple analogy should help here: imagine that a mail exchanger is an airport, and instead of setting up MX records to instruct mailers where to send messages, you're advising your in-laws as to which airport to fly into when they come to visit you.

Say you live in Los Gatos, California. The closest airport for your in-laws to fly into is San Jose, the second closest is San Francisco, and the third Oakland. (We'll ignore other factors such as price of the ticket, Bay Area traffic, etc.) Don't see the parallel? Then picture it like this:

```
los-gatos.ca.us.    IN    MX    1 san-jose.ca.us.
los-gatos.ca.us.    IN    MX    2 san-francisco.ca.us.
los-gatos.ca.us.    IN    MX    3 oakland.ca.us.
```

The MX list is just an ordered list of destinations that tells mailers (your in-laws) where to send messages (fly) if they want to reach a given email destination (your house). The preference value tells them how desirable it is to use that destination; think of it as a logical "distance" from the eventual destination (in any units you choose), or simply as a "top 10"–style ranking of the proximity of those mail exchangers to the final destination.

With this list, you're saying, "Try to fly into San Jose, and if you can't get there, try San Francisco and Oakland, in that order." It *also* says that if you reach San Francisco, you should take a commuter flight to San Jose. If you wind up in Oakland, you should try to get a commuter to San Jose or at least to San Francisco.

What makes a good mail exchanger, then? The same qualities that make a good airport:

Size
> You wouldn't want to fly into tiny Reid-Hillview Airport to get to Los Gatos, because the airport's not equipped to handle large planes or many people. (You'd probably be better off landing a big jet on Interstate 280 than at Reid-Hillview.) Likewise, you don't want to use an emaciated, underpowered host as a mail exchanger; it won't be able to handle the load.

Uptime
> You know better than to fly through Denver International Airport in the winter, right? Then you should know better than to use a host that's rarely up or available as a mail exchanger.

Connectivity
> If your relatives are flying in from far away, you've got to make sure they can get a direct flight to at least one of the airports in the list you give them. You can't tell them their only choices are San Jose and Oakland if they're flying in from Helsinki. Similarly, you've got to make sure that at least one of your hosts' mail exchangers is reachable to anyone who might conceivably send you mail.

Management and administration
> How well an airport is managed has a bearing on your safety while flying into or just through the airport and on how easy it is to use. Think of these factors when choosing a mail exchanger. The privacy of your mail, the speed of its delivery

during normal operations, and how well your mail is treated when your hosts go down all hinge on the quality of the administrators who manage your mail exchangers.

Keep this example in mind because we'll refer to it again later.

The MX Algorithm

That's the basic idea behind MX records and mail exchangers, but there are a few more wrinkles you should know about. To avoid routing loops, mailers need to use a slightly more complicated algorithm than what we've described when they determine where to send mail.*

Imagine what would happen if mailers didn't check for routing loops. Let's say you send mail from your workstation to *nuts@oreilly.com*, raving (or raging) about the quality of this book. Unfortunately, *ora.oreilly.com* is down at the moment. No problem! Recall *oreilly.com*'s MX records:

```
oreilly.com.    IN    MX    0  ora.oreilly.com.
oreilly.com.    IN    MX    10 ruby.oreilly.com.
oreilly.com.    IN    MX    10 opal.oreilly.com.
```

Your mailer falls back and sends your message to *ruby.oreilly.com*, which is up. *ruby.oreilly.com*'s mailer then tries to forward the mail on to *ora.reilly.com* but can't because *ora.oreilly.com* is down. Now what? Unless *ruby.oreilly.com* checks the sanity of what she is doing, she'll try to forward the message to *opal.oreilly.com* or maybe even to herself. That's certainly not going to help get the mail delivered. If *ruby.oreilly.com* sends the message to herself, we have a mail-routing loop. If *ruby.oreilly.com* sends the message to *opal.oreilly.com*, *opal.oreilly.com* will either send it back to *ruby.oreilly.com* or send it to herself, and we again have a mail-routing loop.

To prevent this from happening, mailers discard certain MX records before they decide where to send a message. A mailer sorts the list of MX records by preference value and looks in the list for the canonical domain name of the host on which it's running. If the local host appears as a mail exchanger, the mailer discards that MX record and all MX records in which the preference value is equal or higher (that is, equally or less-preferred mail exchangers). That prevents the mailer from sending messages to itself or to mailers "farther" from the eventual destination.

Let's think about this in the context of our airport analogy. This time, imagine you're an airline passenger (a message) trying to get to Greeley, Colorado. You can't get a direct flight to Greeley, but you can fly to either Fort Collins or Denver (the two next-highest mail exchangers). Since Fort Collins is closer to Greeley, you opt to fly to Fort Collins.

* This algorithm is based on RFC 2821, which describes how Internet mail routing works.

Now, once you've arrived in Fort Collins, there's no sense in flying to Denver, away from your destination (a lower-preference mail exchanger). (And flying from Fort Collins to Fort Collins would be silly, too.) So the only acceptable flight to get you to your destination is now a Fort Collins-Greeley flight. You eliminate flights to less-preferred destinations to prevent frequent-flyer looping and wasteful travel time.

One caveat: most mailers will look *only* for their local host's *canonical* domain name in the list of MX records. They don't check for aliases (domain names on the left side of CNAME records). Unless you always use canonical names in your MX records, there's no guarantee that a mailer will be able to find itself in the MX list, and you'll run the risk of having your mail loop.

If you do list a mail exchanger by an alias, and it unwittingly tries to deliver mail to itself, most mailers will detect the loop and bounce the mail with an error. Here's the error message from recent versions of *sendmail*:

```
554 MX list for movie.edu points back to relay.isp.com
554 <root@movie.edu>... Local configuration error
```

This replaces the quainter "I refuse to talk to myself" error older versions of *sendmail* emitted. The moral: in an MX record, always use the mail exchanger's canonical name.

One more caveat: the hosts you list as mail exchangers *must* have address records. A mailer needs to find an address for each mail exchanger you name or else it can't attempt delivery there.

To go back to our *oreilly.com* example, when *ruby.oreilly.com* received the message from your workstation, her mailer would have checked the list of MX records:

```
oreilly.com.    IN   MX   0  ora.oreilly.com.
oreilly.com.    IN   MX   10 ruby.oreilly.com.
oreilly.com.    IN   MX   10 opal.oreilly.com.
```

Finding the local host's domain name in the list at preference value 10, *ruby.oreilly.com*'s mailer discards all the records at preference value 10 or higher (the records in bold):

```
oreilly.com.    IN   MX   0  ora.oreilly.com.
oreilly.com.    IN   MX   10 ruby.oreilly.com.
oreilly.com.    IN   MX   10 opal.oreilly.com.
```

leaving only:

```
oreilly.com.    IN   MX   0  ora.oreilly.com.
```

Since *ora.oreilly.com* is down, *ruby.oreilly.com* defers delivery until later and queues the message.

What happens if a mailer finds *itself* at the highest preference (lowest preference value) and has to discard the whole MX list? Some mailers attempt delivery directly to the destination host's IP address as a last-ditch effort. In most mailers, however, it's an error. It may indicate that DNS thinks the mailer should be processing (not just forwarding) mail for the destination, but the mailer hasn't been configured to know that. Or it may indicate that the administrator has ordered the MX records incorrectly by using the wrong preference values.

Say, for example, the folks who run *acme.com* add an MX record to direct mail addressed to *acme.com* to a mailer at their Internet service provider:

```
acme.com.    IN    MX    10 mail.isp.net.
```

Most mailers need to be configured to identify their aliases and the names of other hosts for which they process mail. Unless the mailer on *mail.isp.net* is configured to recognize email addressed to *acme.com* as local mail, it assumes it's being asked to relay the mail and attempts to forward the mail to a mail exchanger closer to the final destination.* When it looks up the MX records for *acme.com*, it finds itself as the most-preferred mail exchanger and bounces the mail back to the sender with the familiar error:

```
554 MX list for acme.com points back to mail.isp.net
554 <root@acme.com>... Local configuration error
```

Many versions of *sendmail* use class *w* or fileclass *w* as the list of local destinations. Depending on your *sendmail.cf* file, adding an alias can be as easy as adding the line:

```
Cw acme.com
```

to *sendmail.cf*.

You may have noticed that we tend to use multiples of 10 for our preference values. Ten is convenient because it allows you to insert other MX records temporarily at intermediate values without changing the other weights, but otherwise there's nothing magical about it. We could just as easily have used increments of 1 or 100; the effect would have been the same.

DNS and Email Authentication

In addition to using MX records stored in DNS to determine where to send mail, some modern mail servers can now use other data in DNS to authenticate a message's sender. In particular, several recently proposed email authentication mechanisms use resource records to store critical information. While a complete description of any of these proposals is beyond the scope of this book, we'd like to introduce you to the most widely deployed of them, with a particular emphasis on how it uses DNS.

---

* Unless, of course, *mail.isp.net*'s mailer is configured not to relay mail for unknown domains. In this case, it simply rejects the mail.

The Sender Policy Framework

We'll cover SPF, the Sender Policy Framework, both because it's the most widely deployed of these authentication mechanisms and because it's fairly simple to describe. SPF allows a company's postmaster—maybe with the cooperation of his friendly DNS administrator—to specify which mail servers are allowed to send email addressed from the organization's domain names. It's a little like the opposite function of the MX record: an MX record tells a mailer to send mail addressed to a particular domain name *to* particular mail servers, while SPF information tells a mailer which mail servers can send mail addressed *from* a particular domain name.*

Here's a simple example: Say O'Reilly Media's postmaster knows that all legitimate *oreilly.com* email is sent from one of two SMTP servers, *smtp1.oreilly.com* and *smtp2.oreilly.com*. He can advertise this fact in DNS by adding a TXT record to the domain name *oreilly.com* (or by asking whomever administers the *oreilly.com* zone to do it for him). Here's one possible TXT record that accomplishes this:

```
oreilly.com.  IN  TXT  "v=spf1 +a:smtp1.oreilly.com +a:smtp2.oreilly.com -all"
```

The tag *v=spf1* at the beginning of the record-specific data identifies this TXT record as an SPF record. This is needed because TXT records can be used for many purposes, including human-readable comments, and you wouldn't want Internet mail servers trying to interpret your comments as SPF instructions. If SPF takes off, it will eventually receive its own, dedicated record type, SPF, and the tag will become unnecessary.

The next two fields specify that mail addressed from *oreilly.com* can come from any of the IP addresses of the hosts *smtp1.oreilly.com* or *smtp2.oreilly.com*. The leading plus signs are qualifiers, and indicate that email from these hosts' IP addresses should be *allowed*. There are four possible qualifiers:

+   Pass. A mailer that matches is a valid sender.

−   Fail. A mailer that matches is not a valid sender.

~   SoftFail. A mailer that matches probably isn't a valid sender, so the message should be carefully scrutinized.

?   Neutral. Has no effect.

The default is + (pass), so the plus signs could have been omitted. The final field, *−all*, tells mailers to deny (fail) every other sender of *oreilly.com* email.

There are other ways to specify a domain name's valid senders. Since *oreilly.com*'s two MX records list *smtp1.oreilly.com* and *smtp2.oreilly.com*, the postmaster can instead add this shorter TXT record:

```
oreilly.com.  IN  TXT  "v=spf1 +mx -all"
```

---

* In fact, SPF is descended from a proposal called "Reverse MX," by Hadmut Danisch.

Without a colon and a domain name argument, "mechanisms" such as *a* and *mx* use the domain name in the owner field. Just plain *+mx*, then, is the same as *+mx:oreilly.com* in this record.

Here's a list of common mechanisms used in SPF TXT records:

a   Specifies the domain name of a mail server whose address or addresses are allowed to send email from the owner domain name.

mx Specifies a domain name whose mail exchangers are allowed to send email from the owner domain name.

ip4 Specifies the IP(v4) address of a mail server that is allowed to send email from the owner domain name. Can also specify a network in CIDR notation (e.g., 192.168.0.0/24). Note that all four octets of the network *must* be specified.

ip6 Specifies the IPv6 address of a mail server that is allowed to send email from the owner domain name. Can also specify an IPv6 network in RFC 3513 notation.

ptr Requires that a PTR record exist for the sending mail server's address. The PTR record must map the address to a domain name that ends in the domain name in the owner field of the TXT record or the argument specified after the colon. For example, *+ptr:oreilly.com* requires that a sending mail server's address reverse-map to a domain name ending in *oreilly.com*.

SPF records also support a *redirect* modifier, which allows multiple domain names to share a common set of SPF instructions. For example, say the administrator of *oreilly.com* wants the *ca.oreilly.com* and *ma.oreilly.com* domain names to use the same rules he's established for *oreilly.com*. Rather than duplicate *oreilly.com*'s TXT record, he can add these TXT records:

```
ca.oreilly.com.  IN  TXT  "v=spf1 redirect=oreilly.com"
ma.oreilly.com.  IN  TXT  "v=spf1 redirect=oreilly.com"
```

These tell mailers to refer to the SPF records for *oreilly.com* when determining which are valid mailers for *ca.oreilly.com* and *ma.oreilly.com*. Now if the administrator needs to modify his SPF instructions, he must only change one TXT record.

The *include* mechanism is a similar construct, designed to let administrators refer to SPF instructions configured by someone else. For example, if the *oreilly.com* administrator also wants to allow any legitimate senders of *isp.net* email to send *oreilly.com* email, he can amend the *oreilly.com* TXT record to read:

```
oreilly.com.  IN  TXT  "v=spf1 +mx include:isp.net -all"
```

Note that the separator between *include* and its argument is a colon, while the separator between *redirect* and its argument is an equals sign.

A couple of miscellaneous hints: It's a good idea to use *?all* or *~all* in your SPF records in the beginning because it can be surprisingly difficult to enumerate all the valid sources of your domain name's email. You may have remote employees running their own mail servers, mobile workers sending email from PDAs with company email addresses, and many others. You don't want to inadvertently cut them off.

If your SPF records are very long and complex, they may exceed the maximum length of a TXT record's data, 255 bytes. In that case, you can break the record into multiple TXT records, each beginning with the *v=spf1* tag. They'll be concatenated before evaluation.

Two final notes of caution: Remember that, even if you publish SPF information, only mail servers with SPF support will look it up and use it. Right now, that's a very small proportion of the Internet's mailers. (Still, there's no harm in publishing SPF records, so why not?) And be aware that SPF may change, may never become a standard, and may be superseded by other mechanisms.

## CHAPTER 6

Configuring Hosts

They were indeed a queer-looking party that
assembled on the bank—the birds with draggled
feathers, the animals with their fur clinging close to
them, and all dripping wet, cross, and uncomfortable.

Now that you or someone else in your organization has set up nameservers for your zones, you'll want to configure the hosts on your network to use them. That involves configuring those hosts' resolvers, which you can do by telling the resolvers which nameservers to query and which domain names to search. This chapter covers these topics and describes configuring the resolver in many common versions of Unix and in Microsoft's Windows 2000, 2003, and XP (which are basically the same).

The Resolver

We introduced resolvers way back in Chapter 2, but we didn't say much more about them. The resolver, you'll remember, is the client half of the Domain Name System. It's responsible for translating a program's request for host information into a query to a nameserver and for translating the response into an answer for the program.

We haven't done any resolver configuration yet, because the occasion for it hasn't arisen. When we set up our nameservers in Chapter 4, the resolver's default behavior worked just fine for our purposes. But if we'd needed the resolver to do more than or behave differently from the default, we would have had to configure the resolver.

There's one thing we should mention up front: what we'll be describing in the next few sections is the behavior of the vanilla BIND 8.4.6 resolver in the absence of other naming services. Not all resolvers behave quite this way; some vendors still ship resolvers based on earlier versions of the BIND code, and some have implemented special resolver functionality that lets you modify the resolver algorithm. Whenever we think it's important, we'll point out differences between the behavior of the 8.4.6 BIND resolver and that of earlier resolvers, particularly the 4.8.3 and 4.9 resolvers, which many vendors were shipping when we last updated this book. We'll cover various vendors' extensions later in this chapter.

Resolver Configuration

So what exactly does the resolver allow you to configure? Most resolvers let you configure at least three aspects of the resolver's behavior: the local domain name, the search list, and the nameserver(s) that the resolver queries. Many Unix vendors also allow you to configure other resolver behavior through nonstandard extensions to DNS. Sometimes these extensions are necessary to cope with other software, such as Sun's Network Information Service (NIS); sometimes they're simply value added by the vendor.[*]

Almost all resolver configuration is done in the file */etc/resolv.conf* (this might be */usr/etc/resolv.conf* or something similar on your host—check the *resolver* manual page, usually in section 4 or 5, to make sure). There are five main configuration directives you can use in *resolv.conf*: the *domain* directive, the *search* directive, the *nameserver* directive, the *sortlist* directive, and the *options* directive. These directives control the behavior of the resolver. There are other, vendor-specific directives available on some versions of Unix; we'll discuss them at the end of this chapter.

The Local Domain Name

The local domain name is the domain name in which the resolver resides. In most situations, it's the domain name of the zone in which you'd find the host running the resolver. For example, the resolver on the host *toystory.movie.edu* would probably use *movie.edu* as its local domain name.

The resolver uses the local domain name to interpret domain names that aren't fully qualified. For example, when you add an entry such as:

```
relay bernie
```

to your *.rhosts* file, the name *relay* is assumed to be in your local domain. This makes a lot more sense than allowing access to a user called *bernie* on every host on the Internet whose domain name starts with *relay*. Other authorization files such as *hosts.equiv* and *hosts.lpd* work the same way.

Normally, the local domain name is determined from the host's *hostname*; the local domain name is everything after the first "." in the name. If the name doesn't contain a ".", the local domain is assumed to be the root domain. So the *hostname asylum.sf.ca.us* implies a local domain name of *sf.ca.us*, while the *hostname dogbert*

---

[*] NIS used to be called "Yellow Pages" or "YP," but its name was changed to NIS because the British phone company had a copyright on the name Yellow Pages.

implies a root local domain—which probably isn't correct, given that there are very few hosts with single-label domain names.[*]

You can also set the local domain name with the *domain* directive in *resolv.conf*. If you specify the *domain* directive, it overrides deriving the local domain name from the *hostname*.

The *domain* directive has a very simple syntax, but you must get it right because the resolver doesn't report errors. The keyword *domain* starts the line in column one, followed by whitespace (one or more blanks or tabs), then the name of the local domain. The local domain name should be written without a trailing dot, like this:

```
domain colospgs.co.us
```

In older versions of the BIND resolver (those before BIND 4.8.3), trailing spaces *are not allowed* on the line and will cause your local domain to be set to a name ending with one or more spaces, which is almost certainly not what you want. And there's yet another way to set the local domain name—via the LOCALDOMAIN environment variable. LOCALDOMAIN is handy because you can set it on a per-user basis. For example, you might have a big, massively parallel box in your corporate computing center that employees from all over the world can access. Each employee may do most of her work in a different company subdomain. With LOCALDOMAIN, each employee can set her local domain name appropriately in her shell startup file.

Which method should you use—*hostname*, the *domain* directive, or LOCALDOMAIN? We prefer using *hostname* primarily because that's the way Berkeley does it, and it seems "cleaner" in that it requires less explicit configuration. Also, some Berkeley software, particularly software that uses the *ruserok( )* library call to authenticate users, allows short hostnames in files such as *hosts.equiv* only if *hostname* is set to the full domain name.

If you run software that can't tolerate long *hostnames*, though, you can use the *domain* directive. The *hostname* command will continue to return a short name, and the resolver will fill in the domain from *resolv.conf*. You may even find occasion to use LOCALDOMAIN on a host with lots of users.

The Search List

The local domain name, whether derived from *hostname* or *resolv.conf*, also determines the default search list. The search list was designed to make users' lives a little easier by saving them some typing. The idea is to search one or more domains for names typed at the command line that might be incomplete—that is, that might not be fully qualified domain names.

---

[*] There are actually some single-label domain names that point to addresses, such as *cc*.

Most Unix networking commands that take a domain name as an argument, such as *telnet*, *ftp*, *rlogin*, and *rsh*, apply the search list to those arguments.

Both the way the default search list is derived and the way it is applied changed from BIND 4.8.3 to BIND 4.9. If your resolver is an older make, you'll still see the 4.8.3 behavior, but if you have a newer model, including BIND 8.4.7,* you'll see the improvements in the 4.9 resolver.

With any BIND resolver, a user can indicate that a domain name is fully qualified by adding a trailing dot to it.† For example, the trailing dot in the command:

```
% telnet ftp.ora.com.
```

means "Don't bother searching any other domains; this domain name is fully qualified." This is analogous to the leading slash in full pathnames in the Unix and MS-DOS filesystems. Pathnames without a leading slash are interpreted as relative to the current working directory, while pathnames with a leading slash are absolute, anchored at the root.

The BIND 4.9 and later search list

With BIND 4.9 and later resolvers, the default search list includes just the local domain name. So, if you configure a host with:

```
domain cv.hp.com
```

the default search list contains just *cv.hp.com*. Also, the search list is usually applied *after* the name is tried as-is—a change from earlier resolvers. As long as the argument you type has at least one dot in it, it's looked up exactly as you typed it *before* any element of the search list is appended. If that lookup fails, the search list is applied. Even if the argument has no dots in it (that is, it's a single label name), it's tried as-is after the resolver appends the elements of the search list.

Why is it better to try the argument *literatim* first? From experience, BIND's developers found that, more often than not, if a user bothered to type in a name with even a single dot in it, he was probably typing in a fully qualified domain name without the trailing dot. Better to see right away whether the name was a fully qualified domain name than to create nonsense domain names unnecessarily by appending the elements of the search list to it.

Therefore, with a 4.9 or newer resolver, a user typing:

```
% telnet pronto.cv.hp.com
```

---

* Though the ISC added lots of new functionality to the nameservers in BIND 8 and 9, the resolver in these newer versions of BIND is nearly identical to the BIND 4.9 resolver.

† Note that we said that the resolver can handle a trailing dot. Some programs, particularly some mail user agents, don't deal correctly with a trailing dot in email addresses. They choke even before they hand the domain name in the address to the resolver.

causes *pronto.cv.hp.com* to be looked up first because the name contains three dots, which is certainly more than one. If the resolver doesn't find an address for *pronto.cv.hp.com*, it then tries *pronto.cv.hp.com.cv.hp.com*.

A user typing:

```
% telnet asap
```

on the same host causes the resolver to look up *asap.cv.hp.com* first, because the name doesn't contain a dot, and then just *asap*.

Note that application of the search list stops as soon as a prospective domain name turns up the data being looked up. In the *asap* example, the search list would never get around to looking up just plain *asap* if *asap.cv.hp.com* resolved to an address.

The BIND 4.8.3 search list

With BIND 4.8.3 resolvers, the default search list includes the local domain name and the domain names of each of its parent domains with two or more labels. Therefore, on a host running a 4.8.3 resolver and configured with:

```
domain cv.hp.com
```

the default search list contains first *cv.hp.com*, the local domain name; then *hp.com*, the local domain's parent; but not *com* because it has only one label.* The name is looked up as-is, after the resolver appends each element of the search list, and only if the name typed contains at least one dot. Thus, a user typing:

```
% telnet pronto.cv.hp.com
```

causes lookups of *pronto.cv.hp.com.cv.hp.com* and *pronto.cv.hp.com.hp.com* before the resolver looks up *pronto.cv.hp.com* by itself. A user typing:

```
% telnet asap
```

on the same host causes the resolver to look up *asap.cv.hp.com* and *asap.hp.com*, but not just *asap* because the name typed ("asap") contains no dots.

The search Directive

What if you don't like the default search list you get when you set your local domain name? In all modern resolvers, you can set the search list explicitly, domain name by domain name, in the order you want the domains searched. You do this with the *search* directive.

---

* One reason older BIND resolvers didn't append just the top-level domain name is that there were—and still are—very few hosts at the second level of the Internet's namespace, so tacking on just *com* or *edu* to *foo* is unlikely to result in the domain name of a real host. Also, looking up the address of a *foo.com* or *foo.edu* might well require sending a query to a root nameserver, which taxes the roots and can be time-consuming.

The syntax of the *search* directive is very similar to that of the *domain* directive, except that it can take multiple domain names as arguments. The keyword *search* starts the line in column one, followed by a space or a tab, followed in turn by one to six domain names in the order you want them searched.* The first domain name in the list is interpreted as the local domain name, so the *search* and *domain* directives are mutually exclusive. If you use both in *resolv.conf*, the one that appears last overrides the other.

For example, the directive:

```
search corp.hp.com paloalto.hp.com hp.com
```

instructs the resolver to search the *corp.hp.com* domain first, then *paloalto.hp.com*, and then the parent of both domains, *hp.com*.

This directive might be useful on a host whose users access hosts in both *corp.hp.com* and *paloalto.hp.com* frequently. On the other hand, on a BIND 4.8.3 resolver, the directive:

```
search corp.hp.com
```

causes the resolver to skip searching the local domain's parent domain when the search list is applied. (On a 4.9 or later resolver, the parent domain's name usually isn't in the search list, so this is no different from the default behavior.) This might be useful if the host's users access hosts only in the local domain, or if connectivity to the parent nameservers isn't good (because it minimizes unnecessary queries to the parent nameservers).

 If you use the *domain* directive with a BIND 4.8.3 resolver and update the resolver to version 4.9 or later, users who relied on your local domain's parent being in the search list may believe the resolver has suddenly broken. You can restore the old behavior by using the *search* directive to configure your resolver to use the same search list that it would have built before. For example, under BIND 4.9, BIND 8, or BIND 9, you can replace *domain nsr.hp.com* with *search nsr.hp.com hp.com* and get the same functionality.

The nameserver Directive

Back in Chapter 4, we talked about two types of nameservers: primary nameservers and slave nameservers. But what if you don't want to run a nameserver on a host, yet still want to use DNS? Or, for that matter, what if you *can't* run a nameserver on a host (because the operating system doesn't support it, for example)? Surely, you don't have to run a nameserver on *every* host, right?

---

* BIND 9 resolvers actually support eight elements in the search list.

No, of course you don't. By default, the resolver looks for a nameserver running on the local host—which is why we could use *nslookup* on *toystory.movie.edu* and *wormhole.movie.edu* right after we configured their nameservers. You can, however, instruct the resolver to look to another host for name service. This configuration is called a *DNS client* in the *BIND Operations Guide*.

The *nameserver* directive (yep, all one word) tells the resolver the IP address of a nameserver to query. For example, the line:

```
nameserver 15.32.17.2
```

instructs the resolver to send queries to the nameserver running at the IP address 15.32.17.2 instead of to the local host. This means that on hosts not running nameservers, you can use the *nameserver* directive to point them at a remote nameserver. Typically, you configure the resolvers on your hosts to query your own nameservers.

However, since many nameserver administrators don't restrict queries, you can configure your resolver to query someone else's nameserver. Of course, configuring your host to use someone else's nameserver without first asking permission is presumptuous, if not downright rude, and using one of your own usually gives you better performance, so we'll consider this only an emergency option.

You can also configure the resolver to query the host's local nameserver using either the local host's IP address or the zero address. The zero address, 0.0.0.0, is interpreted by most TCP/IP implementations to mean "this host." The host's real IP address, of course, also means "this host." On hosts that don't understand the zero address, you can use the loopback address, 127.0.0.1.

Now what if the nameserver your resolver queries is down? Isn't there any way to specify a backup? Do you just fall back to using the host table?

The resolver allows you to specify up to three (count 'em, three) nameservers by using multiple *nameserver* directives. The resolver queries those nameservers, in the order listed, until it receives an answer or times out. For example, the lines:

```
nameserver 15.32.17.2
nameserver 15.32.17.4
```

tell the resolver to first query the nameserver at 15.32.17.2, and if it doesn't respond, to query the nameserver at 15.32.17.4. Be aware that the number of nameservers you configure dictates other aspects of the resolver's behavior, too.

If you use multiple *nameserver* directives, *don't* use the loopback address! There's a bug in some Berkeley-derived TCP/IP implementations that can cause problems with BIND if the local nameserver is down. The resolver's connected datagram socket won't rebind to a new local address if the local nameserver isn't running, and consequently the resolver sends query packets to the fallback remote nameservers with a source address of 127.0.0.1. When the remote nameservers try to reply, they end up sending the reply packets to themselves.

One nameserver configured

If there's only one nameserver configured,[*] the resolver queries that nameserver with a timeout of five seconds. The timeout is the length of time the resolver will wait for a response from the nameserver before sending another query. If the resolver encounters an error that indicates the nameserver is really down or unreachable, or if it times out, it doubles the timeout and queries the nameserver again. The errors that could cause this include:

- Receipt of an *ICMP port unreachable* message, which means that no nameserver is listening on the nameserver port

- Receipt of an *ICMP host unreachable* or *network unreachable* message, which means that queries can't be sent to the destination IP address

If the domain name or data doesn't exist, the resolver doesn't retry the query. Theoretically, at least, each nameserver should have an equivalent "view" of the namespace; there's no reason to believe one and not another. So if one nameserver tells you that a given domain name doesn't exist or that the type of data you're looking for doesn't exist for the domain name you specified, any other nameserver should give you the same answer.[†] If the resolver receives a network error each time it sends a query (for a total of four errors[‡]), it falls back to using the host table. Note that these are *errors*, not timeouts. If it times out on even one query, the resolver returns a null answer and does not fall back to */etc/hosts*.

More than one nameserver configured

With more than one nameserver configured, the behavior is a little different. Here's what happens: the resolver starts by querying the first nameserver in the list, with a

---

[*] When we say "one nameserver configured," that means either one *nameserver* directive in *resolv.conf* or no *nameserver* directive and a nameserver running locally.

[†] Caching and the latency of DNS's zone transfer mechanism make this a small fib; cached records may differ temporarily from records in authoritative data, and a primary nameserver can have authority for a zone and have different data from a slave that also has authority for the zone. (The primary may have just loaded new zone data from disk, while the slave may not have had time to transfer the new zone data from its master. Both nameservers return authoritative answers for the zone, but the primary may know about a brand-new host that the slave doesn't yet know about.)

[‡] Two for BIND 8.2.1 and newer resolvers.

timeout of five seconds, just as in the single nameserver case. If the resolver times out or receives a network error, it falls back to the next nameserver, waiting the same five seconds for that nameserver. Unfortunately, the resolver won't receive many of the possible errors; the socket the resolver uses is "unconnected" because it must be able to receive responses from any of the nameservers it queries, and unconnected sockets don't receive ICMP error messages. If the resolver queries all the configured nameservers to no avail, it updates the timeouts and cycles through them again.

The resolver timeout for the next round of queries is based on the number of nameservers configured in *resolv.conf*. The timeout for the second round of queries is 10 seconds divided by the number of nameservers configured, rounded down. Each successive round's timeout is double the previous timeout. After three sets of retransmissions (a total of four timeouts for every nameserver configured), the resolver gives up trying to query nameservers.

In BIND 8.2.1, the ISC changed the resolver to send only one set of retries, or a total of two queries to each nameserver in *resolv.conf*. This was intended to reduce the amount of time a user would have to wait for the resolver to return if none of the nameservers was responding.

For you mathophobes, Table 6-1 shows what the timeouts look like when you have one, two, or three nameservers configured.

Table 6-1. Resolver timeouts in BIND 4.9 to 8.2

	Nameservers configured		
Retry	1	2	3
0	5s	(2x) 5s	(3x) 5s
1	10s	(2x) 5s	(3x) 3s
2	20s	(2x) 10s	(3x) 6s
3	40s	(2x) 20s	(3x) 13s
Total	75s	80s	81s

For BIND 8.2 and later resolvers, Table 6-2 shows the default timeout behavior.

Table 6-2. Resolver timeouts in BIND 8.2.1 and later

	Nameservers configured		
Retry	1	2	3
0	5s	(2x) 5s	(3x) 5s
1	10s	(2x) 5s	(3x) 3s
Total	15s	20s	24s

So if you configure three servers, the resolver queries the first server with a timeout period of five seconds. If that query times out, the resolver queries the second server with the same timeout, and similarly for the third. If the resolver cycles through all three servers, it doubles the timeout period and divides by three (to three seconds, 10/3 rounded down) and queries the first server again.

Do these times seem awfully long? Remember, this describes a worst-case scenario. With properly functioning nameservers running on tolerably fast hosts, your resolvers should get their answers back in well under a second. Only if all the configured nameservers are really busy, or if they or your network are down, will the resolver ever make it all the way through the retransmission cycle and give up.

What does the resolver do after it gives up? It times out and returns an error. Typically, this results in an error message like:

```
% telnet tootsie
tootsie: Host name lookup failure
```

Of course, it may take about 75 seconds before this message appears, so be patient.

The sortlist Directive

The *sortlist* directive is a mechanism in BIND 4.9 and later resolvers that lets you specify subnets and networks for the resolver to prefer if it receives multiple addresses as the result of a query. In some cases, you'll want your host to use a particular network to get to certain destinations. For example, say your workstation and your NFS server have two network interfaces each: one on a standard 100 Mbps Ethernet segment, subnet 128.32.1/24, and one on a gigabit Ethernet segment, subnet 128.32.42/24. If you leave your workstation's resolver to its own devices, it's anybody's guess which of the NFS server's IP addresses you'll use when you mount a filesystem from the server—presumably, the first one in a reply packet from the nameserver. To make sure you try the interface on the gigabit Ethernet first, you can add a *sortlist* directive to *resolv.conf* that sorts the address on 128.32.42/24 to the preferred position in the structure passed back to programs:

```
sortlist 128.32.42.0/255.255.255.0
```

The argument after the slash is the subnet mask for the subnet in question. To prefer an entire network, you can omit the slash and the subnet mask:

```
sortlist 128.32.0.0
```

The resolver then assumes you mean the entire network 128.32/16. (The resolver derives the default unsubnetted net mask for the network from the first two bits of the IP address.)

And, of course, you can specify several (up to 10) subnets and networks to prefer over others:

```
sortlist 128.32.42.0/255.255.255.0 15.0.0.0
```

The resolver sorts any addresses in a reply that match these arguments into the order in which they appear in the directive, and appends addresses that don't match to the end.

The options Directive

The *options* directive was introduced with BIND 4.9 and lets you tweak several internal resolver settings. The first is the debug flag, RES_DEBUG. The directive:

```
options debug
```

sets RES_DEBUG, producing lots of exciting debugging information on standard output, assuming your resolver was configured with DEBUG defined. (Actually, that may not be a good assumption because most vendors compile their stock resolvers without DEBUG defined.) This is very useful if you're attempting to diagnose a problem with your resolver or with name service in general, but very annoying otherwise.

The second setting you can modify is *ndots*, which sets the minimum number of dots a domain name argument must have for the resolver to look it up before applying the search list. By default, one or more dots will do; this is equivalent to *ndots:1*. The resolver first tries the domain name as typed as long as the name has any dots in it. You can raise the threshold if you believe your users are more likely to type partial domain names that will need the search list applied. For example, if your local domain name is *mit.edu*, and your users are accustomed to typing:

```
% ftp prep.ai
```

and having *mit.edu* automatically appended to produce *prep.ai.mit.edu*, you may want to raise *ndots* to 2 so that your users won't unwittingly cause lookups to the root nameservers for names in the top-level *ai* domain. You could do this with:

```
options ndots:2
```

BIND 8.2 introduced four new resolver options: *attempts*, *timeout*, *rotate*, and *no-check-names*. *attempts* allows you to specify how many queries the resolver should send to each nameserver in *resolv.conf* before giving up. If you think the new default value, 2, is too low for your nameservers, you can boost it back to 4, the default value before BIND 8.2.1, with:

```
options attempts:4
```

The maximum value is 5.

timeout allows you to specify the initial timeout for a query to a nameserver in *resolv.conf*. The default value is five seconds. If you'd like your resolver to retransmit more quickly, you can lower the timeout to two seconds with:

```
options timeout:2
```

The maximum value is 30 seconds. For the second and successive rounds of queries, the resolver still doubles the initial timeout and divides by the number of nameservers in *resolv.conf*.

rotate lets your resolver use all the nameservers in *resolv.conf*, not just the first one. In normal operation, if your resolver's first nameserver is healthy, it'll service all your resolver's queries. Unless that nameserver gets very busy or goes down, your resolver will never query the second or third nameservers in *resolv.conf*. If you'd like to spread the load around, you can set:

```
options rotate
```

to have each instance of the resolver rotate the order in which it uses the nameservers in *resolv.conf*. In other words, an instance of the resolver still queries the first nameserver in *resolv.conf* first, but for the next domain name it looks up, it queries the second nameserver first, and so on.

Note that many programs can't take advantage of this because they initialize the resolver, look up a name, then exit. Rotation has no effect on repeated *ping* commands, for example, because each *ping* process initializes the resolver, queries the first nameserver in *resolv.conf*, and then exits before using the resolver again. Each successive invocation of *ping* has no idea which nameserver the previous one used—or even that *ping* was run earlier. But long-lived processes that send lots of queries, such as a *sendmail* daemon, can take advantage of rotation.

Rotation can also make debugging trickier. If you use it, you'll never be sure which nameserver in *resolv.conf* your *sendmail* daemon queried when it received that funky response.

no-check-names, finally, allows you to turn off the resolver's name checking, which is on by default.[*] These routines examine domain names in responses to make sure they adhere to Internet host-naming standards, which allow only alphanumerics and dashes in hostnames. You'll need to set this if you want your users to be able to resolve domain names with underscores or nonalphanumeric characters in them.

If you want to specify multiple options, combine them on a single line in *resolv.conf*, like so:

```
options attempts:4 timeout:2 ndots:2
```

Comments

Also introduced with BIND 4.9 resolvers (and it's about time, if you ask us), is the ability to put comments in the *resolv.conf* file. Lines that begin with a pound sign or

---

[*] In all resolvers that support it, from BIND 4.9.4 on.

semicolon in the first column are interpreted as comments and ignored by the resolver.

A Note on the 4.9 Resolver Directives

If you're just moving to a BIND 4.9 resolver, be careful when using the new directives. You may still have older resolver code statically linked into programs on your host. Often, this isn't a problem because Unix resolvers ignore directives they don't understand. However, don't count on all programs on your host obeying the new directives.

If you're running on a host with programs that include really old resolver code that doesn't understand the *search* directive (i.e., older than 4.8.3) but you still want to use *search* with programs that can take advantage of it, here's a trick: use both a *domain* directive and a *search* directive in *resolv.conf*, with the *domain* directive first. Old resolvers will read the *domain* directive and ignore the *search* directive because they won't recognize it. New resolvers will read the *domain* directive, but the *search* directive will override its behavior.

Sample Resolver Configurations

So much for theory—let's now go over what *resolv.conf* files look like on real hosts. Resolver configuration needs vary depending on whether a host runs a local nameserver, so we'll cover both cases: hosts with local nameservers and hosts with remote nameservers.

Resolver Only

We, as the administrators of *movie.edu*, have just been asked to configure a professor's new standalone workstation, which doesn't run a nameserver. Deciding which domain the workstation belongs in is easy: there's only *movie.edu* to choose from. However, she is working with researchers at Pixar on new shading algorithms, so perhaps it'd be wise to put *pixar.com* in her workstation's search list. The *search* directive:

```
search movie.edu pixar.com
```

makes *movie.edu* her workstation's local domain name and searches *pixar.com* for names not found in *movie.edu*.

The new workstation is on the 192.249.249/24 network, so the closest nameservers are *wormhole.movie.edu* (192.249.249.1) and *toystory.movie.edu* (192.249.249.3). As a rule, you should configure hosts to use the closest nameserver available first. (The closest possible nameserver is a nameserver on the local host; the next closest is a nameserver on the same subnet or network.) In this case, both nameservers are equally close, but we know that *wormhole.movie.edu* is bigger (it's a faster host, with more capacity). So the first *nameserver* directive in *resolv.conf* should be:

```
nameserver 192.249.249.1
```

Since this particular professor is known to get awfully vocal when she has problems with her computer, we'll also add *toystory.movie.edu* (192.249.249.3) as a backup nameserver. That way, if *wormhole.movie.edu* is down for any reason, the professor's workstation can still get name service (assuming *toystory.movie.edu* and the rest of the network are up).

The *resolv.conf* file ends up looking like this:

```
search movie.edu pixar.com
nameserver 192.249.249.1
nameserver 192.249.249.3
```

Hidden Primaries

There's another good reason to configure the resolver to query *wormhole.movie.edu*, the secondary, first. Or rather there's a good reason to configure the resolver *not* to query the primary first. We edit the zone datafile on the primary on a daily basis, and there's always the chance that we'll reload and find that we've made some mistake and introduced a syntax error. If that happens, our primary may begin returning SERVFAIL answers to queries in *movie.edu* or its reverse-mapping zones.

To avoid this situation, some organizations run their primary nameservers *hidden*. No resolvers are configured to query the primary (in fact, in some cases the primary is configured to reject queries from any IP addresses other than those of its secondaries). The resolvers query the secondaries or caching-only nameservers. A syntax error in a zone datafile won't be transferred to the secondaries because the primary won't answer authoritatively until the error is fixed. The primary also isn't listed in the NS records of the zones it's authoritative for. That way, an interruption in service caused by a typo in *named.conf* or a zone datafile won't cause a loss of service to the resolvers.

Local Nameserver

Next, we have to configure the university mail hub, *postmanrings2x.movie.edu*, to use domain name service. *postmanrings2x.movie.edu* is shared by all groups in *movie.edu*. We've recently configured a nameserver on the host to help cut down the load on the other nameservers, so we should make sure the resolver queries the nameserver on the local host first.

The simplest resolver configuration for this case is no configuration at all: don't create a *resolv.conf* file, and let the resolver default to using the local nameserver. The *hostname* should be set to the full domain name of the host so that the resolver can determine the local domain name.

If we decide we need a backup nameserver—a prudent decision—we can use *resolv.conf*. Whether we configure a backup nameserver depends largely on the reliability of the local nameserver. A good implementation of the BIND nameserver will keep running for longer than some operating systems, so there may be no need for a backup. If the local nameserver has a history of problems, though—for example, it hangs occasionally and stops responding to queries—it's a good idea to add a backup nameserver.

To add a backup nameserver, just list the local nameserver first in *resolv.conf* (at the host's IP address or the zero address, 0.0.0.0—either will do), then one or two backup nameservers. Remember not to use the loopback address unless you know your system's TCP/IP stack doesn't have the problem we mentioned earlier.

Since we'd rather be safe than sorry, we're going to add two backup nameservers. *postmanrings2x.movie.edu* is on the 192.249.249/24 network, too, so *toystory.movie.edu* and *wormhole.movie.edu* are its closest nameservers (besides its own). We'll reverse the order in which they're queried from the previous resolver-only example to help balance the load between the two.* And because we'd rather not wait the full five seconds for the resolver to try the second nameserver, we'll lower the timeout to two seconds. The *resolv.conf* file ends up looking like this:

```
domain movie.edu
nameserver 0.0.0.0
nameserver 192.249.249.3
nameserver 192.249.249.
options timeout:2
```

Minimizing Pain and Suffering

Now that you've configured your host to use DNS, what's going to change? Will your users be forced to type long domain names? Will they have to change their mail addresses and mailing lists?

Thanks to the search list, much of this will continue working as before. There are some exceptions, though, and some notable differences in the way that some programs behave when they use DNS. We'll try to cover all the common ones.

---

* Unless we were running a hidden primary. Of course, with our primary hidden, we'd probably want another secondary to help answer queries.

Differences in Service Behavior

As you've seen earlier in this chapter, programs such as *telnet*, *ftp*, *rlogin*, and *rsh* apply the search list to domain name arguments that aren't dot-terminated. That means that if you're in *movie.edu* (i.e., your local domain name is *movie.edu*, and your search list includes *movie.edu*), you can type either:

```
% telnet misery
```

or:

```
% telnet misery.movie.edu
```

or even:

```
% telnet misery.movie.edu.
```

and get to the same place. The same holds true for the other services, too. There's one other behavioral difference you may benefit from: because a nameserver may return more than one IP address when you look up an address, modern versions of Telnet, FTP, and web browsers try to connect to the first address returned, and if the connection is refused or times out, for example, they try the next, and so on:

```
% ftp tootsie
ftp: connect to address 192.249.249.244: Connection timed out
Trying 192.253.253.244...
Connected to tootsie.movie.edu.
220 tootsie.movie.edu FTP server (Version 16.2 Fri Apr 26
    18:20:43 GMT 1991) ready.
Name (tootsie: guest):
```

And remember that with the *resolv.conf sortlist* directive, you can even control the order in which your applications try those IP addresses.

One oddball service is NFS. The *mount* command can handle domain names just fine, and you can put domain names into */etc/fstab* (your vendor may call it */etc/checklist*), too. But watch out for */etc/exports* and */etc/netgroup*. */etc/exports* controls which filesystems you allow various clients to NFS-mount. You can also assign a name to a group of hosts in *netgroup* and then allow them access via *exports* using the name of the group.

Unfortunately, older versions of NFS don't really use DNS to check *exports* or *netgroup*; the client tells the NFS server its identity in a Remote Procedure Call (RPC) packet. Consequently, the client's identity is whatever the client claims it is, and the identity a host uses in Sun RPC is the local host's *hostname*. So the name you use in either file needs to match the client's *hostname*, which isn't necessarily its domain name.

Electronic Mail

Some electronic mail programs, including *sendmail*, also don't work as expected; *sendmail* doesn't use the search list quite the same way that other programs do. Instead, when configured to use a nameserver, it uses a process called *canonicalization* to convert names in electronic mail addresses to fully qualified domain names.

In canonicalization, *sendmail* applies the search list to a name and looks up data of type ANY, which matches any type of record. *sendmail* uses the same rule newer resolvers do: if the name to canonicalize has at least one dot in it, check the name as-is first. If the nameserver queried finds a CNAME record (an alias), *sendmail* replaces the name looked up with the canonical name the alias points to and canonicalizes *that* (in case the target of the alias is itself an alias). If the nameserver queried finds an A record (an address), *sendmail* uses the domain name that resolved to the address as the canonical name. If the nameserver doesn't find an address but does find one or more MX records, one of the following actions is performed:

- If the search list has not yet been appended, *sendmail* uses the domain name that resolved to the MX record(s) as the canonical name.

- If one or more elements of the search list have been appended, *sendmail* notes that the domain name is a potential canonical name and continues appending elements of the search list. If a subsequent element of the search list turns up an address, the domain name that turned up the address is the canonical name. Otherwise, the domain name that found the first MX record is used as the canonical name.[*]

sendmail uses canonicalization several times when processing an SMTP message; it canonicalizes the destination address and several fields in the SMTP headers.[†]

sendmail also sets macro *$w* to the canonicalized *hostname* when the *sendmail* daemon starts up. So even if you set your *hostname* to a short, single-part name, *sendmail* canonicalizes the *hostname* using the search list defined in *resolv.conf*. *sendmail* then adds macro *$w* and all aliases for *$w* encountered during canonicalization to class *$=w*, the list of the mail server's other names.

This is important because class *$=w* names are the only names *sendmail* recognizes, by default, as the local host's name. *sendmail* will attempt to forward mail that's addressed to a domain name it thinks isn't local. So, for example, unless you configure *sendmail* to recognize all of the host's aliases (by adding them to class *w* or fileclass *w*,

---

[*] All this complexity is necessary to deal with wildcard MX records, which we'll discuss in Chapter 17.

[†] Some older versions of *sendmail* use a different technique for doing canonicalization: they apply the search list and query the nameserver for CNAME records for the name in question. CNAME matches only CNAME records. If a record is found, the name is replaced with the domain name on the right side of the CNAME record.

as we showed in Chapter 5), the host will try to forward messages that arrive addressed to anything other than the canonical domain name.

There's another important implication of class $=w$, which is that *sendmail* recognizes only the contents of class $=w$ as the local host's name in MX lists. Consequently, if you use anything other than a name you're sure is in $=w$ on the right side of an MX record, you run the risk that the host will not recognize it. This can cause mail to loop and then be returned to the sender.

One last note on *sendmail*: when you start running a nameserver, if you're running an older version of *sendmail* (before version 8), you should set the *I* option in your *sendmail.cf* file. Option *I* determines what *sendmail* does if a lookup for a destination host fails. When using */etc/hosts*, a failed lookup is fatal. If you search the host table once for a name and don't find it, it's doubtful it'll miraculously appear later, so the mailer may as well return the message. When using DNS, however, a lookup failure may be temporary, because of intermittent networking problems, for example. Setting option *I* instructs *sendmail* to queue mail if a lookup fails instead of returning it to the sender. Just add *OI* to your *sendmail.cf* file to set option *I*.

Updating .rhosts, hosts.equiv, etc.

Once you start using DNS, you may also need to disambiguate hostnames in your host's authorization files. Entries that use simple, one-part hostnames will now be assumed to be in the local domain. For example, the *lpd.allow* file on *wormhole.movie.edu* might include:

```
wormhole
toystory
monsters-inc
shrek
mash
twins
```

If we move *mash* and *twins* into the *comedy.movie.edu* zone, though, they won't be allowed to access *lpd*; the entries in *lpd.allow* allow only *mash.movie.edu* and *twins.movie.edu*. So we have to add the proper domain names to hostnames outside the *lpd* server's local domain:

```
wormhole
toystory
monsters-inc
shrek
mash.comedy.movie.edu
twins.comedy.movie.edu
```

Here are some other files you should check for hostnames in need of domain-ification:

```
hosts.equiv
.rhosts
X0.hosts
sendmail.cf
```

Sometimes, simply running these files through a canonicalization filter—a program that translates hostnames to domain names using the search list—is enough to disambiguate them. Here's a very short canonicalization filter in Perl to help you out:

```
#!/usr/bin/perl -ap
# Expects one hostname per line, in the first field (a la .rhosts,
# X0.hosts)

s/$F[0]/$d/ if ($d)=gethostbyname $F[0];
```

Providing Aliases

Even if you cover all your bases and convert all your *.rhosts*, *hosts.equiv*, and *sendmail.cf* files after you configure your host to use DNS, your users will still have to adjust to using domain names. Hopefully, their confusion will be minimal and more than offset by the benefits of DNS.

One way to make your users' lives less confusing after configuring DNS is to provide aliases for well-known hosts that are no longer reachable using their familiar names. For example, our users are accustomed to typing *telnet doofy* or *rlogin doofy* to get to the bulletin board system run by the movie studio on the other side of town. Now they'll have to start using *doofy*'s full domain name, *doofy.maroon.com*. But most of our users don't know the full domain name, and it'll be some time before we can tell all of them and they get used to it.

Luckily, BIND lets you define aliases for your users. All we need to do is set the environment variable HOSTALIASES to the pathname of a file that contains mappings between aliases and domain names. For example, to set up a system-wide alias for *doofy*, we can set HOSTALIASES to */etc/host.aliases* in the system's shell startup files and add:

```
doofy    doofy.maroon.com
```

to */etc/host.aliases*. The alias file format is simple: the alias starts the line in column one, followed by whitespace and then the domain name that corresponds to the alias. The domain name is written without a trailing dot, and the alias can't contain any dots.

Now when our users type *telnet doofy* or *rlogin doofy*, the resolver transparently substitutes *doofy.maroon.com* for *doofy* in the nameserver query. The message the users see now looks something like:

```
Trying...
Connected to doofy.maroon.com.
Escape character is '^]'.
IRIX System V.3 (sgi)
login:
```

If the resolver falls back to using */etc/hosts*, though, our HOSTALIASES won't have any effect. So we should also keep a similar alias in */etc/hosts*.

With time, and perhaps a little instruction, the users will start to associate the full domain name they see in the *telnet* banner with the bulletin board they use.

With HOSTALIASES, if you know the domain names your users are likely to have trouble with, you can save them a little frustration. If you don't know which hosts they're trying to get to, you can let your users create their own alias files, and have each user point the HOSTALIASES variable in his shell startup file to his personal alias file.

Additional Configuration Files

In addition to configuring the resolver for DNS queries, you may be able to configure which service is used to obtain name and address information. The most common file used by vendors is *nsswitch.conf*, which we will cover here. Some vendors use *irs.conf* or *netsvc.conf*. Check your system's manual pages for details on these files.

nsswitch.conf

/etc/nsswitch.conf is used to configure the order in which a number of different sources are checked. You select the database you want to configure by specifying a keyword. For naming services, the database name is *hosts*. The possible sources for the *hosts* database are *dns*, *nis*, *nisplus*, and *files* (which refers to */etc/hosts* in this case). Configuring the order in which the sources are consulted is a simple matter of listing them after the database name in that order. For example:

```
hosts: dns files
```

has the resolver try DNS (i.e., query a nameserver) first, then check */etc/hosts*. By default, resolution moves from one source to the next (e.g., falls back to */etc/hosts* from DNS) if the first source isn't available or the name being looked up isn't found. You can modify this behavior by specifying a *condition* and an *action* in square brackets between the sources. The possible conditions are:

UNAVAIL
: The source hasn't been configured (in DNS's case, there is no *resolv.conf* file, and there is no nameserver running on the local host).

NOTFOUND
: The source can't find the name in question (for DNS, the name looked up or the type of data looked up doesn't exist).

TRYAGAIN
: The source is busy, but might respond next time (for example, the resolver has timed out while trying to look up a name).

SUCCESS
: The requested name was found in the specified source.

For each criterion, you can specify that the resolver should either *continue* and fall back to the next source or simply *return*. The default action is *return* for *SUCCESS* and *continue* for all the other conditions.

For example, if you want your resolver to stop looking up a domain name if it receives an NXDOMAIN (no such domain name) answer, but to check */etc/hosts* if DNS isn't available, you can use:

```
hosts:  dns [NOTFOUND=return] files
```

The Windows XP Resolver

We'll cover the resolver in Windows XP because most modern Windows resolvers—Windows 2000, Windows Server 2003—look similar and act similarly. This resolver can be a little tough to find; its configuration is well hidden. To get to it, click on *Start*, then *Control Panel*, then *Network and Internet Connections*, then *Network Connections*. This brings up the window shown in Figure 6-1.

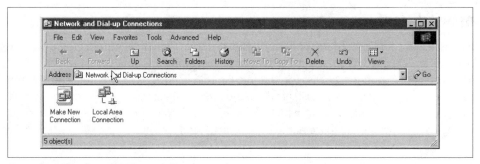

Figure 6-1. Windows XP Network Connections

Right-click on *Local Area Connection* and choose *Properties*. This brings up a window like the one shown in Figure 6-2.

Double-click on *Internet Protocol (TCP/IP)*. This posts the basic resolver configuration window shown in Figure 6-3.

If you check the *Obtain DNS server address automatically* radio button, the resolver queries the nameservers that the local DHCP server tells it to use. If you check the *Use the following DNS server addresses* radio button, the resolver queries the nameservers you specify in the *Preferred DNS server* and *Alternate DNS server* fields.[*]

---

[*] More kudos to Microsoft for clarifying its labels. In previous versions of Windows, nameservers were sometimes labeled *Primary DNS* and *Secondary DNS*. This sometimes misled users into listing the primary and slave (secondary) nameservers for some zone or another in those fields. Besides, "DNS" is an abbreviation for "Domain Name System," not "domain nameserver."

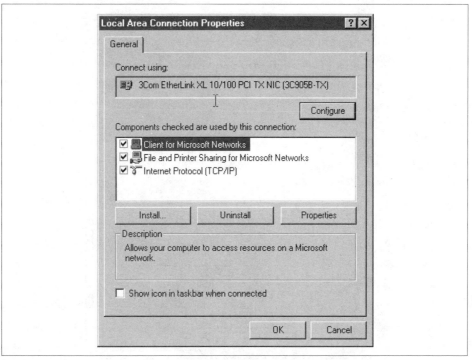

Figure 6-2. Windows XP Local Area Connection Properties

To get at more advanced resolver configuration, click on (what else?) the *Advanced...* button. Click on the *DNS* tab, and you'll see the window in Figure 6-4.

If you've specified the addresses of nameservers to query in the basic resolver configuration window, you'll see them again at the top of this window, under *DNS server addresses, in order of use:*. The buttons allow you to add, edit, remove, and reorder the nameservers listed. There doesn't seem to be a limit to the number of nameservers you can list, but it doesn't make much sense to list more than three.

The Windows XP resolver uses an aggressive retransmission algorithm first introduced in Windows NT 4.0 SP4: the resolver sends its first query to the first nameserver in the *DNS Server Search Order*. However, the resolver waits only one second before retransmitting the query and retransmits simultaneously to the first nameserver configured for each of the network adapters on the host. If after two more seconds the resolver doesn't receive a response, it simultaneously queries *all* the nameservers configured for *all* of the host's adapters—statically configured, configured via DHCP, whatever. If none of those nameservers responds in four seconds, the resolver retransmits to all the nameservers again. It keeps doubling the timeout and retransmitting for a total of 4 retransmissions and 15 seconds. (See the Windows 2000 DNS white paper, at *http://www.microsoft.com/windows2000/docs/w2kdns.doc*, for details.)

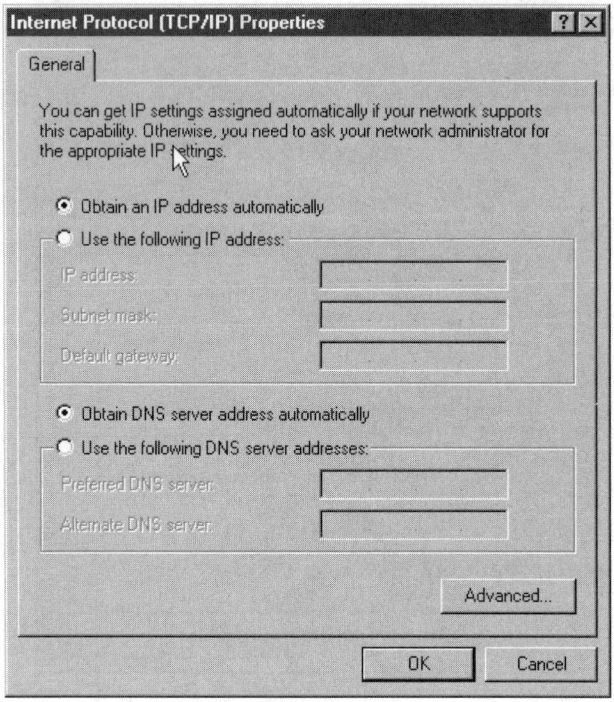

Figure 6-3. Basic Windows XP resolver configuration

Since it's possible, in these days of split namespaces, to get two different answers from two different nameservers, the Windows XP resolver temporarily ignores negative answers (no such domain name and no such data) while querying multiple nameservers. Only if it receives a negative answer from a nameserver configured for each interface does it return a negative answer. If the resolver receives even a single positive answer from a nameserver, it returns that.

Checking the *Append primary and connection specific DNS suffixes* radio button has the resolver use the primary DNS suffix and the connection-specific DNS suffixes as the search list. The DNS suffix specific to this connection is set in this window, in the field to the right of *DNS suffix for this connection*, or via a DHCP option sent by the DHCP server. The primary DNS suffix, on the other hand, is set in the Control Panel by clicking on *System* (from the Classic view), choosing the *Computer Name* tab, then clicking on *Change…*, then clicking on *More…*. This brings up the window shown in Figure 6-5.

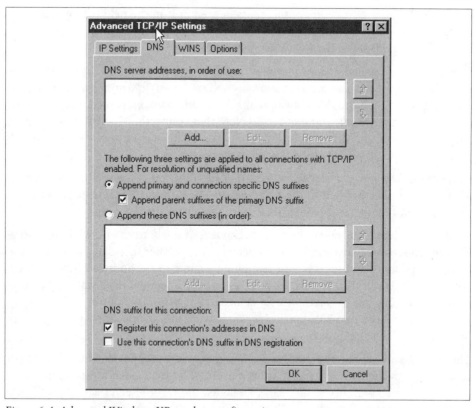

Figure 6-4. Advanced Windows XP resolver configuration

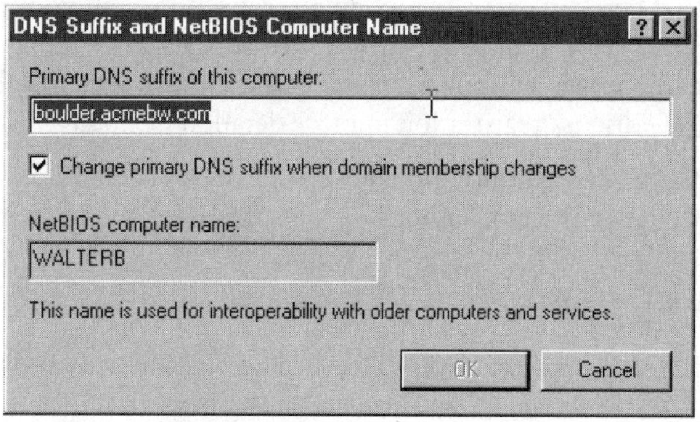

Figure 6-5. Configuring the primary DNS suffix in Windows XP

To set the *Primary DNS suffix of this computer*, enter it in the field below that label. By default, on computers that are members of an Active Directory domain, the primary DNS suffix is set to the AD domain's name.

The checkbox labeled *Append parent suffixes of the primary DNS suffix* (see Figure 6-4) configures the resolver to use a BIND 4.8.3–style search list derived from the primary DNS suffix. So if your primary DNS suffix is *fx.movie.edu*, the search list will contain *fx.movie.edu* and *movie.edu*. Note that connection-specific DNS suffixes aren't "devolved" (in Microsoft's words) into a search list, but if they're configured, connection-specific suffixes are included in the search list.

Checking the *Append these DNS suffixes (in order)* button configures the resolver to use the search list specified in the fields below. As with the list of nameservers, you can add, edit, remove, and reorder these with the buttons and arrows.

Finally, it's worth mentioning the two checkboxes at the bottom of the window. *Register this connection's addresses in DNS* determines whether this client will try to use dynamic update to add an A record mapping its name to the address of this connection, and a PTR record mapping the address back to a name if it's a statically configured address. *Use this connection's suffix in DNS registration* controls whether that update will use the domain name associated with this connection or the primary DNS suffix for this computer.

This feature—automatic registration—is designed to ensure that the domain name of your Windows client always points to its current IP address, even if that address was delivered by a DHCP server. (For DHCP clients, the DHCP server actually adds the PTR record mapping the client's IP address back to its domain name.) It's also the death knell of WINS, the Windows Internet Name Service, the proprietary—and much maligned—Microsoft NetBIOS naming service. Once all your clients are running modern versions of Windows, they'll all use dynamic update to keep their name-to-address mappings current, and you can drive a wooden stake through the heart of WINS. We discuss registration in more detail in Chapter 17.

Allowing clients to dynamically update zones presents certain, er, challenges, though, which we'll explore in Chapter 17.

Caching

The Windows XP resolver stores every record it receives in a shared cache available to all programs on the system. The resolver also obeys the TTL field of resource records it caches, up to a maximum of 24 hours by default. So if a record specifies a

TTL longer than that, the resolver rounds down to 24 hours. This maximum TTL is configurable with a Registry setting:

```
MaxCacheTtl
HKEY_LOCAL_MACHINE\SYSTEM\CurrentControlSet\Services\DNSCache\Parameters
Data type: REG_DWORD

Default value: 86,400 seconds (= 24 hours)
```

The Windows XP resolver also supports negative caching. Windows XP caches negative responses for 15 minutes by default. This negative caching timeout is also configurable with a Registry setting:

```
MaxNegativeCacheTtl
HKEY_LOCAL_MACHINE\SYSTEM\CurrentControlSet\Services\DNSCache\Parameters
Data type: REG_DWORD

Default value: 900 seconds (= 15 minutes)
```

To disable negative caching altogether, set this value to 0.

To view the resolver's cache, use *ipconfig /displaydns*. To clear the cache, type *ipconfig /flushdns*. To disable caching on Windows XP, you can use the command:

```
C:\> net stop dnscache
```

However, this lasts only until the next reboot. To disable caching permanently, go to *Services* (in the *Administrative Tools* program group) and set the DNS Client service's *Startup type* to *Disabled*.

Subnet Prioritization

This feature is analogous to the BIND resolver's address-sorting feature. When the resolver receives multiple address records for the same domain name, it examines the IP address in each record and adjusts the order of the records before returning the list to the calling application: any records with IP addresses on the same subnets as the host on which the resolver is running are moved to the top of the list. Since most applications use addresses in the order returned by the resolver, this behavior causes traffic to remain on local networks.

For example, Movie U. has two mirrored web servers on two different subnets:

```
www.movie.edu.    IN  A  192.253.253.101
www.movie.edu.    IN  A  192.249.249.101
```

Let's say the resolver on *toystory.movie.edu* (192.249.249.3) sends a query and receives these records. It sorts the record with address 192.249.249.101 to the top of the list because *toystory* shares a network with that address.

Note that this behavior defeats the round-robin feature implemented by most nameservers. *Round robin* refers to the nameserver behavior of rotating the order of multiple address records in successive responses to distribute the load among the servers (again taking advantage of the behavior of most applications to use the first address in the list returned by the resolver). With subnet prioritization enabled, the order of the records is subject to shuffling by the resolver. You can disable subnet prioritization with a Registry setting:

```
PrioritizeRecordData
HKEY_LOCAL_MACHINE\SYSTEM\CurrentControlSet\Services\DNSCache\Parameters
Data type: REG_DWORD
Range: 0 - 1
Default value: 1 (Subnet prioritization enabled)
```

## CHAPTER 7

Maintaining BIND

*"Well, in our country," said Alice, still panting a little,
"you'd generally get to somewhere else—if you ran
very fast for a long time as we've been doing."
"A slow sort of country!" said the Queen. "Now, here,
you see, it takes all the running you can do, to keep in
the same place. If you want to get somewhere else, you
must run at least twice as fast as that!"*

This chapter discusses a number of related topics pertaining to nameserver maintenance. We'll talk about controlling nameservers, modifying zone datafiles, and keeping the root hints file up to date. We'll list common *syslog* error messages and explain the statistics BIND keeps.

This chapter doesn't cover troubleshooting problems. Maintenance involves keeping your data current and watching over your nameservers as they operate. Troubleshooting involves putting out fires—those little DNS emergencies that flare up periodically. Firefighting is covered in Chapter 14.

Controlling the Nameserver

Traditionally, administrators have controlled the BIND nameserver, *named*, with Unix signals. The nameserver interprets the receipt of certain signals as instructions to take particular actions, such as reloading all the primary zones that have changed. However, there are a limited number of signals available, and signals offer no means of passing along additional information such as the domain name of a particular zone to reload.

In BIND 8.2, the ISC introduced a method of controlling the nameserver by sending messages to it on a special control channel. The control channel can be either a Unix domain socket or a TCP port that the nameserver listens on for messages. Because the control channel isn't limited to a finite number of discrete signals, it's more flexible and powerful. The ISC says that the control channel is the way of the future and that administrators should use it, rather than signals, for all nameserver management.

You send messages to a nameserver via the control channel using a program called *ndc* (in BIND 8) or *rndc* (in BIND 9). Prior to BIND 8.2, *ndc* was simply a shell script that allowed you to substitute convenient arguments (such as *reload*) for signals (such as *HUP*). We'll talk about that version of *ndc* later in this chapter.

ndc and controls (BIND 8)

Executed without arguments, *ndc* will try to communicate with a nameserver running on the local host by sending messages through a Unix domain socket. The socket is usually called */var/run/ndc*, though some operating systems use a different pathname. The socket is normally owned by root and is readable and writable only by the owner. BIND 8.2 and later nameservers create the Unix domain socket when they start up. You can specify an alternate pathname or permissions for the socket using the *controls* statement. For example, to change the socket's path to */etc/ndc* and group ownership to *named*, and to make the socket readable and writable by both owner and group, you can use:

```
controls {
    unix "/etc/ndc" perm 0660 owner 0 group 53;    // group 53 is "named"
};
```

The permission value must be specified as an octal quantity (with a leading zero to indicate its octalness). If you're not familiar with this format, see the *chmod(1)* manual page. The owner and group values must also be numeric.

The ISC recommends, and we agree, that you restrict access to the Unix domain socket to administrative personnel authorized to control the nameserver.

You can also use *ndc* to send messages across a TCP socket to a nameserver, possibly remote from the host that you're running *ndc* on. To use this mode of operation, run *ndc* with the −*c* command-line option, specifying the name or address of the nameserver, a slash, and the port on which it's listening for control messages. For example:

```
# ndc -c 127.0.0.1/953
```

To configure your nameserver to listen on a particular TCP port for control messages, use the *controls* statement:

```
controls {
    inet 127.0.0.1 port 953 allow { localhost; };
};
```

By default, BIND 8 nameservers don't listen on any TCP ports. BIND 9 nameservers listen on port 953 by default, so we're using that port here. We're configuring the nameserver to listen only on the local loopback address for messages, and to allow only messages from the local host. Even this isn't especially prudent because anyone

with a login on the local host can control the nameserver. If we felt even more impru-
dent (and we don't advise this), we could widen the allow-access list and let the
nameserver listen on all local network interfaces by specifying:

```
controls {
    inet * port 953 allow { localnets; };
};
```

ndc supports two modes of operation, interactive and noninteractive. In noninteractive mode, you specify the command to the nameserver on the command line. For
example:

```
# ndc reload
```

If you don't specify a command on the command line, you enter interactive mode:

```
# ndc
Type   help -or-   /h   if you need help.
ndc>
```

/h gives you a list of commands that *ndc* (not the nameserver) understands. These
apply to *ndc*'s operation, not the nameserver's:

```
ndc> /h
        /h(elp)              this text
        /e(xit)              leave this program
        /t(race)             toggle tracing (protocol and system events)
        /d(ebug)             toggle debugging (internal program events)
        /q(uiet)             toggle quietude (prompts and results)
        /s(ilent)            toggle silence (suppresses nonfatal errors)
ndc>
```

For example, the */d* command induces *ndc* to produce debugging output (e.g., what
it's sending to the nameserver and what it's getting in response). It has no effect on
the nameserver's debugging level. For that, see the *debug* command, described later.

Note that */e,* not */x* or */q,* exits *ndc.* That's a little counterintuitive.

help tells you the commands at your disposal. These control the nameserver:

```
ndc> help
getpid
status
stop
exec
reload [zone] ...
reconfig [-noexpired] (just sees new/gone zones)
dumpdb
stats
trace [level]
notrace
querylog
qrylog
help
quit
ndc>
```

There are two commands that aren't listed here, though you can still use them: *start* and *restart*. They're not listed because *ndc* is telling you what commands the nameserver—as opposed to *ndc*—understands. The nameserver can't perform a *start* command because to do so it would need to be running (and if it's running, it doesn't need to be started). It can't perform a *restart* command either, because if it exited, it would have no way to start a new instance of itself (it wouldn't be around to do it). None of this prevents *ndc* from doing a *start* or *restart*, though.

Here's what those commands do:

getpid
> Prints the nameserver's current process ID.

status
> Prints lots of useful status information about the nameserver, including its version, its debug level, the number of zone transfers running, and whether query logging is on.

start
> Starts the nameserver. If you need to start *named* with any command-line arguments, you can specify these after *start*. For example, *start –c /usr/local/etc/named.conf*.

stop
> Causes the nameserver to exit, writing dynamic zones to their zone datafiles.

restart
> Stops and then starts the nameserver. As with *start*, you can specify command-line arguments for *named* after the command.

exec
> Stops and then starts the nameserver. Unlike *restart*, however, you can't specify command-line options for *named*; the nameserver just starts a new copy of itself with the same command-line arguments.

reload
> Reloads the nameserver. Send this command to a primary nameserver after modifying its configuration file or one or more of its zone datafiles. You can also specify one or more domain names of zones as arguments to *reload*; if you do, the nameserver will reload only these zones.

reconfig [–noexpired]
> Tells the nameserver to check its configuration file for new or deleted zones. Send this command to a nameserver if you've added or deleted zones but haven't changed any existing zones' data. Specifying the *–noexpired* flag tells the nameserver not to bother you with error messages about zones that have expired. This can come in handy if your nameserver is authoritative for thousands of zones and you want to avoid seeing a flurry of expiration messages you already know about.

dumpdb

> Dumps a copy of the nameserver's internal database to *named_dump.db* in the nameserver's current directory.

stats

> Appends the nameserver's statistics to *named.stats* in the nameserver's current directory.

trace [level]

> Appends debugging information to *named.run* in the nameserver's current directory. Specifying higher debug levels increases the amount of detail in the debugging information. For information on what is logged at each level, see Chapter 13.

notrace

> Turns off debugging.

querylog (or qrylog)

> Toggles logging all queries with *syslog*. Logging takes place at priority LOG_INFO. *named* must be compiled with QRYLOG defined (it's defined by default).

quit

> Ends the control session.

rndc and controls (BIND 9)

BIND 9, like BIND 8, uses the *controls* statement to determine how the nameserver listens for control messages. The syntax is the same, except that only the *inet* substatement is allowed. (BIND 9.3.2 doesn't support Unix domain sockets for the control channel yet, and the ISC suggests BIND 9 probably never will.)

With BIND 9, you can leave out the port specification, and the nameserver will default to listening on port 953. You must also add a *keys* specification:

```
controls {
        inet * allow { any; } keys { "rndc-key"; };
};
```

This determines which cryptographic key *rndc* users must authenticate themselves with to send control messages to the nameserver. If you leave the *keys* specification out, you'll see this message after the nameserver starts:

```
Jan 13 18:22:03 terminator named[13964]: type 'inet' control channel
has no 'keys' clause; control channel will be disabled
```

The key or keys specified in the *keys* substatement must be defined in a *key* statement:

```
key "rndc-key" {
        algorithm hmac-md5;
        secret "Zm9vCg==";
};
```

The *key* statement can go directly in *named.conf*, but if your *named.conf* file is world-readable, it's safer to put it in a different file that's not world-readable and include that file in *named.conf*:

```
include "/etc/rndc.key";
```

The only algorithm currently supported is HMAC-MD5, a technique for using the fast MD5 secure hash algorithm to do authentication.* The secret is simply the base-64 encoding of a password that *named* and authorized *rndc* users will share. You can generate the secret using programs such as *mmencode* or *dnssec-keygen* from the BIND distribution, as described in Chapter 11.

For example, you can use *mmencode* to generate the base-64 encoding of *foobarbaz*:

```
% mmencode
foobarbaz
CmZvb2JhcmJh
```

To use *rndc*, you need to create an *rndc.conf* file to tell *rndc* which authentication keys to use and which nameservers to use them with. *rndc.conf* usually lives in */etc*. Here's a simple *rndc.conf* file:

```
options {
        default-server localhost;
        default-key "rndc-key";
};

key "rndc-key" {
        algorithm hmac-md5;
        secret "Zm9vCg==";
};
```

The syntax of the file is very similar to the syntax of *named.conf*. In the *options* statement, you define the default nameserver to send control messages to (which you can override on the command line) and the name of the default key to present to remote nameservers (which you can also override on the command line).

The syntax of the *key* statement is the same as that used in *named.conf*, described earlier. The name of the key in *rndc.conf*, as well as the secret, must match the key definition in *named.conf*.

> Remember that since you're storing keys (which are essentially passwords) in *rndc.conf* and *named.conf*, you should make sure that neither file is readable by users who aren't authorized to control the nameserver.

---

* See RFCs 2085 and 2104 for more information on HMAC-MD5.

If your version of BIND comes with *rndc-confgen*, you can let the tool do most of the work for you. Simply run:

```
# rndc-confgen > /etc/rndc.conf
```

Here is what you'll see in */etc/rndc.conf*:

```
# Start of rndc.conf
key "rndc-key" {
    algorithm hmac-md5;
    secret "4XErjUEy/qgnDuBvHohPtQ==";
};

options {
    default-key "rndc-key";
    default-server 127.0.0.1;
    default-port 953;
};
# End of rndc.conf

# Use with the following in named.conf,
# adjusting the allow list as needed:
#
# key "rndc-key" {
#     algorithm hmac-md5;
#     secret "4XErjUEy/qgnDuBvHohPtQ==";
# };
#
# controls {
#     inet 127.0.0.1 port 953
#         allow { 127.0.0.1; } keys { "rndc-key"; };
# };
# End of named.conf
```

As indicated by the comment, the second half of this file belongs in */etc/named.conf*. Move those lines to */etc/named.conf* and remove the comment character at the beginning of the line. As mentioned earlier, you may want to keep the key in a file outside of */etc/named.conf* for security reasons. Also, notice that the *controls* substatement allows access only to 127.0.0.1. You may need to adjust this list.

Using rndc to control multiple servers

If you're using *rndc* to control only a single nameserver, its configuration is straightforward. You define an authentication key using identical *key* statements in *named.conf* and *rndc.conf*. Then you define your nameserver as the default server to control with the *default-server* substatement in the *rndc.conf options* statement, and define the key as the default key using the *default-key* substatement. Then run *rndc* as:

```
# rndc reload
```

If you have multiple nameservers to control, you can associate each with a different key. Define the keys in separate *key* statements, and then associate each key with a different server in a *server* statement:

```
server localhost {
    key "rndc-key";
};

server wormhole.movie.edu {
    key "wormhole-key";
};
```

Then run *rndc* with the *–s* option to specify the server to control:

```
# rndc -s wormhole.movie.edu reload
```

If you haven't associated a key with a particular nameserver, you can still specify which key to use on the command line with the *–y* option:

```
# rndc -s wormhole.movie.edu -y rndc-wormhole reload
```

Finally, if your nameserver is listening on a nonstandard port for control messages (i.e., a port other than 953), you must use the *–p* option to tell *rndc* which port to connect to:

```
# rndc -s toystory.movie.edu -p 54 reload
```

New rndc commands

In BIND 9.0.0, *rndc* supported only the *reload* command. BIND 9.3.2 supports most of the *ndc* commands, plus many new ones. Here's a list and brief descriptions of each:

reload
> Same as the *ndc* command.

refresh zone
> Schedules an immediate refresh for the specified zone (i.e., an SOA query to the zone's master).

retransfer zone
> Immediately retransfers the specified zone without checking the serial number.

freeze zone
> Suspends dynamic updates to the specified zone. Covered in Chapter 10.

thaw zone
> Resumes dynamic updates to the specified zone. Covered in Chapter 10.

reconfig
> Same as the *ndc* command.

stats
> Same as the *ndc* command.

querylog
> Same as the *ndc* command.

dumpdb

> Same as the *ndc* command. Also allows you to specify whether to dump just cache with the *–cache* option, authoritative zones with the *–zones* option, or both with the *–all* option.

stop

> Same as the *ndc* command.

halt

> Same as *stop*, but doesn't save pending dynamic updates.

trace

> Same as the *ndc* command.

notrace

> Same as the *ndc* command.

flush

> Flushes (empties) the nameserver's cache.

flushname name

> Flushes all records attached to the specified domain name from the nameserver's cache.

status

> Same as the *ndc* command.

recursing

> Dump information about the recursive queries currently being processed to the file *named.recursing* in the current working directory.

Using Signals

Now, back in the old days, all we had to control the nameserver with were signals. If you're stuck in the past (with a version of BIND older than 8.2), you need to use signals to manage your nameserver. The following table is a list of the signals you can send to a nameserver; it includes which *ndc* command each is equivalent to. If you have the shell script version of *ndc* (from BIND 4.9 to 8.1.2), you don't have to pay attention to the signal names because *ndc* will translate the commands into the appropriate signals. With BIND 9, you must use *rndc* for all activities (except reloading and stopping the server) because the signal mechanism for other features is no longer supported.

Signal	BIND 8 signals	ndc equivalent	BIND 9 signals	rndc equivalent
HUP	Reloads the server	*ndc reload*	Reloads the server	*rndc reload*
INT	Dumps the database	*ndc dumpdb*	Stops the server	*rndc dumpdb*
ILL	Dumps the statistics	*ndc stats*	Not supported	*rndc stats*
USR1	Increments the trace level	*ndc trace*	Not supported	*rndc trace*
USR2	Turns off tracing	*ndc notrace*	Not supported	*rndc notrace*

Signal	BIND 8 signals	ndc equivalent	BIND 9 signals	rndc equivalent
WINCH	Toggles query logging	*ndc querylog*	Not supported	*rndc querylog*
TERM	Stops the server	*ndc stop*	Stops the server	*rndc stop*

So, to toggle query logging with an older version of *ndc*, you can use:

```
# ndc querylog
```

just as you would with the newer version of *ndc*. Under the hood, though, this *ndc* is tracking down *named*'s PID and sending it the WINCH signal.

If you don't have *ndc*, you'll have to do what *ndc* does by hand: find *named*'s process ID and send it the appropriate signal. The BIND nameserver leaves its process ID in a disk file called the *PID file*, making it easier to chase the critter down; you don't have to use *ps*. The most common path for the PID file is */var/run/named.pid*. On some systems, the PID file is */etc/named.pid*. Check the *named* manual page to see which directory *named.pid* is in on your system. Since the nameserver's process ID is the only thing in the PID file, sending a HUP signal can be as simple as:

```
# kill -HUP `cat /var/run/named.pid`
```

If you can't find the PID file, you can always find the process ID with *ps*. On a BSD-based system, use:

```
% ps -ax | grep named
```

On a SYS V–based system, use:

```
% ps -ef | grep named
```

However, you may find more than one *named* process running if you use *ps* on some platforms. For example, multithreaded builds of *named* running on Linux show up as multiple processes. If the *ps* output shows multiple nameservers, you can use the *pstree* program to determine which is the parent. This may seem like stating the obvious, but you should send signals only to the *parent* nameserver process.

Updating Zone Datafiles

Something is always changing on your network—new workstations arrive, you finally retire or sell the relic, or you move a host to a different network. Each change means that zone datafiles must be modified. Should you make the changes manually? Or should you wimp out and use a tool to help you?

First, we'll discuss how to make the changes manually. Then, we'll talk about a tool to help out: *h2n*. Actually, we recommend that you use a tool to create the zone datafiles; we were kidding about that wimp stuff, okay? Or at least use a tool to increment the serial number for you. The syntax of zone datafiles lends itself to making mistakes. It doesn't help that the address and pointer records are in different files, which must agree with each other. However, even when you use a tool, it is critical to know what goes on when the files are updated, so we'll start with the manual method.

Adding and Deleting Hosts

After creating your zone datafiles initially, it should be fairly apparent what you need to change when you add a new host. We'll go through the steps here in case you weren't the one to set up those files or if you'd just like a checklist to follow. Make these changes to your *primary* nameserver's zone datafiles. If you make the changes to your *slave* nameserver's backup zone datafiles, the slave's data will change, but the next zone transfer will overwrite it.

- Update the serial number in *db.DOMAIN*. The serial number is likely to be at the top of the file, so it's easy to do first and reduces the chance that you'll forget.
- Add any A (address), CNAME (alias), and MX (mail exchanger) records for the host to the *db.DOMAIN* file. We added the following resource records to the *db.movie.edu* file when a new host (*cujo*) was added to our network:

```
cujo  IN  A   192.253.253.5  ; cujo's internet address
      IN MX   10 cujo        ; if possible, mail directly to cujo
      IN MX   20 toystory    ; otherwise, deliver to our mail hub
```

- Update the serial number and add PTR records to each *db.ADDR* file for which the host has an address. *cujo* only has one address, on network 192.253.253/24; therefore, we added the following PTR record to the *db.192.253.253* file:

```
5  IN PTR cujo.movie.edu.
```

- Reload the primary nameserver; this forces it to load the new information:

```
# rndc reload
```

- If you have a snazzy BIND 9.1 or newer nameserver, you can reload just the zone you changed:

```
# rndc reload movie.edu
```

The primary nameserver will load the new zone data. Slave nameservers will load this new data sometime within the time interval defined in the SOA record for refreshing their data. With version 8 or 9 masters and slaves, the slaves pick up the new data quickly because the primary notifies the slaves of changes within 15 minutes of the change. To delete a host, remove the resource records from *db.DOMAIN* and from each *db.ADDR* file pertaining to that host. Increment the serial number in each zone datafile you changed and reload your primary nameserver.

SOA Serial Numbers

Each zone datafile has a serial number. Every time you change the data in a zone datafile, you must increment the serial number. If you don't increment the serial number, slave nameservers for the zone won't pick up the updated data.

Incrementing the serial number is simple. If the original zone datafile had this SOA record:

```
movie.edu. IN SOA toystory.movie.edu. al.movie.edu. (
                        100     ; Serial
                        3h      ; Refresh
                        1h      ; Retry
                        1w      ; Expire
                        1h )    ; Negative caching TTL
```

the updated zone datafile would have this SOA record:

```
movie.edu. IN SOA toystory.movie.edu. al.movie.edu. (
                        101     ; Serial
                        3h      ; Refresh
                        1h      ; Retry
                        1w      ; Expire
                        1h )    ; Negative caching TTL
```

This simple change is the key to distributing the zone data to all your slaves. Failing to increment the serial number is the most common mistake made when updating a zone. The first few times you make a change to a zone datafile, you'll remember to update the serial number because the process is new, and you're paying close attention. After modifying the zone datafile becomes second nature, you'll make some "quickie" little change, forget to update the serial number...and none of the slaves will pick up the new zone data. That's why you should use a tool that updates the serial number for you! It could be *h2n* or something you write yourself, but it's a good idea to use a tool.

There are several good ways to manage serial numbers. The most obvious is just to use a counter: increment the serial number by one each time you modify the file. Another method is to derive the serial number from the date. For example, you can use the eight-digit number formed by YYYYMMDD. Suppose today is January 15, 2005. In this form, your serial number would be 20050115. This scheme allows only one update per day, though, and that may not be enough. Add another two digits to this number to indicate how many times the file has been updated that day. The first number for January 15, 2005 is then 2005011500. The next modification that day changes the serial number to 2005011501. This scheme allows 100 updates per day. It also lets you know when you last incremented the serial number in the zone datafile. *h2n* generates the serial number from the date if you use the *–y* option. Whatever scheme you choose, the serial number must fit in a 32-bit, unsigned integer.

Starting Over with a New Serial Number

What do you do if the serial number on one of your zones accidentally becomes very large and you want to change it back to a more reasonable value? There is a way that works with all versions of BIND, a way that works with version 4.8.1 and later, and another that works with 4.9 and later.

The way that always works with all versions is to purge your slaves of any knowledge of the old serial number. Then you can start numbering from one (or any convenient point). Here's how. First, change the serial number on your primary server and restart it; now the primary server has the new integer serial number. Log onto one of your slave nameserver hosts and kill the *named* process with the command *rndc stop*. Remove its backup zone datafiles (e.g., *rm bak.movie.edu bak.192.249.249 bak.192.253.253*) and start up your slave nameserver. Since the backup copies were removed, the slave must load a new version of the zone datafiles—picking up the new serial numbers. Repeat this process for each slave server. If any of your slave nameservers aren't under your control, you'll have to contact their administrators to get them to do the same.

If all your slaves run a version of BIND newer than 4.8.1 (and we pray you're not using 4.8.1) but older than BIND 8.2, you can take advantage of the special serial number 0. If you set a zone's serial number to 0, each slave will transfer the zone the next time it checks. In fact, the zone will be transferred *every* time the slave checks, so don't forget to increment the serial number once all the slaves have synchronized on serial number 0. But there is a limit to how far you can increment the serial number. Read on.

The other method of fixing the serial number (with 4.9 and later slaves) is easier to understand if we first cover some background material. The DNS serial number is a 32-bit unsigned integer whose value ranges from 0 to 4,294,967,295. The serial number uses *sequence space arithmetic*, which means that for any serial number, half the numbers in the number space (2,147,483,647 numbers) are less than the serial number, and half the numbers are larger.

Let's go over an example of sequence space numbers. Suppose the serial number is 5. Serial numbers 6 through (5 + 2,147,483,647) are larger than serial number 5, and serial numbers (5 + 2,147,483,649) through 4 are smaller. Notice that the serial number wrapped around to 4 after reaching 4,294,967,295. Also notice that we didn't include the number (5 + 2,147,483,648), because this is exactly halfway around the number space and can be larger or smaller than 5, depending on the implementation. To be safe, don't use it.

Now back to the original problem. If your zone serial number is 25,000, and you want to start numbering at 1 again, you can speed through the serial number space in two steps. First, add the largest increment possible to your serial number (25,000 + 2,147,483,647 = 2,147,508,647). If the number you come up with is larger than 4,294,967,295 (the largest 32-bit value), you'll have wrap around to the beginning of the number space by subtracting 4,294,967,296 from it. After changing the serial number, you must wait for all your slaves to pick up a new copy of the zone. Second, change the zone serial number to its target value (1), which is now *larger* than the current serial number (2,147,508,647). After the slaves pick up a new copy of the zone, you're done!

Additional Zone Datafile Entries

After you've been running a nameserver for a while, you may want to add data to your nameserver to help you manage your zone. Have you ever been stumped when someone asked you *where* one of your hosts is? Maybe you don't even remember what kind of host it is. Administrators have to manage larger and larger populations of hosts these days, making it easy to lose track of this information. The nameserver can help you out. And if one of your hosts is acting up, and someone notices remotely, the nameserver can help that person get in touch with you.

So far in the book, we've covered SOA, NS, A, CNAME, PTR, and MX records. These records are critical to everyday operation: nameservers need them to operate, and applications look up data of these types. DNS defines many more record types, though. The next most useful resource record types are TXT and RP; these can tell you a host's location and responsible person. For a list of common (and not-so-common) resource records, see Appendix A.

General text information

TXT stands for TeXT. These records are simply a list of strings, each less than 256 characters in length.

TXT records can be used for anything you want; one use lists a host's location:

```
cujo  IN  TXT  "Location: machine room dog house"
```

BIND TXT records have a 2 KB limit. You can specify the TXT record as a single string or as multiple strings:

```
cujo  IN  TXT  "Location:" "machine room dog house"
```

Responsible Person

Domain administrators will undoubtedly develop a love/hate relationship with the Responsible Person, or RP, record. The RP record can be attached to any domain name, internal or leaf, and indicates who is responsible for that host or zone. This enables you to locate the miscreant responsible for the host peppering you with DNS queries, for example. But it also leads people to you when one of your hosts acts up.

The record takes two arguments as its record-specific data: an electronic mail address in domain name format and a domain name pointing to additional data about the contact. The electronic mail address is in the same format the SOA record uses: it substitutes a "." for the "@". The next argument is a domain name, which must have a TXT record associated with it. The TXT record then contains free-format information about the contact, such as full name and phone number. If you omit either field, you must specify the root domain (".") as a placeholder instead.

Here are some example RP (and associated) records:

```
shrek       IN  RP   root.movie.edu.  hotline.movie.edu.
            IN  RP   snewman.movie.edu.  sn.movie.edu.
hotline     IN  TXT  "Movie U. Network Hotline, (415) 555-4111"
sn          IN  TXT  "Sommer Newman, (415) 555-9612"
```

Note that TXT records for *root.movie.edu* and *snewman.movie.edu* aren't necessary because they're only the domain name encoding of electronic mail addresses, not real domain names.

Generating Zone Datafiles from the Host Table

As you saw in Chapter 4, we defined a process for converting host-table information into zone data. We've written a tool in Perl to automate this process, called *h2n*.[*] Using a tool to generate your data has one big advantage: there will be no syntax errors or inconsistencies in your zone datafiles—assuming *h2n* is written correctly! One common inconsistency is to have an A (address) record for a host but no corresponding PTR (pointer) record, or the other way around. Because this data is in separate zone datafiles, it is easy to err.

What does *h2n* do? Given the */etc/hosts* file and some command-line options, *h2n* creates the datafiles for your zones. As a system administrator, you keep the host table current. Each time you modify the host table, you run *h2n* again. *h2n* rebuilds each zone datafile from scratch, assigning each new file the next higher serial number. It can be run manually or from *cron* each night. If you use *h2n*, you'll never again have to worry about forgetting to increment the serial number.

First, *h2n* needs to know the domain name of your forward-mapping zone and your network numbers. (*h2n* can figure out the names of your reverse-mapping zones from your network numbers.) These map conveniently into the zone datafile names: *movie.edu* zone data goes in *db.movie*, and network 192.249.249/24 data goes into *db.192.249.249*. The domain name of your forward-mapping zone and your network number are specified with the *–d* and *–n* options, as follows:

–d domain name
> The domain name of your forward-mapping zone.

–n network number
> The network number of your network. If you are generating files for several networks, use several *–n* options on the command line. Omit trailing zeros and netmask specifications from the network numbers.

---

[*] In case you've forgotten how to get *h2n*, see the Preface.

The *h2n* command requires the *–d* flag and at least one *–n* option; they have no default values. For example, to create the datafile for the zone *movie.edu*, which consists of two networks, give the command:

```
% h2n -d movie.edu -n 192.249.249 -n 192.253.253
```

For greater control over the data, you can use other options:

–s server

> The nameservers for the NS records. As with *–n*, use several *–s* options if you have multiple primary or slave nameservers. A version 8 or 9 server will NOTIFY this list of servers when a zone changes. The default is the host that runs *h2n*.

–h host

> The host for the MNAME field of the SOA record. *host* must be the primary nameserver to ensure proper operation of the NOTIFY feature. The default is the host that runs *h2n*.

–u user

> The mail address of the person in charge of the zone data. This defaults to *root* on the host that runs *h2n*.

–o other

> Other SOA values, not including the serial number, as a colon-separated list. These default to 10800:3600:604800:86400.

–f file

> Reads the *h2n* options from the named *file* rather than from the command line. If you have lots of options, keep them in a file.

–v 4|8

> Generates configuration files for BIND 4 or 8; version 8 is the default. Since BIND 9's configuration file format is basically the same as BIND 8's, you can use *–v 8* for a BIND 9 nameserver.

–y

> Generates the serial number from the date.

Here is an example that uses all the options mentioned so far:

```
% h2n -f opts
```

Here are the contents of file *opts*:

```
-d movie.edu
-n 192.249.249
-n 192.253.253
-s toystory.movie.edu
-s wormhole
-u al
-h toystory
-o 10800:3600:604800:86400
-v 8
-y
```

If an option requires a hostname, you can provide either a full domain name (e.g., *toystory.movie.edu*) or just the host's name (e.g., *toystory*). If you give the hostname only, *h2n* forms a complete domain name by adding the domain name given with the *–d* option. (If a trailing dot is necessary, *h2n* adds it too.)

There are more options to *h2n* than we've shown here. For the complete list of options, you'll have to look at the manual page.

Of course, some kinds of resource records aren't easy to generate from */etc/hosts*; the necessary data simply isn't there. You may need to add these records manually. But since *h2n* always rewrites zone datafiles, won't your changes be overwritten?

Well, *h2n* provides a "back door" for inserting this kind of data. Put these special records in a file named *spcl.DOMAIN*, where *DOMAIN* is the first label of the domain name of your zone. When *h2n* finds this file, it "includes" it by adding the line:

```
$INCLUDE spcl.DOMAIN
```

to the end of the *db.DOMAIN* file. (The $INCLUDE control statement is described later in this chapter.) For example, the administrator of *movie.edu* may add extra MX records into the file *spcl.movie* so that users can mail to *movie.edu* directly instead of sending mail to hosts within *movie.edu*. Upon finding this file, *h2n* puts the line:

```
$INCLUDE spcl.movie
```

at the end of the zone datafile *db.movie*.

Keeping the Root Hints Current

As we explained in Chapter 4, the root hints file tells your nameserver where the servers for the root zone are. It must be updated periodically. The root nameservers don't change very often, but they do change. A good practice is to check your root hints file every month or two. In Chapter 4, we told you to get the file by FTP'ing to *ftp.rs.internic.net*. And that's probably the best way to keep current.

If you have a copy of *dig*, a query tool included in the BIND distribution (and covered in Chapter 12), you can retrieve the current list of root nameservers by running:

```
% dig @a.root-servers.net . ns > db.cache
```

Organizing Your Files

Back when you first set up your zones, organizing your files was simple: you put them all in a single directory. There was one configuration file and a handful of zone datafiles. Over time, though, your responsibilities grew. More networks were added and hence more *in-addr.arpa* zones. Maybe you delegated a few subdomains. You started backing up zones for other sites. After a while, an *ls* of your nameserver directory no longer fit on a single screen. It's time to reorganize. BIND has a few features that will help with this reorganization.

BIND nameservers support a configuration file statement, called *include*, which allows you to insert the contents of a file into the current configuration file. This lets you take a very large configuration file and break it into smaller pieces.

Zone datafiles (for all BIND versions) support two* control statements: $ORIGIN and $INCLUDE. The $ORIGIN statement changes a zone datafile's origin, and $INCLUDE inserts a new file into the current zone datafile. These control statements are not resource records; they facilitate the maintenance of DNS data. In particular, they make it easier for you to divide your zone into subdomains by allowing you to store the data for each subdomain in a separate file.

Using Several Directories

One way to organize your zone datafiles is to store them in separate directories. If your nameserver is a primary for several sites' zones (both forward- and reverse-mapping), you can store each site's zone datafiles in its own directory. Another arrangement might be to store all the primary zones' datafiles in one directory and all the backup zone datafiles in another. Let's look at what the configuration file might look like if you chose to split up your primary and slave zones:

```
options { directory "/var/named"; };
//
// These files are not specific to any zone
//
zone "." {
        type hint;
        file "db.cache";
};
zone "0.0.127.in-addr.arpa" {
        type master;
        file "db.127.0.0";
};
//
// These are our primary zone files
//
zone "movie.edu" {
        type master;
        file "primary/db.movie.edu";
};
zone "249.249.192.in-addr.arpa" {
        type master;
        file "primary/db.192.249.249";
};
zone "253.253.192.in-addr.arpa" {
```

---

* Three if you count $TTL, which BIND 8.2 and later nameservers support.

```
        type master;
        file "primary/db.192.253.253";
};
//
// These are our slave zone files
//
zone "ora.com" {
        type slave;
        file "slave/bak.ora.com";
        masters { 198.112.208.25; };
};
zone "208.112.192.in-addr.arpa" {
        type slave;
        file "slave/bak.198.112.208";
        masters { 198.112.208.25; };
};
```

Another variation on this division is to break the configuration file into three files: the main file, a file that contains all the *primary* entries, and a file that contains all the *secondary* entries. Here's what the main configuration file might look like:

```
options { directory "/var/named"; };
//
// These files are not specific to any zone
//
zone "." {
        type hint;
        file "db.cache";
};
zone "0.0.127.in-addr.arpa" {
        type master;
        file "db.127.0.0";
};

include "named.conf.primary";
include "named.conf.slave";
```

Here is *named.conf.primary*:

```
//
// These are our primary zone files
//
zone "movie.edu" {
        type master;
        file "primary/db.movie.edu";
};
zone "249.249.192.in-addr.arpa" {
        type master;
        file "primary/db.192.249.249";
};
zone "253.253.192.in-addr.arpa" {
        type master;
        file "primary/db.192.253.253";
};
```

Here is *named.conf.slave*:

```
//
// These are our slave zone files
//
zone "ora.com" {
        type slave;
        file "slave/bak.ora.com";
        masters { 198.112.208.25; };
};
zone "208.112.192.in-addr.arpa" {
        type slave;
        file "slave/bak.198.112.208";
        masters { 198.112.208.25; };
};
```

You might think the organization would be better if you put the configuration file with the *primary* directives into the *primary* subdirectory by adding a new *directory* directive to change to this directory, and remove the *primary/* from each filename because the nameserver is now running in that directory. Then you could make comparable changes in the configuration file with the *secondary* lines. Unfortunately, that doesn't work. BIND allows you to define only a single working directory. Things get rather confusing when the nameserver keeps switching around to different directories: backup zone datafiles end up in the last directory the nameserver changed to, for example.

Changing the Origin in a Zone Datafile

With BIND, the default origin for the zone datafiles is the second field of the *zone* statement in the *named.conf* file. The origin is a domain name that is automatically appended to all names in the file that don't end in a dot. This origin can be changed in the zone datafile with the $ORIGIN control statement. In the zone datafile, $ORIGIN is followed by a domain name. (Don't forget the trailing dot if you use the full domain name!) From this point on, all names that don't end in a dot have the new origin appended. If your zone (e.g., *movie.edu*) has a number of subdomains, you can use the $ORIGIN statement to reset the origin and simplify the zone datafile. For example:

```
$ORIGIN classics.movie.edu.
maltese        IN  A  192.253.253.100
casablanca     IN  A  192.253.253.101

$ORIGIN comedy.movie.edu.
mash           IN  A  192.253.253.200
twins          IN  A  192.253.253.201
```

We cover creating subdomains in more depth in Chapter 9.

Including Other Zone Datafiles

Once you've subdivided your zone like this, you might find it more convenient to keep each subdomain's records in separate files. The $INCLUDE control statement lets you do this:

```
$ORIGIN classics.movie.edu.
$INCLUDE db.classics.movie.edu

$ORIGIN comedy.movie.edu.
$INCLUDE db.comedy.movie.edu
```

To simplify the file even further, you can specify the included file and the new origin on a single line:

```
$INCLUDE db.classics.movie.edu classics.movie.edu.
$INCLUDE db.comedy.movie.edu   comedy.movie.edu.
```

When you specify the origin and the included file on a single line, the origin change applies only to the particular file that you're including. For example, the *comedy.movie.edu* origin applies only to the names in *db.comedy.movie.edu*. After *db.comedy.movie.edu* has been included, the origin returns to what it was before $INCLUDE, even if there was an $ORIGIN control statement within *db.comedy.movie.edu*.

Changing System File Locations

BIND allows you to change the name and location of the following system files: *named.pid*, *named-xfer*, *named_dump.db*, and *named.stats*. Most of you will not need to use this feature; don't feel obligated to change the names or locations of these files just because you can.

If you do change the location of the files written by the nameserver (*named.pid*, *named_dump.db*, or *named.stats*), for security reasons you should choose a directory that is not world-writable. While we don't know of any break-ins caused by writing these files, you should follow this guideline just to be safe.

named.pid's full path is usually */var/run/named.pid or /etc/named.pid*. One reason you might change the default location of this file is if you find yourself running more than one nameserver on a single host. Yikes! Why would someone do that? Well, Chapter 10 gives an example of running two nameservers on one host (and explains the rationale behind it). You can specify a different *named.pid* file in the configuration file for each server:

```
options { pid-file "server1.pid"; };
```

named-xfer's path is usually */usr/sbin/named-xfer or /etc/named-xfer*. You'll remember that *named-xfer* is used by a slave nameserver for inbound zone transfers. One reason you might change the default location is to build and test a new version of

BIND in a local directory; your test version of *named* can be configured to use the local version of *named-xfer*:

```
options { named-xfer "/home/rudy/named/named-xfer"; };
```

Since BIND 9 doesn't use *named-xfer*, of course, there's not much call for this substatement with BIND 9.

The nameserver writes *named_dump.db* into its current directory when you tell it to dump its database. Here's an example of how to change the location of the dump file:

```
options { dump-file "/home/rudy/named/named_dump.db"; };
```

The nameserver writes *named.stats* into its current directory when you tell it to dump statistics. Here's an example of how to change its location:

```
options { statistics-file "/home/rudy/named/named.stats"; };
```

Logging

BIND supports extensive logging, which consists of writing information to a debug file and sending information to *syslog*. Extensive logging has its costs, though; there's a lot to learn before you can effectively configure this subsystem. If you don't have time to experiment with logging, use the defaults and come back to this topic later. Most of you won't need to change the default logging behavior.

There are two main concepts in logging: *channels* and *categories*. A channel specifies where logged data goes: to *syslog*, to a file, to *named*'s standard error output, or to the bit bucket. A category specifies what data is logged. In the BIND source code, most messages the nameserver logs are categorized according to the function of the code they relate to. For example, a message produced by the part of BIND that handles dynamic updates is probably in the *update* category. We'll give you a list of the categories shortly.

Each category of data can be sent to a single channel or to multiple channels. In Figure 7-1, queries are logged to a file while zone transfer data is both logged to a file and to *syslog*.

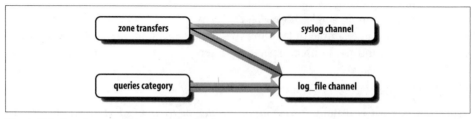

Figure 7-1. Logging categories to channels

Channels allow you to filter by message severity. Here's the list of severities, from most severe to least:

```
critical
error
warning
notice
info
debug [level]
dynamic
```

The top five severities (*critical*, *error*, *warning*, *notice*, and *info*) are the familiar severity levels used by *syslog*. The other two (*debug* and *dynamic*) are unique to BIND.

debug is nameserver debugging for which you can specify a debug level. If you omit the debug level, the level is assumed to be 1. If you specify a debug level, you will see messages of that level when nameserver debugging is turned on (e.g., if you specify "debug 3," you will see level 3 debugging messages even when you send only one trace command to the nameserver). If you specify *dynamic* severity, the nameserver will log messages that match its debug level. (For example, if you send one trace command to the nameserver, it logs messages from level 1. If you send three trace commands to the nameserver, it logs messages from levels 1 through 3.) The default severity is *info*, which means that you won't see debug messages unless you specify the severity.

 You can configure a channel to log both debug messages and *syslog* messages to a file. However, the converse is not true: you cannot configure a channel to log both debug messages and *syslog* messages with *syslog*; debug messages can't be sent to *syslog*.

Let's configure a couple of channels to show you how this works. The first channel will go to *syslog* and log with facility *daemon*, sending those messages of severity *info* and above. The second channel will go to a file, logging debug messages at any level as well as *syslog* messages. Here is the *logging* statement:

```
logging {
  channel my_syslog {
    syslog daemon;
    // Debug messages will not be sent to syslog, so
    // there is no point to setting the severity to
    // debug or dynamic; use the lowest syslog level: info.
    severity info;
  };
  channel my_file {
    file "/tmp/log.msgs";
    // Set the severity to dynamic to see all the debug messages.
    severity dynamic;
  };
};
```

Now that we've configured a couple of channels, we have to tell the nameserver exactly what to send to those channels. Let's implement what was pictured in Figure 7-1, with zone transfers going to *syslog* and to the file, and queries going to the file. The category specification is part of the *logging* statement, so we'll build on the previous *logging* statement:

```
logging {
  channel my_syslog {
     syslog daemon;
     severity info;
  };
  channel my_file {
     file "/tmp/log.msgs";
     severity dynamic;
  };

  category xfer-out { my_syslog; my_file; };
  category queries { my_file; };
};
```

With this *logging* statement in your configuration file, start your nameserver and send it a few queries. If nothing is written to *log.msgs*, you may have to turn on nameserver debugging to get queries logged:

```
# rndc trace
```

Now if you send your nameserver some queries, they're logged to *log.msgs*. But look around the nameserver's working directory: there's a new file called *named.run*. It has all the other debugging information written to it. You didn't want all this other debugging, though; you just wanted the transfers and queries. How do you get rid of *named.run*?

There's a special category we haven't told you about: *default*. If you don't specify any channels for a category, BIND sends those messages to whichever channel the *default* category is assigned to. Let's change the *default* category to discard all logging messages (there's a channel called *null* for this purpose):

```
logging {
  channel my_syslog {
     syslog daemon;
     severity info;
  };
  channel my_file {
     file "/tmp/log.msgs";
     severity dynamic;
  };

  category default { null; };
  category xfer-out { my_syslog; my_file; };
  category queries { my_file; };
};
```

Now start your server, turn on debugging to level 1 (if necessary), and send some queries. The queries end up in *log.msgs*, and *named.run* is created but stays empty. Great! We're getting the hang of this after all.

A few days pass. One of your coworkers notices that the nameserver is sending much fewer messages to *syslog* than it used to. What happened?

Well, the *default* category is set up, by default, to send messages to both *syslog* and to the debug file (*named.run*). When you assigned the *default* category to the *null* channel, you turned off the other *syslog* messages, too. Here's what we should have used:

```
category default { my_syslog; };
```

This sends the *syslog* messages to *syslog* but does not write debug or *syslog* messages to a file.

Remember, we said you'd have to experiment for a while with logging to get exactly what you want. We hope this example gives you a hint of what you might run into. Now, let's go over the details of logging.

The logging Statement

Here's the syntax of the *logging* statement. It's rather intimidating. We'll go over some more examples as we explain what each substatement means:

```
logging {
  [ channel channel_name {
    ( file path_name
      [ versions ( number | unlimited ) ]
      [ size size_spec ]
    | syslog ( kern | user | mail | daemon | auth | syslog | lpr |
               news | uucp | cron | authpriv | ftp |
               local0 | local1 | local2 | local3 |
               local4 | local5 | local6 | local7 )
    | stderr
    | null );

    [ severity ( critical | error | warning | notice |
                 info  | debug [ level ] | dynamic ); ]
    [ print-category yes_or_no; ]
    [ print-severity yes_or_no; ]
    [ print-time yes_or_no; ]
  }; ]

  [ category category_name {
    channel_name; [ channel_name; ... ]
  }; ]
  ...
};
```

Here are the default channels. The nameserver creates these channels even if you don't want them. You can't redefine these channels; you can only add more of them.

```
channel default_syslog {
    syslog daemon;         // send to syslog's daemon facility
    severity info;         // only send severity info and higher
};

channel default_debug {
    file "named.run";      // write to named.run in the
                           // working directory
    severity dynamic;      // log at the server's current debug level
};

channel default_stderr {   // writes to stderr
    stderr;                // only BIND 9 lets you define your own stderr
                           // channel, though BIND 8 has the built-in
                           // default_stderr channel.
    severity info;         // only send severity info and higher
};

channel null {
    null;                  // toss anything sent to this channel
};
```

If you don't assign channels to the categories *default*, *panic*, *packet*, and *eventlib*, a BIND 8 nameserver assigns them these channels by default:

```
logging {
    category default { default_syslog; default_debug; };
    category panic { default_syslog; default_stderr; };
    category packet { default_debug; };
    category eventlib { default_debug; };
};
```

A BIND 9 nameserver uses this as the default logging statement:

```
logging {
    category default {
        default_syslog;
        default_debug;
    };
};
```

As we mentioned earlier, the *default* category logs to both *syslog* and to the debug file (which by default is *named.run*). This means that all *syslog* messages of severity *info* and above are sent to *syslog*, and when debugging is turned on, the *syslog* messages and debug messages are written to *named.run*.

Channel Details

A channel may be defined to go to a file, to *syslog*, or to null.

File channels

If a channel goes to a file, you must specify the file's pathname. Optionally, you can specify how many versions of the file can exist at one time and how big the file may grow.

If you specify that there can be three versions, BIND will retain *file*, *file.0*, *file.1*, and *file.2*. After the nameserver starts or after it is reloaded, it moves *file.1* to *file.2*, *file.0* to *file.1*, *file* to *file.0*, and starts writing to a new copy of *file*. If you specify unlimited versions, BIND will keep 99 versions.

If you specify a maximum file size, the nameserver stops writing to the file after it reaches the specified size. Unlike the *versions* substatement (mentioned in the last paragraph), the file is not rolled over and a new file opened when the specified size is reached. The nameserver just stops writing to the file. If you do not specify a file size, the file grows indefinitely.

Here is an example file channel using the *versions* and *size* substatements:

```
logging{
  channel my_file {
      file "log.msgs" versions 3 size 10k;
      severity dynamic;
  };
};
```

The size can include a scaling factor, as in the example. *K* or *k* is kilobytes; *M* or *m* is megabytes; *G* or *g* is gigabytes.

It's important to specify the severity as either *debug* or *dynamic* if you want to see debug messages. The default severity is *info*, which shows you only *syslog* messages.

syslog channels

If a channel goes to *syslog*, you can specify the facility to be any of the following: *kern*, *user*, *mail*, *daemon*, *auth*, *syslog*, *lpr*, *news*, *uucp*, *cron*, *authpriv*, *ftp*, *local0*, *local1*, *local2*, *local3*, *local4*, *local5*, *local6*, or *local7*. The default is *daemon*, and we recommend that you either use that or one of the local facilities.

Here's an example *syslog* channel that uses the facility *local0* instead of *daemon*:

```
logging {
    channel my_syslog {
        syslog local0;       // send to syslog's local0 facility
        severity info;       // only send severity info and higher
    };
};
```

stderr channel

There is a predefined channel called *default_stderr* for any messages you'd like written to the *stderr* file descriptor of the nameserver. With BIND 8, you cannot configure any other file descriptors to use *stderr*. With BIND 9, you can.

null channel

There is a predefined channel called *null* for messages you want to throw away.

Data formatting for all channels

The BIND logging facility also allows you some control over the formatting of messages. You can add a timestamp, a category, and a severity level to the messages.

Here's an example debug message that has all the extra goodies:

```
01-Feb-1998 13:19:18.889 config: debug 1: source = db.127.0.0
```

The category for this message is *config*, and the severity is *debug* level 1.

Here's an example channel configuration that includes all three additions:

```
logging {
  channel my_file {
     file "log.msgs";
     severity debug;
     print-category yes;
     print-severity yes;
     print-time yes;
  };
};
```

There isn't much point in adding a timestamp for messages to a *syslog* channel because *syslog* adds the time and date itself.

Category Details

Both BIND 8 and BIND 9 have lots of categories—lots! Unfortunately, they're different categories. We'll list them here so you can see them all. Rather than trying to figure out which you want to see, we recommend that you configure your nameserver to print out all its log messages with their category and severity, and then pick out the ones you want to see. We'll show you how to do this after describing the categories.

BIND 8 categories

default
>   If you don't specify any channels for a category, the *default* category is used. In that sense, *default* is synonymous with all categories. However, there are some messages that didn't end up in a category. So, even if you specify channels for

each category individually, you'll still want to specify a channel for the *default* category for all the uncategorized messages.

If you do not specify a channel for the *default* category, one will be specified for you:

```
category default { default_syslog; default_debug; };
```

cname

CNAME errors (e.g., "…has CNAME and other data").

config

High-level configuration file processing.

db

Database operations.

eventlib

System events; must point to a single file channel. The default is:

```
category eventlib { default_debug; };
```

insist

Internal consistency check failures.

lame-servers

Detection of bad delegation.

load

Zone loading messages.

maintenance

Periodic maintenance events (e.g., system queries).

ncache

Negative caching events.

notify

Asynchronous zone change notifications.

os

Problems with the operating system.

packet

Decodes of packets received and sent; must point to a single file channel. The default is:

```
category packet { default_debug; };
```

panic

Problems that cause the shutdown of the server. These problems are logged both in the *panic* category and in their native category. The default is:

```
category panic { default_syslog; default_stderr; };
```

parser

Low-level configuration file processing.

queries
> Query logging.

response-checks
> Malformed responses, unrelated additional information, etc.

security
> Approved/unapproved requests.

statistics
> Periodic reports of activities.

update
> Dynamic update events.

update-security
> Unapproved dynamic updates. (In 8.4.0, these were moved into their own category so that administrators could more easily filter them out.)

xfer-in
> Zone transfers from remote nameservers to the local nameserver.

xfer-out
> Zone transfers from the local nameserver to remote nameservers.

BIND 9 categories

default
> As with BIND 8, BIND 9's *default* category matches all categories not specifically assigned to channels. However, BIND 9's *default* category, unlike BIND 8's, doesn't match BIND's messages that aren't categorized. Those are part of the category listed next.

general
> The *general* category contains all BIND messages that aren't explicitly classified.

client
> Processing client requests.

config
> Configuration file parsing and processing.

database
> Messages relating to BIND's internal database; used to store zone data and cache records.

dnssec
> Processing DNSSEC-signed responses.

lame-servers
> Detection of bad delegation (re-added in BIND 9.1.0; before that, lame server messages were logged to *resolver*).

network

> Network operations.

notify

> Asynchronous zone change notifications.

queries

> Query logging (added in BIND 9.1.0).

resolver

> Name resolution, including the processing of recursive queries from resolvers.

security

> Approved/unapproved requests.

update

> Dynamic update events.

update-security

> Unapproved dynamic updates. See note under the like-named BIND 8 category (added in 9.3.0).

xfer-in

> Zone transfers from remote nameservers to the local nameserver.

xfer-out

> Zone transfers from the local nameserver to remote nameservers.

Viewing all category messages

A good way to start your foray into logging is to configure your nameserver to log all its messages to a file, including the category and severity, and then pick out which messages you are interested in.

Earlier, we listed the categories that are configured by default. Here they are for BIND 8:

```
logging {
    category default { default_syslog; default_debug; };
    category panic { default_syslog; default_stderr; };
    category packet { default_debug; };
    category eventlib { default_debug; };
};
```

And here's the category for BIND 9:

```
logging {
    category default { default_syslog; default_debug; };
};
```

By default, the category and severity are not included with messages written to the *default_debug* channel. In order to see all the log messages, with their category and severity, you'll have to configure each category yourself.

Here's a BIND 8 *logging* statement that does just that:

```
logging {
  channel my_file {
     file "log.msgs";
     severity dynamic;
     print-category yes;
     print-severity yes;
  };

  category default  { default_syslog; my_file; };
  category panic    { default_syslog; my_file; };
  category packet   { my_file; };
  category eventlib { my_file; };
  category queries  { my_file; };
};
```

(A BIND 9 *logging* statement wouldn't have *panic*, *packet*, or *eventlib* categories.)

Notice that we've defined each category to include the channel *my_file*. We also added one category that wasn't in the previous default logging statement: *queries*. Queries aren't printed unless you configure the *queries* category.

Start your server, and turn on debugging to level 1. You'll then see messages in *log.msgs* that look like the following. (BIND 9 shows only the query message because it doesn't generate these debug messages anymore.)

```
queries: info: XX /192.253.253.4/foo.movie.edu/A
default: debug 1: req: nlookup(foo.movie.edu) id 4 type=1 class=1
default: debug 1: req: found 'foo.movie.edu' as 'foo.movie.edu' (cname=0)
default: debug 1: ns_req: answer -> [192.253.253.4].2338 fd=20 id=4 size=87
```

Once you've determined the messages that interest you, configure your server to log only those messages.

Keeping Everything Running Smoothly

A significant part of maintenance is being aware that something is wrong before it becomes a real problem. If you catch a problem early, chances are it'll be that much easier to fix. As the old adage says, an ounce of prevention is worth a pound of cure.

This isn't quite troubleshooting—we'll devote an entire chapter to troubleshooting later—think of it more as "pre-troubleshooting." Troubleshooting (the pound of cure) is what you have to do after your problem has developed complications and you need to identify the problem by its symptoms.

The next two sections deal with preventative maintenance: looking periodically at the *syslog* file and at the BIND nameserver statistics to see whether any problems are developing. Consider this a nameserver's medical checkup.

Common Syslog Messages

There are a large number of *syslog* messages that *named* can emit. In practice, you'll see only a few of them. We'll cover the most common *syslog* messages here, excluding reports of syntax errors in zone datafiles.

Every time you start *named*, it sends out a message at priority LOG_NOTICE. For a BIND 8 nameserver, it looks like this:

```
Jan 10 20:48:32 toystory named[3221]: starting.  named 8.2.3 Tue May 16 09:39:40
MDT 2000 cricket@huskymo.boulder.acmebw.com:/usr/local/src/bind-8.2.3/src/bin/
named
```

For BIND 9, it's significantly abridged:

```
Jul 27 16:18:41 toystory named[7045]: starting BIND 9.3.2
```

This message logs the fact that *named* started at this time and tells you the version of BIND you're running as well as who built it and where (for BIND 8). Of course, this is nothing to be concerned about. It *is* a good place to look if you're not sure what version of BIND your operating system supports.

Every time you send the nameserver a reload command, a BIND 8 nameserver sends out this message at priority LOG_NOTICE:

```
Jan 10 20:50:16 toystory named[3221]: reloading nameserver
```

Here's the BIND 9 nameservers log:

```
Jul 27 16:27:45 toystory named[7047]: loading configuration from
                    '/etc/named.conf'
```

These messages simply tell you that *named* reloaded its database (as a result of a reload command) at this time. Again, this is nothing to be concerned about. This message will most likely be of interest when you are tracking down how long a bad resource record has been in your zone data or how long a whole zone has been missing because of a mistake during an update.

Here's another message you may see shortly after your nameserver starts:

```
Jan 10 20:50:20 toystory named[3221]: cannot set resource limits on
                    this system
```

This means that your nameserver thinks your operating system does not support the *getrlimit( )* and *setrlimit( )* system calls, which are used when you try to define *coresize*, *datasize*, *stacksize*, or *files*. It doesn't matter whether you're actually using any of these substatements in your configuration file; BIND will print the message anyway. If you are not using these substatements, ignore the message. If you are, and you think your operating system actually does support *getrlimit( )* and *setrlimit( )*, you'll have to recompile BIND with HAVE_GETRUSAGE defined. This message is logged at priority LOG_INFO.

If you run your nameserver on a host with many network interfaces (especially virtual network interfaces), you may see this message soon after startup or even after your nameserver has run well for a while:

```
Jan 10 20:50:31 toystory named[3221]: fcntl(dfd, F_DUPFD, 20): Too
            many open files
Jan 10 20:50:31 toystory named[3221]: fcntl(sfd, F_DUPFD, 20): Too
            many open files
```

This means that BIND has run out of file descriptors. BIND uses a fair number of file descriptors: two for each network interface it's listening on (one for UDP and one for TCP), and one for opening zone datafiles. If that's more than the limit your operating system places on processes, BIND won't be able to get any more file descriptors, and you'll see this message. The priority depends on which part of BIND fails to get the file descriptor: the more critical the subsystem, the higher the priority.

The next step is either to get BIND to use fewer file descriptors, or to raise the limit the operating system places on the number of file descriptors BIND can use:

- If you don't need BIND listening on all your network interfaces (particularly the virtual ones), use the *listen-on* substatement to configure BIND to listen only on those interfaces it needs to. See Chapter 10 for details on the syntax of *listen-on*.

- If your operating system supports *getrlimit()* and *setrlimit()* (as just described), configure your nameserver to use a larger number of files with the *files* substatement. See Chapter 10 for details on using the *files* substatement.

- If your operating system places too restrictive a limit on open files, raise that limit before you start *named* with the *ulimit* command.

Every time a nameserver loads a zone, it sends out a message at priority LOG_INFO:

```
Jan 10 21:49:50 toystory named[3221]: zone movie.edu/IN
            loaded serial 2005011000
```

This tells you when the nameserver loaded the zone, the class of the zone (in this case, IN), and the serial number in the zone's SOA record.

About every hour, a BIND 8 nameserver sends a snapshot of the current statistics at priority LOG_INFO:

```
Feb 18 14:09:02 toystory named[3565]: USAGE 824681342 824600158
            CPU=13.01u/3.26s CHILDCPU=9.99u/12.71s
Feb 18 14:09:02 toystory named[3565]: NSTATS 824681342 824600158
            A=4 PTR=2
Feb 18 14:09:02 toystory named[3565]: XSTATS 824681342 824600158
            RQ=6 RR=2 RIQ=0 RNXD=0 RFwdQ=0 RFwdR=0 RDupQ=0 RDupR=0
            RFail=0 RFErr=0 RErr=0 RTCP=0 RAXFR=0 RLame=0 Ropts=0
            SSysQ=2 SAns=6 SFwdQ=0 SFwdR=0 SDupQ=5 SFail=0 SFErr=0
            SErr=0 RNotNsQ=6 SNaAns=2 SNXD=1
```

(BIND 9 doesn't send out the statistics as a log message.) The first two numbers for each message are times. If you subtract the second number from the first number, you'll find out how many seconds your server has been running. (You'd think the nameserver could do that for you.) The CPU entry tells you how much time your server has spent in user mode (13.01 seconds) and system mode (3.26 seconds). Then it tells you the same statistic for child processes. The NSTATS message lists the types of queries your server has received and the counts for each. The XSTATS message lists additional statistics. The statistics under NSTATS and XSTATS are explained in more detail later in this chapter.

If BIND finds a name that doesn't conform to RFC 952, it logs a *syslog* error:

```
Jul 24 20:56:26 toystory named[1496]: ID_4.movie.edu IN:
                          bad owner name (check-names)
```

This message is logged at level LOG_ERROR. See Chapter 4 for the host-naming rules.

Another *syslog* message, sent at priority LOG_ERROR, is a message about the zone data:

```
Jan 10 20:48:38 toystory2 named[3221]: ts2 has CNAME
                          and other data (invalid)
```

This message means that there's a problem with your zone data. For example, you may have entries like these:

```
ts2             IN  CNAME toystory2
ts2             IN  MX    10 toystory2
toystory2       IN  A     192.249.249.10
toystory2       IN  MX    10 toystory2
```

The MX record for *ts2* is incorrect and triggers the message just listed. *ts2* is an alias for *toystory2*, which is the canonical name. As described earlier, when a nameserver looks up a name and finds a CNAME, it replaces the original name with the canonical name and then tries looking up the canonical name. Thus, when the server looks up the MX data for *ts2*, it finds a CNAME record and then looks up the MX record for *toystory2*. Since the server follows the CNAME record for *ts2*, it never uses the MX record for *ts2*; in fact, this record is illegal. In other words, all resource records for a host have to use the canonical name; it's an error to use an alias in place of the canonical name.

The following message indicates that a BIND 8 slave was unable to reach any master server when it tried to do a zone transfer:

```
Jan 10 20:52:42 wormhole named[2813]: zoneref: Masters for
                          secondary zone "movie.edu" unreachable
```

BIND 9 slaves say:

```
Jul 27 16:50:55 toystory named[7174]: transfer of 'movie.edu/IN'
                          from 192.249.249.3#53: failed to connect: timed out
```

This message is sent at priority LOG_NOTICE on BIND 8, and LOG_ERROR on BIND 9, and is sent only the first time the zone transfer fails. When the zone transfer finally succeeds, BIND tells you that the zone transferred by issuing another *syslog* message. When this message first appears, you don't need to take any immediate action. The nameserver will continue attempting to transfer the zone according to the retry period in the SOA record. After a few days (or half the expire time), you might check that the server was able to transfer the zone. Or, you can verify that the zone transferred by checking the timestamp on the backup zone datafile. When a zone transfer succeeds, a new backup file is created. When a nameserver finds a zone is up to date, it "touches" the backup file (*à la* the Unix *touch* command). In both cases, the timestamp on the backup file is updated, so go to the slave and give the command *ls –l /usr/local/named/db**. This tells you when the slave last synchronized each zone with the master server. We'll cover how to troubleshoot slaves failing to transfer zones in Chapter 14.

If you are watching the *syslog* messages, you'll see a LOG_INFO *syslog* message when the slave picks up the new zone data or when a tool such as *nslookup* transfers a zone:

```
Mar  7 07:30:04 toystory named[3977]: client 192.249.249.1#1076:
                transfer of 'movie.edu/IN':AXFR started
```

If you're using the *allow-transfer* substatement (explained in Chapter 11) to limit which servers can load zones, you may see this message saying *denied* instead of *started*:

```
Jul 27 16:59:26 toystory named[7174]: client 192.249.249.1#1386:
                zone transfer 'movie.edu/AXFR/IN' denied
```

You'd see this *syslog* message only if you capture LOG_INFO *syslog* messages:

```
Jan 10 20:52:42 wormhole named[2813]: Malformed response
                from 192.1.1.1
```

Most often, this message means that some bug in a nameserver caused it to send an erroneous response packet. The error probably occurred on the remote nameserver (192.1.1.1) rather than the local server (*wormhole*). Diagnosing this kind of error involves capturing the response packet in a network trace and decoding it. Decoding DNS packets manually is beyond the scope of this book, so we won't go into much detail. You'd see this type of error if the response packet said it contained several answers in the answer section (such as four address resource records), yet the answer section contained only a single answer. The only course of action is to notify the administrator of the offending host via email (assuming you can get the name of the host by looking up the address). You would also see this message if the underlying network altered (damaged) the UDP response packets in some way. Checksumming UDP packets is optional, so this error might not be caught at a lower level.

A BIND 8 *named* logs this message when you try to sneak records into your zone datafile that belong in another zone:

```
Jun 13 08:02:03 toystory named[2657]: db.movie.edu:28: data "foo.bar.edu"
                outside zone "movie.edu" (ignored)
```

A BIND 9 *named* logs:

```
Jul 27 17:07:01 toystory named[7174]: dns_master_load:
                db.movie.edu:28: ignoring out-of-zone data
```

For instance, if we tried to use this zone data:

```
shrek       IN A  192.249.249.2
toystory    IN A  192.249.249.3

; Add this entry to the nameserver's cache
foo.bar.edu.  IN A  10.0.7.13
```

we'd be adding data for the *bar.edu* zone into our *movie.edu* zone datafile. This *syslog* message is logged at priority LOG_WARNING.

Earlier in the book, we said that you couldn't use a CNAME in the data portion of a resource record. BIND 8 will catch this misuse:

```
Jun 13 08:21:04 toystory named[2699]: "movie.edu IN NS" points to a
                                      CNAME (mi.movie.edu)
```

BIND 9 doesn't catch it as of 9.3.0.

Here is an example of the offending resource records:

```
@                         IN  NS     toystory.movie.edu.
                          IN  NS     mi.movie.edu.
toystory.movie.edu.       IN  A      192.249.249.3
monsters-inc.movie.edu.   IN  A      192.249.249.4
mi.movie.edu.             IN  CNAME monsters-inc.movie.edu.
```

The second NS record should have listed *monsters-inc.movie.edu* instead of *mi.movie. edu*. This *syslog* message won't show up immediately when you start your nameserver.

 You'll only see the *syslog* message when the offending data is looked up. This *syslog* message is logged by a BIND 8 server at priority LOG_INFO.

The following message indicates that your nameserver may be guarding itself against one type of network attack:

```
Jun 11 11:40:54 toystory named[131]: Response from unexpected source
                                     ([204.138.114.3].53)
```

Your nameserver sent a query to a remote nameserver, but the response that came wasn't returned from any of the addresses your nameserver had listed for the remote nameserver. The potential security breach is this: an intruder causes your nameserver to query a remote nameserver, and at the same time the intruder sends responses (pretending the responses are from the remote nameserver) that the intruder hopes your nameserver will add to its cache. Perhaps he sends along a false PTR record, pointing the IP address of one of his hosts to the domain name of a host you trust.

Once the false PTR record is in your cache, the intruder uses one of the BSD "r" commands (e.g., *rlogin*) to gain access to your system.

Less paranoid admins will realize that this situation can also happen if a parent zone's nameserver knows about only one of the IP addresses of a multihomed nameserver for a child zone. The parent tells your nameserver the one IP address it knows, and when your server queries the remote nameserver, the remote nameserver responds from the other IP address. This shouldn't happen if BIND is running on the remote nameserver host, because BIND makes every effort to use the same IP address in the response as the query was sent to. This *syslog* message is logged at priority LOG_INFO.

Here's an interesting *syslog* message:

```
Jun 10 07:57:28 toystory named[131]: No root name servers for
          class 226
```

The only classes defined to date are: class 1, Internet (IN); class 3, Chaos (CH); and class 4, Hesiod (HS). What's class 226? That's exactly what your nameserver is saying with this *syslog* message: something is wrong because there's no class 226. What can you do about it? Nothing, really. This message doesn't give you enough information; you don't know who the query is from or what the query was for. Then again, if the class field is corrupted, the domain name in the query may be garbage too. The actual cause of the problem could be a broken remote nameserver or resolver, or a corrupted UDP datagram. This *syslog* message is logged at priority LOG_INFO.

This message might appear if you are backing up some other zone:

```
Jun 7 20:14:26 wormhole named[29618]: Zone "253.253.192.in-addr.arpa"
          (class 1) SOA serial# (3345) rcvd from [192.249.249.10]
          is < ours (563319491)
```

Ah, the pesky admin for *253.253.192.in-addr.arpa* changed the serial number format and neglected to tell you about it. Some thanks you get for running a slave for this zone, huh? Drop the admin a note to see if this change was intentional or just a typo. If the change was intentional, or if you don't want to contact the admin, then you have to deal with it locally—kill your slave, remove the backup copy of this zone, and restart your server. This procedure removes all knowledge your slave had of the old serial number, at which point it's quite happy with the new serial number. This *syslog* message is logged at priority LOG_NOTICE.

By the way, if that pesky admin was running a BIND 8 or 9 nameserver, then he must have missed (or ignored) a message his server logged, telling him that he'd rolled the zone's serial number back. On a BIND 8 nameserver, the message looks like:

```
Jun 7 19:35:14 toystory named[3221]: WARNING: new serial number < old
          (zp->z_serial < serial)
```

On a BIND 9 nameserver, it looks like:

```
Jun 7 19:36:41 toystory named[9832]: dns_zone_load: zone movie.edu/IN: zone
serial has gone backwards
```

This message is logged at LOG_NOTICE.

You might want to remind him of the wisdom of checking *syslog* after making any changes to the nameserver.

This BIND 8 message will undoubtedly become familiar to you:

```
Aug 21 00:59:06 toystory named[12620]: Lame server on 'foo.movie.edu'
        (in 'MOVIE.EDU'?): [10.0.7.125].53 'NS.HOLLYWOOD.LA.CA.US':
        learnt (A=10.47.3.62,NS=10.47.3.62)
```

Under BIND 9, it looks like this:

```
Jan 15 10:20:16 toystory named[14205]: lame server on 'foo.movie.edu' (in
        'movie.EDU'?): 10.0.7.125#53
```

"Aye, Captain, she's sucking mud!" There's some mud out there in the Internet waters in the form of bad delegations. A parent nameserver is delegating a subdomain to a child nameserver, and the child nameserver is not authoritative for the subdomain. In this case, the *edu* nameserver is delegating *movie.edu* to 10.0.7.125, and the nameserver on this host is not authoritative for *movie.edu*. Unless you know the admin for *movie.edu*, there's probably nothing you can do about this. The *syslog* message is logged at LOG_INFO.

If your configuration file has:

```
logging { category queries { default_syslog; }; };
```

you will get a LOG_INFO *syslog* message for every query your nameserver receives:

```
Feb 20 21:43:25 toystory named[3830]:
        XX /192.253.253.2/carrie.movie.edu/A
Feb 20 21:43:32 toystory named[3830]:
        XX /192.253.253.2/4.253.253.192.in-addr.arpa/PTR
```

The format has changed slightly in BIND 9, though:

```
Jan 13 18:32:25 toystory named[13976]: client 192.253.253.2#1702:
        query: carrie.movie.edu IN A +
Jan 13 18:32:42 toystory named[13976]: client 192.253.253.2#1702:
        query: 4.253.253.192.in-addr.arpa IN PTR +
```

These messages include the IP address of the host that made the query as well as the query itself. On a BIND 8.2.1 or later nameserver, recursive queries are marked with XX+ instead of XX. A BIND 9 nameserver marks recursive queries with a + and nonrecursive queries with a – character. BIND 8.4.3 and later and 9.3.0 and later even mark EDNS0 queries and TSIG-signed queries with *E* and *S*, respectively. (We'll talk about EDNS0 in Chapter 10 and TSIG in Chapter 11.)

Make sure you have lots of disk space if you log all the queries to a busy nameserver. (On a running server, you can toggle query logging on and off with the *querylog* command.)

Starting with BIND 8.1.2, you might see this set of *syslog* messages:

```
May 19 11:06:08 named[21160]: bind(dfd=20, [10.0.0.1].53):
                Address already in use
May 19 11:06:08 named[21160]: deleting interface [10.0.0.1].53
May 19 11:06:08 named[21160]: bind(dfd=20, [127.0.0.1].53):
                Address already in use
May 19 11:06:08 named[21160]: deleting interface [127.0.0.1].53
May 19 11:06:08 named[21160]: not listening on any interfaces
May 19 11:06:08 named[21160]: Forwarding source address
                is [0.0.0.0].1835
May 19 11:06:08 named[21161]: Ready to answer queries.
```

On BIND 9 nameservers, that looks like:

```
Jul 27 17:15:58 toystory named[7357]: listening on IPv4 interface lo, 127.0.0.1#53
Jul 27 17:15:58 toystory named[7357]: binding TCP socket: address in use
Jul 27 17:15:58 toystory named[7357]: listening on IPv4 interface eth0,
      206.168.194.122#53
Jul 27 17:15:58 toystory named[7357]: binding TCP socket: address in use
Jul 27 17:15:58 toystory named[7357]: listening on IPv4 interface eth1,
      206.168.194.123#53
Jul 27 17:15:58 toystory named[7357]: binding TCP socket: address in use
Jul 27 17:15:58 toystory named[7357]: couldn't add command channel 0.0.0.0#953:
address in use
```

What has happened is that you had a nameserver running, and you started up a second nameserver without killing the first one. Unlike what you might expect, the second nameserver continues to run; it just isn't listening on any interfaces.

Understanding the BIND Statistics

Periodically, you should look over the statistics on some of your nameservers, if only to see how busy they are. We'll now show you an example of the nameserver statistics and discuss what each line means. Nameservers handle many queries and responses during normal operation, so first we need to show you what a typical exchange might look like.

Reading the explanations for the statistics is hard without a mental picture of what goes on during a lookup. To help you understand the nameserver's statistics, Figure 7-2 shows what might happen when an application tries to look up a domain name. The application, FTP, queries a local nameserver. The local nameserver had previously looked up data in this zone and knows where the remote nameservers are. It queries each of the remote nameservers—one of them twice—trying to find the answer. In the meantime, the application times out and sends yet another query, asking for the same information.

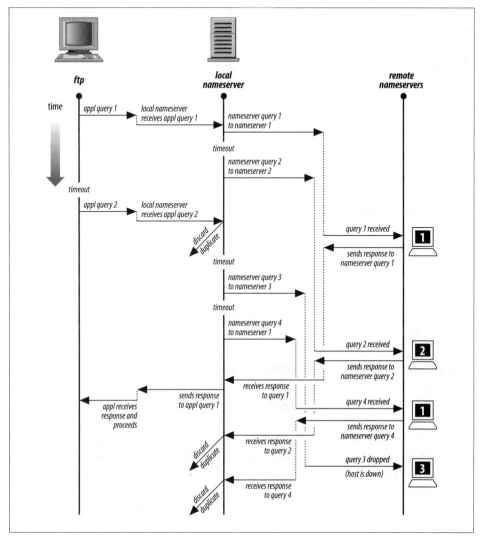

Figure 7-2. Example query/response exchange

Keep in mind that even though a nameserver has sent a query to a remote nameserver, the remote nameserver may not receive the query right away. The query might be delayed or lost by the underlying network, or perhaps the remote nameserver host might be busy with another application.

Notice that a BIND nameserver is able to detect duplicate queries only while it is still trying to answer the original query. The local nameserver detects the duplicate query from the application because the local nameserver is still working on it. But remote nameserver 1 does not detect the duplicate query from the local nameserver because it answered the previous query. After the local nameserver receives the first response from remote nameserver 1, all other responses are discarded as duplicates. This dialog required the following exchanges:

Exchange	Number
Application to local nameserver	2 queries
Local nameserver to application	1 response
Local nameserver to remote nameserver 1	2 queries
Remote nameserver 1 to local nameserver	2 responses
Local nameserver to remote nameserver 2	1 query
Remote nameserver 2 to local nameserver	1 response
Local nameserver to remote nameserver 3	1 query
Remote nameserver 3 to local nameserver	0 responses

These exchanges would make the following contributions to the local nameserver's statistics:

Statistic	Cause
2 queries received	From the application on the local host
1 duplicate query	From the application on the local host
1 answer sent	To the application on the local host
3 responses received	From remote nameservers
2 duplicate responses	From remote nameservers
2 A queries	Queries for address information

In our example, the local nameserver received queries only from an application, yet it sent queries to remote nameservers. Normally, the local nameserver would also receive queries from remote nameservers (that is, in addition to asking remote servers for information it needs to know, the local server would also be asked by remote servers for information they need to know), but we didn't show any remote queries for the sake of simplicity.

BIND 8 statistics

Now that you've seen a typical exchange between applications and nameservers, as well as the statistics it generated, let's go over a more extensive example of the statistics. To get the statistics from your BIND 8 nameserver, use *ndc*:

```
# ndc stats
```

Wait a few seconds, look at the file *named.stats* in the nameserver's working directory. If the statistics are not dumped to this file, your server may not have been compiled with STATS defined and, thus, may not be collecting statistics. Following are the statistics from one of Paul Vixie's BIND 4.9.3 nameservers. BIND 8 nameservers have all of the same items listed here except for RnotNsQ, and the items are arranged in a different order. BIND 9 nameservers, as of 9.1.0, keep an entirely different set of statistics, which we'll show you in the next section.

```
+++ Statistics Dump +++ (800708260) Wed May 17 03:57:40 1995
746683     time since boot (secs)
392768     time since reset (secs)
14         Unknown query types
268459     A queries
3044       NS queries
5680       CNAME queries
11364      SOA queries
1008934    PTR queries
44         HINFO queries
680367     MX queries
2369       TXT queries
40         NSAP queries
27         AXFR queries
8336       ANY queries
++ Name Server Statistics ++
(Legend)
      RQ    RR    RIQ   RNXD    RFwdQ
      RFwdR RDupQ RDupR RFail   RFErr
      RErr  RTCP  RAXFR RLame   ROpts
      SSysQ SAns  SFwdQ SFwdR   SDupQ
      SFail SFErr SErr  RNotNsQ SNaAns
      SNXD
(Global)
   1992938 112600 0 19144 63462 60527 194 347 3420 0  5 2235 27 35289 0
   14886 1927930 63462 60527 107169  10025 119 0 1785426 805592  35863
[15.255.72.20]
   485 0 0 0 0  0 0 0 0 0  0 0 0 0  0 485 0 0 0  0 0 0 0 485  0
[15.255.152.2]
   441 137 0 1 2 108 0 0 0 0  0 0 0 0 0  13 439 85 7 84  0 0 0 0 431  0
[15.255.152.4]
   770 89 0 1 4  69 0 0 0 0  0 0 0 0 0  14 766 68 5 7  0 0 0 0 755  0
... <lots of entries deleted>
```

If your BIND 8 nameserver doesn't include any per–IP address sections after "(Global)," you need to set *host-statistics* to yes in your *options* statement if you want to track per-host statistics:

```
options {
    host-statistics yes;
};
```

However, keeping host statistics requires a fair amount of memory, so you may not want to do it routinely unless you're trying to build a profile of your nameserver's activity.

Let's look at these statistics one line at a time.

```
+++ Statistics Dump +++ (800708260) Wed May 17 03:57:40 1995
```

This is when this section of the statistics was dumped. The number in parentheses (800708260) is the number of seconds since the Unix epoch, which was January 1, 1970. Mercifully, BIND converts that into a real date and time for you: May 17, 1995, 3:57:40 a.m.

```
746683    time since boot (secs)
```

This is how long the local nameserver has been running. To convert to days, divide by 86,400 ($60 \times 60 \times 24$, the number of seconds in a day). This server has been running for about 8.5 days.

```
392768    time since reset (secs)
```

This is how long the local nameserver has run since the last reload. You'll probably see this number differ from the time since boot only if the server is a primary nameserver for one or more zones. Nameservers that are slaves for a zone automatically pick up new data with zone transfers and are not usually reloaded. Since *this* server has been reset, it is probably the primary nameserver for some zone.

```
14        Unknown query types
```

This nameserver received 14 queries for data of a type it didn't recognize. Either someone is experimenting with new types, there is a defective implementation somewhere, or Paul needs to upgrade his nameserver.

```
268459    A queries
```

There have been 268,459 address lookups. Address queries are normally the most common type of query.

```
3044      NS queries
```

There have been 3,044 nameserver queries. Internally, nameservers generate NS queries when they are trying to look up servers for the root zone. Externally, applications such as *dig* and *nslookup* can also be used to look up NS records.

```
5680      CNAME queries
```

Some versions of *sendmail* make CNAME queries in order to canonicalize a mail address (replace an alias with the canonical name). Other versions of *sendmail* use ANY queries instead (we'll get to those shortly). Otherwise, the CNAME lookups are most likely from *dig* or *nslookup*.

```
11364     SOA queries
```

SOA queries are made by slave nameservers to check if their zone data is current. If the data is not current, an AXFR query follows to cause the zone transfer. Since this set of statistics does show AXFR queries, we can conclude that slave nameservers load zone data from this server.

```
1008934   PTR queries
```

The pointer queries map addresses to names. Many kinds of software look up IP addresses: *inetd*, *rlogind*, *rshd*, network management software, and network-tracing software.

```
44      HINFO queries
```

The host-information queries are most likely from someone interactively looking up HINFO records.

```
680367  MX queries
```

Mailers such as *sendmail* make mail exchanger queries as part of the normal electronic mail delivery process.

```
2369    TXT queries
```

Some application must be making text queries for this number to be this large. It might be a tool like *Harvest*, which is an information search-and-retrieval technology developed at the University of Colorado.

```
40      NSAP queries
```

This is a relatively new record type used to map domain names to OSI Network Service Access Point addresses.

```
27      AXFR queries
```

Slave nameservers make AXFR queries to initiate zone transfers.

```
8336    ANY queries
```

ANY queries request records of any type for a name. *sendmail* is the most common program to use this query type. Since *sendmail* looks up CNAME, MX, and address records for a mail destination, it will make a query for ANY record type so that all the resource records are cached right away at the local nameserver.

The rest of the statistics are kept on a per-host basis. If you look over the list of hosts your nameserver has exchanged packets with, you'll find out just how garrulous your nameserver is: you'll see hundreds or even thousands of hosts in the list. While the size of the list is impressive, the statistics themselves are only somewhat interesting. We'll explain *all* the statistics, even the ones with zero counts, although you'll probably find only a handful of the statistics useful. To make the statistics easier to read, you'll need a tool to expand the statistics because the output format is rather compact. We wrote a tool called *bstat* to do just this. Here's what its output looks like:

```
hpcvsop.cv.hp.com
        485 queries received
        485 responses sent to this name server
        485 queries answered from our cache
relay.hp.com
        441 queries received
        137 responses received
          1 negative response received
          2 queries for data not in our cache or authoritative data
```

```
        108 responses from this name server passed to the querier
         13 system queries sent to this name server
        439 responses sent to this name server
         85 queries sent to this name server
          7 responses from other name servers sent to this name server
         84 duplicate queries sent to this name server
        431 queries answered from our cache
hp.com
        770 queries received
         89 responses received
          1 negative response received
          4 queries for data not in our cache or authoritative data
         69 responses from this name server passed to the querier
         14 system queries sent to this name server
        766 responses sent to this name server
         68 queries sent to this name server
          5 responses from other name servers sent to this name server
          7 duplicate queries sent to this name server
        755 queries answered from our cache
```

In the raw statistics (not the *bstat* output), each host's IP address is followed by a table of counts. The column heading for this table is the cryptic legend at the beginning. The legend is broken into several lines, but the host statistics are all on a single line. In the following section, we'll explain briefly what each column means as we look at the statistics for one of the hosts this nameserver conversed with—15.255.152.2 (*relay.hp.com*). For the sake of our explanation, we'll first show you the column heading from the legend (e.g., RQ) followed by the count for this column for *relay*.

RQ 441

> RQ is the count of queries received from *relay*. These queries were made because *relay* needed information about a zone served by this nameserver.

RR 137

> RR is the count of responses received from *relay*. These are responses to queries made from this nameserver. Don't try to correlate this number to RQ, because they are not related. RQ counts questions asked by *relay*; RR counts answers that *relay* gave to this nameserver (because this nameserver asked *relay* for information).

RIQ 0

> RIQ is the count of inverse queries received from *relay*. Inverse queries were originally intended to map addresses to names, but that function is now handled by PTR records. Older versions of *nslookup* use an inverse query on startup, so you may see a nonzero RIQ count.

RNXD 1

> RNXD is the count of "no such domain" answers received from *relay*.

RFwdQ 2

RFwdQ is the count of queries received (RQ) from *relay* that need further processing before they can be answered. This count is much higher for hosts that configure their resolver (with *resolv.conf*) to send all queries to your nameserver.

RFwdR 108

RFwdR is the count of responses received (RR) from *relay* that answer the original query and are passed back to the application that made the query.

RDupQ 0

RDupQ is the count of duplicate queries from *relay*. You'll see duplicates only when the resolver is configured (with *resolv.conf*) to query this nameserver.

RDupR 0

RDupR is the count of duplicate responses from *relay*. A response is a duplicate when the nameserver can no longer find the original query in its list of pending queries that caused the response.

RFail 0

RFail is the count of SERVFAIL responses from *relay*. A SERVFAIL response indicates some sort of server failure. Server failure responses often occur because the remote server reads a zone datafile and finds a syntax error. Any queries for data in the zone with the erroneous zone datafile results in a server failure answer from the remote nameserver. This is probably the most common cause of SERVFAIL responses. Server failure responses also occur when the remote nameserver tries to allocate more memory and can't, or when the remote slave nameserver's zone data expires.

RFErr 0

RFErr is the count of FORMERR responses from *relay*. FORMERR means that the remote nameserver said the local nameserver's query had a format error.

RErr 0

RErr is the count of errors that aren't either SERVFAIL or FORMERR.

RTCP 0

RTCP is the count of queries received on TCP connections from *relay*. (Most queries use UDP.)

RAXFR 0

RAXFR is the count of zone transfers initiated. The count indicates that *relay* is not a slave for any zones served by this nameserver.

RLame 0

RLame is the count of lame delegations received. If this count is not 0, it means that some zone is delegated to the nameserver at this IP address, and the nameserver is not authoritative for the zone.

ROpts 0

ROpts is the count of packets received with IP options set.

SSysQ 13

SSysQ is the count of system queries sent to *relay*. System queries are queries that are *initiated* by the local nameserver. Most system queries will go to root nameservers because system queries are used to keep the list of root nameservers up to date. But system queries are also used to find the address of a nameserver if the address record timed out before the nameserver record did. Since *relay* is not a root nameserver, these queries must have been sent for the latter reason.

SAns 439

SAns is the count of answers sent to *relay*. This nameserver answered 439 out of the 441 (RQ) queries *relay* sent to it. I wonder what happened to the two queries it didn't answer...

SFwdQ 85

SFwdQ is the count of queries that are sent (forwarded) to *relay* when the answer is not in this nameserver's zone data or cache.

SFwdR 7

SFwdR is the count of responses from a nameserver that are sent (forwarded) to *relay*.

SDupQ 84

SDupQ is the count of duplicate queries sent to *relay*. It's not as bad as it looks, though. The duplicate count is incremented if the query is sent to any other nameserver first. So *relay* might have answered all the queries it received the first time it received them, and the query still counted as a duplicate because it was sent to some other nameserver before *relay*.

SFail 0

SFail is the count of SERVFAIL responses sent to *relay*.

SFErr 0

SFErr is the count of FORMERR responses sent to *relay*.

SErr 0

SErr is the count of *sendto( )* system calls that failed when the destination was *relay*.

RNotNsQ 0

RNotNsQ is the count of queries received that are not from port 53, the nameserver port. Prior to BIND 8, all nameserver queries came from port 53. Any queries from ports other than 53 came from a resolver. BIND 8 nameservers query from ports other than 53, however, which makes this statistic useless since you can no longer distinguish resolver queries from nameserver queries. Hence, BIND 8 dropped RNotNsQ from its statistics.

SNaAns 431

SNaAns is the count of nonauthoritative answers sent to *relay*. Out of the 439
answers (SAns) sent to *relay*, 431 are from cached data.

SNXD 0

SNXD is the count of "no such domain" answers sent to *relay*.

BIND 9 statistics

BIND 9.1.0 is the first version of BIND 9 to keep statistics. You use *rndc* to induce
BIND 9 to dump its statistics:

```
% rndc stats
```

The nameserver dumps statistics, as a BIND 8 nameserver would, to a file called
named.stats in its working directory. However, those statistics look completely different from BIND 8's. Here are the contents of the stats file from one of our BIND 9
nameservers:

```
+++ Statistics Dump +++ (979436130)
success 9
referral 0
nxrrset 0
nxdomain 1
recursion 1
failure 1
--- Statistics Dump --- (979436130)
+++ Statistics Dump +++ (979584113)
success 651
referral 10
nxrrset 11
nxdomain 17
recursion 296
failure 217
--- Statistics Dump --- (979584113)
```

The nameserver appends a new statistics block (the section between "+++ Statistics
Dump +++" and "--- Statistics Dump ---") each time it receives a *stats* command.
The number in parentheses (979436130) is, as in earlier stats files, the number of seconds since the Unix epoch. Unfortunately, BIND doesn't convert the value for you,
but you can use the *date* command to convert it to something more readable. For
example, to convert 979584113 seconds since the Unix epoch (January 1, 1970), you
can use:

```
% date -d '1970-01-01 979584113 sec'
Mon Jan 15 18:41:53 MST 2001
```

Let's now go through these statistics one line at a time:

success 651
> This is the number of successful queries the nameserver handled. Successful queries are those that didn't result in referrals or errors.

referral 10
> This is the number of queries the nameserver handled that resulted in referrals.

nxrrset 11
> This is the number of queries the nameserver handled that resulted in responses saying that the type of record the querier requested didn't exist for the domain name it specified.

nxdomain 17
> This is the number of queries the nameserver handled that resulted in responses saying that the domain name the querier specified didn't exist.

recursion 296
> This is the number of queries the nameserver received that required recursive processing to answer.

failure 217
> This is the number of queries the nameserver received that resulted in errors other than those covered by *nxrrset* and *nxdomain*.

These are obviously not nearly as many statistics as a BIND 8 nameserver keeps, but future versions of BIND 9 will probably record more.

Using the BIND statistics

Is your nameserver "healthy"? How do you know what a "healthy" operation looks like? From a single snapshot, you can't really say whether a nameserver is healthy. You have to watch the statistics generated by your server over a period of time to get a feel for what sorts of numbers are normal for your configuration. These numbers will vary markedly among nameservers depending on the mix of applications generating lookups, the type of server (primary, slave, caching-only), and the level of the zones in the namespace it is serving.

One thing to watch for in the statistics is how many queries per second your nameserver receives. Take the number of queries received and divide by the number of seconds the nameserver has been running. Paul's BIND 4.9.3 nameserver received 1,992,938 queries in 746,683 seconds, or approximately 2.7 queries per second—not a very busy server.* If the number you come up with for your nameserver seems out of line, look at which hosts are making all the queries and decide if it makes sense for them to be making all those queries. At some point, you may decide that you need more nameservers to handle the load. We'll cover that situation in the next chapter.

---

* Recall that the root nameservers, which run plain vanilla BIND, can handle thousands of queries per second.

## CHAPTER 8

Growing Your Domain

"What size do you want to be?" it asked.
"Oh, I'm not particular as to size," Alice hastily
replied; "only one doesn't like changing so often, you
know…"
"Are you content now?" said the Caterpillar.
"Well, I should like to be a little larger, sir, if you
wouldn't mind…"

How Many Nameservers?

We set up two nameservers in Chapter 4. Two servers are as few as you'll ever want to run and, depending on the size of your network, you may need to run many more. It is not uncommon to run four or more nameservers, with one of them off-site. How many nameservers are enough? You'll have to decide that based on your network. Here are some guidelines to help out:

- Run at least one nameserver on each network or subnet you have. This removes routers as a point of failure. Make the most of any multihomed hosts you may have because they are (by definition) attached to more than one network.

- If you have a file server and some diskless nodes, run a nameserver on the file server to serve this group of machines.

- Run nameservers near, but not necessarily on, large multiuser computers. The users and their processes probably generate a lot of queries, and, as an administrator, you will work harder to keep a multiuser host up. But balance their needs against the risk of running a nameserver—a security-critical server—on a system to which lots of people have access.

- Run at least one nameserver off-site. This makes your data available when your network isn't. You might argue that it's useless to look up an address when you can't reach the host. Then again, the off-site nameserver may be available if your network is reachable, but your other nameservers are down. If you have a close relationship with an organization on the Internet—say another university, your ISP, or a business partner—they may be willing to run a slave for you.

Figure 8-1 presents a sample topology to show you how this might work.

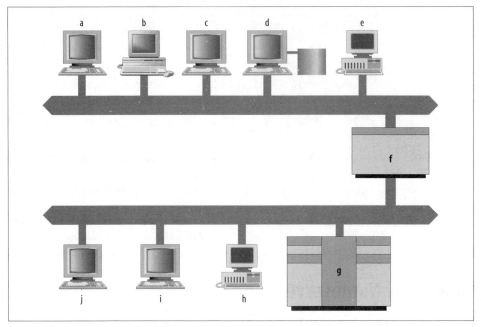

Figure 8-1. Sample network topology

Notice that if you follow our guidelines, there are still a number of places you can choose to run a nameserver. Host *d*, the file server for hosts *a*, *b*, *c*, and *e*, could run a nameserver. Host *g*, a big, multiuser host, is another good candidate. But probably the best choice is host *f*, the smaller host with interfaces on both networks. You'll need to run only one nameserver, instead of two, and it will run on a closely watched host. If you want more than one nameserver on either network, you can also run one on *d* or *g*.

Where Do I Put My Nameservers?

In addition to giving you a rough idea of how many nameservers you'll need, these criteria should help you decide *where* to run nameservers (e.g., on file servers and multihomed hosts). But there are other important considerations when choosing the right host.

Other factors to keep in mind are the host's connectivity, the host's security, the software it runs (BIND and otherwise), and maintaining the homogeneity of your nameservers:

Connectivity

It's important that nameservers be well connected. Running a nameserver on the fastest, most reliable host on your network won't do you any good if the host is mired in some backwater subnet of your network behind a slow, flaky serial line. Try to find a host close to your link to the Internet (if you have one), or find a well-connected Internet host to act as a slave for your zone. On your own network, try to run nameservers near the network's topological hubs.

It's doubly important that your primary nameserver be well connected. The primary needs good connectivity to all the slaves that update from it, for reliable zone transfers. And, like any nameserver, it will benefit from fast, reliable networking.

Security

Since you would undoubtedly prefer that hackers not commandeer your nameserver to assist them in attacking your own hosts or other networks across the Internet, it's important to run your nameserver on a secure host. Don't run a nameserver on a big, multiuser system if you can't trust its users. If you have certain computers that are dedicated to hosting network services but don't permit general logins, those are good candidates for running nameservers. If you have only one or a few really secure hosts, consider running the primary nameserver on one of those because its compromise would be more significant than the compromise of the slaves.

Software

Another factor to consider in choosing a host for a nameserver is the software the host runs. Software-wise, the best candidate for a nameserver is a host running a vendor-supported version of BIND 9.2 or 9.3 and a robust implementation of TCP/IP (preferably based on 4.3 or 4.4 BSD Unix's networking—we're Berkeley snobs). You can compile your own 9.2 or 9.3 BIND from the sources—it's not hard, and the latest versions are very reliable—but you'll probably have a tough time getting your vendor to support it. If you absolutely can't run BIND 9, you may be able to get away with running your vendor's port of older BIND code, such as 8.2 or 8.3, which gives you the benefit of your vendor's support, for what that's worth.

Homogeneity

One last thing to take into account is the homogeneity of your nameservers. As much as you might believe in operating system "standards," hopping between different versions of Unix can be frustrating and confusing. Avoid running nameservers on lots of different platforms if you can. You can waste a lot of time porting your scripts (or ours!) from one operating system to another or looking for the location of *nslookup* or *named.conf* on three different Unixes. Moreover, different vendors' versions of Unix tend to support different versions of BIND, which can cause all sorts of frustration. If you need the security features of BIND 9 on all your nameservers, for example, choose a platform that supports BIND 9 for all your nameservers.

Though these are really secondary considerations—it's more important to have a nameserver on a given subnet than to have it running on the perfect host—do keep these criteria in mind when making a choice.

Capacity Planning

If you have heavily populated networks or users who do a lot of nameserver-intensive work, you may find you need more nameservers than we've recommended to handle the load. Likewise, our recommendations may be fine for a little while, but as people add hosts to your networks or install new nameserver-intensive programs, you may find your nameservers bogged down by queries.

Just which tasks are "nameserver-intensive"? Surfing the Web can be, as can sending electronic mail, especially to large mailing lists. Programs that make lots of remote procedure calls to different hosts can also be nameserver-intensive. Even running certain graphical user environments can tax your nameserver. X Windows-based user environments, for example, query the nameserver to check access lists (among other things).

The astute (and precocious) among you may be asking, "But how do I know when my nameservers are overloaded? What do I look for?" An excellent question!

Memory utilization is probably the most important aspect of a nameserver's operation to monitor. *named* can get very large on a nameserver that is authoritative for many zones. If *named*'s size, plus the size of the other processes you run, exceeds the size of your host's real memory, your host may swap furiously ("thrash") and not get anything done. Even if your host has more than enough memory to run all its processes, large nameservers are slow to start and reload.

Another criterion you can use to measure the load on your nameserver is the load the *named* process places on the host's CPU. Correctly configured nameservers don't use much CPU time, so high CPU usage is often symptomatic of a configuration error. Programs such as *top* can help you characterize your nameserver's average CPU utilization.[*]

Unfortunately, there are no universal rules when it comes to acceptable CPU utilization. We offer a rough rule of thumb, though: 5 percent average CPU utilization is

---

[*] *top* is a very handy program, written by Bill LeFebvre, that gives you a continuous report of which processes are sucking up the most CPU time on your host. It's included with many versions of Unix and Linux. If your operating system doesn't include *top*, you can find the most recent version at *http://www.unixtop.org/*.

probably acceptable; 10 percent is a bit high, unless the host is dedicated to providing name service.

To get an idea of what normal figures are, here's what *top* might show for a relatively quiet nameserver:

```
last pid: 14299; load averages: 0.11, 0.12, 0.12        18:19:08
68 processes: 64 sleeping, 3 running, 1 stopped
Cpu states: 11.3% usr, 0.0% nice, 15.3% sys, 73.4% idle, 0.0% intr, 0.0% ker
Memory: Real: 8208K/13168K act/tot Virtual: 16432K/30736K act/tot Free: 4224K

  PID USERNAME PRI NICE   SIZE   RES STATE  TIME   WCPU    CPU COMMAND
   89 root       1    0 2968K 2652K sleep 5:01  0.00%  0.00% named
```

Okay, that's *really* quiet. Here's what *top* shows on a busy (though not overloaded) nameserver:

```
load averages: 0.30, 0.46, 0.44                  system: relay 16:12:20
39 processes: 38 sleeping, 1 waiting
Cpu states: 4.4% user, 0.0% nice, 5.4% system, 90.2% idle, 0.0% unk5, 0.0% unk6,
0.0% unk7, 0.0% unk8
Memory: 31126K (28606K) real, 33090K (28812K) virtual, 54344K free Screen #1/ 3

  PID USERNAME PRI NICE SIZE   RES   STATE   TIME WCPU   CPU  COMMAND
21910 root       1    0 2624K 2616K sleep 146:21  0.00% 1.42% /etc/named
```

Another statistic to look at is the number of queries the nameserver receives per minute (or second, if you have a busy nameserver). Again, there are no absolutes here: a fast processor running FreeBSD can probably handle thousands of queries per second without breaking a sweat, while an older box running an outdated version of Unix might have problems with more than a few queries a second.

To check the volume of queries your nameserver is receiving, it's easiest to look at the nameserver's internal statistics. You can configure the server to write the statistics at regular intervals. For example, you can configure your nameserver to dump statistics every hour (actually, that's the default for BIND 8 servers), and compare the number of queries received between hours:

```
options {
        statistics-interval 60;
};
```

BIND 9 nameservers don't support the *statistics-interval* substatement, but you can use *rndc* to tell a BIND 9 nameserver to dump statistics on the hour—for example, in *crontab*:

```
0 * * * *  /usr/local/sbin/rndc stats
```

You should pay special attention to peak periods. For example, Monday morning is often busy because many people like to respond to mail they've received over the weekend first thing on Mondays.

You might also want to take a sample starting just after lunch, when people are returning to their desks and getting back to work—all at about the same time. Of course, if your organization is spread across several time zones, you'll have to use your best judgment to determine a busy time.

Here's a snippet from the *syslog* file on a BIND 8 nameserver:

```
Aug  1 11:00:49 toystory named[103]: NSTATS 965152849 959476930 A=8 NS=1
SOA=356966 PTR=2 TXT=32 IXFR=9 AXFR=204
Aug  1 11:00:49 toystory named[103]: XSTATS 965152849 959476930 RR=3243 RNXD=0
RFwdR=0 RDupR=0 RFail=20 RFErr=0 RErr=11 RAXFR=204 RLame=0 ROpts=0 SSysQ=3356

SAns=391191 SFwdQ=0 SDupQ=1236 SErr=0
RQ=458031
 RIQ=25 RFwdQ=0 RDupQ=0 RTCP=101316
SFwdR=0 SFail=0 SFErr=0 SNaAns=34482 SNXD=0 RUQ=0 RURQ=0 RUXFR=10 RUUpd=34451
Aug  1 12:00:49 toystory named[103]: NSTATS 965156449 959476930 A=8 NS=1
SOA=357195 PTR=2 TXT=32 IXFR=9 AXFR=204
Aug  1 12:00:49 toystory named[103]: XSTATS 965156449 959476930 RR=3253 RNXD=0
RFwdR=0 RDupR=0 RFail=20 RFErr=0 RErr=11 RAXFR=204 RLame=0 ROpts=0 SSysQ=3360

SAns=391444 SFwdQ=0 SDupQ=1244 SErr=0
RQ=458332
RIQ=25 RFwdQ=0 RDupQ=0 RTCP=101388
SFwdR=0 SFail=0 SFErr=0 SNaAns=34506 SNXD=0 RUQ=0 RURQ=0 RUXFR=10 RUUpd=34475
```

The number of queries received is dumped in the *RQ* field (in bold). To calculate the number of queries received in the hour, just subtract the first *RQ* value from the second one: 458332 − 458031 = 301.

Even if your host is fast enough to handle the volume of queries it receives, you should make sure the DNS traffic isn't placing undue load on your network. On most LANs, DNS traffic will be too small a proportion of the network's bandwidth to worry about. Over slow leased lines or dial-up connections, though, DNS traffic could consume enough bandwidth to merit concern.

To get a rough estimate of the volume of DNS traffic on your LAN, multiply the number of queries received (RQ) plus the number of answers sent (SAns) in an hour by 800 bits (100 bytes, a rough average size for a DNS message), and divide by 3,600 (seconds per hour) to find the bandwidth utilized. This should give you a feeling for how much of your network's bandwidth is being consumed by DNS traffic.[*]

To give you an idea of what's normal, the last NSFNET traffic report (in April 1995) showed that DNS traffic constituted just over five percent of the total traffic volume (in bytes) on its backbone. The NSFNET's figures were based on actual traffic sampling,

---

[*] For a nice package that automates the analysis of BIND's statistics, look for Marco d'Itri's *bindgraph* in the DNS Resources Directory's tools page, *http://www.dns.net/dnsrd/tools.html*.

not calculations like ours using the nameserver's statistics.* If you want to get a more accurate idea of the traffic your nameserver is receiving, you can always do your own traffic sampling with a LAN protocol analyzer.

If you find that your nameservers are overworked, what then? First, it's a good idea to make sure that your nameservers aren't being bombarded with queries by a misbehaving program. To do that, you'll need to find the sources of all the queries.

If you're running a BIND 8 nameserver, you can find out which resolvers and nameservers are querying your nameserver just by dumping the server's statistics. BIND 8 nameservers keep statistics on a host-by-host basis, which is really useful in tracking down heavy users of your nameserver. BIND 8.2 or newer nameservers don't keep these statistics by default; to induce them to keep host-by-host statistics, use the *host-statistics* substatement in your *options* statement, like this:†

```
options {
    host-statistics yes;
};
```

For example, take these statistics:

```
+++ Statistics Dump +++ (829373099) Fri Apr 12 23:24:59 1996
970779    time since boot (secs)
471621    time since reset (secs)
0    Unknown query types
185108    A queries
6    NS queries
69213    PTR queries
669    MX queries
2361    ANY queries
++ Name Server Statistics ++
(Legend)
        RQ      RR      RIQ     RNXD    RFwdQ
        RFwdR   RDupQ   RDupR   RFail   RFErr
        RErr    RTCP    RAXFR   RLame   ROpts
        SSysQ   SAns    SFwdQ   SFwdR   SDupQ
        SFail   SFErr   SErr    RNotNsQ SNaAns
        SNXD
(Global)
    257357 20718 0 8509 19677  19939 1494 21 0 0  0 7 0 1 0
    824 236196 19677 19939 7643  33 0 0 256064 49269  155030
  [15.17.232.4]
    8736 0 0 0 717  24 0 0 0 0  0 0 0 0 0  0 8019 0 717 0
    0 0 0 8736 2141  5722
  [15.17.232.5]
    115 0 0 0 8  0 21 0 0 0  0 0 0 0 0  0 86 0 1 0  0 0 0 115 0  7
```

---

* We're not sure how representative of the current state of the Internet these numbers are, because it's extremely difficult to wheedle equivalent numbers out of the commercial backbone providers that succeeded the NSFNET.

† BIND 9 doesn't support the *host-statistics* substatement—or keeping per-host statistics, for that matter.

```
[15.17.232.8]
    66215 0 0 0 6910   148 633 0 0 0   0 5 0 0 0   0 58671 0 6695 0
    15 0 0 66215 33697   6541
[15.17.232.16]
    31848 0 0 0 3593   209 74 0 0 0   0 0 0 0 0   0 28185 0 3563 0
    0 0 0 31848 8695   15359
[15.17.232.20]
    272 0 0 0 0   0 0 0 0 0   0 0 0 0 0   0 272 0 0 0   0 0 0 272 7   0
[15.17.232.21]
    316 0 0 0 52   14 3 0 0 0   0 0 0 0 0   0 261 0 51 0   0 0 0 316 30   30
[15.17.232.24]
    853 0 0 0 65   1 3 0 0 0   0 2 0 0 0   0 783 0 64 0   0 0 0 853 125   337
[15.17.232.33]
    624 0 0 0 47   1 0 0 0 0   0 0 0 0 0   0 577 0 47 0   0 0 0 624 2   217
[15.17.232.94]
    127640 0 0 0 1751   14 449 0 0 0   0 0 0 0 0   0 125440 0 1602 0
    0 0 0 127640 106   124661
[15.17.232.95]
    846 0 0 0 38   1 0 0 0 0   0 0 0 0 0   0 809 0 37 0   0 0 0 846 79   81
-- Name Server Statistics --
--- Statistics Dump --- (829373099) Fri Apr 12 23:24:59 1996
```

After the *Global* entry, each host is broken out by IP address in brackets. Looking at the legend, you can see that the first field in each record is RQ, or queries received. That gives us a good reason to look at hosts 15.17.232.8, 15.17.232.16, and 15.17.232.94, which appear to be responsible for about 88 percent of our queries.

If you're running a BIND 9 nameserver, the only way to find out which resolvers and nameservers are sending all those darned queries is to turn on nameserver debugging. (We'll cover this in depth in Chapter 13.) All you're really interested in is the source IP addresses of the queries your nameserver is receiving. When poring over the debugging output, look for hosts sending repeated queries, especially for the same or similar information. That may indicate a misconfigured or buggy program running on the host or a foreign nameserver pelting your nameserver with queries.

If all the queries appear to be legitimate, add a new nameserver. Don't put the nameserver just anywhere, though; use the information from the debugging output to help you decide where it's best to run one. If DNS traffic is gobbling up your bandwidth, it won't help to choose a host at random and create a nameserver there. You need to consider which hosts are sending most of the queries, then figure out how to best provide them name service. Here are some hints to help you decide:

- Look for queries from resolvers on hosts that share the same file server. You could run a nameserver on that file server.

- Look for queries from resolvers on large, multiuser hosts. You could run a nameserver there.

- Look for queries from resolvers on another subnet. Those resolvers should be configured to query a nameserver on their local subnet. If there isn't one on that subnet, create one.

- Look for queries from resolvers on the same switch. If you connect a nameserver to the switch, the traffic won't need to traverse the rest of the network.

- Look for queries from hosts connected to each other via another, lightly loaded network. You could run a nameserver on the other network.

Adding More Nameservers

When you need to create new nameservers for your zones, the simplest recourse is to add slaves. You already know how—we went over it in Chapter 4—and once you've set up one slave, cloning it is a piece of cake. However, you can run into trouble by adding slaves indiscriminately.

If you run a large number of slave servers for a zone, the primary nameserver can take quite a beating serving all of the slaves' zone transfers. There are a number of remedies for this problem, as described in the sections that follow:

- Make more primary master nameservers.
- Direct some of the slave nameservers to load from other slave nameservers.
- Create caching-only nameservers.
- Create "partial-slave" nameservers.

Primary Master and Slave Servers

Creating more primaries means extra work for you because you have to keep */etc/named.conf* and the zone datafiles synchronized manually. Whether this is preferable to your other alternatives is your call. You can use tools such as *rdist* or *rsync*[*] to simplify the process of distributing the files. A *distfile*[†] to synchronize files between primaries might be as simple as the following:

```
dup-primary:

# copy named.conf file to dup'd primary

/etc/named.conf  -> wormhole
    install ;

# copy contents of /var/named (zone data files, etc.) to dup'd primary

/var/named -> wormhole
    install ;
```

---

[*] *rsync* is a remote file synchronization program that transmits only the differences between files. You can find out more about it at *http://rsync.samba.org*.

[†] The file *rdist* reads to find out which files to update.

or for multiple primaries:

```
dup-primary:

primaries = ( wormhole carrie )
/etc/named.conf  -> {$primaries}
    install ;

/var/named -> {$primaries}
    install ;
```

You can even have *rdist* trigger your nameserver's reload using the *special* option by adding lines such as:

```
special /var/named/* "rndc reload" ;
special /etc/named.conf "rndc reload" ;
```

These tell *rdist* to execute the quoted command if any of the files change.

You can also have some of your slaves load from other slaves. Slave nameservers can load zone data from other slave nameservers instead of loading from a primary master nameserver. The slave nameserver can't tell if it is loading from a primary or from another slave. The only requirement is that the nameserver serving the zone transfer is authoritative for the zone. There's no trick to configuring this. Instead of specifying the IP address of the primary in the slave's configuration file, you simply specify the IP address of another slave.

Here are the contents of the file *named.conf*:

```
// this slave updates from wormhole, another
// slave
zone "movie.edu" {
            type slave;
            masters { 192.249.249.1; };
            file "bak.movie.edu";
};
```

When you go to this second level of distribution, though, keep in mind that it can take up to twice as long for the data to percolate from the primary nameserver to all the slaves. Remember that the refresh interval is the period after which the slave nameservers will check to make sure that their zone data is still current. Therefore, it can take the first-level slave servers the entire length of the refresh interval before they get a new copy of the zone from the primary master server. Similarly, it can take the second-level slave servers the entire refresh interval to get a new copy of the zone from the first-level slave servers. The propagation time from the primary master server to all of the slave servers can therefore be twice the refresh interval.

One way to avoid this is to use the NOTIFY mechanism. This feature is on by default, and will trigger zone transfers soon after the zone is updated on the primary master. We'll discuss NOTIFY in more detail in Chapter 10.

If you decide to configure your network with two (or more) tiers of slave nameservers, be careful to avoid updating loops. If we configured *wormhole* to update from *monsters-inc* and then accidentally configured *monsters-inc* to update from *wormhole*, neither would ever get data from the primary. They would merely check their out-of-date serial numbers against each other and perpetually decide that they were both up to date.

Caching-Only Servers

Creating *caching-only nameservers* is another alternative when you need more servers. Caching-only nameservers are nameservers not authoritative for any zones (except *0.0.127.in-addr.arpa*). The name doesn't imply that primary and slave nameservers don't cache—they do—but rather that the *only* function this server performs is looking up data and caching it. As with primary and slave nameservers, a caching-only nameserver needs a root hints file and a *db.127.0.0* file. The *named.conf* file for a caching-only server contains these lines:

```
options {
    directory "/var/named";  // or your data directory
};

zone "0.0.127.in-addr.arpa" {
    type master;
    file "db.127.0.0";
};

zone "." {
    type hint;
    file "db.cache";
};
```

A caching-only nameserver can look up domain names inside and outside your zone, as can primary and slave nameservers. The difference is that when a caching-only nameserver initially looks up a name within your zone, it ends up asking one of your zone's primary master or slave nameservers for the answer. A primary or slave answers the same question out of its authoritative data. Which primary or slave does the caching-only server ask? As with nameservers outside of your zone, it finds out which nameservers serve your zone from one of the nameservers for your parent zone. Is there any way to prime a caching-only nameserver's cache so it knows which hosts run primary and slave nameservers for your zone? No, there isn't. You can't use *db.cache*: the *db.cache* file is only for root nameserver hints. And actually, it's better that your caching-only nameservers find out about your authoritative nameservers from your parent zone's nameservers: you keep your zone's delegation information up to date. If you hard-wired a list of authoritative nameservers on your caching-only nameservers, you might forget to update it.

A caching-only nameserver's real value comes after it builds up its cache. Each time it queries an authoritative nameserver and receives an answer, it caches the records in the answer. Over time, the cache will grow to include the information most often requested by the resolvers querying the caching-only nameserver. And you avoid the overhead of zone transfers: a caching-only nameserver doesn't need to do them.

Partial-Slave Servers

In between a caching-only nameserver and a slave nameserver is another variation: a nameserver that is a slave for only a few of the local zones. We call this a *partial-secondary nameserver* (although probably nobody else does). Suppose *movie.edu* had 20 /24-sized (the old Class C) networks (and a corresponding 20 *in-addr.arpa* zones). Instead of creating a slave server for all 21 zones (all the *in-addr.arpa* subdomains plus *movie.edu*), we can create a partial-slave server for *movie.edu* and only those *in-addr.arpa* zones the host itself is in. If the host had two network interfaces, its nameserver would be a slave for three zones: *movie.edu* and the two *in-addr.arpa* zones.

Let's say we scare up the hardware for another nameserver. We'll call the new host *zardoz.movie.edu*, with IP addresses 192.249.249.9 and 192.253.253.9. We'll create a partial-slave nameserver on *zardoz* with this *named.conf* file:

```
options {
    directory "/var/named";
};

zone "movie.edu" {
    type slave;
    masters { 192.249.249.3; };
    file "bak.movie.edu";
};

zone "249.249.192.in-addr.arpa" {
    type slave;
    masters { 192.249.249.3; };
    file "bak.192.249.249";
};

zone "253.253.192.in-addr.arpa" {
    type slave;
    masters { 192.249.249.3; };
    file "bak.192.253.253";
};
```

```
zone "0.0.127.in-addr.arpa" {
    type master;
    file "db.127.0.0";
};

zone "." {
    type hint;
    file "db.cache";
};
```

This server is a slave for *movie.edu* and only two of the 20 *in-addr.arpa* zones. A "full" slave would have 21 different *zone* statements in *named.conf*.

What's so useful about a partial-slave nameserver? They're not much work to administer because their *named.conf* files don't change much. On a nameserver authoritative for all the *in-addr.arpa* zones, we'd need to add and delete *in-addr.arpa* zones as our network changed. That can be a surprising amount of work on a large network.

A partial slave can still answer most of the queries it receives, though. Most of these queries will be for data in *movie.edu* and the two *in-addr.arpa* zones. Why? Because most of the hosts querying the nameserver are on the two networks to which it's connected, 192.249.249/24 and 192.253.253/24. And those hosts probably communicate primarily with other hosts on their own network. This generates queries for data within the *in-addr.arpa* zone that corresponds to the local network.

Registering Nameservers

When you get around to setting up more and more nameservers, a question may strike you—do I need to register *all* of my primary and slave nameservers with my parent zone? The answer is no. Only those servers you want to make available to nameservers outside your zone need to be registered with your parent. For example, if you run nine nameservers for your zone, you may choose to tell the parent zone about only four of them. Within your network, you use all nine servers. Five of those nine servers, however, are queried only by resolvers on hosts that are configured to query them (in *resolv.conf*, for example). Their parent zone's nameservers don't delegate to them, so they'll never be queried by remote nameservers. Only the four servers registered with your parent zone are queried by other nameservers, including caching-only and partial-slave nameservers on your network. This setup is shown in Figure 8-2.

Besides being able to pick and choose which of your nameservers are hammered by outside queries, there's a technical motivation for registering only some of your zone's nameservers: there is a limit to how many servers will fit in a UDP-based response message. In practice, around 10 nameserver records should fit. Depending on the data (how many servers' names are in the same domain), you can get more or

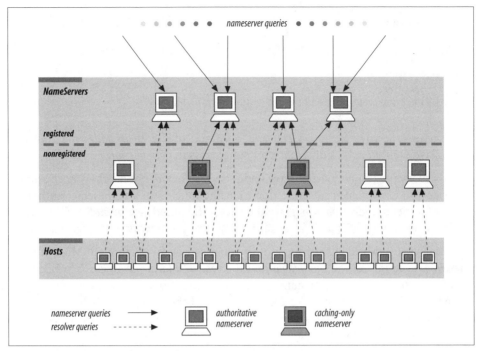

Figure 8-2. Registering only some of your nameservers

fewer.* There's not much point in registering more than 10 nameservers, anyway; if none of those 10 servers can be reached, it's unlikely the destination host can be reached.

If you've set up a new authoritative nameserver, and you decide it should be registered, make a list of the parents of the zones for which it's authoritative. You'll need to contact the administrators for each parent zone. For example, let's say we want to register the nameserver we just set up on *zardoz*. To get this slave registered in all the right zones, we'll need to contact the administrators of *edu* and *in-addr.arpa*. (For help determining who runs your parent zones, turn back to Chapter 3.)

When you contact the administrators of a parent zone, be sure to follow the process they specify (if any) on their web site. If there's no standard modification process, you'll have to send them the domain name of the zone (or zones) for which the new nameserver is authoritative. If the new nameserver is in the new zone, you'll also need to give them the IP address(es) of the new nameserver. In fact, if there's no official format for submitting the information, it's often best just to send your parent the

---

* The domain names of the Internet's root nameservers were changed because of this. All the roots were moved into the same domain, *root-servers.net*, to take maximum advantage of domain-name compression and to allow information about as many roots as possible to be stored in a single UDP packet.

complete list of registered nameservers for the zone, plus any addresses necessary, in zone datafile format. This avoids any potential confusion.

Since our networks were originally assigned by the InterNIC, we used the Network Modification form at *http://www.arin.net/library/templates/netmod.txt* to change our registration. If they hadn't had a template for us to use, our message to the administrator of *in-addr.arpa* might have read something like this:

```
Howdy!

I've just set up a new slave name server on zardoz.movie.edu for the
249.249.192.in-addr.arpa and 253.253.192.in-addr.arpa zones. Would you
please add NS records for this name server to the in-addr.arpa zone?
That would make our delegation information look like:

253.253.192.in-addr.arpa. 86400 IN NS toystory.movie.edu.
253.253.192.in-addr.arpa. 86400 IN NS wormhole.movie.edu.
253.253.192.in-addr.arpa. 86400 IN NS zardoz.movie.edu.

249.249.192.in-addr.arpa. 86400 IN NS toystory.movie.edu.
249.249.192.in-addr.arpa. 86400 IN NS wormhole.movie.edu.
249.249.192.in-addr.arpa. 86400 IN NS zardoz.movie.edu.

Thanks!

Albert LeDomaine
al@movie.edu
```

Notice that we specified explicit TTLs on the NS records. That's because our parent nameservers aren't authoritative for those records; *our* nameservers are. By including them, we're indicating our choice of a TTL for our zone's delegation. Of course, our parent may have other ideas about what the TTL should be.

In this case, glue data—A records for each of the nameservers—isn't necessary because the domain names of the nameservers aren't within the *in-addr.arpa* zones. They're within *movie.edu*, so a nameserver that was referred to *toystory.movie.edu* or *wormhole.movie.edu* can still find their addresses by following delegation to the *movie.edu* nameservers.

Is a partial-slave nameserver a good nameserver to register with your parent zone? Actually, it's not ideal because it's authoritative for only some of your *in-addr.arpa* zones. Administratively, it may be easier to register only servers that slave all the local zones; that way, you don't need to keep track of which nameservers are authoritative for which zones. All your parent zones can delegate to the same set of nameservers: your primary master and your "full" slaves.

If you don't have many nameservers, though, or if you're good at remembering which nameservers are authoritative for which zones, go ahead and register a partial-slave.

Caching-only nameservers, on the other hand, must *never* be registered. A caching-only nameserver rarely has complete information for any given zone; it just has the bits and pieces of the zone that it has looked up recently. If a parent nameserver mistakenly refers a foreign nameserver to a caching-only nameserver, the foreign nameserver sends the caching-only nameserver a nonrecursive query. The caching-only nameserver might have the data cached, but then again, it might not.* If it doesn't have the data, it refers the querier to the best nameservers it knows (those closest to the domain name in the query)—which may include the caching-only nameserver itself! The poor foreign nameserver may never get an answer. This kind of misconfiguration—actually, delegating a zone to any nameserver not authoritative for that zone—is known as *lame delegation*.

Changing TTLs

An experienced zone administrator needs to know how to set the time to live on his zone's data to his best advantage. The TTL on a resource record, remember, is the length of time for which any nameserver can cache that record. So if the TTL for a particular resource record is 3,600 seconds and a server outside your network caches that record, it will have to remove the entry from its cache after an hour. If it needs the same data after the hour is up, it'll have to query one of your nameservers again.

When we introduced TTLs, we emphasized that your choice of a TTL would dictate how current you would keep copies of your data, at the cost of increased load on your nameservers. A low TTL would mean that nameservers outside your network would have to get data from your nameservers often and that the data would therefore be kept current. On the other hand, your nameservers would be peppered by the nameservers' queries.

You don't *have* to choose a TTL once and for all, though. You can—and experienced administrators do—change TTLs periodically to suit your needs.

Suppose we know that one of our hosts is about to be moved to another network. This host houses the *movie.edu* film library, a large collection of files our site makes available to hosts on the Internet. During normal operation, outside nameservers cache the address of our host according to the default TTL set in the $TTL control statement, or for pre–BIND 8.2 nameservers, in the SOA record. (We set the default TTL for *movie.edu* to three hours in our sample zone datafiles.) A nameserver caching the old address record just before the change could have the wrong address for as long as three hours. A loss of connectivity for three hours is unacceptable, though. What can we do to minimize the loss of connectivity? We can lower the TTL so that

---

* More importantly, even if the caching-only nameserver had the answer cached, it would respond non-authoritatively. The nameserver that was referred to it, expecting an authoritative answer, would ignore the response.

---

outside servers cache the address record for a shorter period. By reducing the TTL, we force the outside servers to update their data more frequently, which means that any changes we make when we actually move the system will be propagated to the outside world quickly. How short can we make the TTL? Unfortunately, we can't safely use a TTL of 0, which should mean "don't cache this record at all." Some older BIND version 4 nameservers can't cope with a TTL of 0. Small TTLs, like 30 seconds, are okay, though. The easiest change is to lower the TTL in the $TTL control statement in the *db.movie.edu* file. If you don't place an explicit TTL on resource records in the zone datafiles, the nameserver applies this to each resource record. If you lower the default TTL, though, the new, lower default applies to all zone data, not just the address of the host being moved. The drawback to this approach is that your nameserver will be answering a lot more queries because the querying servers will cache all the data in your zone for a shorter period. A better alternative is to put a different TTL only on the affected address record.

To add an explicit TTL on an individual resource record, place it before the IN in the class field. The TTL value is in seconds by default, but you can also specify units of *m* (minutes), *h* (hours), *d* (days), and *w* (weeks), just as you could in the $TTL control statement. Here's an example of an explicit TTL from *db.movie.edu*:

```
cujo  1h IN  A    192.253.253.5 ; explicit TTL of 1 hour
```

When giving out answers, a slave supplies the same TTL a primary master does; that is, if a primary gives out a TTL of one hour for a particular record, a slave will, too. The slave doesn't decrement the TTL according to how long it has been since it loaded the zone. So, if the TTL of a single resource record is set smaller than the default, both the primary and slave nameservers give out the resource record with the same, smaller TTL. If the slave nameserver has reached the expiration time for the zone, it expires the whole zone. It will never expire an individual resource record within a zone.

So BIND allows you to put a small TTL on an individual resource record if you know that the data is going to change shortly. Thus, any nameserver caching that data caches it only for a brief time. Unfortunately, while the nameserver makes tagging records with a small TTL possible, most administrators don't take the time to do it. When a host changes addresses, you often lose connectivity to it for a while.

More often than not, the host having its address changed is not one of the main hubs on the site, so the outage affects few people. If one of the mail hubs or a major web server or *ftp* archive—like the film library—is moving, though, a day's loss of connectivity may be unacceptable. In cases like this, the administrator should plan ahead and reduce the TTL on the data to be changed.

Remember that the TTL on the affected data will need to be lowered *before* the change takes place. Reducing the TTL on a workstation's address record and changing the workstation's address simultaneously may do you little or no good; the address record may have been cached seconds before you made the change and may linger until the old TTL times out. You must also be sure to factor in the time it'll take your slaves to load from your primary. For example, if your default TTL is 12 hours and your refresh interval is 3 hours, be sure to lower the TTLs at least 15 hours ahead of time, so that by the time you move the host, all the old, longer TTL records will have timed out. Of course, if all your slaves are using NOTIFY, the slaves shouldn't take the full refresh interval to synch up.

Changing Other SOA Values

We briefly mentioned increasing the refresh interval as a way to offload your primary nameserver. Let's discuss refresh in a little more detail and go over the remaining SOA values, too.

The *refresh* value, you'll remember, controls how often a slave checks whether its zone data is up to date. The *retry* value then becomes the refresh time after the first failure to reach a master nameserver. The *expire* value determines how long zone data can be held before it's discarded, when a master is unreachable. Finally, on pre–BIND 8.2 nameservers, the *minimum TTL* sets how long zone information may be cached. On newer nameservers, the last SOA field is the negative caching TTL.

Suppose we decide we want the slaves to pick up new information every hour instead of every three hours. We change the refresh value to one hour in each of the zone datafiles (or with the –o option to *h2n*). Since retry is related to refresh, we should probably reduce retry, too—to every 15 minutes or so. Typically, retry is less than refresh, but that's not required.* Although lowering the refresh value speeds up the distribution of zone data, it also increases the load on the nameserver from which data is being transferred because the slaves will check more often. The added load isn't much, though; each slave makes a single SOA query during each zone's refresh interval to check its master's copy of the zone. So with two slave nameservers, changing the refresh time from three hours to one hour generates only four more queries (per zone) to the master in any three-hour span.

If all your slaves run BIND 8 or 9, and you use NOTIFY, of course, refresh doesn't mean as much. But if you have even one BIND version 4 slave, your zone data may take up to the full refresh interval to reach it.

Some versions of BIND may refresh *more often* than the refresh interval. All modern versions of BIND (from version 4.9 on) will wait a random number of seconds between one-half (for BIND 8) or three-quarters (BIND 9) of the refresh interval and the full refresh interval to check serial numbers.

Expiration times on the order of a week—longer if you frequently have problems reaching your updating source—are common. The expiration time should always be

---

* Actually, BIND 8 servers will warn you if refresh is set to less than 10 times the retry interval.

much larger than the retry and refresh intervals; if the expiration time is smaller than the refresh interval, your slaves will expire their data before trying to load new data. BIND 8 complains if you set an expiration time less than refresh plus retry, less than twice retry, less than seven days, or greater than six months. (BIND 9 doesn't complain—yet.) Choosing an expiration time that meets all BIND 8's criteria is a good idea in most situations.

If your zone's data doesn't change much, you might consider raising its default TTL. Default TTLs are commonly a few hours to one day. One day is about the longest value that makes sense for a TTL. If it's longer than that, you may find yourself unable to change bad, cached data in a reasonable amount of time.

Planning for Disasters

It's a fact of life on a network that things go wrong. Hardware fails, software has bugs, and people occasionally make mistakes. Sometimes this results in minor inconveniences, like having a few users lose connections. Sometimes the results are catastrophic and involve the loss of important data and gainful employment.

Because the Domain Name System relies so heavily on the network, it is vulnerable to network outages. Thankfully, the design of DNS takes into account the imperfection of networks: it allows for multiple, redundant nameservers; retransmission of queries; retrying zone transfers; and so on.

DNS doesn't protect itself from every conceivable calamity, though. There are types of network failures—some of them quite common—that DNS doesn't or can't protect against. But with a small investment of time and money, you can minimize the threat of these problems.

Outages

Power outages, for example, are relatively common in many parts of the world. In some parts of the United States, thunderstorms or tornadoes may cause a site to lose power, or to have only intermittent power, for an extended period. Elsewhere, typhoons, volcanoes, or construction work may interrupt your electrical service. And you never know when those of you in California might lose power in a rolling blackout from a lack of electrical capacity.

If all your hosts are down, of course, you don't need name service. Quite often, however, sites have problems when power is *restored*. Following our recommendations, they run their nameservers on file servers and big, multiuser machines. And when the power comes up, those machines are naturally the last to boot because all those disks need to be checked and fixed first! Which means that all the on-site hosts that are quick to boot do so without the benefit of name service.

This can cause all sorts of wonderful problems, depending on how your hosts' start-up files are written. Unix hosts often execute some variant of:

```
/usr/sbin/ifconfig lan0 inet `hostname` netmask 255.255.128.0 up
/usr/sbin/route add default site-router 1
```

to bring up their network interface and add a default route. Using hostnames in commands (`hostname` expands to the local hostname, and *site-router* is the name of the local router) is admirable because it allows administrators to change devices' IP addresses without changing all the startup files on-site.

Unfortunately, the *route* command fails without name service. The *ifconfig* command fails only if the local host's name and IP address don't appear in the host's */etc/hosts* file, so it's a good idea to leave at least that data in each host's */etc/hosts*.

By the time the startup sequence reaches the *route* command, the network interface will be up, and the host will try to use name service to map the name of the router to an IP address. And since the host has no default route until the *route* command is executed, the only nameservers it can reach are those on the local subnet.

If the booting host can reach a working nameserver on its local subnet, it can execute the *route* command successfully. Quite often, however, one or more of the nameservers it can reach aren't yet running. What happens then depends on the contents of *resolv.conf*.

BIND resolvers fall back to the host table only if there is just one nameserver listed in *resolv.conf* (or if no nameserver is listed, and the resolver defaults to using a nameserver on the local host). If only one nameserver is configured, the resolver queries it, and if the network returns an error each time the resolver sends a query, the resolver falls back to searching the host table. The errors that cause the resolver to fall back include:

- Receipt of an ICMP port unreachable message
- Receipt of an ICMP network unreachable message
- Inability to send the UDP packet (e.g., because networking is not yet running on the local host)[*]

If the host running the one configured nameserver isn't running at all, though, the resolver doesn't receive any errors. The nameserver is effectively a black hole. After about 75 seconds of trying, the resolver just times out and returns a null answer to the application that called it. Only if the nameserver host has actually started networking—but not yet started the nameserver—does the resolver get an error: an ICMP port unreachable message.

---

[*] Check Chapter 6 for vendor-specific enhancements to and variants of this resolver algorithm.

Overall, the single-nameserver configuration does work if you have nameservers available on each network, but not as elegantly as we might like. If the local nameserver hasn't come up when a host on its network reboots, the *route* command fails.

This may seem awkward, but it's not nearly as bad as what happens with multiple nameservers. With multiple servers listed in *resolv.conf*, BIND never falls back to the host table after the primary network interface has been *ifconfig*'ed. The resolver simply loops through the nameservers, querying them until one answers, or the 75-plus-second timeout is reached.

This is especially problematic during bootup. If none of the configured nameservers is available, the resolver times out without returning an IP address, and adding the default route fails.

Recommendations

Our recommendation, as primitive as it sounds, is to hardcode the IP address of the default router into the startup file or an external file (many systems use */etc/defaultrouter*). This ensures that your host's networking starts correctly.

An alternative is to list just a single, reliable nameserver on your host's local network in *resolv.conf*. This allows you to use the name of the default router in the startup file, as long as you make sure that the router's name appears in */etc/hosts* (in case your reliable nameserver isn't running when the host reboots). Of course, if the host running the reliable nameserver isn't running when your host reboots, all bets are off. You won't fall back to */etc/hosts* because there won't be any networking running to return an error to your host.

If your vendor's version of BIND allows configuration of the order in which services are queried or falls back from DNS to */etc/hosts* if DNS doesn't find an answer, take advantage of it! In the former case, you can configure the resolver to check */etc/hosts* first, and then keep a "stub" */etc/hosts* file on each host, including the default router and the local host's name. In the latter situation, just make sure such a "stub" */etc/hosts* exists; no other configuration should be necessary.

However, there's some danger in using */etc/hosts* files: unless you take care to keep the files up to date, the information in them may become stale. Maintaining stub */etc/hosts* files on many hosts is a great application for *rsync*.

And what if your default route is added correctly but the nameservers still haven't come up? This can affect *sendmail*, NFS, and a slew of other services. *sendmail* won't canonicalize hostnames correctly without DNS, and your NFS mounts may fail.

The best solution to this problem is to run a nameserver on a host with uninterruptible power. If you rarely experience extended power loss, battery backup might be enough. If your outages are longer, and name service is critical to you, you should consider an uninterruptible power system (UPS) with a generator of some kind.

If you can't afford luxuries like these, you might just try to track down the fastest-booting host around and run a nameserver on it. Hosts with filesystem journaling should boot especially quickly because they usually don't need to check and repair their disks. Hosts with small filesystems should also boot quickly because they don't have many disks to check.

Once you've located the right host, you'll need to make sure the host's IP address appears in the resolver configurations of all of your hosts that need full-time name service. You'll probably want to list the backed-up host last because during normal operation, hosts should use the nameserver closest to them. Then, after a power failure, your critical applications will still have name service, albeit with a small sacrifice in performance.

Coping with Disaster

When disaster strikes, it really helps to know what to do. Knowing to duck under a sturdy table or desk during an earthquake can save you from being pinned under a toppling monitor. Knowing how to turn off your gas can save your house from conflagration.

Likewise, knowing what to do in a network disaster (or even just a minor mishap) can help you keep your network running. Living out in California, as we do, we have some first-hand experience with disaster, and some suggestions.

Long Outages (Days)

If you lose network connectivity for a long time, your nameservers may begin to have problems. If they lose connectivity to the root nameservers for an extended period, they'll stop resolving queries outside their authoritative zone data. If the slaves can't reach their master, sooner or later they'll expire the zone.

In case your name service really goes haywire because of the connectivity loss, it's a good idea to keep a site-wide or workgroup */etc/hosts* around. In times of dire need, you can move *resolv.conf* to *resolv.bak*, kill the local nameserver (if there is one), and just use */etc/hosts*. It's not flashy, but it'll get you by.

As for slaves, you can reconfigure a slave that can't reach its master to temporarily run as a primary. Just edit *named.conf* and change the *type* substatement in the *zone* statement from *slave* to *master*, then delete the *masters* substatement. If more than one slave for the same zone is cut off, you can configure one as a primary temporarily and reconfigure the others to load from the temporary primary.

Really Long Outages (Weeks)

If an extended outage cuts you off from the Internet—say for a week or more—you may need to restore connectivity to root nameservers artificially to get things working again. Every nameserver needs to talk to a root nameserver occasionally. It's a bit like therapy: the nameserver needs to contact a root periodically to regain its perspective on the world.

To provide root name service during a long outage, you can set up your own root nameservers, *but only temporarily*. Once you're reconnected to the Internet, you *must* shut off your temporary root servers. The most obnoxious vermin on the Internet are nameservers that believe they're root nameservers but don't know anything about most top-level domains. A close second is the Internet nameserver configured to query—and report—a false set of root nameservers.

That said, and with our alibis in place, here's what you have to do to configure your own root nameserver. First, you need to create *db.root*, the root zone datafile. The root zone will delegate to the highest-level zones in your isolated network. For example, if *movie.edu* were to be isolated from the Internet, we might create a *db*.root file for *toystory* that looks like this:

```
$TTL 1d
. IN SOA toystory.movie.edu. al.movie.edu. (
                1       ; Serial
                3h      ; Refresh
                1h      ; Retry
                1w      ; Expire
                1h )    ; Negative TTL

   IN NS toystory.movie.edu. ; toystory is the temp. root

; Our root only knows about movie.edu and our two
; in-addr.arpa domains

movie.edu. IN NS toystory.movie.edu.
           IN NS wormhole.movie.edu.

249.249.192.in-addr.arpa. IN NS toystory.movie.edu.
                          IN NS wormhole.movie.edu.

253.253.192.in-addr.arpa. IN NS toystory.movie.edu.
                          IN NS wormhole.movie.edu.

toystory.movie.edu.    IN A 192.249.249.3
wormhole.movie.edu.    IN A 192.249.249.1
                       IN A 192.253.253.1
```

Then, we need to add the appropriate line to *toystory*'s *named.conf* file:

```
// Comment out hints zone
// zone . {
//              type hint;
```

```
//                      file "db.cache";
//              };

zone "." {
                type master;
                file "db.root";
};
```

We then update all of our nameservers (except the new, temporary root) with a *db.cache* file that includes just the temporary root nameserver (it's best to move the old root hints file aside; we'll need it later, once connectivity is restored).

Here are the contents of the file *db.cache*:

```
.  99999999  IN  NS  toystory.movie.edu.

toystory.movie.edu.  99999999   IN  A  192.249.249.3
```

This process keeps *movie.edu* name resolution going during the outage. Once Internet connectivity is restored, we can delete the root zone statement from *named.conf*, uncomment the hint *zone* statement on *toystory*, then restore the original root hints files on all other nameservers.

## CHAPTER 9

Parenting

The way Dinah washed her children's faces was this: first she held the poor thing down by its ear with one paw, and then with the other paw she rubbed its face all over, the wrong way, beginning at the nose: and just now, as I said, she was hard at work on the white kitten, which was lying quite still and trying to purr— no doubt feeling that it was all meant for its good.

Once your domain reaches a certain size, or you decide you need to distribute the management of parts of your domain to various entities within your organization, you'll want to divide the domain into subdomains. These subdomains will be the children of your current domain in the namespace; your domain will be the parent. If you delegate responsibility for your subdomains to another organization, each becomes its own zone, separate from its parent zone. We like to call the management of your subdomains—your children—*parenting*.

Good parenting starts with carving up your domain sensibly, choosing appropriate names for your subdomains, and delegating the subdomains to create new zones. A responsible parent also works hard at maintaining the relationship between his zone and its children; he ensures that delegation from parent to child is current and correct.

Good parenting is vital to the success of your network, especially as name service becomes critical to navigating between sites. Incorrect delegation to a child zone's nameservers can render a site effectively unreachable, while the loss of connectivity to the parent zone's nameservers can leave a site unable to reach any hosts outside the local zone.

In this chapter, we present our views on when to create subdomains, and we go over how to create and delegate them in some detail. We also discuss management of the parent/child relationship and, finally, how to manage the process of carving up a large domain into smaller subdomains with minimal disruption and inconvenience.

When to Become a Parent

Far be it from us to *tell* you when you should become a parent, but we will be so bold as to offer you some guidelines. You may find some compelling reason to implement subdomains that isn't on our list, but here are some common reasons:

- A need to delegate or distribute management of your domain to a number of organizations
- The large size of your domain: dividing it would make it easier to manage and reduce the load on your authoritative nameservers
- A need to distinguish hosts' organizational affiliations by including them in particular subdomains

Once you've decided to have children, the next question to ask yourself is, naturally, how many children to have.

How Many Children?

Of course, you won't simply say, "I want to create four subdomains." Deciding how many subdomains to implement is really choosing the organizational affiliations of those subdomains. For example, if your company has four branch offices, you might decide to create four subdomains, each of which corresponds to a branch office.

Should you create subdomains for each site, for each division, or even for each department? You have a lot of latitude in your choice because of DNS's scalability. You can create a few large subdomains or many small subdomains. There are trade-offs whichever you choose, though.

Delegating to a few large subdomains isn't much work for the parent, because there's not much delegation to keep track of. However, you wind up with larger subdomains, which require more memory to load and faster nameservers, and administration isn't as distributed. If you implement site-level subdomains, for example, you may force autonomous or unrelated groups at a site to share a single zone and a single point of administration.

Delegating to many smaller subdomains can be a headache for the parent's administrator. Keeping delegation data current involves keeping track of which hosts run nameservers and which zones they're authoritative for. The data changes each time a subdomain adds a new nameserver or the address of a nameserver for the subdomain changes. If the subdomains are all administered by different people, that means more administrators to train, more relationships for the parent's administrator to maintain, and more overhead for the organization overall. On the other hand, the subdomains are smaller and easier to manage, and the administration is more widely distributed, allowing closer management of zone data.

Given the advantages and disadvantages of either alternative, it may seem difficult to make a choice. Actually, there's probably a natural division in your organization. Some companies manage computers and networks at the site level; others have decentralized, relatively autonomous workgroups that manage everything themselves. Here are a few basic rules to help you find the right way to carve up your namespace:

- Don't shoehorn your organization into a weird or uncomfortable structure. Trying to fit 50 independent, unrelated U.S. divisions into four regional subdomains may save you work (as the administrator of the parent zone), but it won't help your reputation. Decentralized, autonomous operations demand different zones: that's the *raison d'être* of the Domain Name System.

- The structure of your domain should mirror the structure of your organization, especially your organization's *support* structure. If departments run networks, assign IP addresses, and manage hosts, they should also manage the subdomains.

- If you're not sure or can't agree about how the namespace should be organized, try to come up with guidelines for when a group within your organization can carve off its own subdomain (for example, how many hosts are needed to create a new subdomain and what level of support the group must provide) and grow the namespace organically, but only as needed.

What to Name Your Children

Once you've decided how many subdomains you'd like to create and what they correspond to, you must choose names for them. Rather than unilaterally deciding on your subdomains' names, it's considered polite to involve your future subdomain administrators and their constituencies in the decision. In fact, you can leave the decision entirely to them if you like.

This can lead to problems, though. It's preferable to use a relatively consistent naming scheme across your subdomains. This practice makes it easier for users in one subdomain, or outside your domain entirely, to guess or remember your subdomain names and to figure out in which domain a particular host or user lives.

Leaving the decision to the locals can result in naming chaos. Some will want to use geographical names; others will insist on organizational names. Some will want to abbreviate; others will want to use full names.

Therefore, it's often best to establish a naming convention before choosing subdomain names. Here are some suggestions from our experience:

- In a dynamic company, the names of organizations can change frequently. Naming subdomains organizationally in a climate like this can be disastrous. One month the Relatively Advanced Technology group seems stable enough, the next month they've been merged into the Questionable Computer Systems organization, and the following quarter they're all sold to a German conglomerate. Meanwhile, you're stuck with well-known hosts in a subdomain whose name no longer has any meaning.

- Geographical names are more stable than organizational names but sometimes aren't as well known. You may know that your famous Software Evangelism Business Unit is in Poughkeepsie or Waukegan, but people outside your company may have no idea where it is (and might have trouble spelling either name).

- Don't sacrifice readability for convenience. Two-letter subdomain names may be easy to type, but impossible to recognize. Why abbreviate "Italy" to "it" and have it confused with your Information Technology organization when for a paltry three more letters you can use the full name and eliminate any ambiguity?

- Too many companies use cryptic, inconvenient domain names. The general rule seems to be the larger the company, the more indecipherable the domain names. Buck the trend: make the names of your subdomains obvious!

- Don't use existing or reserved top-level domain names as subdomain names. It might seem sensible to use two-letter country abbreviations for your international subdomains or to use organizational top-level domain names like *net* for your networking organization, but doing so can cause nasty problems. For example, naming your Communications Department's subdomain *com* might impede your ability to communicate with hosts under the top-level *com* domain. Imagine the administrators of your *com* subdomain naming their new Sun workstation *sun* and their new HP 9000 *hp* (they aren't the most imaginative folks): users anywhere within your domain sending mail to friends at *sun.com* or *hp.com* could have their letters end up in your *com* subdomain because the name of your parent zone may be in some of your hosts' search lists.[*]

How to Become a Parent: Creating Subdomains

Once you've decided on names, creating the child domains is easy. But first, you must decide how much autonomy you're going to give your subdomains. Odd that you have to decide that *before* you actually create them....

Thus far, we've assumed that if you create a subdomain, you'll want to delegate it to another organization, thereby making it a separate zone from the parent. Is this always true, though? Not necessarily.

Think carefully about how the computers and networks within a subdomain are managed when choosing whether to delegate it. It doesn't make sense to delegate a subdomain to an entity that doesn't manage its own hosts or networks. For example, in a

---

[*] Actually, not all mailers have this problem, but some popular versions of *sendmail* do. It all depends on which form of canonicalization they do, as we discussed in the section "Local Nameserver" in Chapter 6.

large corporation, the Personnel Department probably doesn't run its own computers: the MIS (Management Information Systems) or IT (Information Technology— same animal as MIS) Department manages them. So while you may want to create a subdomain for personnel, delegating management for that subdomain to it is probably wasted effort.

Creating a Subdomain in the Parent's Zone

You can create a subdomain without delegating it, however. How? By creating resource records that refer to the subdomain within the parent's zone. For example, *movie.edu* has a host that stores its complete database of employee and student records, called *brazil*. To put *brazil* in the *personnel.movie.edu* domain, we can add records to *db.movie.edu*.

Partial contents of file *db.movie.edu*:

```
brazil.personnel       IN  A      192.253.253.10
                       IN  MX     10 brazil.personnel.movie.edu.
                       IN  MX     100 postmanrings2x.movie.edu.
employeedb.personnel   IN  CNAME  brazil.personnel.movie.edu.
db.personnel           IN  CNAME  brazil.personnel.movie.edu.
```

Now users can log into *db.personnel.movie.edu* to get to the employee database. We can make this setup especially convenient for Personnel Department employees by adding *personnel.movie.edu* to their PCs' or workstations' search lists; they'd need to type only *telnet db* to get to the right host.

We can make this more convenient for ourselves by using the $ORIGIN control statement to change the origin to *personnel.movie.edu* so that we can use shorter names.

Partial contents of file *db.movie.edu*:

```
$ORIGIN personnel.movie.edu.
brazil     IN A     192.253.253.10
           IN MX    10 brazil.personnel.movie.edu.
           IN MX    100 postmanrings2x.movie.edu.
employeedb IN CNAME brazil.personnel.movie.edu.
db         IN CNAME brazil.personnel.movie.edu.
```

If we had a few more records, we could create a separate file for them and use $INCLUDE to include it in *db.movie.edu* and change the origin at the same time.

Notice there's no SOA record for *personnel.movie.edu*? There's no need for one because the *movie.edu* SOA record indicates the start of authority for the entire *movie.edu* zone. Since there's no delegation to *personnel.movie.edu*, it's part of the *movie.edu* zone.

Creating and Delegating a Subdomain

If you decide to delegate your subdomains—to send your children out into the world, as it were—you'll need to do things a little differently. We're in the process of doing it now, so you can follow along with us.

We need to create a new subdomain of *movie.edu* for our special-effects lab. We've chosen the name *fx.movie.edu*—short, recognizable, unambiguous. Because we're delegating *fx.movie.edu* to administrators in the lab, it'll be a separate zone. The hosts *bladerunner* and *outland*, both within the special-effects lab, will serve as the zone's nameservers (*bladerunner* will serve as the primary). We've chosen to run two nameservers for the zone for redundancy; a single *fx.movie.edu* nameserver would be a single point of failure that could effectively isolate the entire special-effects lab. Since there aren't many hosts in the lab, though, two nameservers should be enough.

The special-effects lab is on *movie.edu*'s new 192.253.254/24 network.

Partial contents of */etc/hosts*:

```
192.253.254.1 movie-gw.movie.edu movie-gw
# fx primary
192.253.254.2 bladerunner.fx.movie.edu bladerunner br
# fx slave
192.253.254.3 outland.fx.movie.edu outland
192.253.254.4 starwars.fx.movie.edu starwars
192.253.254.5 empire.fx.movie.edu empire
192.253.254.6 jedi.fx.movie.edu jedi
```

First, we create a zone datafile that includes records for all the hosts that will live in *fx.movie.edu*.

Contents of file *db.fx.movie.edu*:

```
$TTL 1d
@  IN  SOA  bladerunner.fx.movie.edu. hostmaster.fx.movie.edu. (
                  1       ; serial
                  3h      ; refresh
                  1h      ; retry
                  1w      ; expire
                  1h )    ; negative caching TTL

     IN  NS  bladerunner
     IN  NS  outland

; MX records for fx.movie.edu
     IN  MX  10 starwars
     IN  MX  100 wormhole.movie.edu.

; starwars handles bladerunner's mail
; wormhole is the movie.edu mail hub

bladerunner  IN  A    192.253.254.2
             IN  MX   10 starwars
             IN  MX   100 wormhole.movie.edu.
```

```
br              IN  CNAME    bladerunner

outland         IN  A    192.253.254.3
                IN  MX   10 starwars
                IN  MX   100 wormhole.movie.edu.

starwars        IN  A    192.253.254.4
                IN  MX   10 starwars
                IN  MX   100 wormhole.movie.edu.

empire          IN  A    192.253.254.5
                IN  MX   10 starwars
                IN  MX   100 wormhole.movie.edu.

jedi            IN  A    192.253.254.6
                IN  MX   10 starwars
                IN  MX   100 wormhole.movie.edu.
```

Then, we create the *db.192.253.254* file:

```
$TTL 1d
@  IN  SOA  bladerunner.fx.movie.edu. hostmaster.fx.movie.edu. (
                1        ; serial
                3h       ; refresh
                1h       ; retry
                1w       ; expire
                1h )     ; negative caching TTL

        IN   NS    bladerunner.fx.movie.edu.
        IN   NS    outland.fx.movie.edu.

1       IN   PTR   movie-gw.movie.edu.
2       IN   PTR   bladerunner.fx.movie.edu.
3       IN   PTR   outland.fx.movie.edu.
4       IN   PTR   starwars.fx.movie.edu.
5       IN   PTR   empire.fx.movie.edu.
6       IN   PTR   jedi.fx.movie.edu.
```

Notice that the PTR record for *1.254.253.192.in-addr.arpa* points to *movie-gw. movie.edu*. That's intentional. The router connects to the other *movie.edu* networks, so it really doesn't belong in *fx.movie.edu*, and there's no requirement that all the PTR records in *254.253.192.in-addr.arpa* map into a single zone—though they should correspond to the canonical names for those hosts.

Next, we create an appropriate *named.conf* file for the primary nameserver:

```
options {
                directory "/var/named";
};

zone "0.0.127.in-addr.arpa" {
                type master;
                file "db.127.0.0";
};
```

```
zone "fx.movie.edu" {
             type master;
             file "db.fx.movie.edu";
};

zone "254.253.192.in-addr.arpa" {
             type master;
             file "db.192.253.254";
};

zone "." {
             type hint;
             file "db.cache";
};
```

Of course, if we use *h2n*, we can just run:

```
% h2n -v 8 -d fx.movie.edu -n 192.253.254 -s bladerunner -s outland \
-u hostmaster.fx.movie.edu -m 10:starwars -m 100:wormhole.movie.edu
```

and save ourselves some typing. *h2n* creates essentially the same *db.fx.movie.edu*, *db.192.253.254*, and *named.conf* files.

Now we need to configure *bladerunner*'s resolver. Actually, this may not require creating *resolv.conf*. If we set *bladerunner*'s *hostname* to its new domain name, *bladerunner.fx.movie.edu*, the resolver can derive the local domain name from the fully qualified domain name. By default, of course, the resolver will configure the local nameserver.

Next, we start up the *named* process on *bladerunner* and check for *syslog* errors. If *named* starts okay, and there are no *syslog* errors that need tending to, we'll use *nslookup* to look up a few hosts in *fx.movie.edu* and in *254.253.192.in-addr.arpa*:

```
Default Server:  bladerunner.fx.movie.edu
Address:  192.253.254.2

> jedi
Server:  bladerunner.fx.movie.edu
Address:  192.253.254.2

Name:    jedi.fx.movie.edu
Address:  192.253.254.6

> set type=mx
> empire
Server:  bladerunner.fx.movie.edu
Address:  192.253.254.2

empire.fx.movie.edu      preference = 10,
                         mail exchanger = starwars.fx.movie.edu
empire.fx.movie.edu      preference = 100,
                         mail exchanger = wormhole.movie.edu
fx.movie.edu     nameserver = outland.fx.movie.edu
fx.movie.edu     nameserver = bladerunner.fx.movie.edu
```

```
starwars.fx.movie.edu    internet address = 192.253.254.4
wormhole.movie.edu       internet address = 192.249.249.1
wormhole.movie.edu       internet address = 192.253.253.1
bladerunner.fx.movie.edu      internet address = 192.253.254.2
outland.fx.movie.edu     internet address = 192.253.254.3

> ls -d fx.movie.edu
[bladerunner.fx.movie.edu]
$ORIGIN fx.movie.edu.
@                    1D IN SOA       bladerunner hostmaster (
                                     1              ; serial
                                     3H             ; refresh
                                     1H             ; retry
                                     1W             ; expiry
                                     1H )           ; minimum

                     1D IN NS        bladerunner
                     1D IN NS        outland
                     1D IN MX        10 starwars
                     1D IN MX        100 wormhole.movie.edu.
bladerunner          1D IN A         192.253.254.2
                     1D IN MX        10 starwars
                     1D IN MX        100 wormhole.movie.edu.
br                   1D IN CNAME     bladerunner
empire               1D IN A         192.253.254.5
                     1D IN MX        10 starwars
                     1D IN MX        100 wormhole.movie.edu.
jedi                 1D IN A         192.253.254.6
                     1D IN MX        10 starwars
                     1D IN MX        100 wormhole.movie.edu.
outland              1D IN A         192.253.254.3
                     1D IN MX        10 starwars
                     1D IN MX        100 wormhole.movie.edu.
starwars             1D IN A         192.253.254.4
                     1D IN MX        10 starwars
                     1D IN MX        100 wormhole.movie.edu.
@                    1D IN SOA       bladerunner hostmaster (
                                     1              ; serial
                                     3H             ; refresh
                                     1H             ; retry
                                     1W             ; expiry
                                     1H )           ; minimum

> set type=ptr
> 192.253.254.3
Server:  bladerunner.fx.movie.edu
Address:  192.253.254.2

3.254.253.192.in-addr.arpa      name = outland.fx.movie.edu

> ls -d 254.253.192.in-addr.arpa.
[bladerunner.fx.movie.edu]
$ORIGIN 254.253.192.in-addr.arpa.
@               1D IN SOA       bladerunner.fx.movie.edu. hostmaster.fx.movie.edu. (
```

```
                        1              ; serial
                        3H             ; refresh
                        1H             ; retry
                        1W             ; expiry
                        1H )           ; minimum

            1D IN NS    bladerunner.fx.movie.edu.
            1D IN NS    outland.fx.movie.edu.
1           1D IN PTR   movie-gw.movie.edu.
2           1D IN PTR   bladerunner.fx.movie.edu.
3           1D IN PTR   outland.fx.movie.edu.
4           1D IN PTR   starwars.fx.movie.edu.
5           1D IN PTR   empire.fx.movie.edu.
6           1D IN PTR   jedi.fx.movie.edu.
@           1D IN SOA   bladerunner.fx.movie.edu. hostmaster.fx.movie.edu. (
                        1              ; serial
                        3H             ; refresh
                        1H             ; retry
                        1W             ; expiry
                        1H )           ; minimum
> exit
```

The output looks reasonable, so it's now safe to set up a slave nameserver for *fx. movie.edu* and then delegate *fx.movie.edu* from *movie.edu*.

An fx.movie.edu Slave

Setting up the slave nameserver for *fx.movie.edu* is simple: copy *named.conf*, *db.127.0.0*, and *db.cache* over from *bladerunner*, and edit *named.conf* and *db.127.0.0* according to the instructions in Chapter 4.

Contents of file *named.conf*:

```
options {
            directory "/var/named";
};

zone "0.0.127.in-addr.arpa" {
            type master;
            file "db.127.0.0";
};

zone "fx.movie.edu" {
            type slave;
            masters { 192.253.254.2; };
            file "bak.fx.movie.edu";
};

zone "254.253.192.in-addr.arpa" {
            type slave;
            masters { 192.253.254.2; };
            file "bak.192.253.254";
};
```

```
zone "." {
                type hint;
                file "db.cache";
};
```

Like *bladerunner*, *outland* really doesn't need a *resolv.conf* file, as long as its *hostname* is set to *outland.fx.movie.edu*.

Again, we start *named* and check for errors in the *syslog* output. If the *syslog* output is clean, we'll look up a few records in *fx.movie.edu*.

On the movie.edu Primary Nameserver

All that's left now is to delegate the *fx.movie.edu* subdomain to the new *fx.movie.edu* nameservers on *bladerunner* and *outland*. We add the appropriate NS records to *db. movie.edu*.

Partial contents of file *db.movie.edu*:

```
fx    86400    IN    NS    bladerunner.fx.movie.edu.
      86400    IN    NS    outland.fx.movie.edu.
```

According to RFC 1034, the domain names in the resource record–specific portion of NS records (the right side, containing *bladerunner.fx.movie.edu* and *out-land.fx.movie.edu*) must be the canonical domain names for the nameservers. A remote nameserver following delegation expects to find one or more address records attached to that domain name, not an alias (CNAME) record. Actually, the RFC extends this restriction to any type of resource record that includes a domain name as its value; all must specify the canonical domain name.

These two records alone aren't enough, though. Do you see the problem? How can a nameserver outside of *fx.movie.edu* look up information within *fx.movie.edu*? Well, a *movie.edu* nameserver would refer it to the nameservers authoritative for *fx. movie.edu*, right? That's true, but the NS records in *db.movie.edu* give only the *names* of the *fx.movie.edu* nameservers. The foreign nameserver needs the IP addresses of the *fx.movie.edu* nameservers in order to send queries to them. Who can give it those addresses? Only the *fx.movie.edu* nameservers. A real chicken-and-egg problem!

The solution is to include the addresses of the *fx.movie.edu* nameservers in the *movie.edu* zone datafile. While these aren't strictly part of the *movie.edu* zone, delegation to *fx.movie.edu* won't work without them. Of course, if the nameservers for *fx.movie.edu* weren't within *fx.movie.edu*, these addresses—called *glue records*—wouldn't be necessary. A foreign nameserver would be able to find the address it needed by querying other nameservers.

So, with the glue records, the added records look like the following.

Partial contents of file *db.movie.edu*:

```
fx      86400   IN   NS    bladerunner.fx.movie.edu.
        86400   IN   NS    outland.fx.movie.edu.
   bladerunner.fx.movie.edu.  86400  IN  A  192.253.254.2
   outland.fx.movie.edu.      86400  IN  A  192.253.254.3
```

Don't include unnecessary glue records in the file. BIND 8 and 9 nameservers automatically ignore any glue you include that isn't strictly necessary and log the fact that they've ignored the record(s) to *syslog*. For example, if we had an NS record for *movie.edu* that pointed to an off-site nameserver, *ns-1.isp.net*, and we made the mistake of including its address in *db.movie.edu* on the *movie.edu* primary nameserver, we'd see a message like this in *named*'s *syslog* output:

```
Aug  9 14:23:41 toystory named[19626]: dns_master_load:
db.movie.edu:55: ignoring out-of-zone data
```

Also, remember to keep the glue up to date. If *bladerunner* gets a new network interface, and hence another IP address, you should add another A record to the glue data.

We might also want to include aliases for any hosts moving into *fx.movie.edu* from *movie.edu*. For example, if we move *plan9.movie.edu*, a server with an important library of public-domain special-effects algorithms, into *fx.movie.edu*, we should create an alias in *movie.edu* pointing the old domain name to the new one. In the zone datafile, the record looks like this:

```
plan9           IN    CNAME   plan9.fx.movie.edu.
```

This allows people outside *movie.edu* to reach *plan9* even though they're using its old domain name, *plan9.movie.edu*.

Don't get confused about the zone in which this alias belongs. The *plan9* alias record is actually in the *movie.edu* zone, so it belongs in the file *db.movie.edu*. An alias pointing *p9.fx.movie.edu* to *plan9.fx.movie.edu*, on the other hand, is in the *fx.movie.edu* zone and belongs in *db.fx.movie.edu*. If you put a record in the zone datafile that's outside the zone the file describes, the nameserver will ignore it, as shown earlier in the unnecessary glue example.

Delegating an in-addr.arpa Zone

We almost forgot to delegate the *254.253.192.in-addr.arpa* zone! This is a little trickier than delegating *fx.movie.edu* because we don't manage the parent zone.

First, we need to figure out what *254.253.192.in-addr.arpa*'s parent zone is and who runs it. Figuring this out may take some sleuthing; we covered how to do this in Chapter 3.

As it turns out, the *192.in-addr.arpa* zone is *254.253.192.in-addr.arpa*'s parent. And, if you think about it, that makes some sense. There's no reason for the administrators of *in-addr.arpa* to delegate *253.192.in-addr.arpa* to a separate authority, because unless 192.253/16 is all one big CIDR block, networks like 192.253.253/24 and 192.253.254/24 don't have anything in common with each other. They may be managed by totally unrelated organizations.

To find out who runs *192.in-addr.arpa*, we can use *nslookup* or *whois*, as we demonstrated in Chapter 3. Here's how to use *nslookup* to find the administrator:

```
% nslookup
Default Server: toystory.movie.edu
Address: 0.0.0.0#53

> set type=soa
> 192.in-addr.arpa.
Server:        toystory.movie.edu
Address:       0.0.0.0#53

Non-authoritative answer:
192.in-addr.arpa
        origin = chia.arin.net
        mail addr = bind.arin.net
        serial = 2005112714
        refresh = 1800
        retry = 900
        expire = 691200
        minimum = 10800

Authoritative answers can be found from:
192.in-addr.arpa        nameserver = chia.arin.net.
192.in-addr.arpa        nameserver = dill.arin.net.
192.in-addr.arpa        nameserver = basil.arin.net.
192.in-addr.arpa        nameserver = henna.arin.net.
192.in-addr.arpa        nameserver = indigo.arin.net.
192.in-addr.arpa        nameserver = epazote.arin.net.
192.in-addr.arpa        nameserver = figwort.arin.net.
chia.arin.net   has AAAA address 2001:440:2000:1::21
basil.arin.net  internet address = 192.55.83.32
henna.arin.net  internet address = 192.26.92.32
indigo.arin.net internet address = 192.31.80.32
```

So ARIN is responsible for *192.in-addr.arpa* (remember them from Chapter 3?). All that's left is for us to submit the form at *http://www.arin.net/library/templates/net-end-user.txt* to request registration of our reverse-mapping zone.

Adding a movie.edu Slave

If the special-effects lab gets big enough, it may make sense to put a *movie.edu* slave somewhere on the 192.253.254/24 network. That way, a larger proportion of DNS queries from *fx.movie.edu* hosts can be answered locally. It seems logical to make one of the existing *fx.movie.edu* nameservers into a *movie.edu* slave, too—that way, we can better use an existing nameserver instead of setting up a brand-new nameserver.

We've decided to make *bladerunner* a slave for *movie.edu*. This won't interfere with *bladerunner*'s primary mission as the primary nameserver for *fx.movie.edu*. A single nameserver, given enough memory, can be authoritative for literally thousands of zones. One nameserver can load some zones as a primary and others as a slave.[*]

The configuration change is simple: we add one statement to *bladerunner*'s *named.conf* file to tell *named* to load the *movie.edu* zone from the IP address of the *movie.edu* primary nameserver, *toystory.movie.edu*.

Contents of file *named.conf*:

```
options {
    directory "/var/named";
};

zone "0.0.127.in-addr.arpa" {
    type master;
    file "db.127.0.0";
};

zone "fx.movie.edu" {
    type master;
    file "db.fx.movie.edu";
};

zone "254.253.192.in-addr.arpa" {
    type master;
    file "db.192.253.254";
};

zone "movie.edu" {
    type slave;
    masters { 192.249.249.3; };
    file "bak.movie.edu";
};

zone "." {
    type hint;
    file "db.cache";
};
```

Subdomains of in-addr.arpa Domains

Forward-mapping domains aren't the only domains you can divide into subdomains and delegate. If your *in-addr.arpa* namespace is large enough, you may need to divide it, too. Typically, you divide the domain that corresponds to your network number

---

[*] Clearly, though, a nameserver can't be both the primary and a slave for a single zone. Either the nameserver gets the data for a given zone from a local zone datafile (and is a primary for the zone) or from another nameserver (and is a slave for the zone).

into subdomains that correspond to your subnets. How that works depends on the type of network you have and on your network's subnet mask.

Subnetting on an Octet Boundary

Since Movie U. has just three /24 (Class C–sized) networks, one per segment, there's no particular need to subnet those networks. However, our sister university, Altered State, has a Class B–sized network, 172.20/16. Its network is subnetted between the third and fourth octet of the IP address; that is, its subnet mask is 255.255.255.0. It's already created a number of subdomains of its domain: *altered.edu*, including *fx.altered.edu* (okay, we copied them); *makeup.altered.edu*; and *foley.altered.edu*. Since each department also runs its own subnet (its Special Effects department runs subnet 172.20.2/24, Makeup runs 172.20.15/24, and Foley runs 172.20.25/24), it'd like to divvy up its *in-addr.arpa* namespace appropriately, too.

Delegating *in-addr.arpa* subdomains is no different from delegating subdomains of forward-mapping domains. Within its *db.172.20* zone datafile, it needs to add NS records like these:

```
2     86400    IN    NS    gump.fx.altered.edu.
2     86400    IN    NS    toystory.fx.altered.edu.
15    86400    IN    NS    prettywoman.makeup.altered.edu.
15    86400    IN    NS    priscilla.makeup.altered.edu.
25    86400    IN    NS    blowup.foley.altered.edu.
25    86400    IN    NS    muppetmovie.foley.altered.edu.
```

These records delegate the subdomain that corresponds to each subnet to the correct nameserver in each subdomain.

A few important notes: the Altered States administrators can use only the third octet of the subnet in the owner name field because the default origin in this file is *20.172.in-addr.arpa*. They need to use the fully qualified domain names of the nameservers in the right side of the NS records, though, to avoid having the origin appended. And they *don't* need glue address records because the names of the nameservers they delegated the zone to don't end in the domain name of the zone.

Subnetting on a Nonoctet Boundary

What do you do about networks that aren't subnetted neatly on octet boundaries, like subnetted /24 (Class C–sized) networks? In these cases, you can't delegate along lines that match the subnets. This forces you into one of two situations: you have multiple subnets per *in-addr.arpa* zone, or you have multiple *in-addr.arpa* zones per subnet. Neither is particularly pleasing.

/8 (Class A–sized) and /16 (Class B–sized) networks

Let's take the case of the /8 (Class A–sized) network 15/8, subnetted with the subnet mask 255.255.248.0 (a 13-bit subnet field and an 11-bit host field, or 8,192 subnets of 2,048 hosts). In this case, the subnet 15.1.200.0, for example, extends from 15.1.200.0 to 15.1.207.255. Therefore, the delegation for that single subdomain in *db.15*, the zone datafile for *15.in-addr.arpa*, might look like this:

```
200.1.15.in-addr.arpa.    86400    IN    NS    ns-1.cns.hp.com.
200.1.15.in-addr.arpa.    86400    IN    NS    ns-2.cns.hp.com.
201.1.15.in-addr.arpa.    86400    IN    NS    ns-1.cns.hp.com.
201.1.15.in-addr.arpa.    86400    IN    NS    ns-2.cns.hp.com.
202.1.15.in-addr.arpa.    86400    IN    NS    ns-1.cns.hp.com.
202.1.15.in-addr.arpa.    86400    IN    NS    ns-2.cns.hp.com.
203.1.15.in-addr.arpa.    86400    IN    NS    ns-1.cns.hp.com.
203.1.15.in-addr.arpa.    86400    IN    NS    ns-2.cns.hp.com.
204.1.15.in-addr.arpa.    86400    IN    NS    ns-1.cns.hp.com.
204.1.15.in-addr.arpa.    86400    IN    NS    ns-2.cns.hp.com.
205.1.15.in-addr.arpa.    86400    IN    NS    ns-1.cns.hp.com.
205.1.15.in-addr.arpa.    86400    IN    NS    ns-2.cns.hp.com.
206.1.15.in-addr.arpa.    86400    IN    NS    ns-1.cns.hp.com.
206.1.15.in-addr.arpa.    86400    IN    NS    ns-2.cns.hp.com.
207.1.15.in-addr.arpa.    86400    IN    NS    ns-1.cns.hp.com.
207.1.15.in-addr.arpa.    86400    IN    NS    ns-2.cns.hp.com.
```

That's a lot of delegation for one subnet!

Luckily, BIND 8.2 and later, as well as BIND 9.1.0 and later, nameservers support a control statement called $GENERATE, which lets you create a group of resource records that differ only by a numerical iterator. For example, you can create the 16 NS records just listed using these two $GENERATE control statements:[*]

```
$GENERATE 200-207 $.1.15.in-addr.arpa.  86400  IN  NS  ns-1.cns.hp.com.
$GENERATE 200-207 $.1.15.in-addr.arpa.  86400  IN  NS  ns-2.cns.hp.com.
```

The syntax is fairly simple: when the nameserver reads the control statement, it iterates over the range specified as the first argument, replacing any dollar signs ($) in the template that follows the first argument with the current iterator.

/24 (Class C–sized) networks

In the case of a subnetted /24 (Class C–sized) network, say 192.253.254/24, subnetted with the mask 255.255.255.192, you have a single *in-addr.arpa* zone, *254.253. 192.in-addr.arpa*, that corresponds to subnets 192.253.254.0/26, 192.253.254.64/26, 192.253.254.128/26, and 192.253.254.192/26. This can be a problem if you want to let different organizations manage the reverse-mapping information that corresponds to each subnet. You can solve this in one of three ways, none of which is pretty.

---

[*] Older BIND 8 nameservers are syntactically challenged and require that you omit the class ("IN") field.

Solution 1. The first solution is to administer the *254.253.192.in-addr.arpa* zone as a single entity and not even try to delegate. This requires either cooperation between the administrators of the four subnets involved or the use of a tool such as Webmin (*http://www.webmin.com/*) to allow each of the four administrators to take care of his own data.

Solution 2. The second is to delegate at the *fourth* octet. That's even nastier than the /8 delegation we just showed you. You'll need at least a couple of NS records per IP address in the file *db.192.253.254*, like this:

```
1.254.253.192.in-addr.arpa.     86400    IN    NS    ns1.foo.com.
1.254.253.192.in-addr.arpa.     86400    IN    NS    ns2.foo.com.

2.254.253.192.in-addr.arpa.     86400    IN    NS    ns1.foo.com.
2.254.253.192.in-addr.arpa.     86400    IN    NS    ns2.foo.com.

...

65.254.253.192.in-addr.arpa.    86400    IN    NS    relay.bar.com.
65.254.253.192.in-addr.arpa.    86400    IN    NS    gw.bar.com.

66.254.253.192.in-addr.arpa.    86400    IN    NS    relay.bar.com.
66.254.253.192.in-addr.arpa.    86400    IN    NS    gw.bar.com.

...

129.254.253.192.in-addr.arpa.   86400    IN    NS    mail.baz.com.
129.254.253.192.in-addr.arpa.   86400    IN    NS    www.baz.com.

130.254.253.192.in-addr.arpa.   86400    IN    NS    mail.baz.com.
130.254.253.192.in-addr.arpa.   86400    IN    NS    www.baz.com.
```

and so on, all the way down to *254.254.253.192.in-addr.arpa*.

You can pare that down substantially using $GENERATE:

```
$GENERATE 0-63 $.254.253.192.in-addr.arpa.    86400   IN  NS  ns1.foo.com.
$GENERATE 0-63 $.254.253.192.in-addr.arpa.    86400   IN  NS  ns2.foo.com.

$GENERATE 64-127 $.254.253.192.in-addr.arpa.  86400   IN  NS  relay.bar.com.
$GENERATE 64-127 $.254.253.192.in-addr.arpa.  86400   IN  NS  gw.bar.com.

$GENERATE 128-191 $.254.253.192.in-addr.arpa. 86400   IN  NS  mail.baz.com.
$GENERATE 128-191 $.254.253.192.in-addr.arpa. 86400   IN  NS  www.baz.com.
```

Of course, in *ns1.foo.com*'s *named.conf*, you'd also expect to see:

```
zone "1.254.253.192.in-addr.arpa" {
            type master;
            file "db.192.253.254.1";
};
```

```
zone "2.254.253.192.in-addr.arpa" {
        type master;
        file "db.192.253.254.2";
};
```

and in *db.192.253.254.1*, just the one PTR record:

```
$TTL 1d
@   IN   SOA   ns1.foo.com.   root.ns1.foo.com.   (
                        1        ; Serial
                        3h       ; Refresh
                        1h       ; Retry
                        1w       ; Expire
                        1h       ; Negative caching TTL

    IN   NS   ns1.foo.com.
    IN   NS   ns2.foo.com.

    IN   PTR   thereitis.foo.com.
```

Note that the PTR record is attached to the zone's domain name because the zone's domain name corresponds to just one IP address. Now, when a *254.253.192.in-addr.arpa* nameserver receives a query for the PTR record for *1.254.253.192.in-addr.arpa*, it refers the querier to *ns1.foo.com* and *ns2.foo.com*, which respond with the one PTR record in the zone.

Solution 3. Finally, there's a clever technique that obviates the need to maintain a separate zone datafile for each IP address.[*] The organization responsible for the overall /24 network creates CNAME records for each domain name in the zone, pointing to domain names in new subdomains, which are then delegated to the proper nameservers. These new subdomains can be called just about anything, but names such as *0-63*, *64-127*, *128-191*, and *192-255* clearly indicate the range of addresses each subdomain will reverse-map. Each subdomain then contains only the PTR records in the range for which the subdomain is named.

Partial contents of file *db.192.253.254*:

```
1.254.253.192.in-addr.arpa.   IN   CNAME   1.0-63.254.253.192.in-addr.arpa.
2.254.253.192.in-addr.arpa.   IN   CNAME   2.0-63.254.253.192.in-addr.arpa.

...

0-63.254.253.192.in-addr.arpa.    86400    IN    NS    ns1.foo.com.
0-63.254.253.192.in-addr.arpa.    86400    IN    NS    ns2.foo.com.

65.254.253.192.in-addr.arpa. IN  CNAME 65.64-127.254.253.192.in-addr.arpa.
66.254.253.192.in-addr.arpa. IN  CNAME 66.64-127.254.253.192.in-addr.arpa.
```

---

[*] We first saw this explained by Glen Herrmansfeldt of CalTech in the newsgroup *comp.protocols.tcp-ip.domains*. It's now codified as RFC 2317.

```
...

64-127.254.253.192.in-addr.arpa.     86400   IN   NS   relay.bar.com.
64-127.254.253.192.in-addr.arpa.     86400   IN   NS   gw.bar.com.

129.254.253.192.in-addr.arpa.   IN   CNAME   129.128-191.254.253.192.in-addr.arpa.
130.254.253.192.in-addr.arpa.   IN   CNAME   130.128-191.254.253.192.in-addr.arpa.

...

128-191.254.253.192.in-addr.arpa.    86400   IN   NS   mail.baz.com.
128-191.254.253.192.in-addr.arpa.    86400   IN   NS   www.baz.com.
```

Again, you can abbreviate this with $GENERATE:

```
$GENERATE 1-63 $ IN CNAME $.0-63.254.253.192.in-addr.arpa.

0-63.254.253.192.in-addr.arpa.     86400   IN   NS   ns1.foo.com.
0-63.254.253.192.in-addr.arpa.     86400   IN   NS   ns2.foo.com.

$GENERATE 65-127 $ IN CNAME $.64-127.254.253.192.in-addr.arpa.

64-127.254.253.192.in-addr.arpa.   86400   IN   NS   relay.bar.com.
64-127.254.253.192.in-addr.arpa.   86400   IN   NS   gw.bar.com.
```

The zone datafile for *0-63.254.253.192.in-addr.arpa*, *db.192.253.254.0-63*, can contain just PTR records for IP addresses 192.253.254.1 through 192.253.254.63.

Partial contents of file *db.192.253.254.0-63*:

```
$TTL 1d
@    IN   SOA   ns1.foo.com.    root.ns1.foo.com.   (
                         1       ; Serial
                         3h      ; Refresh
                         1h      ; Retry
                         1w      ; Expire
                         1h )    ; Negative caching TTL

     IN   NS    ns1.foo.com.
     IN   NS    ns2.foo.com.

1    IN   PTR   thereitis.foo.com.
2    IN   PTR   setter.foo.com.
3    IN   PTR   mouse.foo.com.
...
```

The way this setup works is a little tricky, so let's go over it. A resolver requests the PTR record for *1.254.253.192.in-addr.arpa*, causing its local nameserver to go look up that record. The local nameserver ends up asking a *254.253.192.in-addr.arpa* nameserver, which responds with the CNAME record indicating that *1.254.253.192.in-addr.arpa* is actually an alias for *1.0-63.254.253.192.in-addr.arpa* and that the PTR record is attached to that name. The response also includes NS records telling the local nameserver that the authoritative nameservers for *0-63.254.253.192.in-addr.arpa* are *ns1.foo.com* and *ns2.foo.com*. The local nameserver then queries either *ns1.foo.com* or *ns2.foo.com* for the PTR record for *1.0-63.254.253.192.in-addr.arpa*, and receives the PTR record.

Good Parenting

Now that the delegation to the *fx.movie.edu* nameservers is in place, we—responsible parents that we are—should check that delegation using *host*. What? We haven't given you *host* yet? A version of *host* for many Unix variants is available from *http://www.weird.com/~woods/projects/host.html*.

To build *host*, first extract it:

```
% zcat host.tar.Z | tar -xvf -
```

Then build it on your system:

```
% make
```

host makes it easy to check delegation. With *host,* you can look up the NS records for your zone on your parent zone's nameservers. If those look good, you can use *host* to query each nameserver listed for the zone's SOA record. The query is nonrecursive, so the nameserver queried doesn't query other nameservers to find the SOA record. If the nameserver replies, *host* checks the reply to see whether the *aa*—authoritative answer—bit in the reply message is set. If it is, the nameserver checks to make sure that the message contains an answer. If both these criteria are met, the nameserver is flagged as authoritative for the zone. Otherwise, the nameserver is not authoritative, and *host* reports an error.

Why all the fuss over bad delegation? Incorrect delegation slows name resolution and causes the propagation of old and erroneous nameserver information. Remote nameservers will waste time following your bad NS records, only to receive responses from your nameservers indicating that they aren't, in fact, authoritative for the zone. The remote nameservers will be forced to query a nameserver listed in another NS record, which means resolving names will take longer. Worse, those remote nameservers will cache those bogus NS records and return them in responses to other nameservers, compounding the problem.

Using host

If our little lecture has convinced you of the importance of maintaining correct delegation, you'll be eager to learn how to use *host* to ensure that you don't join the ranks of the miscreants.

The first step is to use *host* to look up your zone's NS records on a nameserver for your parent zone and make sure they're correct. Here's how we'd check the *fx.movie.edu* NS records on one of the *movie.edu* nameservers:

```
% host -t ns fx.movie.edu. toystory.movie.edu.
```

If everything's okay with the NS records, we'll simply see the NS records in the output:

```
fx.movie.edu name server bladerunner.fx.movie.edu
fx.movie.edu name server outland.fx.movie.edu
```

(The format of the output may vary with the version of *host* you use, but the gist is the same.) This tells us that all the NS records delegating *fx.movie.edu* from *toystory.movie.edu* are correct.

Next, we'll use *host*'s "SOA check" mode to query each nameserver in the NS records for the *fx.movie.edu* zone's SOA record. This also checks whether the response was authoritative.

```
% host -C fx.movie.edu.
```

Normally, this produces a list of the nameservers for *fx.movie.edu*, along with the contents of the *fx.movie.edu* zone's SOA record on each nameserver:

```
Nameserver bladerunner.fx.movie.edu:
    fx.movie.edu SOA bladerunner.fx.movie.edu. hostmaster.fx.movie.edu. 1 10800 3600
608400 3600
Nameserver outland.fx.movie.edu:
    fx.movie.edu SOA bladerunner.fx.movie.edu. hostmaster.fx.movie.edu. 1 10800 3600
608400 3600
```

If one of the *fx.movie.edu* nameservers—say *outland*—is misconfigured, we might see this:

```
Nameserver bladerunner.fx.movie.edu:
    fx.movie.edu SOA bladerunner.fx.movie.edu. hostmaster.fx.movie.edu. 1 10800 3600
608400 3600
nxdomain.com has no SOA record
```

This (subtly) indicates that the nameserver on *outland* is running, but isn't authoritative for *fx.movie.edu*.

If one of the *fx.movie.edu* nameservers weren't running at all, we'd see:

```
Nameserver bladerunner.fx.movie.edu:
    fx.movie.edu SOA bladerunner.fx.movie.edu. hostmaster.fx.movie.edu. 1 10800 3600
608400 3600
;; connection timed out; no servers could be reached
```

In this case, the *connection timed out* message indicates that *host* sent *outland* a query and didn't get a response back in an acceptable amount of time.

While we could have checked the *fx.movie.edu* delegation using *nslookup* or *dig*, *host*'s powerful command-line options make the task especially easy.

Managing Delegation

If the special-effects lab gets bigger, we may find that we need additional nameservers. We dealt with setting up new nameservers in Chapter 8 and even went over what information to send to the parent zone's administrator. But we never explained what the parent needs to do.

It turns out that the parent's job is relatively easy, especially if the administrators of the subdomain send complete information. Imagine that the special-effects lab expands to a new network, 192.254.20/24. It has a passel of new, high-powered graphics workstations. One of them, *alien.fx.movie.edu*, will act as the new network's nameserver.

The administrators of *fx.movie.edu* (we delegated it to the folks in the lab) send their parent zone's administrators (that's us) a short note:

```
Hi!

We've just set up alien.fx.movie.edu (192.254.20.3) as a name
server for fx.movie.edu.  Would you please update your
delegation information?  I've attached the NS records you'll
need to add.

Thanks,

Arty Segue
ajs@fx.movie.edu

----- cut here -----

fx.movie.edu.  86400  IN  NS  bladerunner.fx.movie.edu.
fx.movie.edu.  86400  IN  NS  outland.fx.movie.edu.
fx.movie.edu.  86400  IN  NS  alien.fx.movie.edu.

bladerunner.fx.movie.edu.  86400  IN  A  192.253.254.2
outland.fx.movie.edu.      86400  IN  A  192.253.254.3
alien.fx.movie.edu.        86400  IN  A  192.254.20.3
```

Our job as the *movie.edu* administrator is straightforward: add the NS and A records to *db.movie.edu*.

What if we're using *h2n* to create our nameserver data? We can stick the delegation information into the *spcl.movie* file, which *h2n* $INCLUDEs at the end of the *db.movie* file it creates.

The final step for the *fx.movie.edu* administrator is to send a similar message to *hostmaster@arin.net* (the administrator of the *192.in-addr.arpa* zone), requesting that the *20.254.192.in-addr.arpa* subdomain be delegated to *alien.fx.movie.edu*, *bladerunner.fx.movie.edu*, and *outland.fx.movie.edu*.

Managing delegation with stubs

If you're running a recent BIND nameserver, you don't have to manage delegation information manually. BIND 8 and 9 nameservers support an experimental feature called *stub zones*, which enable a nameserver to pick up changes to delegation information automatically.

A nameserver that's configured as a stub for a zone periodically sends discrete queries for the zone's SOA and NS records, as well as any necessary glue A records. The nameserver then uses the NS records to delegate the zone from its parent, and the SOA record governs how often the nameserver does these queries. Now, when the administrators of a subdomain make changes to the subdomain's nameservers, they simply update their NS records (and increment the serial number in the SOA record, of course). The parent zone's authoritative nameservers, configured as stub for the child zone, pick up the updated records within the refresh interval.

On the *movie.edu* nameservers, here's what we'd add to *named.conf*:

```
zone "fx.movie.edu" {
            type stub;
            masters { 192.253.254.2; };
            file "stub.fx.movie.edu";
};
```

Note that, if we're running BIND 9 nameservers, we must configure all *movie.edu* nameservers—including slaves—as stubs for *fx.movie.edu*. BIND 9 nameservers don't "promote" the *fx.movie.edu* delegation information into the parent zone, so the *fx.movie.edu* zone's delegation isn't included in zone transfers. Making all the *movie.edu* nameservers stubs for the subdomain keeps them synchronized.

Managing the Transition to Subdomains

We won't lie to you: the *fx.movie.edu* example we showed you was unrealistic for several reasons. The main one is the magical appearance of the special-effects lab's hosts. In the real world, the lab would have started out with a few hosts, probably in the *movie.edu* zone. After a generous endowment, an NSF grant, or a corporate gift, the lab might expand a little and a few more computers might be purchased. Sooner or later, the lab would have enough hosts to warrant the creation of a new subdomain. By that point, however, many of the original hosts would be well known by their names in *movie.edu*.

We briefly touched on using CNAME records in the parent zone (in our *plan9.movie.edu* example) to help people adjust to a host's change of domain. But what happens when you move a whole network or subnet into a new subdomain?

The strategy we recommend uses CNAME records in much the same way but on a larger scale. Using a tool such as *h2n*, you can create CNAMEs for hosts *en masse*. This allows users to continue using the old domain names for any of the hosts that have moved. When they telnet or *ftp* (or whatever) to those hosts, however, the command reports that they're connected to a host in *fx.movie.edu*:

```
% telnet plan9
Trying...
```

```
Connected to plan9.fx.movie.edu.
Escape character is '^]'.

HP-UX plan9.fx.movie.edu A.09.05 C 9000/735 (ttyu1)

login:
```

Some users, of course, don't notice subtle changes like this, so you should also do some public relations work and notify folks of the change.

On *fx.movie.edu* hosts running old versions of *sendmail*, we may also need to configure *sendmail* to accept mail addressed to the new domain names. Modern versions of *sendmail* canonicalize the hostnames in message headers using a nameserver before sending the messages. This turns a *movie.edu* alias into a canonical name in *fx.movie.edu*. If, however, the *sendmail* on the receiving end is older and hardcodes the local host's domain name, we have to change the name to the new domain name by hand. This usually requires a simple change to class *w* or fileclass *w* in *sendmail.cf*; see the section "What's a Mail Exchanger, Again?" in Chapter 5.

How do you create all these aliases? You simply tell *h2n* to create the aliases for hosts on the *fx.movie.edu* networks (192.253.254/24 and 192.254.20/24) and indicate (in the */etc/hosts* file) the new domain names of the hosts. For example, using the *fx.movie.edu* host table, we can easily generate the aliases in *movie.edu* for all the hosts in *fx.movie.edu*.

Partial contents of file */etc/hosts*:

```
192.253.254.1 movie-gw.movie.edu movie-gw
# fx primary
192.253.254.2 bladerunner.fx.movie.edu bladerunner br
# fx slave
192.253.254.3 outland.fx.movie.edu outland
192.253.254.4 starwars.fx.movie.edu starwars
192.253.254.5 empire.fx.movie.edu empire
192.253.254.6 jedi.fx.movie.edu jedi
192.254.20.3  alien.fx.movie.edu alien
```

h2n's –*c* option takes a zone's domain name as an argument. When *h2n* finds any hosts in that zone on networks it's building data for, it creates aliases for them in the current zone (specified with –*d*). So by running:

```
% h2n -d movie.edu -n 192.253.254 -n 192.254.20 \
-c fx.movie.edu -f options
```

(where *options* contains other command-line options for building data from other *movie.edu* networks), we can create aliases in *movie.edu* for all *fx.movie.edu* hosts.

Removing Parent Aliases

Although parent-level aliases are useful for minimizing the impact of moving your hosts, they're also a crutch of sorts. Like a crutch, they'll restrict your freedom.

They'll clutter up your parent namespace even though one of your motivations for implementing a subdomain was to make the parent zone smaller. And they'll prevent you from using the names of hosts in the subdomain as names for hosts in the parent zone.

After a grace period—which should be well advertised to users—you should remove all the aliases, with the possible exception of aliases for extremely well-known Internet hosts. During the grace period, users can adjust to the new domain names and modify scripts, *.rhosts* files, and the like. But don't get suckered into leaving all those aliases in the parent zone; they defeat part of the purpose of DNS because they prevent you and your subdomain administrator from naming hosts autonomously.

You might want to leave CNAME records for well-known Internet hosts or central network resources intact because of the potential impact of a loss of connectivity. On the other hand, rather than moving the well-known host or central resource into a subdomain at all, it might be better to leave it in the parent zone.

h2n gives you an easy way to delete the aliases you created so simply with the *–c* option, even if the records for the subdomain's hosts are mixed in the host table or on the same network as hosts in other zones. The *–e* option takes a zone's domain name as an argument and tells *h2n* to exclude (hence *e*) all records containing that domain name on networks it would otherwise create data for. This command, for example, deletes all the CNAME records for *fx.movie.edu* hosts created earlier while still creating an A record for *movie-gw.movie.edu* (which is on the 192.253.254/24 network):

```
% h2n -d movie.edu -n 192.253.254 -n 192.254.20 \
-e fx.movie.edu -f options
```

The Life of a Parent

That's a lot of parental advice to digest in one sitting, so let's recap the highlights of what we've talked about. The lifecycle of a typical parent goes something like this:

- You have a single zone, with all your hosts in that zone.

- You break your zone into a number of subdomains, some of them in the same zone as the parent, if necessary. You provide CNAME records in the parent zone for well-known hosts that have moved into subdomains.

- After a grace period, you delete any remaining CNAME records.

- You handle subdomain delegation updates, either manually or by using stub zones, and periodically check delegation.

Okay, now that you know all there is to parenting, let's go on to talk about more advanced nameserver features. You may need some of these tools to keep those kids in line.

## CHAPTER 10

Advanced Features

"What's the use of their having names," the Gnat said,
"if they won't answer to them?"

The latest BIND nameservers, versions 8.4.7 and 9.3.2, have *lots* of new features. Some of the most prominent introductions are support for dynamic updates, asynchronous zone change notification (called "NOTIFY" for short), and incremental zone transfer. Of the rest, the most important are related to security: they let you tell your nameserver whom to answer queries from, whom to serve zone transfers to, and whom to permit dynamic updates from. Many of the security features aren't necessary inside a corporate network, but the other mechanisms will help out administrators of any nameservers.

In this chapter, we'll cover these features and suggest how they might come in handy in your DNS infrastructure. (We do save some of the hardcore firewall material 'til the next chapter, though.)

Address Match Lists and ACLs

Before we introduce the new features, however, we'd better cover address match lists. BIND 8 and 9 use address match lists for nearly every security feature and for some features that aren't security-related at all.

An *address match list* is a list (what else?) of terms that specifies one or more IP addresses. The elements in the list can be individual IP addresses, IP prefixes, or a named address match list (more on those shortly).* An IP prefix has the format:

        network in dotted-octet format/bits in netmask

For example, the network 15.0.0.0 with the network mask 255.0.0.0 (eight contiguous ones) is written 15/8. Traditionally, this would have been thought of as the

---

* And if you're running a BIND 9 nameserver or BIND 8 from version 8.3.0 on, address match lists can include IPv6 addresses and IPv6 prefixes. These are described later in the chapter.

"class A" network 15. The network consisting of IP addresses 192.168.1.192 through 192.168.1.255, on the other hand, would be written 192.168.1.192/26 (network 192. 168.1.192 with the netmask 255.255.255.192, which has 26 contiguous ones). Here's an address match list comprising those two networks:

```
15/8; 192.168.1.192/26;
```

A named address match list is just that: an address match list with a name. To be used within another address match list, a named address match list must have been previously defined in *named.conf* with an *acl* statement. The *acl* statement has a simple syntax:

```
acl name { address_match_list; };
```

This just makes the name equivalent to that address match list from now on. Although the name of the statement, *acl*, suggests "access control list," you can use the named address match list anywhere an address match list is accepted, including some places that don't have anything to do with access control.

Whenever you use one or more of the same terms in a few access control lists, it's a good idea to use an *acl* statement to associate them with a name. You can then refer to the name in the address match list. For example, let's call 15/8 what it is: "HP-NET." And we'll call 192.168.1.192/26 "internal":

```
acl "HP-NET" { 15/8; };
```

```
acl "internal" { 192.168.1.192/26; };
```

Now we can refer to these address match lists by name in other address match lists. This not only cuts down on typing and simplifies managing your address match lists, it makes the resulting *named.conf* file more readable.

We prudently enclosed the names of our ACLs in quotes to avoid collisions with words BIND reserves for its own use. If you're sure your ACL names don't conflict with reserved words, you don't need the quotes.

There are four predefined named address match lists:

none
    No IP addresses

any
    All IP addresses

localhost
    Any of the IP addresses of the local host (i.e., the one running the nameserver)

localnets
    Any of the networks the local host has a network interface on (found by using each network interface's IP address and using the netmask to mask off the host bits in the address)

DNS Dynamic Update

The world of the Internet—and of TCP/IP networking in general—has become a much more dynamic place. Most large corporations use DHCP to control IP address assignment. Nearly all ISPs assign addresses to dial-up and cable modem customers using DHCP. To keep up, DNS needed to support the dynamic addition and deletion of records. RFC 2136 introduced this mechanism, called DNS Dynamic Update.

BIND 8 and 9 support the dynamic update facility described in RFC 2136. This permits authorized updaters to add and delete resource records from a zone for which a nameserver is authoritative. An updater can find the authoritative nameservers for a zone by retrieving the zone's NS records. If the nameserver receiving an authorized update message is not the primary master for the zone, it forwards the update "upstream" to its master server, a process referred to as *update forwarding*. If this next server, in turn, is a slave for the zone, it also forwards the update upstream. Only the primary nameserver for a zone, after all, has a writable copy of the zone data; all the slaves get their copies of the zone data from the primary, either directly or indirectly (through other slaves). Once the primary has processed the dynamic update and modified the zone, the slaves can get a new copy of it via zone transfers.

Dynamic update permits more than the simple addition and deletion of records. Updaters can add or delete individual resource records, delete RRsets (a set of resource records with the same domain name, class, and type, such as all the addresses of *www.movie.edu*), or even delete all records associated with a given domain name. An update can also stipulate that certain records exist or not exist in the zone as a prerequisite to the update's taking effect. For example, an update can add the address record:

```
armageddon.fx.movie.edu.  300  IN  A  192.253.253.15
```

only if the domain name *armageddon.fx.movie.edu* isn't currently being used or only if *armageddon.fx.movie.edu* currently has no address records.

> A note on update forwarding: BIND nameservers didn't implement update forwarding before 9.1.0, so it's particularly important when using BIND nameservers older than 9.1.0 that you make sure the update is sent directly to the primary nameserver for the zone you're trying to update. You can do this by ensuring that the primary nameserver for the zone is listed in the MNAME field of the zone's SOA record. Most dynamic update routines use the MNAME field as a hint to tell them which authoritative nameserver to send the update to.

For the most part, dynamic update functionality is used by programs such as DHCP servers that assign IP addresses automatically to computers and then need to register the resulting name-to-address and address-to-name mappings. Some of these programs use the new *ns_update()* resolver routine to create update messages and send them to an authoritative server for the zone that contains the domain name.

It's also possible to create updates manually with the command-line program *nsupdate*, which is part of the standard BIND distribution. *nsupdate* reads one-line commands and translates them into an update message. Commands can be specified on standard input (the default) or in a file, whose name must be given as an argument to *nsupdate*. Commands not separated by a blank line are incorporated into the same update message, as long as there's room.

nsupdate understands the following commands:

prereq yxrrset domain name type [rdata]
: Makes the existence of an RRset of type *type* owned by *domain name* a prerequisite for performing the update specified in successive *update* commands. If *rdata* is specified, it must also match.

prereq nxrrset domain name type
: Makes the nonexistence of an RRset of type *type* owned by *domain name* a prerequisite for performing the update specified.

prereq yxdomain domain name
: Makes the existence of the specified domain name a prerequisite for performing the update.

prereq nxdomain domain name
: Makes the nonexistence of the specified domain name a prerequisite for performing the update.

update delete domain name [type] [rdata]
: Deletes the domain name specified or, if *type* is also specified, deletes the RRset specified or, if *rdata* is also specified, deletes the record matching *domainname*, *type*, and *rdata*.

update add domain name ttl [class] type rdata
: Adds the record specified to the zone. Note that the TTL, in addition to the type and resource record–specific data, must be included, but the class is optional and defaults to IN.

So, for example, the command:

```
% nsupdate
> prereq nxdomain mib.fx.movie.edu.
> update add mib.fx.movie.edu. 300 A 192.253.253.16
> send
```

tells the server to add an address for *mib.fx.movie.edu* only if the domain name does not already exist. Note that BIND 8 versions of *nsupdate* before 8.4.5 use a blank line as a cue to send the update instead of the *send* command. Subtle, eh?

The following command checks to see whether *mib.fx.movie.edu* already has MX records and, if it does, deletes them and adds two in their place:

```
% nsupdate
> prereq yxrrset mib.fx.movie.edu. MX
> update delete mib.fx.movie.edu. MX
> update add mib.fx.movie.edu. 600 MX 10 mib.fx.movie.edu.
> update add mib.fx.movie.edu. 600 MX 50 postmanrings2x.movie.edu.
> send
```

As with queries, the nameservers that process dynamic updates answer them with DNS messages that indicate whether the update was successful and, if not, what went wrong. Updates may fail for many reasons: for example, because the nameserver wasn't actually authoritative for the zone being updated, because a prerequisite wasn't satisfied, or because the updater wasn't allowed.

There are some limitations to what you can do with dynamic update: you can't delete a zone entirely (though you can delete everything in it except the SOA record and one NS record), and you can't add new zones.

Dynamic Update and Serial Numbers

When a nameserver processes a dynamic update, it's changing a zone and must increment that zone's serial number to signal the change to the zone's slaves. This is done automatically. However, the nameserver doesn't necessarily increment the serial number for each dynamic update.

BIND 8 nameservers defer updating a zone's serial number for as long as 5 minutes or 100 updates, whichever comes first. The deferral is intended to deal with a mismatch between a nameserver's ability to process dynamic updates and its ability to transfer zones: the latter may take significantly longer for large zones. When the nameserver does finally increment the zone's serial number, it sends a NOTIFY announcement (described later in this chapter) to tell the zone's slaves that the serial number has changed.

BIND 9 nameservers update the serial number once for each dynamic update that is processed.

Dynamic Update and Zone Datafiles

Since a dynamic update makes a permanent change to a zone, a record of it needs to be kept on disk. But rewriting a zone datafile each time a record is added to or deleted from the zone can be prohibitively onerous for a nameserver. Writing a zone datafile takes time, and the nameserver could conceivably receive tens or hundreds of dynamic updates each second.

Instead, when they receive dynamic updates, both BIND 8 and 9 nameservers simply append a short record of the update to a logfile.* The change takes effect immediately in the copy of the zone the nameservers maintain in memory, of course. But the nameservers can wait and write the entire zone to disk only at a designated interval (hourly, usually). BIND 8 nameservers then delete the logfile because it's no longer needed. (At that point, the copy of the zone in memory is the same as that on disk.) BIND 9 nameservers, however, leave the logfile because they also use it for incremental zone transfers, which we'll cover later in this chapter. (BIND 8 nameservers keep incremental zone transfer information in another file.)

On BIND 8 nameservers, the name of the logfile is constructed by appending *.log* to the name of the zone datafile. On BIND 9 nameservers, the name of the logfile—also called a *journal file*—is the name of the zone datafile concatenated with *.jnl*. So when you start using dynamic update, don't be surprised to see these files appear alongside your zone datafiles: it's totally normal.

On a BIND 8 nameserver, the logfiles should disappear hourly (though they may reappear very quickly if your nameserver receives lots of updates) as well as when the nameserver exits gracefully. On a BIND 9 nameserver, the logfiles won't disappear at all. Both nameservers incorporate the record of the changes in the logfile into the zone if the logfile exists when the nameserver starts.

In case you're interested, BIND 8's logfiles are human-readable and contain entries like this:

```
;BIND LOG V8
[DYNAMIC_UPDATE] id 8761 from [192.249.249.3].1148 at 971389102 (named pid 17602):
zone:   origin movie.edu class IN serial 2000010957
update: {add} almostfamous.movie.edu. 600 IN A 192.249.249.215
```

BIND 9's logfiles, unfortunately, aren't human-readable. Well, not to these humans, anyway.

Update Access Control Lists

Given the fearsome control that dynamic updates obviously give an updater over a zone, you clearly need to restrict them, if you use them at all. By default, neither BIND 8 nor BIND 9 nameservers allow dynamic updates to authoritative zones. In order to use dynamic updates, you add an *allow-update* or *update-policy* substatement to the *zone* statement of the zone that you'd like to allow updates to.

---

* This idea will seem familiar to anyone who's ever used a journaling filesystem.

allow-update takes an address match list as an argument. The address or addresses matched by the list are the only addresses allowed to update the zone. It's prudent to make this access control list as restrictive as possible:

```
zone "fx.movie.edu" {
    type master;
    file "db.fx.movie.edu";
    allow-update { 192.253.253.100; }; // just our DHCP server
};
```

An updater authorized using *allow-update* can make any change to the zone: delete any record (except the SOA record) or add any records.

TSIG-Signed Updates

Given that BIND 9.1.0 and later slave nameservers can forward updates, what's the use of an IP address–based access control list? If the primary nameserver allows updates from its slaves' addresses, then any forwarded update is allowed, regardless of the original sender. That's not good.[*]

Well, first, you can control which updates are forwarded. The *allow-update-forwarding* substatement takes an address match list as an argument. Only updates from IP addresses that match the address match list will be forwarded. So the following *zone* statement forwards only those updates from the Special Effects Department's subnet:

```
zone "fx.movie.edu" {
    type slave;
    file "bak.fx.movie.edu";
    allow-update-forwarding { 192.253.254/24; };
};
```

Still, when you use update forwarding, you should also use transaction signatures (TSIG)–signed dynamic updates. We won't cover TSIG in depth until Chapter 11, but all you need to know for now is that TSIG-signed dynamic updates bear the cryptographic signature of the signer. If they're forwarded, the signature is forwarded with them. The signature, when verified, tells you the name of the key used to sign the update. The name of the key looks like a domain name, and it's often just the domain name of the host the key is installed on.

With BIND 8.2 and later nameservers, an address match list can include the name of one or more TSIG keys:

```
zone "fx.movie.edu" {
    type master;
    file "db.fx.movie.edu";
```

---

[*] BIND 9.1.0 and later nameservers go so far as to warn you that IP address–based access control lists are insecure if you try to use them.

```
allow-update { key dhcp-server.fx.movie.edu.; }; // allow only updates
                                                 // signed by the DHCP
                                                 // server's TSIG key
};
```

This allows an updater who signs an update with the TSIG key *dhcp-server.fx.movie.edu*
to make any change to the *fx.movie.edu* zone. Unfortunately, there's no way to further
restrict the updater with that TSIG key to a list of source IP addresses.

BIND 9 supports a finer-grained access control mechanism than *allow-update*, also
based on TSIG signatures. This mechanism uses the new *update-policy zone* substatement. *update-policy* lets you specify which keys are allowed to update which records
in the zone. It's meaningful only for primary nameservers because the slaves are
expected to forward the updates.

The update is specified by the name of the key used to sign it and by the domain
name and type of records it attempts to update. *update-policy*'s syntax looks like the
following:

```
(grant | deny) identity nametype string [types]
```

grant and *deny* have the obvious meanings: allow or disallow the specified dynamic
update. *identity* refers to the name of the TSIG key used to sign the update. *nametype* is one of:

name

> Matches when the domain name being updated is the same as the string speci-
> fied in the *string* field.

subdomain

> Matches when the domain name being updated is a subdomain of (i.e., ends in)
> the string specified in the *string* field. (The domain name must still be in the
> zone, of course.)

wildcard

> Matches when the domain name being updated matches the wildcard expres-
> sion specified in the *string* field.

self

> Matches when the domain name being updated is the same as the name in the
> *identity* (not *string*!) field—that is, when the domain name being updated is the
> same as the name of the key used to sign the update. If *nametype* is *self*, the
> *string* field is ignored. And even though it looks redundant (as we'll see in the
> example in a moment), you still have to include the *string* field when using a
> *nametype* of *self*.

string, naturally, is a domain name appropriate to the *nametype* specified. For example, if you specify *wildcard* as the *nametype*, the *string* field should contain a wildcard label.

The *types* field is optional and can contain any valid record type (or multiple types, separated by spaces) except NSEC. (ANY is a convenient shorthand for "all types but NSEC.") If you leave *types* out, it matches all record types except SOA, NS, RRSIG, and NSEC.

 A note on the precedence of *update-policy* rules: the first match (not the closest match) in an *update-policy* substatement is the one that applies to a dynamic update.

So, if the host *mummy.fx.movie.edu* uses a key called *mummy.fx.movie.edu* to sign its dynamic updates, we can restrict *mummy.fx.movie.edu* to updating its own records with the following:

```
zone "fx.movie.edu" {
    type master;
    file "db.fx.movie.edu";
    update-policy { grant mummy.fx.movie.edu. self mummy.fx.movie.edu.; };
};
```

or just its own address records with this:

```
zone "fx.movie.edu" {
    type master;
    file "db.fx.movie.edu";
    update-policy { grant mummy.fx.movie.edu. self mummy.fx.movie.edu. A; };
};
```

More generally, we can restrict all our clients to updating only their own address records using:

```
zone "fx.movie.edu" {
    type master;
    file "db.fx.movie.edu";
    update-policy { grant *.fx.movie.edu. self fx.movie.edu. A; };
};
```

We can allow our DHCP server to use the key *dhcp-server.fx.movie.edu* to update any A, TXT, and PTR records attached to domain names in *fx.movie.edu* with:

```
zone "fx.movie.edu" {
    type master;
    file "db.fx.movie.edu";
    update-policy {
        grant dhcp-server.fx.movie.edu. wildcard *.fx.movie.edu. A TXT PTR;
    };
};
```

In case you're wondering, the difference between:

```
grant dhcp-server.fx.movie.edu. subdomain fx.movie.edu.
```

and:

```
grant dhcp-server.fx.movie.edu. wildcard *.fx.movie.edu.
```

is that the former allows the key *dhcp-server.fx.movie.edu* to modify records attached to *fx.movie.edu* (for example, the zone's NS records) while the latter doesn't. Since the DHCP server has no business modifying any records attached to the domain name of the zone, the second is the more secure option.

Here's a more complicated example: to enable all clients to change any records, except SRV records, that are owned by the same domain name as their key name, but to allow *matrix.fx.movie.edu* to update SRV, A, and CNAME records associated with Active Directory (in the *_udp.fx.movie.edu*, *_tcp.fx.movie.edu*, *_sites.fx.movie.edu*, and *_msdcs.fx.movie.edu* subdomains), you can use:

```
zone "fx.movie.edu" {
    type master;
    file "db.fx.movie.edu";
    update-policy {
        grant matrix.fx.movie.edu. subdomain _udp.fx.movie.edu. SRV CNAME A;
        grant matrix.fx.movie.edu. subdomain _tcp.fx.movie.edu. SRV CNAME A;
        grant matrix.fx.movie.edu. subdomain _sites.fx.movie.edu. SRV CNAME A;
        grant matrix.fx.movie.edu. subdomain _msdcs.fx.movie.edu. SRV CNAME A;
        deny *.fx.movie.edu. self *.fx.movie.edu. SRV;
        grant *.fx.movie.edu. self *.fx.movie.edu. ANY;
    };
};
```

Since the rules in the *update-policy* substatement are evaluated in the order in which they appear, clients can't update their SRV records, though they can update any other record types they own.

If you'd like to take advantage of TSIG-signed dynamic updates but don't have any software that can send them, you can use newer versions of *nsupdate*; see Chapter 11 for that.

DNS NOTIFY (Zone Change Notification)

Traditionally, BIND slaves have used a polling scheme to determine when they need a zone transfer. The polling interval is called the *refresh interval*. Other parameters in the zone's SOA record govern other aspects of the polling mechanism.

But with this polling scheme, it can take up to the refresh interval before a slave detects and transfers new zone data from its master nameserver. That kind of latency can wreak havoc in a dynamically updated environment. Wouldn't it be nice if the primary nameserver could tell its slave servers when the information in the zone changed? After all, the primary nameserver knows the data has changed; someone reloaded the data or it received and processed a dynamic update. The primary could send notification right after processing the reload or update instead of waiting for the refresh interval to pass.[*]

RFC 1996 proposed a mechanism that would allow primary nameservers to notify their slaves of changes to a zone's data. BIND 8 and 9 implement this scheme, which is called DNS NOTIFY.

DNS NOTIFY works like this: when a primary nameserver notices that the serial number of a zone has changed, it sends a special announcement to all the slave nameservers for that zone. The primary nameserver determines which servers are the slaves for the zone by looking at the list of NS records in the zone and taking out the record that points to the nameserver listed in the MNAME field of the zone's SOA record as well as the domain name of the local host.

When does the nameserver notice a change? Restarting a primary nameserver causes it to notify all its slaves as to the current serial number of all of its zones because the primary has no way of knowing whether its zone datafiles were edited before it started. Reloading one or more zones with new serial numbers causes a nameserver to notify the slaves of those zones. And a dynamic update that causes a zone's serial number to increment also causes notification.

The special NOTIFY announcement is identified by its opcode in the DNS header. The opcode for most queries is QUERY. NOTIFY messages, including announcements and responses, have a special opcode, NOTIFY (duh). Other than that, NOTIFY messages look very much like a response to a query for a zone's SOA record: they include the SOA record of the zone whose serial number has changed, and the authoritative answer bit is set.

When a slave receives a NOTIFY announcement for a zone from one of its configured master nameservers, it responds with a NOTIFY response. The response tells the master that the slave received the NOTIFY announcement so that the master can stop sending it NOTIFY announcements for the zone. The slave then proceeds just as if the refresh timer for that zone had expired: it queries the master nameserver for the SOA record for the zone that the master claims has changed. If the serial number is higher, the slave transfers the zone.

Why doesn't the slave simply take the master's word that the zone has changed? It's possible that a miscreant could forge NOTIFY announcements to slaves, causing lots of unnecessary zone transfers and amounting to a denial-of-service attack against a master nameserver.

If the slave actually transfers the zone, RFC 1996 says that it should issue its own NOTIFY announcements to the other authoritative nameservers for the zone. The

---

[*] Actually, in the case of reloading a zone, the nameserver may not send the NOTIFY messages right away. To avoid causing a flurry of refresh queries from slaves, BIND nameservers reloading zones wait a fraction of each zone's refresh interval before sending NOTIFY messages for that zone.

idea is that the primary master may not be able to notify all the slave nameservers for the zone itself because it's possible some slaves can't communicate directly with the primary (they use another slave as their master). However, while BIND 8.2.3 and later and all BIND 9 nameservers implement this, earlier versions of BIND 8 don't. Older BIND 8 slaves don't send NOTIFY messages unless explicitly configured to do so.

Here's how that works in practice. On our network, *toystory.movie.edu* is the primary nameserver for *movie.edu*, and *wormhole.movie.edu* and *zardoz.movie.edu* are slaves, as shown in Figure 10-1.

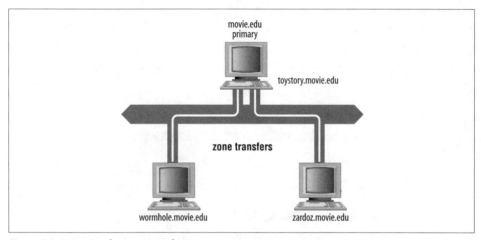

Figure 10-1. movie.edu zone transfers

When we edit and reload or dynamically update *movie.edu* on *toystory.movie.edu*, *toystory.movie.edu* sends NOTIFY announcements to *wormhole.movie.edu* and *zardoz.movie.edu*. Both slaves respond to *toystory.movie.edu*, telling it that they've received the notification. They then check to see whether *movie.edu*'s serial number has incremented and, when they find it has, perform a zone transfer. If *wormhole.movie.edu* and *zardoz.movie.edu* are running BIND 8.2.3 or later or BIND 9, after they transfer the new version of the zone, they also send NOTIFY announcements to tell each other about the change. But since *wormhole.movie.edu* isn't *zardoz.movie.edu*'s master nameserver for *movie.edu*, and the converse isn't true either, both slaves just ignore each other's NOTIFY announcements.

BIND nameservers log information about NOTIFY messages to *syslog*. Here's what BIND 8 running on *toystory.movie.edu* logged after we reloaded *movie.edu*:

```
Oct 14 22:56:34 toystory named[18764]: Sent NOTIFY for "movie.edu IN SOA 2000010958"
(movie.edu); 2 NS, 2 A
Oct 14 22:56:34 toystory named[18764]: Received NOTIFY answer (AA) from 192.249.249.1
for "movie.edu IN SOA"
Oct 14 22:56:34 toystory named[18764]: Received NOTIFY answer (AA) from 192.249.249.9
for "movie.edu IN SOA"
```

The first message shows us the NOTIFY announcement that *toystory.movie.edu* sent, informing the two slaves (2 NS) that the serial number of *movie.edu* is now 2000010958. The next two lines show the slave nameservers confirming their receipt of the notification.

A BIND 9 nameserver would have logged just:

```
Oct 14 22:56:34 toystory named[18764]: zone movie.edu/IN: sending notifies (serial
2000010958)
```

Let's also look at a more complicated zone transfer scheme. In Figure 10-2, *a* is the primary nameserver for the zone and *b*'s master server, but *b* is *c*'s master server. Moreover, *b* has two network interfaces.

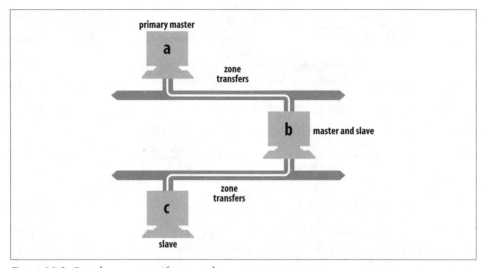

Figure 10-2. Complex zone transfer example

In this scenario, *a* notifies both *b* and *c* after the zone is updated. Then *b* checks to see whether the zone's serial number has incremented and initiates a zone transfer. However, *c* ignores *a*'s NOTIFY announcement because *a* is not *c*'s configured master nameserver (*b* is). If *b* is running BIND 8.2.3 or later, or BIND 9, or is explicitly configured to notify *c*, then after *b*'s zone transfer completes, it sends a NOTIFY announcement to *c*, which prompts *c* to check the serial number *b* holds for the zone. If *c* is also running BIND 8.2.3 or later or BIND 9, it sends *b* a NOTIFY announcement after its zone transfer finishes, which *b*, naturally, ignores.

Note also that if there's any possibility that *c* will receive a NOTIFY announcement from *b*'s other network interface, *c* must be configured with both network interfaces' addresses in the zone's *masters* substatement, or else *c* will ignore NOTIFY announcements from the unknown interface.

BIND 4 slave nameservers and other nameservers that don't support NOTIFY will respond with a Not Implemented (NOTIMP) error. Note that the Microsoft DNS Server *does* support DNS NOTIFY.

In both BIND 8 and 9, DNS NOTIFY is on by default, but you can turn off NOTIFY globally with the substatement:

```
options {
    notify no;
};
```

You can also turn on or off NOTIFY for a particular zone. For example, say we know that all the slave nameservers for our *fx.movie.edu* zone are running BIND 4 and therefore don't understand NOTIFY announcements. The *zone* statement:

```
zone "fx.movie.edu" {
    type master;
    file "db.fx.movie.edu";
    notify no;
};
```

avoids sending useless NOTIFY announcements to the slaves for *fx.movie.edu*. A zone-specific NOTIFY setting overrides any global setting for that zone. Unfortunately, neither BIND 8 nor BIND 9 allows you to turn off NOTIFY announcements on a server-by-server basis.

BIND 8 and 9 even have a provision for adding servers besides those in your zone's NS records to your "NOTIFY list." For example, you may have one or more unregistered slave nameservers (described in Chapter 8), and you'd like them to pick up changes to the zone quickly. Or you may have an older BIND 8 slave for the zone that is the master server for another slave and needs to send NOTIFY messages to the slave.

To add a server to your NOTIFY list, use the *also-notify* substatement of the *zone* statement:

```
zone "fx.movie.edu" {
    type slave;
    file "bak.fx.movie.edu";
    notify yes;
    also-notify { 15.255.152.4; }; // This is a BIND 8 slave, which
                                   // must be explicitly configured
                                   // to notify its slave
};
```

In BIND 8.2.2 and later nameservers, you can specify *also-notify* as an *options* substatement as well. This applies to all zones for which NOTIFY is on (and which don't have their own *also-notify* substatements).

Beginning in BIND 8.3.2 and 9.1.0, you can specify *explicit* as an argument to the *notify* substatement; this suppresses NOTIFY messages to all nameservers except those in the *also-notify* list. For example, these two substatements tell the nameserver to send NOTIFY messages only to the slave at 192.249.249.20:

```
options {
    also-notify { 192.249.249.20; };
    notify explicit;
};
```

You can also use the *allow-notify* substatement to tell your nameserver to accept NOTIFY messages from nameservers other than just the configured master nameservers for a zone:

```
options {
    allow-notify { 192.249.249.17; }; // let 192.249.249.17 send NOTIFY msgs
};
```

As an *options* substatement, *allow-notify* affects all slave zones. When specified as a *zone* substatement, *allow-notify* overrides any global *allow-notify* for just that zone.

Incremental Zone Transfer (IXFR)

With dynamic update and NOTIFY, our zones are updated according to the changing state of the network, and those changes quickly propagate to all the authoritative nameservers for those zones. The picture's complete, right?

Not quite. Imagine you run a large zone that's dynamically updated with frightening frequency. That's easy to envision: you might have a big zone to begin with, including thousands of clients, when all of a sudden management decides to implement Active Directory and DHCP. Now each of your clients updates its own address record in the zone, and the Domain Controllers update the records that tell clients which services they run. (There's much more to come on Active Directory in Chapter 17.)

Each time your primary nameserver receives an update that increments the zone's serial number, it sends a NOTIFY announcement to its slaves. And each time they receive NOTIFY announcements, the slaves check the serial number of the zone on their master server and, possibly, transfer the zone. If that zone is large, the transfer will take some time; another update could arrive in the interim. Your slaves could be transferring zones in perpetuity! At the very least, your nameservers will spend a lot of time transferring the whole zone when the change to the zone is probably very small (e.g., the addition of a client's address record).

Incremental zone transfer, or IXFR for short, solves this problem by allowing slave nameservers to tell their master servers which version of a zone they currently hold and to request just the changes to the zone between that version and the current one. This can dramatically reduce the size and duration of a zone transfer.

An incremental zone transfer request has a query type of IXFR instead of AXFR (the type of query that initiates a full zone transfer), and it contains the slave's current

SOA record from the zone in the authority section of the message. When the master nameserver receives an incremental zone transfer request, it looks for the record of the changes to the zone between the slave's version of the zone and the version the master holds. If that record is missing, the master sends a full zone transfer. Otherwise, it sends just the differences between the versions of the zone.

IXFR Limitations

Sound good? It is! But IXFR has a few limitations that you should know about. First, IXFR didn't work well until BIND 8.2.3. All BIND 9 nameservers have IXFR implementations that work well and interoperate with BIND 8.2.3.

Next, IXFR traditionally has worked only when you're modifying your zone data with dynamic updates, not by making manual changes. Dynamic updates leave a record of the changes made to the zone and the serial number changes they correspond to—exactly what a master nameserver needs to send to a slave that requests IXFR. But a nameserver that reloads an entire zone datafile would have to compute the differences between that zone and the previous zone, like doing a *diff* between the versions. This meant that, to take maximum advantage of IXFR, you needed to modify your zone only by using dynamic update, and never edit the zone datafile by hand.

IXFR from Differences

BIND 9.3.0 introduced support for calculating IXFR responses by comparing a zone datafile with the version of the zone it has in memory. This means that you can now (or again) edit zone datafiles manually. You do have to take precautions, however, to make sure the file you're editing contains the latest version of the zone and dynamic updates are refused while you're working on the file. (Dynamic updates could change the in-memory version of the zone so that the file no longer reflected its state.)

To turn on this feature, use the *ixfr-from-differences* substatement. You can use it within an *options* or *zone* statement. Here's how you would turn on the feature for all zones:

```
options {
    directory "/var/named";
    ixfr-from-differences yes;
};
```

To force the nameserver to write a new version of a zone's datafile and suspend processing of dynamic updates to the zone, use *rndc*'s new *freeze* command:

```
% rndc freeze zone [class [view]]
```

To tell the nameserver to reread the zone datafile and resume processing of dynamic updates for the zone, use *rndc thaw*:

```
% rndc thaw zone [class [view]]
```

You probably shouldn't keep a zone frozen for too long, especially if you might be missing important updates.

IXFR Files

BIND 8 nameservers maintain an IXFR log of changes to the zone separate from the dynamic update logfile. Like the dynamic update logfile, the IXFR logfile is updated every time the nameserver receives an update. Unlike the dynamic update logfile, the IXFR logfile is never deleted, though the nameserver can be configured to trim it when it exceeds a particular size. The name of the BIND 8 IXFR logfile, by default, is the name of the zone datafile with *.ixfr* appended to it.

BIND 9 nameservers use the dynamic update logfile, or *journal file*, to assemble IXFR responses and to maintain the integrity of the zone. Since a primary nameserver never knows when it may need the record of a particular change to the zone, it doesn't delete the journal file. A BIND 9 slave saves the journal file even if it receives an AXFR of the zone because it may serve as a master nameserver to one or more slaves, too.

BIND 8 IXFR Configuration

Configuring IXFR in BIND 8 is fairly straightforward. First, you need an *options* substatement called *maintain-ixfr-base* on your master nameserver that tells it to maintain IXFR logfiles for all zones—even those the nameserver is a slave for because those in turn may have slaves that want IXFRs:

```
options {
    directory "/var/named";
    maintain-ixfr-base yes;
};
```

You then need to tell your slaves to request IXFRs from that master nameserver. You do that with a new *server* substatement, *support-ixfr*:

```
server 192.249.249.3 {
    support-ixfr yes;
};
```

That's about it, unless you want to rename the IXFR logfile on the master. That's done with a new *zone* statement, *ixfr-base*:

```
zone "movie.edu" {
    type master;
    file "db.movie.edu";
    ixfr-base "ixfr.movie.edu";
};
```

Oh, and you can configure the nameserver to trim the IXFR logfile after it exceeds a particular size:[*]

```
options {
    directory "/var/named";
    maintain-ixfr-base yes;
    max-ixfr-log-size 1M;     // trim IXFR log to 1 megabyte
};
```

Once the IXFR logfile exceeds the specified limit by 100 KB, the nameserver trims it back to that size. The 100 KB of "slush" prevents the logfile from reaching the limit and then being trimmed back after each successive update.

Using the *many-answers* zone transfer format can make zone transfers even more efficient. We'll cover *many-answers* zone transfers later in this chapter.

BIND 9 IXFR Configuration

It's even easier to configure IXFR in a BIND 9 master nameserver because you don't have to do a thing: it's on by default. If you need to turn it off for a particular slave server (and you probably won't because a slave must request an incremental zone transfer), use the *provide-ixfr server* substatement, which defaults to *yes*:

```
server 192.249.249.1 {
    provide-ixfr no;
};
```

You can also use *provide-ixfr* as an *options* substatement, in which case it applies to all slaves that don't have an explicit *provide-ixfr* substatement of their own in a *server* statement.

Since BIND 9 master nameservers send *many-answers* zone transfers by default, you don't need any special *transfer-format* configuration.

More useful is the *request-ixfr* substatement, which can be used in either an *options* or a *server* statement. If you have a mix of IXFR-capable and IXFR-impaired masters, you can tailor your slave's zone transfer requests to match the capabilities of its masters:

```
options {
    directory "/var/named";
    request-ixfr no;
};

server 192.249.249.3 {
    request-ixfr yes;     // of our masters, only toystory supports IXFR
};
```

---

[*] Before BIND 8.2.3, you need to specify the number of bytes, rather than just "1M," because of a bug.

From BIND 9.3.0 on, BIND 9 nameservers support configuring the maximum size of a journal file with the *max-journal-size options* substatement.

Forwarding

Certain network connections discourage sending large volumes of traffic off-site, per-haps because it's a slow link with high delay; a remote office's satellite connection to the company's network is an example. In these situations, you'll want to limit the off-site DNS traffic to the bare minimum. BIND provides a mechanism to do this: *forwarders*.

Forwarders are also useful if you need to shunt name resolution to a particular nameserver. For example, if only one of the hosts on your network has Internet con-nectivity, and you run a nameserver on that host, you can configure your other nameservers to use it as a forwarder so that they can look up Internet domain names. (More on this use of forwarders when we discuss firewalls in Chapter 11.)

If you designate one or more servers at your site as forwarders, your nameservers will send all their off-site queries to the forwarders first. The idea is that the forwarders handle all the off-site queries generated at the site, building up a rich cache of infor-mation. For any given query in a remote zone, there is a high probability that the for-warder can answer the query from its cache, avoiding the need for the other servers to send queries off-site. You don't do anything to a nameserver to make it a for-warder; you modify all the *other* servers at your site to direct their queries through the forwarders.

A primary or slave nameserver's mode of operation changes slightly when it is config-ured to use a forwarder. If a resolver requests records that are already in the nameserver's authoritative data or cached data, the nameserver answers with that information; this part of its operation hasn't changed. However, if the records aren't in its database, the nameserver sends the query to a forwarder and waits a short period for an answer before resuming normal operation and starting the iterative name resolution process. This mode of operation is called *forward first*. What the nameserver is doing differently here is sending a *recursive* query to the forwarder, expecting it to find the answer. At all other times, the nameserver sends out only *nonrecursive* queries to other nameservers.

For example, here is the BIND 8 and 9 *forwarders* substatement for nameservers in *movie.edu*. Both *wormhole.movie.edu* and *toystory.movie.edu* are the site's forward-ers. We add this *forwarders* substatement to every nameserver's configuration file except the ones for the forwarders themselves:

```
options {
    forwarders { 192.249.249.1; 192.249.249.3; };
};
```

When you use forwarders, try to keep your site configuration simple. You could end up with configurations that are really twisted.

 Avoid chaining your forwarders. Don't configure nameserver A to forward to server B, and server B to forward to server C (or, worse yet, back to server A). This can cause long resolution delays and creates a brittle configuration, in which the failure of any forwarder in the chain impairs or breaks name resolution.

A More Restricted Nameserver

You may want to restrict your nameservers even further—stopping them from even *trying* to contact an off-site server if their forwarder is down or doesn't respond. You can do this by configuring your nameservers to use *forward-only* mode. A nameserver in forward-only mode is a variation on a nameserver that uses forwarders. It still answers queries from its authoritative data and cached data. However, it relies *completely* on its forwarders; it doesn't try to contact other nameservers to find information if the forwarders don't give it an answer. Here is an example of what the configuration file of a nameserver in forward-only mode would contain:

```
options {
    forwarders { 192.249.249.1; 192.249.249.3; };
    forward only;
};
```

If you use forward-only mode, you must have forwarders configured. Otherwise, it doesn't make sense to have forward-only mode set. If you configure a nameserver in forward-only mode and run a version of BIND older than 8.2.3, you might want to consider including the forwarders' IP addresses more than once. That would look like:

```
options {
    forwarders { 192.249.249.1; 192.249.249.3;
        192.249.249.1; 192.249.249.3; };
    forward only;
};
```

This nameserver contacts each forwarder only once, and it waits a short time for the forwarder to respond. Listing the forwarders multiple times directs the nameserver to *retransmit* queries to the forwarders and increases the overall length of time that the forward-only nameserver will wait for an answer from forwarders.

 In our experience, forward-only mode actually provides more predictable name resolution than forward-first mode (which is the default). It takes so long for the queries to forwarders to time out that by the time the nameserver starts iterative name resolution, the resolver that sent the original query has often given up already or is on the verge of giving up. The result is that resolvers get inconsistent resolution results: Some queries, which resolve quickly, are answered, but others time out.

Forward Zones

Traditionally, using forwarders has been an all-or-nothing proposition: either you use forwarders to resolve every query your nameserver can't answer itself, or you don't use forwarders at all. However, there are some situations in which it would be nice to have more control over forwarding. For example, maybe you'd like to resolve certain domain names using a particular forwarder but resolve other domain names iteratively.

BIND 8.2 introduced a new feature, *forward zones*, that allows you to configure your nameserver to use forwarders only when looking up certain domain names. (BIND 9's support for forward zones was added in 9.1.0.) For example, you can configure your nameserver to shunt all queries for domain names ending in *pixar.com* to a pair of Pixar's nameservers:

```
zone "pixar.com" {
    type forward;
    forwarders { 138.72.10.20; 138.72.30.28; };
};
```

Why would you ever configure this explicitly rather than letting your nameserver follow delegation from the *com* nameservers to the *pixar.com* nameservers? Well, imagine that you have a private connection to Pixar, and you're told to use a special set of nameservers, reachable only from your network, to resolve all *pixar.com* domain names.

Even though forwarding rules are specified in the *zone* statement, they apply to all domain names that end in the domain name specified. That is, regardless of whether the domain name you're looking up, *foo.bar.pixar.com*, is in the *pixar.com* zone, the rule applies to it because it ends in *pixar.com* (or is in the *pixar.com* domain, if you prefer).

There's another variety of forward zone, in a way the opposite of the kind we just showed you. These allow you to specify which queries *don't* get forwarded. Therefore, it applies only to nameservers with forwarders specified in the *options* statement, which would normally apply to all queries.

These forward zones are configured using a *zone* statement, but not of type *forward*. Instead, these are normal zones—master, slave, or stub—with a *forwarders* substatement. To "undo" the forwarding configured in the *options* statement, we specify an empty list of forwarders:

```
options {
    directory "/var/named";
    forwarders { 192.249.249.3; 192.249.249.1; };
};

zone "movie.edu" {
    type slave;
    masters { 192.249.249.3; };
```

```
        file "bak.movie.edu";
        forwarders {};
    };
```

Wait a minute—why would you need to disable forwarding in a zone you're authoritative for? Wouldn't you just answer the query and not use a forwarder?

Remember, the forwarding rules apply to queries for all domain names that end in the domain name of the zone. So this forwarding rule really applies only to queries for domain names in delegated subdomains of *movie.edu*, such as *fx.movie.edu*. Without the forwarding rule, this nameserver would have forwarded a query for *matrix.fx.movie.edu* to the nameservers at 192.249.249.3 and 192.249.249.1. With the forwarding rule, it instead uses the subdomain's NS records from the *movie.edu* zone and queries the *fx.movie.edu* nameservers directly.

Forward zones are enormously helpful in dealing with Internet firewalls, as we'll see in Chapter 11.

Forwarder Selection

On BIND 8 nameservers from 8.2.3 on, and BIND 9 nameservers from 9.3.0 on, you don't need to list forwarders more than once. These nameservers don't necessarily query the forwarders in the order listed; they interpret the nameservers in the list as "candidate" forwarders and choose which one to query first based on roundtrip time, the time it took to respond to previous queries.

This is a real benefit if a forwarder fails, especially the first one in the list. Older versions of BIND would keep blindly querying the failed forwarder and waiting before querying the next in the list. These newer versions of BIND quickly realize that the forwarder isn't responding and will try another.

Views

BIND 9 introduced *views*, another mechanism that's very useful in firewalled environments. Views allow you to present one nameserver configuration to one community of hosts and a different configuration to another community. This is particularly handy if you're running a nameserver on a host that receives queries from both your internal hosts and hosts on the Internet (we'll cover this in the next chapter).

If you don't configure any views, BIND 9 automatically creates a single, implicit view that it shows to all hosts that query it. To explicitly create a view, you use the *view* statement, which takes the name of the view as an argument:

```
view "internal" {
};
```

Although the name of the view can be just about anything, using a descriptive name is always a good idea. And while quoting the name of the view isn't necessary, it's helpful to do so to avoid conflict with words BIND reserves for its own use ("internal," for example). The *view* statement must come after any *options* statement, though not necessarily right after it.

You can select which hosts "see" a particular view using the *match-clients view* substatement, which takes an address match list as an argument. If you don't specify a community of hosts with *match-clients*, the view applies to all hosts.

Let's say we're setting up a special view of the *fx.movie.edu* zone on our nameservers that we want only the Special Effects department to see. We could create a view visible only to hosts on our subnet:

```
view "internal" {
    match-clients { 192.253.254/24; };
};
```

If you want to make that a little more readable, you can use an *acl* statement:

```
acl "fx-subnet" { 192.253.254/24; };

view "internal" {
    match-clients { "fx-subnet"; };
};
```

Just be sure you define the ACL *outside* the view because you can't use *acl* statements inside views.

You can also specify who sees a view using the *match-destinations view* substatement, which, like *match-clients,* takes an address match list as an argument. *match-destinations* applies to nameservers with multiple IP addresses: clients querying one of a server's IP address, might see one view, while those querying another address see a different view. *match-clients* and *match-destinations* can be used in combination, too, to select queries from a particular client and those sent to a particular address. There's even a *match-recursive-only* Boolean substatement that will let you select only recursive or nonrecursive queries.

What can you put inside a *view* statement? Almost anything (well, except for *acl* statements). You can define zones with *zone* statements, describe remote nameservers with *server* statements, and configure TSIG keys with *key* statements. You can use most *options* substatements within a view, but if you do, don't enclose them in an *options* statement; just use them "raw" in the *view* statement:

```
acl "fx-subnet" { 192.253.254/24; };

view "internal" {
    match-clients { "fx-subnet"; };
    recursion yes;  // turn recursion on for this view
                    // (it's off globally, in the options statement)
};
```

Any configuration option you specify within a view overrides the like-named global option (e.g., one in the *options* statement) for hosts that match *match-clients*.

For a complete list of what's supported inside the *view* statement on the version of BIND 9 you run (because it changes from release to release), see the file *doc/misc/options* in the BIND distribution.

To give you an idea of the power of views, here's the Special Effects lab's full *named.conf* file:

```
options {
    directory "/var/named";
};

acl "fx-subnet" { 192.253.254/24; };

view "internal" {  // internal view of our zones

    match-clients { "fx-subnet"; };

    zone "fx.movie.edu" {
        type master;
        file "db.fx.movie.edu";
    };

    zone "254.253.192.in-addr.arpa" {
        type master;
        file "db.192.253.254";
    };
};

view "external" {  // view of our zones for the rest of the world

    match-clients { any; };  // implicit
    recursion no;            // outside of our subnet, they shouldn't be
                             // requesting recursion
    zone "fx.movie.edu" {
        type master;
        file "db.fx.movie.edu.external";  // external zone datafile
    };

    zone "254.253.192.in-addr.arpa" {
        type master;
        file "db.192.253.254.external";   // external zone datafile
    };
};
```

Notice that each view has an *fx.movie.edu* and a *254.253.192.in-addr.arpa* zone, but the zone datafiles are different in the internal and external views. This allows us to show the outside world a different "face" than we see internally.

The order of the *view* statements is important because the first view that a host's IP address matches is the one that dictates what it sees. If the external view were listed first in the configuration file, it would occlude the internal view because the external view matches all addresses.

One last note on views (before we use them in the next chapter, anyway): if you configure even one *view* statement, all your *zone* statements must appear within explicit views.

Round-Robin Load Distribution

Nameservers released since BIND 4.9 have formalized some load distribution functionality that has existed in patches to BIND for some time. Bryan Beecher wrote patches to BIND 4.8.3 to implement what he called "shuffle address records." These were address records of a special type that the nameserver rotated between responses. For example, if the domain name *foo.bar.baz* had three "shuffled" IP addresses, 192.168.1.1, 192.168.1.2, and 192.168.1.3, an appropriately patched nameserver would give them out first in the order:

```
192.168.1.1 192.168.1.2 192.168.1.3
```

then in the order:

```
192.168.1.2 192.168.1.3 192.168.1.1
```

and then in the order:

```
192.168.1.3 192.168.1.1 192.168.1.2
```

before starting all over with the first order and repeating the rotation ad infinitum.

This functionality is enormously useful if you have a number of equivalent network resources, such as mirrored FTP servers, web servers, or terminal servers, and you'd like to spread the load among them. You establish one domain name that refers to the group of resources and configure clients to access that domain name, and the nameserver distributes requests among the IP addresses you list.

BIND 8 and 9 do away with the shuffle address record as a separate record type, subject to special handling. Instead, a modern nameserver rotates addresses for any domain name that has more than one A record. (In fact, the nameserver will rotate any type of record as long as a given domain name has more than one of them.)* So the records:

```
foo.bar.baz.    60    IN    A    192.168.1.1
foo.bar.baz.    60    IN    A    192.168.1.2
foo.bar.baz.    60    IN    A    192.168.1.3
```

accomplish on a BIND 8 or 9 nameserver just what the shuffle address records did on a patched 4.8.3 server. The BIND documentation calls this process *round-robin*.

---

* Actually, until BIND 9, PTR records weren't rotated. BIND 9 rotates all record types.

It's a good idea to reduce the records' time to live, too, as we did in this example. This ensures that if the addresses are cached on an intermediate nameserver that doesn't support round-robin, they'll time out of the cache quickly. If the intermediate nameserver looks up the name again, your authoritative nameserver can round-robin the addresses again.

Note that this is really load distribution, not load balancing, because the nameserver gives out the addresses in a completely deterministic way without regard to the actual load or capacity of the servers servicing the requests. In our example, the server at address 192.168.1.3 could be a 486DX33 running Linux and the other two servers HP9000 Superdomes, and the Linux box would still get a third of the queries. Listing a higher-capacity server's address multiple times won't help because BIND eliminates duplicate records.

Multiple CNAMEs

Back in the heyday of BIND 4 nameservers, some folks set up round-robin using multiple CNAME records instead of multiple address records:

```
foo1.bar.baz.   60   IN   A       192.168.1.1
foo2.bar.baz.   60   IN   A       192.168.1.2
foo3.bar.baz.   60   IN   A       192.168.1.3
foo.bar.baz.    60   IN   CNAME   foo1.bar.baz.
foo.bar.baz.    60   IN   CNAME   foo2.bar.baz.
foo.bar.baz.    60   IN   CNAME   foo3.bar.baz.
```

This probably looks odd to those of you who are used to our harping on the evils of mixing anything with a CNAME record. But BIND 4 nameservers didn't recognize this as the configuration error it is and simply returned the CNAME records for *foo.bar.baz* in round-robin order.[*]

BIND 8 nameservers, on the other hand, are more vigilant and catch this error. You can, however, explicitly configure them to allow multiple CNAME records for a single domain name with:

```
options {
    multiple-cnames yes;
};
```

Not that we think you *should*, however.

BIND 9 nameservers don't notice the multiple CNAME problem until version 9.1.0. BIND versions from 9.1.0 on detect the problem but don't give you the option of allowing multiple CNAME records with the *multiple-cnames* statement. We think

---

[*] The right way to do this, in case you're wondering, is to attach the addresses of *foo1.bar.baz*, *foo2.bar.baz*, and *foo3.bar.baz* directly to the domain name *foo.bar.baz*.

that's the right approach: attaching multiple CNAME records to a single domain name is a violation of the DNS standards (in particular RFC 2181). Don't do it.

The rrset-order Substatement

There are certain times when you'd rather the nameserver didn't use round-robin. For example, maybe you'd like to designate one web server as a backup to another. To do this, the nameserver should always return the backup's address after the primary web server's address. But you can't do that with round-robin; it'll just rotate the order of the addresses in successive responses.

BIND 8.2 and later nameservers and BIND 9.3.0 and later nameservers allow you to turn off round-robin for certain domain names and types of records. For example, if we want to ensure that the address records for *www.movie.edu* are always returned in the same order, we'd use this *rrset-order* substatement:

```
options {
    rrset-order {
        class IN type A name "www.movie.edu" order fixed;
    };
};
```

We should probably lower the TTL on *www.movie.edu*'s address records, too, so a nameserver that cached the records wouldn't round-robin them for long.

The *class*, *type*, and *name* settings determine which records the specified order applies to. The class defaults to IN, type to ANY, and name to *—in other words, any records. So the statement:

```
options {
    rrset-order {
        order random;
    };
};
```

applies a random order to all records returned by the nameserver. The name setting may contain a wildcard as its leftmost label, as in:

```
options {
    rrset-order {
        type A name "*.movie.edu" order cyclic;
    };
};
```

Only one *rrset-order* substatement is permitted, but it can contain multiple order specifications. The first order specification to match a set of records in a response applies.

rrset-order supports three (count 'em, three!) different orders:

fixed
> Always returns matching records in the same order

random
> Returns matching records in random order

cyclic
> Returns matching records in cyclic (round-robin) order

Unfortunately, BIND 9.3.2 doesn't yet support the *fixed* order completely.[*]

The default behavior is:

```
options {
    rrset-order {
        class IN type ANY name "*" order cyclic;
    };
};
```

Configuring *rrset-order* is far from a complete solution, unfortunately, because resolver and nameserver caching can interfere with its operation. A better long-term solution is the SRV record, which we'll discuss in Chapter 17.

Nameserver Address Sorting

Sometimes, neither round-robin nor any other configurable order is what you want. When you are contacting a host that has multiple network interfaces and hence multiple IP addresses, choosing a particular interface based on your host's address may give you better performance. No *rrset-order* substatement can do that for you.

If the multihomed host is local and shares a network or subnet with your host, one of the multihomed host's addresses is "closer." If the multihomed host is remote, you may see better performance using one interface instead of another, but often it doesn't matter much which address is used. In days long past, net 10 (the former ARPAnet "backbone") was always closer than any other remote address. The Internet has improved drastically since those days, so you won't often see a marked performance improvement when using one network over another for remote multihomed hosts, but we'll cover that case anyway.

Before we get into address sorting by a nameserver, you should first look at whether address sorting by the resolver better suits your needs. (See the section "The sortlist Directive" in Chapter 6.) Since your resolver and nameserver may be on different networks, it often makes more sense for the resolver to sort addresses optimally for its

---

[*] Fixed order works only if you happen to have your records in DNSSEC's sorted order. See Chapter 11 for details on DNSSEC's sorting.

host. Address sorting at the nameserver works fairly well, but it can be hard to optimize for every resolver it services.

In an uncommon turn of events, the nameserver's address-sorting feature was *removed* in early versions of BIND 8, primarily because of the developers' insistence that it had no place in the nameserver. The feature was restored—and in fact enhanced—in BIND 8.2. BIND 9.1.0 was the first BIND 9 release to support address sorting.

The key to address sorting is an *options* substatement called *sortlist*. The *sortlist* substatement takes an address match list as an argument. Unlike address match lists used as access control lists, though, *sortlist*'s has a very specialized interpretation. Each entry in the address match list is itself an address match list with either one or two elements.

If an entry has only one element, it's used to check the IP address of a querier. If the querier's address matches, then the nameserver sorts addresses in a response to that querier so that any addresses that match the element are first. Confusing? Here's an example:

```
options {
    sortlist {
        { 192.249.249/24; };
    };
};
```

The only entry in this sort list has just one element. This sort list sorts addresses on the network 192.249.249/24 to the beginning of responses to queriers that are also on that network. So if the client at 192.249.249.101 looks up a domain name that owns two addresses, 192.249.249.87 and 192.253.253.87, the nameserver will sort 192.249.249.87 to the beginning of the response.

If an entry has two elements, the first element is used to match the IP address of a querier. If the querier's address matches, the nameserver sorts addresses in a response to that querier so that any addresses that match the second element come first. The second element can actually be a whole address match list of several elements, in which case the first address added to the response is the one that matches first in the list. Here's a simple example:

```
options {
    sortlist {
        { 192.249.249/24; { 192.249.249/24; 192.253.253/24; }; };
    };
};
```

This sort list applies to queriers on 192.249.249/24 and sends them addresses on their own network first, followed by addresses on 192.253.253/24.

The elements in the sort list specification can just as easily be subnets or even individual hosts:

```
options {
    sortlist {
        { 15.1.200/21;        // if the querier is on 15.1.200/21
            { 15.1.200/21;    // then prefer addresses on that subnet
            15/8; };          // or at least on 15/8
        };
    };
};
```

Preferring Nameservers on Certain Networks

BIND 8's topology feature is somewhat similar to *sortlist*, but it applies only to the process of choosing nameservers. (BIND 9 doesn't support topology as of 9.3.2.) Earlier in the book, we described how BIND chooses between a number of nameservers that are authoritative for the same zone by selecting the nameserver with the lowest round-trip time. But we lied—a little. BIND 8 actually places remote nameservers in 64-millisecond bands when comparing RTT. The first band is actually only 32 milliseconds wide (there! we did it again), from 0 to 32 milliseconds. The next extends from 33 to 96 milliseconds, and so on. The bands are designed so that nameservers on different continents are always in different bands.

The idea is to favor nameservers in lower bands but to treat servers in the same band as equivalent. If a nameserver compares two remote servers' RTTs, and one is in a lower band, the nameserver chooses to query the nameserver in the lower band. But if the remote servers are in the same band, the nameserver checks to see whether one of the remote servers is topologically closer.

So topology lets you introduce an element of fudge into the process of choosing a nameserver to query. It lets you favor nameservers on certain networks over others. Topology takes as an argument an address match list, where the entries are networks, listed in the order in which the local nameserver should prefer them (highest to lowest). Therefore:

```
topology {
    15/8;
    172.88/16;
};
```

tells the local nameserver to prefer nameservers on the network 15/8 over other nameservers, and nameservers on the network 172.88/16 over nameservers on networks other than 15/8. So if the nameserver has a choice between a nameserver on network 15/8, a nameserver on 172.88/16, and a nameserver on 192.168.1/24, assuming all three have RTT values in the same band, it will choose to query the nameserver on 15/8.

You can also negate entries in the topology address match list to penalize nameservers on certain networks. The earlier in the address match list the negated entry matches, the greater the penalty. You might use this to keep your nameserver from querying remote nameservers on a network that's particularly flaky, for example.

A Nonrecursive Nameserver

By default, BIND resolvers send recursive queries, and, by default, BIND nameservers do the work required to answer them. (If you don't remember how recursion works, see Chapter 2.) In the process of finding the answers to recursive queries, the nameserver builds up a cache of nonauthoritative information from other zones.

In some situations, it's undesirable for nameservers to do the extra work required to answer a recursive query or to build up a cache of data. The root nameservers are an example of one of these situations. The root nameservers are so busy that they can't expend the extra effort necessary to find the answers to recursive queries. Instead, they send a response based only on the authoritative data they have. The response may contain the answer, but it more likely contains a referral to other nameservers. And since the root servers do not support recursive queries, they don't build up a cache of nonauthoritative data, which is good because their caches would be huge.*

You can induce a BIND nameserver to run in nonrecursive mode with the following configuration (config) file statement:

```
options {
    recursion no;
};
```

Now the server will respond to recursive queries as if they were nonrecursive.

In conjunction with *recursion no*, there is one more configuration option necessary if you want to prevent your nameserver from building a cache:

```
options {
    fetch-glue no;
};
```

This stops the server from fetching missing glue when constructing the additional data section of a response. BIND 9 nameservers don't fetch glue, so the *fetch-glue* substatement is obsolete in BIND 9.

If you choose to make one of your servers nonrecursive, don't list that nameserver in any host's *resolv.conf* file. While you can make your nameserver nonrecursive, there is no corresponding option to make your resolver work with a nonrecursive

---

* Note that a root nameserver doesn't normally receive recursive queries unless a nameserver's administrator configured it to use the root server as a forwarder, a host's administrator configured its resolver to use the root server as a nameserver, or a user pointed *nslookup* or *dig* at the root server. All of these happen more often than you'd expect, though.

nameserver.* If your nameserver needs to continue to serve one or more resolvers, you can use the *allow-recursion* substatement, available in BIND 8.2.1 and later (including BIND 9). *allow-recursion* takes an address match list as an argument; any queriers that match can send recursive queries, but everyone else is treated as if recursion were off:

```
options {
    allow-recursion { 192.253.254/24; };  // Only resolvers on the FX
                                           // subnet should be sending
                                           // recursive queries
};
```

allow-recursion's default is to provide recursion to any IP address.

Also, don't list a nonrecursive nameserver as a forwarder. When a nameserver is using another server as a forwarder, it forwards *recursive* queries to the forwarder. Use *allow-recursion* to permit just authorized nameservers to use your forwarder instead.

You *can* list a nonrecursive nameserver as one of the servers authoritative for your zone data (i.e., you can tell a parent nameserver to refer queries about your zone to this server). This works because nameservers send nonrecursive queries between themselves.

Avoiding a Bogus Nameserver

In your term as nameserver administrator, you might find some remote nameserver that responds with bad information—old, incorrect, badly formatted, or even deliberately deceptive. You can attempt to find an administrator to fix the problem. Or you can save yourself some grief and configure your nameserver not to ask questions of this server, which is possible with BIND 8, and BIND 9.1.0 and later. Here is the configuration file statement:

```
server 10.0.0.2 {
    bogus yes;
};
```

Of course, you fill in the correct IP address.

If you tell your nameserver to stop talking to a server that is the only server for a zone, don't expect to be able to look up names in that zone. Hopefully, there are other servers for that zone that can provide good information.

An even more potent way of shutting out a remote nameserver is to put it on your *blackhole* list. Your nameserver won't query nameservers on the list, *and* it won't

---

* In general. Of course, programs designed to send nonrecursive queries, or programs that can be configured to send nonrecursive queries, such as *nslookup* or *dig*, will still work.

respond to their queries.* *blackhole* is an *options* substatement that takes an address match list as an argument:

```
options {

    /* Don't waste your time trying to respond to queries from RFC 1918
       private addresses */

    blackhole {
        10/8;
        172.16/12;
        192.168/16;
    };
};
```

This prevents your nameserver from trying to respond to any queries it might receive from RFC 1918 private addresses. There are no routes on the Internet to these addresses, so trying to reply to them is a waste of CPU cycles and bandwidth.

The *blackhole* substatement is supported on BIND 8 versions after 8.2 and on BIND 9 after 9.1.0.

System Tuning

While for many nameservers BIND's default configuration values work just fine, yours may be one of those that need some further tuning. In this section, we discuss all the various dials and switches available to you to tune your nameserver.

Zone Transfers

Zone transfers can place a heavy load on a nameserver. Consequently, BIND has mechanisms for limiting the zone transfer load that your slave nameservers place on their master servers.

Limiting transfers requested per nameserver

On a slave nameserver, you can limit the number of zones the server requests from a single master nameserver. This will make the administrator of your master nameserver happy because his host won't be pounded for zone transfers if all the zones change—important if hundreds of zones are involved.

The config file statement is:

```
options {
    transfers-per-ns 2;
};
```

---

* And we really mean *won't respond*. Whereas queriers disallowed by an *allow-query* access control list get a response back indicating that their query was refused, queries on the *blackhole* list get nothing back. Nada.

In BIND 9, you can also set the limit on a server-by-server basis instead of globally. To do this, use the *transfers* substatement inside a *server* statement, where the server is the nameserver you'd like to specify the limit for:

```
server 192.168.1.2 {
    transfers 2;
};
```

This overrides any global limit set in the *options* statement. The default limit is two active zone transfers per master nameserver. That limit may seem small, but it works. Here's what happens: suppose your nameserver needs to load four zones from a master nameserver. Your nameserver starts transferring the first two zones and waits to transfer the third and fourth zones. After one of the first two zone transfers completes, the nameserver begins transferring the third zone. After another transfer completes, the nameserver starts transferring the fourth zone. The net result is the same as before when there were limits—all the zones are transferred—but the work is spread out.

When may you need to increase this limit? You might notice that it is taking too long to synch up with the master nameserver, and you know that the reason is the serializing of transfers—not just that the network between the hosts is slow. This probably matters only if you're maintaining hundreds or thousands of zones. You also need to make sure that the master nameserver and the networks in between can handle the additional workload of more simultaneous zone transfers.

Limiting the total number of zone transfers requested

The last limit dealt with the zone transfers requested from a single master nameserver. This limit deals with multiple master nameservers. BIND lets you limit the total number of zones your nameserver can request at any one time. The default limit is 10. As we explained previously, your nameserver pulls only two zones from any single master server by default. If your nameserver is transferring two zones from each of five master servers, your server has hit the limit and will postpone any further transfers until one of the current transfers finishes.

The BIND 8 and 9 *named.conf* file statement is:

```
options {
    transfers-in 10;
};
```

If your host or network cannot handle 10 active zone transfers, you should decrease this number. If you run a server that supports hundreds or thousands of zones, and your host and network can support the load, you might want to raise this limit. If you raise this limit, you may also need to raise the limit for the number of transfers per nameserver. (For example, if your nameserver loads from only four remote nameservers, and your nameserver will start only two transfers per remote nameserver, your server will have at most eight active zone transfers. Increasing the limit for the total number of zone transfers won't have any effect unless you also increase the per-nameserver limit.)

Limiting the total number of zone transfers served

BIND 9 nameservers can also limit the number of zone transfers they'll *serve* simultaneously. This is arguably more useful than limiting the number you'll request because without it you'd have to rely on the kindness of the administrators who run your slave nameservers not to overload your master server. Here's the BIND 9 statement:

```
options {
    transfers-out 10;
};
```

The default limit is 10.

Limiting the duration of a zone transfer

BIND also lets you limit the duration of an inbound zone transfer. By default, zone transfers are limited to 120 minutes, or 2 hours. The idea is that a zone transfer taking longer than 120 minutes is probably hung and won't complete, and the process is taking up resources unnecessarily. If you'd like a smaller or larger limit, perhaps because you know that your nameserver is a slave for a zone that normally takes more than 120 minutes to transfer, you can use this statement:

```
options {
    max-transfer-time-in 180;
};
```

You can even place a limit on transfers of a particular zone by using the *max-transfer-time-in* substatement inside a *zone* statement. For example, if you know that the *rinkydink.com* zone always takes a long time (say three hours) to transfer, either because of its size or because the links to the master nameserver are so slow, but you'd still like a shorter time limit (maybe an hour) on other zone transfers, you could use:

```
options {
    max-transfer-time-in 60;
};

zone "rinkydink.com" {
    type slave;
    file "bak.rinkydink.com";
    masters { 192.168.1.2; };
    max-transfer-time-in 180;
};
```

In BIND 9, there's also a *max-transfer-time-out* substatement that can be used the same way (either within an *options* statement or a *zone* statement). It controls how long an outbound zone transfer (i.e., a transfer to a slave) can run and has the same default value (120 minutes) as *max-transfer-time-in*.

BIND 9 nameservers even let you limit zone transfer idle time, the length of time since the zone transfer made any progress. The two configuration substatements, *max-transfer-idle-in* and *max-transfer-idle-out*, control how long an inbound and an outbound zone transfer can be idle, respectively. Like the transfer time limits, both can be used as either an *options* substatement or a *zone* substatement. The default limit on idle time is 60 minutes.

Limiting the frequency of zone transfers

It's possible to set a zone's refresh interval so low as to cause undue work for that zone's slave nameservers. For example, if your nameserver is a slave for thousands of zones, and the administrators of some of those zones set their refresh intervals to very small values, your nameserver may not be able to keep up with all the refreshing it needs to do. (If you run a nameserver that's a slave for that many zones, be sure to read the later section "Limiting SOA queries"; you may also need to tune the number of SOA queries allowed.) On the other hand, it's possible for an inexperienced administrator to set her zone's refresh interval so high as to cause prolonged inconsistencies between the zone's primary and slave nameservers.

BIND versions 9.1.0 and later let you limit the refresh interval with *max-refresh-time* and *min-refresh-time*. These substatements bracket the refresh value for all master, slave, and stub zones if used as an *options* substatement, or just for a particular zone if used as a *zone* substatement. Both take a number of seconds as an argument:

```
options {
    max-refresh-time 86400;    // refresh should never be more than a day
    min-refresh-time 1800;     // or less than 30 minutes
};
```

BIND 9.1.0 and later nameservers also let you limit the retry interval with the *max-retry-time* and *min-retry-time* substatements, which use the same syntax.

More efficient zone transfers

A zone transfer, as we said earlier, comprises many DNS messages sent end-to-end over a TCP connection. Traditional zone transfers put only a single resource record in each DNS message. That's a waste of space: you need a full header on each DNS message, even though you're carrying only a single record. It's like being the only person in a Chevy Suburban. A TCP-based DNS message can carry many more records: its maximum size is a whopping 64 KB!

BIND 8 and 9 nameservers understand a new zone transfer format, called *many-answers*. The *many-answers* format puts as many records as possible into a single DNS message. The result is that a *many-answers* zone transfer takes less bandwidth because there's less overhead and less CPU time because less time is spent unmarshaling DNS messages.

The *transfer-format* substatement controls which zone transfer format the nameserver uses for zones for which it is a master. That is, it determines the format of the zones that your nameserver transfers to its slaves. *transfer-format* is both an *options* substatement and a *server* substatement; as an *options* substatement, *transfer-format* controls the nameserver's global zone transfer format. BIND 8's default is to use the old *one-answer* zone transfer format for interoperability with BIND 4 nameservers. BIND 9's default is to use the *many-answers* format. The statement:

```
options {
    transfer-format many-answers;
};
```

configures the nameserver to use the *many-answers* format for zone transfers to all slave servers, unless a *server* statement such as the following explicitly says otherwise:

```
server 192.168.1.2 {
    transfer-format one-answer;
};
```

If you'd like to take advantage of the new, more efficient zone transfers, do one of the following:

- Set your nameserver's global zone transfer format to *many-answers* (or don't add one at all if you're running BIND 9) if most of your slaves run BIND 8, BIND 9, or the Microsoft DNS Server, which also understands the format.[*]

- Set your nameserver's global zone transfer format to *one-answer* if most of your slaves run BIND 4. Then use the *transfer-format server* substatement to adjust the global setting for exceptional servers.

Remember that if you run BIND 9, you'll need to add an explicit *server* statement for all BIND 4 slaves to change their transfer formats to *one-answer*.

Resource Limits

Sometimes you just want to tell the nameserver to stop being so greedy: don't use more than this much memory, don't open more than this many files. With BIND 8 and 9, you can impose many such limits.

Changing the data segment size limit

Some operating systems place a default limit on the amount of memory a process can use. If your OS ever prevents your nameserver from allocating additional memory, the server will panic or exit. Unless your nameserver handles an extremely large amount of data or the limit is very small, you won't run into this limit. But if you do,

---

[*] Beware older versions of the Microsoft DNS Server, which can't handle *many-answers* zone transfers that include DNS messages over 16 KB. If some of your slaves run this version, upgrade them or stick with the *one-answer* format until they're upgraded.

BIND 8 as well as BIND 9.1.0 and later nameservers have configuration options to change the system's default limit on data segment size. You might use these options to set a higher limit for *named* than the default system limit.

For both BIND 8 and 9, the statement is:

```
options {
    datasize size
};
```

size is an integer value, specified in bytes by default. You can specify a unit other than bytes by appending a character: k (kilobyte), m (megabyte), or g (gigabyte). For example, "64m" is 64 megabytes.

 Not all systems support increasing the data segment size for individual processes. If your system doesn't, the nameserver issues a *syslog* message at level LOG_WARNING to tell you that this feature is not implemented.

Changing the stack size limit

In addition to allowing you to change the limit on the size of the nameserver's data segment, BIND 8 and BIND 9.1.0 and later nameservers let you adjust the limit the system places on the amount of memory the *named* process's stack can use. Here's the syntax:

```
options {
    stacksize size;
};
```

where *size* is specified as in *datasize*. Like *datasize*, this feature works only on systems that permit a process to modify the stack size limit.

Changing the core size limit

If you don't appreciate *named*'s leaving huge core files lying around on your filesystem, you can at least make them smaller using *coresize*. Conversely, if *named* hasn't been able to dump an entire core file because of a tight operating system limit, you may be able to raise that limit with *coresize*.

coresize's syntax is:

```
options {
    coresize size;
};
```

Again, as with *datasize*, this feature works only on operating systems that let processes modify the limit on core file size and doesn't work on versions of BIND 9 before 9.1.0.

Changing the open files limit

If your nameserver is authoritative for a lot of zones, the *named* process opens lots of files when it starts up—one per authoritative zone, assuming you use backup zone datafiles with the zones you're a slave for. Likewise, if the host running your nameserver has lots of virtual network interfaces,* *named* requires one file descriptor per interface. Most Unix operating systems place a limit on the number of files any process can open concurrently. If your nameserver tries to open more files than this limit permits, you'll see this message in your *syslog* output:

```
named[pid]: socket(SOCK_RAW): Too many open files
```

If your operating system also permits changing that limit on a per-process basis, you can increase it using BIND's *files* substatement:

```
options {
    files number;
};
```

The default is *unlimited* (which is also a valid value), although this just means that the nameserver doesn't place a limit on the number of concurrently open files; the operating system may, however. And though we know you're sick of our saying it, BIND 9 doesn't support this until 9.1.0.

Limiting the number of clients

BIND 9 lets you restrict the number of clients your nameserver can serve concurrently. You can apply a limit to the number of recursive clients (resolvers plus nameservers using your nameserver as a forwarder) with the *recursive-clients* substatement:

```
options {
    recursive-clients 5000;
};
```

The default limit is 1000. If you find your nameserver refusing recursive queries and logging, as shown by an error message like this one:

```
Sep 22 02:26:11 toystory named[13979]: client 192.249.249.151#1677: no more
recursive clients: quota reached
```

you may want to increase the limit. Conversely, if you find your nameserver struggling to keep up with the deluge of recursive queries it receives, you can lower the limit.

You can also apply a limit to the number of concurrent TCP connections your nameserver will process (for zone transfers and TCP-based queries) with the *tcp-clients* substatement. TCP connections consume considerably more resources than UDP

---

* Chapter 14 describes better solutions to the "too many open files" problem than bumping up the limit on files.

because the host needs to track the state of the TCP connection. The default limit is 100.

Limiting SOA queries

BIND 8.2.2 and later nameservers let you limit the number of outstanding SOA queries your nameserver allows. If your nameserver is a slave for thousands of zones, it may have many queries for the SOA records of those zones pending at any one time. Tracking each query requires a small but finite amount of memory, so, by default, BIND 8 nameservers limit outstanding SOA queries to four. If you find that your nameserver can't keep up with its duties as a slave, you may need to raise the limit with the *serial-queries* substatement:

```
options {
    serial-queries 1000;
};
```

serial-queries is obsolete in BIND 9. BIND 9 limits the rate at which serial queries are sent (to 20 per second), not the number of outstanding queries. This limit can be adjusted with the *serial-query-rate options* substatement, which takes an integer (number of queries per second) as an argument.

Maintenance Intervals

BIND nameservers have always done periodic housekeeping, such as refreshing zones for which the server is a slave. With BIND 8 and 9, you can control how often these chores happen or whether they happen at all.

Cleaning interval

All nameservers passively remove stale entries from the cache. Before a nameserver returns a record to a querier, it checks to see whether the TTL on that record has expired. If it has, the nameserver starts the resolution process to find more current data. However, relying entirely on this mechanism can result in an unnecessarily large cache. A nameserver may cache a lot of records in a flurry of name resolution and then just let those records spoil in the cache, taking up valuable memory even though the records are stale.

To deal with this, BIND nameservers actively walk through the cache and remove stale records once per cleaning interval. This helps minimize the amount of memory used by the cache. On the other hand, the cleaning process takes CPU time, and on very slow or very busy nameservers, you may not want it running often.

By default, the cleaning interval is 60 minutes. You can tune the interval with the *cleaning-interval* substatement to the *options* statement. For example:

```
options {
    cleaning-interval 120;
};
```

sets the cleaning interval to 120 minutes. To turn off cache cleaning entirely, set the cleaning interval to 0.

Interface interval

We've said already that BIND, by default, listens on all of a host's network interfaces. BIND 8 and 9 nameservers are actually smart enough to notice when a network interface on the host they're running on comes up or goes down. To do this, they periodically scan the host's network interfaces. This happens once each interface interval, which is 60 minutes by default. If you know that the host your nameserver runs on has no dynamic network interfaces, you can disable scanning for new interfaces to avoid the unnecessary hourly overhead by setting the interface interval to 0:

```
options {
    interface-interval 0;
};
```

On the other hand, if your host brings up or tears down network interfaces more often than every hour, you may want to reduce the interval.

Statistics interval

Okay, adjusting the statistics interval—the frequency with which the BIND 8 nameserver dumps statistics to the statistics file—won't have much effect on performance. But it fits better here, with the other maintenance intervals, than anywhere else in the book.

The syntax of the *statistics-interval* substatement is exactly analogous to the other maintenance intervals:

```
options {
    statistics-interval 60;
};
```

And as with the other maintenance intervals, the default is 60 minutes, and a setting of 0 disables the periodic dumping of statistics. Because BIND 9 doesn't write statistics to *syslog*, it doesn't have a configurable statistics interval.

TTLs

Internally, BIND trims TTL values on cached records to reasonable values. BIND 8 and 9 nameservers make the limits configurable.

In BIND 8.2 or later and all BIND 9 nameservers, you can limit the TTL on cached negative information with the *max-ncache-ttl options* substatement. This was designed as a safety net for people who upgraded to 8.2 and its new negative caching scheme (RFC 2308 and all that, described in Chapter 4). This new nameserver caches negative information according to the last field of the zone's SOA record, and many zone admins still use that field for the default TTL for the zone—probably much too long for negative information. So a prudent nameserver administrator can use a substatement such as:

```
options {
    max-ncache-ttl 3600;   // 3600 seconds is one hour
};
```

to trim larger negative caching TTLs to one hour. The default is 10,800 seconds (3 hours). Without this precaution, it's possible that someone looking up a brand-new record could get a negative answer (maybe because the new record hadn't yet reached the zone's slaves), and her nameserver would cache that answer for an inordinately long time, rendering the record unresolvable.

BIND 9 nameservers also let you configure the upper limit of the TTL on cached records with the *max-cache-ttl* substatement. The default is one week. BIND 8 nameservers trim TTLs to one week, too, but they don't let you configure the limit.

Finally, there's what's referred to as the *lame TTL*, which isn't really a TTL at all. Instead, it's the amount of time your nameserver remembers that a given remote nameserver isn't authoritative for a zone that's delegated to it. This prevents your nameserver from wasting valuable time and resources asking that nameserver for information about a domain name it knows nothing about. BIND 8 nameservers after 8.2 and BIND 9 nameservers newer than 9.1.0 let you tune the lame TTL with the *lame-ttl options* substatement. The default lame TTL is 600 seconds (10 minutes), with a maximum of 30 minutes. You can even turn off the caching of lame nameservers with a value of 0, though that strikes us as a Very Bad Thing.

Compatibility

Now, to wrap things up, we'll cover some configuration substatements related to your nameserver's compatibility with resolvers and other nameservers.

The *rfc2308-type1* substatement controls the format of the negative answers your nameserver sends. By default, BIND 8 and 9 nameservers include only the SOA record in a negative response from a zone. Another legitimate format for that response includes the zone's NS records, too, but some older nameservers misinterpret such a response as a referral. If for some odd reason (odd because we can't think of one) you want to send those NS records as well, use:

```
options {
    rfc2308-type1 yes;
};
```

rfc2308-type1 is first supported in BIND 8.2; BIND 9 doesn't support it.

Older nameservers can also cause problems when you send them cached negative responses. Before the days of negative caching, all negative responses were, naturally, authoritative. But some nameserver implementers added a check to their servers:

they'd accept only authoritative negative responses. Then, with the advent of negative caching, negative responses could be nonauthoritative. Oops!

The *auth-nxdomain options* substatement lets your nameserver falsely claim that a negative answer from its cache is actually authoritative, just so one of these older nameservers will believe it. By default, BIND 8 nameservers have *auth-nxdomain* on (set to yes); BIND 9 nameservers turn it off by default.

When some adventurous souls ported BIND 8.2.2 to Windows NT, they found they needed the nameserver to treat a carriage return and a newline at the end of a line (Windows' end-of-line sequence) the same way it treated just a newline (Unix's end-of-line). For that behavior, use:

```
options {
    treat-cr-as-space yes;
};
```

BIND 9 ignores this option because it always treats a carriage return and a newline the same way as a newline by itself.

Finally, if you run a BIND nameserver that's configured as a slave to Microsoft DNS Servers with Active Directory–integrated zones, you may see an error message in *syslog* informing you that the zones' serial numbers have decreased. This is a side effect of the replication mechanism Active Directory uses and isn't cause for alarm. If you want to squelch the message, you can use BIND 9.3.0's new *multi-master zone* substatement to tell your slave that the IP addresses in the *masters* substatement actually belong to multiple nameservers, not to multiple interfaces on a single nameserver:

```
zone "_msdcs.domain.com" {
    type slave;
    masters { 10.0.0.2; 10.0.0.3; };
    file "bak._msdcs.domain.com";
    multi-master yes;
};
```

The ABCs of IPv6 Addressing

Before we cover the next two topics, which include how domain names map to IPv6 addresses and vice versa, we'd better describe the representation and structure of IPv6 addresses. As you probably know, IPv6 addresses are 128 bits long. The preferred representation of an IPv6 address is eight groups of as many as four hexadecimal digits, separated by colons; for example:

```
2001:db80:0123:4567:89ab:cdef:0123:4567
```

The first group of hex digits (2001, in this example) represents the most significant (or highest-order) 16 bits of the address.

Groups of digits that begin with one or more zeros don't need to be padded to four places, so you can also write the previous address as:

```
2001:db80:123:4567:89ab:cdef:123:4567
```

Each group must contain at least one digit, though, unless you're using the :: notation. The :: notation allows you to compress sequential groups of zeros. This comes in handy when you're specifying just an IPv6 prefix. For example:

```
2001:db80:dead:beef::
```

specifies the first 64 bits of an IPv6 address as *2001:db80:dead:beef* and the remaining 64 as zeros.

You can also use :: at the beginning of an IPv6 address to specify a suffix. For example, the IPv6 loopback address is commonly written as:

```
::1
```

or 127 zeros followed by a single one. You can even use :: in the middle of an address as a shorthand for contiguous groups of zeros:

```
2001:db80:dead:beef::1
```

You can use the :: shorthand only once in an address, since more than one could be ambiguous.

IPv6 prefixes are specified in a format similar to IPv4's CIDR notation. As many bits of the prefix as are significant are expressed in the standard IPv6 notation, followed by a slash and a decimal count of exactly how many significant bits there are. So the following three prefix specifications are equivalent (though obviously not equivalently terse):

```
2001:db80:dead:beef:0000:00f1:0000:0000/96
2001:db80:dead:beef:0:f1:0:0/96
2001:db80:dead:beef:0:f1::/96
```

The IPv6 equivalent of an IPv4 network number is called a *global routing prefix*. These are a variable number of high-order bits of the IPv6 address used to identify a particular network. All global unicast addresses have global routing prefixes that begin with the binary value 001. These are assigned by address registries or Internet service providers. The global routing prefix itself may be hierarchical, with an address registry responsible for allocating lower-order bits to various ISPs, and ISPs responsible for allocating the lowest-order bits of the prefix to its customers.

After the global routing prefix, IPv6 addresses may contain another variable number of bits that identify the particular subnet within a network, called the *subnet ID*. The remaining bits of the address identify a particular network interface and are referred to as the *interface ID*.

Here's a diagram from RFC 3513 that shows how these parts fit together:

```
|        n bits        |  m bits  |      128-n-m bits        |
+----------------------+----------+--------------------------+
| global routing prefix | subnet ID |      interface ID        |
+----------------------+----------+--------------------------+
```

According to RFC 3177, which recommends how IPv6 addresses should be allo-cated to sites:

- Home network subscribers should receive a /48 prefix.
- Small and large enterprises should receive a /48 prefix.
- Very large subscribers could receive a /47 or slightly shorter prefix.

Addresses and Ports

Since IPv4 is relatively simple compared to IPv6, let's cover the nameserver's IPv4 con-figuration together with IPv6. BIND 8.4.0 and later and all BIND 9 nameservers can use both IPv4 and IPv6 as a transport; that is, they can send and receive queries and responses over IPv4 and IPv6. Both nameservers also support similar substatements to configure which network interfaces and ports they listen on and send queries from.

Configuring the IPv4 Transport

You can specify which network interface your BIND 8 or BIND 9 nameserver listens on for queries using the *listen-on* substatement. In its simplest form, *listen-on* takes an address match list as an argument:

```
options {
    listen-on { 192.249.249/24; };
};
```

The nameserver listens on any of the local host's network interfaces whose addresses match the address match list. To specify an alternate port (one other than 53) to lis-ten on, use the *port* modifier:

```
options {
    listen-on port 5353 { 192.249.249/24; };
};
```

In BIND 9, you can even specify a different port for each network interface:

```
options {
    listen-on { 192.249.249.1 port 5353; 192.253.253.1 port 1053; };
};
```

Note that there's no way to configure most resolvers to query a nameserver on an alter-nate port, so this nameserver might not be as useful as you'd think. Still, it can serve zone transfers because you can specify an alternate port in a *masters* substatement:

```
zone "movie.edu" {
    type slave;
```

```
        masters port 5353 { 192.249.249.1; };
        file "bak.movie.edu";
};
```

Or, if your BIND 9 nameserver has multiple master nameservers, each listening on a different port, you can use something like:

```
zone "movie.edu" {
    type slave;
    masters { 192.249.249.1 port 5353; 192.253.253.1 port 1053; };
    file "bak.movie.edu";
};
```

BIND 9 even allows you to send your NOTIFY messages to alternate ports. To tell your master nameserver to notify all its slave nameservers on the same oddball port, use:

```
also-notify port 5353 { 192.249.249.9; 192.253.253.9; }; // zardoz's two addresses
```

To notify each on a different port, use:

```
also-notify { 192.249.249.9 port 5353; 192.249.249.1 port 1053; };
```

If your slave nameserver needs to use a particular local network interface to send queries—perhaps because one of its master nameservers recognizes it by only one of its many addresses—use the *query-source* substatement:

```
options {
    query-source address 192.249.249.1;
};
```

Note that the argument isn't an address match list; it's a single IP address. You can also specify a particular source port to use for queries:

```
options {
    query-source address 192.249.249.1 port 53;
};
```

BIND's default behavior is to use whichever network interface the route to the destination points out and a random, unprivileged port, i.e.:

```
options {
    query-source address * port *;
};
```

Note that *query-source* applies only to UDP-based queries; TCP-based queries always choose the source address according to the routing table and use a random source port.

There's an analogous *transfer-source* substatement that controls the source address to use for zone transfers. In BIND 9, it also applies to a slave nameserver's SOA queries and to forwarded dynamic updates:

```
options {
    transfer-source 192.249.249.1;
};
```

As with *query-source*, the argument is just a single IP address, but with no *address* keyword. With BIND 8, there's no *port* modifier. With BIND 9, you can specify a source port:

```
options {
    transfer-source 192.249.249.1 port 1053;
};
```

However, that source port applies only to UDP-based traffic (i.e., SOA queries and forwarded dynamic updates).

transfer-source can also be used as a *zone* substatement, in which case it applies only to transfers (and, for BIND 9, SOA queries and dynamic updates) of that zone:

```
zone "movie.edu" {
    type slave;
    masters { 192.249.249.3; };
    file "bak.movie.edu";
    transfer-source 192.249.249.1; // always use IP address on same network
                                    // for transfers of movie.edu
};
```

Finally, as of BIND 9.1.0, there's even a substatement that lets you control which address you send NOTIFY messages from, called *notify-source*. This comes in handy with multihomed nameservers because, by default, slaves accept only NOTIFY messages for a zone from IP addresses in that zone's *masters* substatement. *notify-source*'s syntax is similar to the syntax of the other *-source* substatements; for example:

```
options {
    notify-source 192.249.249.1;
};
```

As with *transfer-source*, *notify-source* can specify a source port and can be used as a *zone* statement to apply only to that zone:

```
zone "movie.edu" {
    type slave;
    masters { 192.249.249.3; };
    file "bak.movie.edu";
    notify-source 192.249.249.1 port 5353;
};
```

If you can't control the IP address from which NOTIFY messages are sent (because you don't administer the master server, for example), you can either include all the master's IP addresses in your zone's *masters* substatement, or you can use the *allow-notify* substatement to explicitly permit NOTIFY messages from addresses not listed in *masters*.

Configuring the IPv6 Transport

By default, a BIND 9 nameserver won't listen for IPv6-based queries. To configure it to listen on the local host's IPv6 network interfaces, use the *listen-on-v6* substatement:

```
options {
    listen-on-v6 { any; };
};
```

Before BIND 9.3.0, the *listen-on-v6* substatement accepted only *any* and *none* as arguments. You can also configure a BIND nameserver to listen on an alternate port—or even multiple ports—with the *port* modifier:

```
options {
    listen-on-v6 port 1053 { any; };
};
```

To listen on more than one IPv6 interface or port, use multiple *listen-on-v6* substatements. The default port is, of course, 53.

You can also determine which IPv6 address your nameserver uses as the source address for outgoing queries with the *transfer-source-v6* substatement, as in:

```
options {
    transfer-source-v6 222:10:2521:1:210:4bff:fe10:d24;
};
```

or, also specifying a source port:

```
options {
    transfer-source-v6 222:10:2521:1:210:4bff:fe10:d24 port 53;
};
```

Only BIND 9 supports setting the source port, as in the second example. The default is to use the source address corresponding to whichever network interface the route points out and a random, unprivileged source port. As with *transfer-source*, you can use *transfer-source-v6* as a *zone* substatement. And the source port applies only to SOA queries and forwarded dynamic updates.

Finally, BIND 9.1.0 and later let you determine which IPv6 address to use in NOTIFY messages, à la the *notify-source* substatement. The IPv6 substatement is called, not surprisingly, *notify-source-v6*:

```
options {
    notify-source-v6 222:10:2521:1:210:4bff:fe10:d24;
};
```

As with *transfer-source-v6*, you can specify a source port and use the substatement in a *zone* statement.

EDNS0

UDP-based DNS messages have traditionally been limited to 512 bytes. This limit was instituted to prevent fragmentation, which in the early days of the Internet was costly and unreliable. Times have changed, though, and most paths on the Internet can accommodate much larger UDP datagrams.

Thanks to new developments in DNS, such as DNSSEC and IPv6 support, the average response is getting larger. Responses from signed zones, in particular, can easily exceed the 512-byte limit, which can cause costly retries over TCP.

The Extension Mechanisms for DNS, version 0, referred to as EDNS0, introduces a simple signaling system to DNS. Using this system, a resolver or nameserver can tell another nameserver that it can handle a DNS message larger than 512 bytes. (In fact, the sender can signal other capabilities, too, as we'll see in the next chapter.)

BIND nameservers have supported EDNS0 since versions 9.0.0 and 8.3.0. These nameservers send EDNS0 signaling information by default, and try to negotiate a UDP-based DNS message size of 4,096 bytes. If they receive a response that indicates that the nameserver they're talking to doesn't understand EDNS0, they'll fall back to using messages that adhere to the old 512-byte limit.

This technique generally works well, but occasionally you'll run across a nameserver that reacts badly to EDNS0 probes. To cope with these nameservers, you can use the new *edns server* substatement to turn off EDNS0 for that nameserver:

```
server 10.0.0.1 {
    edns no;
};
```

This is supported in BIND 9.2.0 and later and BIND 8.3.2 and later nameservers.

BIND 9.3.0 and later and 8.4.0 and later also allow you to configure the size of the UDP-based DNS messages your nameserver will negotiate with the *edns-udp-size* *options* substatment:

```
options {
    directory "/var/named";
    edns-udp-size 512;
};
```

This can be useful if your firewall doesn't understand that DNS messages can exceed 512 bytes in size and keeps dropping legitimate messages. (Of course, we think you should upgrade your firewall, but you may need to resort to this in the interim.) The maximum value for *edns-udp-size* is 4096; the minimum is 512.

IPv6 Forward and Reverse Mapping

Clearly, the existing A record won't accommodate IPv6's 128-bit addresses; BIND expects an A record's record-specific data to be a 32-bit address in dotted-octet format.

The IETF came up with a simple solution to this problem, described in RFC 1886. A new address record, AAAA, was used to store a 128-bit IPv6 address, and a new IPv6 reverse-mapping domain, *ip6.int*, was introduced. This solution was straightforward enough to implement in BIND 4. Unfortunately, not everyone liked the simple solution, so it came up with a much more complicated one. This solution, which we'll describe shortly, involved the new A6 and DNAME records and required a complete overhaul of the BIND nameserver to implement. Then, after much acrimonious debate, the IETF decided that the new A6/DNAME scheme required too much overhead, was prone to failure, and was of unproven usefulness. At least temporarily, it moved the RFC that describes A6 records off the IETF standards track to experimental status, deprecated the use of DNAME records in reverse-mapping zones, and trotted old RFC 1886 back out. Everything old is new again.

For now, the AAAA record is the way to handle IPv6 forward mapping. The use of *ip6.int* is deprecated, however, mostly for political reasons; it's been replaced by *ip6.arpa*. In the interest of preparing you for all possible futures, including one in which A6 and DNAME make a dramatic comeback, we'll cover both methods.

AAAA and ip6.arpa

The easy way to handle IPv6 forward mapping, described in RFC 1886, is with an address record that's four times as long as an A record. That's the AAAA (pronounced "quad A") record. The AAAA record takes as its record-specific data the textual format of an IPv6 address, as described earlier. So, for example, you'd see AAAA records like this one:

```
ipv6-host    IN    AAAA    2001:db80:1:2:3:4:567:89ab
```

RFC 1886 also established *ip6.int*, now replaced by *ip6.arpa*, a new reverse-mapping namespace for IPv6 addresses. Each level of subdomain under *ip6.arpa* represents four bits of the 128-bit address, encoded as a hexadecimal digit just like in the record-specific data of the AAAA record. The least significant (lowest-order) bits appear at the far left of the domain name. Unlike the format of addresses in AAAA records, omitting leading zeros is not allowed, so there are always 32 hexadecimal digits and 32 levels of subdomain below *ip6.arpa* in a domain name corresponding to a full IPv6 address. The domain name that corresponds to the address in the previous example is:

```
b.a.9.8.7.6.5.0.4.0.0.0.3.0.0.0.2.0.0.0.1.0.0.0.0.8.b.d.1.0.0.2.ip6.arpa.
```

These domain names have PTR records attached, just as the domain names under *in-addr.arpa* do:

```
b.a.9.8.7.6.5.0.4.0.0.0.3.0.0.0.2.0.0.0.1.0.0.0.0.8.b.d.1.0.0.2.ip6.arpa.  IN  PTR
mash.ip6.movie.edu.
```

A6, DNAMEs, Bitstring Labels, and ip6.arpa

That's the easy way. The more difficult—and now only experimental—way of handling IPv6 forward and reverse mapping uses two new record types, A6 and DNAME records. A6 and DNAME records are described in RFCs 2874 and 2672, respectively. Version 9.0.0 was the first version of BIND to support these records.

There's no guarantee that this method of doing IPv6 forward and reverse mapping will ever reemerge as the standard, and the latest versions of BIND don't even support it fully. You may be wasting your time in reading this section, just as we may have wasted our time in writing it. We're leaving it here because fashion is cyclical, and A6 and friends may yet make a comeback.

If you want to experiment with A6 and bitstring labels, dig out a BIND 9.2.x nameserver. The ISC removed support for bitstring labels in 9.3.0, and advises that A6 is "no longer fully supported." Also, note that bitstring labels can also cause interoperability problems with some DNS software.

The main reason a replacement for the AAAA record and *ip6.int* reverse-mapping scheme was sought was because they make network renumbering difficult. For example, if an organization were to change ISPs, it would have to change all the AAAA records in its zone datafiles because some of the bits of an IPv6 address are an identifier for the ISP.* Or imagine an ISP changing address registries: this would wreak havoc with its customers' zone data.

A6 records and forward mapping

To make renumbering easier, A6 records can specify only a part of an IPv6 address, such as the last 64 bits (maybe the interface ID) assigned to a host's network interface, and then refer to the remainder of the address by a symbolic domain name. This allows zone administrators to specify only the part of the address under their control. To build an entire address, a resolver or nameserver must follow the chain of A6 records from a host's domain name to the address registry's ID. And that chain may branch if a site network is connected to multiple ISPs or if an ISP is connected to multiple address registries.

For example, the A6 record:

```
$ORIGIN movie.edu.
drunkenmaster  IN   A6   64   ::0210:4bff:fe10:0d24  subnet1.v6.movie.edu.
```

---

* And, of course, the new ISP might use a different address registry, which would mean more bits to change.

specifies the final 64 bits of *drunkenmaster.movie.edu*'s IPv6 address (64 is the number of bits of the prefix *not* specified in this A6 record) and that the remaining 64 bits can be found by looking up an A6 record at *subnet1.v6.movie.edu*.

subnet1.v6.movie.edu, in turn, specifies the last 16 bits of the 64-bit prefix (the subnet ID) that we didn't specify in *drunkenmaster.movie.edu*'s A6 address, as well as the domain name of the next A6 record to look up:

```
$ORIGIN v6.movie.edu.
subnet1  IN  A6  48  0:0:0:1::  movie-u.isp-a.net.
subnet1  IN  A6  48  0:0:0:1::  movie.isp-b.net.
```

The first 48 bits of the prefix in *subnet1.v6.movie.edu*'s record-specific data are set to 0 because they're not significant here.

In fact, these records tell us to look up *two* A6 records next, one at *movie-u.isp-a.net* and one at *movie.isp-b.net*. That's because Movie U. has connections to two ISPs, ISP A and ISP B. In ISP A's zone, we might find:

```
$ORIGIN isp-a.net.
movie-u  IN  A6   40  0:0:21::  isp-a.rir-1.net.
```

indicating an eight-bit pattern within the global routing prefix field set by ISP A for the Movie U. network. (Remember, the global routing prefix field can be hierarchical, too, comprising both an identifier for our ISP assigned to it by its address registry *and* our ISP's identifier for our network.) Since the ISP assigns some bits of the global routing prefix to us but has the rest of the prefix assigned by its address registry, we'd expect to see only our bits in our ISP's zone data. The remainder of the prefix appears in an A6 record in its address registry's zone.

In ISP B's zone, we might find the following record showing us the bits that ISP assigns for our network:

```
$ORIGIN isp-b.net.
movie  IN  A6  40  0:0:42::  isp-b.rir-2.net.
```

In the address registries' zones, we might find the next four bits of the IPv6 address:

```
$ORIGIN rir-1.net.
isp-a  IN  A6  36  0:0:0500::  rir-2.top-level-v6.net.
```

and:

```
$ORIGIN rir-2.net.
isp-b  IN  A6  36  0:0:0600::  rir-1.top-level-v6.net.
```

Finally, in the top-level IPv6 address registry's zone, we might find these records showing us the bits of the prefix assigned to RIR 1 and RIR 2:

```
$ORIGIN top-level-v6.net.
rir-1  IN  A6  0  2001:db80::2
rir-2  IN  A6  0  2001:db80::6
```

By following this chain of A6 records, a nameserver can assemble all 128 bits of *drunkenmaster.movie.edu*'s two IPv6 addresses. These turn out to be:

```
2001:db80:2521:1:210:4bff:fe10:d24
2001:db80:6642:1:210:4bff:fe10:d24
```

The first of these uses a route through RIR 1 and ISP A to the Movie U. network, and the second uses a route through RIR 2 and ISP B. (We're connected to two ISPs for redundancy.) Note that if RIR 1 changes its prefix assignment for ISP A, it needs to change only the A6 record for *isp-a.rir-1.net* in its zone data; the change "cascades" into all A6 chains that go through ISP A. This makes the management of addressing on IPv6 networks very convenient and makes changing ISPs easy, too.

You can probably already see some of the potential problems with A6 records. Resolving a domain name to a single IPv6 address may require several independent queries (to look up A6 records for an RIR's domain name, an ISP's domain name, and so on). Completing all of those queries may take many times longer than resolving a domain name's single AAAA record, and if any one of the "subresolutions" fails, the overall resolution process fails.

 If a nameserver appears in an NS record and owns one or more A6 records, those A6 records should specify all 128 bits of the IPv6 address. This helps avoid deadlock problems, in which a resolver or nameserver needs to talk to a remote nameserver to resolve part of that nameserver's IPv6 address.

DNAME records and reverse mapping

Now that you've seen how forward mapping works with A6 records, let's look at how reverse-mapping IPv6 addresses works. As with A6 records, unfortunately, this isn't nearly as simple as *ip6.arpa*.

Reverse-mapping IPv6 addresses involves DNAME records, described in RFC 2672, and bitstring labels, introduced in RFC 2673. DNAME records are a little like wildcard CNAME records. They're used to substitute one suffix of a domain name with another. For example, if we previously used the domain name *movieu.edu* at Movie U. but have since changed to *movie.edu*, we can replace the old *movieu.edu* zone with this one:

```
$TTL 1d
@   IN  SOA     toystory.movie.edu.  root.movie.edu. (
    2000102300
    3h
    30m
    30d
    1h  )
```

```
IN  NS    toystory.movie.edu.
IN  NS    wormhole.movie.edu.

IN  MX    10 postmanrings2x.movie.edu.

IN  DNAME  movie.edu.
```

The DNAME record in the *movieu.edu* zone applies to any domain name that ends in *movieu.edu* except *movieu.edu* itself. Unlike the CNAME record, the DNAME record can coexist with other record types owned by the same domain name as long as they aren't CNAME or other DNAME records. The owner of the DNAME record may not have any subdomains, though.

When the *movieu.edu* nameserver receives a query for any domain name that ends in *movieu.edu*, say *cuckoosnest.movieu.edu*, the DNAME record tells it to "synthesize" an alias from *cuckoosnest.movieu.edu* to *cuckoosnest.movie.edu*, replacing *movieu.edu* with *movie.edu*:

```
cuckoosnest.movieu.edu.  IN  CNAME  cuckoosnest.movie.edu.
```

It's a little like *sed*'s "s" (substitute) command. The *movieu.edu* nameserver replies with this CNAME record. If it's responding to a newer nameserver, it also sends the DNAME record in the response, and the recipient nameserver can then synthesize its own CNAME records from the cached DNAME.

Bitstring labels are the other half of the magic involved in IPv6 reverse mapping. Bitstring labels are simply a compact way to represent a long sequence of binary (i.e., one-bit) labels in a domain name. Say you want to permit delegation between any two bits of an IP address. This might compel you to represent each bit of the address as a label in a domain name. But that would require over 128 labels for a domain name that represented an IPv6 address! Oy! That exceeds the limit on the number of labels in a normal domain name!

Bitstring labels concatenate the bits in successive labels into a shorter hexadecimal, octal, binary, or dotted-octet string. The string is encapsulated between the tokens "\[" and "]" to distinguish it from a traditional label, and begins with one letter that determines the base of the string: *b* for binary, *o* for octal, and *x* for hexadecimal.

Here are the bitstring labels that correspond to *drunkenmaster.movie.edu*'s two IPv6 addresses:

```
\[x2001db802521000102104bfffe100d24]
\[x2001db806642000102104bfffe100d24]
```

Notice that the most significant bit begins the string, as in the text representation of an IPv6 address, but in the opposite order of the labels in the *in-addr.arpa* domain. Despite this, these two bitstring labels are simply a different encoding of traditional domain names that begin:

```
0.0.1.0.0.1.0.0.1.0.1.1.0.0.0.0.0.0.0.0.1.0.0.0.0.1.1.1.1.1.1.1...
```

Also note that all 32 hex digits in the address are present; you can't drop leading zeros, because there are no colons to separate groups of four digits.

Bitstring labels can also represent parts of IPv6 addresses, in which case you need to specify the number of significant bits in the string, separated from the string by a slash. So RIR 1's portion of the global routing prefix is \[x2001db802/36].

Together, DNAMEs and bitstring labels are used to match portions of a long domain name that encode an IPv6 address and to iteratively change the domain name looked up to a domain name in a zone under the control of the organization that manages the host with that IPv6 address.

Imagine we're reverse-mapping \[x2001db806642000102104bfffe100d24].ip6.arpa, the domain name that corresponds to *drunkenmaster.movie.edu*'s network interface (when reached through RIR 2 and ISP B). The root nameservers would probably refer our nameserver to the *ip6.arpa* nameservers, which contain these records:

```
$ORIGIN ip6.arpa.
\[x2001db802/36]   IN   DNAME    ip6.rir-1.net.
\[x2001db806/36]   IN   DNAME    ip6.rir-2.net.
```

The second of these matches the beginning of the domain name we're looking up, so the *ip6.arpa* nameservers reply to our nameserver with an alias that says:

```
\[x2001db806642000102104bfffe100d24].ip6.arpa.  IN  CNAME
\[x642000102104bfffe100d24].ip6.rir-2.net.
```

Notice that the first nine hex digits (the most significant 36 bits) of the address are stripped off, and the end of the target of the alias is now *ip6.rir-2.net*, since we know this address belongs to RIR 2. In *ip6.rir-2.net*, we find:

```
$ORIGIN ip6.rir-2.net.
\[x6/4]  IN   DNAME    ip6.isp-b.net.
```

This turns the domain name in our new query:

```
\[x642000102104bfffe100d24].ip6.rir-2.net
```

into:

```
\[x42000102104bfffe100d24].ip6.isp-b.net
```

Next, our nameserver queries the *ip6.isp-b.net* nameservers for the new domain name. This record in the *ip6.isp-b.net* zone:

```
$ORIGIN ip6.isp-b.net.
\[x42/8]   IN   DNAME    ip6.movie.edu.
```

turns the domain name we're looking up into:

```
\[x000102104bfffe100d24].ip6.movie.edu
```

The *ip6.movie.edu* zone, finally, contains the PTR record that gives us the domain name of the host we're after:

```
$ORIGIN ip6.movie.edu.
\[x000102104bfffe100d24/80] IN   PTR   drunkenmaster.ip6.movie.edu.
```

(Though we could have used another DNAME just for subnet1, we didn't.)

Mercifully, as a zone administrator you'll probably only be responsible for maintaining PTR records like the ones in *ip6.movie.edu*. Even if you work for an RIR or ISP, creating DNAME records that extract the appropriate bits of the global routing prefix from your customers' addresses isn't too tough. And you gain the convenience of using a single zone datafile for your reverse-mapping information, even though each of your hosts has multiple addresses and can switch ISPs without changing all of your zone datafiles.

CHAPTER 11
Security

*"I hope you've got your hair well fastened on?" he
continued, as they set off.*

"Only in the usual way," Alice said, smiling.

*"That's hardly enough," he said, anxiously. "You see
the wind is so very strong here. It's as strong as soup."*

*"Have you invented a plan for keeping the hair from
being blown off?" Alice enquired.*

*"Not yet," said the Knight. "But I've got a plan for
keeping it from falling off."*

Why should you care about DNS security? Why go to the trouble of securing a service that mostly maps names to addresses? Let us tell you a story.

In July 1997, during two periods of several days, users around the Internet who typed *www.internic.net* into their web browsers thinking they were going to the InterNIC's web site instead ended up at a web site belonging to the AlterNIC. (The AlterNIC runs an alternate set of root nameservers that delegate to additional top-level domains with names like *med* and *porn*.) How'd it happen? Eugene Kashpureff, then affiliated with the AlterNIC, had run a program to "poison" the caches of major nameservers around the world, making them believe that *www.internic.net*'s address was actually the address of the AlterNIC web server.

Kashpureff hadn't made any attempt to disguise what he had done; the web site that users reached was plainly the AlterNIC's, not the InterNIC's. But imagine someone poisoning your nameserver's cache to direct *www.amazon.com* or *www.wellsfargo.com* to his own web server, conveniently located well outside local law enforcement jurisdiction. Further, imagine your users typing in their credit card numbers and expiration dates. Now you get the idea.

Protecting your users against these kinds of attacks requires DNS security. DNS security comes in several flavors. You can secure transactions—the queries, responses, and other messages your nameserver sends and receives. You can secure your nameserver, refusing queries, zone transfer requests, and dynamic updates from unauthorized addresses, for example. You can even secure zone data by digitally signing it.

Since DNS security is one of the most complicated topics in DNS, we'll start you off easy and build up to the hard stuff.

TSIG

BIND 8.2 introduced a new mechanism for securing DNS messages called *transaction signatures*, or TSIG for short. TSIG uses shared secrets and a one-way hash function to authenticate DNS messages, particularly responses and updates.

TSIG, now codified in RFC 2845, is relatively simple to configure, light-weight for resolvers and nameservers to use, and flexible enough to secure DNS messages (including zone transfers) and dynamic updates. (Contrast this with the DNS Security Extensions, which we'll discuss at the end of this chapter.)

With TSIG configured, a nameserver or updater adds a TSIG record to the additional data section of a DNS message. The TSIG record "signs" the DNS message, proving that the message's sender had a cryptographic key shared with the receiver and that the message wasn't modified after it left the sender.[*]

One-Way Hash Functions

TSIG provides authentication and data integrity through the use of a special type of mathematical formula called a *one-way hash function*. A one-way hash function, also known as a cryptographic checksum or message digest, computes a fixed-size hash value based on arbitrarily large input. The magic of a one-way hash function is that each bit of the hash value depends on each and every bit of the input. Change a single bit of the input, and the hash value changes dramatically and unpredictably—so unpredictably that it's "computationally infeasible" to reverse the function and find an input that produces a given hash value.

TSIG uses a one-way hash function called MD5. In particular, it uses a variant of MD5 called HMAC-MD5. HMAC-MD5 works in a keyed mode in which the 128-bit hash value depends not only on the input, but also on a key.

---

[*] Cryptography wonks may argue that TSIG "signatures" aren't really signatures in a cryptographic sense because they don't provide nonrepudiation. Since either holder of the shared key can create a signed message, the recipient of a signed message can't claim that only the sender could have sent it (the recipient could have forged it himself).

The TSIG Record

We won't cover the TSIG record's syntax in detail because you don't need to know it: TSIG is a "meta-record" that never appears in zone data and is never cached by a resolver or nameserver. A signer adds the TSIG record to a DNS message, and the recipient removes and verifies the record before doing anything further, such as caching the data in the message.

You should know, however, that the TSIG record includes a hash value computed over the entire DNS message as well as some additional fields. (When we say "computed over," we mean that the raw, binary DNS message and the additional fields are fed through the HMAC-MD5 algorithm to produce the hash value.) The hash value is keyed with a secret shared between the signer and the verifier. Verifying the hash value proves both that the DNS message was signed by a holder of the shared secret and that it wasn't modified after it was signed.

The additional fields in the TSIG record include the time the DNS message was signed. This helps combat replay attacks, in which a hacker captures a signed, authorized transaction (say a dynamic update deleting an important resource record) and replays it later. The recipient of a signed DNS message checks the time signed to make sure it's within the allowable "fudge" (another field in the TSIG record).

Configuring TSIG

Before using TSIG for authentication, we need to configure one or more TSIG keys on either end of the transaction. For example, if we want to use TSIG to secure zone transfers between the master and slave nameservers for *movie.edu*, we need to configure both nameservers with a common key:

```
key toystory-wormhole.movie.edu. {
    algorithm hmac-md5;
    secret "skrKc4Twy/cIgIykQu7JZA==";
};
```

The argument to the *key* statement in this example, *toystory-wormhole.movie.edu*, is actually the name of the key, though it looks like a domain name. (It's encoded in the DNS message in the same format as a domain name.) The TSIG RFC suggests you name the key after the two hosts that use it. The RFC also suggests that you use different keys for each pair of hosts. This prevents the disclosure of one key from compromising all of your communications, and limits the use of each key.

It's important that the name of the key—not just the binary data the key points to—be identical on both ends of the transaction. If it's not, the recipient tries to verify the TSIG record and finds it doesn't know the key that the TSIG record says was used to compute the hash value. That causes errors such as the following:

```
Jan  4 16:05:35 wormhole named[86705]: client 192.249.249.1#4666: request has invalid
signature: TSIG tsig-key.movie.edu: tsig verify failure (BADKEY)
```

The algorithm, for now, is always *hmac-md5*. The secret is the base 64 encoding of the binary key. You can create a base-64-encoded key using the *dnssec-keygen* program included in BIND 9 or the *dnskeygen* program included in BIND 8. Here's how you'd create a key using *dnssec-keygen*, the easier of the two to use:

```
# dnssec-keygen -a HMAC-MD5 -b 128 -n HOST toystory-wormhole.movie.edu.
Ktoystory-wormhole.movie.edu.+157+28446
```

The *–a* option takes as an argument the name of the algorithm the key will be used with. (That's necessary because *dnssec-keygen* can generate other kinds of keys, as you'll see in the section "The DNS Security Extensions.") The *–b* option takes the length of the key as its argument; the RFC recommends using keys 128 bits long. The *–n* option takes as an argument HOST, the type of key to generate. (DNSSEC uses ZONE keys.) The final argument is the name of the key.

dnssec-keygen and *dnskeygen* both create files in their working directories that contain the keys generated. *dnssec-keygen* prints the base name of the files to its standard output. In this case, *dnssec-keygen* created the files *Ktoystory-wormhole.movie. edu.+157+28446.key* and *Ktoystory-wormhole.movie.edu.+157+28446.private*. You can extract the key from either file. The funny numbers (157 and 28446), in case you're wondering, are the key's DNSSEC algorithm number (157 is HMAC-MD5) and the key's fingerprint (28446), a hash value computed over the key to identify it. The fingerprint isn't particularly useful in TSIG, but DNSSEC supports multiple keys per zone, so identifying which key you mean by its fingerprint is important.

Ktoystory-wormhole.movie.edu.+157+28446.key contains:

```
toystory-wormhole.movie.edu. IN KEY 512 3 157 skrKc4Twy/cIgIykQu7JZA==
```

and *Ktoystory-wormhole.movie.edu.+157+28446.private* contains:

```
Private-key-format: v1.2
Algorithm: 157 (HMAC_MD5)
Key: skrKc4Twy/cIgIykQu7JZA==
```

If you prefer, you can choose your own key and encode it in base 64 using *mmencode*:

```
% mmencode
foobarbaz
Zm9vYmFyYmF6
```

Since the actual binary key is, as the substatement implies, a secret, we should take care in transferring it to our nameservers (e.g., by using *ssh*) and make sure that not just anyone can read it. We can do that by making sure our *named.conf* file isn't world-readable or by using the *include* statement to read the *key* statement from another file, which isn't world-readable:

```
include "/etc/dns.keys.conf";
```

There's one last problem that we see cropping up frequently with TSIG: time synchronization. The timestamp in the TSIG record is useful for preventing replay attacks, but it tripped us up initially because the clocks on our nameservers weren't synchronized. (They need to be synchronized to within five minutes, the default value for "fudge.") That produced error messages like the following:

```
wormhole named[86705]: client 192.249.249.1#54331: request has invalid signature:
TSIG toystory-wormhole.movie.edu.: tsig verify failure (BADTIME)
```

We quickly remedied the problem using NTP, the network time protocol.*

Using TSIG

Now that we've gone to the trouble of configuring our nameservers with TSIG keys, we should probably configure them to use those keys for something. In BIND 8.2 and later and all BIND 9 nameservers, we can secure queries, responses, zone transfers, and dynamic updates with TSIG.

The key to configuring this is the *server* statement's *keys* substatement, which tells a nameserver to sign queries and zone transfer requests sent to a particular remote nameserver. This *server* substatement, for example, tells the local nameserver, *wormhole.movie.edu*, to sign all such requests sent to 192.249.249.1 (*toystory.movie.edu*) with the key *toystory-wormhole.movie.edu*:

```
server 192.249.249.1 {
    keys { toystory-wormhole.movie.edu.; };
};
```

If you're only concerned about zone transfers (and not about general query traffic, for example), you can specify the key in the *masters* substatement for any slave zones:

```
zone "movie.edu" {
    type slave;
    masters { 192.249.249.1 key toystory-wormhole.movie.edu.; };
    file "bak.movie.edu";
};
```

Now, on *toystory.movie.edu*, we can restrict zone transfers to those signed with the *toystory-wormhole.movie.edu* key:

```
zone "movie.edu" {
    type master;
    file "db.movie.edu";
    allow-transfer { key toystory-wormhole.movie.edu.; };
};
```

toystory.movie.edu also signs the zone transfer, which allows *wormhole.movie.edu* to verify it.

---

* See the Network Time Protocol web site at *http://www.ntp.org/* for information on NTP.

You can also restrict dynamic updates with TSIG using the *allow-update* and *update-policy* substatements, as we showed you in the last chapter.

The *nsupdate* programs shipped with BIND 8.2 and later and BIND 9 support, sending TSIG-signed dynamic updates. If you have the key files created by *dnssec-keygen* lying around, you can specify either of those as an argument to *nsupdate*'s *–k* option. Here's how you'd do that with BIND 9's version of *nsupdate*:

```
% nsupdate -k Ktoystory-wormhole.movie.edu.+157+28446.key
```

or:

```
% nsupdate -k Ktoystory-wormhole.movie.edu.+157+28446.private
```

With the BIND 8.2 or later *nsupdate*, the syntax is a little different: *–k* takes a directory and a key name as an argument, separated by a colon:

```
% nsupdate -k /var/named:toystory-wormhole.movie.edu.
```

If you don't have the files around (maybe you're running *nsupdate* from another host), you can still specify the key name and the secret on the command line with the BIND 9 *nsupdate*:

```
% nsupdate -y toystory-wormhole.movie.edu.:skrKc4Twy/cIgIykQu7JZA==
```

The name of the key is the first argument to the *–y* option, followed by a colon and the base-64-encoded secret. You don't need to quote the secret because base-64 values can't contain shell metacharacters, but you can if you like.

Michael Fuhr's Net::DNS Perl module also lets you send TSIG-signed dynamic updates and zone transfer requests. For more information on Net::DNS, see Chapter 15.

Now that we have a handy mechanism for securing DNS transactions, let's talk about securing our whole nameserver.

Securing Your Nameserver

BIND 8 and 9 support a wide variety of security mechanisms. These features are particularly important if your nameserver is running on the Internet, but they're also useful on purely internal nameservers.

We'll start by discussing measures you should take on all nameservers for which security is important. Then we'll describe a model in which your nameservers are split into two communities, one for serving only resolvers and one for answering other nameservers' queries.

BIND Version

One of the most important ways you can enhance the security of your nameserver is to run a recent version of BIND. All versions of BIND 8 before 8.4.7 and all versions of BIND 9 older than 9.3.2 are susceptible to at least a few known attacks. Check the ISC's list of vulnerabilities in various BIND versions at *http://www.isc.org/sw/bind/bind-security.php* for updates.

But don't stop there: new attacks are being thought up all the time, so you'll have to do your best to keep abreast of BIND's vulnerabilities and the latest "safe" version of BIND. One good way to do that is to read the *comp.protocols.dns.bind* newsgroup or its mailing list equivalent, *bind-users*, regularly. If you'd prefer less noise, there's always the *bind-announce* mailing list, which carries only announcements of patches and new releases of BIND.[*]

There's another aspect of BIND's version relevant to security: if a hacker can easily find out which version of BIND you're running, he may be able to tailor his attacks to that version of BIND. And, wouldn't you know it, since about BIND 4.9, BIND nameservers have replied to a certain query with their version. If you look up TXT records in the CHAOSNET class attached to the domain name *version.bind*, BIND graciously returns something like this:

```
% dig txt chaos version.bind.

; <<>> DiG 9.3.2 <<>> txt chaos version.bind.
;; global options:  printcmd
;; Got answer:
;; ->>HEADER<<- opcode: QUERY, status: NOERROR, id: 14286
;; flags: qr aa rd; QUERY: 1, ANSWER: 1, AUTHORITY: 1, ADDITIONAL: 0

;; QUESTION SECTION:
;version.bind.                  CH      TXT

;; ANSWER SECTION:
version.bind.           0       CH      TXT     "9.3.2"

;; AUTHORITY SECTION:
version.bind.           0       CH      NS      version.bind.

;; Query time: 17 msec
;; SERVER: 192.168.0.1#53(192.168.0.1)
;; WHEN: Sat Jan  7 16:14:39 2006
;; MSG SIZE  rcvd: 62
```

To address this, BIND versions 8.2 and later let you tailor your nameserver's response to the *version.bind* query:

```
options {
    version "None of your business";
};
```

---

[*] We described how to subscribe to *bind-users* back in Chapter 3. To subscribe to *bind-announce*, the instructions are the same.

Of course, receiving a response like "None of your business" will tip off the alert hacker to the fact that you're likely running BIND 8.2 or better, but that still leaves a number of possibilities. If you'd rather the reply was less obvious, you can use "version none" with BIND 9.3.0 and later:

```
options {
    directory "/var/named";
    version none;
};
```

Now your nameserver will respond to version queries like this:

```
; <<>> DiG 9.3.2 <<>> txt chaos version.bind.
;; global options:  printcmd
;; Got answer:
;; ->>HEADER<<- opcode: QUERY, status: NOERROR, id: 21957
;; flags: qr aa rd; QUERY: 1, ANSWER: 0, AUTHORITY: 1, ADDITIONAL: 0

;; QUESTION SECTION:
;version.bind.                  CH      TXT

;; AUTHORITY SECTION:
version.bind.          86400    CH      SOA     version.bind. hostmaster.version.
bind. 0 28800 7200 604800 86400

;; Query time: 2 msec
;; SERVER: 192.168.0.1#53(192.168.0.1)
;; WHEN: Sat Jan  7 16:16:43 2006
;; MSG SIZE  rcvd: 77
```

Restricting Queries

Back in the old days of BIND 4, administrators had no way to control who could look up names on their nameservers. That makes a certain amount of sense; the original idea behind DNS was to make information easily available all over the Internet.

The neighborhood is not such a friendly place anymore, though. In particular, people who run Internet firewalls may have a legitimate need to hide certain parts of their namespace from most of the world while making it available to a limited audience.

The BIND 8 and 9 *allow-query* substatement lets you apply an IP address-based access control list to queries. The ACL can apply to queries for data in a particular zone or to any queries received by the nameserver. In particular, the ACL specifies which IP addresses are allowed to send queries to the server.

Restricting all queries

The global form of the *allow-query* substatement looks like this:

```
options {
    allow-query { address_match_list; };
};
```

So to restrict our nameserver to answering queries from the three main Movie U. networks, we'd use:

```
options {
        allow-query { 192.249.249/24; 192.253.253/24; 192.253.254/24; };
};
```

Restricting queries in a particular zone

BIND 8 and 9 also allow you to apply an ACL to a particular zone. In this case, just use *allow-query* as a substatement to the *zone* statement for the zone you want to protect:

```
acl "HP-NET" { 15/8; };

zone "hp.com" {
        type slave;
        file "bak.hp.com";
        masters { 15.255.152.2; };
        allow-query { "HP-NET"; };
};
```

Any kind of authoritative nameserver, master or slave, can apply an ACL to the zone.[*] Zone-specific ACLs take precedence over a global ACL for queries in that zone. The zone-specific ACL may even be more permissive than the global ACL. If there's no zone-specific ACL defined, any global ACL will apply.

Preventing Unauthorized Zone Transfers

Arguably even more important than controlling who can query your nameserver is ensuring that only your real slave nameservers can transfer zones from your nameserver. Users on remote hosts that can query your nameserver's zone data can only look up records (e.g., addresses) for domain names they already know, one at a time. Users who can start zone transfers from your server can list all the records in your zones. It's the difference between letting random folks call your company's switchboard and ask for John Q. Cubicle's phone number and sending them a copy of your corporate phone directory.

BIND 8 and 9's *allow-transfer* substatement lets administrators apply an ACL to zone transfers. *allow-transfer* restricts transfers of a particular zone when used as a *zone* substatement and restricts all zone transfers when used as an *options* substatement. It takes an address match list as an argument.

---

[*] In fact, you can even use an *allow-query* substatement with a stub zone.

The slave servers for our *movie.edu* zone have the IP addresses 192.249.249.1 and 192.253.253.1 (*wormhole.movie.edu*) and 192.249.249.9 and 192.253.253.9 (*zardoz.movie.edu*). The following *zone* statement:

```
zone "movie.edu" {
        type master;
        file "db.movie.edu";
        allow-transfer { 192.249.249.1; 192.253.253.1; 192.249.249.9; 192.253.253.9; };
};
```

allows only those slaves to transfer *movie.edu* from the primary master nameserver. Note that because the default for BIND 8 or 9 is to allow zone transfer requests from any IP address, and because hackers can just as easily transfer the zone from your slaves, you should probably also have a *zone* statement like this on your slaves:

```
zone "movie.edu" {
        type slave;
        masters { 192.249.249.3; };
        file "bak.movie.edu";
        allow-transfer { none; };
};
```

BIND 8 and 9 also let you apply a global ACL to zone transfers. This applies to any zones that don't have their own explicit ACLs defined as *zone* substatements. For example, we might want to limit all zone transfers to our internal IP addresses:

```
options {
        allow-transfer { 192.249.249/24; 192.253.253/24; 192.253.254/24; };
};
```

Finally, as we mentioned earlier in the chapter, those newfangled BIND 8.2 and later and BIND 9 nameservers let you restrict zone transfers to slave nameservers that include a correct transaction signature with their request. On the master nameserver, you need to define the key in a *key* statement and then specify the key in the address match list:

```
key toystory-wormhole. {
        algorithm hmac-md5;
        secret "UNd5xYLjzOFPkoqWRymtgI+paxW927LU/gTrDyulJRI=";
};

zone "movie.edu" {
        type master;
        file "db.movie.edu";
        allow-transfer { key toystory-wormhole.; };
};
```

On the slave's end, you need to configure the slave to sign zone transfer requests with the same key:

```
key toystory-wormhole. {
        algorithm hmac-md5;
        secret "UNd5xYLjzOFPkoqWRymtgI+paxW927LU/gTrDyulJRI=";
};
```

```
server 192.249.249.3 {
    keys { toystory-wormhole.; };   // sign all requests to 192.249.249.3
                                     // with this key
};

zone "movie.edu" {
    type slave;
    masters { 192.249.249.3; };
    file "bak.movie.edu";
};
```

For a primary nameserver accessible from the Internet, you probably want to limit zone transfers to just your slave nameservers. You probably don't need to worry about securing zone transfers from nameservers inside your firewall, unless you're worried about your own employees listing your zone data.

Running BIND with Least Privilege

Running a network server like BIND as the root user can be dangerous, and BIND normally runs as root. If a hacker finds a vulnerability in the nameserver through which he can read or write files, he'll have unfettered access to the filesystem. If he can exploit a flaw that allows him to execute commands, he'll execute them as root.

BIND 8.1.2 and later and all BIND 9 nameservers include code that allows you to change the user and group the nameserver runs as. This allows you to run the nameserver with what's known as *least privilege*: the minimal set of rights it needs to do its job. That way, if someone breaks into your host through the nameserver, at least that person won't have root privileges.

These nameservers also include an option that allows you to *chroot()* the nameserver: to change its view of the filesystem so that its root directory is actually a particular directory on your host's filesystem. This effectively traps your nameserver in this directory, along with any attackers who successfully compromise your nameserver's security.

Here are the command-line options that implement these features:

−*u* Specifies the username or user ID the nameserver changes to after starting, e.g., *named −u bind*.

−*g* Specifies the group or group ID the nameserver changes to after starting, e.g., *named −g other*. If you specify −*u* without −*g*, the nameserver uses the user's primary group. BIND 9 nameservers always change to the user's primary group, so they don't support −*g*.

−*t* Specifies the directory for the nameserver to *chroot()* to.

If you opt to use the −*u* and −*g* options, you'll have to decide what user and group to use. Your best bet is to create a new user and group for the nameserver to run as, such as *bind* or *named*. Since the nameserver reads *named.conf* before giving up root privileges, you don't have to change that file's permissions. However, you may have to change the permissions and ownership of your zone datafiles so that the user the nameserver runs as can read them. If you use dynamic update, you'll have to make the zone datafiles for dynamically updated zones writable by the nameserver.

If your nameserver is configured to log to files (instead of to *syslog*), make sure that those files exist and are writable by the nameserver before starting the server.

The *–t* option takes a little more specialized configuration. In particular, you need to make sure that all the files *named* uses are present in the directory you're restricting the server to. Here's a procedure to set up your *chroot*ed environment, which we'll assume lives under */var/named:*[*]

1. Create the */var/named* directory, if it doesn't exist. Create *dev*, *etc*, *lib*, *usr*, and *var* subdirectories. Within *usr*, create an *sbin* subdirectory. Within *var*, create subdirectories named *named* and *run*:

   ```
   # mkdir /var/named
   # cd /var/named
   # mkdir -p dev etc lib usr/sbin var/named var/run
   ```

2. Copy *named.conf* to */var/named/etc/named.conf*:

   ```
   # cp /etc/named.conf etc
   ```

3. If you're running BIND 8, copy the *named-xfer* binary to the *usr/sbin/* or *etc* sub-directory (depending on whether you found it in */usr/sbin* or */etc*):

   ```
   # cp /usr/sbin/named-xfer usr/sbin
   ```

   Alternatively, you can put it wherever you like under */var/named* and use the *named-xfer* substatement to tell *named* where to find it. Just remember to strip */var/named* off of the pathname because when *named* reads *named.conf*, */var/named* will look like the root of the filesystem. (If you're running BIND 9, skip this step because BIND 9 doesn't use *named-xfer*.)

4. Create *dev/null* in the *chroot*ed environment:[†]

   ```
   # mknod dev/null c 2 2
   ```

5. If you're running BIND 8, copy the standard shared C library and the loader to the *lib* subdirectory:

   ```
   # cp /lib/libc.so.6 /lib/ld-2.1.3.so lib
   ```

   The pathnames may vary on your operating system. BIND 9 nameservers are self-contained, so you don't need to copy libraries.

6. Edit your startup files to start *syslogd* with an additional option and option argument: *–a /var/named/dev/log*. On many modern versions of Unix, *syslogd* is

---

[*] This procedure is based on FreeBSD, so if you use a different operating system, your mileage may vary.

[†] The arguments to *mknod* needed to create *dev/null* will vary depending on the operating system.

started from */etc/rc* or */etc/rc.d/init.d/syslog*. When *syslogd* restarts next, it creates */var/named/dev/log*, and *named* logs to it.

If your *syslogd* doesn't support the *–a* option, use the *logging* statement described in Chapter 7 to log to files in the *chroot*ed directory.

7. If you're running BIND 8 and use the *–u* or *–g* options, create *passwd* and *group* files in the *etc* subdirectory to map the arguments of *–u* and *–g* to their numeric values (or just use numeric values as arguments):

```
# echo "named:x:42:42:named:/:" > etc/passwd
# echo "named::42" > etc/group
```

Then add the entries to the system's */etc/passwd* and */etc/group* files. If you're running BIND 9, you can *just* add the entries to the system's */etc/passwd* and */etc/group* files because BIND 9 nameservers read the information they need before calling *chroot( )*.

8. Finally, edit your startup files to start *named* with the *–t* option and option argument: *–t /var/named*. Similar to *syslogd*, many modern versions of Unix start *named* from */etc/rc* or */etc/rc.d/init.d/named*.

If you're hooked on using *ndc* to control your BIND 8 nameserver, you can continue to do so as long as you specify the pathname to the Unix domain socket as the argument to *ndc*'s *–c* option:

```
# ndc -c /var/named/var/run/ndc reload
```

rndc will continue to work as before with your BIND 9 nameserver because it just talks to the server via port 953.

Split-Function Nameservers

Nameservers really have two major roles: answering iterative queries from remote nameservers and answering recursive queries from local resolvers. If we separate these roles, dedicating one set of nameservers to answering iterative queries and another to answering recursive queries, we can more effectively secure those nameservers.

"Advertising" nameserver configuration

Some of your nameservers answer nonrecursive queries from other nameservers on the Internet because these nameservers appear in NS records delegating your zones to them. We'll call these nameservers *advertising* nameservers, because their role is to advertise your zones to the Internet.

There are special measures you can take to secure your advertising nameservers. But first, you should make sure that these nameservers don't receive any recursive queries (that is, you don't have any resolvers configured to use these servers and no nameservers use them as forwarders). Some of the precautions we'll take—like making the server respond nonrecursively even to recursive queries—preclude your resolvers from using these servers. If you do have resolvers using your advertising nameservers, consider establishing another class of nameservers to serve just your resolvers or using the *two nameservers in one* configuration, both described later in this chapter.

Once you know your nameserver answers queries only from other nameservers, you can turn off recursion. This eliminates a major vector of attack: the most common spoofing attacks involve inducing the target nameserver to query nameservers under the hacker's control by sending the target a recursive query for a domain name in a zone served by the hacker's servers. To turn off recursion, use the following statement on a BIND 8 or 9 nameserver:

```
options {
        recursion no;
};
```

You should also restrict zone transfers of your zones to known slave servers, as described in the earlier section "Preventing Unauthorized Zone Transfers." Finally, you might also want to turn off glue fetching. Some nameservers will automatically try to resolve the domain names of any nameservers in NS records; to prevent this from happening and keep your nameserver from sending any queries of its own, use this on a BIND 8 nameserver (BIND 9 nameservers don't support glue fetching):

```
options {
        fetch-glue no;
};
```

"Resolving" nameserver configuration

We'll call a nameserver that serves one or more resolvers or that is configured as another nameserver's forwarder a *resolving* nameserver. Unlike an advertising nameserver, a resolving nameserver can't refuse recursive queries. Consequently, we have to configure it a little differently to secure it. Since we know our nameserver should receive queries only from our own resolvers, we can configure it to deny queries from any but our resolvers' IP addresses.

This *allow-query* substatement restricts queries to just our internal network:

```
options {
        allow-query { 192.249.249/24; 192.253.253/24; 192.253.254/24; };
};
```

With this configuration, the only resolvers that can send our nameserver recursive queries and induce them to query other nameservers are our own internal resolvers, which are presumably relatively benign.

There's one other option we can use to make our resolving nameserver a little more secure: *use-id-pool*:

```
options {
        use-id-pool yes;
};
```

use-id-pool was introduced in BIND 8.2. It tells our nameserver to take special care to use random message IDs in queries. Normally, the message IDs aren't random enough to prevent brute-force attacks that try to guess the IDs our nameserver has outstanding in order to spoof a response.

The ID pool code became a standard part of BIND 9, so you don't need to specify it on a BIND 9 nameserver.

Two Nameservers in One

What if you have only one nameserver to advertise your zones and serve your resolvers, and you can't afford the additional expense of buying another computer to run a second nameserver on? There are still a few options open to you. Two are single-server solutions that take advantage of the flexibility of BIND 8 and 9. One of these configurations allows anyone to query the nameserver for information in zones it's authoritative for, but only our internal resolvers can query the nameserver for other information. While this doesn't prevent remote resolvers from sending our nameserver recursive queries, those queries have to be in its authoritative zones so they won't induce our nameserver to send additional queries.

Here's a *named.conf* file to do that:

```
acl "internal" {
    192.249.249/24; 192.253.253/24; 192.253.254/24; localhost;
};

acl "slaves" {
    192.249.249.1; 192.253.253.1; 192.249.249.9; 192.253.253.9;
};

options {
    directory "/var/named";
    allow-query { "internal"; };
    use-id-pool yes;
};

zone "movie.edu" {
    type master;
    file "db.movie.edu";
    allow-query { any; };
    allow-transfer { "slaves"; };
};

zone "249.249.192.in-addr.arpa" {
    type master;
    file "db.192.249.249";
    allow-query { any; };
    allow-transfer { "slaves"; };
};
```

```
zone "." {
    type hint;
    file "db.cache";
};
```

Here, the more permissive zone-specific ACLs apply to queries in the nameserver's authoritative zones, but the more restrictive global ACL applies to all other queries.

If we were running BIND 8.2.1 or newer, or any version of BIND 9, we could simplify this configuration somewhat using the *allow-recursion* substatement:

```
acl "internal" {
    192.249.249/24; 192.253.253/24; 192.253.254/24; localhost;
};

acl "slaves" {
    192.249.249.1; 192.253.253.1; 192.249.249.9; 192.253.253.9;
};

options {
    directory "/var/named";
    allow-recursion { "internal"; };
    use-id-pool yes;
};

zone "movie.edu" {
    type master;
    file "db.movie.edu";
    allow-transfer { "slaves"; };
};

zone "249.249.192.in-addr.arpa" {
    type master;
    file "db.192.249.249";
    allow-transfer { "slaves"; };
};

zone "." {
    type hint;
    file "db.cache";
};
```

We don't need the *allow-query* substatements anymore: although the nameserver may receive queries from outside our internal network, it'll treat those queries as nonrecursive, regardless of whether they are or not. Consequently, external queries won't induce our nameserver to send any queries. This configuration also doesn't suffer from a gotcha the previous setup is susceptible to: if your nameserver is authoritative for a parent zone, it may receive queries from remote nameservers resolving domain names in a delegated subdomain of the zone. The *allow-query* solution will refuse those legitimate queries, but the *allow-recursion* solution won't.

Another option is to run two *named* processes on a single host. One is configured as an advertising nameserver, another as a resolving nameserver. Since we have no way of telling remote servers or configuring resolvers to query one of our nameservers on a port other than 53, the default DNS port, we have to run these servers on different IP addresses.

Of course, if your host already has more than one network interface, that's no problem. Even if it has only one, the operating system may support IP address aliases. These allow you to attach more than one IP address to a single network interface. One *named* process can listen on each. Finally, if the operating system doesn't support IP aliases, you can still bind one *named* against the network interface's IP address and one against the loopback address. Only the local host will be able to send queries to the instance of *named* listening on the loopback address, but that's fine if the local host's resolver is the only one you need to serve.

First, here's the *named.conf* file for the advertising nameserver, listening on the network interface's IP address:

```
acl "slaves" {
    192.249.249.1; 192.253.253.1; 192.249.249.9; 192;253.253.9;
};

options {
    directory "/var/named-advertising";
    recursion no;
    fetch-glue no;
    listen-on { 192.249.249.3; };
    pid-file "/var/run/named.advertising.pid";
};

zone "movie.edu" {
    type master;
    file "db.movie.edu";
    allow-transfer { "slaves"; };
};

zone "249.249.192.in-addr.arpa" {
    type master;
    file "db.192.249.249";
    allow-transfer { "slaves"; };
};
```

Next, here's the *named.conf* file for the resolving nameserver, listening on the loopback address:

```
options {
    directory "/var/named-resolving";
    listen-on { 127.0.0.1; };
    pid-file "/var/run/named.resolving.pid";
    use-id-pool yes;
};
```

```
zone "." {
    type hint;
    file "db.cache";
};
```

Note that we didn't need an ACL for the resolving nameserver because it's only listening on the loopback address and can't receive queries from other hosts. (If our resolving nameserver were listening on an IP alias or a second network interface, we could use *allow-query* to prevent others from using our nameserver.) We turn off recursion on the advertising nameserver, but we must leave it on the resolving nameserver. We also give each nameserver its own PID file so that the servers don't try to use the same default filename for their PID files, and we give each nameserver its own directory so debug files and statistics files are saved in separate locations.

To use the resolving nameserver listening on the loopback address, the local host's *resolv.conf* file must include the following:

```
nameserver 127.0.0.1
```

as the first *nameserver* directive.

If you're running BIND 9, you can even consolidate the two nameserver configurations into one using views:

```
options {
    directory "/var/named";
};

acl "internal" {
    192.249.249/24; 192.253.253/24; 192.253.254/24; localhost;
};

view "internal" {
    match-clients { "internal"; };
    recursion yes;

    zone "movie.edu" {
        type master;
        file "db.movie.edu";
    };

    zone "249.249.192.in-addr.arpa" {
        type master;
        file "db.192.249.249";
    };

    zone "." {
        type hint;
        file "db.cache";
    };
};
```

```
view "external" {
    match-clients { any; };
    recursion no;

    zone "movie.edu" {
        type master;
        file "db.movie.edu";
    };

    zone "249.249.192.in-addr.arpa" {
        type master;
        file "db.192.249.249";
    };

    zone "." {
        type hint;
        file "db.cache";
    };
};
```

It's a fairly simple configuration: two views, internal and external. The internal view, which applies only to our internal network, has recursion on. The external view, which applies to everyone else, has recursion off. The zones *movie.edu* and *249.249.192.in-addr.arpa* are defined identically in both views. You could do a lot more with it—define different versions of the zones internally and externally, for example—but we'll hold off on that until the next section.

DNS and Internet Firewalls

The Domain Name System wasn't designed to work with Internet firewalls. It's a testimony to the flexibility of DNS and of its BIND implementation that you can configure DNS to work with, or even through, an Internet firewall.

That said, configuring BIND to work in a firewalled environment, although not difficult, takes a good, complete understanding of DNS and a few of BIND's more obscure features. Describing it also requires a large portion of this chapter, so here's a roadmap.

We'll start by describing the two major families of Internet firewall software: packet filters and proxies. The capabilities of each family have a bearing on how you'll need to configure BIND to work through the firewall. Next, we'll detail the two most common DNS architectures used with firewalls, forwarders and internal roots, and describe the advantages and disadvantages of each. We'll then introduce a solution using a new feature, forward zones, which combines the best of internal roots and forwarders. Finally, we'll discuss split namespaces and the configuration of the bastion host, the host at the core of your firewall system.

Types of Firewall Software

Before you start configuring BIND to work with your firewall, it's important to understand what your firewall is capable of. Your firewall's capabilities will influence your choice of DNS architecture and determine how you implement it. If you don't know the answers to the questions in this section, track down someone in your organization who does know and ask. Better yet, work with your firewall's administrator when designing your DNS architecture to ensure it will coexist with the firewall.

Note that this is far from a complete explanation of Internet firewalls. These few paragraphs describe only the two most common types of Internet firewalls and only in enough detail to show how the differences in their capabilities affect nameservers. For a comprehensive treatment of Internet firewalls, see *Building Internet Firewalls* by Elizabeth D. Zwicky, Simon Cooper, and D. Brent Chapman (O'Reilly).

Packet filters

The first type of firewall we'll cover is the *packet-filtering firewall*. Packet-filtering firewalls operate largely at the transport and network levels of the TCP/IP stack (layers three and four of the OSI reference model, if you dig that). They decide whether to route a packet based on packet-level criteria such as the transport protocol (e.g., whether it's TCP or UDP), the source and destination IP address, and the source and destination port (see Figure 11-1).

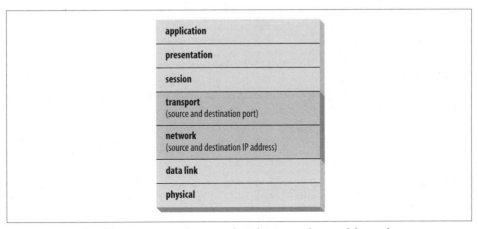

Figure 11-1. Packet filters operate at the network and transport layers of the stack

What's most important to us about packet-filtering firewalls is that you can typically configure them to allow DNS traffic selectively between hosts on the Internet and your internal hosts. That is, you can let an arbitrary set of internal hosts communicate with Internet nameservers. Some packet-filtering firewalls can even permit your nameservers to query nameservers on the Internet, but not vice versa. All router-based

Internet firewalls are packet-filtering firewalls. Checkpoint's FireWall-1, Cisco's PIX, and Juniper's NetScreen are popular commercial packet-filtering firewalls.

A Gotcha with BIND 8 or 9 and Packet-Filtering Firewalls

BIND 4 nameservers always sent queries from port 53, the well-known port for DNS servers, to port 53. Resolvers, on the other hand, usually send queries from high-numbered ports (above 1023) to port 53. Though nameservers clearly have to send their queries *to* the DNS port on a remote host, there's no reason they have to send the queries *from* the DNS port. And, wouldn't you know it, BIND 8 and 9 nameservers don't send queries from port 53 by default. Instead, they send queries from high-numbered ports, the same as resolvers do.

This can cause problems with packet-filtering firewalls that are configured to allow nameserver-to-nameserver traffic but not resolver-to-nameserver traffic, because they typically expect nameserver-to-nameserver traffic to originate from port 53 and terminate at port 53.

There are two solutions to this problem:

- Reconfigure the firewall to allow your nameserver to send and receive queries from ports other than 53 (assuming this doesn't compromise the security of the firewall by allowing packets from Internet hosts to high-numbered ports on internal nameservers).
- Configure BIND to revert to its old behavior with the *query-source* substatement.

query-source takes as arguments an address specification and an optional port number. For example, the statement:

```
options { query-source address * port 53; };
```

tells BIND to use port 53 as the source port for queries sent from all local network interfaces. You can use a nonwildcard address specification to limit the addresses that BIND will send queries from. For example, on *wormhole.movie.edu*, the statement:

```
options { query-source address 192.249.249.1 port *; };
```

tells BIND to send all queries from the 192.249.249.1 address (i.e., not from 192.253. 253.1) and to use a dynamic, high-numbered port.

The use of *query-source* with a wildcard address is broken in BIND 9 before 9.1.0, though you can tell an early BIND 9 nameserver to send all queries from a particular address's port 53.

Proxies

Proxies operate at the application protocol level, several layers higher in the OSI reference model than most packet filters (see Figure 11-2). In a sense, they "understand" the application protocol in the same way that a server for that particular application does. An FTP proxy, for example, can make the decision to allow or deny a particular FTP operation, such as a *RETR* (a *get*) or a *STOR* (a *put*).

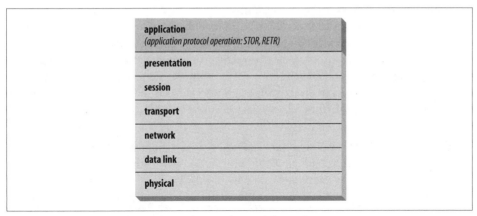

Figure 11-2. Proxies operate at the application layer of the stack

The bad news, and what's important for our purposes, is that most proxy-based firewalls handle only TCP-based application protocols. DNS, of course, is largely UDP-based. This implies that if you run a proxy-based firewall, your internal hosts will likely not be able to communicate directly with nameservers on the Internet.

The original Firewall Toolkit from Trusted Information Systems (now part of McAfee) was a suite of proxies for common Internet protocols such as Telnet, FTP, and HTTP. Secure Computing's Sidewinder firewall products are also based on proxies, as are Symantec's firewalls.

Note that these two categories of firewall are really just generalizations. The state of the art in firewalls changes very quickly. New packet filter–based firewalls can inspect application protocol-layer data, while some proxy-based firewalls include DNS proxies. Which family your firewall falls into is important only because it *suggests* what that firewall is capable of; what's more important is whether your particular firewall will let you permit DNS traffic between arbitrary internal hosts and the Internet.

A Bad Example

The simplest configuration is to allow DNS traffic to pass freely through your firewall (assuming you can configure your firewall to do that). That way, any internal nameserver can query any nameserver on the Internet, and any Internet nameserver can query any of your internal nameservers. You don't need any special configuration.

Unfortunately, this is a really bad idea, for two main reasons:

Version control
> The developers of BIND are constantly finding and fixing security-related bugs in the BIND code. Consequently, it's important to run a recent version of BIND, especially on nameservers directly exposed to the Internet. If one or just a few of your nameservers communicate directly with nameservers on the Internet, upgrading them to a new version is easy. If any of the nameservers on your network can communicate directly with nameservers on the Internet, upgrading all of them is vastly more difficult.

Possible vector for attack
> Even if you're not running a nameserver on a particular host, a hacker might be able to take advantage of your allowing DNS traffic through your firewall to attack that host. For example, a co-conspirator working on the inside could set up a Telnet daemon listening on the host's DNS port, allowing the hacker to telnet right in.

For the rest of this chapter, we'll try to set a good example.

Internet Forwarders

Given the dangers of allowing bidirectional DNS traffic through the firewall unrestricted, most organizations limit the internal hosts that can "talk DNS" to the Internet. In a proxy-based firewall, or any firewall without the ability to pass DNS traffic, the only hosts that can communicate with Internet nameservers are the bastion hosts (see Figure 11-3).

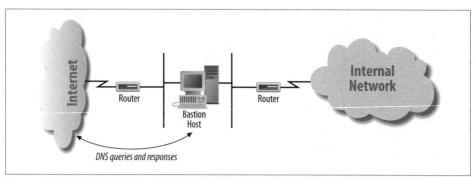

Figure 11-3. A small network, showing the bastion host

In a packet-filtering firewall, the firewall's administrator can configure the firewall to let any set of internal nameservers communicate with Internet nameservers. Often, this is a small set of hosts that run nameservers under the direct control of the network administrator (see Figure 11-4).

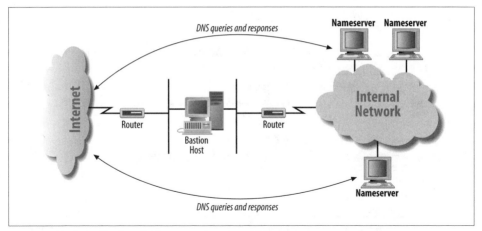

Figure 11-4. A small network, showing select internal nameservers

Internal nameservers that can directly query nameservers on the Internet don't require any special configuration. Their root hints files contain the Internet's root nameservers, which enables them to resolve Internet domain names. Internal nameservers that *can't* query nameservers on the Internet, however, need to know to forward queries they can't resolve to one of the nameservers that can. This is done with the *forwarders* substatement, introduced in Chapter 10.

Figure 11-5 illustrates a common forwarding setup, with internal nameservers forwarding queries to a nameserver running on a bastion host.

At Movie U., we put in a firewall to protect ourselves from the Big Bad Internet several years ago. Ours is a packet-filtering firewall, and we negotiated with our firewall administrator to allow DNS traffic between Internet nameservers and two of our nameservers, *toystory.movie.edu* and *wormhole.movie.edu*. Here's how we configured the other internal nameservers at the university. For our BIND 8 and 9 nameservers, we used the following:

```
options {
    forwarders { 192.249.249.1; 192.249.249.3; };
    forward only;
};
```

We vary the order in which the forwarders appear to help spread the load between them, though that's not necessary with BIND 8.2.3 and later or 9.3.0 and later nameservers, which choose a forwarder to query according to roundtrip time.

When an internal nameserver receives a query for a name it can't resolve locally, such as an Internet domain name, it forwards that query to one of our forwarders, which can resolve the name using nameservers on the Internet. Simple!

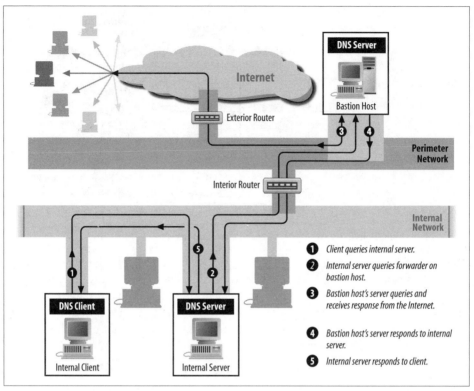

Figure 11-5. Using forwarders

The trouble with forwarding

Unfortunately, it's a little too simple. Forwarding starts to get in the way once you delegate subdomains or build an extensive network. To explain what we mean, take a look at part of the configuration file on *zardoz.movie.edu*:

```
options {
    directory "/var/named";
    forwarders { 192.249.249.1; 192.253.253.3; };
};

zone "movie.edu" {
    type slave;
    masters { 192.249.249.3; };
    file "bak.movie.edu";
};
```

zardoz.movie.edu is a slave for *movie.edu* and uses our two forwarders. What happens when *zardoz.movie.edu* receives a query for a name in *fx.movie.edu*? As an authoritative *movie.edu* nameserver, *zardoz.movie.edu* has the NS records that delegate *fx.movie.edu* to its authoritative nameservers. But it's also been configured to forward queries it can't resolve locally to *toystory.movie.edu* and *wormhole.movie.edu*. Which will it do?

It turns out that *zardoz.movie.edu* ignores the delegation information and forwards the query to *toystory.movie.edu*. That works because *toystory.movie.edu* receives the recursive query and asks an *fx.movie.edu* nameserver on *zardoz.movie.edu*'s behalf. But it's not particularly efficient because *zardoz.movie.edu* could easily have sent the query directly.

Now imagine that the scale of the network is much larger: a corporate network that spans continents, with tens of thousands of hosts and hundreds or thousands of nameservers. All the internal nameservers that don't have direct Internet connectivity—the vast majority of them—use a small set of forwarders. What's wrong with this picture?

Single point of failure

If the forwarders fail, your nameservers lose the ability to resolve both Internet domain names and internal domain names that they don't have cached or stored as authoritative data.

Concentration of load

The forwarders have an enormous query load placed on them. This is both because of the large number of internal nameservers that use them, and because the queries are recursive and require a good deal of work to answer.

Inefficient resolution

Imagine two internal nameservers, authoritative for *west.acmebw.com* and *east.acmebw.com*, respectively, both on the same network segment in Boulder, Colorado. Both are configured to use the company's forwarder in Bethesda, Maryland. For the *west.acmebw.com* nameserver to resolve a name in *east.acmebw.com*, it sends a query to the forwarder in Bethesda. The forwarder in Bethesda then sends a query back to Boulder to the *east.acmebw.com* nameserver, the original querier's neighbor. The *east.acmebw.com* nameserver replies by sending a response back to Bethesda, which the forwarder sends back to Boulder.

In a traditional configuration with root nameservers, the *west.acmebw.com* nameserver would have quickly learned that an *east.acmebw.com* nameserver was next door and would favor it (because of its low roundtrip time). Using forwarders short-circuits the normally efficient resolution process.

The upshot is that forwarding is fine for small networks and simple namespaces, but probably inadequate for large networks and complex namespaces. We found this out the hard way at Movie U., as our network grew, and we were forced to find an alternative.

Using forward zones

We can solve the previous problem using the forward zones introduced in BIND 8.2 and 9.1.0.* We change *zardoz.movie.edu*'s configuration to this:

```
options {
    directory "/var/named";
    forwarders { 192.249.249.1; 192.253.253.3; };
};

zone "movie.edu" {
    type slave;
    masters { 192.249.249.3; };
    file "bak.movie.edu";
    forwarders {};
};
```

Notice the *forwarders* substatement with the null list of forwarders. Now, if *zardoz.movie.edu* receives a query for a domain name ending in *movie.edu* but outside the *movie.edu* zone (e.g., in *fx.movie.edu*), it ignores the forwarders configured in the *options* statement and sends iterative queries.

With this configuration, *zardoz.movie.edu* still sends queries for domain names in our reverse-mapping zones to our forwarders. To relieve that load, we can add a few *zone* statements to *named.conf*:

```
zone "249.249.192.in-addr.arpa" {
    type stub;
    masters { 192.249.249.3; };
    file "stub.192.249.249";
    forwarders {};
};

zone "253.253.192.in-addr.arpa" {
    type stub;
    masters { 192.249.249.3; };
    file "stub.192.253.253";
    forwarders {};
};

zone "254.253.192.in-addr.arpa" {
    type stub;
    masters { 192.253.254.2; };
    file "stub.192.253.254";
    forwarders {};
};

zone "20.254.192.in-addr.arpa" {
    type stub;
```

---

* This particular variation of conditional forwarding, however, didn't work in BIND 9 until 9.2.0 because of a bug.

```
        masters { 192.253.254.2; };
        file "stub.192.254.20";
        forwarders {};
};
```

These new *zone* statements bear some explaining. First of all, they configure Movie U.'s reverse-mapping zones as stubs. That makes our nameserver track the NS records for those zones by periodically querying the master nameservers for those zones. The *forwarders* substatement then turns off forwarding for domain names in the reverse-mapping domains. Now, instead of querying the forwarders for, say, the PTR record for *2.254.253.192.in-addr.arpa*, *zardoz.movie.edu* will query one of the *254.253.192.in-addr.arpa* nameservers directly.

We'll need *zone* statements like these on all our internal nameservers, which implies that we'll need all our nameservers to run some version of BIND 8 after 8.2 or 9.2.0.

This gives us a fairly robust resolution architecture that minimizes our exposure to the Internet: it uses efficient, robust iterative name resolution to resolve internal domain names, and forwarders only when necessary to resolve Internet domain names. If our forwarders fail, or we lose our connection to the Internet, we only lose our ability to resolve Internet domain names.

Internal Roots

If you want to avoid the scalability problems of forwarding, you can set up your own root nameservers. These internal roots will serve only the nameservers in your organization. They'll know only about the portions of the namespace relevant to your organization.

What good are they? By using an architecture based on root nameservers, you gain the scalability of the Internet's namespace (which should be good enough for most companies), plus redundancy, distributed load, and efficient resolution. You can have as many internal roots as the Internet has roots—13 or so—whereas having that many forwarders may be an undue security exposure and a configuration burden. Most of all, the internal roots don't get used frivolously. Nameservers need to consult an internal root only when they time out the NS records for your top-level zones. Using forwarders, nameservers may have to query a forwarder once *per resolution*.

The moral of our story is that if you have, or intend to have, a large namespace and lots of internal nameservers, internal root nameservers will scale better than any other solution.

Where to put internal root nameservers

Since nameservers "lock on" to the closest root nameserver by favoring the one with the lowest roundtrip time, it pays to pepper your network with internal root nameservers. If your organization's network spans the United States, Europe, and the

Pacific Rim, consider locating at least one internal root nameserver on each continent. If you have three major sites in Europe, give each of them an internal root.

Forward-mapping delegation

Here's how an internal root nameserver is configured. An internal root delegates directly to any zones you administer. For example, on the *movie.edu* network, the root zone's datafile contains:

```
movie.edu.   86400  IN  NS  toystory.movie.edu.
             86400  IN  NS  wormhole.movie.edu.
             86400  IN  NS  zardoz.movie.edu.
toystory.movie.edu.   86400  IN  A  192.249.249.3
wormhole.movie.edu.   86400  IN  A  192.249.249.1
                      86400  IN  A  192.253.253.1
zardoz.movie.edu.     86400  IN  A  192.249.249.9
                      86400  IN  A  192.253.253.9
```

On the Internet, this information appears in the *edu* nameservers' zone datafiles. On the *movie.edu* network, of course, there aren't any *edu* nameservers, so you delegate directly to *movie.edu* from the root.

Notice that this doesn't contain delegation to *fx.movie.edu* or to any other subdomain of *movie.edu*. The *movie.edu* nameservers know which nameservers are authoritative for all *movie.edu* subdomains, and all queries for information in those subdomains pass through the *movie.edu* nameservers, so there's no need to delegate them here.

in-addr.arpa delegation

We also need to delegate from the internal roots to the *in-addr.arpa* zones that correspond to the networks at the university:

```
249.249.192.in-addr.arpa.   86400  IN  NS  toystory.movie.edu.
                            86400  IN  NS  wormhole.movie.edu.
                            86400  IN  NS  zardoz.movie.edu.
253.253.192.in-addr.arpa.   86400  IN  NS  toystory.movie.edu.
                            86400  IN  NS  wormhole.movie.edu.
                            86400  IN  NS  zardoz.movie.edu.
254.253.192.in-addr.arpa.   86400  IN  NS  bladerunner.fx.movie.edu.
                            86400  IN  NS  outland.fx.movie.edu.
                            86400  IN  NS  alien.fx.movie.edu.
20.254.192.in-addr.arpa.    86400  IN  NS  bladerunner.fx.movie.edu.
                            86400  IN  NS  outland.fx.movie.edu.
                            86400  IN  NS  alien.fx.movie.edu.
```

Notice that we *did* include delegation for the *254.253.192.in-addr.arpa* and the *20.254. 192.in-addr.arpa* zones, even though they correspond to the *fx.movie.edu* zone. We don't need to delegate to *fx.movie.edu* because we already delegated to its parent, *movie.edu*. The *movie.edu* nameservers delegate to *fx.movie.edu*, so, by transitivity, the roots delegate to *fx.movie.edu*. Since neither of the other *in-addr.arpa* zones is a parent of *254.253.192.in-addr.arpa* or *20.254.192.in-addr.arpa*, we need to delegate both zones from the root. As we explained earlier, we don't need to add address records for the three Special Effects nameservers, *bladerunner.fx.movie.edu, outland.fx.movie.edu*, and *alien.fx.movie.edu*, because a remote nameserver can already find their addresses by following delegation from *movie.edu*.

The db.root file

All that's left is to add an SOA record for the root zone and NS records for this internal root nameserver and any others:

```
$TTL 1d
.  IN  SOA  rainman.movie.edu.  hostmaster.movie.edu.  (
                1    ; serial
                3h   ; refresh
                1h   ; retry
                1w   ; expire
                1h ) ; negative caching TTL

    IN  NS  rainman.movie.edu.
    IN  NS  awakenings.movie.edu.

rainman.movie.edu.    IN  A  192.249.249.254
awakenings.movie.edu. IN  A  192.253.253.254
```

rainman.movie.edu and *awakenings.movie.edu* are the hosts running the internal root nameservers. We shouldn't run an internal root on a bastion host, because of the danger of the root becoming corrupt by caching external data.

So the whole *db.root* file (by convention, we call the root zone's datafile *db.root*) looks like this:

```
$TTL 1d
.  IN  SOA  rainman.movie.edu.  hostmaster.movie.edu.  (
                1    ; serial
                3h   ; refresh
                1h   ; retry
                1w   ; expire
                1h ) ; negative caching TTL

    IN  NS  rainman.movie.edu.
    IN  NS  awakenings.movie.edu.

rainman.movie.edu.    IN  A  192.249.249.254
awakenings.movie.edu. IN  A  192.253.253.254

movie.edu.  IN  NS  toystory.movie.edu.
            IN  NS  wormhole.movie.edu.
            IN  NS  zardoz.movie.edu.

toystory.movie.edu.    IN  A  192.249.249.3
wormhole.movie.edu.    IN  A  192.249.249.1
                       IN  A  192.253.253.1
```

```
zardoz.movie.edu.        IN  A  192.249.249.9
                         IN  A  192.253.253.9

249.249.192.in-addr.arpa.  IN  NS  toystory.movie.edu.
                           IN  NS  wormhole.movie.edu.
                           IN  NS  zardoz.movie.edu.
253.253.192.in-addr.arpa.  IN  NS  toystory.movie.edu.
                           IN  NS  wormhole.movie.edu.
                           IN  NS  zardoz.movie.edu.
254.253.192.in-addr.arpa.  IN  NS  bladerunner.fx.movie.edu.
                           IN  NS  outland.fx.movie.edu.
                           IN  NS  alien.fx.movie.edu.
20.254.192.in-addr.arpa.   IN  NS  bladerunner.fx.movie.edu.
                           IN  NS  outland.fx.movie.edu.
                           IN  NS  alien.fx.movie.edu.
```

The *named.conf* file on both the internal root nameservers, *rainman.movie.edu* and *awakenings.movie.edu*, contains the lines:

```
zone "." {
    type master;
    file "db.root";
};
```

This replaces a *zone* statement of type *hint*—a root nameserver doesn't need a root hints file to tell it where the other roots are; it can find that in *db.root*. Did we really mean that each root nameserver is a primary for the root zone? No, the root zone is just like any zone, so you'll probably have one primary nameserver and the rest slaves.

If you don't have a lot of idle hosts sitting around that you can turn into internal roots, don't despair! Any internal nameserver (i.e., one that's not running on a bastion host or outside your firewall) can serve double duty as an internal root *and* as an authoritative nameserver for whatever other zones you need it to load. Remember, a single nameserver can be authoritative for many, many zones, including the root zone.

Configuring other internal nameservers

Once you've set up internal root nameservers, configure all your nameservers on hosts anywhere on your internal network to use them. Any nameserver running on a host without direct Internet connectivity (i.e., behind the firewall) should list the internal roots in its root hints file:

```
; Internal root hints file, for Movie U. hosts without direct
; Internet connectivity
;
; Don't use this file on a host with Internet connectivity!
;

.  99999999  IN  NS  rainman.movie.edu.
   99999999  IN  NS  awakenings.movie.edu.
```

```
rainman.movie.edu.       99999999  IN  A  192.249.249.254
awakenings.movie.edu.    99999999  IN  A  192.253.253.254
```

Nameservers running on hosts using this root hints file can resolve domain names in *movie.edu* and in Movie U.'s *in-addr.arpa* domains, but not outside those domains.

How internal nameservers use internal roots

To tie together how this whole scheme works, let's go through an example of name resolution on an internal caching-only nameserver using these internal root nameservers. First, the internal nameserver receives a query for a domain name in *movie.edu*, say the address of *gump.fx.movie.edu*. If the internal nameserver doesn't have any "better" information cached, it starts by querying an internal root nameserver. If it has communicated with the internal roots before, it has a round-trip time associated with each, telling it which of the internal roots responded to it most quickly. It then sends a nonrecursive query to that internal root for *gump.fx.movie.edu*'s address. The internal root answers with a referral to the *movie.edu* nameservers on *toystory.movie.edu*, *wormhole.movie.edu*, and *zardoz.movie.edu*. The caching-only nameserver follows up by sending another nonrecursive query to one of the *movie.edu* nameservers for *gump.fx.movie.edu*'s address. The *movie.edu* nameserver responds with a referral to the *fx.movie.edu* nameservers. The caching-only nameserver sends the same nonrecursive query for *gump.fx.movie.edu*'s address to one of the *fx.movie.edu* nameservers and finally receives a response.

Contrast this with the way a forwarding setup works. Let's imagine that instead of using internal root nameservers, our caching-only nameserver is configured to forward queries first to *toystory.movie.edu* and then to *wormhole.movie.edu*. In that case, the caching-only nameserver checks its cache for the address of *gump.fx.movie.edu* and, not finding it, forwards the query to *toystory.movie.edu*. Then *toystory.movie.edu* queries an *fx.movie.edu* nameserver on the caching-only nameserver's behalf and returns the answer. Should the caching-only nameserver need to look up another name in *fx.movie.edu*, it still asks the forwarder, even though the forwarder's response to the query for *gump.fx.movie.edu*'s address probably contains the names and addresses of the *fx.movie.edu* nameservers.

Mail from internal hosts to the Internet

But wait! That's not all internal roots will do for you. We talked about getting mail to the Internet without changing *sendmail*'s configuration all over the network.

Wildcard records are the key to getting mail to work—specifically, wildcard MX records. Let's say that we want mail to the Internet to be forwarded through *postmanrings2x.movie.edu*, the Movie U. bastion host, which has direct Internet connectivity. Adding the following records to *db.root* gets the job done:

```
*        IN    MX    5 postmanrings2x.movie.edu.
*.edu.   IN    MX    10 postmanrings2x.movie.edu.
```

We need the *.edu MX record in addition to the * record because of wildcard production rules, which you can read more about in the section "Wildcards" in Chapter 16. Basically, since there is explicit data for *movie.edu* in the zone, the first wildcard won't match *movie.edu* or any other subdomains of *edu*. We need another, explicit wildcard record in *edu* to match subdomains of *edu* besides *movie.edu*.

Now mailers on our internal *movie.edu* hosts will send mail addressed to Internet domain names to *postmanrings2x.movie.edu* for forwarding. For example, mail addressed to *nic.ddn.mil* matches the first wildcard MX record:

```
% nslookup -type=mx nic.ddn.mil.      Matches the MX record for *
Server:  rainman.movie.edu
Address: 192.249.249.19

nic.ddn.mil
      preference = 5, mail exchanger = postmanrings2x.movie.edu
postmanrings2x.movie.edu    internet address = 192.249.249.20
```

Mail addressed to *vangogh.cs.berkeley.edu* matches the second MX record:

```
% nslookup -type=mx vangogh.cs.berkeley.edu.      Matches the MX record for *.edu
Server:  rainman.movie.edu
Address: 192.249.249.19

vangogh.cs.berkeley.edu
      preference = 10, mail exchanger = postmanrings2x.movie.edu
postmanrings2x.movie.edu    internet address = 192.249.249.20
```

Once the mail has reached *postmanrings2x.movie.edu*, our bastion host, *postmanrings2x.movie.edu*'s mailer looks up the MX records for these addresses itself. Since *postmanrings2x.movie.edu* resolves the destination's domain name in the Internet's namespace instead of the internal namespace, it will find the real MX records for the domain name and deliver the mail. No changes to *sendmail*'s configuration are necessary.

Mail to specific Internet domain names

Another nice perk of this internal root scheme is that it enables you to forward mail addressed to certain Internet domain names through particular bastion hosts, if you have more than one. We can choose, for example, to send all mail addressed to recipients in the *uk* domain to our bastion host in London first and then out onto the Internet. This can be very useful if we want our mail to travel across our own network as far as possible or if we're billed for our usage of some network in the United Kingdom.

Movie U. has a private network connection to our sister university in London near Pinewood Studios. For security reasons, we'd like to send mail addressed to correspondents in the United Kingdom. across our private link and then through the Pinewood host. So we add the following wildcard records to *db.root*:

```
; holygrail.movie.ac.uk is at the other end of our U.K. Internet link
*.uk.    IN    MX    10 holygrail.movie.ac.uk.
holygrail.movie.ac.uk.    IN    A    192.168.76.4
```

Now mail addressed to users in subdomains of *uk* will be forwarded to the host *holygrail.movie.ac.uk* at our sister university, which presumably has facilities to forward that mail to other points in the United Kingdom.

The trouble with internal roots

Unfortunately, just as forwarding has its problems, internal root architectures have their limitations. Chief among these is the fact that your internal hosts can't see the Internet namespace. On some networks, this isn't an issue because most internal hosts don't have any direct Internet connectivity. The few that do can have their resolvers configured to use a nameserver on a bastion host. Some of these hosts will probably need to run proxy servers to allow other internal hosts access to services on the Internet.

On other networks, however, the Internet firewall or other software may require that all internal hosts be able to resolve names in the Internet's namespace. For these networks, an internal root architecture won't work.

A Split Namespace

Many organizations would like to advertise different zone data to the Internet than they advertise internally. In most cases, much of the internal zone data is irrelevant to the Internet because of the organization's Internet firewall. The firewall may not allow direct access to most internal hosts and may also translate internal, unregistered IP addresses into a range of IP addresses registered to the organization. Therefore, the organization might need to trim out irrelevant information from the external view of the zone or change internal addresses to their external equivalents.

Unfortunately, BIND doesn't support automatic filtering and translation of zone data. Consequently, many organizations manually create what have become known as *split namespaces*. In a split namespace, the real namespace is available only internally, while a pared-down, translated version of it called the *shadow namespace* is visible to the Internet.

The shadow namespace contains the name-to-address and address-to-name mappings of only those hosts on your perimeter network (i.e., outside your firewall) or accessible from the Internet through the firewall. The addresses advertised may be the translated equivalents of internal addresses. The shadow namespace may also contain one or more MX records to direct mail from the Internet through the firewall to a mail server.

Since Movie U. has an Internet firewall that greatly limits access from the Internet to the internal network, we elected to create a shadow namespace. For the zone *movie.edu*, the only information we need to give out is about the domain name *movie.edu* (an SOA record and a few NS records); the bastion host (*postmanrings2x.movie.edu*); our new external nameserver, *ns.movie.edu*; and our external web server, *www.movie.edu*. The address of the external interface on the bastion host is 200.1.4.2, the address of the nameserver is 200.1.4.3, and the address of the web server is 200.1.4.4. The shadow *movie.edu* zone datafile looks like this:

```
$TTL 1d
@   IN   SOA   ns.movie.edu.     hostmaster.movie.edu. (
                          1    ; Serial
                          3h   ; Refresh
                          1h   ; Retry
                          1w   ; Expire
                          1h ) ; Negative caching TTL

     IN   NS    ns.movie.edu.
     IN   NS    ns1.isp.net.         ; our ISP's name server is a movie.edu slave

     IN   A     200.1.4.4    ; for people who try to access http://movie.edu
     IN   MX    10 postmanrings2x.movie.edu.
     IN   MX    100 mail.isp.net.

www            IN   A     200.1.4.4

postmanrings2x IN   A     200.1.4.2
               IN   MX    10 postmanrings2x.movie.edu.
               IN   MX    100 mail.isp.net.

;postmanrings2x.movie.edu handles mail addressed to ns.movie.edu
ns             IN   A     200.1.4.3
               IN   MX    10 postmanrings2x.movie.edu.
               IN   MX    100 mail.isp.net.

*              IN   MX    10 postmanrings2x.movie.edu.
               IN   MX    100 mail.isp.net.
```

Note that there's no mention of any of the subdomains of *movie.edu*, including any delegation to the nameservers for those subdomains. The information simply isn't necessary because there's nothing in any of the subdomains that you can get to from the Internet, and inbound mail addressed to hosts in the subdomains is caught by the wildcard.

The *db.200.1.4* file, which we need in order to reverse-map the two Movie U. IP addresses that hosts on the Internet might see, looks like this:

```
$TTL 1d
@   IN   SOA   ns.movie.edu.     hostmaster.movie.edu. (
                          1    ; Serial
                          3h   ; Refresh
```

```
                    1h   ; Retry
                    1w   ; Expire
                    1h ) ; Negative caching TTL

    IN    NS    ns.movie.edu.
    IN    NS    ns1.isp.net.

2   IN    PTR   postmanrings2x.movie.edu.
3   IN    PTR   ns.movie.edu.
4   IN    PTR   www.movie.edu.
```

One precaution we have to take is to make sure that the resolvers on our bastion host, on our mail server, and on our web server aren't configured to use the server on *ns.movie.edu*. Since that server can't see the real, internal *movie.edu*, using it renders these hosts unable to map internal domain names to addresses or internal addresses to names.

Configuring the bastion host

The bastion host is a special case in a split namespace configuration. It has a foot in each environment: one network interface connects it to the Internet and another connects it to the internal network. Now that we have split our namespace in two, how can our bastion host see both the Internet namespace and our real internal namespace? If we configure it with the Internet's root nameservers in its root hints file, it will follow delegation from the Internet's *edu* nameservers to an external *movie.edu* nameserver with shadow zone data. It would be blind to our internal namespace, which it needs to see to log connections, deliver inbound mail, and more. On the other hand, if we configure it with our internal roots, it won't see the Internet's namespace, which it clearly needs to do in order to function as a bastion host. What to do?

If we have internal nameservers that can resolve both internal and Internet domain names—using forward zones per the configuration earlier in this chapter, for example—we can simply configure the bastion host's resolver to query those nameservers. But if we use forwarding internally, depending on the type of firewall we're running, we may also need to run a forwarder on the bastion host itself. If the firewall won't pass DNS traffic, we'll need to run at least a caching-only nameserver, configured with the Internet roots, on the bastion host so that our internal nameservers will have somewhere to forward their unresolved queries.

If our internal nameservers don't support forward zones, the nameserver on our bastion host must be configured as a slave or stub for *movie.edu* and any *in-addr.arpa* zones in which it needs to resolve addresses. This way, if it receives a query for a domain name in *movie.edu*, it uses its local authoritative data to resolve the name (in the case of a slave zone) or follows internal NS records to the authoritative nameservers (for a stub zone). (If our internal nameservers support forward zones and are configured correctly, the nameserver on our bastion host will never receive queries for names in *movie.edu*.) If the domain name is in a delegated subdomain of *movie.edu*, it follows NS records that are in the *movie.edu* zone data or received from a *movie.edu* nameserver to query an internal nameserver for the name. Therefore, it doesn't need to be configured as a slave or stub for any *movie.edu* subdomains, such as *fx.movie.edu*, just the "topmost" zone (see Figure 11-6).

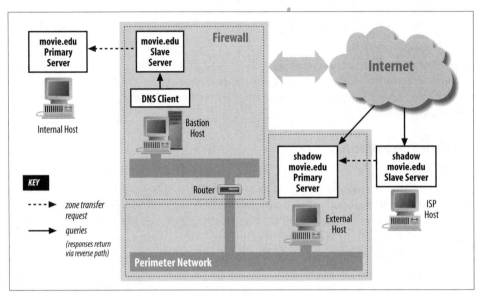

Figure 11-6. A split DNS solution

The *named.conf* file on our bastion host looks like this:

```
options {
    directory "/var/named";
};

zone "movie.edu" {
    type slave;
    masters { 192.249.249.3; };
    file "bak.movie.edu";
};

zone "249.249.192.in-addr.arpa" {
    type slave;
    masters { 192.249.249.3; };
    file "bak.192.249.249";
};
```

```
zone "253.253.192.in-addr.arpa" {
    type slave;
    masters { 192.249.249.3; };
    file "bak.192.253.253";
};

zone "254.253.192.in-addr.arpa" {
    type slave;
    masters { 192.253.254.2; };
    file "bak.192.253.254";
};

zone "20.254.192.in-addr.arpa" {
    type slave;
    masters { 192.253.254.2; };
    file "bak.192.254.20";
};

zone "." {
    type hint;
    file "db.cache";
};
```

Protecting zone data on the bastion host

Unfortunately, loading these zones on the bastion host also exposes them to the possibility of disclosure on the Internet, which we were trying to avoid by splitting the namespace in the first place. But we can protect the zone data using the *allow-query* substatement, discussed earlier in the chapter. With *allow-query*, we can place a global access list on our zone data. Here's the new *options* statement from our *named.conf* file:

```
options {
    directory "/var/named";
    allow-query { 127/8; 192.249.249/24; 192.253.253/24;
        192.253.254/24; 192.254.20/24; };
};
```

Don't forget to include the loopback address in the list, or the bastion host's resolver may not get answers from its own nameserver!

The final configuration

Finally, we need to apply the other security precautions we discussed earlier to our bastion host's nameserver. In particular, we should:

- Restrict zone transfers
- Use the ID pool feature (on BIND 8.2 or newer nameservers but not BIND 9)
- (Optionally) Run BIND *chroot*ed and with least privilege

In the end, our *named.conf* file ends up looking like this:

```
acl "internal" {
    127/8; 192.249.249/24; 192.253.253/24;
    192.253.254/24; 192.254.20/24;
};

options {
    directory "/var/named";
    allow-query { "internal"; };
    allow-transfer { none; };
};

zone "movie.edu" {
    type slave;
    masters { 192.249.249.3; };
    file "bak.movie.edu";
};

zone "249.249.192.in-addr.arpa" {
    type slave;
    masters { 192.249.249.3; };
    file "bak.192.249.249";
};

zone "253.253.192.in-addr.arpa" {
    type slave;
    masters { 192.249.249.3; };
    file "bak.192.253.253";
};

zone "254.253.192.in-addr.arpa" {
    type slave;
    masters { 192.253.254.2; };
    file "bak.192.253.254";
};

zone "20.254.192.in-addr.arpa" {
    type slave;
    masters { 192.253.254.2; };
    file "bak.192.254.20";
};

zone "." {
    type hint;
    file "db.cache";
};
```

Using views on the bastion host

If we're running BIND 9 on our bastion host, we can use views to safely present the shadow *movie.edu* to the outside world on the same nameserver that resolves Internet domain names. That may obviate the need to run an external nameserver on *ns.movie.edu*. If not, it'll give us an additional nameserver to advertise the external *movie.edu*.

This configuration is very similar to one shown in the "Views" section in Chapter 10:

```
options {
    directory "/var/named";
};

acl "internal" {
    127/8; 192.249.249/24; 192.253.253/24; 192.253.254/24; 192.254.20/24;
};

view "internal" {
    match-clients { "internal"; };
    recursion yes;

    zone "movie.edu" {
        type slave;
        masters { 192.249.249.3; };
        file "bak.movie.edu";
     };

    zone "249.249.192.in-addr.arpa" {
        type slave;
        masters { 192.249.249.3; };
        file "bak.192.249.249";
    };

    zone "253.253.192.in-addr.arpa" {
        type slave;
        masters { 192.249.249.3; };
        file "bak.192.253.253";
    };

    zone "254.253.192.in-addr.arpa" {
        type slave;
        masters { 192.253.254.2; };
        file "bak.192.253.254";
    };

    zone "20.254.192.in-addr.arpa" {
        type slave;
        masters { 192.253.254.2; };
        file "bak.192.254.20";
    };
```

```
    zone "." {
        type hint;
        file "db.cache";
    };
};

acl "ns1.isp.net" { 199.11.28.12; };

view "external" {
    match-clients { any; };
    recursion no;

    zone "movie.edu" {
        type master;
        file "db.movie.edu.external";
        allow-transfer { "ns1.isp.net"; };
    };

    zone "4.1.200.in-addr.arpa" {
        type master;
        file "db.200.1.4";
        allow-transfer { "ns1.isp.net"; };
    };

    zone "." {
        type hint;
        file "db.cache";
    };
};
```

Notice that the internal and external views present different versions of *movie.edu*: one loaded from the primary nameserver for the internal *movie.edu* and one loaded from the zone datafile *db.movie.edu.external*. If there were more than a few zones in our external view, we probably would have used a different subdirectory for our external zone datafiles than we used for the internal zone datafiles.

The DNS Security Extensions

TSIG, which we described earlier in this chapter, is well suited to securing the communications between two nameservers or between an updater and a nameserver. However, it won't protect you if one of your nameservers is compromised: if someone breaks into the host that runs one of your nameservers, he may also gain access to its TSIG keys. Moreover, because TSIG uses shared secrets, it isn't practical to configure TSIG among many nameservers. You couldn't use TSIG to secure your nameservers' communications with arbitrary nameservers on the Internet because you can't distribute and manage that many keys.

The most common way to deal with key management problems like these is to use *public-key cryptography*. The DNS Security Extensions (DNSSEC), described in

RFCs 4033, 4034, and 4035, use public-key cryptography to enable zone administrators to digitally sign their zone data, thereby proving its authenticity.

> We'll describe the DNS Security Extensions in their current form as described by RFCs 4033 through 4035. These RFCs reflect substantial changes in DNSSEC since its original version, described in RFC 2065 (and in the previous edition of this book). However, the IETF's DNSEXT working group is still working on DNSSEC and may change aspects of it before it becomes a standard.
>
> Also know that though BIND 8 provided preliminary support of DNSSEC as early as BIND 8.2,[*] DNSSEC wasn't really usable before BIND 9, and it isn't implemented as described in this section (and in the latest RFCs) until 9.3.0. Consequently, we'll use BIND 9.3.2 in our examples. If you want to use DNSSEC, you really shouldn't use anything older.

Public-Key Cryptography and Digital Signatures

Public-key cryptography solves the key distribution problem by using asymmetric cryptographic algorithms. In an asymmetric cryptographic algorithm, one key is used to decrypt data that another has encrypted. These two keys—a *key pair*—are generated at the same time using a mathematical formula. That's the only easy way to find two keys that have this special asymmetry (one decrypts what the other encrypts): it's very difficult to determine one key given the other. (In the most popular asymmetric cryptographic algorithm, RSA, that determination involves factoring very large numbers, a notoriously hard problem.)

In public-key cryptography, an individual first generates a key pair. Then, one key of the key pair is made public (e.g., published in a directory), while the other is kept private. Someone who wants to communicate securely with that individual can encrypt a message with the individual's public key and then send the encrypted message to the individual. (Or he could even post the message to a newsgroup or on a web site.) If the recipient has kept his private key private, only he can decrypt the message.

Conversely, the individual can encrypt a message with his private key and send it to someone. The recipient can verify that it came from that individual by attempting to decrypt it with the individual's public key. If the message decrypts to something reasonable (i.e., not gibberish), and the sender kept his private key to himself, the individual must have encrypted it. Successful decryption also proves that the message wasn't modified in transit (e.g., while passing through a mail server), because if it

---

[*] In particular, BIND 8 can't follow a chain of trust. It can verify SIG records only in zones it has *trusted-keys* statements for.

had been, it wouldn't have decrypted correctly. So the recipient has authenticated the message.

Unfortunately, encrypting large amounts of data with asymmetric encryption algorithms tends to be slow—much slower than encryption using symmetric encryption algorithms. But when using public-key encryption for authentication (and not for privacy), we don't have to encrypt the whole message. Instead, we run the message through a one-way hash function first. Then we can encrypt just the hash value, which represents the original data. We attach the encrypted hash value, now called a *digital signature*, to the message we want to authenticate. The recipient can still authenticate the message by decrypting the digital signature and running the message through his own copy of the one-way hash function. If the hash values match, the message is authentic. We call the process of computing the hash value and encrypting it *signing*, and the process of validating the digital signature *verifying*. The process of signing and verifying a message is shown in Figure 11-7.

The DNSKEY Record

In the DNS Security Extensions, each signed zone has a key pair associated with it. The zone's private key is stored somewhere safe, often in a file on the primary nameserver's filesystem. The zone's public key is advertised as a new type of record attached to the domain name of the zone, the DNSKEY record.

The previous version included a general-purpose KEY record: you could use the record to store different kinds of cryptographic keys, not just zones' public keys for use with DNSSEC. However, the revised DNSSEC uses the DNSKEY record only to store a zone's public key.

A DNSKEY record looks like this:

```
movie.edu. IN DNSKEY 257 3 5 AQPWA4BRyjB3eqYNy/oykeGcSXjl+HQK9CciAxJfMcS1vEuwz9c
+QG7s EJnQuH5B9i5o/ja+DVitY3jpXNa12mEn
```

The owner is the domain name of the zone that owns this public key. The first field after the type, 257, is the flags field. The flags field is two bytes long and encodes a set of two one-bit values:

```
  0   1   2   3   4   5   6   7   8   9   0   1   2   3   4   5
+---+---+---+---+---+---+---+---+---+---+---+---+---+---+---+---+
|                           |ZK |                           |SEP|
+---+---+---+---+---+---+---+---+---+---+---+---+---+---+---+---+
```

The first seven bits (0 through 6) and bits 8 through 14 are reserved and must have a value of 0.

The eighth bit encodes the type of key:

0   This is not a DNS zone key and can't be used to verify signed zone data.

1   This is a DNS zone key. The DNSKEY record's owner name is the domain name of the zone.

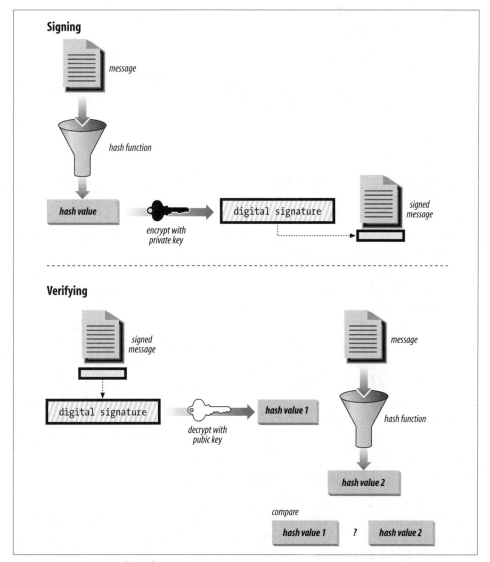

Figure 11-7. Signing and verifying a message

The last bit (15) is the Secure Entry Point (SEP) flag, which has an experimental use documented in RFC 3757. We'll discuss it in more detail later in the chapter.

In the DNSKEY record shown earlier, the flags field (the first field in the record after the type) says that this DNSKEY is *movie.edu*'s zone key.

The next field in the record, which in the example has the value 3, is called the *protocol field*. This is a holdover from the older version of DNSSEC, when you could use KEY records for different purposes. In the current version of DNSSEC, however, you can use DNSKEY records only with DNSSEC, so this field is always set to 3, which historically indicated a DNSSEC key.

The next (third) field in the DNSKEY record, which here has the value 5, is the *algorithm field*. DNSSEC can work with a number of public-key encryption algorithms, so you need to identify which algorithm a zone uses and which algorithm this key is used with here. The following values are defined:

0
> Reserved.

1
> RSA/MD5. The use of RSA/MD5 is no longer recommended, mostly due to recently discovered shortcomings in the MD5 one-way hash algorithm.

2
> Diffie-Hellman. Diffie-Hellman can't be used to sign zones, but it can be used for other DNSSEC-related purposes.

3
> DSA/SHA-1. The use of DSA/SHA-1 (in addition to any mandatory algorithm) is optional.

4
> Reserved for an elliptic curve-based public-key algorithm.

5
> RSA/SHA-1. The use of RSA/SHA-1 is mandatory.

253–254
> Private. These algorithm numbers are reserved for private use per RFC 4034.

255
> Reserved.

We'll use RSA/SHA-1 keys in our examples, naturally.

The final field in the DNSKEY record is the public key itself, encoded in base 64. DNSSEC supports keys of many lengths, as we'll see shortly when we generate the *movie.edu* public key. The longer the key, the more secure (because it's harder to find the corresponding private key), but the longer it takes to sign zone data with the private key and verify it with the public key, and the longer the DNSKEY record and signatures created.

The RRSIG Record

If the DNSKEY record stores a zone's public key, then there must be a new record to store the corresponding private key's signature, right? Sure enough, that's the RRSIG record. The RRSIG record stores the private key's digital signature on an *RRset*. An RRset is a group of resource records with the same owner, class, and type; for example, all of *wormhole.movie.edu*'s address records make up an RRset. Likewise, all of *movie. edu*'s MX records are another RRset.

Why sign RRsets rather than individual records? It saves time. There's no way to look up just one of *wormhole.movie.edu*'s address records; a nameserver will always return them as a group. So why go to the trouble of signing each one individually when you can sign them together?

Here's the RRSIG record that "covers" *wormhole.movie.edu*'s address records:

```
wormhole.movie.edu.        86400   RRSIG  A 5 3 86400 20060219233605 (
                                   20060120233605 3674 movie.edu.
                                   ZZP9AV28r824SZJqyIT+3WKkMQgcu1YTuFzp
                                   LgU3EN4USgpJhLZbYBqTHL77mipET5aJr80d
                                   RxZvfFHHYV6UGw== )
```

The owner name is *wormhole.movie.edu*, the same as the owner of the records signed. The first field after the type, which holds the value A, is called the *type covered*. That tells us which of *wormhole.movie.edu*'s records were signed—in this case, its address records. There would be a separate RRSIG record for each type of record *wormhole.movie.edu* might own.

The second field, which has the value 5, is the *algorithm field*. This is one of the same values used in the DNSKEY record's algorithm field, so 5 means RSA/SHA-1. If you generate an RSA/SHA-1 key and use it to sign your zone, you'll get RSA/SHA-1 signatures, naturally. If you sign your zone with multiple types of keys, say an RSA/SHA-1 key and a DSA key, you'll end up with two RRSIG records for each RRset, one with an algorithm number of 5 (RSA/SHA-1) and one with an algorithm number of 3 (DSA).*

The third field is called the *labels field*. It indicates how many labels there are in the owner name of the records signed. *wormhole.movie.edu* obviously has three labels, so the labels field contains 3. When would the labels field ever differ from the number of labels in the RRSIG's owner? When the RRSIG record covered a wildcard record of some type. We won't cover the nuances of wildcards in signed zones in this book.

The fourth field is the *original TTL* on the records in the RRset that was signed. (All the records in an RRset are supposed to have the same TTL.) The TTL needs to be stored here because a nameserver caching the RRset that this RRSIG record covers will decrement the TTLs on the cached records. Without the original TTL, it's impossible to reconstruct the original address records to feed them through the one-way hash function to verify the digital signature.

The next two fields are the signature expiration and inception fields, respectively. They're both stored as an unsigned integer number of seconds since the Unix epoch,

---

* You might sign your zone with two different algorithms' keys so that people whose software preferred DSA could verify your data while people who supported only RSA/SHA-1 could use RSA/SHA-1.

January 1, 1970, but in the RRSIG record's text representation, they're presented in the format YYYYMMDDHHMMSS for convenience. (The signature expiration time for the RRSIG record we showed you earlier is just after 11:36 p.m. on February 19, 2006.) The signature inception time is usually the time you ran the program to sign your zone. You choose the signature expiration time when you run that program, too. After the signature's expiration, the RRSIG record is no longer valid and can't be used to verify the RRset. Bummer. This means you have to re-sign your zone data periodically to keep the signatures valid. Fun. Thankfully, re-signing takes much less work than signing it for the first time.

The next (seventh) field in the RRSIG record, which in this record contains 3674, is the *key tag* field. The key tag is a fingerprint derived from the public key that corresponds to the private key that signed the zone. If the zone has more than one public key (and yours probably will), DNSSEC verification software uses the key tag to determine which key to use to verify this signature.

The eighth field, which contains *movie.edu*, is the *signer's name* field. As you'd expect, it's the domain name of the public key that a verifier should use to check the signature. It, together with the key tag, identifies the DNSKEY record to use. The signer's name field is always the domain name of the zone the signed records are in.

The final field is the *signature field*. This is the digital signature of the zone's private key on the signed records and the right side of the RRSIG record itself, minus this field. Like the key in the DNSKEY record, this signature is encoded in base 64.

The NSEC Record

DNSSEC introduces another new record type: the NSEC record. We'll explain what it's for.

What happens if you look up a domain name that doesn't exist in a signed zone? If the zone weren't signed, the nameserver would simply respond with the "no such domain name" response code. But how do you sign a response code? If you signed the whole response message, it would be difficult to cache. You need something unique to sign, something that proves that the domain name you looked up doesn't exist.

The NSEC record solves the problem of signing negative responses. It spans a gap between two consecutive domain names in a zone, telling you which domain name comes next after a given domain name—hence the name of the record: "Next SECure."

But doesn't the notion of "consecutive domain names" imply a canonical order to the domain names in a zone? Why, yes, it does.

To order the domain names in a zone, you begin by sorting by the rightmost label in those domain names, then by the next label to the left, and so on. Labels are sorted case-insensitively and lexicographically (by dictionary order), with numbers coming before letters and nonexistent labels before numbers (in other words, *movie.edu* would come before *0.movie.edu*). So the domain names in *movie.edu* sort to the following:

```
movie.edu
carrie.movie.edu
cujo.movie.edu
fx.movie.edu
bladerunner.fx.movie.edu
outland.fx.movie.edu
horror.movie.edu
localhost.movie.edu
mi.movie.edu
misery.movie.edu
monsters-inc.movie.edu
shining.movie.edu
shrek.movie.edu
toys.movie.edu
toystory.movie.edu
wh.movie.edu
wh249.movie.edu
wh253.movie.edu
wormhole.movie.edu
```

Notice that just as *movie.edu* comes before *carrie.movie.edu*, *fx.movie.edu* precedes *bladerunner.fx.movie.edu*.

Once the zone is in canonical order, the NSEC records make sense. Here's one NSEC record (the first, in fact) from *movie.edu*:

```
movie.edu.                    NSEC    carrie.movie.edu. NS SOA MX RRSIG NSEC DNSKEY
```

This record says that the next domain name in the zone after *movie.edu* is *carrie. movie.edu*, which we can see from our sorted list of domain names. It also says that *movie.edu* has NS records, an SOA record, MX records, RRSIG records, an NSEC record, and a DNSKEY record.

The last NSEC record in a zone is special. Since there's really no next domain name after the last one, the last NSEC record wraps around to the first record in the zone:

```
wormhole.movie.edu.           NSEC    movie.edu. A RRSIG NSEC
```

In other words, to indicate that *wormhole.movie.edu* is the last domain name in the zone, we say that the next domain name is *movie.edu*, the first domain name in the zone. Call it circular logic.

So how do NSEC records provide authenticated negative responses? Well, if you look up *www.movie.edu* internally, you get back the *wormhole.movie.edu* NSEC record, telling you that there's no *www.movie.edu* because there are no domain names in the zone after *wormhole.movie.edu*. Similarly, if you try to look up TXT records for *movie.edu*, you get the first NSEC record we showed you, which tells you there are no TXT records for *movie.edu*, just NS, SOA, MX, RRSIG, NSEC, and DNSKEY records.

An RRSIG record covering the NSEC record accompanies it in the response, authenticating the nonexistence of the domain name or type of data you asked for.

It's important that the NSEC records, *in toto*, identify specifically what doesn't exist in the zone. A single catch-all record that simply says "That doesn't exist" could be sniffed off the wire and replayed to claim falsely that existing domain names or records don't actually exist.

For those of you worried about the prospects of adding these new records to your zone and keeping them up to date manually—"Uh-oh, now that I've added a host, I've got to adjust my NSEC records"—take heart: BIND provides a tool to add NSEC and RRSIG records for you automatically.

Some of you may also worry about the information NSEC records reveal about your zone. A hacker could, for example, look up the NSEC record attached to the domain name of your zone to find the record types attached to that domain name and the lexicographically next domain name, then repeat the process to learn all the domain names and RRsets in the zone. That, unfortunately, is an unavoidable side effect of signing your zone. Just repeat this mantra: "My zone data is secure, but public."

The DS Record and the Chain of Trust

There's one more aspect of DNSSEC theory that we should discuss: the chain of trust. (No, this isn't some touchy-feely team-building exercise.) So far, each RRset in our signed zone has an RRSIG record associated with it. To let others verify those RRSIG records, our zone advertises its public key to the world in a DNSKEY record. But imagine if someone breaks into our primary nameserver. What's to keep her from generating her own key pair? Then she could modify our zone data, resign our zone with her newly generated private key, and advertise her newly generated public key in a DNSKEY record.

To combat this problem, our public key is "certified" by a higher authority. This higher authority attests to the fact that the *movie.edu* public key in our DNSKEY record really belongs to the organization that owns and runs the zone, and not to some random yahoo. Before certifying us, this higher authority demanded some sort of proof that we were who we said we were and that we were the duly authorized administrators of *movie.edu*.

This higher authority is our parent zone, *edu*. When we generated our key pair and signed our zone, we also sent our public key to the administrators of *edu*, along with proof of our identity and of our positions as the Two True Administrators of *movie.edu*.*

---

* In fact, only the Swedish top-level zone, *se*, currently signs its zone and can sign DNSKEY records.

They indicated their approval of our credentials and of our public key by inserting a DS record to the *edu* zone, then signing the record with their private key. Here are the resulting records:

```
movie.edu.              86400   DS      15480 5 1 (
                                        F340F3A05DB4D081B6D3D749F300636DCE3D
                                        6C17 )
                        86400   RRSIG   DS 5 2 86400 20060219234934 (
                                        20060120234934 23912 edu.
                                        Nw4xLOhtFoPOcE6ECIC8GgpJKtGWstzkOuH6
                                        nd2cz28/24j4kz1Ahznr/+g5oU3AADyv86EK
                                        CnWZtyOeqnfhMZ3UWOyyPcF3wy73tYLQ/KjN
                                        gPm1VPQA/Sl3smauJsFW7/YPaoQuxcnREPWf
                                        YWInWvWx12IiPKfkVU3FOEbosBA= )
```

DS stands for *delegation signer*. The DS record identifies the public key authorized to sign the *movie.edu* zone's data. The first field after the type is a key tag, as in the RRSIG record, that helps identify the DNSKEY record authorized to do the signing. The second field is another algorithm field, as in both the DNSKEY and RRSIG records, also used to help identify the relevant DNSKEY record in case we used multiple cryptographic algorithms. The third field is the *digest type field*, which tells a verifier which digest mechanism to use to verify the *digest*, the final field. The only currently supported digest type is 1, for an SHA-1 digest. The digest is a 20-byte, hexadecimal-encoded, one-way hash of the *movie.edu* DNSKEY record.*

Accompanying the DS record is an RRSIG record, showing that the administrators of the *edu* zone signed the *movie.edu* DS record, thereby vouching for it.

When following a referral from the *edu* nameservers to the *movie.edu* servers and verifying the *movie.edu* DNSKEY record, a nameserver first verifies the RRSIG record covering the DS record. Assuming the RRSIG verified, the nameserver looks up DNSKEY records attached to *movie.edu* and looks for one matching the key tag and algorithm listed in the DS record. Once the correct DNSKEY record was identified, the nameserver runs the record through the one-way hash algorithm and checks whether the digest matches the digest from the DS record. If it does, the DNSKEY record is authentic, and the nameserver can use it to verify the RRSIG record covering the DNSKEY RRset or other RRsets signed by the corresponding private key.

What if someone breaks into the *edu* zone's primary nameserver? The *edu* zone's DNSKEY record is certified by a DS record in the root zone, so they can't simply replace it or any data signed by it. And the root zone? Well, the root zone's public key is very widely known and configured on every nameserver that supports DNSSEC.†

---

* Our sources tell us (OK, one of our technical reviewers, but didn't "sources" sound cool?) that an upcoming version of BIND will move to SHA-256 to address weaknesses in SHA-1.

† This reminds us of the tale of the man who asks the priest what holds the Earth up. The priest tells him that the Earth rests on the back of a turtle, which holds it up. The man then asks what the turtle rests on. "On the back of an elephant," replies the priest. "But what," the man asks, "does the elephant rest on?" The frustrated priest snaps back, "It's elephants all the way down!"

That is, the root zone's public key *will* be configured on every nameserver once DNS-SEC is widely implemented. Right now, neither the root zone nor the *edu* zone is signed, and neither has a key pair. Until DNSSEC is widely implemented, though, it's possible to use DNSSEC piecemeal.

Islands of security

Let's say we want to begin using DNSSEC at Movie U. to improve the security of our zone data. We've signed the *movie.edu* zone but can't have *edu* certify our DNSKEY record because they haven't signed their zone yet and don't have a key pair. How can other nameservers on the Internet verify our zone data? How can our own nameservers verify our zone data, for that matter?

BIND 9 nameservers provide a mechanism for specifying the public key that corresponds to a particular zone in the *named.conf* file: the *trusted-keys* statement. Here's the *trusted-keys* statement for *movie.edu*:

```
trusted-keys {
    movie.edu. 257 3 5 "AQPWA4BRyjB3eqYNy/oykeGcSXjl+HQK9CciAxJfMcS1vEuwz9c
+QG7s EJnQuH5B9i5o/ja+DVitY3jpXNa12mEn";
};
```

It's basically the DNSKEY record without the class and type fields and with the key itself quoted. The domain name of the zone may be quoted, but it's not necessary. If *movie.edu* had more than one public key—say a DSA key—we could include it, too:

```
trusted-keys {
    movie.edu. 257 3 5 "AQPWA4BRyjB3eqYNy/oykeGcSXjl+HQK9CciAxJfMcS1vEuwz9c
+QG7s EJnQuH5B9i5o/ja+DVitY3jpXNa12mEn";
    movie.edu. 257 3 3 "AMnD8GXACuJ5GVnfCJWmRydg2A6JptSm6tjH7QoL81SfBY/kcz1Nbe
    Hh z4l9AT1GG2kAZjGLjHO7BZHY+joz6iYMPRCDaPOIt9LO+SRfBNZg62P4 aSPT5zVQPahDIMZmTIvv
    O7FV6IaTV+cQiKQl6noro8uTk4asCADrAHwO iVjzjaYpoFF5AsBOcJU18fzDiCNBUbOVqE1mKFuRA/K
    1KyxM2vJ3U7IS tooIgACiCfHkYK5r3qFbMvF1GrjyVwfwCC4NcMsqEXIT8IEI/YYIgFt4 Ennh";
};
```

This *trusted-keys* statement enables a BIND 9 nameserver to verify any records in the *movie.edu* zone. The nameserver can also verify any records in child zones such as *fx.movie.edu*, assuming their DNSKEY records are certified by a DS record and accompanying RRSIG record in *movie.edu*. In other words, *movie.edu* becomes a *trust anchor*, below which our nameserver can verify any signed zone data.

Delegating to unsigned zones

A DS record indicates that a particular delegated subdomain is signed and authorizes a particular DNSKEY record to verify signed data. But what if a subdomain isn't signed?

Unsigned subdomains won't have DS records in the parent zone. They also won't have RRSIG records covering their DS records, of course. The NS records that implement the delegation will have one or more associated NSEC records, though, and the NSEC records will be covered with RRSIG records.

If there are any glue address records, they won't have NSEC records or RRSIG records because these records really belong to the subdomain.

What happens to name resolution when a nameserver follows delegation from a signed zone to an unsigned zone depends on the security policy of the querying nameserver. The nameserver might accept responses from the unsigned zone or insist that those responses be signed.

DO, AD, and CD

You've now seen examples of the four new DNSSEC record types, so you know how long they can be. But the classical limit on the length of a UDP-based DNS message is just 512 bytes. Including all those RRSIGs would cause a lot of truncated responses.

To cope with this, DNSSEC requires support for EDNS0, which we introduced in Chapter 10. EDNS0 allows the use of UDP-based DNS messages as long as 4,096 bytes. DNSSEC also uses a new EDNS0 flag, called the DO flag, for *DNSSEC OK*, as an indication that a querier supports DNSSEC and wants DNSSEC-related records in the response. Through this use of the DO flag, nameservers don't needlessly include a bunch of useless records in responses to queriers that don't support DNSSEC.

DNSSEC uses two other flags in queries: AD and CD. Both are part of the standard DNS query header; they were allocated from previously unused space.*

AD stands for Authenticated Data. It's set by DNSSEC-capable nameservers in responses only if they've verified all the DNSSEC-related records included in the message. A nameserver returning any records that failed to verify, or simply weren't from a signed zone, would clear the AD bit.

The AD bit is designed to allow resolvers that query a nameserver that supports DNSSEC but can't themselves verify DNSSEC records to determine whether a response has been validated. However, these resolvers should only trust the setting of the AD bit if their communications channel to the nameserver is secure—using IPSEC or TSIG, for example.

The CD bit, on the other hand, is meant for use by resolvers that *can* verify DNSSEC records. CD, which is an abbreviation for Checking Disabled, tells the nameserver not to bother verifying DNSSEC records on the resolver's behalf because it can handle the job itself.

---

* Previously unused but precious: there were only three unused bits in the header; AD and CD use two of them.

How the Records Are Used

Let's go through what a DNSSEC-capable nameserver does to verify a record in *movie.edu*. In particular, let's see what happens when it looks up the address of *wormhole.movie.edu*. We'll use *dig*, since we can't set the DO bit with *nslookup*.

First, of course, the nameserver sends a query for the address:

```
% dig +dnssec +norec wormhole.movie.edu.

; <<>> DiG 9.3.2 <<>> +dnssec +norec wormhole.movie.edu.
; (1 server found)
;; global options:  printcmd
;; Got answer:
;; ->>HEADER<<- opcode: QUERY, status: NOERROR, id: 32579
;; flags: qr aa ra; QUERY: 1, ANSWER: 3, AUTHORITY: 4, ADDITIONAL: 3

;; OPT PSEUDOSECTION:
; EDNS: version: 0, flags: do; udp: 4096
;; QUESTION SECTION:
;wormhole.movie.edu.            IN      A

;; ANSWER SECTION:
wormhole.movie.edu.    86400   IN      A       192.253.253.1
wormhole.movie.edu.    86400   IN      A       192.249.249.1
wormhole.movie.edu.    86400   IN      RRSIG   A 5 3 86400 20060219233605
20060120233605 3674 movie.edu.
ZZP9AV28r824SZJqyIT+3WKkMQgcu1YTuFzpLgU3EN4USgpJhLZbYBqT
HL77mipET5aJr8OdRxZvfFHHYV6UGw==

;; AUTHORITY SECTION:
movie.edu.             86400   IN      NS      outland.fx.movie.edu.
movie.edu.             86400   IN      NS      wormhole.movie.edu.
movie.edu.             86400   IN      NS      toystory.movie.edu.
movie.edu.             86400   IN      RRSIG   NS 5 2 86400 20060219233605
20060120233605 3674 movie.edu. bwiM/R56VVVOpHrzIERVADLat7BoTR+eeFuCfgYc/
GMXecdTxnUahLig RKsbNSsY+Uz8RVkcewFSiExExFoqwA==

;; ADDITIONAL SECTION:
toystory.movie.edu.    86400   IN      A       192.249.249.3
toystory.movie.edu.    86400   IN      RRSIG   A 5 3 86400 20060219233605
20060120233605 3674 movie.edu. hlz+W41UlcfIaCMdzoKVAuTPjnyqZhxY3TKOOm/
2i7FPAkfnVyWMyTwG iBns7Z1ws6QVj7+ZedDFx7xs+VOIyw==

;; Query time: 13 msec
;; SERVER: 127.0.0.1#53(127.0.0.1)
;; WHEN: Fri Jan 20 16:52:54 2006
;; MSG SIZE  rcvd: 474
```

Notice that we had to specify *+dnssec* on the command line. That sets the DO flag we just described, telling the nameserver to include DNSSEC records in the response. You can see that the DO flag is set in *dig*'s output: look for the line that begins with *; EDNS:*.

The flags show that DO was set, and that the maximum UDP message size was negotiated to a full 4,096 bytes.

Also notice that the response includes three RRSIG records: one covering the records in the answer section, one covering the records in the authority section, and one covering *toystory.movie.edu*'s address record in the additional section.

To verify the RRSIG records, the nameserver must look up *movie.edu*'s DNSKEY record. But before using the key, it must verify the key—unless, of course, the nameserver has previously verified it or knows the *movie.edu* public key from a *trusted-keys* statement. Verifying the key may require additional queries: one to an *edu* nameserver for the *movie.edu* DS record and the RRSIG records covering it, and possibly a query to a root nameserver for the *edu* DS record and its associated RRSIG records.

DNSSEC and Performance

It should be evident from this *dig* output that DNSSEC increases the average size of a DNS message; that it requires substantially more computational horsepower from nameservers verifying zone data; that verification can entail several successive queries, each of which may result in additional data that requires verifying; and that signing a zone increases its size substantially—current estimates are that signing multiplies the size of a zone by a factor of three to four. Each effect has its consequences:

- Verifying zone data involves decryption and consumes computational resources.
- The longer the chain of trust, the longer verification takes.
- The longer the chain of trust, the greater the chance of misconfiguration.
- Larger, signed zones mean larger *named* processes, which consume more memory and take longer to start.

In fact, DNSSEC's complexity meant that BIND 8's architecture couldn't support DNSSEC completely. DNSSEC also provided part of the impetus for developing BIND 9 and for ensuring it supported multiprocessor hosts. If you're planning on signing your zones, make sure your authoritative nameservers have enough memory to load the new, larger zones. If your nameservers are resolving more records in signed zones, make sure they have enough processor power to verify all those digital signatures.

Zone-Signing Keys and Key-Signing Keys

In practice, administrators are expected to use two types of keys per zone: *zone-signing keys* (ZSKs) and *key-signing keys* (KSKs). An administrator signs his zone data with the zone-signing key (duh) and publishes the corresponding public key in a DNSKEY record. The key-signing key also appears in the DNSKEY records, and the administrator uses the private key-signing key to sign just the DNSKEY records.

The SEP flag in the DNSKEY record serves as a hint to software to determine which of a zone's DNSKEY records corresponds to the key-signing key (the one with the SEP flag set). When we generate our key pair, we'll specify which one is the key-signing key.

Why bother with two keys for a zone? Cryptography wonks know that the more data encrypted using a cryptographic key, the greater the danger that someone will crack it. In the case of public-key cryptography, that means determining the corresponding private key. Zone-signing keys are used all the time: every time you modify your zone, you re-sign it. With a large zone, there's lots of available encrypted data subject to cryptanalysis. Consequently, you must generate new zone-signing keys frequently. If that entails resubmitting your DNSKEY record to your parent zone's administrators, having them replace your zone's DS record and re-signing it, that'll take a lot of time and effort. Using separate zone-signing and key-signing keys allows you to re-sign your zone data without involving your parent zone's administrators. You'll only need to contact them if you rotate your key-signing key, which doesn't need to be done as often because it isn't used to encrypt much data (just enough to produce an RRSIG for the DNSSEC RRset).

Signing a Zone

Okay, now you have the theoretical background you need to actually sign your zone. We'll show you how we signed *movie.edu*. Remember, we used the BIND 9.3.2 tools, which support the newest version of DNSSEC.

Generating your key pairs

First, we generated a KSK key pair for *movie.edu*:[*]

```
# cd /var/named
# dnssec-keygen -f KSK -a RSASHA1 -b 512 -n ZONE movie.edu.
Kmovie.edu.+005+15480
```

Next, we generated a ZSK key pair (we don't need to specify a *–f* option because this is the default):

```
# dnssec-keygen -a RSASHA1 -b 512 -n ZONE movie.edu.
Kmovie.edu.+005+03674
```

We ran *dnssec-keygen* in our nameserver's working directory. That's mostly for convenience: the zone datafiles are in this directory, so we won't need to use full pathnames as arguments. If we want to use dynamic update with DNSSEC, however, the keys must be in the nameserver's working directory.

---

[*] We're using relatively short key lengths in these examples to keep the DNSKEY and RRSIG records short. You should use longer keys, at least 1,024 bits.

The *–f KSK* option sets the SEP flag in the DNSKEY record. To leave the flag clear, omit the option.

Recall *dnssec-keygen*'s other options from the TSIG section of this chapter (oh, so long ago):

–a The cryptographic algorithm to use, in this case RSA/SHA-1. We could also have used DSA, but RSA/SHA-1 is mandatory.

–b The length of the keys to generate, in bits. RSA/SHA-1 keys can be anywhere from 512 to 4,096 bits long. DSA keys can be 512 to 1,024 bits long, as long as the length is divisible by 64.

–n The type of key. DNSSEC keys are always zone keys.

The only nonoption argument is the domain name of the zone, *movie.edu*. The *dnssec-keygen* program prints the basename of the files it's written the keys to. The numbers at the end of the basename (005 and 15494), as we explained in the "TSIG" section, are the key's DNSSEC algorithm number as used in the DNSKEY record (005 is RSA/SHA-1), and the key's fingerprint, used to distinguish one key from another when multiple keys are associated with the same zone.

The public key is written to the file *basename.key* (e.g., *Kmovie.edu.+005+15480.key*). The private key is written to the file *basename.private* (e.g., *Kmovie.edu.+005+15480. private*). Remember to protect the private key; anyone who knows the private key can forge signed zone data. *dnssec-keygen* does what it can to help you: it makes the *.private* file readable and writable only by the user who ran the program.

Signing your zone

Before signing our zone, we had to add the DNSKEY records to our plain-Jane zone datafile:

```
# cat "$INCLUDE Kmovie.edu.+005+15480.key" >> db.movie.edu
# cat "$INCLUDE Kmovie.edu.+005+03674.key" >> db.movie.edu
```

Then, we signed the zone with *dnssec-signzone*:

```
# dnssec-signzone -o movie.edu. db.movie.edu
db.movie.edu.signed
```

We used the *–o* option to specify the origin in the zone datafile, because *dnssec-signzone* doesn't read *named.conf* to determine which zone the file describes. The only nonoption argument is the name of the zone datafile. If the name of our zone datafile had been the same as the domain name of the zone, we could have omitted the *–o* option.

dnssec-signzone is smart enough to look at the SEP field in the DNSKEY records to determine which key to sign which records with. It'll sign the whole zone with the ZSK and just the DNSKEY records with both the ZSK and the KSK.

This produces a new zone datafile, *db.movie.edu.signed*, which begins like this:

```
; File written on Fri Jan 20 16:36:05 2006
; dnssec_signzone version 9.3.2
movie.edu.              86400    IN SOA  toystory.movie.edu. al.movie.edu. (
                                         2006011700 ; serial
                                         10800      ; refresh (3 hours)
                                         3600       ; retry (1 hour)
                                         604800     ; expire (1 week)
                                         3600       ; minimum (1 hour)
                                         )
                        86400    RRSIG   SOA 5 2 86400 20060219233605 (
                                         20060120233605 3674 movie.edu.
                                         joujDnvBovW1h+GJ2ZEhvmXQTGqVL4cZBCHM
                                         ByFitPRLINe/dKj8VCZg87ZUHQ/eAZSSGDuw
                                         XVIlT46ByG5AOg== )
                        86400    NS      outland.fx.movie.edu.
                        86400    NS      wormhole.movie.edu.
                        86400    NS      toystory.movie.edu.
                        86400    RRSIG   NS 5 2 86400 20060219233605 (
                                         20060120233605 3674 movie.edu.
                                         bwiM/R56VVVOpHrzIERVADLat7BoTR+eeFuC
                                         fgYc/GMXecdTxnUahLigRKsbNSsY+Uz8RVkc
                                         ewFSiExExFoqwA== )
                        86400    MX      10 postmanrings2x.movie.edu.
                        86400    RRSIG   MX 5 2 86400 20060219233605 (
                                         20060120233605 3674 movie.edu.
                                         rm7ROIb451iK49+bRhch4pIP11F4xZMWtqll
                                         8rQ9tKIOg+jTunNXxix5XnyVKoMQwoa8C5Tu
                                         ZFeDcbHNOUB5ow== )
                        3600     NSEC    misery.movie.edu. NS SOA MX RRSIG NSEC DNSKEY
                        3600     RRSIG   NSEC 5 2 3600 20060219233605 (
                                         20060120233605 3674 movie.edu.
                                         V4ipZI5SHGdFNOVEFn43gsRdYffUH6COrPxn
                                         RNfUMv6gfgwkythXXr5rxONTOSfa+Dp4CZrC
                                         qwn+CLryUN8vZg== )
                        86400    DNSKEY  256 3 5 (
                                         AQO/T4DRCAbi1diCB+UT4fDOeCvsa+1NKkO8
                                         UJMF5TlfRvokChybhHaDG5U98xw4XgAO1/4R
                                         gSlAcSDvhQeKu9n9
                                         ) ; key id = 3674
                        86400    DNSKEY  257 3 5 (
                                         AQPWA4BRyjB3eqYNy/oykeGcSXjl+HQK9Cci
                                         AxJfMcS1vEuwz9c+QG7sEJnQuH5B9i5o/ja+
                                         DVitY3jpXNa12mEn
                                         ) ; key id = 15480
                        86400    RRSIG   DNSKEY 5 2 86400 20060219233605 (
                                         20060120233605 3674 movie.edu.
                                         b35F2azzAY6QDghakORqJzPacmAhcsw3lDoA
                                         zKCFPQRnqVpwl4l7tAgKw2T1Cy9GPmdHMTBx
                                         foODB2smQQJjog== )
```

```
         86400   RRSIG   DNSKEY 5 2 86400 20060219233605 (
                         20060120233605 15480 movie.edu.
                         J267HbxKdzGq6iIKywZT6xOFQY7Ev1JWYWEc
                         PKRyZLY2WQ9S3roOrIUGJRIhHS5oBtzN1gOK
                         3DL2edi1Hgy+OA== )
```

Believe it or not, those are just the records attached to the domain name *movie.edu*. The zone datafile as a whole more than quintupled in length and quadrupled in size. Oy!

Finally, we turned on DNSSEC support on our nameserver[*] and changed the *zone* statement in *named.conf* so that *named* would load the new zone datafile:

```
options {
    directory "/var/named";
    dnssec-enable yes;
};

zone "movie.edu" {
    type master;
    file "db.movie.edu.signed";
};
```

Then we reloaded the zone and checked *syslog*.

dnssec-signzone does take some options that we didn't use:

−*s*, −*e*

These options specify the signature inception and expiration times to use in RRSIG records. The signature inception and expiration fields default to "now" and "30 days from now," respectively. Both options accept either an absolute time as an argument, in the form YYYYMMDDHHMMSS, or an offset. For −*s*, the offset is calculated from the current time. For −*e*, the offset is calculated from the start time.

−*i*

Specifies as an option argument the cycle period for resigning records (which we'll cover in a minute). This was the −*c* option before BIND 9.1.0.

−*f*

Specifies as an option argument the name of the file to write the signed zone to. The default is the name of the zone datafile with *.signed* concatenated.

−*k*

Specifies the key to be used as the key-signing key. The default is to use any private keys corresponding to DNSKEY records with the SEP flag set.

You can also specify, as a second nonoption argument, which private key to use to sign the zone. By default, *dnssec-signzone* signs the zone with each of the zone's private keys

---

[*] This assumes our nameserver was compiled with the −*with-openssl=yes* option. If not, we'd need to rerun *configure* with that option (see Appendix C) and recompile.

in the directory. If you specify the name of one or more files that contain the zone's private keys as arguments, it will sign using only those keys.

Remember, you'll need to re-sign the zone each time you change the zone data, though you certainly don't need to generate a new key pair each time. You can re-sign the zone by running *dnssec-signzone* on the signed zone data:

```
# dnssec-signzone -o movie.edu -f db.movie.edu.signed.new db.movie.edu.signed
# mv db.movie.edu.signed db.movie.edu.signed.bak
# mv db.movie.edu.signed.new db.movie.edu.signed
# rndc reload movie.edu
```

The program is smart enough to recalculate NSEC records, sign new records, and re-sign records whose signature expiration times are approaching. By default, *dnssec-signzone* resigns records whose signatures expire within 7.5 days (a quarter of the difference between the default signature inception and expiration times). If you specify different inception and expiration times, *dnssec-signzone* adjusts the re-signing cycle time accordingly. Or you can simply specify a cycle time with the *–i* (formerly the *–c*) option.

Sending your keys to be signed

Next, we sent our KSK to the administrator of our parent zone to sign. Conveniently, *dnssec-signzone* created a *keyset file* for us when we ran it. This is a small file, called *keyset-movie.edu*, which contains all of the DNSKEY records in our zone. The contents look like this:

```
$ORIGIN .
movie.edu              3600    IN DNSKEY 257 3 5 (
                                AQPWA4BRyjB3eqYNy/oykeGcSXjl+HQK9Cci
                                AxJfMcS1vEuwz9c+QG7sEJnQuH5B9i5o/ja+
                                DVitY3jpXNa12mEn
                                ) ; key id = 15480
```

dnssec-signzone even creates a DS record for the *edu* administrators to insert into the *edu* zone and writes it to the file *dsset-movie.edu.* * The *dsset* file contains:

```
movie.edu.             IN DS 15480 5 1 F340F3A05DB4D081B6D3D749F300636DCE3D6C17
```

Then, we sent our *keyset* file off to our parent zone's administrators to sign. Since the message included proof of our identity,[†] they added it to the *edu* zone and re-signed the zone. The resulting records in the *edu* zone datafile look like this:

```
movie.edu.             86400   IN NS   outland.fx.movie.edu.
                       86400   IN NS   wormhole.movie.edu.
```

---

* At this point, it's unclear whether the administrator of a signed zone should submit a *keyset* file or a *dsset* file to his parent zone's administrator. Either will do: the parent zone's administrator can generate a DS record from a DNSKEY record. For now, we'll guess that we'd submit a *keyset* file.

† Since top-level zones haven't started signing zones yet, there's still some question as to how they'll require us to authenticate ourselves. The use of cryptographically signed email messages is a possibility.

```
                86400    IN NS   toystory.movie.edu.
                86400    DS      15480 5 1 (
                                 F340F3A05DB4D081B6D3D749F300636DCE3D
                                 6C17 )
                86400    RRSIG   DS 5 2 86400 20060219234934 (
                                 20060120234934 23912 edu.
                                 Nw4xLOhtFoPOcE6ECIC8GgpJKtGWstzkOuH6
                                 nd2cz28/24j4kz1Ahznr/+g5oU3AADyv86EK
                                 CnWZtyOeqnfhMZ3UWOyyPcF3wy73tYLQ/KjN
                                 gPm1VPQA/Sl3smauJsFW7/YPaoQuxcnREPWf
                                 YWInWvWx12IiPKfkVU3FOEbosBA= )
                86400    NSEC    edu. NS DS RRSIG NSEC
                86400    RRSIG   NSEC 5 2 86400 20060219234934 (
                                 20060120234934 23912 edu.
                                 LpOmh/SZMonQUBUil5MYfIrxld5g6pVeyTxl
                                 deDvJ7OIMdI+XOvXmRI3RgmKaRJKYBr4BcNO
                                 jrNU8fQo5Ox5WvEeKn1St1NvdB62/Nqjfz6F
                                 I+LNXe6diq1uDZZUB3hx5PF+Flp28D75KHnZ
                                 5YE9+vVJryOHHsGawklSrUAJAUg= )
```

Note the RRSIG record covering the DS record. This indicates the *edu* zone's certification of our DS record, and thus our KSK's DNSKEY record.

If we didn't care about getting our DNSKEY record signed, we could have skipped this step. However, then only nameservers with a *trusted-keys* entry for *movie.edu* could verify our data.

Signing a parent zone

Signing a zone that's a parent to one or more subzones is straightforward. If the subzones aren't signed, there's really nothing different to do: run *dnssec-signzone* to sign the parent zone, just as you normally would. The records that make up delegation to unsigned subzones won't be changed. For example, here's what the delegation to the unsigned *fx.movie.edu* looked like after we signed *movie.edu*:

```
fx.movie.edu.                   86400    IN NS   alien.fx.movie.edu.
                                86400    IN NS   outland.fx.movie.edu.
                                86400    IN NS   bladerunner.fx.movie.edu.
                                3600     NSEC    misery.movie.edu. NS RRSIG NSEC
                                3600     RRSIG   NSEC 5 3 3600 20060220215231 (
                                                 20060121215231 3674 movie.edu.
                                                 maFMyIVEdjg5BUTKMUyCZvBu6ZrtrQwJyJRo
                                                 9A9PDO3bTpWcpCAp4QOcQ5FwQcveIq15LMit
                                                 CWyOwN745dJ86Q== )
alien.fx.movie.edu.             86400    IN A    192.254.20.3
bladerunner.fx.movie.edu. 86400 IN A             192.253.254.2
outland.fx.movie.edu.           86400    IN A    192.253.254.3
```

Note the NSEC record attached to *fx.movie.edu*: the domain name "counts" as far as NSEC records are concerned, but neither the NS records nor the glue A records are signed. Only the NSEC record itself is signed.

If the *fx.movie.edu* administrators sign their zone, they need to submit only their *keyset* or *dsset* file to us (in some sufficiently secure fashion), just as we submitted ours to the *edu* administrators. If the *keyset* file is present in the working directory when we sign *movie.edu*, we can use the –g option to tell *dnssec-signzone* to create an *fx.movie.edu* DS record automatically. Otherwise, we can add the DS record from the *dsset* file manually and re-sign *movie.edu*. Here's how the signed delegation ends up looking:

```
fx.movie.edu.           86400   IN NS   alien.fx.movie.edu.
                        86400   IN NS   outland.fx.movie.edu.
                        86400   IN NS   bladerunner.fx.movie.edu.
                        86400   DS      2847 5 1 (
                                        F495606120C4927FB4BEB04D0C354BBE5ED8
                                        CA31 )
                        86400   RRSIG   DS 5 3 86400 20060220230640 (
                                        20060121230640 3674 movie.edu.
                                        OuZCLrqLZlaEgePAxzhUCneV6FyOq6hQwRWF
                                        4bsHPrvIrLMIuftxfB8M3mmgkKlpOlJIJFvH
                                        Qc4RUfYOGkMkdg== )
                        3600    NSEC    misery.movie.edu. NS DS RRSIG NSEC
                        3600    RRSIG   NSEC 5 3 3600 20060220230640 (
                                        20060121230640 3674 movie.edu.
                                        TUTCnZFvrOYqCD7HOOMTxRs3kAb5OkR74YP3
                                        ZxaBN9SOXxokkeUwHIlWq4JxFJrlZJjMaamp
                                        uKf+WSgdF+v3iA== )
```

Notice that the NS records still aren't signed (because technically they belong to the child zone), but the DS record is.

DNSSEC and Dynamic Update

dnssec-signzone isn't the only way to sign zone data. The BIND 9 nameserver is capable of signing dynamically updated records on the fly.[*] Color us impressed!

As long as the private key for a secure zone is available in the nameserver's working directory (in the correctly named *.private* file), a BIND 9 nameserver signs any records that are added via dynamic update. If any records are added to or deleted from the zone, the nameserver adjusts (and re-signs) the neighboring NSEC records, too.

Let's show you this in action. First, we'll look up a domain name that doesn't yet exist in *movie.edu*:

```
% dig +dnssec perfectstorm.movie.edu.

; <<>> DiG 9.3.2 <<>> +dnssec perfectstorm.movie.edu.
; (1 server found)
;; global options:  printcmd
;; Got answer:
```

---

[*] Yet another DNSSEC capability BIND 8 doesn't have.

```
;; ->>HEADER<<- opcode: QUERY, status: NXDOMAIN, id: 47491
;; flags: qr aa rd ra; QUERY: 1, ANSWER: 0, AUTHORITY: 6, ADDITIONAL: 1

;; OPT PSEUDOSECTION:
; EDNS: version: 0, flags: do; udp: 4096
;; QUESTION SECTION:
;perfectstorm.movie.edu.                    IN       A

;; AUTHORITY SECTION:
movie.edu.                  3600    IN      SOA     toystory.movie.edu. al.movie.edu.
2006011700 10800 3600 604800 3600
movie.edu.                  3600    IN      RRSIG   SOA 5 2 86400 20060219233605
20060120233605 3674 movie.edu. joujDnvBovW1h+GJ2ZEhvmXQTGqVL4cZBCHMByFitPRLINe/
dKj8VCZg 87ZUHQ/eAZSSGDuwXVIlT46ByG5AOg==
movie.edu.                  3600    IN      NSEC    misery.movie.edu. NS SOA MX RRSIG
NSEC DNSKEY
movie.edu.                  3600    IN      RRSIG   NSEC 5 2 3600 20060219233605
20060120233605 3674 movie.edu.
V4ipZI5SHGdFNOVEFn43gsRdYffUH6COrPxnRNfUMv6gfgwkythXXr5r
xoNTOSfa+Dp4CZrCqwn+CLryUN8vZg==
misery.movie.edu.           3600    IN      NSEC    monsters-inc.movie.edu. A RRSIG NSEC
misery.movie.edu.           3600    IN      RRSIG   NSEC 5 3 3600 20060219233605
20060120233605 3674 movie.edu. AFTF8DBjDtIzM/QkEajY4lUkbuEyDM5yt/
Kpe++Jrp1K1kArUSdGPuxj xDZUXujbRzPY6JoAOgBO4bU8UDx2tA==

;; Query time: 16 msec
;; SERVER: 127.0.0.1#53(127.0.0.1)
;; WHEN: Fri Jan 20 17:02:51 2006
;; MSG SIZE  rcvd: 502
```

Notice *misery.movie.edu*'s NSEC record, indicating that the domain name doesn't exist. Now we'll use *nsupdate* to add an address record for *perfectstorm.movie.edu*:

```
% nsupdate
> update add perfectstorm.movie.edu. 3600 IN A 192.249.249.91
> send
```

Now let's look up *perfectstorm.movie.edu* again:

```
% dig +dnssec perfectstorm.movie.edu.

; <<>> DiG 9.3.2 <<>> +dnssec perfectstorm.movie.edu.
; (1 server found)
;; global options:  printcmd
;; Got answer:
;; ->>HEADER<<- opcode: QUERY, status: NOERROR, id: 52846
;; flags: qr aa rd ra; QUERY: 1, ANSWER: 3, AUTHORITY: 4, ADDITIONAL: 6

;; OPT PSEUDOSECTION:
; EDNS: version: 0, flags: do; udp: 4096
;; QUESTION SECTION:
;perfectstorm.movie.edu.         IN      A

;; ANSWER SECTION:
perfectstorm.movie.edu. 3600    IN      A       192.249.249.91
```

```
perfectstorm.movie.edu. 3600    IN      RRSIG   A 5 3 3600 20060220010558
20060121000558 3674 movie.edu.
Fdp9EwdP6ze2siolli7wtYRgZdts+A+HTt5g8uqsgBavMml3TKFe+ba3
ppXvFosGHD7j3i6r1rfYUBF+aupEnQ==
perfectstorm.movie.edu. 3600    IN      RRSIG   A 5 3 3600 20060220010558
20060121000558 15480 movie.edu. o46m/V762W9OHqZ1R5mCTFSBYagjCqgpuIwflg/
O6QvX9Ce67WSoHD3/ YjSh5oag5eSmAAn2iozZYVCLSoIzjA==

;; AUTHORITY SECTION:
movie.edu.              86400   IN      NS      outland.fx.movie.edu.
movie.edu.              86400   IN      NS      wormhole.movie.edu.
movie.edu.              86400   IN      NS      toystory.movie.edu.
movie.edu.              86400   IN      RRSIG   NS 5 2 86400 20060219233605
20060120233605 3674 movie.edu. bwiM/R56VVVOpHrzIERVADLat7BoTR+eeFuCfgYc/
GMXecdTxnUahLig RKsbNSsY+Uz8RVkcewFSiExExFoqwA==

;; ADDITIONAL SECTION:
wormhole.movie.edu.     86400   IN      A       192.253.253.1
wormhole.movie.edu.     86400   IN      A       192.249.249.1
toystory.movie.edu.     86400   IN      A       192.249.249.3
wormhole.movie.edu.     86400   IN      RRSIG   A 5 3 86400 20060219233605
20060120233605 3674 movie.edu.
ZZP9AV28r824SZJqyIT+3WKkMQgcu1YTuFzpLgU3EN4USgpJhLZbYBqT
HL77mipET5aJr80dRxZvfFHHYV6UGw==
toystory.movie.edu.     86400   IN      RRSIG   A 5 3 86400 20060219233605
20060120233605 3674 movie.edu. hlz+W41UlcfIaCMdzoKVAuTPjnyqZhxY3TKOOm/
2i7FPAkfnVyWMyTwG iBns7Z1ws6QVj7+ZedDFx7xs+VOIyw==

;; Query time: 18 msec
;; SERVER: 127.0.0.1#53(127.0.0.1)
;; WHEN: Fri Jan 20 17:06:22 2006
;; MSG SIZE  rcvd: 713
```

Not only was an address record added, but there is also an RRSIG record generated from *movie.edu*'s ZSK.[*] The signature expiration is set to 30 days from the update by default, but you can change it with the *sig-validity-interval* substatement, which takes a number of days as an argument:[†]

```
options {
    sig-validity-interval 7;  // We want RRSIGs on updated records to last a week
};
```

The signature inception is always set to one hour before the update to allow for verifiers with clocks that may be slightly skewed from ours.

---

[*] As well as one from the KSK. That's a bug.

[†] Before BIND 9.1.0, *sig-validity-interval* interpreted its argument as seconds, not days.

If we look up *perfectstorm2.movie.edu* (though how there'd be a sequel to *that* movie I don't know), we find the following:

```
% dig +dnssec perfectstorm2.movie.edu.

; <<>> DiG 9.3.2 <<>> +dnssec perfectstorm2.movie.edu.
; (1 server found)
;; global options:  printcmd
;; Got answer:
;; ->>HEADER<<- opcode: QUERY, status: NXDOMAIN, id: 8402
;; flags: qr aa rd ra; QUERY: 1, ANSWER: 0, AUTHORITY: 8, ADDITIONAL: 1

;; OPT PSEUDOSECTION:
; EDNS: version: 0, flags: do; udp: 4096
;; QUESTION SECTION:
;perfectstorm2.movie.edu.       IN      A

;; AUTHORITY SECTION:
movie.edu.              3600    IN      SOA     toystory.movie.edu. al.movie.edu.
2006011701 10800 3600 604800 3600
movie.edu.              3600    IN      RRSIG   SOA 5 2 86400 20060220010558
20060121000558 3674 movie.edu.
vwiC+zBzw8VFmrmFnARkNPLLmYEbSJRCiCsqjnvwVc5CMSzXu6kBkatN bWE9Iqd//
brLiOA3E9GO2BM3j+5Wkg==
movie.edu.              3600    IN      RRSIG   SOA 5 2 86400 20060220010558
20060121000558 15480 movie.edu.
HVlniwE8N8Fy+IdRSmTLw3XTVyLaeOeOr26C5MAkzNoMr3OzRrDfbZUm
4+N1a6gC9P+EMzUYM1yflVQFs3Cehg==
movie.edu.              3600    IN      NSEC    misery.movie.edu. NS SOA MX RRSIG
NSEC DNSKEY
movie.edu.              3600    IN      RRSIG   NSEC 5 2 3600 20060219233605
20060120233605 3674 movie.edu.
V4ipZI5SHGdFNOVEFn43gsRdYffUH6COrPxnRNfUMv6gfgwkythXXr5r
xONTOSfa+Dp4CZrCqwn+CLryUN8vZg==
perfectstorm.movie.edu. 3600    IN      NSEC    shining.movie.edu. A RRSIG NSEC
perfectstorm.movie.edu. 3600    IN      RRSIG   NSEC 5 3 3600 20060220010558
20060121000558 3674 movie.edu. EC/HwFtyrDtcf27QYvnSrJTypnAg3LsimFH+lTO/VbB/
dD7WzjOam1Yy +/SF3u6nrJ1nV2hZBgSqmYB9plpM3Q==
perfectstorm.movie.edu. 3600    IN      RRSIG   NSEC 5 3 3600 20060220010558
20060121000558 15480 movie.edu.
H2XwAMRYkxsv721q0fOQk7g7j1SPPurKNGBDqlEDpeLnRkde8NHtlFOx
VbqWDsWzq15sxoV4NRZyK14cQcbG7Q==

;; Query time: 14 msec
;; SERVER: 127.0.0.1#53(127.0.0.1)
;; WHEN: Fri Jan 20 17:15:58 2006
;; MSG SIZE  rcvd: 726
```

Notice the second NSEC record: it was added automatically when we added *perfectstorm.movie.edu*'s address record because *perfectstorm.movie.edu* was a new domain name in the zone. Sweet!

As impressive as this is, you should be careful when allowing dynamic updates to signed zones. You should make sure that you use strong authentication (e.g., TSIG) to authenticate the updates, or you'll give a hacker an easy backdoor to use to modify your "secure" zone. And you should ensure you have enough horsepower for the task: normally, dynamic updates don't take much to process. But dynamic updates to a secure zone require the recalculation of NSEC records and, more significantly, asymmetric encryption (to calculate new RRSIG records), so you should expect your nameserver to take longer and need more resources to process them.

Changing Keys

Though we said you don't need to generate a new key each time you sign your zone, there are occasions when you'll need to create a new key, either because you've "used up" a private key or, worse, because one of your private keys has been cracked.

After a certain amount of use, it becomes dangerous to continue signing records with a private key. While there's no simple rule to tell you when a private key's time is up, here are some guidelines:

- The longer your key, the harder it is to crack. Long keys don't need to be changed as often as short keys.

- The more valuable it would be for a hacker to spoof your zone data, the more time and money he will spend trying to crack one of your private keys. If the integrity of your zone data is particularly crucial, change keys frequently.

Since *movie.edu* isn't a high-value target, we change our zone-signing key pair every six months. We're only a university, after all. If we were more concerned about our zone data, we would use longer keys or change keys more frequently.

Unfortunately, rolling over to a new key isn't as easy as just generating a new key and replacing the old one with it. If you did that, you'd leave nameservers that had cached your zone's data with no way to retrieve your zone-signing DNSKEY record and verify that data. So rolling over to a new key is a multistep process:

1. At least one TTL before the set of RRSIG records signed with your old ZSK expire, generate a new ZSK pair.
2. Add the new DNSKEY record to your zone data.
3. Sign your zone data with the new private key and *without* the old private key, but leave the old DNSKEY record in the zone.
4. After all records signed with the old private key have expired, remove the old DNSKEY record from the zone and re-sign it with the new private key.

Let's go through the process. First, we generated a new key pair:

```
# dnssec-keygen -a RSA -b 512 -n ZONE movie.edu.
Kmovie.edu.+005+15494
```

Next, we added the new DNSKEY record to the zone data:

```
# cat Kmovie.edu.+005+15494.key >> db.movie.edu.signed
```

We had to tell *dnssec-signzone* the keys to sign to zone with, and specify the KSK:

```
# dnssec-signzone -o movie.edu -k Kmovie.edu.+005+15480 db.movie.edu.signed
Kmovie.edu.+005.15494
```

This will sign the zone with the new ZSK and leave the set of RRSIG records signed with the old ZSK in the zone, but won't regenerate RRSIGs with the old ZSK. Here's how the resulting file began:

```
; File written on Tue Feb 21 02:41:09 2006
; dnssec_signzone version 9.3.2
movie.edu.              86400   IN SOA  toystory.movie.edu. al.movie.edu. (
                                        2006022100 ; serial
                                        10800      ; refresh (3 hours)
                                        3600       ; retry (1 hour)
                                        604800     ; expire (1 week)
                                        3600       ; minimum (1 hour)
                                        )
                        86400   RRSIG   SOA 5 2 86400 20060220210704 (
                                        20060121210704 3674 movie.edu.
                                        otYTiIHqJ4KOc6M5JZ9uC8q7AvXO1Gjp5FXJ
                                        5SRO+UL/ilAZXGSfJSCJrUDetb7ROH27NqHe
                                        yKujxcec69FoLw== )
                        86400   RRSIG   SOA 5 2 86400 20060320094111 (
                                        20060221094111 15494 movie.edu.
                                        zD/IGbzgO3sB5sPvYbb3vLmvULRQO5fV21Yz
                                        DO8gq2E+v575ag469h+J2Dzs6XheMxShmIpk
                                        YwjYxgMLcc1SjA== )
```

Although the zone includes two DNSKEY records, the other records in the zone (such as the SOA record, shown here) were signed only by the new private key, with key tag 15494. The old RRSIG records, generated from the private key with key tag 3674, were still included because they were still valid—but not for much longer. Note the expirations of the two RRSIG records covering the SOA record: key tag 3674's RRSIG record expires a month earlier because it wasn't regenerated.

After the old RRSIG records expired, we deleted the old DNSKEY record and the key files (so the signer wouldn't use them) and re-signed the zone with just the new ZSK and the KSK:

```
# dnssec-signzone -o movie.edu db.movie.edu.signed
# mv db.movie.edu.signed.signed db.movie.edu.signed
```

That removed the old, invalid RRSIGs and re-signed the DNSKEY RRset with the KSK.

Changing KSKs is similar, and doesn't need to be done as often:

1. At least one TTL before its RRSIG covering the DNSKEY RRset expires, generate a new KSK pair.

2. Add the new KSK's DNSKEY record to the zone.

3. Re-sign the DNSKEY RRset with both KSKs (specifying multiple –k options to *dnssec-signzone*).

4. Submit your new KSK to your parent zone's administrators to certify.

5. After the TTL of the DS RRset in your parent zone has passed, you can remove the old KSK from your zone and re-sign the zone without it.

We're guessing that after reading this, you'll probably decide to use the longest keys available just to avoid ever needing to roll your keys over.

What Was That All About?

We realize that DNSSEC is a bit, er, daunting. (We nearly fainted the first time we saw it.) But it's designed to do something very important: make DNS spoofing much, much harder. And as people do more and more business over the Internet, knowing you're really getting where you thought you were going becomes crucial.

That said, we realize that DNSSEC and the other security measures we've described in this chapter aren't for all of you. (Certainly they're not *all* for all of you.) You should balance your need for security against the cost of implementing it, in terms of the burden it places both on your infrastructure and on your productivity.

nslookup and dig

> *"Don't stand chattering to yourself like that," Humpty Dumpty said, looking at her for the first time, "but tell me your name and your business."*
>
> *"My name is Alice, but—"*
>
> *"It's a stupid name enough!" Humpty Dumpty interrupted impatiently. "What does it mean?"*
>
> *"Must a name mean something?" Alice asked doubtfully.*
>
> *"Of course it must," Humpty Dumpty said with a short laugh…*

To be proficient at troubleshooting nameserver problems, you'll need a troubleshooting tool to send DNS queries, one that gives you complete control. We'll cover *nslookup* in this chapter because it's distributed with BIND and with many vendors' operating systems. That doesn't mean it's the best DNS troubleshooting tool available, though. *nslookup* has its faults—so many, in fact, that it's now deprecated (geekish for "officially out of favor") in the BIND 9 distribution. We'll cover it anyway because it's pervasive. We'll also cover *dig*, which provides similar functionality and doesn't suffer from *nslookup*'s deficiencies.

Note that this chapter isn't comprehensive; there are aspects of *nslookup* and *dig* (mostly obscure and seldom used) that we won't cover. You can always consult the manual pages for those.

Is nslookup a Good Tool?

Much of the time, you'll use *nslookup* to send queries in the same way the resolver sends them. Sometimes, though, you'll use *nslookup* to query other nameservers as a nameserver would instead. The way you use it will depend on the problem you're trying to debug. You might wonder, "How accurately does *nslookup* emulate a resolver or a nameserver? Does *nslookup* actually use the BIND resolver library routines?" No, *nslookup* uses its own routines for querying nameservers, but those routines are based on the resolver routines. Consequently, *nslookup*'s behavior is very similar to the resolver's behavior, but it does differ slightly. We'll point out some of those differences. As for emulating nameserver behavior, *nslookup* allows us to query another server with the same query message that a nameserver would use, but the retransmission scheme is quite different. Like a nameserver, though, *nslookup* can transfer a copy of the zone data. So *nslookup* doesn't emulate either the resolver or the nameserver exactly, but it does emulate them well enough to make a decent troubleshooting tool. Let's delve into those differences we alluded to.

Multiple Servers

nslookup talks to only one nameserver at a time. This is the biggest difference between *nslookup*'s behavior and the resolver's behavior. The resolver uses each *nameserver* directive in *resolv.conf*. If there are two *nameserver* directives in *resolv.conf*, the resolver tries the first nameserver, then the second, then the first, then the second, until it receives a response or gives up. The resolver does this for every query. On the other hand, *nslookup* tries the first nameserver in *resolv.conf* and keeps retrying until it finally gives up on the first nameserver and tries the second. Once it gets a response, it locks onto that server and doesn't try the next. However, you *want* your troubleshooting tool to talk to only one nameserver so you can reduce the number of variables when analyzing a problem. If *nslookup* used more than one nameserver, you wouldn't have as much control over your troubleshooting session. So talking to only one server is the right thing for a troubleshooting tool to do.

Timeouts

The *nslookup* timeouts match the resolver timeouts when the resolver is querying only one nameserver. A nameserver's timeouts, however, are based on how quickly the remote server answered the last query, a dynamic measure. *nslookup*'s timeouts will never match a nameserver's timeouts, but that's not a problem either. When you're querying remote nameservers with *nslookup*, you probably care only what the response was, not how long it took.

The Search List

nslookup implements a search list just as the resolver code does. *nslookup*, however, uses either the abridged BIND search list that includes just the local domain name or the one specified in the last *search* entry in */etc/resolv.conf*. Nameservers don't implement search lists, so, to act like a nameserver, the *nslookup* search function must be turned off—more on that later.

Zone Transfers

nslookup does zone transfers just like a nameserver. Unlike a nameserver, however, *nslookup* does not check SOA serial numbers before pulling the zone data; if you want to do that, you'll have to do it manually.

Using NIS and /etc/hosts

This last point doesn't compare *nslookup* to the resolver or nameserver but to ways of looking up names in general. As distributed from the Internet Software Consortium, *nslookup* uses only DNS; it won't use NIS or */etc/hosts*. Most applications can use DNS, NIS, or */etc/hosts*, depending on how the system is configured. Don't count on *nslookup* to help you find your lookup problem unless your host is really configured to use nameservers.*

Interactive Versus Noninteractive

Let's start our tutorial on *nslookup* by looking at how to start it and how to exit from it. You can run *nslookup* either interactively or noninteractively. If you only want to look up one record for one domain name, use the noninteractive form. If you plan on doing something more extensive, such as changing nameservers or options, use an interactive session.

To start an interactive session, just type *nslookup*:

```
% nslookup
Default Server:  toystory.movie.edu
Address:  0.0.0.0#53

> ^D
```

If you need help, type *?* or *help*.† When you want to exit, type ^D (Ctrl-D) or *exit*. If you try to exit from *nslookup* by interrupting it with ^C (or whatever your interrupt character is), you won't get very far. *nslookup* catches the interrupt, stops whatever it is doing (like a zone transfer), and gives you the > prompt.

For a noninteractive lookup, include the name you are looking up on the command line:

```
% nslookup carrie
Server:  toystory.movie.edu
Address:  0.0.0.0#53

Name:    carrie.movie.edu
Address: 192.253.253.4
```

---

* Or your vendor's *nslookup* has been enhanced to query NIS servers and check */etc/hosts*, like the one in HP-UX.
† The help function isn't implemented in BIND 9's *nslookup* as of 9.3.2.

Option Settings

nslookup has its own set of dials and knobs, called *options*. All of the option settings can be changed. We'll discuss here what each of the options means, and we'll use the rest of the chapter to show you how to use them.

```
% nslookup
Default Server:  bladerunner.fx.movie.edu
Address:  0.0.0.0#53

> set all
Default Server:  bladerunner.fx.movie.edu
Address:  0.0.0.0

Set options:
   nodebug        defname        search         recurse
   nod2           novc           noignoretc     port=53
   querytype=A    class=IN       timeout=5      retry=4
   root=a.root-servers.net.
   domain=fx.movie.edu
   srchlist=fx.movie.edu

> ^D
```

For BIND 9.3.2, a few of the options have been removed or changed:

```
   novc                 nodebug          nod2
   search               recurse
   timeout = 0          retry = 3        port = 53
   querytype = A        class = IN
   srchlist = fx.movie.edu
```

Before we get into the options, we need to cover the introductory lines. The default nameserver is *bladerunner.fx.movie.edu*. This means that *nslookup* will query *bladerunner* unless we specify another nameserver. The address 0.0.0.0 means "this host." When *nslookup* is using address 0.0.0.0 or 127.0.0.1 as its nameserver, it is using the server running on the local system—in this case, *bladerunner*.

The options come in two flavors: Boolean and value. The options that do not have an equals sign after them are Boolean options. They have the interesting property of being either "on" or "off." The value options can take on different, well, values. How can we tell which Boolean options are on and which are off? The option is off when a "no" precedes the option's name. *nodebug* means that debugging is off. As you might guess, the *search* option is on.

How you change Boolean or value options depends on whether you are using *nslookup* interactively. In an interactive session, you change an option with the *set* command, as in *set debug* or *set domain=classics.movie.edu*. From the command line, you omit the word *set* and precede the option with a hyphen, as in *nslookup –debug* or *nslookup –domain=classics.movie.edu*. An option can be abbreviated to its shortest unique prefix, e.g., *nodeb* for *nodebug*. In addition to its abbreviation, the *querytype* option can also be called simply *type*.

Let's go through each option:

[no]debug
Debugging is turned off by default. If it is turned on, the nameserver shows time-outs and displays the response messages. See *[no]d2* for a discussion of debug level 2.

[no]defname
(This option is no longer supported as of 9.3.2.) Before search lists existed, the BIND resolver code added only the local domain name to names without *any* dots in them; this option selects that behavior. *nslookup* can implement the pre-search list behavior (with *search* off and *defname* on) or the search list behavior (with *search* on).

[no]search
The *search* option supersedes the local domain name (*defname*) option. That is, *defname* applies only if *search* is turned off. By default, *nslookup* appends the domain names in the search list (*srchlist*) to names that don't end in a dot.

[no]recurse
nslookup sends recursive queries by default. This turns on the recursion-desired bit in query messages. The BIND resolver sends recursive queries in the same way. Nameservers, however, send out nonrecursive queries to other nameservers.

[no]d2
Debugging at level 2 is turned off by default. If it is turned on, you see the query messages sent out in addition to the regular debugging output. Turning on *d2* also turns on *debug*. Turning off *d2* turns off *d2* only; *debug* is left on. Turning off *debug* turns off both *debug* and *d2*.

[no]vc
By default, *nslookup* sends queries using UDP datagrams instead of over a virtual circuit (TCP). Most BIND resolvers send queries over UDP, so the default *nslookup* behavior matches the resolver. As some resolvers can be instructed to use TCP, so can *nslookup*.

[no]ignoretc
(This option is no longer supported as of 9.3.2.) By default, *nslookup* doesn't ignore truncated messages. If a message is received that has the "truncated" bit set—indicating that the nameserver couldn't fit all the important information in the UDP response datagram—*nslookup* doesn't ignore it; it retries the query using a TCP connection instead of UDP. Again, this matches the BIND resolver's behavior. The reason for retrying the query using a TCP connection is that TCP responses can be many times larger than UDP responses.

port=53

Nameservers listen on port 53. You can start a nameserver on another port—for debugging purposes, for example—and *nslookup* can be directed to use that port.

querytype=A

By default, *nslookup* looks up A (address) resource record types. In addition, if you type in an IP address (and the *nslookup* query type is A or PTR), *nslookup* inverts the address, appends *in-addr.arpa*, and looks up PTR records instead.

class=IN

The only class that matters is Internet (IN). Well, there is the Hesiod (HS) class, too, if you are an MITer or run Ultrix.

timeout=5

If the nameserver doesn't respond within 5 seconds, *nslookup* resends the query and doubles the timeout (to 10, 20, and then 40 seconds). Most BIND resolvers use the same timeouts when querying a single nameserver.

retry=4

Send the query four times before giving up. After each retry, the timeout value is doubled. Again, this matches most BIND resolvers' behavior.

root=a.root-servers.net

(This option is no longer supported as of 9.3.2.) There is a convenience command called *root* that switches your default nameserver to the server named here. Executing the *root* command from a modern *nslookup*'s prompt is equivalent to executing *server a.root-servers.net*. Older versions use *nic.ddn.mil* (old) or even *sri-nic.arpa* (ancient) as the default root nameserver. You can change the default root server with *set root=server*.

domain=fx.movie.edu

(This option is no longer supported as of 9.3.2.) This is the default domain name to append if the *defname* option is on.

srchlist=fx.movie.edu

If *search* is on, these are the domain names appended to names that do not end in a dot. The domain names are listed in the order in which they are tried, separated by a slash.

The .nslookuprc File

 .nslookuprc is no longer supported as of 9.3.2.

You can set up new default *nslookup* options in an *.nslookuprc* file. *nslookup* looks for an *.nslookuprc* file in your home directory when it starts up, in both interactive and noninteractive modes. The *.nslookuprc* file can contain any legal *set* commands, one per line. This is useful, for example, if your old *nslookup* still thinks *sri-nic.arpa* is a root nameserver. You can set the default root nameserver to a real, current root with a line like this in your *.nslookuprc* file:

```
set root=a.root-servers.net.
```

You might also use *.nslookuprc* to set your search list to something other than your host's default search list or to change the timeouts *nslookup* uses.

Avoiding the Search List

nslookup implements the same search list as the resolver. When you're debugging, though, the search list can get in your way. You may need to turn off the search list completely (*set nosearch*) or add a trailing dot to the fully qualified domain name you are looking up. We prefer the latter, as you'll see in our examples.

Common Tasks

There are little chores you'll come to use *nslookup* for almost every day: finding the IP address or MX records for a given domain name, or querying a particular nameserver for data. We'll cover these first, before moving on to the more occasional stuff.

Looking Up Different Record Types

By default, *nslookup* looks up the address for a domain name, or the domain name for an address. You can look up any record type by changing the *querytype*, as we show in this example:

```
% nslookup
Default Server:  toystory.movie.edu
Address:  0.0.0.0#53

> misery                    Look up address
Server:  toystory.movie.edu
Address:  0.0.0.0#53

Name:    misery.movie.edu
Address:  192.253.253.2

> 192.253.253.2            Look up domain name
Server:  toystory.movie.edu
Address:  0.0.0.0#53

Name:    misery.movie.edu
Address:  192.253.253.2
```

```
> set q=mx              Look up MX records
> wormhole
Server:  toystory.movie.edu
Address:  0.0.0.0#53

wormhole.movie.edu      preference = 10, mail exchanger = wormhole.movie.edu
wormhole.movie.edu      internet address = 192.249.249.1
wormhole.movie.edu      internet address = 192.253.253.1

> set q=any             Look up records of any type
> monsters-inc
Server:  toystory.movie.edu
Address:  0.0.0.0#53

monsters-inc.movie.edu      internet address = 192.249.249.4
monsters-inc.movie.edu      preference = 10, mail exchanger = monsters-inc.movie.edu
monsters-inc.movie.edu      internet address = 192.249.249.4
```

These are only a few of the valid DNS record types, of course. For a more complete list, see Appendix A.

Authoritative Versus Nonauthoritative Answers

If you've used *nslookup* before, you might have noticed something peculiar: the first time you look up a remote domain name, the answer is authoritative, but the second time you look up the same name, it is nonauthoritative. Here's an example:

```
% nslookup
Default Server:  toystory.movie.edu
Address:  0.0.0.0#53

> slate.mines.colorado.edu.
Server:  toystory.movie.edu
Address:  0.0.0.0#53

Name:    slate.mines.colorado.edu
Address:  138.67.1.3

> slate.mines.colorado.edu.
Server:  toystory.movie.edu
Address:  0.0.0.0#53

Non-authoritative answer:
Name:    slate.mines.colorado.edu
Address:  138.67.1.3
```

While this looks odd, it really isn't. What's happening here is that the first time the local nameserver looks up *slate.mines.colorado.edu*, it contacts the nameserver for *mines.colorado.edu*, and the *mines.colorado.edu* server then responds with an authoritative answer. The local nameserver, in effect, passes the authoritative response directly back to *nslookup*. It also caches the response. The second time you look up *slate.mines.colorado.edu*, the nameserver answers out of its cache, which results in the answer "non-authoritative."*

Notice that we terminated the domain name with a trailing dot each time we looked it up. The response would have been the same if we'd left off the trailing dot. There are times when it's critical that you use the trailing dot while debugging, and times when it's not. Rather than stopping to decide if *this* name needs a trailing dot, we always add one if we know the name is fully qualified, except, of course, if we've turned off the search list.

Switching Nameservers

Sometimes you want to query another nameserver directly: you may think it is misbehaving, for example. You can switch servers with *nslookup* using the *server* or *lserver* command. The difference between *server* and *lserver* is that *lserver* queries your local nameserver—the one you started out with—to get the address of the server you want to switch to; *server* uses the default nameserver instead of the local server. This difference is important because the server you just switched to may not be responding, as we'll show in this example:

```
% nslookup
Default Server:  toystory.movie.edu
Address:  0.0.0.0#53
```

When we start up, our first nameserver, *toystory.movie.edu*, becomes our *lserver*. This will matter later on in this session.

```
> server galt.cs.purdue.edu.
Default Server:  galt.cs.purdue.edu
Address:  128.10.2.39#53

> cs.purdue.edu.
Server:  galt.cs.purdue.edu
Address:  128.10.2.39#53

*** galt.cs.purdue.edu can't find cs.purdue.edu.: Query refused
```

At this point, we try to switch back to our original nameserver. But the nameserver running on *galt.cs.purdue.edu* refuses to look up *toystory.movie.edu*'s address:

```
> server toystory.movie.edu.
*** Can't find address for server toystory.movie.edu.: Query refused
```

---

* BIND 9 nameservers, interestingly, show even the first responses as nonauthoritative.

Instead of being stuck, though, we use the *lserver* command to have our local nameserver look up *toystory.movie.edu*'s address:

```
> lserver toystory.movie.edu.
Default Server:  toystory.movie.edu
Address:  192.249.249.3#53

> ^D
```

Since the nameserver on *galt.cs.purdue.edu* refused to respond, it wasn't possible to look up the address of *toystory.movie.edu* to switch back to using *toystory*'s nameserver. Here's where *lserver* comes to the rescue: the local nameserver, *toystory*, was still responding, so we used it. Instead of using *lserver*, we also could have recovered using *toystory*'s IP address directly: *server 192.249.249.3*.

You can even change servers on a per-query basis. To specify that you'd like *nslookup* to query a particular nameserver for information about a given domain name, you can specify the server as the second argument on the line, after the domain name to look up, like so:

```
% nslookup
Default Server:  toystory.movie.edu
Address:  192.249.249.3#53

> saturn.sun.com. ns.sun.com.
Name Server:  ns.sun.com
Address:  192.9.9.3#53

Name:     saturn.sun.com
Addresses: 192.9.25.2

> ^D
```

And, of course, you can change servers from the command line. You can specify the server to query as the argument after the domain name to look up, like this:

```
% nslookup -type=mx fisherking.movie.edu. toystory.movie.edu.
```

This instructs *nslookup* to query *toystory.movie.edu* for MX records for *fisherking.movie.edu*.

Finally, to specify an alternate default nameserver and enter interactive mode, you can use a hyphen in place of the domain name to look up:

```
% nslookup - toystory.movie.edu.
```

Less Common Tasks

Let's move on to some tricks you'll probably use less often but are still handy to have in your repertoire. Most of these will be helpful when you are trying to troubleshoot a DNS or BIND problem; they'll enable you to grub around in the messages the resolver sees and mimic a BIND nameserver querying another nameserver or transferring zone data.

Showing the Query and Response Messages

If you need to, you can direct *nslookup* to show you the queries it sends out and the responses it receives. Turning on *debug* shows the responses. Turning on *d2* shows the queries as well. When you want to turn off debugging completely, you have to use *set nodebug* because *set nod2* turns off only level 2 debugging. After the following trace, we'll explain some parts of the output. If you want, pull out your copy of RFC 1035, turn to page 25, and read along with our explanation.

```
% nslookup
Default Server:  toystory.movie.edu
Address:  0.0.0.0#53

> set debug
> wormhole
Server:  toystory.movie.edu
Address:  0.0.0.0#53

------------
Got answer:
    HEADER:
        opcode = QUERY, id = 6813, rcode = NOERROR
        header flags:  response, auth. answer, want recursion,
        recursion avail.  questions = 1,  answers = 2,
        authority records = 2,  additional = 3

    QUESTIONS:
        wormhole.movie.edu, type = A, class = IN
    ANSWERS:
    -> wormhole.movie.edu
        internet address = 192.253.253.1
        ttl = 86400 (1D)
    -> wormhole.movie.edu
        internet address = 192.249.249.1
        ttl = 86400 (1D)
    AUTHORITY RECORDS:
    -> movie.edu
        nameserver = toystory.movie.edu
        ttl = 86400 (1D)
    -> movie.edu
        nameserver = wormhole.movie.edu
        ttl = 86400 (1D)
    ADDITIONAL RECORDS:
    -> toystory.movie.edu
        internet address = 192.249.249.3
        ttl = 86400 (1D)
    -> wormhole.movie.edu
        internet address = 192.253.253.1
        ttl = 86400 (1D)
```

```
     ->  wormhole.movie.edu
         internet address = 192.249.249.1
         ttl = 86400 (1D)


     ------------
     Name:    wormhole.movie.edu
     Addresses:  192.253.253.1, 192.249.249.1

     > set d2
     > wormhole
     Server:  toystory.movie.edu
     Address:  0.0.0.0#53
```

This time the query is also shown.

```
     ------------
     SendRequest(  ), len 36
         HEADER:
             opcode = QUERY, id = 6814, rcode = NOERROR
             header flags:  query, want recursion
             questions = 1,  answers = 0,  authority records = 0,
          additional = 0

         QUESTIONS:
             wormhole.movie.edu, type = A, class = IN


     ------------
     ------------
     Got answer (164 bytes):
```

The answer is the same as above.

The lines between the dashes are the query and response messages. As promised, we'll go through the contents of the messages. DNS packets comprise five sections: header, question, answer, authority, and additional.

Header section

> The header section is present in every query and response message. The operation code *nslookup* reports is always QUERY. There are other opcodes for asynchronous notification of zone changes (NOTIFY) and for dynamic updates (UPDATE), but *nslookup* doesn't see those because it just sends regular queries and receives responses.

> The ID in the header associates a response with a query and detects duplicate queries or responses. You have to look in the header flags to see which messages are queries and which are responses. The string *want recursion* means that this is a recursive query. The string *auth. answer* means that this response is authoritative. In other words, the response is from the nameserver's authoritative data, not from its cache. The response code, *rcode*, can be one of *no error, server failure, name error* (also known as *nxdomain* or *nonexistent domain*), *not implemented*, or *refused*. The *server failure, name error, not implemented*, and *refused*

response codes cause the *nslookup* "Server failed," "Nonexistent domain," "Not implemented," and "Query refused" errors, respectively. The last four entries in the header section are counters: they indicate how many resource records there are in each of the next four sections.

Question section

There is always one question in a DNS message; it includes the domain name and the requested record type and class. There is never more than one question in a DNS message; the capability of handling more than one would require a redesign of the message format. For one thing, the single authority bit would have to be changed because the answer section could contain a mix of authoritative and nonauthoritative answers. In the present design, setting the authoritative answer bit means that the nameserver is authoritative for the zone that contains the domain name in the question section.

Answer section

This section contains the resource records that answer the question. There can be more than one resource record in the response. For example, if the host is multihomed, there will be more than one address resource record.

Authority section

The authority section is where nameserver records are returned. When a response refers the querier to some other nameservers, those nameservers are listed here.

Additional section

The additional records section adds information that may complete the information included in other sections. For instance, if a nameserver is listed in the authority section, the nameserver's address may be included in the additional records section. After all, to contact the nameserver, you need to have its address.

Querying Like a BIND Nameserver

You can make *nslookup* send out the same query message a nameserver would. Nameservers' query messages aren't that much different from resolvers' query messages in the first place. The primary difference in the query messages is that resolvers request recursive resolution and nameservers seldom do. Requesting recursion is the default with *nslookup*, so you have to explicitly turn it off. Another difference in operation between a resolver and a nameserver is that the resolver applies the search list, and the nameserver doesn't. By default, *nslookup* applies the search list, so that must be explicitly turned off as well. Of course, judicious use of the trailing dot will have the same effect.

In raw *nslookup* terms, this means that to query like a resolver, you use *nslookup*'s default settings. To query like a nameserver, use *set norecurse* and *set nosearch*. On the command line, that's *nslookup –norecurse –nosearch*.

When a BIND nameserver receives a query, it looks for the answer in its authoritative data and in its cache. If it doesn't have the answer, and it is authoritative for the zone, the nameserver responds that the name doesn't exist or that there are no records of the type sought. If the nameserver doesn't have the answer and it is not authoritative for the zone, it starts walking up the namespace looking for NS records. There are always NS records somewhere higher in the namespace. As a last resort, it uses the NS records for the root zone, the highest level.

If the nameserver has received a nonrecursive query, it responds to the querier by returning the NS records that it found. On the other hand, if the original query was a recursive query, the nameserver queries the remote nameservers in the NS records that it found. When the nameserver receives a response from one of the remote nameservers, it caches the response and, if necessary, repeats this process. The remote server's response either has the answer to the question or contains a list of nameservers lower in the namespace and closer to the answer.

Let's assume for our example that we are trying to satisfy a recursive query. When we ask the nameserver on *toystory.movie.edu* about *www.usps.gov* (the United States Postal Service), it doesn't find any NS records until the *gov* zone. From there, we switch servers to a *gov* nameserver and ask the same question. It directs us to the *usps.gov* servers. We then switch to a *usps.gov* nameserver and ask the same question:

```
% nslookup
Default Server:  toystory.movie.edu
Address:  0.0.0.0#53

> set norec          Query like a nameserver: turn off recursion
> set nosearch       Turn off the search list
> set nodefname      Turn off appending the local domain (only for older nslookups)
> www.usps.gov       We don't need to dot-terminate since we've turned off search
Server:  toystory.movie.edu
Address:  0.0.0.0#53

Name:    www.usps.gov
Served by:
- G.GOV.ZONEEDIT.COM
        66.135.32.100
        gov
- F.GOV.ZONEEDIT.COM
        66.197.185.229
        gov
- E.GOV.ZONEEDIT.COM
        82.165.40.134
        gov
- D.GOV.ZONEEDIT.COM
        209.97.207.48
        gov
```

```
        - C.GOV.ZONEEDIT.COM
                69.72.142.35
                gov
        - B.GOV.ZONEEDIT.COM
                206.51.224.229
                gov
        - A.GOV.ZONEEDIT.COM
                216.55.155.29
                gov
```

Switch to a *gov* nameserver (you may have to turn on recursion again temporarily if your nameserver doesn't have the address of the *gov* nameserver already cached):

```
> server g.gov.zoneedit.com
Default Server:  g.gov.zoneedit.com
Address:  66.135.32.100#53
```

Ask the same question of the *gov* nameserver. It will refer us to nameservers closer to our desired answer:

```
> www.usps.gov
Server:  g.gov.zoneedit.com
Address:  66.135.32.100#53

Name:    www.usps.gov
Served by:
- DNS072.usps.gov
        56.0.72.25
        usps.gov
- DNS096.usps.gov
        56.0.96.25
        usps.gov
- DNS141.usps.gov
        56.0.141.25
        usps.gov
```

Switch to a *usps.gov* nameserver—any of them will do:

```
> server dns096.usps.gov
Default Server:  dns096.usps.gov
Address:  56.0.96.25#53

> www.usps.gov
Server:  dns096.usps.gov
Address:  56.0.96.25#53

Name:    www.usps.gov
Address:  56.0.134.23
```

Hopefully, this example gives you a feeling for how nameservers look up domain names. If you need to refresh your understanding of what this looks like graphically, flip back to Figures 2-12 and 2-13.

Before we move on, notice that we asked each of the servers the very same question: "What's the address of *www.usps.gov*?" What do you think would happen if the *gov* nameserver had already cached *www.usps.gov*'s address itself? The *gov* nameserver would have answered the question out of its cache instead of referring you to the *usps.gov* nameservers. Why is this significant? Suppose you messed up a particular host's address in your zone. Someone points it out to you, and you clean up the problem. Even though your nameserver now has the correct data, some remote sites find the old, messed-up data when they look up the domain name of the host. One of the nameservers that serves a zone higher up in the namespace, such as a nameserver for a top-level zone, has cached the incorrect data; when it receives a query for that host's address, it returns the incorrect data instead of referring the querier to your nameservers. What makes this problem hard to track down is that only one of the higher-up nameservers has cached the incorrect data, so only some of the remote lookups get the wrong answer—the ones that use this server. Fun, huh? Eventually, though, the higher-up nameserver will time out the old record. Thankfully, most TLD nameservers have recursion turned off and consequently don't cache data. A few, unfortunately, still do.

Zone Transfers

nslookup can be used to transfer a whole zone using the *ls* command. This feature is useful for troubleshooting, for figuring out how to spell a remote host's domain name, or for just counting how many hosts are in some remote zone. Since the output can be substantial, *nslookup* allows you to redirect the output to a file. If you want to bail out in the middle of a transfer, you can interrupt it by typing your interrupt character.

Beware: some nameservers won't let you pull a copy of their zones, either for security reasons or to limit the load placed on them. On today's Internet, administrators must defend their turf.

Let's look at the *movie.edu* zone. As you can see in the following output, all the zone data is listed; the SOA record is listed twice, which is an artifact of how the data is exchanged during the zone transfer. Since some *nslookups* show you only address and nameserver records by default, we specify the *–d* option to retrieve the whole zone:

```
% nslookup
Default Server:  toystory.movie.edu
Address:  0.0.0.0#53

> ls -d movie.edu.
[toystory.movie.edu]
$ORIGIN movie.edu.
```

```
@                     1D IN SOA      toystory al (
                                     2000091400    ; serial
                                     3H            ; refresh
                                     1H            ; retry
                                     4W2D          ; expiry
                                     1H )          ; minimum

                      1D IN NS       toystory
                      1D IN NS       wormhole
wormhole              1D IN A        192.249.249.1
                      1D IN A        192.253.253.1
wh249                 1D IN A        192.249.249.1
shrek                 1D IN A        192.249.249.2
toys                  1D IN CNAME    toystory
cujo                  1D IN TXT      "Location:" "machine" "room" "dog" "house"
wh253                 1D IN A        192.253.253.1
wh                    1D IN CNAME    wormhole
shining               1D IN A        192.253.253.3
toystory              1D IN A        192.249.249.3
localhost             1D IN A        127.0.0.1
fx                    1D IN NS       bladerunner.fx
bladerunner.fx        1D IN A        192.253.254.2
fx                    1D IN NS       outland.fx
outland.fx            1D IN A        192.253.254.3
fx                    1D IN NS       huskymo.boulder.acmebw.com.
                      1D IN NS       tornado.acmebw.com.
me                    1D IN CNAME    monsters-inc
carrie                1D IN A        192.253.253.4
monsters-inc          1D IN A        192.249.249.4
misery                1D IN A        192.253.253.2
@                     1D IN SOA      toystory al (
                                     2000091400    ; serial
                                     3H            ; refresh
                                     1H            ; retry
                                     4W2D          ; expiry
                                     1H )          ; minimum
```

Now let's say you missed a record in the beginning of the zone data, one that flew off the top of your screen. *nslookup* lets you save the listing of a zone to a file:

```
> ls -d movie.edu > /tmp/movie.edu    List all data into /tmp/movie.edu
[toystory.movie.edu]
Received 25 answers (25 records).
```

Some versions of *nslookup* even support a built-in *view* command that sorts and displays the contents of a zone listing from interactive mode. In the latest BIND 8 releases, though, *view* is broken, and it isn't supported by BIND 9's *nslookup* as of 9.3.2.

Troubleshooting nslookup Problems

The last thing you want is to have problems with your troubleshooting tool. Unfortunately, some types of failures render *nslookup* nearly useless. Other types of *nslookup* failures are (at best) confusing, because they don't give you any clear information to work with. While there may be a few problems with *nslookup* itself, most of the problems you encounter will be caused by nameserver configuration and operation. We'll cover these problems here.

Looking Up the Right Data

This isn't really a problem per se, but it can be awfully confusing. If you use *nslookup* to look up a type of record for a domain name, and the domain name exists but records of the type you're looking for don't, you'll get an error like this:

```
% nslookup
Default Server:  toystory.movie.edu
Address:  0.0.0.0#53

> movie.edu.
Server:  toystory.movie.edu
Address:  0.0.0.0#53

*** No address (A) records available for movie.edu.
```

So what types of records do exist? Just type *set type=any* to find out:

```
> set type=any
> movie.edu.
Server:  toystory.movie.edu
Address:  0.0.0.0#53

movie.edu
        origin = toystory.movie.edu
        mail addr = al.shrek.movie.edu
        serial = 42
        refresh = 10800 (3H)
        retry   = 3600 (1H)
        expire  = 604800 (7D)
        minimum ttl = 86400 (1D)
movie.edu    nameserver = toystory.movie.edu
movie.edu    nameserver = wormhole.movie.edu
movie.edu    nameserver = zardoz.movie.edu
movie.edu    preference = 10, mail exchanger = postmanrings2x.movie.edu
postmanrings2x.movie.edu        internet address = 192.249.249.66
```

No Response from Server

What could have gone wrong if your nameserver can't look up its own name?

```
% nslookup
Default Server: toystory.movie.edu
Address: 0.0.0.0#53

> toystory
Server: toystory.movie.edu
Address: 0.0.0.0#53

*** toystory.movie.edu can't find toystory: No response from server
```

The "no response from server" error message means exactly that: the resolver didn't get back a response. *nslookup* doesn't necessarily look up anything when it starts up. If you see that the address of your nameserver is 0.0.0.0, then *nslookup* grabbed the system's hostname (what the *hostname* command returns) for the *Default Server* field and gave you its prompt. It's only when you try to look up something that you find there is no nameserver responding. In this case, it's pretty obvious there's no server running: a nameserver ought to be able to look up its own name. If you are looking up some remote information, though, the nameserver could fail to respond because it's still trying to look up the data, and *nslookup* gave up waiting. How can you tell the difference between a nameserver that isn't running and a nameserver that is running but didn't respond? You can use the *ls* command to figure it out:

```
% nslookup
Default Server: toystory.movie.edu
Address: 0.0.0.0#53

> ls foo.          Try to list a nonexistent zone
*** Can't list domain foo.: No response from server
```

In this case, no nameserver is running. If the host couldn't be reached, the error would be timed out. If a nameserver is running, you'll see this error message:

```
% nslookup
Default Server: toystory.movie.edu
Address: 0.0.0.0#53

> ls foo.
[toystory.movie.edu]
*** Can't list domain foo.: No information
```

That is, unless there's a top-level *foo* zone in your world.

No PTR Record for Nameserver's Address

Here's one of *nslookup*'s most annoying problems: something went wrong, and *nslookup* exited on startup:

```
% nslookup
*** Can't find server name for address 192.249.249.3: Non-existent host/domain
*** Default servers are not available
```

The "nonexistent domain" message means that the name *3.249.249.192.in-addr.arpa* doesn't exist. In other words, *nslookup* couldn't map 192.249.249.3, the address of its nameserver, to a domain name. But didn't we just say that *nslookup* doesn't look up anything when it starts up? In the configuration we showed you before, *nslookup* didn't look up anything, but that's not a rule. If you create a *resolv.conf* that includes one or more *nameserver* directives, *nslookup* tries to reverse-map the address to get the nameserver's domain name. In the preceding example, there *is* a nameserver running on 192.249.249.3, but it said there are no PTR records for the address 192.249.249.3. Obviously, the reverse-mapping zone is messed up, at least for the domain name *3.49.249.192.in-addr.arpa*.

The "default servers are not available" message in the example is misleading. After all, there is a nameserver available to say the address doesn't exist. More often, you'll see the error "no response from server" if the nameserver isn't running on the host or the host can't be reached. Only then does the "default servers are not available" message make sense.

Query Refused

Refused queries can cause problems at startup, and they can cause lookup failures during a session. Here's what it looks like when *nslookup* exits on startup because of a refused query:

```
% nslookup
*** Can't find server name for address 192.249.249.3: Query refused
*** Default servers are not available
%
```

Access lists can cause *nslookup* startup problems. When *nslookup* attempts to find the domain name of its nameserver using a PTR query, the query can be refused. If you think the problem is an access list, make sure you allow the host you're running on to query the nameserver. Check any *allow-query* substatements for the IP address of the local host or the loopback address, if you're running *nslookup* on the same host as the nameserver.

First resolv.conf Nameserver Not Responding

Here is another twist on the last problem:

```
% nslookup
*** Can't find server name for address 192.249.249.3: No response from server
Default Server:  wormhole.movie.edu
Address:  192.249.249.1
```

This time, the first nameserver listed in *resolv.conf* did not respond. We had a second *nameserver* directive in *resolv.conf*, though, and the second server did respond. From now on, *nslookup* will send queries only to *wormhole.movie.edu*; it won't try the nameserver at 192.249.249.3 again.

Finding Out What Is Being Looked Up

We've been waving our hands in the last examples, claiming that *nslookup* was looking up the nameserver's address, but we didn't prove it. Here is our proof. This time, when we started up *nslookup*, we turned on *d2* debugging from the command line. This causes *nslookup* to print out the query messages it sent, as well as when the query timed out and was retransmitted:

```
% nslookup -d2
------------
SendRequest(), len 44
    HEADER:
        opcode = QUERY, id = 1, rcode = NOERROR
        header flags:  query, want recursion
        questions = 1,  answers = 0,  authority records = 0,
        additional = 0

    QUESTIONS:
        3.249.249.192.in-addr.arpa, type = PTR, class = IN

------------
timeout (5 secs)
timeout (10 secs)
timeout (20 secs)
timeout (40 secs)
SendRequest failed

*** Can't find server name for address 192.249.249.3: No response from server
*** Default servers are not available
```

As you can see by the timeouts, it took 75 seconds for *nslookup* to give up. Without the debugging output, you wouldn't have seen anything printed to the screen for 75 seconds; it'd look as if *nslookup* had hung.

Unspecified Error

You can run into a rather unsettling problem called an "unspecified error." We have an example of this error here. We've included only the tail end of the output because we just want to talk about the error at this point (you'll find the whole *nslookup* session that produced this segment in Chapter 14):

```
Authoritative answers can be found from:
(root)  nameserver = NS.NIC.DDN.MIL
(root)  nameserver = B.ROOT-SERVERS.NET
(root)  nameserver = E.ROOT-SERVERS.NET
(root)  nameserver = D.ROOT-SERVERS.NET
(root)  nameserver = F.ROOT-SERVERS.NET
(root)  nameserver = C.ROOT-SERVERS.NET
(root)  nameserver =
*** Error: record size incorrect (1050690 != 65519)

*** relay.hp.com can't find .: Unspecified error
```

What happened here is that there was too much data to fit into a UDP datagram. The nameserver stopped filling in the response when it ran out of room. The nameserver didn't set the truncation bit in the response packet, or *nslookup* would have retried the query over a TCP connection; the nameserver must have decided that enough of the "important" information fit. You won't see this kind of error very often. You'll see it if you create too many NS records for a zone, so don't create too many. (Advice like this makes you wonder why you bought this book, right?) How many is "too many" depends on how well the domain names in the packet can be "compressed," which, in turn, depends on how many nameservers' names end in the same domain name. The root nameservers were renamed to end in *root-servers.net* for this very reason: to allow more root nameservers (13) on the Internet. As a rule of thumb, don't go over 10 NS records. As for what caused *this* error, you'll have to read Chapter 14. Those of you who just read Chapter 9 may know already.

Best of the Net

System administrators have a thankless job. There are certain questions, usually quite simple ones, that users ask over and over again. And sometimes, when in a creative mood, sysadmins come up with clever ways to help their users. When the rest of us discover their ingenuity, we can only sit back, smile admiringly, and wish we had thought of it ourselves. Here is one such case, where a system administrator found a way to communicate the solution to the sometimes vexing puzzle of how to end an *nslookup* session:

```
% nslookup
Default Server:  envy.ugcs.caltech.edu
Address:  131.215.134.135
```

```
> quit
Server:  envy.ugcs.caltech.edu
Addresses:  131.215.134.135, 131.215.128.135

Name:    ugcs.caltech.edu
Addresses:  131.215.128.135, 131.215.134.135
Aliases:  quit.ugcs.caltech.edu
          use.exit.to.leave.nslookup.--.-..ugcs.caltech.edu

> exit
```

Using dig

That's one way to deal with what's arguably a shortcoming in *nslookup*. Another is just to chuck *nslookup* and use *dig*, the Domain Information Groper (a reverse-engineered acronym if we've ever heard one).

We said earlier that *dig* isn't as pervasive as *nslookup*, so we'd better begin by telling you where to get it. You can pick up source for *dig* from the *src/bin/dig* directory (BIND 8), or the *bin/dig* directory (BIND 9) of the BIND distribution. If you build the whole distribution, you'll build a nice, new copy of *dig*, too.

With *dig*, you specify all aspects of the query you'd like to send on the command line; there's no interactive mode. You specify the domain name you want to look up as an argument, and the type of query you want to send (e.g., *a* for address records, *mx* for MX records) as another argument; the default is to look up address records. You specify the nameserver you'd like to query after an "@." You can use either a domain name or an IP address to designate a nameserver. The default is to query the nameservers in *resolv.conf*.

dig is smart about arguments, too. You can specify the arguments in any order you like, and *dig* will figure out that *mx* is probably the type of records, not the domain name, you want to look up.*

One major difference between *nslookup* and *dig* is that *dig* doesn't apply the search list, so always use fully qualified domain names as arguments to *dig*. The following:

    % dig plan9.fx.movie.edu

looks up address records for *plan9.fx.movie.edu* using the first nameserver in *resolv.conf*, while:

    % dig acmebw.com mx

looks up MX records for *acmebw.com* on the same nameserver, and:

    % dig @wormhole.movie.edu. movie.edu. soa

queries *wormhole.movie.edu* for the SOA record of *movie.edu*.

---

* Actually, early BIND 9 versions of *dig* (before 9.1.0) are order-impaired and require that you specify the domain name argument before the type. You can specify the server to query anywhere, though.

dig's Output Format

dig shows you the complete DNS response message in all its glory, with the various sections (header, question, answer, authority, and additional) clearly called out, and with resource records in those sections printed in master file format. This can come in handy if you need to use some of your troubleshooting tool's output in a zone datafile or in your root hints file. For example, the output produced by:

```
% dig @a.root-servers.net ns .
```

looks like this:

```
; <<>> DiG 8.3 <<>> @a.root-servers.net . ns
; (1 server found)
;; res options: init recurs defnam dnsrch
;; got answer:
;; ->>HEADER<<- opcode: QUERY, status: NOERROR, id: 6
;; flags: qr aa rd; QUERY: 1, ANSWER: 13, AUTHORITY: 0, ADDITIONAL: 13
;; QUERY SECTION:
;;      ., type = NS, class = IN

;; ANSWER SECTION:
.                       6D IN NS        A.ROOT-SERVERS.NET.
.                       6D IN NS        H.ROOT-SERVERS.NET.
.                       6D IN NS        C.ROOT-SERVERS.NET.
.                       6D IN NS        G.ROOT-SERVERS.NET.
.                       6D IN NS        F.ROOT-SERVERS.NET.
.                       6D IN NS        B.ROOT-SERVERS.NET.
.                       6D IN NS        J.ROOT-SERVERS.NET.
.                       6D IN NS        K.ROOT-SERVERS.NET.
.                       6D IN NS        L.ROOT-SERVERS.NET.
.                       6D IN NS        M.ROOT-SERVERS.NET.
.                       6D IN NS        I.ROOT-SERVERS.NET.
.                       6D IN NS        E.ROOT-SERVERS.NET.
.                       6D IN NS        D.ROOT-SERVERS.NET.

;; ADDITIONAL SECTION:
A.ROOT-SERVERS.NET.     6D IN A         198.41.0.4
H.ROOT-SERVERS.NET.     6D IN A         128.63.2.53
C.ROOT-SERVERS.NET.     6D IN A         192.33.4.12
G.ROOT-SERVERS.NET.     6D IN A         192.112.36.4
F.ROOT-SERVERS.NET.     6D IN A         192.5.5.241
B.ROOT-SERVERS.NET.     6D IN A         128.9.0.107
J.ROOT-SERVERS.NET.     5w6d16h IN A    198.41.0.10
K.ROOT-SERVERS.NET.     5w6d16h IN A    193.0.14.129
L.ROOT-SERVERS.NET.     5w6d16h IN A    198.32.64.12
M.ROOT-SERVERS.NET.     5w6d16h IN A    202.12.27.33
I.ROOT-SERVERS.NET.     6D IN A         192.36.148.17
E.ROOT-SERVERS.NET.     6D IN A         192.203.230.10
D.ROOT-SERVERS.NET.     6D IN A         128.8.10.90

;; Total query time: 116 msec
;; FROM: toystory.movie.edu to SERVER: a.root-servers.net  198.41.0.4
;; WHEN: Fri Sep 15 09:47:26 2000
;; MSG SIZE  sent: 17  rcvd: 436
```

Let's examine this output section by section.

The first line, beginning with the master file comment character (;) and <<>> DiG 8.3 <<>>, simply parrots the options we specified in the command line, namely, that we were interested in the NS records that *a.root-servers.net* had for the root zone.

The next line, (1 server found), tells us that when *dig* looked up the addresses associated with the domain name we specified after the @, *a.root-servers.net*, it found one. (If *dig* finds more than three, the maximum number of nameservers most resolvers can query, it'll report three.)

The line beginning with ->> HEADER <<- is the first part of the header of the reply message that *dig* received from the remote nameserver. The opcode in the header is always QUERY, just as it is with *nslookup*. The status is NOERROR; it can be any of the statuses (stati?) mentioned in the earlier section "Showing the Query and Response Messages." The ID is the message ID, a 16-bit number used to match responses to queries.

The flags tell us a bit more about the response. *qr* indicates that the message was a response, not a query. *dig* decodes responses, not queries, so *qr* will always be present. Not so with *aa* or *rd*, though. *aa* indicates that the response was authoritative, and *rd* indicates that the recursion-desired bit was set in the query (because the responding nameserver just copies the bit from the query to the response). Most of the time *rd* is set in the query, you'll also see *ra* set in the response, indicating that recursion was available from the remote nameserver. However, *a.root-servers.net* is a root nameserver and has recursion disabled, like we showed you in Chapter 11, so it handles recursive queries the same as it does iterative queries. So it ignores the *rd* bit and correctly indicates that recursion wasn't available by leaving *ra* unset.

The last fields in the header indicate that *dig* asked 1 question and received 13 records in the answer section, 0 records in the authority section, and 13 records in the additional data section.

The line after the line that contains QUERY SECTION: shows us the query *dig* sent: for the NS records in the IN class for the root zone. After ANSWER SECTION:, we see the 13 NS records for the root nameservers, and after ADDITIONAL SECTION:, we have the 13 A records that correspond to those 13 root nameservers. If the response had included an authority section, we'd have seen that, too, after AUTHORITY SECTION:.

At the very end, *dig* includes summary information about the query and response. The first line shows how long it took the remote nameserver to return the response after *dig* sent the query. The second line shows from which host you sent the query and to which nameserver you sent it. The third line is a timestamp showing when the response was received. And the fourth line shows the size of the query and the response, in bytes.

Zone Transfers with dig

As with *nslookup*, you can use *dig* to initiate zone transfers. Unlike *nslookup*, though, *dig* has no special command to request a zone transfer. Instead, you simply specify *axfr* (as the query type) and the domain name of the zone as arguments. Remember that you can transfer a zone only from a nameserver that's authoritative for the zone.

So to transfer the *movie.edu* zone from *wormhole.movie.edu*, you can use:

```
% dig @wormhole.movie.edu movie.edu axfr

; <<>> DiG 8.3 <<>> @wormhole.movie.edu movie.edu axfr
; (1 server found)
$ORIGIN movie.edu.
@                    1D IN SOA       toystory al (
                                     2000091402      ; serial
                                     3H              ; refresh
                                     1H              ; retry
                                     1W              ; expiry
                                     1H )            ; minimum

                     1D IN NS        toystory
                     1D IN NS        wormhole
                     1D IN NS        outland.fx
outland.fx           1D IN A         192.253.254.3
wormhole             1D IN A         192.249.249.1
                     1D IN A         192.253.253.1
wh249                1D IN A         192.249.249.1
shrek                1D IN A         192.249.249.2
toys                 1D IN CNAME     toystory
cujo                 1D IN TXT       "Location:" "machine" "room" "dog" "house"
wh253                1D IN A         192.253.253.1
wh                   1D IN CNAME     wormhole
shining              1D IN A         192.253.253.3
toystory             1D IN A         192.249.249.3
localhost            1D IN A         127.0.0.1
fx                   1D IN NS        bladerunner.fx
bladerunner.fx       1D IN A         192.253.254.2
fx                   1D IN NS        outland.fx
outland.fx           1D IN A         192.253.254.3
me                   1D IN CNAME     monsters-inc
carrie               1D IN A         192.253.253.4
monsters-inc            1D IN A         192.249.249.4
misery               1D IN A         192.253.253.2
@                    1D IN SOA       toystory al (
                                     2000091402      ; serial
                                     3H              ; refresh
                                     1H              ; retry
                                     1W              ; expiry
                                     1H )            ; minimum
```

```
;; Received 25 answers (25 records).
;; FROM: toystory.movie.edu to SERVER: wormhole.movie.edu
;; WHEN: Fri Sep 22 11:02:45 2000
```

Note that as with *nslookup*, the SOA record appears twice, at the beginning and the end of the zone. And as with all *dig* output, the results of the zone transfer are printed in master file format, so you can use the output as a zone datafile if you need to.[*]

dig Options

There are too many command-line options to *dig* to show here, so look at *dig*'s manual page for an exhaustive list. Here's a list of the most important ones, though, and what they do:

–x address

> *nslookup* is smart enough to recognize an IP address and look up the appropriate domain name in *in-addr.arpa*, so why not *dig*? If you use the *–x* option, *dig* assumes that the domain name argument you've specified is really an IP address, so it inverts the octets and tacks on *in-addr.arpa*. Using *–x* also changes the default record type looked up to ANY, so you can reverse-map an IP address with *dig –x 10.0.0.1*.

–p port

> Sends queries to the specified port instead of port 53, the default.

+norec[urse]

> Turns off recursion (recursion is on by default).

+vc

> Sends TCP-based queries (queries are UDP by default).

---

[*] Though you'd need to delete the extra SOA record first.

CHAPTER 13

Reading BIND Debugging Output

"O Tiger-lily!" said Alice, addressing herself to one
that was waving gracefully about in the wind, "I wish
you could talk!"
"We can talk," said the Tiger-lily, "when there's
anybody worth talking to."

One of the tools in your troubleshooting toolbox is the nameserver's debugging output. As long as your nameserver has been compiled with DEBUG defined, you can get query-by-query reports of its internal operation. The messages you get are often quite cryptic; they were meant for someone who has the source code to follow. We'll explain some of the debugging output in this chapter. Our goal is to cover just enough for you to follow what the nameserver is doing; we aren't trying to supply an exhaustive compilation of debugging messages.

As you read through the explanations here, think back to material covered in earlier chapters. Seeing this information again, in another context, should help you understand more fully how a nameserver works.

Debugging Levels

The amount of information the nameserver provides depends on the debugging level. The lower the debugging level, the less information you get. Higher debugging levels give you more information, but they also fill up your disk faster. After you've read a lot of debugging output, you'll develop a feel for how much information you'll need to solve any particular problem. Of course, if you can easily recreate the problem, you can start at level 1 and increase the debugging level until you have enough information. For the most basic problem—why a name can't be looked up—level 1 will often suffice, so you should start there.

What Information Is at Each Level?

Here's a list of the information that each debugging level produces for BIND 8 and BIND 9 nameservers. The debugging information is cumulative; for example, level 2 includes all of level 1's debugging information. The data is divided into the following basic areas: starting up, updating the database, processing queries, and maintaining zones. We won't cover updating the nameserver's internal database; problems almost always occur elsewhere. However, *what* the nameserver adds or deletes from its internal database can be a problem, as you'll see in Chapter 14.

BIND 8 and 9 have a whopping 99 debug levels, but most of the debugging messages are logged at just a few of those levels. We'll look at those now.

BIND 8 debugging levels

Level 1

> The information at this level is necessarily brief. Nameservers can process *lots* of queries, which can create *lots* of debugging output. Since the output is condensed, you can collect data over long periods. Use this debugging level for basic startup information and for watching query transactions. You'll see some errors logged at this level, including syntax errors and DNS packet-formatting errors. This level also shows referrals.

Level 2

> Level 2 provides lots of useful stuff: it lists the IP addresses of remote nameservers used during a lookup, along with their round-trip time values; it calls out bad responses; and it tags a response as to which type of query it is answering—a SYSTEM (sysquery) or a USER query. When you are tracking down a problem with a slave server loading a zone, this level shows you the zone values—serial number, refresh time, retry time, expire time, and time left—as the slave checks if it is up to date with its master.

Level 3

> Level 3 debugging becomes much more verbose because it generates lots of messages about updating the nameserver database. Make sure you have enough disk space if you are going to collect debugging output at level 3 or above. At level 3, you also see duplicate queries called out, system queries generated (sysquery), the names of the remote nameservers used during a lookup, and the number of addresses found for each server.

Level 4

> Use level 4 debugging when you want to see the query and response packets *received* by the nameserver. This level also shows the credibility level for cached data.

Level 5

There are a variety of messages at level 5, but none of them is particularly useful for general debugging. This level includes some error messages—for example, when a *malloc()* fails or when the nameserver gives up on a query.

Level 6

Level 6 shows the response sent to the original query.

Level 7

Level 7 shows a few configuration and parsing messages.

Level 8

There is no significant debugging information at this level.

Level 9

There is no significant debugging information at this level.

Level 10

Use level 10 debugging when you want to see the query and response packets sent by the nameserver. The format of these packets is the same format used in level 4. You won't use this level very often because you can see the nameserver response packet with *nslookup* or *dig*.

Level 11

There are only a couple of debugging messages at and above this level, and they are in seldom-traversed code.

BIND 9 debugging levels

Level 1

Level 1 shows you basic nameserver operation: zone loading, maintenance (including SOA queries, zone transfers and zone expiration, and cache cleaning), NOTIFY messages, and high-level tasks dispatched (such as looking up addresses for a nameserver).

Level 2

Level 2 logs multicast requests.

Level 3

Level 3 shows you low-level task creation and operation. Unfortunately, most of these tasks don't have particularly descriptive names (*requestmgr_detach*?), and the arguments they report are awfully cryptic. Level 3 also shows you journal activity, such as when the nameserver writes a record of a zone change to the zone's journal or when the nameserver applies a journal to a zone at startup. Operation of the DNSSEC validator and checking of TSIG signatures also come in at debug level 3.

Level 4

Level 4 logs when a master nameserver falls back to using AXFR because the transferred zone's journal isn't available.

Level 5
> Level 5 logs which view was used while satisfying a particular request.

Level 6
> A handful of outbound zone transfer messages are logged at level 6, including checks of the query that initiated the transfer.

Level 7
> There are only a couple of new debugging messages at this level: logging of journal adds and deletes, and a count of how many bytes were returned by a zone transfer.

Level 8
> Many dynamic update messages are logged at level 8: prerequisite checks, writing journal entries, and rollbacks. Several low-level zone transfer messages also appear here, including a log of resource records sent in a zone transfer.

Level 10
> Level 10 reports a couple of messages about zone timer activity.

Level 20
> Level 20 reports an update to a zone's refresh timer.

Level 90
> Low-level operation of the BIND 9 task dispatcher is logged at level 90.

With BIND 8 and BIND 9, you can configure the nameserver to print out the debug level with the debug message. Just turn on the logging option *print-severity*, as explained in the section "Logging" in Chapter 7.

Keep in mind that this is debugging information; it was used by the authors of BIND to debug the code, so it is not as readable as you might like. You can use it to figure out why the nameserver isn't doing what you think it should be or just to learn how the nameserver operates. However, don't expect nicely designed, carefully formatted output.

Turning On Debugging

Nameserver debugging can be started either from the command line or with control messages. If you need to see the startup information to diagnose your current problem, you'll have to use the command-line option. If you want to start debugging on a nameserver that is already running, or if you want to turn off debugging, you'll have to use controls. The nameserver writes its debugging output to *named.run* in the nameserver's working directory.

Debugging Command-Line Option

When troubleshooting, you sometimes need to see the sortlist, know which interface a file descriptor is bound to, or find out where in the initialization stage the nameserver was when it exited (if the *syslog* error message wasn't clear enough). To see this kind of debugging information, you'll have to start debugging with a command-line option; by the time you send a control message, it will be too late. The command-line option for debugging is *–d level*.

Changing the Debugging Level with Control Messages

If you don't need to see the nameserver's initialization, start your nameserver without the debugging command-line option. You can later turn debugging on and off using *rndc* (or, with BIND 8, *ndc*) to send the appropriate control message to the nameserver process. Here, we set debugging to level 3, then turn off debugging:

```
# rndc trace 3
# rndc notrace
```

And, as you might expect, if you turn on debugging from the command line, you can still use *rndc* to change the nameserver's debug level.

Reading Debugging Output

We'll cover five examples of debugging output. The first example shows the nameserver starting up. The next two examples show successful name lookups. The fourth example shows a slave nameserver keeping its zone up to date. And in the last example, we switch from showing you nameserver behavior to showing you resolver behavior: the resolver search algorithm. After each trace (except the last one), we killed the nameserver and started it again so that each trace started with a fresh, nearly empty cache.

You might wonder why we've chosen to show normal nameserver behavior for all our examples; after all, this chapter is about debugging. We're showing you normal behavior because you have to know what normal operation is before you can track down abnormal operation. Another reason is to help you understand the concepts (retransmissions, roundtrip times, etc.) we described in earlier chapters.

Nameserver Startup (BIND 8, Debug Level 1)

We'll start the debugging examples by watching the nameserver initialize. This first nameserver is a BIND 8 nameserver. We used *–d 1* on the command line, and this is the *named.run* output that resulted:

```
1  Debug level 1
2  Version = named 8.2.3-T7B Mon Aug 21 19:21:21 MDT 2000
3  cricket@abugslife.movie.edu:/usr/local/src/bind-8.2.3-T7B/src/bin/named
```

```
 4  conffile = ./named.conf
 5  starting.  named 8.2.3-T7B Mon Aug 21 19:21:21 MDT 2000
 6  cricket@abugslife.movie.edu:/usr/local/src/bind-8.2.3-T7B/src/bin/named
 7  ns_init(./named.conf)
 8  Adding 64 template zones
 9  update_zone_info('0.0.127.in-addr.arpa', 1)
10  source = db.127.0.0
11  purge_zone(0.0.127.in-addr.arpa,1)
12  reloading zone
13  db_load(db.127.0.0, 0.0.127.in-addr.arpa, 1, Nil, Normal)
14  purge_zone(0.0.127.in-addr.arpa,1)
15  master zone "0.0.127.in-addr.arpa" (IN) loaded (serial 2000091500)
16  zone[1] type 1: '0.0.127.in-addr.arpa' z_time 0, z_refresh 0
17  update_zone_info('.', 3)
18  source = db.cache
19  reloading hint zone
20  db_load(db.cache, , 2, Nil, Normal)
21  purge_zone(,1)
22  hint zone "" (IN) loaded (serial 0)
23  zone[2] type 3: '.' z_time 0, z_refresh 0
24  update_pid_file( )
25  getnetconf(generation 969052965)
26  getnetconf: considering lo [127.0.0.1]
27  ifp->addr [127.0.0.1].53 d_dfd 20
28  evSelectFD(ctx 0x80d8148, fd 20, mask 0x1, func 0x805e710, uap 0x40114344)
29  evSelectFD(ctx 0x80d8148, fd 21, mask 0x1, func 0x8089540, uap 0x4011b0e8)
30  listening on [127.0.0.1].53 (lo)
31  getnetconf: considering eth0 [192.249.249.3]
32  ifp->addr [192.249.249.3].53 d_dfd 22
33  evSelectFD(ctx 0x80d8148, fd 22, mask 0x1, func 0x805e710, uap 0x401143b0)
34  evSelectFD(ctx 0x80d8148, fd 23, mask 0x1, func 0x8089540, uap 0x4011b104)
35  listening on [206.168.194.122].53 (eth0)
36  fwd ds 5 addr [0.0.0.0].1085
37  Forwarding source address is [0.0.0.0].1085
38  evSelectFD(ctx 0x80d8148, fd 5, mask 0x1, func 0x805e710, uap 0)
39  evSetTimer(ctx 0x80d8148, func 0x807cbe8, uap 0x40116158, due 969052990.812648000,
    inter 0.000000000)
40  exit ns_init( )
41  update_pid_file( )
42  Ready to answer queries.
43  prime_cache: priming = 0, root = 0
44  evSetTimer(ctx 0x80d8148, func 0x805bc30, uap 0, due 969052969.000000000, inter 0.
    000000000)
45  sysquery: send -> [192.33.4.12].53 dfd=5 nsid=32211 id=0 retry=969052969
46  datagram from [192.33.4.12].53, fd 5, len 436
47  13 root servers
```

We added the line numbers to the debugging output; you won't see them in yours.
Lines 2–6 give the version of BIND you are running and the name of the configuration file. Version 8.2.3-T 7B was released by ISC (Internet Software Consortium) in
August 2000. We used the configuration file in the current directory, *./named.conf*,
for this run.

Lines 7–23 show BIND reading the configuration file and the zone datafiles. This nameserver is a caching-only nameserver—the only files read are *db.127.0.0* (lines 9–16) and *db.cache* (lines 17–23). Line 9 shows the zone being updated (*0.0.127.inaddr.arpa*), and line 10 shows the file containing the zone data (*db.127.0.0*). Line 11 indicates that any old data for the zone is purged before new data is added. Line 12 says the zone is being reloaded, even though the zone is actually being loaded for the first time. The zone data is loaded during lines 13–15. On lines 16 and 23, *z_time* is the time to check when this zone is up to date; *z_refresh* is the zone refresh time. These values matter only if the nameserver is a slave for the zone.

Lines 25–39 show the initialization of file descriptors. (In this case, they're really socket descriptors.) File descriptors 20 and 21 (lines 27–29) are bound to 127.0.0.1, the loopback address. Descriptor 20 is a datagram socket, and descriptor 21 is a stream socket. File descriptors 22 and 23 (lines 32–34) are bound to the 192.249. 249.3 interface. Each interface address was considered and used; they would not be used if the interface had not been initialized or if the address were already in the list. File descriptor 5 (lines 36–39) is bound to 0.0.0.0, the wildcard address. Most network daemons use only one socket bound to the wildcard address, not sockets bound to individual interfaces. The wildcard address picks up packets sent to any interface on the host. Let's digress for a moment to explain why *named* uses both a socket bound to the wildcard address and sockets bound to specific interfaces.

When *named* receives a request from an application or from another nameserver, it receives the request on one of the sockets bound to a specific interface. If *named* did not have sockets bound to specific interfaces, it would receive the requests on the socket bound to the wildcard address. When *named* sends back a response, it uses the same socket descriptor that the request came in on. Why does *named* do this? When responses are sent out via the socket bound to the wildcard address, the kernel fills in the sender's address with the address of the interface the response was actually sent out on. This address may or may not be the same address that the request was sent to. When responses are sent out via the socket bound to a specific address, the kernel fills in the sender's address with that specific address—the same address the request was sent to. If a nameserver gets a response from an IP address it doesn't know about, the response is tagged a *martian* and discarded. *named* tries to avoid causing martian responses by sending its responses on descriptors bound to specific interfaces, so the address it replies from is the same address the request was sent to. However, when *named* sends out *queries*, it uses the wildcard descriptor because there is no need to use a specific IP address.

Lines 43–47 show the nameserver sending out a system query to find which nameservers are currently serving the root zone. This is known as *priming the cache*. The first server queried sent a response that included 13 nameservers.

The nameserver is now initialized and ready to answer queries.

Nameserver Startup (BIND 9, Debug Level 1)

Here's what a BIND 9 nameserver looks like starting up. When you start the nameserver, BIND 9 logs debug messages to *named.run* in your shell's current directory. Then, after BIND 9 has read the configuration file and switches to the directory in which your database files are stored, it logs debug messages to *named.run* in that directory. Here is the *named.run* from your shell's current directory:

```
1  26-Jun-2005 15:34:23.136 starting BIND 9.3.2 -d1
2  26-Jun-2005 15:34:23.232 loading configuration from '/etc/named.conf'
3  26-Jun-2005 15:34:23.247 no IPv6 interfaces found
4  26-Jun-2005 15:34:23.247 listening on IPv4 interface lo, 127.0.0.1#53
5  26-Jun-2005 15:34:23.248 listening on IPv4 interface eth0, 192.249.249.3#53
6  26-Jun-2005 15:34:23.255 command channel listening on 127.0.0.1#953
```

Lines 1 and 2 show the version of BIND we're running (9.3.2) and the configuration file it's reading.

Line 3 reminds us that our host doesn't have any IP Version 6 network interfaces; if it did, BIND 9 could listen on those interfaces for queries.

Lines 4 and 5 show the nameserver listening on two network interfaces: *lo*, the loopback interface, and *eth0*, the Ethernet interface. BIND 9 displays the address and port in the format *address#port*, unlike BIND 8, which uses *[address].port*. Line 6 shows *named* listening on port 953, the default port, for control messages.

At this point, BIND 9 reads the configuration file and switches to the directory with your database files if your configuration file has an *options* statement that specifies a new directory, like the one shown here:

```
options {
        directory "/var/named";
};
```

Here is the *named.run* from */var/named*:

```
1   26-Jun-2005 15:34:23.255 now using logging configuration from config file
2   26-Jun-2005 15:34:23.256 load_configuration: success
3   26-Jun-2005 15:34:23.256 zone 0.0.127.IN-ADDR.ARPA/IN: starting load
4   26-Jun-2005 15:34:23.258 zone 0.0.127.IN-ADDR.ARPA/IN: loaded
5   26-Jun-2005 15:34:23.258 zone 0.0.127.IN-ADDR.ARPA/IN: journal rollforward completed
    successfully: no journal
6   26-Jun-2005 15:34:23.258 zone 0.0.127.IN-ADDR.ARPA/IN: loaded serial 3
7   26-Jun-2005 15:34:23.258 zone authors.bind/CH: starting load
8   26-Jun-2005 15:34:23.259 zone authors.bind/CH: loaded
9   26-Jun-2005 15:34:23.259 zone hostname.bind/CH: starting load
10  26-Jun-2005 15:34:23.259 zone hostname.bind/CH: loaded
11  26-Jun-2005 15:34:23.259 zone version.bind/CH: starting load
12  26-Jun-2005 15:34:23.259 zone version.bind/CH: loaded
13  26-Jun-2005 15:34:23.260 zone id.server/CH: starting load
14  26-Jun-2005 15:34:23.260 zone id.server/CH: loaded
15  26-Jun-2005 15:34:23.260 dns_zone_maintenance: zone 0.0.127.IN-ADDR.ARPA/IN: enter
16  26-Jun-2005 15:34:23.260 dns_zone_maintenance: zone version.bind/CH: enter
```

```
17   26-Jun-2005 15:34:23.260 dns_zone_maintenance: zone hostname.bind/CH: enter
18   26-Jun-2005 15:34:23.260 dns_zone_maintenance: zone authors.bind/CH: enter
19   26-Jun-2005 15:34:23.260 dns_zone_maintenance: zone id.server/CH: enter
20   26-Jun-2005 15:34:23.263 running
```

Lines 3–6 show the nameserver loading *0.0.127.in-addr.arpa*. The *starting* and *loaded* messages are self-explanatory. The *no journal* message indicates that no journal file was present. (A journal file, described in Chapter 10, is a record of dynamic updates the nameserver received for the zone.)

Lines 7–14 show the nameserver loading the built-in CHAOSNET zones *authors.bind, hostname.bind, version.bind*, and *id.server*.

Finally, lines 15–19 show the nameserver doing maintenance on *its* zones. Zone maintenance is the process that schedules periodic tasks, such as SOA queries for slave and stub zones or NOTIFY messages.

If you are curious about what is in the built-in CHOASNET zones, you can query your nameserver for the zone data, as we did here with a *dig* query for *authors.bind*, record type *any*, class *CHAOSNET*:

```
# dig @wormhole.movie.edu authors.bind any c
; <<>> DiG 9.3.2 <<>> @wormhole.movie.edu authors.bind any ch
; (1 server found)
;; global options:  printcmd
;; Got answer:
;; ->>HEADER<<- opcode: QUERY, status: NOERROR, id: 6822
;; flags: qr aa rd; QUERY: 1, ANSWER: 14, AUTHORITY: 0, ADDITIONAL: 0

;; QUESTION SECTION:
;authors.bind.              CH      ANY

;; ANSWER SECTION:
authors.bind.        0    CH    TXT    "Mark Andrews"
authors.bind.        0    CH    TXT    "James Brister"
authors.bind.        0    CH    TXT    "Ben Cottrell"
authors.bind.        0    CH    TXT    "Michael Graff"
authors.bind.        0    CH    TXT    "Andreas Gustafsson"
authors.bind.        0    CH    TXT    "Bob Halley"
authors.bind.        0    CH    TXT    "David Lawrence"
authors.bind.        0    CH    TXT    "Danny Mayer"
authors.bind.        0    CH    TXT    "Damien Neil"
authors.bind.        0    CH    TXT    "Matt Nelson"
authors.bind.        0    CH    TXT    "Michael Sawyer"
authors.bind.        0    CH    TXT    "Brian Wellington"
authors.bind.        86400    CH    SOA    authors.bind. hostmaster.authors.bind. 0
28800 7200 604800 86400
authors.bind.        0    CH    NS    authors.bind.

;; Query time: 2 msec
;; SERVER: wormhole.movie.edu#53(192.249.249.1)
;; WHEN: Sun Jun 26 16:30:28 2005
;; MSG SIZE  rcvd: 402
```

A Successful Lookup (BIND 8, Debug Level 1)

Suppose you want to watch the nameserver look up a name. Your nameserver wasn't started with debugging. Use *ndc* once to turn on debugging, look up the name, then use it again to turn off debugging, like this:

```
# ndc trace 1
# /etc/ping galt.cs.purdue.edu.
# ndc notrace
```

We did this; here's the resulting *named.run* file:

```
datagram from [192.249.249.3].1162, fd 20, len 36

req: nlookup(galt.cs.purdue.edu) id 29574 type=1 class=1
req: missed 'galt.cs.purdue.edu' as '' (cname=0)
forw: forw -> [198.41.0.10].53 ds=4 nsid=40070 id=29574 2ms retry 4sec
datagram from [198.41.0.10].53, fd 4, len 343

;; ->>HEADER<<- opcode: QUERY, status: NOERROR, id: 40070
;; flags: qr; QUERY: 1, ANSWER: 0, AUTHORITY: 9, ADDITIONAL: 9
;;              galt.cs.purdue.edu, type = A, class = IN
EDU.                    6D IN NS    A.ROOT-SERVERS.NET.
EDU.                    6D IN NS    H.ROOT-SERVERS.NET.
EDU.                    6D IN NS    B.ROOT-SERVERS.NET.
EDU.                    6D IN NS    C.ROOT-SERVERS.NET.
EDU.                    6D IN NS    D.ROOT-SERVERS.NET.
EDU.                    6D IN NS    E.ROOT-SERVERS.NET.
EDU.                    6D IN NS    I.ROOT-SERVERS.NET.
EDU.                    6D IN NS    F.ROOT-SERVERS.NET.
EDU.                    6D IN NS    G.ROOT-SERVERS.NET.
A.ROOT-SERVERS.NET.        5w6d16h IN A    198.41.0.4
H.ROOT-SERVERS.NET.        5w6d16h IN A    128.63.2.53
B.ROOT-SERVERS.NET.        5w6d16h IN A    128.9.0.107
C.ROOT-SERVERS.NET.        5w6d16h IN A    192.33.4.12
D.ROOT-SERVERS.NET.        5w6d16h IN A    128.8.10.90
E.ROOT-SERVERS.NET.        5w6d16h IN A    192.203.230.10
I.ROOT-SERVERS.NET.        5w6d16h IN A    192.36.148.17
F.ROOT-SERVERS.NET.        5w6d16h IN A    192.5.5.241
G.ROOT-SERVERS.NET.        5w6d16h IN A    192.112.36.4
resp: nlookup(galt.cs.purdue.edu) qtype=1
resp: found 'galt.cs.purdue.edu' as 'edu' (cname=0)
resp: forw -> [192.36.148.17].53 ds=4 nsid=40071 id=29574 1ms
datagram from [192.36.148.17].53, fd 4, len 202

;; ->>HEADER<<- opcode: QUERY, status: NOERROR, id: 40071
;; flags: qr rd; QUERY: 1, ANSWER: 0, AUTHORITY: 4, ADDITIONAL: 4
;;   galt.cs.purdue.edu, type = A, class = IN
PURDUE.EDU.             2D IN NS    NS.PURDUE.EDU.
PURDUE.EDU.             2D IN NS    MOE.RICE.EDU.
PURDUE.EDU.             2D IN NS    PENDRAGON.CS.PURDUE.EDU.
PURDUE.EDU.             2D IN NS    HARBOR.ECN.PURDUE.EDU.
NS.PURDUE.EDU.          2D IN A     128.210.11.5
MOE.RICE.EDU.           2D IN A     128.42.5.4
```

```
PENDRAGON.CS.PURDUE.EDU.    2D IN A  128.10.2.5
HARBOR.ECN.PURDUE.EDU.      2D IN A    128.46.199.76
resp: nlookup(galt.cs.purdue.edu) qtype=1
resp: found 'galt.cs.purdue.edu' as 'cs.purdue.edu' (cname=0)
resp: forw -> [128.46.199.76].53 ds=4 nsid=40072 id=29574 8ms
datagram from [128.46.199.76].53, fd 4, len 234

send_msg -> [192.249.249.3].1162 (UDP 20) id=29574
Debug off
```

First, notice that IP addresses, not domain names, are logged—odd for a *nameserver*, don't you think? It's really not that odd, though. If you are trying to debug a problem with looking up names, you don't want the nameserver looking up additional names just to make the debugging output more readable; the extra queries would interfere with the debugging. None of the debugging levels translate IP addresses into domain names. You have to use a tool (like the one we provide later) to convert them for you.

Let's go through this debugging output line by line. This detailed approach is important if you want to understand what each line means. If you turn on debugging, you're probably trying to find out why some name can't be looked up, and you're going to have to figure out what the trace means.

```
datagram from [192.249.249.3].1162, fd 20, len 36
```

A datagram came from the host with IP address 192.249.249.3 (*toystory.movie.edu*). You may see the datagram come from 127.0.0.1 if the sender is on the same host as the nameserver. The sending application used port 1162. The nameserver received the datagram on file descriptor (fd) 20. The startup debugging output, like the one shown earlier, tells you which interface file descriptor 20 is bound to. The length (len) of the datagram was 36 bytes.

```
req: nlookup(galt.cs.purdue.edu) id 29574 type=1 class=1
```

Since the next debugging line starts with *req*, we know that the datagram was a request. The name looked up in the request was *galt.cs.purdue.edu*. The request ID is 29574. The *type=1* means the request is for address information. The *class=1* means the class is IN. You can find a complete list of query types and classes in the header file */usr/ include/arpa/nameser.h*.

```
req: missed 'galt.cs.purdue.edu' as '' (cname=0)
```

The nameserver looked up the requested name and didn't find it. It then tried to find a remote nameserver to ask; none was found until the root zone (the empty quotes). The *cname=0* means the nameserver didn't encounter a CNAME record. If it does see a CNAME record, the canonical name is looked up instead of the original name, and *cname* will be nonzero.

```
forw: forw -> [198.41.0.10].53 ds=4 nsid=40070 id=29574 2ms retry 4sec
```

The query was forwarded to the nameserver (port 53) on host 198.41.0.10 (*j.root-servers.net*). The nameserver used file descriptor 4 (which is bound to the wildcard address) to send the query. The nameserver tagged this query with ID number 40070 (*nsid=40070*) so that it could match the response to the original question. The application used ID number 29574 (*id=29574*), as you saw on the *nlookup* line. The nameserver will wait four seconds before trying the next nameserver.

```
datagram from [198.41.0.10].53, fd 4, len 343
```

The nameserver on *j.root-servers.net* responded. Since the response was a delegation, it is printed in full in the debug log.

```
resp: nlookup(galt.cs.purdue.edu) qtype=1
```

After the information in the response message is cached, the name is looked up again. As mentioned earlier, *qtype=1* means that the nameserver is looking for address information.

```
resp: found 'galt.cs.purdue.edu' as 'edu' (cname=0)
resp: forw -> [192.36.148.17].53 ds=4 nsid=40071 id=29574 1ms
datagram from [192.36.148.17].53, fd 4, len 202
```

The root nameserver responds with a delegation to the *edu* servers. The same query is sent to 192.36.148.17 (*i.root-servers.net*), one of the *edu* servers. *i.root-servers.net* responds with information about the *purdue.edu* servers.

```
resp: found 'galt.cs.purdue.edu' as 'cs.purdue.edu' (cname=0)
```

This time there is some information at the *cs.purdue.edu* level.

```
resp: forw -> [128.46.199.76].53 ds=4 nsid=40072 id=29574 8ms
```

A query is sent to the nameserver on 128.46.199.76 (*harbor.ecn.purdue.edu*). This time the nameserver ID is 40072.

```
datagram from [128.46.199.76].53, fd 4, len 234
```

The nameserver on *harbor.ecn.purdue.edu* responded. We have to look at what happens next to figure out the contents of this response.

```
send_msg -> [192.249.249.3].1162 (UDP 20) id=29574
```

The last response must have contained the address requested, since the nameserver responded to the application (which used port 1162, if you look back at the original query). The response was in a UDP packet (as opposed to a TCP connection), and it used file descriptor 20.

This nameserver was "quiet" when we did this trace; it wasn't handling other queries at the same time. When you do a trace on an active nameserver, though, you won't be so lucky. You'll have to sift through the output and patch together those pieces that pertain to the lookup in which you are interested. It's not that hard, though. Start up your favorite editor, search for the *nlookup* line with the name you looked up, then trace the entries with the same *nsid*. You'll see how to follow the *nsid* in the next BIND 8 trace.

A Successful Lookup (BIND 9, Debug Level 1)

We'll show you the debugging output produced by looking up the same domain name on a BIND 9 nameserver at debug level 1, but it's almost laughably short. Still, as we said, it's important to know what debugging output looks like under correct operation. Anyway, here goes:

```
1  28-Jun-2005 21:14:20.554 createfetch: galt.cs.purdue.edu A
2  28-Jun-2005 21:14:20.568 createfetch: . NS
```

This does in fact show you the query being processed. You will get better data if you turn on query logging to see the actual queries. After adding the following lines to /etc/named.conf:

```
logging {
  category queries {
      default_debug;
  };
};
```

you get the following debug output:

```
1  28-Jun-2005 21:16:36.080 client 192.249.249.3#1090: query: galt.cs.purdue.edu IN A +
2  28-Jun-2005 21:16:36.081 createfetch: galt.cs.purdue.edu A
3  28-Jun-2005 21:16:36.081 createfetch: . NS
```

The first line tells us that a client at IP address 192.249.249.3 (that is, the local host), running on port 1090, sent us a query for *galt.cs.purdue.edu*'s address. The + at the end of the line indicates that recursion was requested. The other lines are logged by the portion of the nameserver that does name resolution to let us know what it's up to.

A Successful Lookup with Retransmissions (BIND 8, Debug Level 1)

Not all lookups are as "clean" as the last one: sometimes the query must be retransmitted. The user doesn't see any difference as long as the lookup succeeds, although a query involving retransmissions will take longer. Following is a trace where there are retransmissions. We converted the IP addresses to domain names after the trace was done. Notice how much easier it is to read with names!

```
1   Debug turned ON, Level 1
2
3   datagram from toystory.movie.edu port 3397, fd 20, len 35
4   req: nlookup(ucunix.san.uc.edu) id 1 type=1 class=1
5   req: found 'ucunix.san.uc.edu' as 'edu' (cname=0)
6   forw: forw -> i.root-servers.net port 53   ds=4 nsid=2 id=1 0ms retry 4 sec
7
8   datagram from i.root-servers.net port 53, fd 4, len 240
    <delegation lines removed>
9   resp: nlookup(ucunix.san.uc.edu) qtype=1
10  resp: found 'ucunix.san.uc.edu' as 'san.uc.edu' (cname=0)
11  resp: forw -> uceng.uc.edu port 53 ds=4 nsid=3 id=1 0ms
12  resend(addr=1 n=0) - > ucbeh.san.uc.edu port 53 ds=4 nsid=3 id=1 0ms
13
```

```
14  datagram from toystory.movie.edu port 3397, fd 20, len 35
15  req: nlookup(ucunix.san.uc.edu) id 1 type=1 class=1
16  req: found 'ucunix.san.uc.edu' as 'san.uc.edu' (cname=0)
17  resend(addr=2 n=0) - > uccba.uc.edu port 53 ds=4 nsid=3 id=1 0ms
18  resend(addr=3 n=0) - > mail.cis.ohio-state.edu port 53 ds=4 nsid=3 id=1 0ms
19
20  datagram from mail.cis.ohio-state.edu port 53, fd 4, len 51
21  send_msg -> toystory.movie.edu (UDP 20 3397) id=1
```

This trace starts out the same way as the last trace (lines 1–11): the nameserver receives a query for *ucunix.san.uc.edu*, sends the query to an *edu* nameserver (*i.root-servers.net*), receives a response that includes a list of nameservers for *uc.edu*, and sends the query to one of the *uc.edu* nameservers (*uceng.uc.edu*).

What's new in this trace are the *resend* lines (lines 12, 17, and 18). The *forw* on line 11 counts as *resend(addr=0 n=0)*; we CS dweebs always start counting at zero. Since *uceng.uc.edu* didn't respond, the nameserver goes on to try *ucbeh.san.uc.edu* (line 12), *uccba.uc.edu* (line 17), and *mail.cis.ohio-state.edu* (line 18). The off-site nameserver on *mail.cis.ohio-state.edu* finally responds (line 20). Notice that you can track all the retransmissions by searching for *nsid=3*; that's important to know, because lots of other queries may be wedged between these.

Also, notice the second datagram from *toystory.movie.edu* (line 14). It has the same port, file descriptor, length, ID, and type as the query on line 3. The application didn't receive a response in time, so it retransmitted its original query. Since the nameserver is still working on the first query transmitted, this one is a duplicate. It doesn't say so in this output, but the nameserver detected the duplicate and dropped it. We can tell because there is no *forw:* line after the *req:* lines, as there was on lines 4–6.

Can you guess what this output might look like if the nameserver has trouble looking up a name? You'd see a lot of retransmissions as the nameserver kept trying to look up the name (which you could track by matching the *nsid=* lines). You'd see the application send a couple more retransmissions, thinking that the nameserver hadn't received the application's first query. Eventually, the nameserver would give up, usually after the application itself gave up.

With a BIND 9.1.0 or later nameserver, you won't see resends until debug level 3, and at that point they'll be very difficult to pick out from BIND 9's other logged messages. Moreover, even at debug level 3, BIND 9.1.0 doesn't tell you *which* nameserver it's resending to.

A Slave Nameserver Checking Its Zone (BIND 8, Debug Level 1)

In addition to tracking down problems with nameserver lookups, you may have to track down why a slave server is not loading from its master. Tracking down this problem can often be done by simply comparing the zone's SOA serial numbers on the two servers using *nslookup* or *dig*, as we'll show in Chapter 14. If your problem is more elusive, you may have to resort to looking at the debugging information. We'll show you what the debugging information should look like if your server is running normally.

This debugging output was generated on a "quiet" nameserver—one not receiving any queries—to show you exactly which lines pertain to zone maintenance. Remember that a BIND 8 slave nameserver uses a child process to transfer the zone data to the local disk before reading it in. While the slave logs its debugging information to *named.run*, the slave's child process logs its debugging information to *xfer.ddt.PID*. The *PID* suffix, by default the process ID of the child process, may be changed to ensure that the filename is unique. Beware—turning on debugging on a slave nameserver will leave *xfer.ddt.PID* files lying around, even if you are only trying to trace a lookup. Our trace is at debugging level 1, and we turned on the BIND 8 logging option *print-time*. Debug level 3 gives you more information, more than you may want if a transfer actually occurs. A debugging level 3 trace of a zone transfer of several hundred resource records can create an *xfer.ddt.PID* file several megabytes in size.

```
21-Feb 00:13:18.026 do_zone_maint for zone movie.edu (class IN)
21-Feb 00:13:18.034 zone_maint('movie.edu')
21-Feb 00:13:18.035 qserial_query(movie.edu)
21-Feb 00:13:18.043 sysquery: send -> [192.249.249.3].53 dfd=5
                    nsid=29790 id=0 retry=888048802
21-Feb 00:13:18.046 qserial_query(movie.edu) QUEUED
21-Feb 00:13:18.052 next maintenance for zone 'movie.edu' in 2782 sec
21-Feb 00:13:18.056 datagram from [192.249.249.3].53, fd 5, len 380
21-Feb 00:13:18.059 qserial_answer(movie.edu, 26739)
21-Feb 00:13:18.060 qserial_answer: zone is out of date
21-Feb 00:13:18.061 startxfer() movie.edu
21-Feb 00:13:18.063 /usr/etc/named-xfer -z movie.edu -f db.movie
                    -s 26738 -C 1 -P 53 -d 1 -l xfer.ddt 192.249.249.3
21-Feb 00:13:18.131 started xfer child 390
21-Feb 00:13:18.132 next maintenance for zone 'movie.edu' in 7200 sec

21-Feb 00:14:02.089 endxfer: child 390 zone movie.edu returned
                    status=1 termsig=-1
21-Feb 00:14:02.094 loadxfer() "movie.edu"
21-Feb 00:14:02.094 purge_zone(movie.edu,1)

21-Feb 00:14:30.049 db_load(db.movie, movie.edu, 2, Nil)
21-Feb 00:14:30.058 next maintenance for zone 'movie.edu' in 1846 sec

21-Feb 00:17:12.478 slave zone "movie.edu" (IN) loaded (serial 26739)
21-Feb 00:17:12.486 no schedule change for zone 'movie.edu'

21-Feb 00:42:44.817 Cleaned cache of 0 RRs
```

```
21-Feb 00:45:16.046 do_zone_maint for zone movie.edu (class IN)
21-Feb 00:45:16.054 zone_maint('movie.edu')
21-Feb 00:45:16.055 qserial_query(movie.edu)
21-Feb 00:45:16.063 sysquery: send -> [192.249.249.3].53 dfd=5
                        nsid=29791 id=0 retry=888050660
21-Feb 00:45:16.066 qserial_query(movie.edu) QUEUED
21-Feb 00:45:16.067 next maintenance for zone 'movie.edu' in 3445 sec
21-Feb 00:45:16.074 datagram from [192.249.249.3].53, fd 5, len 380
21-Feb 00:45:16.077 qserial_answer(movie.edu, 26739)
21-Feb 00:45:16.078 qserial_answer: zone serial is still OK
21-Feb 00:45:16.131 next maintenance for zone 'movie.edu' in 2002 sec
```

Unlike the previous traces, each line in this trace has a timestamp. The timestamp makes it clear which debug statements are grouped together.

This nameserver is a slave for a single zone, *movie.edu*. The line with time 00:13:18.026 shows that it is time to check with the master server. The server queries for the zone's SOA record and compares serial numbers before deciding to load the zone. The lines with times 00:13:18.059 through 00:13:18.131 show the zone's serial number (26739), show that the zone is out of date, and start a child process (pid 390) to transfer the zone. At time 00:13:18.132, a timer is set to expire 7,200 seconds later. This is the amount of time the server allows for a transfer to complete. At time 00:14:02.089, you see the exit status of the child process. The status of 1 indicates that the zone data was successfully transferred. The old zone data is purged (time 00:14:02.094), and the new data is loaded.

The next maintenance (see time 00:14:30.058) is scheduled for 1,846 seconds later. For this zone, the refresh interval is 3,600, but the nameserver chose to check again in 1,846 seconds. Why? The nameserver is trying to avoid having its refresh timer become synchronized. Instead of using 3,600 exactly, it uses a random time between half the refresh interval (1,800) and the full refresh interval (3,600). At 00:45:16.046, the zone is checked again, and this time it is up to date.

If your trace ran long enough, you'd see more lines like the one at 00:42:44.817—one line each hour. What's happening is that the server is making a pass through its cache, freeing any data that has expired to reduce the amount of memory used.

The master server for this zone is a BIND 4 nameserver. If the master is a BIND 8 nameserver, the slave is notified when the zone changes rather than waiting for the refresh interval to pass. The slave server's debug output looks almost exactly the same, but the trigger to check the zone status is a NOTIFY:

```
rcvd NOTIFY(movie.edu, IN, SOA) from [192.249.249.3].1059
qserial_query(movie.edu)
sysquery: send -> [192.249.249.3].53 dfd=5
        nsid=29790 id=0 retry=888048802
```

A Slave Nameserver Checking Its Zone (BIND 9 Debug Level 1)

The equivalent debugging output from a BIND 9.3.1 nameserver at level 1 is, as usual, more concise. Here's what it looks like:

```
04-Jul-2005 15:05:00.059 zone_timer: zone movie.edu/IN: enter
04-Jul-2005 15:05:00.059 zone_maintenance: zone movie.edu/IN: enter
04-Jul-2005 15:05:00.059 queue_soa_query: zone movie.edu/IN: enter
04-Jul-2005 15:05:00.059 soa_query: zone movie.edu/IN: enter
04-Jul-2005 15:05:00.061 refresh_callback: zone movie.edu/IN: enter
04-Jul-2005 15:05:00.062 refresh_callback: zone movie.edu/IN: Serial: new 2005010923,
                                                                  old 2005010922
04-Jul-2005 15:05:00.062 queue_xfrin: zone movie.edu/IN: enter
04-Jul-2005 15:05:00.062 zone movie.edu/IN: Transfer started.
04-Jul-2005 15:05:00.062 zone movie.edu/IN: requesting IXFR from 192.249.249.3#53
04-Jul-2005 15:05:00.063 transfer of 'movie.edu/IN' from 192.249.249.3#53:
                                      connected using 192.249.249.2#1106
04-Jul-2005 15:05:00.070 calling free_rbtdb(movie.edu)
04-Jul-2005 15:05:00.070 zone movie.edu/IN: zone transfer finished: success
04-Jul-2005 15:05:00.070 zone movie.edu/IN: transferred serial 5
04-Jul-2005 15:05:00.070 transfer of 'movie.edu' from 192.249.249.3#53: end of
    transfer
04-Jul-2005 15:05:01.089 zone_timer: zone movie.edu/IN: enter
04-Jul-2005 15:05:01.089 zone_maintenance: zone movie.edu/IN: enter
04-Jul-2005 15:05:19.121 notify_done: zone movie.edu/IN: enter
04-Jul-2005 15:05:19.621 notify_done: zone movie.edu/IN: enter
```

The message at 15:05:00.059 shows the refresh timer popping, causing the nameserver to begin maintenance for the zone on the next line. First, the nameserver queues a query for the SOA record for the IN class zone *movie.edu* (*queue_soa_query* at the same timestamp), which it sends. At 15:05:00.062, the nameserver finds that the master nameserver has a higher serial number than it does (2005010923 to its 2005010922), so it queues an inbound zone transfer (*queue_xfrin*). All of eight milliseconds later (at 15:05:00.070), the transfer is done, and at 15:05:01.089, the nameserver resets the refresh timer (*zone_timer*).

The next three lines show the nameserver doing maintenance on *movie.edu* again. If, for example, some of *movie.edu*'s nameservers were outside the *movie.edu* zone, the nameserver would use this opportunity to look up their addresses (not just A, but also A6 and AAAA records!) so that it could include them in future responses. On the last two lines, our nameserver sends NOTIFY messages—two, to be exact—to the nameservers listed in the NS records for *movie.edu*.

The Resolver Search Algorithm and Negative Caching (BIND 8)

In this trace, we'll show you what the BIND search algorithm and negative caching look like from the perspective of a BIND 8 nameserver. We could look up *galt.cs.purdue.edu* like the last trace, but it wouldn't show the search algorithm. Instead, we will look up *foo.bar*, a name that doesn't exist. In fact, we'll look it up twice:

```
 1  datagram from cujo.horror.movie.edu 1109, fd 6, len 25
 2  req: nlookup(foo.bar) id 19220 type=1 class=1
 3  req: found 'foo.bar' as '' (cname=0)
 4  forw: forw -> D.ROOT-SERVERS.NET 53 ds=7 nsid=2532 id=19220 0ms retry 4sec
 5
 6  datagram from D.ROOT-SERVERS.NET 53, fd 5, len 25
 7  ncache: dname foo.bar, type 1, class 1
 8  send_msg -> cujo.horror.movie.edu 1109 (UDP 6) id=19220
 9
10  datagram from cujo.horror.movie.edu 1110, fd 6, len 42
11  req: nlookup(foo.bar.horror.movie.edu) id 19221 type=1 class=1
12  req: found 'foo.bar.horror.movie.edu' as 'horror.movie.edu' (cname=0)
13  forw: forw -> carrie.horror.movie.edu 53 ds=7 nsid=2533 id=19221 0ms
                                                            retry 4sec
14  datagram from carrie.horror.movie.edu 53, fd 5, len 42
15  ncache: dname foo.bar.horror.movie.edu, type 1, class 1
16  send_msg -> cujo.horror.movie.edu 1110 (UDP 6) id=19221
```

Look up *foo.bar* again:

```
17  datagram from cujo.horror.movie.edu 1111, fd 6, len 25
18  req: nlookup(foo.bar) id 15541 type=1 class=1
19  req: found 'foo.bar' as 'foo.bar' (cname=0)
20  ns_req: answer -> cujo.horror.movie.edu 1111 fd=6 id=15541 size=25 Local
21
22  datagram from cujo.horror.movie.edu 1112, fd 6, len 42
23  req: nlookup(foo.bar.horror.movie.edu) id 15542 type=1 class=1
24  req: found 'foo.bar.horror.movie.edu' as 'foo.bar.horror.movie.edu' (cname=0)
25  ns_req: answer -> cujo.horror.movie.edu 1112 fd=6 id=15542 size=42 Local
```

Let's look at the resolver search algorithm. The first name looked up (line 2) is exactly the name we typed in. Since the name had at least one dot, it is looked up without modification. When that name lookup failed, *horror.movie.edu* was appended to the name and looked up.

Line 7 shows the caching of the negative answer (*ncache*). If the same name is looked up again in the next few minutes (line 19), the nameserver still has the negative response in its cache, so the server can answer immediately that the name doesn't exist. (If you don't believe this hand-waving, compare lines 3 and 19. On line 3, nothing was found for *foo.bar*, but line 19 shows the whole name being found.)

The Resolver Search Algorithm and Negative Caching (BIND 9)

Here's what a BIND 9.3.1 nameserver's debugging output looks like when looking up *foo.bar* twice:

```
04-Jul-2005 15:45:42.944 client cujo.horror.movie.edu#1044: query: foo.bar A +
04-Jul-2005 15:45:42.945 createfetch: foo.bar. A
04-Jul-2005 15:45:42.945 createfetch: . NS
04-Jul-2005 15:45:43.425 client cujo.horror.movie.edu#1044: query:
                                          foo.bar.horror.movie.edu A +
04-Jul-2005 15:45:43.425 createfetch: foo.bar.horror.movie.edu. A
```

This assumes, of course, that you added the following lines to */etc/named.conf* to see the queries:

```
logging {
    category queries {
        default_debug;
    };
};
```

This output is more subtle and succinct than BIND 8's, but you can get the information you need from it. The first line, at 15:45:42.944, shows the initial query for *foo.bar*'s address arriving from the client *cujo.horror.movie.edu* (remember, we ran this through our magic IP-to-name filter, which we'll introduce next). The next two lines show the nameserver dispatching two tasks (*createfetch*) to look up *foo.bar*: the first is the actual task to look up *foo.bar*'s address, while the second is a subsidiary task to look up NS records for the root zone, necessary to complete the *foo.bar* lookup. Once the nameserver has current NS records for the root, it queries a root nameserver for *foo.bar*'s address and gets a response indicating that no top-level domain called *bar* exists. Unfortunately, you don't see that.

The line at 15:45:43.425 shows *cujo.horror.movie.edu* applying the search list, looking up *foo.bar.horror.movie.edu*. This causes the nameserver to dispatch a task (*createfetch*) to look up that domain name.

When we look up *foo.bar* again, we see:

```
04-Jul-2005 15:45:46.557 client cujo.horror.movie.edu#1044: query: foo.bar A +
04-Jul-2005 15:45:46.558 client cujo.horror.movie.edu#1044: query:
                                          foo.bar.horror.movie.edu A +
```

Notice the absence of *createfetch* entries? That's because our nameserver has the negative answers cached.

Tools

Let's wrap up loose ends. We told you about our tool to convert IP addresses to names so that your debugging output is easier to read. Here is such a tool written in Perl:

```
#!/usr/bin/perl -n

use "Socket";

if (/\b)(\d+\.\d+\.\d+\.\d+)\b/) {
$addr = pack('C4', split(/\./, $1));
($name, $rest) = gethostbyaddr($addr, &AF_INET);
if($name) {s/$1/$name/};
}

print;
```

It's best not to pipe *named.run* output into this script with debugging on because the script will generate its own queries to the nameserver.

## CHAPTER 14

Troubleshooting DNS and BIND

"Of course not," said the Mock Turtle. "Why, if a fish came to me, and told me he was going on a journey, I should say, 'With what porpoise?'"

"Don't you mean 'purpose'?" said Alice.

"I mean what I say," the Mock Turtle replied, in an offended tone. And the Gryphon added, "Come, let's hear some of your adventures."

In the last two chapters, we've demonstrated how to use *nslookup* and *dig*, and how to read the nameserver's debugging information. In this chapter, we'll show you how to use these tools—plus traditional Unix networking tools like trusty ol' *ping*—to troubleshoot real-life problems with DNS and BIND.

Troubleshooting, by its nature, is a tough subject to teach. You start with any of a world of symptoms and try to work your way back to the cause. We can't cover the whole gamut of problems you may encounter on the Internet, but we will certainly do our best to show how to diagnose the most common of them. And along the way, we hope to teach you troubleshooting techniques that will be valuable in tracking down more obscure problems that we don't document.

Is NIS Really Your Problem?

Before we launch into a discussion of how to troubleshoot a DNS or BIND problem, we should make sure you know how to tell whether a problem is caused by DNS as opposed to NIS. On hosts running NIS, figuring out whether the culprit is DNS or NIS can be difficult. The stock BSD *nslookup*, for example, doesn't pay any attention to NIS. You can run *nslookup* on a Sun and query the nameserver 'til the cows come home while all the other services are using NIS.

How do you know where to put the blame? Some vendors have modified *nslookup* to use NIS for name service if NIS is configured. The HP-UX *nslookup*, for example, will report that it's querying an NIS server when it starts up:

```
% nslookup
Default NIS Server:  toystory.movie.edu
Address:  192.249.249.3

>
```

A surefire way to decide whether an answer came from NIS is to use *ypcat* to list the *hosts* database. For example, to find out whether *andrew.cmu.edu* is in your NIS hosts map, you could execute:

```
% ypcat hosts | grep andrew.cmu.edu
```

If you find the answer in NIS (and you know NIS is being consulted first), you've found the cause of the problem.

Finally, in the versions of Unix that use the *nsswitch.conf* file, you can determine the order in which the different name services are used by referring to the entry for the *hosts* database in the file. An entry like this, for example, indicates that NIS is being checked first:

```
hosts:    nis dns files
```

while this entry has the name resolver querying DNS first:

```
hosts:    dns nis files
```

For more detailed information on the syntax and semantics of the *nsswitch.conf* file, see Chapter 6.

These hints should help you identify the guilty party or at least exonerate one suspect. If you narrow down the suspects and DNS is still implicated, you'll just have to read this chapter.

Troubleshooting Tools and Techniques

We went over *nslookup*, *dig*, and the nameserver's debugging output in the last two chapters. Before we go on, let's introduce some new tools that can be useful in troubleshooting: *named-xfer*, nameserver database dumps, and query logging.

How to Use named-xfer

named-xfer is the program that BIND 8 nameservers start to perform zone transfers. (BIND 9 nameservers, you'll remember, are multithreaded, so they don't need a separate program to do inbound zone transfers; they just start a new thread.) *named-xfer* checks whether the slave's copy of the zone data is up to date and transfers a new zone if necessary.

In Chapter 13, we showed you the debugging output a BIND 8 slave nameserver logged as it checked its zone. When the slave server transferred the zone, it started a child process (*named-xfer*) to pull the data to the local filesystem. We didn't tell you, however, that you can also start *named-xfer* manually instead of waiting for *named* to start it, and that you can tell it to produce debugging output independent of *named*.

This can be useful if you're tracking down a problem with zone transfers but don't want to wait for *named* to schedule one. To test a zone transfer manually, you need to specify a number of command-line options:

```
% /usr/sbin/named-xfer
Usage error: no domain
Usage: named-xfer
        -z zone_to_transfer
        -f db_file
        [-i ixfr_file]
        [-s serial_no]
        [-d debug_level]
        [-l debug_log_file]
        [-t trace_file]
        [-p port]
        [-S] [-Z]
        [-C class]
        [-x axfr-src]
        [-X axfr-src-v6]
        [-T tsig_info_file]
        servers [-ixfr|-axfr]...
```

This is the output from a BIND 8.4.7 version of *named-xfer*. Earlier versions of *named-xfer* won't have all these options.

When *named* starts *named-xfer*, it specifies the *–z* option (the zone *named* wants to check), the *–f* option (the name of the zone datafile that corresponds to the zone, from *named.conf*), the *–s* option (the zone's serial number on the slave from the current SOA record), and the addresses of the servers the slave was instructed to load from (the IP addresses from the *masters* substatement in the *zone* statement in *named.conf*). If *named* is running in debug mode, it also specifies the debug level for *named-xfer* with the *–d* option. The other options aren't usually necessary to troubleshoot problems; they have to do with incremental zone transfers, TSIG signing zone transfers, and such.

When you run *named-xfer* manually, you can also specify the debug level on the command line with *–d*. (Don't forget, though, that debug levels above 3 produce tons of debugging output if the transfer succeeds!) You can also specify an alternate filename for the debug file with the *–l* option. The default log file is */var/tmp/xfer.ddt.XXXXXX*, where *XXXXXX* is a suffix appended to preserve uniqueness or a file by the same name in */usr/tmp*. And you can specify the name of the host to load from instead of its IP address.

For example, with the following command line, you can see whether zone transfers from *toystory.movie.edu* are working:

```
% /usr/sbin/named-xfer -z movie.edu -f /tmp/db.movie -s 0 toystory.movie.edu.
% echo $?
4
```

In this command, we specified a serial number of 0 because we wanted to force *named-xfer* to attempt a zone transfer even if it wasn't needed. If 0 is higher than *movie.edu*'s serial number on *toystory* (remember, serial numbers use sequence space arithmetic), we'd need to choose a different number. Also, we told *named-xfer* to put the new zone datafile in */tmp* rather than overwrite the zone's working zone datafile.

We can tell if the transfer succeeded by looking at *named-xfer*'s return value. If you're running BIND 8.1.2 or older, your *named-xfer* has four possible return values:

0   The zone data is up to date and no transfer was needed.

1   Indicates a successful transfer.

2   The host(s) *named-xfer* queried can't be reached, or an error occurred and *named-xfer* may have logged an error message to *syslog*.

3   An error occurred and *named-xfer* logged an error message to *syslog*.

As of BIND 8.2, four new return values have been added to accommodate incremental zone transfers:

4   Indicates a successful AXFR (full) zone transfer

5   Indicates a successful IXFR (incremental) zone transfer

6   Indicates that the master nameserver returned an AXFR to *named-xfer*'s IXFR request

7   Indicates that the transfer was refused

It's perfectly legal for a nameserver—even one that supports IXFR—to return a full zone transfer to a request for an incremental zone transfer. For example, the master nameserver may be missing part of the record of the changes made to the zone.

Note that BIND 8.2 and later *named-xfer*s don't use return value 1 anymore. Return value 1 has been replaced by return values 4–7.

What if I Don't Have named-xfer?

If you've upgraded to BIND 9 and don't have a *named-xfer* binary, you can still use *nslookup* or *dig* to do a zone transfer. Either query tool will give you some of the information that *named-xfer* would have given you.

For example, to use *dig* to do the same zone transfer we showed you earlier, you can run:

```
% dig @toystory.movie.edu movie.edu. axfr
```

With *nslookup*, you can change your nameserver and use the *ls –d* command from interactive mode.

Unfortunately, both *dig* and *nslookup* are more limited than *named-xfer* is in reporting errors. If *nslookup* can't transfer a zone, it usually reports an "unspecified error":

```
> ls movie.edu.
[toystory.movie.edu]
*** Can't list domain movie.edu: Unspecified error
```

This could be caused by an *allow-transfer* access list, the fact that *toystory.movie.edu* isn't actually authoritative for *movie.edu*, or a number of other problems. To tell which, you may just have to send other, related queries or check the *syslog* output on the master nameserver.

How to Read a BIND 8 Database Dump

Poring over a dump of the nameserver's internal database—including cached information—can also help you track down problems. The *ndc dumpdb* command causes *named* to dump its authoritative data, cached data, and hints data to *named_dump.db* in BIND's working directory.[*] An example of a *named_dump.db* file follows. The authoritative data and cached entries, mixed together, appear first in the file. At the end of the file is the hints data.

```
; Dumped at Tue Jan  6 10:49:08 1998
;; ++zone table++
; 0.0.127.in-addr.arpa (type 1, class 1, source db.127.0.0)
;    time=0, lastupdate=0, serial=1,
;    refresh=0, retry=3600, expire=608400, minimum=86400
;    ftime=884015430, xaddr=[0.0.0.0], state=0041, pid=0
;; --zone table--
; Note: Cr=(auth,answer,addtnl,cache) tag only shown for non-auth RR's
; Note: NT=milliseconds for any A RR which we've used as a nameserver
; --- Cache & Data ---
$ORIGIN .
.    518375  IN      NS  G.ROOT-SERVERS.NET.    ;Cr=auth [128.8.10.90]
     518375  IN      NS  J.ROOT-SERVERS.NET.    ;Cr=auth [128.8.10.90]
     518375  IN      NS  K.ROOT-SERVERS.NET.    ;Cr=auth [128.8.10.90]
     518375  IN      NS  L.ROOT-SERVERS.NET.    ;Cr=auth [128.8.10.90]
     518375  IN      NS  M.ROOT-SERVERS.NET.    ;Cr=auth [128.8.10.90]
     518375  IN      NS  A.ROOT-SERVERS.NET.    ;Cr=auth [128.8.10.90]
     518375  IN      NS  H.ROOT-SERVERS.NET.    ;Cr=auth [128.8.10.90]
     518375  IN      NS  B.ROOT-SERVERS.NET.    ;Cr=auth [128.8.10.90]
     518375  IN      NS  C.ROOT-SERVERS.NET.    ;Cr=auth [128.8.10.90]
     518375  IN      NS  D.ROOT-SERVERS.NET.    ;Cr=auth [128.8.10.90]
     518375  IN      NS  E.ROOT-SERVERS.NET.    ;Cr=auth [128.8.10.90]
     518375  IN      NS  I.ROOT-SERVERS.NET.    ;Cr=auth [128.8.10.90]
     518375  IN      NS  F.ROOT-SERVERS.NET.    ;Cr=auth [128.8.10.90]
```

[*] BIND 9.1.0 is the first version of BIND 9 to support dumping the database.

```
EDU  86393  IN    SOA A.ROOT-SERVERS.NET.  hostmaster.INTERNIC.NET. (
            1998010500 1800 900 604800 86400 )   ;Cr=addtnl [128.63.2.53]
$ORIGIN  0.127.in-addr.arpa.
0        IN    SOA cujo.movie.edu. root.cujo.movie.edu. (
            1998010600 10800 3600 608400 86400 )         ;Cl=5
         IN    NS cujo.movie.edu.   ;Cl=5
$ORIGIN  0.0.127.in-addr.arpa.
1        IN    PTR localhost.   ;Cl=5
$ORIGIN  EDU.
PURDUE   172787  IN  NS  NS.PURDUE.EDU.            ;Cr=addtnl [192.36.148.17]
         172787  IN  NS  MOE.RICE.EDU.             ;Cr=addtnl [192.36.148.17]
         172787  IN  NS  PENDRAGON.CS.PURDUE.EDU.  ;Cr=addtnl [192.36.148.17]
         172787  IN  NS  HARBOR.ECN.PURDUE.EDU.    ;Cr=addtnl [192.36.148.17]
$ORIGIN  movie.EDU.
;cujo    593   IN  SOA  A.ROOT-SERVERS.NET. hostmaster.INTERNIC. NET. (
;        1998010500 1800 900 604800 86400 );EDU.; NXDOMAIN  ;-$
   ;Cr=auth [128.63.2.53]
$ORIGIN  RICE.EDU.
MOE      172787  IN  A   128.42.5.4          ;NT=84 Cr=addtnl [192.36.148.17]
$ORIGIN  PURDUE.EDU.
CS       86387  IN  NS  pendragon.cs.PURDUE.edu.   ;Cr=addtnl [128.42.5.4]
         86387  IN  NS  ns.PURDUE.edu.             ;Cr=addtnl [128.42.5.4]
         86387  IN  NS  harbor.ecn.PURDUE.edu.     ;Cr=addtnl [128.42.5.4]
         86387  IN  NS  moe.rice.edu.              ;Cr=addtnl [128.42.5.4]
NS       172787  IN  A   128.210.11.5       ;NT=4 Cr=addtnl [192.36.148.17]
$ORIGIN  ECN.PURDUE.EDU.
HARBOR   172787  IN   A  128.46.199.76       ;NT=6 Cr=addtnl [192.36.148.17]
$ORIGIN  CS.PURDUE.EDU.
galt     86387   IN   A  128.10.2.39                 ;Cr=auth [128.42.5.4]
PENDRAGON 172787 IN  A  128.10.2.5          ;NT=20 Cr=addtnl [192.36.148.17]
$ORIGIN  ROOT-SERVERS.NET.
K        604775   IN  A  193.0.14.129        ;NT=10 Cr=answer [128.8.10.90]
A        604775   IN  A  198.41.0.4          ;NT=20 Cr=answer [128.8.10.90]
L        604775   IN  A  198.32.64.12        ;NT=8 Cr=answer [128.8.10.90]
B        604775   IN  A  128.9.0.107         ;NT=9 Cr=answer [128.8.10.90]
M        604775   IN  A  202.12.27.33        ;NT=20 Cr=answer [128.8.10.90]
C        604775   IN  A  192.33.4.12         ;NT=17 Cr=answer [128.8.10.90]
D        604775   IN  A  128.8.10.90         ;NT=11 Cr=answer [128.8.10.90]
E        604775   IN  A  192.203.230.10      ;NT=9 Cr=answer [128.8.10.90]
F        604775   IN  A  192.5.5.241         ;NT=73 Cr=answer [128.8.10.90]
G        604775   IN  A  192.112.36.4        ;NT=14 Cr=answer [128.8.10.90]
H        604775   IN  A  128.63.2.53         ;NT=160 Cr=answer [128.8.10.90]
I        604775   IN  A  192.36.148.17       ;NT=102 Cr=answer [128.8.10.90]
J        604775   IN  A  198.41.0.10         ;NT=21 Cr=answer [128.8.10.90]
; --- Hints ---
$ORIGIN .
.    3600          IN  NS  A.ROOT-SERVERS.NET.   ;Cl=0
     3600          IN  NS  B.ROOT-SERVERS.NET.   ;Cl=0
     3600          IN  NS  C.ROOT-SERVERS.NET.   ;Cl=0
     3600          IN  NS  D.ROOT-SERVERS.NET.   ;Cl=0
     3600          IN  NS  E.ROOT-SERVERS.NET.   ;Cl=0
     3600          IN  NS  F.ROOT-SERVERS.NET.   ;Cl=0
     3600          IN  NS  G.ROOT-SERVERS.NET.   ;Cl=0
     3600          IN  NS  H.ROOT-SERVERS.NET.   ;Cl=0
```

```
     3600          IN  NS  I.ROOT-SERVERS.NET.     ;Cl=0
     3600          IN  NS  J.ROOT-SERVERS.NET.     ;Cl=0
     3600          IN  NS  K.ROOT-SERVERS.NET.     ;Cl=0
     3600          IN  NS  L.ROOT-SERVERS.NET.     ;Cl=0
     3600          IN  NS  M.ROOT-SERVERS.NET.     ;Cl=0
$ORIGIN    ROOT-SERVERS.NET.
K    3600     IN  A   193.0.14.129      ;NT=11 Cl=0
L    3600     IN  A   198.32.64.12      ;NT=9 Cl=0
A    3600     IN  A   198.41.0.4        ;NT=10 Cl=0
M    3600     IN  A   202.12.27.33      ;NT=11 Cl=0
B    3600     IN  A   128.9.0.107       ;NT=1288 Cl=0
C    3600     IN  A   192.33.4.12       ;NT=21 Cl=0
D    3600     IN  A   128.8.10.90       ;NT=1288 Cl=0
E    3600     IN  A   192.203.230.10    ;NT=19 Cl=0
F    3600     IN  A   192.5.5.241       ;NT=23 Cl=0
G    3600     IN  A   192.112.36.4      ;NT=18 Cl=0
H    3600     IN  A   128.63.2.53       ;NT=11 Cl=0
I    3600     IN  A   192.36.148.17     ;NT=21 Cl=0
J    3600     IN  A   198.41.0.10       ;NT=13 Cl=0
```

The nameserver that created this *named_dump.db* file was authoritative only for *0.0. 127.in-addr.arpa*. Only two names have been looked up by this server: *galt.cs.pur- due.edu* and *cujo.movie.edu*. In the process of looking up *galt.cs.purdue.edu*, this server cached not only the address of *galt*, but also the list of nameservers for *pur- due.edu* and the addresses for those servers. The name *cujo.movie.edu*, however, doesn't really exist (nor does the zone *movie.edu*, except in our examples), so the server cached the negative response. In the dump file, the negative response is com- mented out (the line starts with a semicolon), and the reason is listed (NXDO- MAIN) instead of real data. You'll notice the TTL is quite low (593). On BIND 8.2 and later nameservers, negative responses are cached according to the last field in the SOA record, which is usually much smaller than the default TTL for the zone.

The hints section at the bottom of the file contains the data from the *db.cache* file. The TTL of the hints data is decremented, and it may go to 0, but the hints are never discarded.

Note that some of the resource records are followed by a semicolon and *NT=*. You will only see these on the address records of nameservers. The number is the round- trip time calculation that the nameserver keeps so that it knows which nameservers have responded most quickly in the past; the nameserver with the lowest round-trip time will be tried first the next time.

The cached data is easy to pick out: those entries have a tag (*Cr=*) and (sometimes) the IP address of the server the data came from.* The zone data and hint data are

---

* The nameserver prints the IP address of the remote nameserver if it's available. On BIND 8.2 and later nameservers, the IP address is available only if you've turned on *host-statistics*, which we introduced in Chapter 8. On earlier BIND 8 nameservers, it's on by default. *host-statistics* keeps impressive statistics on every nameserver and resolver you've ever communicated with, which is very useful for some purposes (such as figuring out which nameserver your server got a record from) but consumes a fair amount of memory.

tagged with *Cl=*, which is just a count of the level in the domain tree (the root is level 0, *foo* would be level 1, *foo.foo* would be level 2, etc.). Let's digress a moment to explain the concept of credibility.

One of the advances between BIND 4.8.3 and 4.9 was the addition of a credibility measure. This allows a nameserver to make more intelligent decisions about what to do with new data from a remote server.

A 4.8.3 nameserver had only two credibility levels: locally authoritative data and everything else. The locally authoritative data was data from your zone datafiles; your nameserver knew better than to update its internal copy of what came from your zone file. But all data from remote nameservers was considered equal.

Here is a situation that could happen and the way a 4.8.3 server would deal with it. Suppose that your server looked up an address for *toystory.movie.edu* and received an authoritative answer from the *movie.edu* nameserver. (Remember, an authoritative answer is the best you can get.) Sometime later, while looking up *foo.oreilly.com*, your server receives another address record for *toystory.movie.edu*, but this time as part of the delegation information for *oreilly.com* (which *toystory.movie.edu* is a slave for). The 4.8.3 nameserver would update the cached address record for *toystory.movie.edu*, even though the data came from the *com* nameserver instead of the authoritative *movie.edu* nameserver. Of course, the *com* and *movie.edu* nameservers will have exactly the same data for *toystory.movie.edu*, so this won't be a problem, right? Yeah, and it never rains in southern California, either.

A 4.9 or newer nameserver is more intelligent. Like a 4.8.3 nameserver, it still considers your zone data unassailable—beyond any doubt. But a 4.9 or newer nameserver distinguishes among the different data from remote nameservers. Here is the hierarchy of remote data credibility from most credible to least:

auth
> These records are data from authoritative answers—the answer section of a response message with the authoritative answer bit set.

answer
> These records are data from nonauthoritative, or cached, answers—the answer section of a response message without the authoritative answer bit set.

addtnl
> These records are data from the rest of the response message—the authority and additional sections. The authority section of the response contains NS records that delegate a zone to an authoritative nameserver. The additional section contains address records that may complete information in other sections (e.g., address records that go with NS records in the authority section).

There is one exception to this rule: when the nameserver is priming its root nameserver cache, the records that would be at credibility *addtnl* are bumped up to *answer* to make them harder to change accidentally. Notice in the dump that the address records for root nameservers are at credibility *answer*, but the address records for the *purdue.edu* nameservers are at credibility *addtnl*.

In the situation just described, a 4.9 or newer nameserver would not replace the authoritative data (credibility = *auth*) for *toystory.movie.edu* with the delegation data (credibility = *addtnl*) because the authoritative answer would have higher credibility.

How to Read a BIND 9 Database Dump

With BIND 9, the database dump changed significantly. Here is the result of running *rndc dumpdb*. The nameserver dumps its cache data to *named_dump.db* in BIND's working directory. What you don't see in this dump is the authoritative data. To get that, you must run *rndc dumpdb –all*.

```
;
; Start view _default
;
;
; Cache dump of view '_default'
;
$DATE 20050827190436
; authanswer
.               518364    IN NS    A.ROOT-SERVERS.NET.
                518364    IN NS    B.ROOT-SERVERS.NET.
                518364    IN NS    C.ROOT-SERVERS.NET.
                518364    IN NS    D.ROOT-SERVERS.NET.
                518364    IN NS    E.ROOT-SERVERS.NET.
                518364    IN NS    F.ROOT-SERVERS.NET.
                518364    IN NS    G.ROOT-SERVERS.NET.
                518364    IN NS    H.ROOT-SERVERS.NET.
                518364    IN NS    I.ROOT-SERVERS.NET.
                518364    IN NS    J.ROOT-SERVERS.NET.
                518364    IN NS    K.ROOT-SERVERS.NET.
                518364    IN NS    L.ROOT-SERVERS.NET.
                518364    IN NS    M.ROOT-SERVERS.NET.
; glue
A3.NSTLD.COM.         172764    A    192.5.6.32
; glue
C3.NSTLD.COM.         172764    A    192.26.92.32
; glue
D3.NSTLD.COM.         172764    A    192.31.80.32
; glue
E3.NSTLD.COM.         172764    A    192.12.94.32
; glue
G3.NSTLD.COM.         172764    A    192.42.93.32
; glue
H3.NSTLD.COM.         172764    A    192.54.112.32
; glue
L3.NSTLD.COM.         172764    A    192.41.162.32
; glue
M3.NSTLD.COM.         172764    A    192.55.83.32
; glue
```

```
edu.             172764   NS   A3.NSTLD.COM.
                 172764   NS   C3.NSTLD.COM.
                 172764   NS   D3.NSTLD.COM.
                 172764   NS   E3.NSTLD.COM.
                 172764   NS   G3.NSTLD.COM.
                 172764   NS   H3.NSTLD.COM.
                 172764   NS   L3.NSTLD.COM.
                 172764   NS   M3.NSTLD.COM.
; authauthority
cujo.movie.edu.       10796    \-ANY    ;-$NXDOMAIN
; glue
purdue.edu.      172764   NS   NS.purdue.edu.
                 172764   NS   MOE.RICE.edu.
                 172764   NS   HARBOR.ECN.purdue.edu.
                 172764   NS   PENDRAGON.cs.purdue.edu.
; authauthority
cs.purdue.edu.   86364    NS   ns.purdue.edu.
                 86364    NS   moe.rice.edu.
                 86364    NS   ns2.purdue.edu.
                 86364    NS   harbor.ecn.purdue.edu.
                 86364    NS   pendragon.cs.purdue.edu.
; authanswer
galt.cs.purdue.edu.       86364    A    128.10.2.39
; glue
PENDRAGON.cs.purdue.edu. 172764    A    128.10.2.5
; glue
HARBOR.ECN.purdue.edu.    172764    A    128.46.154.76
; glue
NS.purdue.edu.            172764    A    128.210.11.5
; additional
ns2.purdue.edu.            3564     A    128.210.11.57
; glue
MOE.RICE.edu.             172764    A    128.42.5.4
; additional
A.ROOT-SERVERS.NET.       604764    A    198.41.0.4
; additional
B.ROOT-SERVERS.NET.       604764    A    192.228.79.201
; additional
C.ROOT-SERVERS.NET.       604764    A    192.33.4.12
; additional
D.ROOT-SERVERS.NET.       604764    A    128.8.10.90
; additional
E.ROOT-SERVERS.NET.       604764    A    192.203.230.10
; additional
F.ROOT-SERVERS.NET.       604764    A    192.5.5.241
; additional
G.ROOT-SERVERS.NET.       604764    A    192.112.36.4
; additional
H.ROOT-SERVERS.NET.       604764    A    128.63.2.53
; additional
I.ROOT-SERVERS.NET.       604764    A    192.36.148.17
; additional
J.ROOT-SERVERS.NET.       604764    A    192.58.128.30
; additional
```

```
K.ROOT-SERVERS.NET.       604764    A    193.0.14.129
; additional
L.ROOT-SERVERS.NET.       604764    A    198.32.64.12
; additional
M.ROOT-SERVERS.NET.       604764    A    202.12.27.33
;
; Start view _default
;
;
; Address database dump
;
; M3.NSTLD.COM [v4 TTL 6] [v4 success] [v6 unexpected]
;     192.55.83.32 [srtt 20] [flags 00000000] [ttl 1796]
; L3.NSTLD.COM [v4 TTL 6] [v4 success] [v6 unexpected]
;     192.41.162.32 [srtt 20] [flags 00000000] [ttl 1796]
; H3.NSTLD.COM [v4 TTL 6] [v4 success] [v6 unexpected]
;     192.54.112.32 [srtt 27] [flags 00000000] [ttl 1796]
; G3.NSTLD.COM [v4 TTL 6] [v4 success] [v6 unexpected]
;     192.42.93.32 [srtt 15] [flags 00000000] [ttl 1796]
; E3.NSTLD.COM [v4 TTL 6] [v4 success] [v6 unexpected]
;     192.12.94.32 [srtt 17] [flags 00000000] [ttl 1796]
; D3.NSTLD.COM [v4 TTL 6] [v4 success] [v6 unexpected]
;     192.31.80.32 [srtt 10] [flags 00000000] [ttl 1796]
; C3.NSTLD.COM [v4 TTL 6] [v4 success] [v6 unexpected]
;     192.26.92.32 [srtt 28156] [flags 00000000] [ttl 1796]
; A3.NSTLD.COM [v4 TTL 6] [v4 success] [v6 unexpected]
;     192.5.6.32 [srtt 23155] [flags 00000000] [ttl 1796]
; M.ROOT-SERVERS.NET [v4 TTL 86364] [v4 success] [v6 unexpected]
;     202.12.27.33 [srtt 0] [flags 00000000] [ttl 1764]
; L.ROOT-SERVERS.NET [v4 TTL 86364] [v4 success] [v6 unexpected]
;     198.32.64.12 [srtt 16] [flags 00000000] [ttl 1764]
; K.ROOT-SERVERS.NET [v4 TTL 86364] [v4 success] [v6 unexpected]
;     193.0.14.129 [srtt 22] [flags 00000000] [ttl 1764]
; J.ROOT-SERVERS.NET [v4 TTL 86364] [v4 success] [v6 unexpected]
;     192.58.128.30 [srtt 25] [flags 00000000] [ttl 1764]
; I.ROOT-SERVERS.NET [v4 TTL 86364] [v4 success] [v6 unexpected]
;     192.36.148.17 [srtt 19] [flags 00000000] [ttl 1764]
; H.ROOT-SERVERS.NET [v4 TTL 86364] [v4 success] [v6 unexpected]
;     128.63.2.53 [srtt 19] [flags 00000000] [ttl 1764]
; G.ROOT-SERVERS.NET [v4 TTL 86364] [v4 success] [v6 unexpected]
;     192.112.36.4 [srtt 24] [flags 00000000] [ttl 1764]
; F.ROOT-SERVERS.NET [v4 TTL 86364] [v4 success] [v6 unexpected]
;     192.5.5.241 [srtt 17850] [flags 00000000] [ttl 1764]
; E.ROOT-SERVERS.NET [v4 TTL 86364] [v4 success] [v6 unexpected]
;     192.203.230.10 [srtt 7] [flags 00000000] [ttl 1764]
; D.ROOT-SERVERS.NET [v4 TTL 86364] [v4 success] [v6 unexpected]
;     128.8.10.90 [srtt 8] [flags 00000000] [ttl 1764]
; C.ROOT-SERVERS.NET [v4 TTL 86364] [v4 success] [v6 unexpected]
;     192.33.4.12 [srtt 5] [flags 00000000] [ttl 1764]
; B.ROOT-SERVERS.NET [v4 TTL 86364] [v4 success] [v6 unexpected]
;     192.228.79.201 [srtt 24] [flags 00000000] [ttl 1764]
; A.ROOT-SERVERS.NET [v4 TTL 86364] [v4 success] [v6 unexpected]
;     198.41.0.4 [srtt 29] [flags 00000000] [ttl 1764]
;
```

```
;   Unassociated entries
;
;       128.210.11.5 [srtt 47718] [flags 00000000] [ttl 1764]
;       128.10.2.5 [srtt 9] [flags 00000000] [ttl 1764]
;       128.42.5.4 [srtt 2] [flags 00000000] [ttl 1764]
;       128.46.154.76 [srtt 6] [flags 00000000] [ttl 1764]
;
;   Start view _bind
;
;
;   Cache dump of view '_bind'
;
$DATE 20050827190436
;
;   Start view _bind
;
;
;   Address database dump
;
;
;   Unassociated entries
;
;   Dump complete
```

The nameserver that created this *named_dump.db* file was authoritative only for *0.0.
127.in-addr.arpa* (although you won't see that data because we didn't use *rndc
dumpdb –all* to dump the authoritative data). Only two names have been looked up
by this server: *galt.cs.purdue.edu* and *cujo.movie.edu*. In the process of looking up
galt.cs.purdue.edu, this server cached not only the address of *galt*, but also the list of
nameservers for *edu*, *purdue.edu*, *cs.purdue.edu*, and the addresses for those servers.
The name *cujo.movie.edu*, however, doesn't really exist (nor does the zone *movie.edu*,
except in our examples), so the server cached the negative response.

Like BIND 8, BIND 9 tags each data with information about how trustworthy the
data is. The trust measure is displayed in a comment before the actual data. In the
snippet below, the NS record for the root domain is at trust level *authanswer*.

```
;   authanswer
.               518364    IN NS    A.ROOT-SERVERS.NET.
```

Here is a complete list of the trust levels you might see in a database dump:

Trust level	Description
secure	DNSSEC-validated
authanswer	Answer from an authoritative server
authauthority	Data from the authority section of an authoritative response
answer	Answer from a nonauthoritative server
glue	Referral data
additional	Data from the additional section of a response
pending	Subject to DNSSEC validation but has not yet been validated

In the *Address database dump* section of the previous code, the nameserver is displaying some additional data it keeps about other nameservers. Some of the data is associated with the name (whether it does IPv4 or IPv6), and some of the data is associated with the address (the smoothed round-trip time and *flags*, which indicates only EDNS0 support at this point).

The next section is the *Unassociated entries* section. This section is just like the *Address database dump* section, but the data associated with the name has gone away. The only thing left is the data associated with the address. The first entry in the *Address database dump* section (*M3.NSTLD.COM*) has a TTL of 6. In six seconds, the data associated with the name will expire, and the data associated with 192.55.83.32 will be demoted to the *Unassociated entries* section.

Logging Queries

BIND has a feature called *query logging* that can help diagnose certain problems. When query logging is turned on, a running nameserver logs every query to *syslog*. This feature can help you find resolver configuration errors because you can verify that the name you think is being looked up really is the name being looked up.

First, make sure that LOG_INFO messages are being logged by *syslog* for the facility *daemon*. Next, you turn on query logging. This can be done in several ways: for BIND 8, start the nameserver with *–q* on the command line or send an *ndc querylog* command to a running nameserver. For BIND 9.1.0 or later (earlier versions don't support query logging), use *rndc querylog*. You'll start seeing *syslog* messages like this:

```
Feb 20 21:43:25 toystory named[3830]:
                    XX+ /192.253.253.2/carrie.movie.edu/A
Feb 20 21:43:32 toystory named[3830]:
                    XX+ /192.253.253.2/4.253.253.192.in-addr.arpa/PTR
```

Or, if you're running BIND 9, like this:

```
Jan 13 18:32:25 toystory named[13976]: info: client 192.253.253.2#1702: query:
                    carrie.movie.edu IN A
Jan 13 18:32:42 toystory named[13976]: info: client 192.253.253.2#1702: query:
                    4.253.253.192.in-addr.arpa IN PTR
```

These messages include the IP address of the host that made the query, as well as the query itself. Since the first example comes from a BIND 8.2.3 nameserver and these queries are recursive, they begin with XX+. Iterative queries begin with just XX. (Nameservers older than BIND 8.2.1 don't distinguish between recursive and nonrecursive queries.) After enough queries have been logged, you can turn off query logging by sending another *ndc querylog* or *rndc querylog* command to your nameserver.

If you're stuck running an older BIND 9 nameserver, you can still see the queries received in *named*'s debugging output at level 1.

Potential Problem List

Now that we've given you a nice set of tools, let's talk about how you can use them to diagnose real problems. There are some problems that are easy to recognize and correct. We should cover these as a matter of course; they're some of the most common problems because they're caused by some of the most common mistakes. Here are the contestants, in no particular order. We call 'em our "Unlucky Thirteen."

1. Forgot to Increment Serial Number

The main symptom of this problem is that slave nameservers don't pick up any changes you made to the zone's datafile on the primary. The slaves think the zone data hasn't changed because the serial number is still the same.

How do you check whether you remembered to increment the serial number? Unfortunately, that's not so easy. If you don't remember what the old serial number was, and your serial number gives you no indication of when it was updated, there's no direct way to tell whether it's changed.* When you reload the primary, it loads the updated zone file regardless of whether you've changed the serial number. It checks the file's timestamp, sees that it's been modified since it last loaded the data, and reads the file. About the best you can do is to use *nslookup* to compare the data returned by the primary and by a slave. If they return different data, you probably forgot to increment the serial number. If you can remember a recent change you made, you can look for that data. If you can't remember a recent change, you can try transferring the zone from a primary and from a slave, sorting the results, and using *diff* to compare them.

The good news is that, although determining whether the zone was transferred is tricky, making sure the zone is transferred is simple. Just increment the serial number on the primary's copy of the zone datafile and reload the zone on the primary. The slaves should pick up the new data within their refresh interval, or sooner if they use NOTIFY. If you run BIND 9.3 slaves, you can use the new *rndc retransfer* command to force an immediate zone transfer. To force BIND 8 slaves to transfer the new data, you can delete the backup file and restart *named*, or execute *named-xfer* by hand (on the slaves, naturally):

```
# /usr/sbin/named-xfer -z movie.edu -f bak.movie.edu -s 0 toystory.movie.edu
# echo $?
```

If *named-xfer* returns 1 or 4, the zone was transferred successfully. Other return values indicate that no zone was transferred, either because of an error or because the

---

* On the other hand, if you encode the date into the serial number, as many people do (e.g., 2001010500 is the first rev of data on January 5, 2001), you may be able to tell at a glance whether you updated the serial number when you made the change.

slave thought the zone was up to date. (See the earlier section "How to Use named-xfer" for more details.)

There's another variation of the "forgot to increment the serial number" problem. We see it in environments where administrators use tools such as *h2n* to create zone datafiles from the host table. With scripts like *h2n*, it's temptingly easy to delete old zone datafiles and create new ones from scratch. Some administrators do this occasionally because they mistakenly believe that data in the old zone datafiles can creep into the new ones. The problem with deleting the zone datafiles is that, without the old datafile to read for the current serial number, *h2n* starts over at serial number 1. If your zone's serial number on the primary rolls all the way back to 1 from 598 or what have you, the slaves emit a *syslog* error message warning you that something might be wrong:

```
Jun  7 20:14:26 wormhole named[29618]: Zone "movie.edu"
                (class 1) SOA serial# (1) rcvd from [192.249.249.3]
                is < ours (112)
```

So if the serial number on the primary looks suspiciously low, check the serial number on the slaves, too, and compare them:

```
% nslookup
Default Server:  toystory.movie.edu
Address:  192.249.249.3

> set q=soa
> movie.edu.
Server:  toystory.movie.edu
Address:  192.249.249.3

movie.edu
        origin = toystory.movie.edu
        mail addr = al.movie.edu
        serial = 1
        refresh = 10800 (3 hours)
        retry   = 3600 (1 hour)
        expire  = 604800 (7 days)
        minimum ttl = 86400 (1 day)
> server wormhole.movie.edu.
Default Server:  wormhole.movie.edu
Addresses:  192.249.249.1, 192.253.253.1

> movie.edu.
Server:  wormhole.movie.edu
Addresses:  192.249.249.1, 192.253.253.1

movie.edu
        origin = toystory.movie.edu
        mail addr = al.movie.edu
        serial = 112
        refresh = 10800 (3 hours)
        retry   = 3600 (1 hour)
```

```
expire    = 604800 (7 days)
minimum ttl = 86400 (1 day)
```

wormhole.movie.edu, as a *movie.edu* slave, should never have a larger serial number than the primary, so clearly something's amiss.

This problem is really easy to spot, by the way, with the tool we'll write in Chapter 15.

2. Forgot to Reload Primary Nameserver

Occasionally, you may forget to reload your primary nameserver after making a change to the configuration file or to a zone datafile. The nameserver won't know to load the new configuration or the new zone data; it doesn't automatically check the timestamp of the file and notice that it changed. Consequently, any changes you've made won't be reflected in the nameserver's data: new zones won't be loaded, and new records won't percolate out to the slaves.

To check when you last reloaded the nameserver, scan the *syslog* output for the last entry like this for a BIND 9 nameserver:

```
Mar  8 17:22:08 toystory named[22317]: loading configuration from '/etc/named.conf'
```

Or like this for a BIND 8 nameserver:

```
Mar  8 17:22:08 toystory named[22317]: reloading nameserver
```

These messages tell you the last time you sent a reload command to the nameserver. If you killed and then restarted the nameserver, you'll see an entry like this on a BIND 9 nameserver:

```
Mar  8 17:22:08 toystory named[22317]: running
```

On a BIND 8 nameserver, it'd look like:

```
Mar  8 17:22:08 toystory named[22317]: restarted
```

If the time of the restart or reload doesn't correlate with the time you made the last change, reload the nameserver again. And check that you incremented the serial numbers in zone datafiles you changed, too. If you're not sure when you edited the zone datafile, you can check the file modification time by doing a long listing of the file with *ls –l*.

3. Slave Nameserver Can't Load Zone Data

If a slave nameserver can't get the current serial number for a zone from its master nameserver, it logs a message via *syslog*. On a BIND 9 nameserver, that looks like:

```
Sep 25 22:02:38 wormhole named[21246]: refresh_callback: zone
       movie.edu/IN: failure for 192.249.249.3#53: timed out
```

On BIND 8, look for:

```
Jan  6 11:55:25 wormhole named[544]: Err/TO getting serial# for "movie.edu"
```

If you let this problem fester, the slave will expire the zone. A BIND 9 nameserver will report:

```
Sep 25 23:20:20 wormhole named[21246]: zone_expire: zone
      movie.edu/IN: expired
```

A BIND 8 nameserver will log:

```
Mar  8 17:12:43 wormhole named[22261]: secondary zone
      "movie.edu" expired
```

Once the zone has expired, you'll start getting SERVFAIL errors when you query the nameserver for data in the zone:

```
% nslookup robocop wormhole.movie.edu.
Server:  wormhole.movie.edu
Addresses:  192.249.249.1, 192.253.253.1

*** wormhole.movie.edu can't find robocop.movie.edu: Server failed
```

There are three leading causes of this problem: a loss in connectivity to the master server due to network failure, an incorrect IP address for the master server in the configuration file, or a syntax error in the zone datafile on the master server. First, check the configuration file's entry for the zone and see what IP address the slave is attempting to load from:

```
zone "movie.edu" {
                type slave;
                masters { 192.249.249.3; };
                file "bak.movie.edu";
};
```

Make sure that's really the IP address of the master nameserver. If it is, check connectivity to that IP address:

```
% ping 192.249.249.3 -n 10
PING 192.249.249.3: 64 byte packets

----192.249.249.3 PING Statistics----
10 packets transmitted, 0 packets received, 100% packet loss
```

If the master server isn't reachable, make sure that the host the nameserver runs on is really running (e.g., is powered on, etc.), or look for a network problem. If the host is reachable, make sure *named* is running on the host and that you can manually transfer the zone:

```
# /usr/sbin/named-xfer -z movie.edu -f /tmp/db.movie.edu -s 0 192.249.249.3
# echo $?
2
```

A return code of 2 means that an error occurred. Check to see if there is a *syslog* message. In this case, there is a message:

```
Jan  6 14:56:07 zardoz named-xfer[695]: record too short from [192.249.249.3], zone
movie.edu
```

At first glance, this error looks like a truncation problem. The real problem is easier to see if you use *nslookup*:

```
% nslookup - toystory.movie.edu
Default Server:  toystory.movie.edu
Address:  192.249.249.3

> ls movie.edu                     This attempts a zone transfer
[toystory.movie.edu]
*** Can't list domain movie.edu: Query refused
```

What's happening here is that *named* is refusing to allow you to transfer its zone data. The remote server has probably secured its zone data with an *allow-transfer* substatement.

If the master server is responding as not authoritative for the zone, you'll see a message like this from your BIND 9 nameserver:

```
Sep 26 13:29:23 zardoz named[21890]: refresh_callback: zone movie.edu/IN:
    non-authoritative answer from 192.249.249.3#53
```

Or on BIND 8, like this:

```
Jan  6 11:58:36 zardoz named[544]: Err/TO getting serial# for "movie.edu"
Jan  6 11:58:36 zardoz named-xfer[793]: [192.249.249.3] not authoritative for
    movie.edu, SOA query got rcode 0, aa 0, ancount 0, aucount 0
```

If this is the correct master server, the server *should* be authoritative for the zone. This probably indicates that the master had a problem loading the zone, usually because of a syntax error in the zone datafile. Contact the administrator of the master server and have her check her *syslog* output for indications of a syntax error (see the section "5. Syntax Error in Configuration File or Zone Datafile").

4. Added Name to Zone Datafile but Forgot to Add PTR Record

Because mappings of hostnames to IP addresses are disjointed from mappings of IP addresses to hostnames in DNS, it's easy to forget to add a PTR record for a new host. Adding the A record is intuitive, but many people who are used to host tables assume that adding an address record takes care of the reverse mapping, too. That's not true: you need to add a PTR record for the host to the appropriate reverse-mapping zone.

Forgetting to add the PTR record for a host's address usually causes that host to fail authentication checks. For example, users on the host won't be able to *rlogin* to other hosts without specifying a password, and *rsh* or *rcp* to other hosts simply won't work. The servers these commands talk to must be able to map a client's IP address to a domain name to check *.rhosts* and *hosts.equiv*. These users' connections will cause entries like this to be *syslog*ged:

```
Aug 15 17:32:36 toystory inetd[23194]: login/tcp:
    Connection from unknown (192.249.249.23)
```

Also, some network servers on the Internet, including certain FTP servers, deny access to hosts whose IP addresses don't map back to domain names. An attempt to access such a server might produce an error message like this:

```
530- Sorry, we're unable to map your IP address 140.186.66.1 to a hostname
530- in the DNS.  This is probably because your nameserver does not have a
530- PTR record for your address in its tables, or because your reverse
530- nameservers are not registered.  We refuse service to hosts whose
530- names we cannot resolve.
```

That makes the reason you can't use the service pretty evident. Other servers, however, don't bother printing informative messages; they simply deny service.

nslookup is handy for checking whether you've forgotten the PTR record:

```
% nslookup
Default Server:  toystory.movie.edu
Address:  192.249.249.3

> beetlejuice          Check for a name-to-address mapping
Server:  toystory.movie.edu
Address:  192.249.249.3

Name:    beetlejuice.movie.edu
Address:  192.249.249.23

> 192.249.249.23       Now check for a corresponding address-to-name mapping
Server:  toystory.movie.edu
Address:  192.249.249.3

*** toystory.movie.edu can't find 192.249.249.23: Non-existent domain
```

On the primary for *249.249.192.in-addr.arpa*, a quick check of the *db.192.249.249* file will tell you if the PTR record hasn't been added to the zone datafile or if the nameserver hasn't been reloaded. If the nameserver having trouble is a slave for the zone, check that the serial number was incremented on the primary and that the slave has had enough time to load the zone.

5. Syntax Error in Configuration File or Zone Datafile

Syntax errors in a nameserver's configuration file and in zone datafiles are also relatively common (more or less, depending on the experience of the administrator). Generally, an error in the config file will cause the nameserver to fail to load one or more zones. Some typos in the *options* statement will cause the nameserver to fail to start at all and to log an error like this via *syslog* (BIND 9):

```
Sep 26 13:39:30 toystory named[21924]: change directory to '/var/name' failed: file
    not found
Sep 26 13:39:30 toystory named[21924]: options configuration failed: file not found
Sep 26 13:39:30 toystory named[21924]: loading configuration: failure
Sep 26 13:39:30 toystory named[21924]: exiting (due to fatal error)
```

A BIND 8 nameserver logs:

```
Jan  6 11:59:29 toystory named[544]: can't change directory to /var/name: No
    such file or directory
```

Note that you won't see an error message when you try to start *named* on the command line or at boot time, but *named* won't stay running for long.

If the syntax error is in a less important line in the config file—say, in a *zone* statement—only that zone will be affected. Usually, the nameserver won't be able to load the zone at all (say, you misspell "masters" or the name of the zone datafile, or you forget to put quotes around the filename or domain name). This produces *syslog* output from BIND 9 like this:

```
Sep 26 13:43:03 toystory named[21938]: /etc/named.conf:80:
    parse error near 'masters'
Sep 26 13:43:03 toystory named[21938]: loading configuration: failure
Sep 26 13:43:03 toystory named[21938]: exiting (due to fatal error)
```

Or, from BIND 8:

```
Jan  6 12:01:36 toystory named[841]: /etc/named.conf:10: syntax error near
    'movie.edu'
```

If a zone datafile contains a syntax error yet the nameserver succeeds in loading the zone, it either answers as nonauthoritative for *all* data in the zone or returns a SERVFAIL error for lookups in the zone:

```
% nslookup carrie.movie.edu.
Server:  toystory.movie.edu
Address:  192.249.249.3

*** toystory.movie.edu can't find carrie.movie.edu.: Server failed
```

Here's the BIND 9 *syslog* message produced by the syntax error that caused this problem:

```
Sep 26 13:45:40 toystory named[21951]: error: dns_rdata_fromtext: db.movie.edu:11:
    near 'postmanrings2x': unexpected token
Sep 26 13:45:40 toystory named[21951]: error: dns_zone_load: zone movie.edu/IN:
    database db.movie.edu: dns_db_load failed: unexpected token
Sep 26 13:45:40 toystory named[21951]: critical: loading zones: unexpected token
Sep 26 13:45:40 toystory named[21951]: critical: exiting (due to fatal error)
```

Here's BIND 8's error:

```
Jan  6 15:07:46 toystory named[693]: db.movie.edu:11: Priority error
    (postmanrings2x.movie.edu.)
Jan  6 15:07:46 toystory named[693]: master zone "movie.edu" (IN) rejected due
    to errors (serial 1997010600)
```

If you looked in the zone datafile for the problem, you'd find this record:

```
postmanrings2x    IN    MX    postmanrings2x.movie.edu.
```

The MX record is missing the preference field, which causes the error.

Note that unless you correlate the SERVFAIL error or lack of authority (when you expect the nameserver to be authoritative) with a problem or scan your *syslog* file assiduously, you might never notice the syntax error!

Also, an "invalid" hostname can be a syntax error:

```
Jan  6 12:04:10 toystory named[841]: owner name "ID_4.movie.edu" IN (primary)
    is invalid - rejecting
Jan  6 12:04:10 toystory named[841]: db.movie.edu:11: owner name error
Jan  6 12:04:10 toystory named[841]: db.movie.edu:11: Database error near (A)
Jan  6 12:04:10 toystory named[841]: master zone "movie.edu" (IN) rejected
    due to errors (serial 1997010600)
```

6. Missing Dot at the End of a Domain Name in a Zone Datafile

It's *very* easy to leave off trailing dots when editing a zone datafile. Since the rules for when to use them change so often (don't use them in the configuration file, don't use them in *resolv.conf*, do use them in zone datafiles to override $ORIGIN…), it's hard to keep them straight. These resource records:

```
zorba        IN    MX     10 zelig.movie.edu
movie.edu    IN    NS     toystory.movie.edu
```

really don't look that odd to the untrained eye, but they probably don't do what they're intended to. In the *db.movie.edu* file, they'd be equivalent to:

```
zorba.movie.edu.          IN    MX     10 zelig.movie.edu.movie.edu.
movie.edu.movie.edu.      IN    NS     toystory.movie.edu.movie.edu.
```

unless the origin were explicitly changed.

If you omit a trailing dot after a domain name in the resource record's data (as opposed to leaving off a trailing dot in the resource record's *name*), you usually end up with wacky NS or MX records:

```
% nslookup -type=mx zorba.movie.edu.
Server:  toystory.movie.edu
Address:  192.249.249.3

zorba.movie.edu        preference = 10, mail exchanger
                       = zelig.movie.edu.movie.edu
zorba.movie.edu        preference = 50, mail exchanger
                       = postmanrings2x.movie.edu.movie.edu
```

The cause of this should be fairly clear from the *nslookup* output. But if you forget the trailing dot on the domain name field in a record (as in the *movie.edu* NS record just listed), spotting your mistake might not be as easy. If you try to look up the record with *nslookup*, you won't find it under the domain name you thought you used. Dumping your nameserver's database may help you root it out:

```
$ORIGIN edu.movie.edu.
movie    IN    NS     toystory.movie.edu.movie.edu.
```

The $ORIGIN line looks odd enough to stand out.

---

7. Missing Root Hints Data

You're unlikely to run into this problem with BIND 9 because it has built-in root hints.

If, for some reason, you forget to install a root hints file on your nameserver or you accidentally delete it, your nameserver will be unable to resolve names outside of its authoritative data. This behavior is easy to recognize using *nslookup*, but be careful to use full, dot-terminated domain names, or else the search list may cause misleading failures:

```
% nslookup
Default Server:  toystory.movie.edu
Address:  192.249.249.3

> ftp.uu.net.        A lookup of a name outside your nameserver's authoritative data
                     causes a SERVFAIL error...

Server:  toystory.movie.edu
Address:  192.249.249.3

*** toystory.movie.edu can't find ftp.uu.net.: Server failed
```

A lookup of a name in your nameserver's authoritative data returns a response:

```
> wormhole.movie.edu.
Server:  toystory.movie.edu
Address:  192.249.249.3

Name:    wormhole.movie.edu
Addresses:  192.249.249.1, 192.253.253.1

> ^D
```

To confirm your suspicion that the root hints data is missing, check the *syslog* output for an error like this:

```
Jan  6 15:10:22 toystory named[764]: No root nameservers for class IN
```

Class 1, you'll remember, is the IN, or Internet, class. This error indicates that because no root hints data was available, no root nameservers were found.

8. Loss of Network Connectivity

Though the Internet is more reliable today than it was back in the wild and woolly days of the ARPAnet, network outages are still relatively common. Without "lifting the hood" and poking around in debugging output, these failures usually look like poor performance:

```
% nslookup nisc.sri.com.
Server:  toystory.movie.edu
Address:  192.249.249.3

*** Request to toystory.movie.edu timed out ***
```

If you turn on nameserver debugging, though, you may see that your nameserver, anyway, is healthy. It received the query from the resolver, sent the necessary queries, and waited patiently for a response. It just didn't get one. Here's what the debugging output might look like on a BIND 8 nameserver:

```
Debug turned ON, Level 1
```

Here, *nslookup* sends the first query to our local nameserver for the IP address of *nisc.sri.com*. The query is then forwarded to another nameserver, and, when no answer is received, is resent to a different nameserver:

```
datagram from [192.249.249.3].1051, fd 5, len 30
req: nlookup(nisc.sri.com) id 18470 type=1 class=1
req: missed 'nisc.sri.com' as 'com' (cname=0)
forw: forw -> [198.41.0.4].53 ds=7 nsid=58732 id=18470 0ms retry 4 sec
resend(addr=1 n=0) -> [128.9.0.107].53 ds=7 nsid=58732 id=18470 0ms
```

Now *nslookup* is getting impatient, and it queries our local nameserver again. Notice that it uses the same source port. The local nameserver ignores the duplicate query and tries forwarding the query two more times:

```
datagram from [192.249.249.3].1051, fd 5, len 30
req: nlookup(nisc.sri.com) id 18470 type=1 class=1
req: missed 'nisc.sri.com' as 'com' (cname=0)
resend(addr=2 n=0) -> [192.33.4.12].53 ds=7 nsid=58732 id=18470 0ms
resend(addr=3 n=0) -> [128.8.10.90].53 ds=7 nsid=58732 id=18470 0ms
```

nslookup queries the local nameserver again, and the nameserver fires off more queries:

```
datagram from [192.249.249.3].1051, fd 5, len 30
req: nlookup(nisc.sri.com) id 18470 type=1 class=1
req: missed 'nisc.sri.com' as 'com' (cname=0)
resend(addr=4 n=0) -> [192.203.230.10].53 ds=7 nsid=58732 id=18470 0ms
resend(addr=0 n=1) -> [198.41.0.4].53 ds=7 nsid=58732 id=18470 0ms
resend(addr=1 n=1) -> [128.9.0.107].53 ds=7 nsid=58732 id=18470 0ms
resend(addr=2 n=1) -> [192.33.4.12].53 ds=7 nsid=58732 id=18470 0ms
resend(addr=3 n=1) -> [128.8.10.90].53 ds=7 nsid=58732 id=18470 0ms
resend(addr=4 n=1) -> [192.203.230.10].53 ds=7 nsid=58732 id=18470 0ms
resend(addr=0 n=2) -> [198.41.0.4].53 ds=7 nsid=58732 id=18470 0ms
Debug turned OFF
```

On a BIND 9 nameserver, there's considerably less detail at debug level 1. Still, you can see that the nameserver is trying repeatedly to look up *nisc.sri.com*:

```
Sep 26 14:33:27.486 client 192.249.249.3#1028: query: nisc.sri.com A
Sep 26 14:33:27.486 createfetch: nisc.sri.com. A
Sep 26 14:33:32.489 client 192.249.249.3#1028: query: nisc.sri.com A
Sep 26 14:33:32.490 createfetch: nisc.sri.com. A
Sep 26 14:33:42.500 client 192.249.249.3#1028: query: nisc.sri.com A
Sep 26 14:33:42.500 createfetch: nisc.sri.com. A
Sep 26 14:34:02.512 client 192.249.249.3#1028: query: nisc.sri.com A
Sep 26 14:34:02.512 createfetch: nisc.sri.com. A
```

At higher debug levels, you can actually see the timeouts, but BIND 9.3.2 still doesn't show the addresses of the remote nameservers tried.

From the BIND 8 debugging output, you can extract a list of the IP addresses of the nameservers that your nameserver tried to query, and then check your connectivity to them. Odds are, *ping* won't have much better luck than your nameserver did:

```
% ping 198.41.0.4 -n 10    ping first nameserver queried
PING 198.41.0.4: 64 byte packets

----198.41.0.4 PING Statistics----
10 packets transmitted, 0 packets received, 100% packet loss
% ping 128.9.0.107 -n 10    ping second nameserver queried
PING 128.9.0.107: 64 byte packets

----128.9.0.107 PING Statistics----
10 packets transmitted, 0 packets received, 100% packet loss
```

If it does, you should check that the remote nameservers are really running. You might also check whether your Internet firewall is inadvertently blocking your nameserver's queries. If you've upgraded to BIND 8 or 9 recently, see the sidebar "A Gotcha with BIND 8 or 9 and Packet-Filtering Firewalls" in Chapter 11 and see if it applies to you.

If *ping* can't get through either, all that's left to do is locate the break in the network. Utilities like *traceroute* and *ping*'s record route option can be very helpful in determining whether the problem is on your network, the destination network, or somewhere in the middle.

Also, use your own common sense when tracking down the break. In this trace, for example, the remote nameservers your nameserver tried to query are all root nameservers. (You might have had their PTR records cached somewhere, so you could find out their domain names.) Now it's not very likely that each root's local network went down, nor that the Internet's backbone networks collapsed entirely. Occam's razor says that the simplest condition that could cause this behavior—namely, the loss of *your* network's link to the Internet—is most likely the cause.

9. Missing Subdomain Delegation

Even though registrars do their very best to process your requests as quickly as possible, it may take a day or two for your subdomain's delegation to appear in your parent zone's nameservers. If your parent zone isn't one of the generic top-level domains, your mileage may vary. Some parents are quick and responsible, others are slow and inconsistent. Just like in real life, though, you're stuck with them.

Until your zone's delegation appears in your parent zone's nameservers, your nameservers will be able to look up data in the Internet's namespace, but no one out on the Internet (outside of your domain) will know how to look up data in *your* namespace.

That means that even though you may be able to send mail outside of your domain, the recipients won't be able to reply to it. Furthermore, no one will be able to *ssh* to, *ftp* to, or even *ping* your hosts by domain name.

Remember that this applies equally to any *in-addr.arpa* zones you may run. Until their parent zones add delegation to your servers, nameservers on the Internet won't be able to reverse-map addresses on your networks.

To determine whether your zone's delegation has made it into your parent zone's nameservers, query a parent nameserver for the NS records for your zone. If the parent nameserver has the data, any nameserver on the Internet can find it:

```
% nslookup
Default Server:  toystory.movie.edu
Address:  192.249.249.3

> server a.root-servers.net.    Query a root nameserver
Default Server:  a.root-servers.net
Address:  198.41.0.4

> set norecurse                 Instruct the server to answer out of its own data
> set type=ns                   and to look for NS records
> 249.249.192.in-addr.arpa.     for 249.249.192.in-addr.arpa
Server:  a.root-servers.net
Address:  198.41.0.4

192.in-addr.arpa        nameserver = chia.ARIN.NET
192.in-addr.arpa        nameserver = dill.ARIN.NET
192.in-addr.arpa        nameserver = BASIL.ARIN.NET
192.in-addr.arpa        nameserver = henna.ARIN.NET
192.in-addr.arpa        nameserver = indigo.ARIN.NET
192.in-addr.arpa        nameserver = epazote.ARIN.NET
192.in-addr.arpa        nameserver = figwort.ARIN.NET

> server dill.arin.net.    Query an in-addr.arpa nameserver
Server:  dill.arin.net
Address:  192.35.51.32

> 249.249.192.in-addr.arpa.
Server:  dill.arin.net
Address:  192.35.51.32

*** dill.arin.net can't find 249.249.192.in-addr.arpa.: Non-existent domain
```

Here, the delegation clearly hasn't been added yet. You can either wait patiently or, if an unreasonable amount of time has passed since you requested delegation from your parent zone, contact your parent zone's administrator and ask what's up.

10. Incorrect Subdomain Delegation

Incorrect subdomain delegation is another familiar problem on the Internet. Keeping delegation up to date requires human intervention—informing your parent zone's administrator of changes to your set of authoritative nameservers. Consequently, delegation information often becomes inaccurate as administrators make changes without letting their parents know. Far too many administrators believe that setting up delegation is a one-shot deal: they let their parents know which nameservers are authoritative once when they set up their zone and then never talk to them again. They don't even call on Mother's Day.

An administrator may add a new nameserver, decommission another, and change the IP address of a third, all without telling the parent zone's administrator. Gradually, the number of nameservers correctly delegated to by the parent zone dwindles. In the best case, this leads to long resolution times as querying nameservers struggle to find an authoritative nameserver for the zone. If the delegation information becomes badly out of date, and the last authoritative nameserver is brought down for maintenance, the information within and below the zone will be inaccessible.

If you suspect bad delegation from your parent zone to your zone, from your zone to one of your children, or from a remote zone to one of its children, you can check with *nslookup*:

```
% nslookup
Default Server:  toystory.movie.edu
Address:  192.249.249.3

> server a.root-servers.net.      Set server to the parent zone's nameserver that
                                   you suspect has bad delegation
Default Server:  a.root-servers.net
Address:  198.41.0.4

> set type=ns                      Look for NS records
> hp.com.                          for the zone in question
Server:          a.root-servers.net.
Address:         198.41.0.4

Non-authoritative answer:
*** Can't find hp.com.: No answer

Authoritative answers can be found from:
com      nameserver = A.GTLD-SERVERS.NET.
com      nameserver = G.GTLD-SERVERS.NET.
com      nameserver = H.GTLD-SERVERS.NET.
com      nameserver = C.GTLD-SERVERS.NET.
com      nameserver = I.GTLD-SERVERS.NET.
com      nameserver = B.GTLD-SERVERS.NET.
com      nameserver = D.GTLD-SERVERS.NET.
com      nameserver = L.GTLD-SERVERS.NET.
com      nameserver = F.GTLD-SERVERS.NET.
com      nameserver = J.GTLD-SERVERS.NET.
com      nameserver = K.GTLD-SERVERS.NET.
com      nameserver = E.GTLD-SERVERS.NET.
com      nameserver = M.GTLD-SERVERS.NET.
A.GTLD-SERVERS.NET      has AAAA address 2001:503:a83e::2:30
```

```
A.GTLD-SERVERS.NET       internet address = 192.5.6.30
G.GTLD-SERVERS.NET       internet address = 192.42.93.30
H.GTLD-SERVERS.NET       internet address = 192.54.112.30
C.GTLD-SERVERS.NET       internet address = 192.26.92.30
I.GTLD-SERVERS.NET       internet address = 192.43.172.30
B.GTLD-SERVERS.NET       has AAAA address 2001:503:231d::2:30
B.GTLD-SERVERS.NET       internet address = 192.33.14.30
D.GTLD-SERVERS.NET       internet address = 192.31.80.30
L.GTLD-SERVERS.NET       internet address = 192.41.162.30
F.GTLD-SERVERS.NET       internet address = 192.35.51.30
J.GTLD-SERVERS.NET       internet address = 192.48.79.30
K.GTLD-SERVERS.NET       internet address = 192.52.178.30
E.GTLD-SERVERS.NET       internet address = 192.12.94.30
M.GTLD-SERVERS.NET       internet address = 192.55.83.30

> server a.gtld-servers.net.                    Switch to a COM nameserver
Default server: a.gtld-servers.net.
Address: 192.5.6.30#53

> hp.com.                        Ask again
Server:       a.gtld-servers.net.
Address:      192.5.6.30#53

Non-authoritative answer:
hp.com  nameserver = am10.hp.com.
hp.com  nameserver = am3.hp.com.
hp.com  nameserver = ap1.hp.com.
hp.com  nameserver = eu1.hp.com.
hp.com  nameserver = eu2.hp.com.
hp.com  nameserver = eu3.hp.com.

Authoritative answers can be found from:
am10.hp.com      internet address = 15.227.128.50
am3.hp.com       internet address = 15.243.160.50
ap1.hp.com       internet address = 15.211.128.50
eu1.hp.com       internet address = 16.14.64.50
eu2.hp.com       internet address = 16.6.64.50
eu3.hp.com       internet address = 16.8.64.50
```

Let's say you suspect that the delegation to *am10.hp.com* is incorrect. You now query *am10.hp.com* for data in the *hp.com* zone (e.g., the SOA record for *hp.com*) and check the answer:

```
> server am10.hp.com.
Default Server:  am10.hp.com
Addresses:  15.227.128.50

> set norecurse
> set type=soa
> hp.com.
Server:  am10.hp.com
Addresses:  15.227.128.50
```

```
Non-authoritative answer:
hp.com
        origin = charon.core.hp.com
        mail addr = hostmaster.hp.com
        serial = 1008811
        refresh = 3600
        retry = 900
        expire = 604800
        minimum = 600

Authoritative answers can be found from:
hp.com  nameserver = eu3.hp.com.
hp.com  nameserver = am3.hp.com.
hp.com  nameserver = ap1.hp.com.
hp.com  nameserver = eu1.hp.com.
hp.com  nameserver = eu2.hp.com.
am3.hp.com        internet address = 15.243.160.50
ap1.hp.com        internet address = 15.211.128.50
eu1.hp.com        internet address = 16.14.64.50
eu2.hp.com        internet address = 16.6.64.50
eu3.hp.com        internet address = 16.8.64.50
```

If *am10.hp.com* really were authoritative for *hp.com*, it would have responded with an authoritative answer. The administrator of the *hp.com* zone can tell you whether *am10.hp.com* should be an authoritative nameserver for *hp.com*, so that's who you should contact.

Another common symptom of this is a "lame server" error message:

```
Oct 1 04:43:38 toystory named[146]: Lame server on '40.234.23.210.in-addr.arpa'
(in '210.in-addr.arpa'?): [198.41.0.5].53 'RS0.INTERNIC.NET': learnt(A=198.41.0.
21,NS=128.63.2.53)
```

Here's how to read this: your nameserver was referred by the nameserver at 128.63.2.53 to the nameserver at 198.41.0.5 for a name in the domain *210.in-addr.arpa*, specifically *40.234.23.210.in-addr.arpa*. The response from the nameserver at 198.41.0.5 indicated that it wasn't, in fact, authoritative for *210.in-addr.arpa*, and therefore either the delegation that 128.63.2.53 gave you is wrong, or the server at 198.41.0.5 is misconfigured.

11. Syntax Error in resolv.conf

Despite the *resolv.conf* file's simple syntax, people do occasionally make mistakes when editing it. And, unfortunately, lines with syntax errors in *resolv.conf* are silently ignored by the resolver. The result is usually that some part of your intended configuration doesn't take effect: either your local domain name or search list isn't set correctly, or the resolver won't query one of the nameservers you configured it to query. Commands that rely on the search list won't work, your resolver won't query the right nameserver, or it won't query a nameserver at all.

The easiest way to check whether your *resolv.conf* file is having the intended effect is to run *nslookup*. *nslookup* will kindly report the local domain name and search list it derives from *resolv.conf*, plus the nameserver it's querying, when you type *set all*, as we showed you in Chapter 12:

```
% nslookup
Default Server:  toystory.movie.edu
Address:  192.249.249.3

> set all
Default Server:  toystory.movie.edu
Address:  192.249.249.3

Set options:
  novc                nodebug         nod2
  search              recurse
  timeout = 0         retry = 3       port = 53
  querytype = A       class = IN
  srchlist=movie.edu

>
```

Check that the output of *set all* is what you expect, given your *resolv.conf* file. For example, if you set *search fx.movie.edu movie.edu* in *resolv.conf*, you'd expect to see:

```
srchlist=fx.movie.edu/movie.edu
```

in the output. If you don't see what you're expecting, look carefully at *resolv.conf*. If there's nothing obvious, look for unprintable characters (with *vi*'s *set list* command, for example). Watch out for trailing spaces, especially; on older resolvers, a trailing space after the domain name will set the local domain name to include a space. No real top-level domain names actually end with spaces, of course, so all of your non-dot-terminated lookups will fail.

12. Local Domain Name Not Set

Failing to set your local domain name is another old standby gaffe. You can set it implicitly by setting your *hostname* to your host's fully qualified domain name or explicitly in *resolv.conf*. The characteristics of an unset local domain name are straightforward: folks who use single-label names (or abbreviated domain names) in commands get no joy:

```
% telnet br
br: No address associated with name
% telnet br.fx
br.fx: No address associated with name
% telnet br.fx.movie.edu
Trying...
Connected to bladerunner.fx.movie.edu.
Escape character is '^]'.

HP-UX bladerunner.fx.movie.edu A.08.07 A 9000/730 (ttys1)
login:
```

You can use *nslookup* to check this one, much as you do when you suspect a syntax error in *resolv.conf*:

```
% nslookup
Default Server:  toystory.movie.edu
Address:  192.249.249.3

> set all
Default Server:  toystory.movie.edu
Address:  192.249.249.3

Set options:
  novc                  nodebug        nod2
  search                recurse
  timeout = 0           retry = 3      port = 53
  querytype = A         class = IN
  srchlist=
```

Notice that the search list is set. You can also track this down by enabling debugging on the nameserver. (This, of course, requires access to the nameserver, which may not be running on the host that the problem is affecting.) Here's how the debugging output from a BIND 9 nameserver might look after trying those *telnet* commands:

```
Sep 26 16:17:58.824 client 192.249.249.3#1032: query: br A
Sep 26 16:17:58.825 createfetch: br. A
Sep 26 16:18:09.996 client 192.249.249.3#1032: query: br.fx A
Sep 26 16:18:09.996 createfetch: br.fx. A
Sep 26 16:18:18.677 client 192.249.249.3#1032: query: br.fx.movie.edu A
```

On a BIND 8 nameserver, it would look something like this:

```
Debug turned ON, Level 1

datagram from [192.249.249.3].1057, fd 5, len 20
req: nlookup(br) id 27974 type=1 class=1
req: missed 'br' as '' (cname=0)
forw: forw -> [198.41.0.4].53 ds=7 nsid=61691 id=27974 0ms retry 4 sec

datagram from [198.41.0.4].53, fd 5, len 20
ncache: dname br, type 1, class 1
send_msg -> [192.249.249.3].1057 (UDP 5) id=27974

datagram from [192.249.249.3].1059, fd 5, len 23
req: nlookup(br.fx) id 27975 type=1 class=1
req: missed 'br.fx' as '' (cname=0)
forw: forw -> [128.9.0.107].53 ds=7 nsid=61692 id=27975 0ms retry 4 sec

datagram from [128.9.0.107].53, fd 5, len 23
ncache: dname br.fx, type 1, class 1
send_msg -> [192.249.249.3].1059 (UDP 5) id=27975

datagram from [192.249.249.3].1060, fd 5, len 33
req: nlookup(br.fx.movie.edu) id 27976 type=1 class=1
req: found 'br.fx.movie.edu' as 'br.fx.movie.edu' (cname=0)
```

```
req: nlookup(bladerunner.fx.movie.edu) id 27976 type=1 class=1
req: found 'bladerunner.fx.movie.edu' as 'bladerunner.fx.movie.edu'
    (cname=1)
ns_req: answer -> [192.249.249.3].1060 fd=5 id=27976 size=183 Local
Debug turned OFF
```

Contrast this with the debugging output produced by the application of the search list in Chapter 13. The only names looked up here are exactly what the user typed, with no domain names appended at all. Clearly, the search list isn't being applied.

13. Response from Unexpected Source

One problem we've seen increasingly often in the DNS newsgroups is the "response from unexpected source." This was once called a martian response: it's a response that comes from an IP address other than the one your nameserver sent a query to. When a BIND nameserver sends a query to a remote server, BIND conscientiously makes sure that answers come only from the IP addresses on that server. This helps minimize the possibility of accepting spoofed responses. BIND is equally demanding of itself: a BIND server makes every effort to reply via the same network interface that it received a query on.

Here's the error message you'd see upon receiving a possibly unsolicited response:

```
Mar  8 17:21:04 toystory named[235]: Response from unexpected source ([205. 199.4.
131].53)
```

This can mean one of two things: either someone is trying to spoof your nameserver, or—more likely—you sent a query to an older BIND server or a different make of nameserver that's not as assiduous about replying from the same interface it receives queries on.

Transition Problems

With the release of BIND 8, and now BIND 9, many Unix operating systems are updating their resolvers and nameservers. Some features of the most recent versions of BIND, however, may seem like errors to you after you upgrade to a new version. We'll try to give you an idea of some changes you may notice in your nameserver and name service after making the jump.

Resolver Behavior

The changes to the resolver's default search list described in Chapter 6 may seem like a problem to your users. Recall that with a local domain name set to *fx.movie.edu*, your default search list will no longer include *movie.edu*. Therefore, users accustomed to using commands such as *ssh db.personnel* and having the partial domain name expanded to *db.personnel.movie.edu* will have their commands fail. To solve this problem, you can use the *search* directive to define an explicit search list that includes your local domain name's parent. Or just tell your users to expect the new behavior.

Nameserver Behavior

Before Version 4.9, a BIND nameserver would gladly load data in any zone from any zone datafile that the nameserver read as a primary. If you configured the nameserver as the primary for *movie.edu* and told it that the *movie.edu* data was in *db.movie.edu*, you could stick data about *hp.com* in *db.movie.edu*, and your nameserver would load the *hp.com* resource records into the cache. Some books even suggested putting the data for all your *in-addr.arpa* zones in one file. Ugh.

All BIND 4.9 and later nameservers ignore any "out of zone" resource records in a zone datafile. So if you cram PTR records for all your *in-addr.arpa* zones into one file and load it with a single *zone* statement, the nameserver ignores all the records not in the named zone. And that, of course, means loads of missing PTR records and failed *gethostbyaddr()* calls.

BIND does log that it's ignoring the records in *syslog*. The messages look like this in BIND 9:

```
Sep 26 13:48:19 toystory named[21960]: dns_master_load: db.movie.edu:16: ignoring
out-of-zone data
```

and like this in BIND 8:

```
Jan  7 13:58:01 toystory named[231]: db.movie.edu:16: data "hp.com" outside zone
    "movie.edu" (ignored)
Jan  7 13:58:01 toystory named[231]: db.movie.edu:17: data "hp.com" outside zone
    "movie.edu" (ignored)
```

The solution is to use one zone datafile and one *zone* statement per zone.

Interoperability and Version Problems

With the move to BIND 9 and the introduction of Microsoft DNS Server, more interoperability problems are cropping up between nameservers. There are also a handful of problems unique to one version or another of BIND or the underlying operating system. Many of these are easy to spot and correct, and we would be remiss if we didn't cover them.

Zone Transfer Fails Because of Proprietary WINS Record

When a Microsoft DNS Server is configured to consult a WINS server for names it can't find in a given zone, it inserts a special record into the zone datafile. The record looks like this:

```
@   IN   WINS   &IP address of WINS server
```

Unfortunately, WINS is not a standard record type in the IN class. Consequently, if there are BIND slaves that transfer this zone, they'll choke on the WINS record and refuse to load the zone:

```
May 23 15:58:43 toystory named-xfer[386]: "fx.movie.edu IN 65281" - unknown type
(65281)
```

The workaround for this is to configure the Microsoft DNS Server to filter out the proprietary record before transferring the zone. You do this by selecting the zone on the left side of the DNS Manager screen, right-clicking on it, and selecting *Properties*. Click on the *WINS Lookup* tab in the resulting *Zone Properties* window, shown in Figure 14-1.

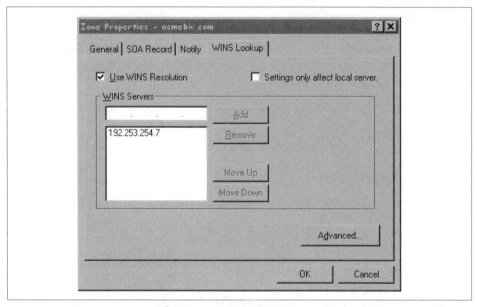

Figure 14-1. Zone Properties window

Checking *Settings only affect local server* filters out the WINS record for that zone. However, if there are any Microsoft DNS Server slaves, they won't see the record either, even though they can use it.

Nameserver Reports "no NS RR for SOA MNAME"

You'll see this error only on BIND 8.1 servers:

```
May 8 03:44:38 toystory named[11680]: no NS RR for SOA MNAME "movie.edu" in
    zone "movie.edu"
```

The 8.1 server was a real stickler about the first field in the SOA record. Remember that one? In Chapter 4, we said that it was, by convention, the domain name of the primary nameserver for the zone. BIND 8.1 assumes it is and checks for a corresponding

NS record pointing the zone's domain name to the server in that field. If there's no such NS record, BIND emits that error message. It will also prevent NOTIFY messages from working correctly. The solution is either to change your MNAME field to the domain name of a nameserver listed in an NS record or to upgrade to a newer version of BIND 8. Upgrading is the better option because BIND 8.1 is so old. The check was removed in BIND 8.1.1.

Nameserver Reports "Too many open files"

On hosts with many IP addresses or a low limit on the maximum number of files a user can open, BIND will report:

```
Dec 12 11:52:06 toystory named[7770]: socket(SOCK_RAW): Too many open files
```

and die.

Since BIND tries to *bind()* to and listen on every network interface on the host, it may run out of file descriptors. This is especially common on hosts that use lots of virtual interfaces, often in support of web hosting. The possible solutions are:

- Use name-based virtual hosting, which doesn't require additional IP addresses.
- Configure your BIND 8 or 9 nameserver to listen on only one or a few of the host's network interfaces using the *listen-on* substatement. If *toystory.movie.edu* is the host we're having this problem with, the following:

```
options {
    listen-on { 192.249.249.3; };
};
```

will tell *named* on *toystory.movie.edu* to *bind()* only to the IP address 192.249. 249.3.

- Reconfigure your operating system to allow a process to open more file descriptors concurrently.

Resolver Reports "asked for PTR, got CNAME"

This is another problem related to BIND's strictness. On some lookups, the resolver logs:

```
Sep 24 10:40:11 toystory syslog: gethostby*.getanswer: asked for
    "37.103.74.204.in-addr.arpa IN PTR", got type "CNAME"
Sep 24 10:40:11 toystory syslog: gethostby*.getanswer: asked for
    "37.103.74.204.in-addr.arpa", got "37.32/27.103.74.204.in-addr.arpa"
```

What happened here is that the resolver asked the nameserver to reverse-map the IP address 204.74.103.37 to a domain name. The server did, but in the process found that *37.103.74.204.in-addr.arpa* was actually an alias for *37.32/27.103.74.204.in-addr.arpa*. That's almost certainly because the folks who run *103.74.204.in-addr.arpa* are using the scheme we described in Chapter 9 to delegate part of their namespace. The BIND

4.9.3-BETA resolver, however, doesn't understand that and flags it as an error, thinking it didn't get the domain name or the type it was after. And, believe it or not, some operating systems ship with the BIND 4.9.3-BETA resolver as their system resolver.

The only solution to this problem is to upgrade to a newer version of the BIND resolver.

Nameserver Startup Fails Because UDP Checksums Disabled

On some hosts running SunOS 4.1.x, you'll see this error:

```
Sep 24 10:40:11 toystory named[7770]: ns_udp checksums NOT turned on: exiting
```

named checked to make sure UDP checksumming was turned on on this system, and it wasn't, so *named* exited. *named* is insistent on UDP checksumming for good reason: it makes copious use of UDP and needs those UDP datagrams to arrive unmolested.

The solution to this problem is to enable UDP checksums on your system. The BIND distribution has documentation on that in *shres/sunos/INSTALL* and *src/port/sunos/shres/ISSUES* (in the BIND 8 distribution).

Other Nameservers Don't Cache Your Negative Answers

You need a keen eye to notice this problem, and, if you're running BIND 8, you'd have to have turned off an important feature to have caused the problem. If you're running BIND 9, though, the feature is turned off by default. If you're running a BIND 8 or 9 nameserver and other resolvers and servers seem to ignore your server's cached negative responses, *auth-nxdomain* is probably off.

auth-nxdomain is an *options* substatement that tells a BIND 8 or 9 nameserver to flag cached negative responses as authoritative, even though they're not. That is, if your nameserver has cached the fact that *titanic.movie.edu* does not exist from the authoritative *movie.edu* nameservers, *auth-nxdomain* tells your server to pass along that cached response to resolvers and servers that query it as though it were the authoritative nameserver for *movie.edu*.

The reason this feature is sometimes necessary is that some nameservers check to make sure that negative responses (such as an NXDOMAIN return code or no records with a NOERROR return code) are marked authoritative. In the days before negative caching, negative responses *had* to be authoritative, so this was a sensible sanity check. With the advent of negative caching, however, a negative response could come from the cache. To make sure that older servers don't ignore such answers, though, or consider them errors, BIND 8 and 9 let you falsely flag those responses as authoritative. In fact, that's the default behavior for a BIND 8 nameserver, so you shouldn't see remote queriers ignoring your BIND 8 server's negative responses unless you've explicitly turned off *auth-nxdomain*. BIND 9 nameservers, on the other hand, have *auth-nxdomain* off by default, so queriers may ignore their responses even if you haven't touched the config file.

TTL Not Set

As we mentioned in Chapter 4, RFC 2308 was published just before BIND 8.2 was released. RFC 2308 changed the semantics of the last field in the SOA record to be the negative-caching TTL and introduced a new control statement, $TTL, to set the default TTL for a zone datafile.

If you upgrade to a BIND 8 nameserver newer than 8.2 without adding the necessary $TTL control statements to your zone datafiles, you'll see messages like this one in your nameserver's *syslog* output:

```
Sep 26 19:34:39 toystory named[22116]: Zone "movie.edu" (file db.movie.edu): No
default TTL ($TTL <value>) set, using SOA minimum instead
```

BIND 8 generously assumes that you just haven't read RFC 2308 yet and is content to use the last field of the SOA record as both the zone's default TTL and its negative-caching TTL. BIND 9 nameservers older than 9.2.0, however, aren't so forgiving:

```
Sep 26 19:35:54 toystory named[22124]: dns_master_load: db.movie.edu:7: no TTL
    specified
Sep 26 19:35:54 toystory named[22124]: dns_zone_load: zone movie.edu/IN:
    database db.movie.edu: dns_db_load failed: no ttl
Sep 26 19:35:54 toystory named[22124]: loading zones: no ttl
Sep 26 19:35:54 toystory named[22124]: exiting (due to fatal error)
```

So before upgrading to BIND 9, be sure that you add the necessary $TTL control statements.

TSIG Errors

As we said in Chapter 11, transaction signatures require time synchronization and key synchronization (the same key on either end of the transaction, plus the same key name) to work. Here are a couple of errors that may arise if you lose time synchronization or use different keys or key names:

- Here's an error you'd see on a BIND 8 nameserver if you had configured TSIG but had too much clock skew between your primary nameserver and a slave:

```
Sep 27 10:47:49 wormhole named[22139]: Err/TO getting serial# for "movie.edu"
Sep 27 10:47:49 wormhole named-xfer[22584]: SOA TSIG verification from server
[192.249.249.3], zone movie.edu: message had BADTIME set (18)
```

  Here, your nameserver tries to check the serial number of the *movie.edu* zone on *toystory.movie.edu* (192.249.249.3). The response from *toystory.movie.edu* doesn't verify because *wormhole.movie.edu*'s clock shows a time difference of more than 10 minutes from the time the response was signed. The *Err/TO* message is just a byproduct of the failure of the TSIG-signed response to verify.

- If you use a different key name on either end of the transaction, even if the data the key name refers to is the same, you'll see an error like this one from your BIND 8 nameserver:

```
Sep 27 12:02:44 wormhole named-xfer[22651]: SOA TSIG verification from server
[209.8.5.250], zone movie.edu: BADKEY(-17)
```

This time, the TSIG-signed response doesn't check out because the verifier can't find a key with the name specified in the TSIG record. You'd see the same error if the key name matched but pointed to different data.

As always, BIND 9 is considerably more closed-mouthed about TSIG failure, reporting only:

```
Sep 27 13:35:42.804 client 192.249.249.1#1115: query: movie.edu SOA
Sep 27 13:35:42.804 client 192.249.249.1#1115: error
```

at debug level 3 for both previous scenarios.

Problem Symptoms

Some problems, unfortunately, aren't as easy to identify as the ones we listed. You'll experience some misbehavior but won't be able to attribute it directly to its cause, often because any of a number of problems can cause the symptoms you see. For cases like this, we'll suggest some of the common causes of these symptoms and ways to isolate them.

Local Name Can't Be Looked Up

The first thing to do when a program such as *ssh* or *ftp* can't look up a local domain name is to use *nslookup* or *dig* to try to look up the same name. When we say "the same name," we mean *literally* the same name: don't add labels and a trailing dot if the user didn't type them. Don't query a different nameserver than the user did.

As often as not, the user mistyped the name or doesn't understand how the search list works and just needs direction. Occasionally, you'll turn up real host configuration errors:

- Syntax errors in *resolv.conf* (problem 11 in the earlier section "Potential Problem List")
- An unset local domain name (problem 12)

You can check for either of these using *nslookup*'s *set all* command.

If *nslookup* points to a problem with the nameserver rather than with the host configuration, check for the problems associated with the type of nameserver. If the nameserver is the primary for the zone, but it isn't responding with data you think it should:

- Check that the zone datafile contains the data in question and that the nameserver has loaded it (problem 2). A database dump can tell you for sure whether the data was loaded.
- Check the configuration file and the pertinent zone datafile for syntax errors (problem 5). Check the nameserver's *syslog* output for indications of those errors.
- Ensure that the records have trailing dots, if they require them (problem 6).

If the nameserver is a slave server for the zone, you should first check whether its master has the correct data. If it does, and the slave doesn't:

- Make sure you've incremented the serial number on the primary (problem 1).
- Look for a problem on the slave in updating the zone (problem 3).

If the primary *doesn't* have the correct data, of course, diagnose the problem on the primary.

If the problem server is a caching-only nameserver:

- Make sure it has its root hints (problem 7).
- Check that your parent zone's delegation to your zone exists and is correct (problems 9 and 10). Remember that to a caching-only server, your zone looks like any other remote zone. Even though the host it runs on may be inside your zone, the caching-only nameserver must be able to locate an authoritative server for your zone from your parent zone's servers.

Remote Names Can't Be Looked Up

If your local lookups succeed but you can't look up domain names outside your local zones, there is a different set of problems to check:

- First, did you just set up your nameservers? You might have omitted the root hints data (problem 7).
- Can you *ping* the remote zone's nameservers? Maybe you can't reach the remote zone's servers because of connectivity loss (problem 8).
- Is the remote zone new? Maybe its delegation hasn't yet appeared (problem 9). Or the delegation information for the remote zone may be wrong or out of date due to neglect (problem 10).
- Does the domain name actually exist on the remote zone's servers (problem 2)? On all of them (problems 1 and 3)?

Wrong or Inconsistent Answer

If you get the wrong answer when looking up a local domain name, or an inconsistent answer depending on which nameserver you ask or when you ask, first check the synchronization between your nameservers:

- Are they all holding the same serial number for the zone? Did you forget to increment the serial number on the primary after you made a change (problem 1)? If you did, the nameservers may all have the same serial number, but they will answer differently out of their authoritative data.

- Did you roll the serial number back to 1 (problem 1 again)? Then the primary's serial number will appear much lower than the slaves' serial numbers.

- Did you forget to reload the primary (problem 2)? Then the primary will return (via *nslookup* or *dig*, for example) a different serial number from the one in the zone datafile.

- Are the slaves having trouble updating from their master(s) (problem 3)? If so, they should have *syslog*ged appropriate error messages.

- Is the nameserver's round-robin feature rotating the addresses of the domain name you're looking up?

If you get these results when looking up a domain name in a remote zone, you should check whether the remote zone's nameservers have lost synchronization. You can use tools such as *nslookup* and *dig* to determine whether the remote zone's administrator forgot to increment the serial number, for example. If the nameservers answer differently from their authoritative data but show the same serial number, the serial number probably wasn't incremented. If the primary's serial number is much lower than the slaves', the primary's serial number was probably accidentally reset. We usually assume a zone's primary nameserver is running on the host listed in the MNAME (first) field of the SOA record.

You probably can't determine conclusively that the primary hasn't been reloaded, though. It's also difficult to pin down updating problems between remote nameservers. In cases like this, if you've determined that the remote nameservers are giving out incorrect data, contact the zone administrator and (gently) relay what you've found. This will help the administrator track down the problem on the remote end.

If you can determine that a parent nameserver—a remote zone's parent, your zone's parent, or even one in your zone—is giving out a bad answer, check whether this is coming from old delegation information. Sometimes this requires contacting both the administrator of the remote zone and the administrator of its parent to compare the delegation and the current, correct list of authoritative nameservers.

If you can't induce the administrator to fix the data or if you can't track down the administrator, you can always use the *bogus server* substatement to instruct your nameserver not to query that particular server.

Lookups Take a Long Time

Slow name resolution is usually due to one of two problems:

- Connectivity loss (problem 8), which you can diagnose with nameserver debugging output and tools such as *ping*
- Incorrect delegation information (problem 10) pointing to the wrong nameservers or the wrong IP addresses

Usually, going over the debugging output and sending a few *ping*s will point to one or the other: either you can't reach the nameservers at all, or you can reach the hosts but the nameservers aren't responding.

Sometimes, though, the results are inconclusive. For example, the parent nameservers delegate to a set of nameservers that don't respond to *ping*s or queries, but connectivity to the remote network seems all right (a *traceroute*, for example, will get you to the remote network's "doorstep"—the last router between you and the host). Is the delegation information so badly out of date that the nameservers have long since moved to other addresses? Are the hosts simply down? Or is there really a remote network problem? Usually, finding out requires a call or a message to the administrator of the remote zone. (Remember, *whois* gives you phone numbers!)

rlogin and rsh to Host Fails Access Check

This is a problem you expect to see right after you set up your nameservers. Users unaware of the change from the host table to domain name service won't know to update their *.rhosts* files. (We covered what needs to be updated in Chapter 6.) Consequently, *rlogin*'s or *rsh*'s access check will fail and deny the user access.

Other causes of this problem are missing or incorrect *in-addr.arpa* delegation (problems 9 and 10) or forgetting to add a PTR record for the client host (problem 4). If you've recently upgraded to BIND 4.9 or newer and have PTR data for more than one *in-addr.arpa* zone in a single zone datafile, your nameserver may be ignoring the out-of-zone data. Any of these situations will result in the same behavior:

```
% rlogin wormhole
Password:
```

In other words, the user is prompted for a password despite having set up password-less access with *.rhosts* or *hosts.equiv*. If you were to look at the *syslog* file on the destination host (*wormhole.movie.edu*, in this case), you'd probably see something like this:

```
May  4 18:06:22 wormhole inetd[22514]: login/tcp: Connection
        from unknown (192.249.249.213)
```

You can tell which problem it is by stepping through the resolution process with your favorite query tool. First, query one of your *in-addr.arpa* zone's parent nameservers for NS records for your *in-addr.arpa* zone. If these are correct, query the nameservers listed for the PTR record corresponding to the IP address of the *rlogin* or *rsh* client. Make sure they all have the PTR record and that the record maps to the right domain name. If not all the nameservers have the record, check for a loss of synchronization between the primary and the slaves (problems 1 and 3).

Access to Services Denied

Sometimes *rlogin* and *rsh* aren't the only services to go. Occasionally, you'll install BIND on your server and your diskless hosts won't boot, and hosts won't be able to mount disks from the server, either.

If this happens, make sure that the case of the domain names your nameservers return agrees with the case your previous name service returned. For example, if you are running NIS and your NIS host maps contain only lowercase names, you should make sure your nameservers also return lowercase domain names. Some programs are case-sensitive and won't recognize names in a different case in a datafile, such as */etc/bootparams* or */etc/exports*.

Can't Get Rid of Old Data

Sometimes, after decommissioning a nameserver or changing a server's IP address, you'll find the old address record lingering around. An old record may show up in a nameserver's cache or in a zone datafile weeks or even months later. The record clearly should have timed out of any caches by now. So why's it still there? Well, there are a few reasons this happens. We'll describe the simpler cases first.

Old delegation information

The first (and simplest) case occurs if a parent zone doesn't keep up with its children or if the children don't inform the parent of changes to the authoritative nameservers for the zone. If the *edu* administrators have this old delegation information for *movie.edu*:

```
$ORIGIN movie.edu.
@       86400   IN  NS    toystory
        86400   IN  NS    wormhole
toystory        86400   IN  A   192.249.249.3
wormhole        86400   IN  A   192.249.249.254 ; wormhole's former
                                                ; IP address
```

the *edu* nameservers will give out the bogus old address for *wormhole.movie.edu*.

This is easily corrected once it's isolated to the parent zone's nameservers: just contact the parent zone's administrator and ask to have the delegation information updated. If your parent zone is one of the gTLDs, you may be able to fix the problem by filling out a form on your registrar's web site to modify the information about the nameserver. If any of the child zone's nameservers have cached the bad data, kill them (to clear out their caches), delete any backup zone datafiles that contain the bad data, and restart them.

Registration of a non-nameserver

This is a problem unique to the gTLD zones: *com*, *net*, and *org*. Sometimes, you'll find the gTLD nameservers giving out stale address information about a host in one of your zones—and not even a nameserver! But why would the gTLD nameservers have information about an arbitrary host in one of your zones?

Here's the answer: you can register hosts in the gTLD zones that aren't nameservers at all, such as your web server. For example, you can register an address for *www.foo.com* through a *com* registrar, and the *com* nameservers will give out that address. You shouldn't, though, because you'll lose a fair amount of control over the address. If you need to change the address, it could take a day or more to push the change through your registrar. If you run the *foo.com* primary nameserver, you can make the change almost instantly.

What have I got?

How do you determine which of these problems is plaguing you? Pay attention to which nameservers are distributing the old data and which zones the data relates to:

- Is the nameserver a gTLD nameserver? Check for a stale, registered address.
- Is the nameserver your parent nameserver but not a gTLD nameserver? Check the parent for old delegation information.

That's about all we can think to cover. It's certainly not a comprehensive list, but we hope it'll help you solve the more common problems you encounter with DNS and give you ideas about how to approach the rest. Boy, if we'd only had a troubleshooting guide when *we* started!

## CHAPTER 15

Programming with the Resolver and Nameserver Library Routines

*"I know what you're thinking about," said
Tweedledum; "but it isn't so, nohow."*

*"Contrariwise," continued Tweedledee, "if it was so, it
might be; and if it were so, it would be; but as it isn't,
it ain't. That's logic."*

I bet you think resolver programming is hard. Contrariwise! It isn't very hard, really. The format of DNS messages is quite straightforward; you don't have to deal with ASN.1* at all, as you do with SNMP. And you have nifty library routines to make parsing DNS messages easy. We've included portions of RFC 1035 in Appendix A. However, you might find it handy to have a copy of RFC 1035 to look at as we go through this chapter; at least have a copy of it nearby when you write your own DNS programs.

Shell Script Programming with nslookup

Before you go off and write a C program to do your DNS chore, you should write the program as a shell script using *nslookup* or *dig*. There are good reasons to start with a shell script:

- You can write the shell script much faster than you can write a C program.
- If you're not comfortable with DNS, you can work out the details of your program's logic with a quick shell script prototype. When you finally write the C program, you can focus on the additional control you have with C rather than spending your time reworking the basic functionality.

---

* ASN.1 stands for Abstract Syntax Notation. ASN.1 is a method of encoding object types, accepted as an international standard by the International Organization for Standardization.

- You might find out that the shell script version does your task well enough so that you don't have to write the C program after all. And not only is it quicker to write shell scripts, but they're easier to maintain if you stick with them for the long run.

If you prefer Perl over plain old shell programming, you can use Perl instead. At the end of this chapter, we'll show you how to use the Perl Net::DNS module written by Michael Fuhr.

A Typical Problem

Before you write a program, you need a problem to solve. Let's suppose you want your network management system to watch over your primary master and slave nameservers. You want it to notify you of several problems: a nameserver that isn't running (it might have died), a nameserver that is not authoritative for a zone it is supposed to be authoritative for (the config file or zone datafile might have been messed up), or a nameserver that has fallen behind in updating its zone data (the primary master's serial number might have been decreased accidentally).

Each problem is easily detectable. If a nameserver is not running on a host, the host sends back an ICMP *port unreachable* message. You can find this out with either a query tool or the resolver routines. Checking whether a nameserver is authoritative for a zone is easy: ask it for the zone's SOA record. If the answer is nonauthoritative or the nameserver does not have the SOA record, there's a problem. You'll have to ask for the SOA record in a *nonrecursive* query so that the nameserver doesn't go off and look up the SOA record from another server. Once you have the SOA record, you can extract the serial number.

Solving This Problem with a Script

This problem requires a program that takes the domain name of a zone as an argument, looks up the nameservers for that zone, and then queries each nameserver for the SOA record for the zone. The response will show whether the nameserver is authoritative, and it will show the zone's serial number. If there is no response, the program needs to determine if there's even a nameserver running on the host. Once you write this program, you should run it on each zone you want to watch over. Since this program looks up the nameservers (by looking up the NS records for the zone), we assume that you have listed all your nameservers in NS records in your zone data. If that's not the case, you will have to change this program to read a list of nameservers from the command line.

Let's write the basic program as a shell script that uses *nslookup*. First, we figure out what the output of *nslookup* looks like so that we can parse it with Unix tools. We'll look up NS records to find out which nameservers are supposed to be authoritative for the zone, both when the server is authoritative for the zone that contains the NS records and when it isn't:

```
% nslookup

Default Server:  relay.hp.com
Address:  15.255.152.2

> set type=ns
```

Find out what the response looks like when the nameserver is not authoritative for the NS records:

```
> mit.edu.

Server:  relay.hp.com
Address:  15.255.152.2

Non-authoritative answer:
mit.edu nameserver = STRAWB.MIT.EDU
mit.edu nameserver = W20NS.MIT.EDU
mit.edu nameserver = BITSY.MIT.EDU

Authoritative answers can be found from:
MIT.EDU nameserver = STRAWB.MIT.EDU
MIT.EDU nameserver = W20NS.MIT.EDU
MIT.EDU nameserver = BITSY.MIT.EDU
STRAWB.MIT.EDU  internet address = 18.71.0.151
W20NS.MIT.EDU   internet address = 18.70.0.160
BITSY.MIT.EDU   internet address = 18.72.0.3
```

Then, find out what the response looks like when the nameserver *is* authoritative for the NS records:

```
> server strawb.mit.edu.

Default Server:  strawb.mit.edu
Address:  18.71.0.151

> mit.edu.

Server:  strawb.mit.edu
Address:  18.71.0.151

mit.edu nameserver = BITSY.MIT.EDU
mit.edu nameserver = STRAWB.MIT.EDU
mit.edu nameserver = W20NS.MIT.EDU
BITSY.MIT.EDU   internet address = 18.72.0.3
STRAWB.MIT.EDU  internet address = 18.71.0.151
W20NS.MIT.EDU   internet address = 18.70.0.160
```

You can see from this output that we can grab the domain names of the nameservers by looking for the lines that contain *nameserver* and saving the last field. When the nameserver wasn't authoritative for the NS records, it printed them twice, so we'll have to weed out duplicates.

Next, we look up the SOA record for the zone, both when the server is authoritative for the zone that contains the SOA record and when it isn't. We turn off *recurse* so the nameserver doesn't go off and query an authoritative nameserver for the SOA:

```
% nslookup

Default Server:  relay.hp.com
Address:  15.255.152.2

> set type=soa

> set norecurse
```

Find out what the response looks like when the nameserver is not authoritative and does not have the SOA record:

```
> mit.edu.

Server:  relay.hp.com
Address:  15.255.152.2

Authoritative answers can be found from:
MIT.EDU nameserver = STRAWB.MIT.EDU
MIT.EDU nameserver = W20NS.MIT.EDU
MIT.EDU nameserver = BITSY.MIT.EDU
STRAWB.MIT.EDU  internet address = 18.71.0.151
W20NS.MIT.EDU   internet address = 18.70.0.160
BITSY.MIT.EDU   internet address = 18.72.0.3
```

Then, find out what the response looks like when the nameserver *is* authoritative for the zone:

```
> server strawb.mit.edu.

Default Server:  strawb.mit.edu
Address:  18.71.0.151

> mit.edu.

Server:  strawb.mit.edu
Address:  18.71.0.151

mit.edu
        origin = BITSY.MIT.EDU
        mail addr = NETWORK-REQUEST.BITSY.MIT.EDU
        serial = 1995
        refresh = 3600 (1H)
        retry   = 900 (15M)
        expire  = 3600000 (5w6d16h)
        minimum ttl = 21600 (6H)
```

When the nameserver was not authoritative for the zone, it returned references to other nameservers. If the nameserver had previously looked up the SOA record and cached it, the nameserver would have returned the SOA record and said that it was nonauthoritative. We need to check for both cases. When the nameserver returns the SOA record and it is authoritative, we can grab the serial number from the line that contains *serial*.

Now we need to see what *nslookup* returns when no nameserver is running on a host. We'll change servers to a host that does not normally run a nameserver and look up an SOA record:

```
% nslookup

Default Server:  relay.hp.com
Address:  15.255.152.2

> server galt.cs.purdue.edu.

Default Server:  galt.cs.purdue.edu
Address:  128.10.2.39

> set type=soa

> mit.edu.

Server:  galt.cs.purdue.edu
Address:  128.10.2.39

*** galt.cs.purdue.edu can't find mit.edu.: No response from server
```

Last, we need to see what *nslookup* returns if a host is not responding. We can test this by switching nameservers to an unused IP address on our LAN:

```
% nslookup

Default Server:  relay.hp.com
Address:  15.255.152.2

> server 15.255.152.100

Default Server:  [15.255.152.100]
Address:  15.255.152.100

> set type=soa

> mit.edu.

Server:  [15.255.152.100]
Address:  15.255.152.100

*** Request to [15.255.152.100] timed-out
```

In the last two cases, the error message was written to *stderr*.[*] We can use that fact when writing our shell script. Now we are ready to compose the shell script. We'll call it *check_soa*:

```
#!/bin/sh
if test "$1" = ""
then
    echo usage: $0 zone
    exit 1
fi
ZONE=$1
#
# Use nslookup to discover the name servers for this zone ($1).
# Use awk to grab the name server's domain names from the nameserver lines.
# (The names are always in the last field.)  Use sort -u to weed out
# duplicates; we don't actually care about collation.
#
SERVERS=`nslookup -type=ns $ZONE |\
                awk '/nameserver/ {print $NF}' | sort -u`
if test "$SERVERS" = ""
then
    #
    # Didn't find any servers.  Just quit silently; nslookup will
    # have detected this error and printed a message.  That will
    # suffice.
    #
    exit 1
fi
#
# Check each server's SOA serial number.  The output from
# nslookup is saved in two temp files: nso.$$ (standard output)
# and nse.$$ (standard error).  These files are rewritten on
# every iteration.  Turn off defname and search since we
# should be dealing with fully qualified domain names.
#
# NOTE: this loop is rather long; don't be fooled.
#
for i in $SERVERS
do
  nslookup >/tmp/nso.$$ 2>/tmp/nse.$$ <<-EOF
    server $i
    set nosearch
    set nodefname
    set norecurse
    set q=soa
    $ZONE
EOF
  #
  # Does this response indicate that the current server ($i) is
  # authoritative?  The server is NOT authoritative if (a) the
```

---

[*] Not all versions of *nslookup* print the last error message for a timeout. Be sure to check what yours prints.

```
# response says so, or (b) the response tells you to find
# authoritative info elsewhere.
#
if egrep "Non-authoritative|Authoritative answers can be" \
                                    /tmp/nso.$$ >/dev/null
then
   echo $i is not authoritative for $ZONE
   continue
fi
#
# We know the server is authoritative; extract the serial number.
#
SERIAL=`cat /tmp/nso.$$ | grep serial | sed -e "s/.*= //"`
if test "$SERIAL" = ""
then
   #
   # We get here if SERIAL is null.  In this case, there should
   # be an error message from nslookup; so cat the "standard
   # error" file.
   #
   cat /tmp/nse.$$
else
   #
   # Report the server's domain name and its serial number.
   #
   echo $i has serial number $SERIAL
fi
done   # end of the "for" loop
#
# Delete the temporary files.
#
rm -f /tmp/nso.$$ /tmp/nse.$$
```

Here is what the output looks like:

```
% check_soa mit.edu

BITSY.MIT.EDU has serial number 1995
STRAWB.MIT.EDU has serial number 1995
W20NS.MIT.EDU has serial number 1995
```

If you are pressed for time, this short tool will solve your problem, and you can go on to other work. If you find that you are checking lots of zones and that this tool is too slow, you'll want to convert it to a C program. Also, if you want more control over the error messages—rather than relying on *nslookup* for error messages—you'll have to write a C program. We'll do that later in this chapter.

C Programming with the Resolver Library Routines

Before writing any code, though, you need to be familiar with the DNS message format and the resolver library routines. In the shell script we just wrote, *nslookup* parsed the DNS message. In a C program, though, you have to do the parsing. Let's start this section on programming by looking at the DNS message format.

DNS Message Format

You've seen the DNS message format before, in Chapter 12. It looks like this:

- Header section
- Question section
- Answer section
- Authority section
- Additional section

The format of the header section is described in RFC 1035 on pages 26–28, and in Appendix A of this book. It looks like this:

```
query identification number (2 octets)
query response (1 bit)
opcode (4 bits)
authoritative answer (1 bit)
truncation (1 bit)
recursion desired (1 bit)
recursion available (1 bit)
reserved (3 bits)
response code (4 bits)
question count (2 octets)
answer record count (2 octets)
name server record count (2 octets)
additional record count (2 octets)
```

You'll also find opcode, response code, type, and class values defined in *arpa/nameser.h*, as well as routines to extract this information from a message. We'll discuss these routines, part of the *nameserver library*, shortly.

The question section is described on pages 28–29 of RFC 1035. It looks like this:

```
domain name (variable length)
query type (2 octets)
query class (2 octets)
```

The answer, authority, and additional sections are described on pages 29–30 of RFC 1035. These sections comprise some number of resource records that look like this:

```
domain name (variable length)
type (2 octets)
```

```
class (2 octets)
TTL (4 octets)
resource data length (2 octets)
resource data (variable length)
```

The header section contains a count of how many of these resource records are in each section.

Domain Name Storage

As you can see, the names stored in the DNS message are of variable length. Unlike C, DNS does not store the names as null-terminated strings. Domain names are stored as a series of length/value pairs ending with an octet of 0. Each label in a domain name is composed of a length octet and a label. A name like *venera.isi.edu* is stored as:

```
6 venera  3  isi  3 edu 0
```

You can imagine how much of a DNS message could be devoted to storing names. The developers of DNS recognized this and came up with a simple way to compress domain names.

Domain Name Compression

Often, an entire domain name or, at least, the trailing labels of a domain name match a name already stored in the message. Domain name compression eliminates the repetition of domain names by storing a pointer to the earlier occurrence of the name instead of inserting the name again. Here is how it works. Suppose a response message already contains the name *venera.isi.edu*. If the name *vaxa.isi.edu* is added to the response, the label *vaxa* is stored, and then a pointer to the earlier occurrence of *isi.edu* is added. So how are these pointers implemented?

The first two bits of the length octet indicate whether a length/label pair or a pointer to a length/label pair follows. If the first two bits are zeros, then the length and label follow. As you may remember from way back in Chapter 2, a label is limited to 63 characters. That's because the length field has only the remaining six bits for the length of the label—enough to represent the lengths 0–63. If the first two bits of the length octet are ones, then what follows is not a length but a pointer. The pointer is the last 6 bits of the length octet *and* the next octet—14 bits in total. The pointer is an offset from the start of the DNS message. Now, when *vaxa.isi.edu* is compressed into a buffer containing only *venera.isi.edu*, this is what results:

```
byte offset: 0 123456 7 890 1 234 5 6 7890 1    2
             -------------+--------------+--------
pkt contents: 6 venera 3 isi 3 edu 0 4 vaxa 0xC0 7
```

The *0xC0* is a byte with the high two bits ones and the rest of the bits zeros. Since the high two bits are ones, this is a pointer instead of a length. The pointer value is 7: the last six bits of the first octet are zeros and the second octet is 7. At offset seven in this buffer, you find the rest of the domain name that begins with *vaxa*, which is *isi.edu*.

In this example, we only showed the compression in two domain names in a buffer, not a whole DNS message. A DNS message would have had a header as well as other fields. This example is intended only to give you an idea of how the domain name compression works. Now the good news: you don't really need to care how names are compressed as long as the library routines do it properly. What you do need to know is how parsing a DNS response message can get messed up if you are off by one byte. For example, try to expand the name starting with byte two instead of byte one. You'll discover that "v" doesn't make a very good length octet or pointer.

The Resolver Library Routines

The resolver library contains the routines that you need to write your application. You'll use these routines to generate queries. You'll use the *nameserver library* routines, explained next, to parse the response.

In case you're wondering why we're not using the BIND 9 resolver routines in our code, BIND 9 includes library routines to perform lots of powerful DNS functions, but they're oriented toward the BIND 9 nameserver's needs and are very complicated to use, we're told. BIND 9 includes the BIND 8 resolver in *lib/bind/resolv* and we will continue to use that for now. A program linked against the BIND 8 library routines will work just fine with a BIND 9 nameserver.

Here are the header files you must include:

```
#include <sys/types.h>
#include <netinet/in.h>
#include <arpa/nameser.h>
#include <resolv.h>
```

Now let's look at the resolver library routines.

herror and h_errno

```
extern int h_errno;
int herror(const char *s)
```

herror is a routine like *perror*, except that it prints out a string based on the value of the external variable *h_errno* instead of *errno*. The only argument is:

s   A string used to identify the error message. If a string *s* is supplied, it is printed first, followed by ":" and a string based on the value of *h_errno*.

Here are the possible values of *h_errno*:

HOST_NOT_FOUND
> The domain name does not exist. The return code in the nameserver response was NXDOMAIN.

TRY_AGAIN
> Either the nameserver is not running, or the nameserver returned SERVFAIL.

NO_RECOVERY
> Either the domain name could not be compressed because it was an invalid domain name (e.g., a name missing a label—*.movie.edu*) or the nameserver returned FORMERR, NOTIMP, or REFUSED.

NO_DATA
> The domain name exists, but there is no data of the requested type.

NETDB_INTERNAL
> There was a library error unrelated to the network or name service. Instead, see *errno* for the problem description.

res_init

```
int res_init(void)
```

res_init reads *resolv.conf* and initializes a data structure called *_res* (more about that later). All the previously discussed routines will call *res_init* if they detect that it hasn't been called previously. Or you can call it on your own; this is useful if you want to change some of the defaults before calling the first resolver library routine. If there are any lines in *resolv.conf* that *res_init* doesn't understand, it ignores them. *res_init* always returns 0, even if the manpage reserves the right to return –1.

res_mkquery

```
int res_mkquery(int op,
                const char *dname,
                int class,
                int type,
                const u_char *data,
                int datalen,
                const u_char *newrr,
                u_char *buf,
                int buflen)
```

res_mkquery creates the query message. It fills in all the header fields, compresses the domain name into the question section, and fills in the other question fields.

The *dname*, *class*, and *type* arguments are the same as for *res_search* and *res_query*. The remaining arguments are:

op

> The "operation" to be performed. This is normally QUERY, but it can be IQUERY (inverse query). However, as we've explained before, IQUERY is seldom used. BIND versions 4.9.4 and later, by default, do not even support IQUERY.

data

> A buffer containing the data for inverse queries. It is NULL when *op* is QUERY.

datalen

> The size of the *data* buffer. If *data* is NULL, then *datalen* is 0.

newrr

> A buffer used for the dynamic update code (covered in Chapter 10). Unless you are playing with this feature, it is always NULL.

buf

> A buffer in which *res_mkquery* places the query message. It should be PACKETSZ or larger, like the answer buffer in *res_search* and *res_query*.

buflen

> The size of the *buf* buffer (e.g., PACKETSZ).

res_mkquery returns the size of the query message or −1 if there was an error.

---

res_query

```
int res_query(const char *dname,
              int class,
              int type,
              u_char *answer,
              int anslen)
```

res_query is one of the "mid-level" resolver routines. It does all the real work in looking up the domain name: it makes a query message by calling *res_mkquery*, sends the query by calling *res_send*, and looks at enough of the response to determine whether your question was answered. In many cases, *res_query* is called by *res_search*, which just feeds it the different domain names to look up. As you'd expect, these two functions have the same arguments. *res_query* returns the size of the response, or it fills in *h_errno* and returns −1 if there was an error or the answer count was 0.

---

res_search

```
int res_search(const char *dname,
               int class,
               int type,
               u_char *answer,
               int anslen)
```

res_search is the "highest level" resolver routine, and is called by *gethostbyname*. *res_search* applies the search algorithm to the domain name passed to it. That is, it takes the domain name it receives (*dname*), "completes" the name (if it's not fully qualified) by adding the various domain names from the resolver search list, and calls *res_query* until it receives a successful response, indicating that it found a valid, fully qualified domain name. In addition to implementing the search algorithm, *res_search* looks in the file referenced by your HOSTALIASES environment variable. (The HOSTALIASES variable was described in Chapter 6.) So it also takes care of any "private" host aliases you might have. *res_search* returns the size of the response or fills in *h_errno* and returns −1 if there was an error or the answer count is 0. (*h_errno* is like *errno*, but for DNS lookups.)

Therefore, the only parameter that's really of interest to *res_search* is *dname*; the others are just passed through to *res_query* and the other resolver routines. The other arguments are:

class
> The class of the data you're looking up. This is almost always the constant C_IN, the Internet class. The class constants are defined in *arpa/nameser.h*.

type
> The type of data you're looking up. Again, this is a constant defined in *arpa/-nameser.h*. A typical value would be T_NS to retrieve a nameserver record, or T_MX to retrieve an MX record.

answer
> A buffer in which *res_search* will place the response message. Its size should be at least PACKETSZ (from *arpa/nameser.h*) bytes.

anslen
> The size of the *answer* buffer (e.g., PACKETSZ).

res_search returns the size of the response or −1 if there was an error.

res_send

```
int res_send(const u_char *msg,
             int msglen,
             u_char *answer,
             int anslen)
```

res_send implements the retry algorithm. It sends the query message, *msg*, in a UDP datagram, but it can also send it over a TCP stream. The response message is stored in *answer*. This routine, of all the resolver routines, is the only one to use black magic (unless you know all about connected datagram sockets). You've seen these arguments before in the other resolver routines:

msg
> The buffer containing the DNS query message

msglen
> The size of the message

answer
> The buffer in which to store the DNS response message

anslen
> The size of the answer message

res_send returns the size of the response or –1 if there was an error. If this routine returns –1 and *errno* is ECONNREFUSED, then there is no nameserver running on the target nameserver host.

You can look at *errno* to see if it is ECONNREFUSED after calling *res_search* or *res_query*. (*res_search* calls *res_query*, which calls *res_send*.) If you want to check *errno* after calling *res_query*, clear *errno* first. That way, you know the current call to *res_send* was the one that set *errno*. However, you don't have to clear *errno* before calling *res_search*. *res_search* clears *errno* itself before calling *res_query*.

The _res Structure

Each resolver routine (i.e., each routine whose name starts with *res_*) uses a common data structure called *_res*. You can change the behavior of the resolver routines by changing *_res*. If you want to change the number of times *res_send* retries a query, you can change the value of the *retry* field. If you want to turn off the resolver search algorithm, you turn off the RES_DNSRCH bit from the *options* mask. You'll find the all-important *_res* structure in *resolv.h*:

```
struct _ _res_state {
      int        retrans;    /* retransmission time interval */
      int        retry;      /* number of times to retransmit */
      u_long     options;    /* option flags - see below. */
      int        nscount;    /* number of name servers */
      struct sockaddr_in
                 nsaddr_list[MAXNS];   /* address of name server */
#define nsaddr nsaddr_list[0]          /* for backward compatibility */
      u_short id;                      /* current packet id */
      char    *dnsrch[MAXDNSRCH+1];    /* components of domain to search */
      char    defdname[MAXDNAME];      /* default domain */
      u_long  pfcode;                  /* RES_PRF_ flags - see below. */
      unsigned ndots:4;                /* threshold for initial abs. query */
      unsigned nsort:4;                /* number of elements in sort_list[] */
      char    unused[3];
      struct {
            struct in_addr  addr;      /* address to sort on */
            u_int32_t       mask;
      } sort_list[MAXRESOLVSORT];
};
```

The *options* field is a simple bit mask of the enabled options. To turn on a feature, turn on the corresponding bit in the options field. Bit masks for each of the options are defined in *resolv.h*; the options are:

RES_INIT

    If this bit is on, *res_init* has been called.

RES_DEBUG

    This bit causes resolver debugging messages to be printed—if the resolver routines were compiled with DEBUG, that is. Off is the default.

RES_AAONLY

Requires the answer to be authoritative, not from a nameserver's cache. It's too bad this isn't implemented, as it would be a useful feature. Given the BIND resolver's design, this feature would have to be implemented in the nameserver, and it's not.

RES_PRIMARY

Query the primary master nameserver only—again, not implemented.

RES_USEVC

Turn on this bit if you'd like the resolver to make its queries over a virtual circuit (TCP) connection instead of with UDP datagrams. As you might guess, there is a performance penalty for setting up and tearing down a TCP connection. Off is the default.

RES_STAYOPEN

If you are making your queries over a TCP connection, turning on this bit causes the connection to be left open, so you can use it to query the same remote nameserver again. Otherwise, the connection is torn down after the query has been answered. Off is the default.

RES_IGNTC

If the nameserver response has the truncation bit set, then the default resolver behavior is to retry the query using TCP. If this bit is turned on, the truncation bit in the response message is ignored, and the query is not retried using TCP. Off is the default.

RES_RECURSE

The default behavior for the BIND resolver is to send recursive queries. Turning off this bit turns off the "recursion desired" bit in the query message. On is the default.

RES_DEFNAMES

The default behavior for the BIND resolver is to append the local domain name to any domain name that does not have a dot in it. Turning off this bit turns off appending the local domain name. On is the default.

RES_DNSRCH

The default behavior for the BIND resolver is to append each element of the search list to a domain name that does not end in a dot. Turning off this bit turns off the search list function. On is the default.

RES_INSECURE1

The default behavior for a 4.9.3 or later BIND resolver is to ignore answers from nameservers that were not queried. Turning on this bit disables this security check. Off (i.e., security check on) is the default.

RES_INSECURE2

The default behavior for a 4.9.3 or later BIND resolver is to ignore answers in which the question section of the response does not match the question section of the original query. Turning on this bit disables this security check. Off (i.e., security check on) is the default.

RES_NOALIASES

The default behavior for the BIND resolver is to use aliases defined in the file specified by the user's HOSTALIASES environment variable. Turning on this bit disables the HOSTALIASES feature for 4.9.3 and later BIND resolvers. Previous resolvers did not allow this feature to be disabled. Off is the default.

RES_USE_INET6

Tells the resolver to return IPv6 addresses (in addition to IPv4 addresses) to the *gethostbyname* function.

RES_ROTATE

Normally, a resolver that sends repeated queries always queries the first nameserver in *resolv.conf* first. With RES_ROTATE set, a BIND 8.2 or later resolver sends its first query to the first nameserver in *resolv.conf*, its second to the second nameserver, and so on. (See the *options rotate* directive in Chapter 6 for details.) The default is not to rotate nameservers.

RES_NOCHECKNAME

Since BIND 4.9.4, resolvers have checked the domain names in responses to make sure they conform to the naming guidelines described in Chapter 4. BIND 8.2 resolvers offer the option of turning off the name-checking mechanism. Off (i.e., name check on) is the default.

RES_KEEPTSIG

This option tells a BIND 8.2 or later resolver not to strip the TSIG record from a signed DNS message. This way, the application that called the resolver can examine it.

RES_BLAST

"Blast" all recursive servers by sending queries to them simultaneously. Not implemented yet.

RES_DEFAULT

This isn't a single option, but rather a combination of the RES_RECURSE, RES_DEFNAMES, and RES_DNSRCH options, all of which are on by default. You normally won't need to set RES_DEFAULT explicitly; it's set for you when you call *res_init*.

The Nameserver Library Routines

The nameserver library contains routines you need to parse response messages. Here are the header files you must include:

```
#include <sys/types.h>
#include <netinet/in.h>
#include <netdb.h>
```

```
#include <arpa/nameser.h>
#include <resolv.h>
```

Following are the nameserver library routines.

ns_get16 and ns_put16

```
u_int ns_get16(const u_char *cp)
void  ns_put16(u_int s, u_char *cp)
```

The DNS messages have fields that are unsigned short integer (type, class, and data length, to name a few). *ns_get16* returns a 16-bit integer pointed to by *cp*, and *ns_put16* assigns the 16-bit value of *s* to the location pointed to by *cp*.

ns_get32 and ns_put32

```
u_long ns_get32(const u_char *cp)
void   ns_put32(u_long l, u_char *cp)
```

These routines are like their 16-bit counterparts except that they deal with a 32-bit integer instead of a 16-bit integer. The TTL (time to live) field of a resource record is a 32-bit integer.

ns_initparse

```
int ns_initparse(const u_char *msg,
                 int msglen,
                 ns_msg *handle)
```

ns_initparse is the first routine you must call before you use the other nameserver library routines. *ns_initparse* fills in the data structure pointed to by *handle*, which is a parameter passed to other routines. The arguments are:

msg
> A pointer to the beginning of the response message buffer

msglen
> The size of the message buffer

handle
> A pointer to a data structure filled in by *ns_initparse*

ns_initparse returns 0 on success and −1 if it fails to parse the message buffer.

ns_msg_base, ns_msg_end, and ns_msg_size

```
const u_char *ns_msg_base(ns_msg handle)
const u_char *ns_msg_end(ns_msg handle)
int ns_msg_size(ns_msg handle)
```

These routines return a pointer to the start of the message, a pointer to the end of the message, and the size of the message. They return the data you passed into *ns_initparse*. The only argument is:

handle

A data structure filled in by *ns_initparse*

ns_msg_count

```
u_int16_t ns_msg_count(ns_msg handle, ns_sect section)
```

ns_msg_count returns a counter from the header section of the response message. Its arguments are:

handle

A data structure filled in by *ns_initparse*

section

An enumerated type that can have the following values:

```
ns_s_qd  /* Query: Question section */
ns_s_zn  /* Update: Zone section */
ns_s_an  /* Query: Answer section */
ns_s_pr  /* Update: Prerequisite section */
ns_s_ns  /* Query: Name Server section */
ns_s_ud  /* Update: Update section */
ns_s_ar  /* Query|Update: Additional records section */
```

ns_msg_get_flag

```
u_int16_t ns_msg_get_flag(ns_msg handle, ns_flag flag)
```

ns_msg_get_flag returns the "flag" fields from the header section of the response message. Its arguments are:

handle

A data structure filled in by *ns_initparse*

flag

An enumerated type that can have the following values:

```
ns_f_qr      /* Question/Response */
ns_f_opcode  /* Operation Code */
ns_f_aa      /* Authoritative Answer */
ns_f_tc      /* Truncation Occurred */
```

```
ns_f_rd      /* Recursion Desired */
ns_f_ra      /* Recursion Available */
ns_f_z       /* Must Be Zero */
ns_f_ad      /* Authentic Data (DNSSEC) */
ns_f_cd      /* Checking Disabled (DNSSEC) */
ns_f_rcode   /* Response Code */
ns_f_max
```

ns_msg_id

```
u_int16_t ns_msg_id(ns_msg handle)
```

ns_msg_id returns the identification from the header section (described earlier) of the response message. The only argument is:

handle
> A data structure filled in by *ns_initparse*

ns_name_compress

```
int ns_name_compress(const char *exp_dn,
                     u_char *comp_dn,
                     size_t length,
                     const u_char **dnptrs,
                     const u_char **lastdnptr)
```

ns_name_compress compresses a domain name. You won't normally call this routine yourself—you'll let *res_mkquery* do it for you. However, if you need to compress a name for some reason, this is the tool to do it. The arguments are:

exp_dn
> The "expanded" domain name that you supply—i.e., a normal, null-terminated string containing a fully qualified domain name.

comp_dn
> The place where *ns_name_compress* will store the compressed domain name.

length
> The size of the *comp_dn* buffer.

dnptrs
> An array of pointers to previously compressed domain names. *dnptrs[0]* points to the beginning of the message; the list ends with a NULL pointer. After you've initialized *dnptrs[0]* to the beginning of the message and *dnptrs[1]* to NULL, *dn_comp* updates the list each time you call it.

lastdnptr
> A pointer to the end of the *dnptrs* array. *ns_name_compress* needs to know where the end of the array is so it doesn't overrun it.

If you want to use this routine, look at how it is used in the BIND source in *src/lib/resolv/res_mkquery.c* (BIND 8) or *res/res_mkquery.c* (BIND 4). It's often easier to see how to use a routine from an example than from an explanation. *ns_name_compress* returns the size of the compressed name or –1 if there was an error.

ns_name_skip

`int ns_name_skip(const u_char **ptrptr, const u_char *eom)`

ns_name_skip is like *ns_name_uncompress*, but instead of uncompressing the name, it just skips over it. The arguments are:

ptrptr

> A pointer to a pointer to the name to skip over. The original pointer is advanced past the name.

eom

> A pointer to the first byte after the message. It is used to make sure that *ns_name_skip* doesn't go past the end of the message.
>
> *ns_name_skip* returns 0 if successful. It returns −1 if it fails to uncompress the name.

ns_name_uncompress

```
int ns_name_uncompress(const u_char *msg,
                       const u_char *eomorig,
                       const u_char *comp_dn,
                       char *exp_dn,
                       size_t length)
```

ns_name_uncompress expands a "compressed" domain name. You'll use this routine if you parse a nameserver response message, as we do in *check_soa*, the C program that follows. The arguments are:

msg

> A pointer to the beginning of your response message.

eomorig

> A pointer to the first byte after the message. It is used to make sure that *ns_name_uncompress* doesn't go past the end of the message.

comp_dn

> A pointer to the compressed domain name within the message.

exp_dn

> The place where *ns_name_uncompress* will store the expanded name. You should always allocate an array of MAXDNAME characters for the expanded name.

length

> The size of the *exp_dn* buffer.

ns_name_uncompress returns the size of the compressed name or −1 if there was an error. You might wonder why *ns_name_uncompress* returns the size of the *compressed* name, not the size of the *expanded* name. It does this because when you call *ns_name_uncompress*, you are parsing a DNS message and need to know how much space the compressed name occupied in the message so that you can skip over it.

ns_parserr

```
int ns_parserr(ns_msg *handle,
               ns_sect section,
               int rrnum,
               ns_rr *rr)
```

ns_parserr extracts information about a response record and stores it in *rr*, which is a parameter passed to other nameserver libarary routines. The arguments are:

handle

    A pointer to a data structure filled in by *ns_initparse*.

section

    The same parameter described in *ns_msg_count*.

rrnum

    A resource record number for the resource records in this section. Resource records start numbering at 0. *ns_msg_count* tells you how many resource records are in this section.

rr

    A pointer to a data structure to be initialized.

ns_parserr returns 0 on success and −1 if it fails to parse the response buffer.

ns_rr routines

```
char *ns_rr_name(ns_rr rr)
u_int16_t ns_rr_type(ns_rr rr)
u_int16_t ns_rr_class(ns_rr rr)
u_int32_t ns_rr_ttl(ns_rr rr)
u_int16_t ns_rr_rdlen(ns_rr rr)
const u_char *ns_rr_rdata(ns_rr rr)
```

These routines return individual fields from a response record. Their only argument is:

rr   A data structure filled in by *ns_parserr*

Parsing DNS Responses

The easiest way to learn how to parse a DNS message is to look at code that already does it. Assuming that you have the BIND source code, the best file to look through is *src/lib/resolv/res_debug.c* (BIND 8) or *lib/bind/resolv/res_debug.c* (BIND 8 resolver in the BIND 9 distribution). (If you're really determined to use BIND 9, you might have to read almost 3,000 lines of *lib/dns/message.c*.) *res_debug.c* contains *fp_query* (or *res_pquery* in BIND 8.2 and later), the function that prints out the DNS messages in the nameserver debugging output. Our sample program traces its parentage to code from this file.

You won't always want to parse the DNS response manually. An intermediate way to parse the response is to call *p_query*, which calls *fp_query*, to print out the DNS message. Then use Perl or *awk* to grab what you need. Cricket has been known to wimp out in this way.

A Sample Program: check_soa

Let's now look at a C program to solve the same problem for which we wrote a shell script earlier.

Here are the header files that are needed, the declarations for external variables, and the declarations of functions. Notice that we use both *h_errno* (for the resolver routines) and *errno*. We limit this program to checking 20 nameservers. You'll rarely see a zone with more than 10 nameservers, so an upper limit of 20 should suffice.

```
/*****************************************************************
 * check_soa -- Retrieve the SOA record from each name server    *
 *      for a given zone and print out the serial number.        *
 *                                                               *
 * usage: check_soa zone                                         *
 *                                                               *
 * The following errors are reported:                            *
 *      o There is no address for a server.                      *
 *      o There is no server running on this host.               *
 *      o There was no response from a server.                   *
 *      o The server is not authoritative for the zone.          *
 *      o The response had an error response code.               *
 *      o The response had more than one answer.                 *
 *      o The response answer did not contain an SOA record.     *
 *      o The expansion of a compressed domain name failed.      *
 *****************************************************************/

/* Various header files */
#include <sys/types.h>
#include <netinet/in.h>
#include <netdb.h>
#include <stdio.h>
#include <errno.h>
#include <arpa/nameser.h>
#include <resolv.h>

/* Error variables */
extern int h_errno;  /* for resolver errors */
extern int errno;    /* general system errors */

/* Our own routines; code included later in this chapter */
void nsError();            /* report resolver errors */
void findNameServers();    /* find a zone's name servers */
void addNameServers();     /* add name servers to our list */
void queryNameServers();   /* grab SOA records from servers */
void returnCodeError();    /* report response message errors */
```

```
/* Maximum number of name servers we will check */
#define MAX_NS 20
```

The main body of the program is small. We have an array of string pointers, *nsList*, to store the names of the nameservers for the zone. We call the resolver function *res_init* to initialize the *_res* structure. It wasn't necessary for this program to call *res_init* explicitly because it would have been called by the first resolver routine that used the *_res* structure. However, if we had wanted to modify the value of any of the *_res* fields before calling the first resolver routine, we would have made the modifications right after calling *res_init*. Next, the program calls *findNameServers* to find all the nameservers for the zone referenced in *argv[1]* and to store them in *nsList*. Last, the program calls *queryNameServers* to query each nameserver in *nsList* for the SOA record for the zone:

```
main(argc, argv)
int argc;
char *argv[];
{
    char *nsList[MAX_NS];  /* list of name servers */
    int  nsNum = 0;        /* number of name servers in list */

    /* sanity check: one (and only one) argument? */
    if(argc != 2){
        (void) fprintf(stderr, "usage: %s zone\n", argv[0]);
        exit(1);
    }

    (void) res_init();

    /*
     * Find the name servers for the zone.
     * The name servers are written into nsList.
     */
    findNameServers(argv[1], nsList, &nsNum);

    /*
     * Query each name server for the zone's SOA record.
     * The name servers are read from nsList.
     */
    queryNameServers(argv[1], nsList, nsNum);

    exit(0);
}
```

The routine *findNameServers* follows. This routine queries the local nameserver for the NS records for the zone. It then calls *addNameServers* to parse the response message and store away all the nameservers it finds. The header files, *arpa/nameser.h* and *resolv.h*, contain declarations we make extensive use of:

```
/****************************************************************
 * findNameServers -- find all of the name servers for the     *
 *     given zone and store their names in nsList.  nsNum is    *
```

```
 *       the number of servers in the nsList array.              *
 ****************************************************************/
void
findNameServers(domain, nsList, nsNum)
char *domain;
char *nsList[];
int  *nsNum;
{
    union {
        HEADER hdr;                /* defined in resolv.h */
        u_char buf[NS_PACKETSZ];   /* defined in arpa/nameser.h */
    } response;                    /* response buffers */
    int responseLen;               /* buffer length */

    ns_msg handle;  /* handle for response message */

    /*
     * Look up the NS records for the given domain name.
     * We expect the domain name to be a fully qualified, so
     * we use res_query().  If we'd wanted the resolver search
     * algorithm, we would have used res_search() instead.
     */
    if((responseLen =
            res_query(domain,       /* the zone we care about   */
                      ns_c_in,      /* Internet class records    */
                      ns_t_ns,      /* Look up name server records*/
                      (u_char *)&response,      /*response buffer*/
                      sizeof(response)))        /*buffer size    */
                                        < 0){   /*If negative    */
        nsError(h_errno, domain); /* report the error        */
        exit(1);                  /* and quit                */
    }

    /*
     * Initialize a handle to this response.  The handle will
     * be used later to extract information from the response.
     */
    if (ns_initparse(response.buf, responseLen, &handle) < 0) {
        fprintf(stderr, "ns_initparse: %s\n", strerror(errno));
        return;
    }

    /*
     * Create a list of name servers from the response.
     * NS records may be in the answer section and/or in the
     * authority section depending on the DNS implementation.
     * Walk through both.  The name server addresses may be in
     * the additional records section, but we will ignore them
     * since it is much easier to call gethostbyname() later
     * than to parse and store the addresses here.
     */

    /*
     * Add the name servers from the answer section.
```

```
     */
    addNameServers(nsList, nsNum, handle, ns_s_an);

    /*
     * Add the name servers from the authority section.
     */
    addNameServers(nsList, nsNum, handle, ns_s_ns);
}

/****************************************************************
 * addNameServers -- Look at the resource records from a       *
 *      section.  Save the names of all name servers.          *
 ****************************************************************/

void
addNameServers(nsList, nsNum, handle, section)
char *nsList[];
int  *nsNum;
ns_msg handle;
ns_sect section;
{
    int rrnum;  /* resource record number */
    ns_rr rr;   /* expanded resource record */

    int i, dup; /* misc variables */

    /*
     * Look at all the resource records in this section.
     */
    for(rrnum = 0; rrnum < ns_msg_count(handle, section); rrnum++)
    {
        /*
         * Expand the resource record number rrnum into rr.
         */
        if (ns_parserr(&handle, section, rrnum, &rr)) {
            fprintf(stderr, "ns_parserr: %s\n", strerror(errno));
        }

        /*
         * If the record type is NS, save the name of the
         * name server.
         */
        if (ns_rr_type(rr) == ns_t_ns) {

            /*
             * Allocate storage for the name.  Like any good
             * programmer should, we test malloc's return value,
             * and quit if it fails.
             */
            nsList[*nsNum] = (char *) malloc (MAXDNAME);
            if(nsList[*nsNum] == NULL){
                (void) fprintf(stderr, "malloc failed\n");
                exit(1);
            }
```

```
                    /* Expand the name server's domain name */
                    if (ns_name_uncompress(
                              ns_msg_base(handle),/* Start of the message    */
                              ns_msg_end(handle), /* End of the message       */
                              ns_rr_rdata(rr),    /* Position in the message */
                              nsList[*nsNum],     /* Result                   */
                              MAXDNAME)           /* Size of nsList buffer    */
                                   < 0) {         /* Negative: error          */
                        (void) fprintf(stderr, "ns_name_uncompress failed\n");
                        exit(1);
                    }

                    /*
                     * Check the domain name we've just unpacked and add it to
                     * the list of name servers if it is not a duplicate.
                     * If it is a duplicate, just ignore it.
                     */
                    for(i = 0, dup=0; (i < *nsNum) && !dup; i++)
                        dup = !strcasecmp(nsList[i], nsList[*nsNum]);
                    if(dup)
                        free(nsList[*nsNum]);
                    else
                        (*nsNum)++;
                }
            }
        }
```

Notice that we don't explicitly check for finding zero nameserver records. We don't need to check because *res_query* flags that case as an error; it returns –1 and sets *her-rno* to *NO_DATA*. If *res_query* returns –1, we call our own routine, *nsError*, to print out an error string from *h_errno* instead of using *herror*. The *herror* routine isn't a good fit for our program because its messages assume you are looking up address data (e.g., if *h_ errno* is *NO_DATA*, the error message is "No address associated with name").

The next routine queries each nameserver that we've found for an SOA record. In this routine, we change the value of several of the *_res* structure fields. By changing the *nsaddr_list* field, we change which nameserver *res_send* queries. We disable the search list by turning off bits in the *options* field; all the domain names that this program handles are fully qualified:

```
/*****************************************************************
 * queryNameServers -- Query each of the name servers in nsList  *
 *      for the SOA record of the given zone.  Report any        *
 *      errors encountered  (e.g., a name server not running or  *
 *      the response not being an authoritative response).  If   *
 * there are no errors, print out the serial number for the zone. *
 *****************************************************************/

void
queryNameServers(domain, nsList, nsNum)
char *domain;
```

```
char *nsList[];
int nsNum;
{
    union {
        HEADER hdr;                 /* defined in resolv.h */
        u_char buf[NS_PACKETSZ];    /* defined in arpa/nameser.h */
    } query, response;              /* query and response buffers */
    int responseLen, queryLen;      /* buffer lengths */

    u_char      *cp;        /* character pointer to parse DNS message */

    struct in_addr saveNsAddr[MAXNS];  /* addrs saved from _res */
    int nsCount;            /* count of addresses saved from _res */
    struct hostent *host;   /* structure for looking up ns addr */
    int i;                  /* counter variable */

    ns_msg handle;  /* handle for response message */
    ns_rr rr;       /* expanded resource record */

    /*
     * Save the _res name server list since
     * we will need to restore it later.
     */
    nsCount = _res.nscount;
    for(i = 0;  i < nsCount; i++)
      saveNsAddr[i] = _res.nsaddr_list[i].sin_addr;

    /*
     * Turn off the search algorithm and turn off appending
     * the local domain name before we call gethostbyname();
     * the name server's domain names will be fully qualified.
     */
    _res.options &= ~(RES_DNSRCH | RES_DEFNAMES);

    /*
     * Query each name server for the zone's SOA record.
     */
    for(nsNum-- ; nsNum >= 0; nsNum--){

        /*
         * First, we have to get the IP address of every name server.
         * So far, all we have are domain names.  We use gethostbyname()
         * to get the addresses, rather than anything fancy.
         * But first, we have to restore certain values in _res
         * because _res affects gethostbyname().  (We altered
         * _res in the previous iteration through the loop.)
         *
         * We can't just call res_init() again to restore
         * these values since some of the _res fields are
         * initialized when the variable is declared, not when
         * res_init() is called.
         */
```

```
    _res.options |= RES_RECURSE;  /* recursion on (default) */
    _res.retry = 4;               /* 4 retries (default)    */
    _res.nscount = nsCount;       /* original name servers  */
    for(i = 0; i < nsCount; i++)
        _res.nsaddr_list[i].sin_addr = saveNsAddr[i];

    /* Look up the name server's address */
    host = gethostbyname(nsList[nsNum]);
    if (host == NULL) {
        (void) fprintf(stderr,"There is no address for %s\n",
                                      nsList[nsNum]);
        continue; /* nsNum for-loop */
    }

    /*
     * Now get ready for the real fun.  host contains IP
     * addresses for the name server we're testing.
     * Store the first address for host in the _res
     * structure.  Soon, we'll look up the SOA record...
     */
    (void) memcpy((void *)&_res.nsaddr_list[0].sin_addr,
       (void *)host->h_addr_list[0], (size_t)host->h_length);
    _res.nscount = 1;

    /*
     * Turn off recursion.  We don't want the name server
     * querying another server for the SOA record; this name
     * server ought to be authoritative for this data.
     */
    _res.options &= ~RES_RECURSE;

    /*
     * Reduce the number of retries.  We may be checking
     * several name servers, so we don't want to wait too
     * long for any one server.  With two retries and only
     * one address to query, we'll wait at most 15 seconds.
     */
    _res.retry = 2;

    /*
     * We want to see the response code in the next
     * response, so we must make the query message and
     * send it ourselves instead of having res_query()
     * do it for us.  If res_query() returned -1, there
     * might not be a response to look at.
     *
     * There is no need to check for res_mkquery()
     * returning -1.  If the compression was going to
     * fail, it would have failed when we called
     * res_query() earlier with this domain name.
     */
    queryLen = res_mkquery(
                ns_o_query,       /* regular query       */
                domain,           /* the zone to look up */
```

```
                    ns_c_in,           /* Internet type        */
                    ns_t_soa,          /* look up an SOA record */
                    (u_char *)NULL,    /* always NULL          */
                    0,                 /* length of NULL       */
                    (u_char *)NULL,    /* always NULL          */
                    (u_char *)&query,/* buffer for the query  */
                    sizeof(query));  /* size of the buffer    */

    /*
     * Send the query message.  If there is no name server
     * running on the target host, res_send( ) returns -1
     * and errno is ECONNREFUSED.  First, clear out errno.
     */
    errno = 0;
    if((responseLen = res_send((u_char *)&query,/* the query  */
                               queryLen,        /* true length*/
                               (u_char *)&response,/*buffer   */
                               sizeof(response)))  /*buf size*/
                               < 0){              /* error  */
        if(errno == ECONNREFUSED) { /* no server on the host */
            (void) fprintf(stderr,
                "There is no name server running on %s\n",
                nsList[nsNum]);
        } else {                    /* anything else: no response */
            (void) fprintf(stderr,
                "There was no response from %s\n",
                nsList[nsNum]);
        }
        continue; /* nsNum for-loop */
    }

    /*
     * Initialize a handle to this response.  The handle will
     * be used later to extract information from the response.
     */
    if (ns_initparse(response.buf, responseLen, &handle) < 0) {
        fprintf(stderr, "ns_initparse: %s\n", strerror(errno));
        return;
    }

    /*
     * If the response reports an error, issue a message
     * and proceed to the next server in the list.
     */
    if(ns_msg_getflag(handle, ns_f_rcode) != ns_r_noerror){
        returnCodeError(ns_msg_getflag(handle, ns_f_rcode),
                                            nsList[nsNum]);
        continue; /* nsNum for-loop */
    }
```

```
/*
 * Did we receive an authoritative response?  Check the
 * authoritative answer bit.  If this name server isn't
 * authoritative, report it, and go on to the next server.
 */
if(!ns_msg_getflag(handle, ns_f_aa)){
    (void) fprintf(stderr,
        "%s is not authoritative for %s\n",
        nsList[nsNum], domain);
    continue; /* nsNum for-loop */
}

/*
 * The response should only contain one answer; if more,
 * report the error, and proceed to the next server.
 */
if(ns_msg_count(handle, ns_s_an) != 1){
    (void) fprintf(stderr,
        "%s: expected 1 answer, got %d\n",
        nsList[nsNum], ns_msg_count(handle, ns_s_an));
    continue; /* nsNum for-loop */
}

/*
 * Expand the answer section record number 0 into rr.
 */
if (ns_parserr(&handle, ns_s_an, 0, &rr)) {
        if (errno != ENODEV){
                fprintf(stderr, "ns_parserr: %s\n",
                        strerror(errno));
        }
}

/*
 * We asked for an SOA record; if we got something else,
 * report the error and proceed to the next server.
 */
if (ns_rr_type(rr) != ns_t_soa) {
    (void) fprintf(stderr,
        "%s: expected answer type %d, got %d\n",
        nsList[nsNum], ns_t_soa, ns_rr_type(rr));
    continue; /* nsNum for-loop */
}

/*
 * Set cp to point the the SOA record.
 */
cp = (u_char *)ns_rr_rdata(rr);

/*
 * Skip the SOA origin and mail address, which we don't
 * care about.  Both are standard "compressed names."
 */
```

```
        ns_name_skip(&cp, ns_msg_end(handle));
        ns_name_skip(&cp, ns_msg_end(handle));

        /* cp now points to the serial number; print it. */
        (void) printf("%s has serial number %d\n",
            nsList[nsNum], ns_get32(cp));

    } /* end of nsNum for-loop */
}
```

Notice that we use recursive queries when we call *gethostbyname*, but nonrecursive queries when we look up the SOA record. *gethostbyname* may need to query other nameservers to find the host's address. But we don't want the nameserver querying another server when we ask it for the SOA record; it's *supposed* to be authoritative for this zone, after all. Allowing the nameserver to ask another server for the SOA record would defeat the error check.

The next two routines print out error messages:

```
/****************************************************************
 * nsError -- Print an error message from h_errno for a failure *
 *     looking up NS records.  res_query() converts the DNS     *
 *     message return code to a smaller list of errors and      *
 *     places the error value in h_errno.  There is a routine   *
 *     called herror() for printing out strings from h_errno    *
 *     like perror() does for errno.  Unfortunately, the        *
 *     herror() messages assume you are looking up address      *
 *     records for hosts.  In this program, we are looking up   *
 *     NS records for zones, so we need our own list of error   *
 *     strings.                                                 *
 ****************************************************************/
void
nsError(error, domain)
int error;
char *domain;
{
    switch(error){
        case HOST_NOT_FOUND:
          (void) fprintf(stderr, "Unknown zone: %s\n", domain);
          break;
        case NO_DATA:
          (void) fprintf(stderr, "No NS records for %s\n", domain);
          break;
        case TRY_AGAIN:
          (void) fprintf(stderr, "No response for NS query\n");
          break;
        default:
          (void) fprintf(stderr, "Unexpected error\n");
          break;
    }
}
```

```
/***************************************************************
 * returnCodeError -- print out an error message from a DNS    *
 *      response return code.                                  *
 ***************************************************************/
void
returnCodeError(rcode, nameserver)
ns_rcode rcode;
char *nameserver;
{
    (void) fprintf(stderr, "%s: ", nameserver);
    switch(rcode){
        case ns_r_formerr:
          (void) fprintf(stderr, "FORMERR response\n");
          break;
        case ns_r_servfail:
          (void) fprintf(stderr, "SERVFAIL response\n");
          break;
        case ns_r_nxdomain:
          (void) fprintf(stderr, "NXDOMAIN response\n");
          break;
        case ns_r_notimpl:
          (void) fprintf(stderr, "NOTIMP response\n");
          break;
        case ns_r_refused:
          (void) fprintf(stderr, "REFUSED response\n");
          break;
        default:
          (void) fprintf(stderr, "unexpected return code\n");
          break;
    }
}
```

To compile this program using the resolver and nameserver routines in *libc*:

```
% cc -o check_soa check_soa.c
```

Or, if you've newly compiled the BIND code as we describe in Appendix C and want to use the latest header files and resolver library:

```
% cc -o check_soa -I/usr/local/src/bind/src/include \
```

```
check_soa.c /usr/local/src/bind/src/lib/libbind.a
```

Here is what the output looks like:

```
% check_soa mit.edu

BITSY.MIT.EDU has serial number 1995
W2ONS.MIT.EDU has serial number 1995
STRAWB.MIT.EDU has serial number 1995
```

If you look back at the shell script output, it looks the same, except that the shell script's output is sorted by the nameserver's name. What you can't see is that the C program ran much faster.

Perl Programming with Net::DNS

If using the shell to parse *nslookup*'s output seems too awkward and writing a C program seems too complicated, consider writing your program in Perl using the Net::DNS module written by Michael Fuhr. You'll find the package at *http://www.perl.com/CPAN-local/modules/by-module/Net/Net-DNS-0.12.tar.gz*.

Net::DNS treats resolvers, DNS messages, sections of DNS messages, and individual resource records as objects and provides methods for setting or querying each object's attributes. We'll examine each object type first, then give a Perl version of our *check_soa* program.

Resolver Objects

Before making any queries, you must first create a resolver object:

```
$res = new Net::DNS::Resolver;
```

Resolver objects are initialized from your *resolv.conf* file, but you can change the default settings by making calls to the object's methods. Many of the methods described in the Net::DNS::Resolver manual page correspond to fields and options in the *_res* structure described earlier in this chapter. For example, if you want to set the number of times the resolver tries each query before timing out, you can call the *$res->retry* method:

```
$res->retry(2);
```

To make a query, call one of the following methods:

```
$res->search
$res->query
$res->send
```

These methods behave like the *res_search*, *res_query*, and *res_send* library functions described in the C programming section, though they take fewer arguments. You must provide a domain name, and you can optionally provide a record type and class (the default behavior is to query for A records in the IN class). These methods return Net::DNS::Packet objects, which we'll describe next. Here are a few examples:

```
$packet = $res->search("terminator");
$packet = $res->query("movie.edu", "MX");
$packet = $res->send("version.bind", "TXT", "CH");
```

Packet Objects

Resolver queries return Net::DNS::Packet objects, whose methods you can use to access the header, question, answer, authority, and additional sections of a DNS message:

```
$header    = $packet->header;
@question  = $packet->question;
```

```
@answer     = $packet->answer;
@authority  = $packet->authority;
@additional = $packet->additional;
```

Header Objects

DNS message headers are returned as Net::DNS::Header objects. The methods described in the Net::DNS::Header manual page correspond to the header fields described in RFC 1035 and in the *HEADER* structure used in C programs. For example, if you want to find out if this is an authoritative answer, call the *$header->aa* method:

```
if ($header->aa) {
    print "answer is authoritative\n";
} else {
    print "answer is not authoritative\n";
}
```

Question Objects

The question section of a DNS message is returned as a list of Net::DNS::Question objects. You can find the name, type, and class of a question object with the following methods:

```
$question->qname
$question->qtype
$question->qclass
```

Resource Record Objects

The answer, authority, and additional sections of a DNS message are returned as lists of Net::DNS::RR objects. You can find the name, type, class, and TTL of an RR object with the following methods:

```
$rr->name
$rr->type
$rr->class
$rr->ttl
```

Each record type is a subclass of Net::DNS::RR and has its own type-specific methods. Here's an example that shows how to get the preference and mail exchanger out of an MX record:

```
$preference = $rr->preference;
$exchanger  = $rr->exchange;
```

A Perl Version of check_soa

Now that we've described the objects Net::DNS uses, let's look at how to use them in a complete program. We've rewritten *check_soa* in Perl:

```perl
#!/usr/local/bin/perl -w

use Net::DNS;

#-----------------------------------------------------------------------
# Get the zone from the command line.
#-----------------------------------------------------------------------

die "Usage:  check_soa zone\n" unless @ARGV == 1;
$domain = $ARGV[0];

#-----------------------------------------------------------------------
# Find all the name servers for the zone.
#-----------------------------------------------------------------------

$res = new Net::DNS::Resolver;

$res->defnames(0);
$res->retry(2);

$ns_req = $res->query($domain, "NS");
die "No name servers found for $domain: ", $res->errorstring, "\n"
    unless defined($ns_req) and ($ns_req->header->ancount > 0);

@nameservers = grep { $_->type eq "NS" } $ns_req->answer;

#-----------------------------------------------------------------------
# Check the SOA record on each name server.
#-----------------------------------------------------------------------

$| = 1;
$res->recurse(0);

foreach $nsrr (@nameservers) {

    #-------------------------------------------------------------------
    # Set the resolver to query this name server.
    #-------------------------------------------------------------------

    $ns = $nsrr->nsdname;
    print "$ns ";

    unless ($res->nameservers($ns)) {
        warn ": can't find address: ", $res->errorstring, "\n";
        next;
    }
```

```
#-------------------------------------------------------------------
# Get the SOA record.
#-------------------------------------------------------------------

$soa_req = $res->send($domain, "SOA");
unless (defined($soa_req)) {
    warn ": ", $res->errorstring, "\n";
    next;
}


#-------------------------------------------------------------------
# Is this name server authoritative for the zone?
#-------------------------------------------------------------------

unless ($soa_req->header->aa) {
    warn "is not authoritative for $domain\n";
    next;
}


#-------------------------------------------------------------------
# We should have received exactly one answer.
#-------------------------------------------------------------------

unless ($soa_req->header->ancount == 1) {
    warn ": expected 1 answer, got ",
         $soa_req->header->ancount, "\n";
    next;
}


#-------------------------------------------------------------------
# Did we receive an SOA record?
#-------------------------------------------------------------------

 unless (($soa_req->answer)[0]->type eq "SOA") {
    warn ": expected SOA, got ",
         ($soa_req->answer)[0]->type, "\n";
    next;
}


#-------------------------------------------------------------------
# Print the serial number.
#-------------------------------------------------------------------

    print "has serial number ", ($soa_req->answer)[0]->serial, "\n";
}
```

Now that you've seen how to write a DNS program using a shell script, a Perl script, and C code, you should be able to write one of your own using the language that best fits your situation.

## CHAPTER 16

Architecture

"Now if you'll only attend, Kitty, and not talk so much, I'll tell you all my ideas about Looking-glass House."

You've now seen bits and pieces of the Movie U. DNS infrastructure: our first primary and slave nameservers in Chapter 4, more slaves in Chapter 8, a delegated subdomain and its associated authoritative nameservers in Chapter 9. In Chapter 11, we introduced external nameservers and forwarders, split namespaces, views, and more. It may be difficult to get a sense of how all these components work together because we introduced them over so many pages. In this chapter, we'll put all of these components together into an overall design for a DNS infrastructure—what we call *DNS architecture*.

DNS architecture focuses on high-level aspects of your nameservers' configuration rather than the contents of your zones. Which nameserver is primary and which is slave for which zones? How are Internet domain names resolved? Who forwards to whom? Which nameserver-based ACLs and firewall rules protect which nameservers?

It's critical that you document your DNS architecture, just as you would your network topology. That documentation can help you identify single points of failure, performance bottlenecks, and security exposures. When name resolution goes awry, it'll be much easier to track down the problem with a thorough understanding of your DNS architecture rather than trying to piece it together from *named.conf* files and *dig* output.

However, digesting a complete DNS architecture all at once can be tough. Let's begin by looking at a small piece of it: external, authoritative nameservers.

External, Authoritative DNS Infrastructure

External, authoritative nameservers play a particularly important role in name resolution: they make your external zone data available to nameservers on the Internet.

When people on the Internet send us email or visit our web site, they rely on data served by these nameservers.

In Chapter 11, we described the nameservers that "advertised" our external zones. One, *ns.movie.edu*, the primary for our external zones, sat outside our firewall on our perimeter network. Our ISP's nameserver, *ns1.isp.net*, acted as a slave for our external zones.

These nameservers, because they're directly exposed to the Internet, require special attention. We should disable recursion on *ns.movie.edu*, because it has no business handling recursive queries. This helps protect it against brute-force denial-of-service attacks, because its capacity to handle nonrecursive queries is many times its capacity to serve recursive queries. We should also limit zone transfers to just our ISP's nameserver, preferably using TSIG. This helps protect the nameserver against denial-of-service attacks in which the attacker simply tries to start numerous concurrent zone transfers. And we can implement ACLs on our router or external firewall to limit the network traffic that our external nameservers are exposed to: minimally, we need to allow inbound UDP and TCP to port 53 and outbound UDP and TCP from our nameserver's port 53.

We might later decide to enhance our external DNS infrastructure by setting up a new primary nameserver for our external zones, this one *inside* the firewall. In fact, using views, we can configure the internal *movie.edu* primary as the primary for the external *movie.edu*, too. This might be more convenient for us as administrators because it allows us to make changes to either the internal or external namespace from the same host. Here's how the primary's *named.conf* file might look:

```
options {
    directory "/var/named";
};

acl "internal" {
    127/8; 192.249.249/24; 192.253.253/24; 192.253.254/24; 192.254.20/24;
};

view "internal" {
    match-clients { "internal"; };
    recursion yes;

    zone "movie.edu" {
        type master;
        file "db.movie.edu.internal";
        forwarders {};
     };

    zone "249.249.192.in-addr.arpa" {
        type master;
        file "db.192.249.249";
    };
```

```
            zone "253.253.192.in-addr.arpa" {
                type master;
                file "db.192.253.253";
            };

            zone "254.253.192.in-addr.arpa" {
                type master;
                file "db.192.253.254";
            };

            zone "20.254.192.in-addr.arpa" {
                type master;
                file "db.192.254.20";
            };

            zone "." {
                type hint;
                file "db.cache";
            };
        };

        key "ns.movie.edu" {
            algorithm hmac-md5;
            secret "JprUYzd+p2TO/B7k9k9Gdg==";
        };

        view "external" {
            match-clients { key "ns.movie.edu"; };
            recursion no;

            zone "movie.edu" {
                type master;
                file "db.movie.edu.external";
            };

            zone "4.1.200.in-addr.arpa" {
                type master;
                file "db.200.1.4";
            };
        };
```

To minimize the traffic we need to allow through the firewall, we can ask our ISP to use our slave nameserver on the DMZ, *ns.movie.edu*, as its master for *movie.edu* and *4.1.200.in-addr.arpa*.

Since we probably don't want to allow queries from nameservers on the Internet to a nameserver inside the firewall, we need to configure the new primary nameserver as a *hidden primary*. This is a primary that, like the unregistered slaves we introduced in Chapter 8, isn't listed in the NS records for our external zones—not the NS records in the zones themselves and not in their parent zones. This prevents any Internet nameserver from trying to query it during the normal name resolution process. All we need to do to configure the new nameserver as a hidden primary is to leave it out of the list of nameservers we register through our registrar and not add any NS records referring to it to our external zones.

Figure 16-1 shows how this works.

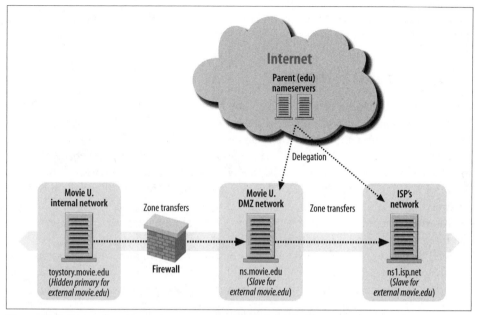

Figure 16-1. External authoritative nameservers, including a hidden primary

We should protect the hidden primary by allowing only DNS traffic between it and our slave nameservers out on the Internet, in order to support NOTIFY messages the primary sends to the slaves, and refresh queries and zone transfer requests from the slaves to the primary. This requires allowing the traffic outlined in Table 16-1.

Table 16-1. Network traffic to allow between hidden primary and slaves

	Source IP address	Source port	Destination IP address	Destination port	Protocol
NOTIFY messages	Primary	Dynamic	Slaves	53	UDP
NOTIFY responses	Slaves	53	Primary	Dynamic	UDP
Refresh queries	Slaves	Dynamic	Primary	53	UDP
Refresh responses	Primary	53	Slaves	Dynamic	UDP
Zone transfer requests	Slaves	Dynamic	Primary	53	TCP, including connection establishment
Zone transfer responses	Primary	53	Slaves	Dynamic	TCP

We can even tighten these rules a little using the *notify-source* and *query-source* substatements to nail down the source UDP ports.

Our views configuration duplicates these restrictions on the primary itself, using TSIG keys rather than IP addresses. (Notice the use of a TSIG key in the external view's *match-clients* substatement.) This gives us redundant, independent mechanisms protecting our primary nameserver—important for "defense in depth."

Forwarder Infrastructure

That's only half of our external DNS infrastructure. We also need to let internal resolvers and nameservers resolve Internet domain names. We can satisfy that requirement by allowing our internal nameservers to query arbitrary nameservers on the Internet, assuming our firewall is capable of that. That can be dangerous, though, for reasons we discussed back in Chapter 11. Consequently, most organizations run forwarders, which basically act as DNS proxy servers. (We introduced them back in Chapter 10.) We'll set up two forwarders, for redundancy, near our connection to the Internet. The forwarders can send queries through our firewall to nameservers on the Internet and receive responses; nameservers on the Internet, however, won't be allowed to query our forwarders. We can enforce this using an *allow-query* ACL in our forwarders' *named.conf* files and state-based UDP filtering on our firewall. As with the ACLs protecting the hidden primary, this gives us defense in depth.

Be sure to run the latest version of BIND, at least 9.3.0, on your internal nameservers to ensure that they choose intelligently between the two forwarders, as described in Chapter 10. Older BIND nameservers (e.g., before 9.3.0) with simpler forwarder selection algorithms can have problems if their first forwarder fails. Since they blindly try the first forwarder each time they forward a query, each forwarded query will take longer to process—sometimes several seconds longer. This can quickly add up on a nameserver processing hundreds of queries per second, even to the point of causing the nameserver to refuse new recursive queries. (Remember the default limit of 1,000 concurrent recursive queries?)

As recommended back in Chapter 11, we'll configure our internal nameservers to forward only queries for domain names outside our internal namespace. Any domain names ending in *movie.edu* should be resolved internally, via iterative queries. On authoritative *movie.edu* nameservers, this requires adding an empty *forwarders* substatement within the *movie.edu zone* statement, like so:

```
zone "movie.edu" {
    type slave;
    masters { 192.249.249.1; };
    file "bak.movie.edu";
    forwarders {};
};
```

On other nameservers, such as the *fx.movie.edu* nameservers, we can add a stub *movie.edu* zone:

```
zone "movie.edu" {
    type stub;
    masters { 192.249.249.1; };
    file "bak.fx.movie.edu";
    forwarders {};
};
```

This gives those nameservers the NS records they need to resolve *movie.edu* domain names—and a rule that tells them to resolve those domain names without relying on the forwarders—without the overhead of zone transfers.

Let's not forget to set up a similar configuration for our reverse-mapping zones, too, if any of them are parent zones. We don't want queries for domain names in our reverse-mapping zones to leak to our forwarders and possibly out to the Internet.

Figure 16-2 shows how this works.

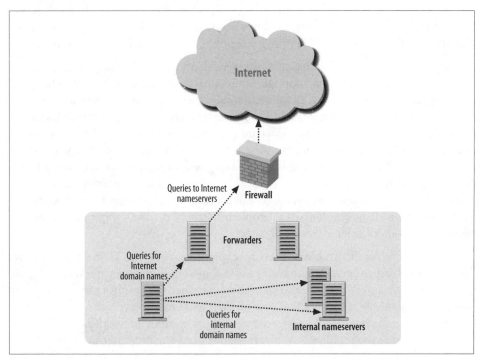

Figure 16-2. Forwarding infrastructure

Could we have saved a few bucks on hardware by using our external authoritative nameservers as forwarders, too? Sure, but that also would have presented a risk. Even if we'd created separate external authoritative and forwarder views, with recursion disabled in the external authoritative view and access to the forwarder view limited to our internal address space, the external nameservers would now be exposed to both queries and responses from arbitrary IP addresses on the Internet. That's twice as many potential vectors hackers can use to attack our external nameservers— nameservers which are now twice as important, because they support both external authoritative name service and forwarding.

Internal DNS Infrastructure

We've already discussed one aspect of our internal DNS architecture: the forwarding configuration. While that's important, there's more to cover. For *movie.edu*, we have a primary nameserver running on *toystory.movie.edu* and slaves on *wormhole.movie.edu* and *zardoz.movie.edu*. For *fx.movie.edu*, *bladerunner.fx.movie.edu* is the primary and *outland.fx.movie.edu* is a slave.

If we can scare up a little extra hardware, we might set up hidden primaries for *movie.edu* and *fx.movie.edu*, too. In our external authoritative DNS infrastructure, a hidden primary configuration is necessary to prevent nameservers on the Internet from trying to query our primary, which is inside the firewall and not reachable from the Internet. Internally, a hidden primary configuration offers different advantages.

Inside the firewall, using a hidden primary helps to insulate our resolvers and nameservers from occasional configuration and data-entry snafus, maintenance-induced outages, and the like. If we accidentally mess up while editing a zone data-file on the *movie.edu* primary and our nameserver starts spewing SERVFAIL responses to *movie.edu* queries, this won't degrade our name service. Our slaves, which answer all queries from resolvers and other internal nameservers, won't be affected. They'll keep responding with the last good version of the zone they trans-ferred, and won't transfer a new copy of the zone until the primary is back up and responding authoritatively. We'll have until *movie.edu*'s expiration time—weeks—to fix the problem. If we can't fix the problem before the zone's expiration time, we should probably consider a change of career.

As time goes on, we'll probably need to expand our internal DNS infrastructure. Let's say we need to provide name service to a new building on campus. Using the guidelines in Chapter 8, we should determine whether the resolvers in the building generate enough queries to warrant setting up a local nameserver. If not—assuming the connection from the building to the rest of the campus network is reliable—we can just configure the building's resolvers to query our existing internal nameservers.

If the building merits its own nameserver, or if the connection to the rest of the net-work is slow or flaky, we can set up a local nameserver. If we expect the local resolv-ers to do most of their queries in *movie.edu*, we can configure the nameserver as a slave for the zone. If the building's link to the campus network is slow, we can omit the NS records in *movie.edu* pointing to the slave to prevent other internal nameserv-ers from trying to query it—making it what's sometimes referred to as a *stealth slave*.

We should also determine which reverse-mapping zones local resolvers will query the most, and whether we should configure the building's nameserver as a slave for them, too.

Operations

While not strictly architectural, it's a good idea to spend some time documenting DNS operations. For example, you can institute a change control process, which can include saving older versions of *named.conf* and zone datafiles, perhaps by checking each modified file in using the Revision Control System, RCS. In fact, before saving a new version of a zone datafile, and certainly before putting the zone into production, you should check its syntax using the *named-checkzone* command, introduced in Chapter 4. Likewise, check the syntax of new *named.conf* files using *named-checkconf*. You can use a script to automate the process of managing zone datafiles, which will:

1. Edit the file
2. Use *named-checkzone* to check the zone datafile
3. If *named-checkzone* exits with errors, reedit the file
4. Otherwise, use *ci -l* to check the file in to RCS

To make it easier to monitor your nameservers, you can aggregate their *syslog* output on a single host. If you haven't reconfigured *named*'s logging, that's a simple matter of adding a line like:

```
daemon.*        @loghost
```

to the *syslog.conf* files on the hosts running your nameservers. If that catches *syslog* messages from network servers you don't want sent, you can easily reconfigure your nameservers to use a unique facility name with a *logging* statement like this:

```
logging {
    channel default_syslog {
        syslog local0;
    };
};
```

Now adding the line:

```
local0.*        @loghost
```

to *syslog.conf* sends only *named*'s *syslog* messages to your log host (assuming you're not using the *local0* facility for anything else).

To ensure that you're notified of important messages your nameservers log, set up a logfile monitor. *swatch** is a popular (and free!) program that scans logfiles for regular

---

* *swatch* is available from *http://swatch.sourceforge.net/*.

expressions you specify and takes action—sends email, pages you—based on rules you establish.

Monitoring *syslog* output won't detect all possible problems, though. In addition, you should probably set up some form of monitoring that uses DNS queries to check the integrity of your namespace. We might use *dnswalk*,[*] a powerful program for checking zone data, for this. We could run *dnswalk* hourly from *cron*, for example:

```
0 * * * *    /usr/bin/dnswalk movie.edu. 2>&1 | mail -s "dnswalk: `date`"
hostmaster@movie.edu
```

If that generates more email than you're interested in, *grep* the output for important error messages and only mail what matches.

Finally—and you experienced system administrators knew this already—you need to back up your nameservers regularly. Nightly backups of your hosts' filesystems may be enough, or you may want to keep copies of important *named.conf* and zone data-files on a central host for easier recovery or just for ready examination. *rsync*, which we introduced in Chapter 8, can come in handy for this task.

Keeping Up with DNS and BIND

As the administrators of many zones and several BIND nameservers, we believe it's critical to keep up with the latest developments. You can do so by subscribing to the BIND Users mailing list or, at minimum, BIND Announce, which we talked about in Chapter 3. Using these resources, you can stay up to date on BIND vulnerabilities, and the availability of patches and new versions of BIND.

Of course, we think a good way to keep up with DNS and BIND is to keep buying the latest edition of this book, too. See you next time!

[*] *dnswalk* is available from *http://sourceforge.net/projects/dnswalk/*.

## CHAPTER 17

Miscellaneous

> *"The time has come," the Walrus said, "To talk of*
> *many things: Of shoes—and ships—and sealing-*
> *wax—Of cabbages—and kings—And why the sea is*
> *boiling hot—And whether pigs have wings."*

It's time we tied up loose ends. We've already covered the mainstream of DNS and BIND, but there's a handful of interesting niches we haven't explored. Some of these may actually be useful to you, such as instructions on how to accommodate Active Directory with BIND; others may just be interesting. We can't in good conscience send you out into the world without completing your education!

Using CNAME Records

We talked about CNAME resource records in Chapter 4. We didn't tell you everything about CNAME records, though; we saved that for this chapter. When you set up your first nameservers, you probably wouldn't have cared about the subtle nuances of the magical CNAME record. Some of this trivia is interesting, some is arcane. We'll let you decide which is which.

CNAMEs Attached to Interior Nodes

If you've ever renamed your zone because of a company reorganization or acquisition, you may have considered creating a single CNAME record that pointed from the zone's old domain name to its new domain name. For instance, if the *fx.movie.edu* zone were renamed *magic.movie.edu*, we'd be tempted to create a single CNAME record to map all the old domain names to the new names:

```
fx.movie.edu.  IN  CNAME  magic.movie.edu.
```

With this in place, you'd expect a lookup of *empire.fx.movie.edu* to result in a lookup of *empire.magic.movie.edu*. Unfortunately, this doesn't work: you can't have a CNAME record attached to an interior node like *fx.movie.edu* if it owns other records. Remember that *fx.movie.edu* has an SOA record and NS records, so attaching a CNAME record to it violates the rule that a domain name be either an alias or a canonical name, not both.

If you're running BIND 9, though, you can use the brand-spanking-new DNAME record (introduced in Chapter 10) to create an alias from your zone's old domain name to its new one:

```
fx.movie.edu.  IN  DNAME  magic.movie.edu.
```

The DNAME record can coexist with other record types at *fx.movie.edu*—like the SOA record and NS records that are undoubtedly there—but you *can't* have any other domain names that end in *fx.movie.edu*. It'll "synthesize" CNAME records from domain names in *fx.movie.edu* to like domain names in *magic.movie.edu* when the names in *fx.movie.edu* are looked up.

If you don't have BIND 9, you'll have to create aliases the old-fashioned way—a CNAME record for each individual domain name within the zone:

```
empire.fx.movie.edu.       IN  CNAME  empire.magic.movie.edu.
bladerunner.fx.movie.edu.  IN  CNAME  bladerunner.magic.movie.edu.
```

If the subdomain isn't delegated, and consequently doesn't have an SOA record and NS records attached, you can also create an alias for *fx.movie.edu*. However, this applies only to the domain name *fx.movie.edu* and not to other domain names in the *fx.movie.edu* zone.

Hopefully, the tool you use to manage your zone datafiles can handle creating CNAME records for you. (*h2n*, which was introduced in Chapter 4, does just that.)

CNAMEs Pointing to CNAMEs

You may have wondered whether it is possible to have an alias (CNAME record) pointing to another alias. This might be useful in situations where an alias points from a domain name outside your zone to a domain name inside your zone. You may not have any control over the alias outside your zone. What if you want to change the domain name it points to? Can you simply add another CNAME record?

The answer is yes: you can chain together CNAME records. The BIND implementation supports it, and the RFCs don't expressly forbid it. But while you can chain CNAME records, is it a wise thing to do? The RFCs recommend against it because of the possibility of creating a CNAME loop and because it slows resolution. You may be able to do it in a pinch, but you probably won't find much sympathy on the Net if something breaks. And all bets are off if a new (non-BIND-based) nameserver implementation emerges.[*]

---

[*] And one has (the Microsoft DNS Server, shipped with server versions of Windows). It also permits CNAMEs that point to CNAMEs, though.

CNAMEs in the Resource Record Data

For any other record besides a CNAME record, you must use canonical domain names in the resource record data. Applications and nameservers won't operate correctly otherwise. As we mentioned back in Chapter 5, for example, *sendmail* recognizes only the canonical name of the local host on the right side of an MX record. If *sendmail* doesn't recognize the local host's name, it won't strip the correct MX records out when paring down the MX list and may try to deliver mail to itself or to less preferred hosts, causing mail to loop.

BIND 8 nameservers log messages like these when they encounter aliases on the right side of a record:

```
Sep 27 07:43:48 toystory named[22139]: "digidesign.com IN NS" points to a CNAME
(ns1.digidesign.com)
Sep 27 07:43:49 toystory named[22139]: "moreland.k12.ca.us IN MX" points to a CNAME
(mail.moreland.k12.ca.us)
```

BIND 9 nameservers, unfortunately, don't seem to notice.

Multiple CNAME Records

One pathological configuration that honestly hadn't occurred to us—and many pathological configurations *have* occurred to us—is multiple CNAME records attached to the same domain name. Some administrators use this with round robin to rotate between RRsets. For example, the records:

```
fullmonty  IN  CNAME  fullmonty1
fullmonty  IN  CNAME  fullmonty2
fullmonty  IN  CNAME  fullmonty3
```

can be used to return all the addresses attached to *fullmonty1*, then all the addresses of *fullmonty2*, then all the addresses of *fullmonty3* on a nameserver that didn't recognize this as the abomination it is. (It violates the "CNAME and other data" rule, for one.)

BIND 4 doesn't recognize this as a misconfiguration; BIND 8 and 9.1.0 and later do. BIND 8 lets you permit it if you want to with:

```
options {
            multiple-cnames yes;
};
```

In BIND 9, there's no option to allow it. The default, naturally, is to disallow it.

Looking Up CNAMEs

At times you may want to look up a CNAME record itself, not data for the canonical name. With *nslookup* or *dig*, this is easy to do. You can either set the query type to *cname*, or set the query type to *any* and then look up the name:

```
% nslookup
Default Server: wormhole
Address: 0.0.0.0

> set query=cname
> toys
Server: wormhole
Address: 0.0.0.0

toys.movie.edu  canonical name = toystory.movie.edu

> set query=any
> toys
Server: wormhole
Address: 0.0.0.0

toys.movie.edu  canonical name = toystory.movie.edu
> exit

% dig toys.movie.edu cname
; <<>> DiG 9.3.2 <<>> toys.movie.edu cname
;; global options:  printcmd
;; Got answer:
;; ->>HEADER<<- opcode: QUERY, status: NOERROR, id: 43984
;; flags: qr aa rd ra; QUERY: 1, ANSWER: 1, AUTHORITY: 3, ADDITIONAL: 4

;; QUESTION SECTION:
;toys.movie.edu.                    IN    CNAME

;; ANSWER SECTION:
toys.movie.edu.         86400 IN CNAME    toystory.movie.edu.
```

Finding Out a Host's Aliases

One thing you can't easily do with DNS is find out a host's aliases. With the host table, it's easy to find both the canonical name of a host and any aliases: no matter which you look up, they're all there, together, on the same line:

```
% grep toystory /etc/hosts
192.249.249.3  toystory.movie.edu toystory toys
```

With DNS, however, if you look up the canonical name, all you get is the canonical name. There's no easy way for the nameserver or the application to know whether aliases exist for that canonical name.

```
% nslookup
Default Server: wormhole
Address: 0.0.0.0
```

```
> toystory
Server:  wormhole
Address:  0.0.0.0

Name:    toystory.movie.edu
Address:  192.249.249.3
```

If you use *nslookup* or *dig* to look up an alias, you'll see that alias and the canonical name. *nslookup* and *dig* report both the alias and the canonical name in the message. But you won't see any other aliases that might point to that canonical name:

```
% nslookup
Default Server:  wormhole
Address:  0.0.0.0

> toys
Server:  wormhole
Address:  0.0.0.0

Name:    toystory.movie.edu
Address:  192.249.249.3
Aliases:  toys.movie.edu

> exit

% dig toys.movie.edu

; <<>> DiG 9.3.2 <<>> toys.movie.edu
;; global options:  printcmd
;; Got answer:
;; ->>HEADER<<- opcode: QUERY, status: NOERROR, id: 29782
;; flags: qr aa rd ra; QUERY: 1, ANSWER: 2, AUTHORITY: 3, ADDITIONAL: 4

;; QUESTION SECTION:
; toys.movie.edu.                    IN    A

;; ANSWER SECTION:
toys.movie.edu.          86400 IN CNAME      toystory.movie.edu.
toystory.movie.edu.      86400 IN A          192.249.249.3
```

About the only way to find out all the CNAMEs for a host is to transfer the whole zone and pick out the CNAME records in which that host is the canonical name:

```
% nslookup
Default Server:  wormhole
Address:  0.0.0.0

> ls -t cname movie.edu
[wormhole.movie.edu]
$ORIGIN movie.edu.
toys                1D IN CNAME     toystory
wh                  1D IN CNAME     wormhole
mi                  1D IN CNAME     monsters-inc
>
```

Even this method shows you the aliases only within that zone; there could be aliases in a different zone, pointing to canonical names in this zone.

Wildcards

Something else we haven't covered in detail yet is DNS *wildcards*. There are times when you want a single resource record to cover any possible name, rather than creating zillions of resource records that are all the same except for the domain name to which they apply. DNS reserves a special character, the asterisk (*), to use in zone datafiles as a wildcard name. It matches any number of labels in a name as long as there isn't an exact match with a name already in the nameserver's database.

Most often, you'd use wildcards to forward mail to non-Internet-connected networks. Suppose our site wasn't connected to the Internet, but we had a host that relayed mail between the Internet and our network. We can add a wildcard MX record to the *movie.edu* zone for Internet consumption that points all our mail to the relay. Here is an example:

```
*.movie.edu.  IN  MX  10 movie-relay.nea.gov.
```

Since the wildcard matches one or more labels, this resource record applies to names such as *toystory.movie.edu*, *empire.fx.movie.edu*, or *casablanca.bogart.classics.movie.edu*. The danger with wildcards is that they clash with search lists. This wildcard also matches *cujo.movie.edu.movie.edu*, making wildcards dangerous to use in our internal zone data. Remember that some versions of *sendmail* apply the search list when looking up MX records:

```
% nslookup
Default Server: wormhole
Address: 0.0.0.0

> set type=mx                          Look up MX records
> cujo.movie.edu                       for cujo
Server: wormhole
Address: 0.0.0.0

cujo.movie.edu.movie.edu               This isn't a real host's name!
    preference = 10, mail exchanger = movie-relay.nea.gov
```

What are other limitations of wildcards? Wildcards do not match domain names for which there is already data. Suppose we *did* use wildcards within our zone data, as in these partial contents of *db.movie.edu*:

```
*     IN  MX  10 mail-hub.movie.edu.
et    IN  MX  10 et.movie.edu.
jaws  IN  A   192.253.253.113
fx    IN  NS  bladerunner.fx.movie.edu.
fx    IN  NS  outland.fx.movie.edu.
```

Mail to *toystory.movie.edu* is sent to *mail-hub.movie.edu*, but mail to *et.movie.edu* is sent directly to *et.movie.edu*. An MX lookup of *jaws.movie.edu* results in a response saying there was no MX data for that domain name. The wildcard doesn't apply because an A record exists. The wildcard also doesn't apply to domain names in *fx.movie.edu* because wildcards don't apply across delegation. Nor does the wildcard apply to the domain name *movie.edu*, because the wildcard amounts to zero or more labels *followed by a dot*, followed by *movie.edu*.

A Limitation of MX Records

While we are on the topic of MX records, let's talk about how they can result in mail taking a longer path than necessary. The MX records are a list of data returned when the domain name of a mail destination is looked up. The list isn't ordered according to which exchanger is closest to the sender. Here is an example of this problem. Your non-Internet-connected network has two hosts that can relay Internet mail to your network. One host is in the United States, and one host is in France. Your network is in Greece. Most of your mail comes from the United States, so you have someone maintain your zone and install two wildcard MX records—the highest preference to the U.S. relay and a lower preference to the relay in France. Since the United States relay is at a higher preference, *all* mail will go through that relay (as long as it is reachable). If someone in France sends you a letter, it will travel across the Atlantic to the United States and back because there is nothing in the MX list to indicate that the French relay is closer to that sender.

Dial-up Connections

Another recent development in networking (recent only relative to DNS's age) that presents a challenge to DNS is the dial-up Internet connection. When the Internet was young, and DNS was born, there was no such thing as a dial-up connection. With the enormous explosion in the Internet's popularity and the propagation of Internet service providers who offer dial-up Internet connectivity to the masses, a whole new breed of problems with name service has been introduced.

The basic goal when setting up DNS to work with dial-up is to enable every host in your network to resolve the domain names of every host it needs to access. (Of course, when your connection to the Internet is down, your hosts probably don't need to resolve Internet domain names.) If you're using dial-on-demand, there's the additional goal of minimizing unnecessary dialouts: if you're looking up the domain name of a host on your local network, that shouldn't require your router to bring up a connection to the Internet.

We'll separate dial-up connections into two categories: manual dial-up, by which we mean a connection to the Internet that must be brought up by a user, and dial-on-demand, which implies the use of a device—often a router, but sometimes just a host running Linux or another server operating system—to connect to the Internet automatically whenever hosts generate traffic bound for the Internet. We'll also describe two scenarios for each category of dial-up: one in which you have just one host dialing up a connection to the Internet, and one in which you have a small network of hosts dialing up a connection. Before we talk about these scenarios, though, let's discuss what causes dialouts and how to avoid them.

What Causes Dialouts

Many users, particularly in Europe, where ISDN is popular, connect to the Internet via dial-on-demand connections. Nearly all of these users want to minimize, if not completely prevent, unnecessary connections to the Internet. Connection setup is often more expensive than successive minutes, and always takes time.

BIND nameservers, unfortunately, aren't terribly well suited to running behind dial-on-demand connections. They periodically send system queries to look up the current list of root nameservers, even when the nameserver isn't resolving domain names. And the operation of the search list can cause the nameserver to query remote nameservers. For example, say your local domain name is *tinyoffice.megacorp.com* and you have a local nameserver authoritative for that zone. Your default search list, on some resolvers, might include:

```
tinyoffice.megacorp.com
megacorp.com
```

Let's say you try to FTP to one of your local systems, *deadbeef.tinyoffice.megacorp.com*, but you misspell it *deadbeer*:

```
% ftp deadbeer
```

Because of your search list, your resolver first looks up *deadbeer.tinyoffice.megacorp.com*. Your local nameserver, authoritative for the *tinyoffice.megacorp.com* zone, can tell that domain name doesn't exist. But then your resolver appends the second domain name in the search list and looks up *deadbeer.megacorp.com*. To figure out whether that domain name exists, your nameserver needs to query a *megacorp.com* server, which requires bringing up the dial-on-demand link.

Avoiding Dialouts

There are several general techniques that can help you minimize unnecessary dialouts. The first, and probably simplest, is to run a version of BIND that supports negative caching (which means any version of BIND 8 or 9). That way, if you mistakenly put *deadbeer* into a configuration file, your nameserver looks up *deadbeer.megacorp.com* once, and then caches the fact that the domain name doesn't exist for the duration of *megacorp.com*'s negative caching TTL.

Another technique is to use a minimal search list. If your local domain name is *tinyoffice.megacorp.com*, you could make do with a search list of just *tinyoffice.megacorp.com*. That way, a typo won't cause a dialout.

Using a modern resolver is also important. The default search list for a post–BIND 4.9 resolver is just the local domain name, which qualifies as "minimal" in our book. And a modern resolver knows to try a domain name with dots as-is, even if it doesn't end in a dot.

Finally, you can use other naming services, such as */etc/hosts*, for local name resolution and configure your resolvers to use DNS only if a name cannot be found in */etc/hosts*. As long as you keep the names of all your local hosts in */etc/hosts*, you won't need to worry about needless connections to the Internet.

Now let's apply these techniques to our scenarios.

Manual Dial-up with One Host

The easiest way to deal with the simple dial-up scenario is to configure your host's resolver to use a nameserver provided by your Internet service provider. Most ISPs run nameservers for their subscribers' use. If you're not sure whether your ISP provides nameservers for your use, or if you don't know what its IP addresses are, check its web site, send an email, or call the provider.

Some operating systems, such as Windows NT, Windows 2000, and Windows XP, let you define a set of nameservers for use with a particular dial-up provider. So, for example, you can configure one set of nameservers to use when you dial up UUNet and another to use when you dial up your office. This is useful if you dial in to multiple ISPs.

This configuration is usually adequate for most casual dial-up users. Name resolution will fail unless the dial-up connection is up, but that's not likely to be a problem because there's no use for Internet name service without Internet connectivity.

Some of you, however, may want to run a nameserver when your dial-up connection is active. It can help your performance by caching domain names you look up frequently, for example. This is easy to set up with a Unix-like operating system such as Linux: you'll typically use a script like *ifup* to bring up your dial-up connection and *ifdown* to bring it down. If that's the case, there are probably also scripts called *ifup-post* and *ifdown-post* that *ifup* and *ifdown* call, respectively, after they've done most of their work. You can start *named* as *named* or with *ndc start* in *ifup-post*, and shut it down with *ndc stop* or *rndc stop* in *ifdown-post*. About the only other thing you'd need to do is set your local domain name in *resolv.conf*. The default resolver behavior, querying a nameserver on the local host, should do fine both when the nameserver's running and when it's not.

Manual Dial-up with Multiple Hosts

The simplest solution to use with the multiple host/manual dial-up scenario is similar to the resolver-only configuration. You can configure your resolvers to use your ISP's nameservers, but also configure the resolvers to check /etc/hosts (or NIS, if you go for that sort of thing) *before* querying a nameserver. Then make sure your /etc/hosts file contains the names of all the hosts on your local network.

If you'd like to run a nameserver locally, you need to modify this configuration only slightly: configure the resolvers to use your local nameserver instead of your ISP's. This gives you the benefits of local caching, but local name resolution will work (via /etc/hosts) even when your connection to the Internet is down. You may as well start and stop the local nameserver from *ifup-post* and *ifdown-post*, as described earlier.

For those of you who really want to use DNS for *all* name resolution, you can forgo the /etc/hosts file and create forward-mapping and reverse-mapping zones on your local nameserver for your hosts. You should trim your resolvers' search lists to the bare minimum, though, to minimize the chance that you'll induce your nameserver to look up some wacky remote domain name.

Dial-on-Demand with One Host

If you have a single host with a dial-on-demand connection to the Internet, your simplest solution is still a resolver-only configuration. Configure your resolver to use your ISP's nameservers, and when the resolver needs to look up a domain name, it'll query one of those nameservers and bring up the link. If there are some domain names that your host looks up routinely as part of "housekeeping," such as *localhost* or *1.0.0.127.in-addr.arpa*, you can add the appropriate entries to /etc/hosts and configure your resolver to check /etc/hosts before querying a nameserver.

If you'd like to run a nameserver locally, make sure it is able to map *localhost* and *1.0.0.127.in-addr.arpa* to 127.0.0.1 and *localhost*, respectively, and trim your search list to the minimum.

If your nameserver brings up the link more than you think it should, try turning on query logging (with *ndc querylog* on a BIND 8 nameserver or *rndc querylog* on a BIND 9.1.0 or later nameserver) and look for the domain names that bring up the link. If many of them are in a single zone, you might consider configuring your local nameserver as a slave for that zone. At least that way, you'll bring up the link at most only once per refresh interval to resolve domain names in the zone.

Dial-on-Demand with Multiple Hosts

The simplest solution in this scenario is exactly the same as the first solution we described earlier in the section "Manual Dialup with Multiple Hosts": a resolver-only configuration with the resolvers configured to check /etc/hosts before querying a nameserver. As with all dial-on-demand configurations, you'll want to trim your search list.

Alternatively, you could try one of the two variants: running a local nameserver and using it as a backup to /etc/hosts, or creating forward- and reverse-mapping zones for the local hosts on the local nameserver.

Running Authoritative Nameservers over Dial-on-Demand

This may sound like a silly subject to some of you—who would run an authoritative nameserver behind a dial-on-demand connection?—but in some parts of the world, where bandwidth and Internet connectivity aren't easy to come by, this is a necessity. And, believe it or not, BIND provides a mechanism to accommodate such nameservers.

If you run an authoritative nameserver behind a dial-on-demand link, you want to concentrate zone maintenance activities into as short a window as possible. If your nameserver is authoritative for 100 zones, you'd rather not have zone refresh timers popping every few minutes and the resulting SOA queries bringing up the dial-on-demand link over and over again.

With BIND 8.2 and newer nameservers and BIND 9.1.0 and later nameservers, you can configure a *heartbeat interval*. The heartbeat interval is how frequently you'd like your nameserver to bring up its dial-on-demand connection, in minutes:

```
options {
    heartbeat-interval 180;     // 3 hours
};
```

The default is 60 minutes, and you can disable zone maintenance by setting the interval to 0.

If you then mark one or more of your zones as dial-up zones, the nameserver will try to concentrate all maintenance of that zone into a short period and to perform the maintenance no more often than the heartbeat interval. For a slave zone, that means inhibiting the normal refresh timer (even ignoring the refresh interval, if it's smaller than the heartbeat interval!) and querying the master for the zone's SOA record only at the heartbeat interval. For a master zone, that means sending out NOTIFY messages, which will presumably bring up the dial-on-demand link and trigger a refresh on the slaves.

To mark all of a nameserver's zones as dial-up zones, use the *dialup* substatement in an *options* statement:

```
options {
    heartbeat-interval 60;
    dialup yes;
};
```

To mark a single zone as a dial-up zone, use the *dialup* substatement in the *zone* statement:

```
zone "movie.edu" {
    type master;
    file "db.movie.edu";
    dialup yes;
};
```

Dial-up zones are also useful in another, perhaps unintended way: on nameservers that serve as slaves for thousands of zones. Some ISPs provide slave service on a large scale but get bitten by miscreants who set their zone's refresh intervals far too low. Their nameservers end up swamped with sending out SOA queries for those zones. By configuring all the zones as dial-up zones and setting the heartbeat interval to something reasonable, ISPs can prevent this.

Network Names and Numbers

The original DNS specifications didn't provide the ability to look up a network name based on a network number—a feature that was provided by the original *HOSTS.TXT* file. Since then, RFC 1101 has defined a system for storing network names; this system also works for subnets and subnet masks, so it goes significantly beyond *HOSTS.TXT*. Moreover, it doesn't require any modification to the nameserver software at all; it's based entirely on the clever use of PTR and A records.

Remember that to map an IP address to a name in DNS, you reverse the IP address, append *in-addr.arpa*, and look up PTR records. This same technique maps a network number to a network name—for example, to map network 15/8 to "HP Internet." To look up the network number, include the network bits and pad them with trailing zeros to make four bytes, and look up PTR data just as you did with a host's IP address. For example, to find the network name for the old ARPAnet, network 10/8, look up PTR data for *0.0.0.10.in-addr.arpa*. You get back an answer like *ARPAnet.ARPA*.

If the ARPAnet is subnetted, you'll also find an address record at *0.0.0.10.in-addr.arpa*. The address would be the subnet mask, 255.255.0.0, for instance. If you were interested in the subnet name instead of the network name, you apply the mask to the IP address and look up the subnet number.

This technique allows you to map the network number to a name. To provide a complete solution, there must be a way to map a network name to its network number. This, again, is accomplished with PTR records. The network name has PTR data that points to the network number (reversed with *in-addr.arpa* appended).

Let's see what the data might look like in HP's zone datafiles (the HP Internet has network number 15/8) and step through mapping a network number to a network name.

Partial contents of the file *db.hp.com*:

```
;
; Map HP's network name to 15.0.0.0.
;
hp-net.hp.com.              IN  PTR 0.0.0.15.in-addr.arpa.
```

Partial contents of the file *db.corp.hp.com*:

```
;
; Map corp's subnet name to 15.1.0.0.
;
corp-subnet.corp.hp.com.  IN  PTR 0.0.1.15.in-addr.arpa.
```

Partial contents of the file *db.15*:

```
;
; Map 15.0.0.0 to hp-net.hp.com.
; HP's subnet mask is 255.255.248.0.
;
0.0.0.15.in-addr.arpa.     IN  PTR hp-net.hp.com.
                           IN  A   255.255.248.0
```

Partial contents of the file *db.15.1*:

```
;
; Map the 15.1.0.0 back to its subnet name.
;
0.0.1.15.in-addr.arpa.     IN  PTR corp-subnet.corp.hp.com.
```

Here's the procedure to look up the subnet name for the IP address 15.1.0.1:

1. Apply the default network mask for the address's class. Address 15.1.0.1 is a Class A address, so the mask is 255.0.0.0. Applying the mask to the IP address makes the network number 15.

2. Send a query (*type=A* or *type=ANY*) for *0.0.0.15.in-addr.arpa*.

3. The query response contains address data. Since there is address data at *0.0.0.15.in-addr.arpa* (the subnet mask, 255.255.248.0), apply the subnet mask to the IP address. This yields 15.1.0.0.

4. Send a query (*type=A* or *type=ANY*) for *0.0.1.15.in-addr.arpa*.

5. The query response does not contain address data, so 15.1.0.0 is not further subnetted.

6. Send a PTR query for *0.0.1.15.in-addr.arpa*.

7. The query response contains the network name for 15.1.0.1: *corp-subnet.corp.hp.com*.

In addition to mapping between network names and numbers, you can also list all the networks for your zone with PTR records:

```
movie.edu.  IN  PTR  0.249.249.192.in-addr.arpa.
            IN  PTR  0.253.253.192.in-addr.arpa.
```

Now for the bad news: despite the fact that RFC 1101 contains everything you need to know to set this up, there's very little software we know of that actually *uses* this type of network name encoding, and very few administrators go to the trouble of adding this information. Until software actually makes use of DNS-encoded network names, about the only reason for setting this up is to show off. But that's a good enough reason for many of us.

Additional Resource Records

There are a number of resource records that we haven't covered yet in this book. Some of these are experimental, but some are on the standards track and are coming into more prevalent use. We'll describe them here to give you a little head start in getting used to them.

AFSDB

AFSDB has a syntax like that of the MX record, and semantics a bit like that of the NS record. An AFSDB record gives either the location of an AFS cell database server or of a DCE cell's authenticated nameserver. The type of server the record points to and the name of the host running the server are contained in the record-specific data portion of the record.

So what's an AFS cell database server? Or AFS, for that matter? AFS originally stood for the Andrew File System, designed by the good folks at Carnegie-Mellon University as part of the Andrew Project. (It's now an IBM product.) AFS is a network filesystem, like NFS, but one that handles the latency of wide area networks much better than NFS does and provides local caching of files to enhance performance. An AFS cell database server runs the process responsible for tracking the location of filesets (groups of files) on various AFS fileservers within a cell (a logical group of hosts). So being able to find the AFS cell database server is the key to finding any file in the cell.

And what's an authenticated nameserver? It holds location information about all sorts of services available within a DCE cell. A DCE cell? That's a logical group of hosts that share services offered by The Open Group's Distributed Computing Environment (DCE).

And now, back to our story. To access another cell's AFS or DCE services across a network, you must first find out where that cell's cell database servers or authenticated nameservers are—hence the new record type. The domain name the record is attached to gives the name of the cell the server knows about. Cells often share names with DNS domains, so this usually doesn't look at all odd.

As we said, the AFSDB record's syntax is like the MX record's syntax. In place of the preference value, you specify the number 1 for an AFS cell database server or 2 for a DCE authenticated nameserver.

In place of the mail exchanger host, you specify the name of the host running the server. Simple!

Suppose an *fx.movie.edu* system administrator sets up a DCE cell (which includes AFS services) because she wants to experiment with distributed processing to speed up graphics rendering. She runs both an AFS cell database server and a DCE nameserver on *bladerunner.fx.movie.edu*, another cell database server on *empire.fx.movie.edu*, and another DCE nameserver on *aliens.fx.movie.edu*. She should set up the AFSDB records as follows:

```
; Our DCE cell is called fx.movie.edu, same as the domain name of the zone
fx.movie.edu.  IN  AFSDB  1 bladerunner.fx.movie.edu.
               IN  AFSDB  2 bladerunner.fx.movie.edu.
               IN  AFSDB  1 empire.fx.movie.edu.
               IN  AFSDB  2 aliens.fx.movie.edu.
```

LOC

RFC 1876 defines an experimental record type, LOC, that allows zone administrators to encode the locations of their computers, subnets, and networks. In this case, location means latitude, longitude, and altitude. Future applications could use this information to produce network maps, assess routing efficiency, and more.

In its basic form, the LOC record takes latitude, longitude, and altitude (in that order) as its record-specific data. Latitude and longitude are expressed in the format:

```
<degrees> [minutes [seconds.<fractional seconds>]] (N|S|E|W)
```

Altitude is expressed in meters.

If you're wondering how in the world you're going to get that data, check out "RFC 1876 Resources" at *http://www.ckdhr.com/dns-loc*. This site, created by Christopher Davis, one of the authors of RFC 1876, is an indispensable collection of information, useful links, and utilities for people creating LOC records.

If you don't have your own Global Positioning System receiver to carry around to all of your computers—and we *know* many of you do—two sites that may come in handy are Tele Atlas's Eagle Geocoding at *http://www.geocode.com/modules.php?name=TestDrive_ Eagle*, which you can use to find the latitude and longitude of most addresses in the United States, and AirNav's Airport Information at *http://www.airnav.com/airports*, which lets you find the elevation of the closest airport to you. If you don't have a major airport near you, don't worry: the database even includes the helipad at your neighborhood hospital!

Here's a LOC record for one of our hosts:

```
huskymo.boulder.acmebw.com.  IN  LOC  40 2 0.373 N 105 17 23.528 W 1638m
```

Optional fields in the record-specific data allow you to specify how large the entity you're describing is, in meters (LOC records can describe networks, after all, which can be quite large), as well as the horizontal and vertical precision. The size defaults to one meter, which is perfect for a single host. Horizontal precision defaults to 10,000 meters, and vertical precision to 10 meters. These defaults represent the size of a typical zip or postal code, the idea being that you can fairly easily find a latitude and longitude given a zip code.

You can also attach LOC records to the names of subnets and networks. If you've taken the time to enter information about the names and addresses of your networks in the format described in RFC 1101 (covered earlier in this chapter), you can attach LOC records to the network names:

```
;
; Map HP's network name to 15.0.0.0.
;
hp-net.hp.com.   IN   PTR 0.0.0.15.in-addr.arpa.
                 IN   LOC 37 24 55.393 N 122 8 37 W 26m
```

SRV

Locating a service or a particular type of server within a zone is a difficult problem if you don't know which host it runs on. Some zone administrators have attempted to solve this problem by using service-specific aliases in their zones. For example, at Movie U., we created the alias *ftp.movie.edu* and pointed it to the domain name of the host that runs our FTP archive:

```
ftp.movie.edu.      IN    CNAME        plan9.fx.movie.edu.
```

This makes it easy for people to guess a domain name that will get them to our FTP archive, and separates the domain name people use to access the archive from the domain name of the host it runs on. If we want to move the archive to a different host, we can simply change the CNAME record.

The experimental SRV record, introduced in RFC 2782, is a general mechanism for locating services. In addition, SRV provides powerful features that allow zone administrators to distribute load and provide backup services, similar to what the MX record provides. In fact, you might think of an SRV record as a generalized MX record, useful for services besides SMTP-based electronic mail.

A unique aspect of the SRV record is the format of the domain name it's attached to. Like service-specific aliases, the domain name to which an SRV record is attached gives the name of the service sought, as well as the protocol it runs over, concatenated with a domain name. The labels representing the service name and the protocol begin with an underscore to distinguish them from labels in the domain name of a host. So, for example:

```
_ftp._tcp.movie.edu
```

represents the SRV records someone *ftp*'ing to *movie.edu* should retrieve in order to find the *movie.edu* FTP servers, while:

```
_http._tcp.www.movie.edu
```

represents the SRV records someone accessing the URL *http://www.movie.edu* should look up in order to find the *www.movie.edu* web servers.

The names of the service and protocol should appear in IANA's list of port number assignments (available at *http://www.iana.org/assignments/port-numbers*) or be unique names used only locally. Don't use the port or protocol *numbers*, just the names.

The SRV record has four resource record–specific fields: *priority*, *weight*, *port*, and *target*. Priority, weight, and port are unsigned 16-bit numbers (between 0 and 65535). Target is a domain name.

Priority

Works very similarly to the preference in an MX record: the lower the number in the priority field, the more desirable the associated target. When searching for hosts offering a given service, clients should try all targets at a lower priority value before trying those at a higher priority value.

Weight

Allows zone administrators to distribute load to multiple targets. Clients should query targets that have the same priority in proportion to their weight. For example, if one target has a priority of 0 and a weight of 1, and another target also has a priority of 0 but a weight of 2, the second target should receive twice as much load (in queries, connections, whatever) as the first. It's up to the service's clients to direct that load: they typically use a system call to choose a random number. If the number is, say, in the top one-third of the range, they try the first target, and if the number is in the bottom two-thirds of the range, they try the second target.

Port

Specifies the port on which the service being sought is running. This allows zone administrators to run servers on nonstandard ports. For example, an administrator can use SRV records to point web browsers at a web server running on port 8000 instead of the standard HTTP port (80).

Target

Specifies the domain name of a host on which the service is running (on the port specified in the port field). Target must be the canonical name of the host (not an alias), with address records attached to it.

So, for the *movie.edu* FTP server, we added these records to *db.movie.edu*:

```
_ftp._tcp.movie.edu.   IN  SRV  1  0  21  plan9.fx.movie.edu.
                       IN  SRV  2  0  21  thing.fx.movie.edu.
```

This instructs SRV-capable FTP clients to try the FTP server on *plan9.fx.movie.edu*'s port 21 first when accessing *movie.edu*'s FTP service, and then to try the FTP server on *thing.fx.movie.edu*'s port 21 if *plan9.fx.movie.edu*'s FTP server isn't available.

The records:

```
_http._tcp.www.movie.edu.   IN  SRV  0  2  80   www.movie.edu.
                            IN  SRV  0  1  80   www2.movie.edu.
                            IN  SRV  1  1  8000 postmanrings2x.movie.edu.
```

direct web queries for *www.movie.edu* (the web site) to port 80 on *www.movie.edu* (the host) and *www2.movie.edu*, with *www.movie.edu* getting twice the queries that *www2.movie.edu* does. If neither is available, the queries will go to *postmanrings2x.movie.edu* on port 8000.

To advertise that a particular service isn't available, use a dot in the target field:

```
_gopher._tcp.movie.edu.  IN  SRV  0  0  0  .
```

Unfortunately, support for the SRV record among clients is, to put it mildly, thin. Certain SIP clients, Windows 2000, Windows XP, and Windows Server 2003 are notable exceptions. (More about Windows support for SRV records later in this chapter.) That's really too bad, given how useful SRV could be. Since SRV isn't widely supported, don't use SRV records in lieu of address records. It's prudent to include at least one address record for the "base" domain name to which your SRV records are attached (that is, the domain name without the labels that begin with underscores), and more if you'd like the load spread between addresses. If you only list a host as a backup in the SRV records, don't include its IP address. Also, if a host runs a service on a nonstandard port, don't include an address record for it since there's no way to redirect clients to a nonstandard port with an A record.

So, for *www.movie.edu*, we included all these records:

```
_http._tcp.www.movie.edu.   IN  SRV  0  2  80   www.movie.edu.
                            IN  SRV  0  1  80   www2.movie.edu.
                            IN  SRV  1  1  8000 postmanrings2x.movie.edu.
www.movie.edu.              IN  A    200.1.4.3 ; the address of www.movie.edu and
                            IN  A    200.1.4.4 ; the address of www2.movie.edu
                                               ; for the benefit of non-SRV aware
                                               ; clients
```

Browsers that can handle SRV records will send twice as many requests to *www. movie.edu* as to *www2.movie.edu*, and will use *postmanrings2x.movie.edu* only if both of the main web servers are unavailable. Browsers that don't use SRV records will have their requests round-robined between the addresses of *www.movie.edu* and *www2.movie.edu*.

ENUM

ENUM, which stands for Telephone Number Mapping, is a new application of DNS; its overall function is to use DNS to map E.164 numbers to URIs.* These URIs might identify a particular VoIP user, an email address, a fax machine, or many other possibilities.

You're probably already familiar with E.164 numbers, though perhaps not by that name. The E.164 recommendation from the International Telecommunication Union, or ITU, specifies the format of world telephone numbers. These formats begin with a country code (such as "1," which actually identifies not a particular country but the North American Dialing Plan, which includes the United States, Canada, and parts of Mexico and the Caribbean), then usually an area code or a city code. The format of the rest of the number is defined locally.

Phone numbers may be written with various forms of punctuation separating the country code and other fields. In the United States, for example, we often write the area code in parentheses, as in (408) 555-1234. Other common formats use dashes, periods, parentheses, or some combination of these. A plus sign ("+") is frequently used before a country code to help identify it.

Mapping an E.164 number to a URI makes it possible, for example, for a caller to reach a VoIP user even though he doesn't know and can't dial the URI that identifies the VoIP user. As long as the caller knows an E.164 number that maps to the correct URI, his phone (or, more likely, some software or device acting on behalf of his phone) can determine the destination URI and make the call. ENUM also allows users of different VoIP networks to communicate without resorting to using the public switched telephone network. And ENUM promises to become a kind of unified directory of methods for communicating with people. Under a single E.164 number, you can list URIs that allow people to contact you via phone, email, fax, and instant messaging, for example.

Translating E.164 Numbers into Domain Names

ENUM uses DNS to map E.164 numbers to URIs, and DNS uses domain names to index data, so we need to write the phone number in a canonical format and translate it into a domain name before looking it up. This requires the following steps:

1. Remove all punctuation separating the digits of the phone number and add a plus sign before the country code. (This converts the phone number "+1-408-555-1234" to the string "+14085551234.") The result is referred to as ENUM's Application Unique String, or AUS, which we'll use later.

---

* URIs are Uniform Resource Identifiers. URLs, or Uniform Resource Locators, such as you'd type into a browser, are a subset of URIs, as are URNs, or Uniform Resource Names.

2. Remove the plus sign and reverse the order of the digits in the number. (This converts the string "+14085551212" to the string "21215558041.")

3. Insert periods after each of the digits in the string and append "e164.arpa." The result is the domain name to be looked up. (This converts the string "2121558041" to the domain name *2.1.2.1.5.5.5.8.0.4.1.e164.arpa.*)

The NAPTR Record

Now that we're turned our E.164 number into a domain name to look up, we need to know what to look up. ENUM stores the information we need in a type of record called a NAPTR record.[*] NAPTR records take six record-specific fields, some of them fairly unusual:

Order

> Similar to an MX record's preference value or an SRV record's priority, this field tells ENUM clients the order in which to use this record relative to the other NAPTR records attached to this domain name. The value is an unsigned, 16-bit integer. The lower the value, the earlier in the order the record should be used.

Preference

> Also an unsigned, 16-bit integer, this field provides ENUM clients with a hint as to which record to use. If an ENUM client supports access using more than one of the URIs listed in a set of NAPTR records with the same value for order, it can use the value of preference to help decide which record to choose, lower preference values indicating greater preference. On the other hand, the client is also free to choose among the record according to its own capabilities and preferences.

Flags

> The "u" flag is the only flag defined in NAPTR records that are used with ENUM. It indicates that this NAPTR record is *terminal*; that is, it maps an E.164 number directly to a URI. As you'll see, NAPTR records can also map to other domain names, which in turn map to URIs.

Service

> The service field for ENUM records always begins with "e2u+" (in uppercase or lowercase—case isn't significant). "e2u" stands for "E.164 to URI." The string after e2u+ indicates the type, and optionally the subtype, of URI this NAPTR record maps to. For example, the e2u+sip service maps E.164 numbers to URIs that begin with "sip:" or "sips:".

---

[*] NAPTR records were actually developed before ENUM and can be used for other purposes, but their only common use today is to support ENUM.

Regular expression

This field contains a substitution expression, much like you'd expect to find in Perl or *sed*. The substitution expression modifies the AUS we derived earlier. The first half of the substitution expression is a POSIX extended regular expression. The second half can contain a combination of bytes to replace a portion of the AUS and back references to portions of the AUS matched between parentheses. The optional flag "i" indicates that the substitution expression should be applied case-insensitively. We show some examples later in this section.

Replacement

For nonterminal NAPTR records, this field specifies the next domain name to look up.

Here are some examples of NAPTR records taken from RFC 3761, which describes ENUM:

```
$ORIGIN 3.8.0.0.6.9.2.3.6.1.4.4.e164.arpa.
    NAPTR 10 100 "u" "E2U+sip"  "!^.*$!sip:info@example.com!" .
    NAPTR 10 101 "u" "E2U+h323" "!^.*$!h323:info@example.com!" .
    NAPTR 10 102 "u" "E2U+msg"  "!^.*$!mailto:info@example.com!" .
```

(Note that in each record, the final record-specific field, replacement, is a single dot, which indicates that there's no replacement domain name.)

These NAPTR records map the E.164 number +441632960083 to three possible URIs. All have the same value for order, but the administrator of the records indicated a preference for the SIP URI.

The regular expression fields look weird enough in a DNS context to warrant some explanation. The exclamation point (!) is used as a delimiter, just as a forward-slash (/) often is. There must be exactly three: one appears before the substitution expression, one between the substitution and the replacement, and one after the replacement and before any flags. You can use any nonnumeric character for the delimiter that's not a valid flag (that is, not the letter "i"). It's prudent to use either "/" or "!" because they're easy to identify.

The extended regular expression matches all or part of the AUS. In the case of these records, "^.*$" matches the entire AUS. "^" anchors the expression to the beginning of the AUS, and "$" to the end. ".*" matches zero or more occurrences of any character. So the expression matches the whole AUS, start to finish. The replacement values simply replace the AUS wholesale with a URI: *sip:info@example.com*, in the first record. Most terminal NAPTR records in ENUM, mercifully, just replace the whole AUS with a URI.

Here's an example of a NAPTR record that uses a back reference to extract part of the AUS and use it in the URI:

```
$ORIGIN 0.5.6.1.e164.arpa.
*    NAPTR 10 100 "u" "E2U+sip" "/^+1650(.*)$/sip:\1@peninsula.sip.sbc.com/" .
```

The extended regular expression uses parentheses to save everything in the AUS after +1650, then uses it in the SIP URI that replaces the AUS. ("\1" is replaced by whatever matched the portion of the regular expression in parentheses, just as in Perl.)

Of course, once an E.164 number has been translated to a URI, it may require additional DNS lookups to map domain names in the URI to IP addresses or other data.

Registering ENUM Domain Names

E.164 numbers, like domain names in DNS, are hierarchical. This makes delegation under *e164.arpa* straightforward: country code–level subdomains of *e164.arpa* will generally be delegated to registries acting on behalf of that country. The registries will then delegate subdomains to carriers or other telecommunications companies.

For example, *9.4.e164.arpa*, the ENUM zone for country code 49, which belongs to Germany, has already been delegated to DENIC—also the registry for the *de* top-level domain. Any user with a German phone number can register NAPTR records under *9.4.e164.arpa* by working through participating DENIC members, who will validate that the user actually owns the number and request that the appropriate NAPTR records be added.

To find out whether your country code's subdomain of *e164.arpa* has been delegated, and, if so, to whom, you can check RIPE's web site at *http://www.ripe.net/enum/request-archives/*.

Privacy and Security Issues with ENUM

There are justifiable concerns about the privacy and security of ENUM data. To be useful, records in the *e164.arpa* namespace must be accessible by anyone. It would be trivial for a spammer to mine all of the email addresses out of that namespace, for example, by walking all possible phone numbers. A hacker might be able to spoof the NAPTR records associated with an E.164 number, redirecting calls made to that number.

DNSSEC can help with the second type of threat. In fact, several of the ENUM RFCs refer to DNSSEC as a possible solution.

Internationalized Domain Names

One shortcoming in the original design of DNS that has become painfully obvious over the years is the character set supported in domain names. While DNS purists may tell you that labels in domain names can contain any binary value, US-ASCII characters are really the only values that are useful and supported by all DNS implementations. As the Internet has expanded internationally, this has meant that companies in countries in which European languages aren't widely spoken have been forced to use ASCII characters for their domain names. Even Europeans have had to transcribe their non-ASCII characters into ASCII; most Germans, for example, reflexively write ä and ö as ae and oe, respectively.

RFC 3490 introduced a method for encoding international characters in the labels of domain names. Because simply inserting non-ASCII characters into domain names doesn't work, most DNS software interprets multibyte characters as a sequence of ASCII characters, for example; these international characters are encoded into ASCII. The resulting ASCII-compatible encoding, or ACE, is basically unintelligible to ordinary humans in the same way that base-64 encodings are. To help distinguish an ACE-encoded label in a domain name from a normal but particularly cryptic ASCII label, ACE encodings include a specific prefix, "xn--," which is now forbidden to appear in a normal, ASCII label. Domain names with one or more labels encoded in ACE are referred to as internationalized domain names, or IDNs.

Rather than trying to accommodate the multitude of language- and script-specific character sets that computers support, RFC 3490 encodes only a single character set, called Unicode, into ASCII. But what a character set it is! Unicode contains tens of thousands of characters from the world's scripts.* In almost all cases, it's possible to transform a string typed in a script-specific character set (say ISO Latin-1) into a Unicode equivalent.

The burden of encoding Unicode into ACE is placed on applications, not on resolvers or nameservers. If a web browser allows a user to type *www.etwas-ähnlich.de* as a URL, it's incumbent upon that web browser to encode the "etwas-ähnlich" label into the equivalent ACE encoding before passing the domain name to the resolver to look up.† In a way, that's good news for you, the administrator, because you don't need to upgrade your resolvers or nameservers. On the other hand, if your Marketing folks drop by with a list of internationalized domain names they want registered, you may end up with a whole lot of very nasty-looking zone data.

For example, say Marketing wants you to register *etwas-ähnlich.de*. DENIC, the registry that runs the top-level *de* zone, requires that you have a zone's nameservers up and running before it'll delegate the zone to you. So you'll need to determine the ACE encoding of *etwas-ähnlich.de*.

There are several web sites that offer simple ACE encoding utilities, among them:

- *http://www.imc.org/idna/*
- *http://www.idnforums.com/converter/*
- *http://josefsson.org/idn.php/*

---

* To learn more about Unicode, see The Unicode Consortium's web site at *http://www.unicode.org/*.
† Since "www" and "com" are simple ASCII labels, they don't need to be encoded.

Using any of these, you can determine that "xn--etwas-hnlich-lcb.de" is the ACE-encoded equivalent of *etwas-ähnlich.de*. In the *named.conf* file on your primary nameserver, you need to add a *zone* statement like this:

```
zone "xn--etwas-hnlich-lcb.de" {
    type master;
    file "db.xn--etwas-hnlich-lcb.de";
};
```

The zone datafile, too, needs to refer to the ACE-encoded domain name:

```
$TTL 1d
xn--etwas-hnlich-lcb.de.   IN    SOA    ns1.xn--etwas-hnlich-lcb.de. (
    hostmaster.xn--etwas-hnlich-lcb.de.
    2006012500 1h 15m 30d 1h )
            IN    NS    ns1.xn--etwas-hnlich-lcb.de.
            IN    NS    ns2.xn--etwas-hnlich-lcb.de.
```

Of course, you can avoid some of this by using nameservers with regular ASCII domain names and by using a different email address in the SOA record.

If you're planning on doing any large-scale manipulation of internationalized domain names, you'll probably need a set of library routines to convert ACE to Unicode and back. There are several available; here are a couple:

- JNIC's *idnkit*, available in the BIND 9 distribution in *contrib/idn/idnkit-1.0-src*
- The GNU IDN Library, or *libidn*, at *http://www.gnu.org/software/libidn/*

A few notes of caution about IDNs. First, support for IDNs in web browsers is spotty. While Firefox and Opera support IDN, Internet Explorer doesn't until IE 7.0, which as of this writing is in beta. Most other programs that take domain names as input, such as mail clients, have no IDN support at all.

There's also concern that IDNs complicate an already tricky problem with *homographs*, different characters whose glyphs (written forms) look the same. This has been a relatively minor problem in the ASCII past, exploited by hackers who take advantage of the fact that it can be difficult to differentiate between "1" and "l" or "0" and "O," and who try to lure you into clicking on a familiar-looking URL like *www.goog1e.com*. IDNs pose a greater threat, because many different Unicode characters appear indistinguishable. Consequently, some newer versions of the browsers that support IDN actually display the ACE version of an IDN label rather than its Unicode equivalent. Yuck.

DNS and WINS

In our first edition—oh, for those simpler days!—we mentioned the close alignment between NetBIOS names and domain names, but noted that, alas, there was no way for DNS to function as a NetBIOS nameserver. Basically, a nameserver would need to support dynamic updates to function as a NetBIOS nameserver.

Of course, BIND 8 and 9 *do* support dynamic updates. Unfortunately, neither NetBIOS clients nor WINS servers send dynamic updates to nameservers. WINS servers accept only the peculiar, proprietary dynamic updates sent by NetBIOS clients. In other words, a WINS server doesn't speak DNS.

However, Microsoft provides a nameserver, the Microsoft DNS Server, which in turn can talk to WINS servers. The Microsoft DNS Server has a nice graphical administration tool, as you would expect from Microsoft, and provides a handy hook into WINS: you can configure the server to query a WINS server for address data if it doesn't find the data in a DNS zone.

This is done by adding a new WINS record to the zone. The WINS record, like the SOA record, is attached to the zone's domain name. It acts as a flag to tell the Microsoft DNS Server to query a WINS server if it doesn't find an address for the name it's looking up. The record:

```
@       0       IN      WINS            192.249.249.39 192.253.253.39
```

tells the Microsoft DNS Server to query the WINS servers running at 192.249.249.39 and 192.253.253.39 (in that order) for the name. The zero TTL is a precaution against the record being looked up and cached.

There's also a companion WINS-R record that allows a Microsoft DNS Server to reverse-map IP addresses using a NetBIOS NBSTAT request. If an *in-addr.arpa* zone contains a WINS-R record such as:

```
@       0       IN      WINS-R          movie.edu
```

and the IP address sought doesn't appear in the zone, the nameserver attempts to send a NetBIOS NBSTAT request to the IP address being reverse-mapped. This amounts to calling a phone number and asking the person on the other end, "What's your name?" The nameserver then appends a dot and the domain name in the record-specific data, in this case ".movie.edu," to the result.

These records provide valuable glue between the two namespaces. Unfortunately, the integration isn't perfect. As they say, the devil is in the details.

The main problem, as we see it, is that only Microsoft DNS Servers support the WINS and WINS-R records. Therefore, if you want lookups in the *fx.movie.edu* zone to be relayed to the Special Effects Department's WINS server, then all *fx.movie.edu* nameservers must be Microsoft DNS Servers. Why? Imagine that the nameservers for *fx.movie.edu* were mixed, with some Microsoft DNS Servers and some BIND nameservers. If a remote nameserver tried to look up a NetBIOS name in *fx.movie.edu*, it would choose which of the *fx.movie.edu* nameservers to query according to round-trip time. If the server it happened to choose were a Microsoft DNS Server, it would be able to resolve the name to a dynamically assigned address. However, if it happened to choose a BIND nameserver, it wouldn't be able to resolve the name.

The best DNS-WINS configuration we've heard of so far puts all WINS-mapped data in its own zone, say *wins.movie.edu*. All the nameservers for *wins.movie.edu* are Microsoft DNS Servers, and the zone *wins.movie.edu* contains just an SOA record, NS records, and a WINS record pointing to the WINS servers for *wins.movie.edu*. This way, there's no chance of inconsistent answers between authoritative servers for the zone.

Reverse-mapping data, of course, can't easily be split into separate zones for BIND and Microsoft nameservers to maintain. So if you want both traditional, PTR record-based reverse mapping and WINS-R-enhanced reverse mapping, you'll need to host your reverse-mapping zones solely on Microsoft DNS Servers.

Another problem is that WINS and WINS-R are proprietary. BIND nameservers don't understand them, and, in fact, a BIND slave that transfers a WINS record from a Microsoft DNS Server primary master will fail to load the zone because WINS is an unknown type. (We discussed this, and how to work around it, in Chapter 14.)

The answer to these problems is the DNS standard dynamic update functionality that was first introduced in BIND 8 (described in Chapter 10) and the support for it in Windows 2000, Windows XP, and Windows Server 2003. Dynamic update allows the addition and deletion of records from a zone, which in turn gives the folks at Microsoft the functionality they need to use DNS as a name service for NetBIOS. So without further ado...

DNS, Windows, and Active Directory

Modern Windows operating systems—by which we mean Windows 2000, Windows XP, and Windows Server 2003—can use standard dynamic updates to register hosts in DNS. For a modern Windows client, registration means adding a name-to-address mapping and an address-to-name mapping for that client—information Windows clients formerly registered with WINS servers. For a Windows server, registration involves adding records to a zone to tell clients which services it's running and where (on which host and port). For example, an Active Directory Domain Controller uses dynamic update to add SRV records that tell Windows clients which services it's running.

How Windows Uses Dynamic Update

So what gets added when a client registers? Let's reboot a Windows client in the Special Effects Lab and see.

Our client is called *mummy.fx.movie.edu*. It has the fixed IP address 192.253.254.13 (it doesn't get its address from our DHCP server). At boot time, the dynamic update routines on the client go through the following steps:

1. Look up the SOA record for *mummy.fx.movie.edu* on the local nameserver. Though there isn't an SOA record for that domain name, the authority section of the response includes the SOA record of the zone that contains *mummy.fx.movie.edu*, which is *fx.movie.edu*.

2. Look up the address of the nameserver in the MNAME field of the SOA record, *bladerunner.fx.movie.edu*.

3. Send a dynamic update to *bladerunner.fx.movie.edu* with two prerequisites: that *mummy.fx.movie.edu* isn't an alias (i.e., doesn't own a CNAME record) and that it doesn't already have an address record pointing to 192.253.254.13. The dynamic update contains no update section; it's just a probe to see what's out there.

4. If *mummy.fx.movie.edu* already points to the correct address, stop. Otherwise, send another dynamic update to *bladerunner.fx.movie.edu* with the prerequisites that *mummy.fx.movie.edu* isn't an alias and doesn't have an address record—any address record—already. If the prerequisites are satisfied, the update adds an address record pointing *mummy.fx.movie.edu* to 192.253.254.13. If *mummy.fx. movie.edu* already has an address record, the client sends an update to delete that address record and add its own.

5. Look up the SOA record for *254.253.192.in-addr.arpa*.

6. Look up the address of the nameserver in the MNAME field of the SOA record (though because the MNAME field contains *bladerunner.fx.movie.edu*, which we looked up recently, and modern Windows OSes have a caching resolver, this shouldn't require another query).

7. Send a dynamic update to *bladerunner.fx.movie.edu* with the prerequisite that *13.254.253.192.in-addr.arpa* isn't an alias. If the prerequisite is satisfied, the update adds a PTR record mapping 192.253.254.13 back to *mummy.fx.movie. edu*. If *13.254.253.192.in-addr.arpa* is an alias, stop.

If we're using the Microsoft DHCP Server included with a modern Windows server operating system, the DHCP server, by default, adds the PTR record. There's also an option in the DHCP server's MMC-based management interface that allows the administrator to specify that the DHCP server add both the PTR record and the A record. If the DHCP server had added the A record, though, it wouldn't have set a prerequisite.

Servers, particularly Domain Controllers, register lots of information in DNS using dynamic update, both when they're first set up and periodically thereafter. (The *netlogon* service, for example, registers its SRV records hourly!) This allows clients to locate services on whichever host and port they're running. Since we just set up an Active Directory domain called *fx.movie.edu*, let's take a look at the records that our Domain Controller, *matrix.fx.movie.edu*, added:

```
fx.movie.edu. 600 IN A 192.253.254.14
ec4caf62-31b2-4773-bcce-7b1e31c04d25._msdcs.fx.movie.edu. 600 IN CNAME matrix.fx.
movie.edu.
gc._msdcs.fx.movie.edu. 600 IN A 192.253.254.14
_gc._tcp.fx.movie.edu. 600 IN SRV 0 100 3268 matrix.fx.movie.edu.
_gc._tcp.Default-First-Site-Name._sites.fx.movie.edu. 600 IN SRV 0 100 3268 matrix.
fx.movie.edu.
_ldap._tcp.gc._msdcs.fx.movie.edu. 600 IN SRV 0 100 3268 matrix.fx.movie.edu.
_ldap._tcp.Default-First-Site-Name._sites.gc._msdcs.fx.movie.edu. 600 IN SRV 0 100
3268 matrix.fx.movie.edu.
_kerberos._tcp.dc._msdcs.fx.movie.edu. 600 IN SRV 0 100 88 matrix.fx.movie.edu.
_kerberos._tcp.Default-First-Site-Name._sites.dc._msdcs.fx.movie.edu. 600 IN SRV 0
100 88 matrix.fx.movie.edu.
_kerberos._tcp.fx.movie.edu. 600 IN SRV 0 100 88 matrix.fx.movie.edu.
_kerberos._tcp.Default-First-Site-Name._sites.fx.movie.edu. 600 IN SRV 0 100 88
matrix.fx.movie.edu.
_kerberos._udp.fx.movie.edu. 600 IN SRV 0 100 88 matrix.fx.movie.edu.
_kpasswd._tcp.fx.movie.edu. 600 IN SRV 0 100 464 matrix.fx.movie.edu.
_kpasswd._udp.fx.movie.edu. 600 IN SRV 0 100 464 matrix.fx.movie.edu.
_ldap._tcp.fx.movie.edu. 600 IN SRV 0 100 389 matrix.fx.movie.edu.
_ldap._tcp.Default-First-Site-Name._sites.fx.movie.edu. 600 IN SRV 0 100 389 matrix.
fx.movie.edu.
_ldap._tcp.pdc._msdcs.fx.movie.edu. 600 IN SRV 0 100 389 matrix.fx.movie.edu.
_ldap._tcp.97526bc9-adf7-4ec8-a096-0dbb34a17052.domains._msdcs.fx.movie.edu. 600 IN
SRV 0 100 389 matrix.fx.movie.edu.
_ldap._tcp.dc._msdcs.fx.movie.edu. 600 IN SRV 0 100 389 matrix.fx.movie.edu.
_ldap._tcp.Default-First-Site-Name._sites.dc._msdcs.fx.movie.edu. 600 IN SRV 0 100
389 matrix.fx.movie.edu.
```

Whoa! That's a lot of records!

These records tell Active Directory clients where the services offered by the Domain Controller, including Kerberos and LDAP, are running.* You can see from the SRV records that they're all running on *matrix.fx.movie.edu*, our only Domain Controller. If we had another Domain Controller, you'd see twice as many records.

The owner names of all the records end in *fx.movie.edu*, the name of the Active Directory domain. If the Active Directory domain was called *ad.movie.edu*, the dynamic update routines would update the zone containing the domain name *ad.movie.edu*, which is *movie.edu*.

---

* For an explanation of the function of each of these records, see the document "How DNS Support for Active Directory Works" at *http://www.microsoft.com/Resources/Documentation/windowsserv/2003/all/techref/en-us/ w2k3tr_addns_how.asp*.

Problems with Active Directory and BIND

While Microsoft's decision to replace WINS with DNS was laudable, the implementation poses some problems for folks who run BIND nameservers. First, Windows clients and DHCP servers have a nasty habit of deleting address records owned by the same domain name as the clients or servers. For example, if we let the users in the Special Effects Lab configure their own computers and choose their computers' names, and one user happens to use a name that is already taken, maybe by one of our rendering servers, his computer will try to delete the conflicting address record (that of the rendering server) and add its own. That's not very sociable.

Luckily, that behavior can be corrected on the client. The client does, in fact, check to see whether the domain name it's using already owns an address record by setting the prerequisite described in the previous section's Step 4. (It just deletes it if it does exist, by default.) But you can follow the instructions in Microsoft Knowledge Base article Q246804 to tell the client not to delete conflicting records. The price? A client can't differentiate between an address being used by a different host with the same domain name and an address that formerly belonged to it, so if the client changes addresses, it can't automatically update the zone.

If you elect to have your Microsoft DHCP Server handle all registration, you don't have the option of leaving conflicting addresses alone. The Microsoft DHCP Server doesn't use prerequisites to detect collisions; it just unceremoniously deletes conflicting address records.

Given the limitations of having the DHCP server handle all the registering, why would anyone consider it? Because if you allow any client to register itself, and you can use only primitive, IP address–based access lists to authorize dynamic updates, you are allowing *any client's address* to dynamically update your zones. Savvier users of those clients can easily fire off a few custom-made dynamic updates to change your zone's MX records or the address of your web server.

Secure Dynamic Update

Surely Microsoft doesn't just live with these problems, right? No, not with the Microsoft DNS Server. The Microsoft DNS Server supports GSS-TSIG, a dialect of TSIG (which we covered in Chapter 11). A client that uses GSS-TSIG negotiates a TSIG key with the help of a Kerberos server, then uses that key to sign a dynamic update. The use of GSS, the Generic Security Service, to retrieve the key means that an administrator doesn't need to hardcode a key on each of his clients.

Since the name of the TSIG key the client uses to sign the update is just the domain name of the client, the nameserver can make sure that only the client that added an address can delete it later, simply by tracking the domain name of the TSIG key used to add a given record. Only an updater with the same TSIG key is allowed to delete that record.

Modern Windows clients try GSS-TSIG-signed dynamic updates if their unsigned dynamic updates are refused. You can also configure them to send signed updates first by following the instructions in Knowledge Base article Q246804, mentioned earlier.

BIND and GSS-TSIG

Unfortunately, BIND nameservers don't yet support GSS-TSIG, so you can't use Windows's secure dynamic update with BIND. A forthcoming version of BIND 9, however, is scheduled to support GSS-TSIG. Once BIND does support GSS-TSIG, you'll be able to use all the update policy rules described in Chapter 10 to control which keys can update which records. A simple set of rules that says:

```
zone "fx.movie.edu" {
    type master;
    file "db.fx.movie.edu";
    update-policy {
        grant *.fx.movie.edu. self *.fx.movie.edu. A;
        grant matrix.fx.movie.edu. self matrix.fx.movie.edu. ANY;
        grant matrix.fx.movie.edu. subdomain fx.movie.edu. SRV CNAME A;
    };
};
```

may someday be enough to let Windows clients and servers register what they need in your zone.

What to Do?

In the meantime, how do you handle the proliferation of Windows and Active Directory on your network? Well, Microsoft would advise you to "upgrade" all your nameservers to the Microsoft DNS Server. But if you like BIND—and we do—you'd probably like some other options.

Handling Windows clients

The first (and probably most common) option for handling your Windows clients is to create a delegated subdomain for all of them to live in. We might call ours *win.fx.movie.edu*. Within *win.fx.movie.edu*, anything goes: clients can stomp on other clients' addresses, and someone may send a bunch of hand-crafted dynamic updates to add bogus records to the zone. The intent is to create a sandbox (or jail, if you prefer) that the clients can't break out of and that they can trash if they want to. If you have kids, you have an intuitive understanding of this concept.

By default, a Windows client will try to register itself in a forward-mapping zone with the same name as its Active Directory domain. So we'll have to do some extra configuration to tell our clients to register in *win.fx.movie.edu* instead of in *fx.movie.edu*. In particular, we'll have to go to a window that resides at My Computer → Properties → Network Identification → Properties → More, uncheck "Change primary DNS suffix when domain membership changes," and type *win.fx.movie.edu* in the field labeled *Primary DNS suffix of this computer*. On all our clients.

Another possibility is to leave your clients in your main production zone (for our lab, that's *fx.movie.edu*) but allow dynamic updates only from the address of the DHCP server. You then configure your DHCP server to assume responsibility for maintaining both A records and PTR records. (You can manually add A and PTR records for hosts that don't use DHCP.)

In this scenario, it's more difficult for the little imps to send their custom dynamic updates to your nameserver because it involves spoofing the address of the DHCP server. It's still possible that someone will bring up a client with a domain name that conflicts with an existing domain name in the zone, though.

If you're willing to consider using a different DHCP server, you can deploy an even more secure solution. The latest versions of the ISC DHCP server support TSIG-signed dynamic updates and use a clever mechanism based on TXT records to avoid name collisions in DHCP clients. When the DHCP server adds an A record on behalf of a DHCP client, it also adds a TXT record to the client's domain name, in which the record-specific data is a one-way hash of the client's MAC address. The resulting records look like this:

```
walktheline       A      192.253.254.237
                  TXT    "313f1778871429e6d240893c1afc163aee"
```

If the DHCP server later tries to add a different A record to that domain name on behalf of a client, it checks whether the client's MAC address hashes to the same value that's stored in the TXT record. If it does, the DHCP server removes the old A record because it belonged to the same client; the client has probably just moved to a new subnet or leased a different address. If it doesn't, the DHCP server won't perform the update because the old A record likely belongs to a different client that happens to have the same domain name.

For more information on the ISC DHCP server, see *http://www.isc.org/sw/dhcp/*.

Handling Windows servers

The main server you need to accommodate with your nameservers is the Domain Controller (or Controllers, if you have more than one). The DC wants to add the passel of records we showed earlier. If it can't add them at setup time, it'll write the records, in master file format, to a file called *System32\Config\netlogon.dns* under the system root.

First, you need to determine which zone you need to update. That's just a matter of finding the zone that contains the Active Directory domain name. If your Active Directory domain has the same name as an existing zone, of course, that's the zone to update. Otherwise, just keep stripping off the leading labels of your Active Directory domain until you get to the domain name of a zone.

Once you have the zone that you need to update, you need to decide how to proceed. If you don't mind letting your Domain Controller dynamically update your zone, just add an appropriate *allow-update* substatement to the *zone* statement and you're done. If you'd rather not allow your DC complete control of the zone, you can leave dynamic updates disabled and let the DC create the *netlogon.dns* file. Then use an $INCLUDE control statement to read the contents of the file into your zone datafile:

```
$INCLUDE netlogon.dns
```

If neither option appeals to you because you want the DC to be able to change its records but don't want it mangling your zone, you still have a trick up your sleeve. You can take advantage of the funny format of the owner names in SRV records and create delegated subdomains called (in our case) *_udp.fx.movie.edu*, *_tcp.fx.movie.edu*, *_sites.fx.movie.edu*, and *_msdcs.fx.movie.edu*. (You might have to turn off name checking for *_msdcs.fx.movie.edu*, because the Domain Controller wants to add an address record to the zone in addition to a slew of SRV records, and the owner name of that record will contain an underscore.) Then let the DC dynamically update these zones, but not your main zone:

```
acl dc { 192.253.254.13; };

zone "_udp.fx.movie.edu" {
    type master;
    file "db._udp.fx.movie.edu";
    allow-update { dc; };
};

zone "_tcp.fx.movie.edu" {
    type master;
    file "db._tcp.fx.movie.edu";
    allow-update { dc; };
};

zone "_sites.fx.movie.edu" {
    type master;
    file "db._sites.fx.movie.edu";
    allow-update { dc; };
};

zone "_msdcs.fx.movie.edu" {
    type master;
    file "db._msdcs.fx.movie.edu";
    allow-update { dc; };
    check-names ignore;
};
```

If your Domain Controllers run Windows Server 2003, you need to add two more zones to that list: *DomainDNSZones.fx.movie.edu* and *ForestDNSZones.fx.movie.edu*:

```
zone "DomainDNSZones.fx.movie.edu" {
    type master;
    file "db.DomainDNSZones.fx.movie.edu";
```

```
        allow-update { dc; };
};

zone "ForestDNSZones.fx.movie.edu" {
    type master;
    file "db.ForestDNSZones.fx.movie.edu";
    allow-update { dc; };
    check-names ignore;
};
```

Now you have the best of both worlds: dynamic registration of services with a safe production zone.

DNS Message Format and Resource Records

This appendix outlines the format of DNS messages and enumerates all the resource record types. The resource records are shown in their textual format, as you would specify them in a zone datafile, and in their binary format, as they appear in DNS messages. You'll find a few resource records here that weren't covered earlier because they are experimental or obsolete.

We've included the portions of RFC 1035, written by Paul Mockapetris, that deal with the textual format of master files (what we called *zone data files* in the book) or with the DNS message format (for those of you who need to parse DNS packets).

Master File Format

(From RFC 1035, pages 33–35)

The format of these files is a sequence of entries. Entries are predominantly line-oriented, though parentheses can be used to continue a list of items across a line boundary, and text literals can contain CRLF within the text. Any combination of tabs and spaces acts as a delimiter between the separate items that make up an entry. The end of any line in the master file can end with a comment. The comment starts with a semicolon (;).

The following entries are defined:

    blank[comment]

    $ORIGIN domain-name [comment]

    $INCLUDE *file-name* [*domain-name*] [*comment*]

    domain-name rr [*comment*]

    blank rr [*comment*]

Blank lines, with or without comments, are allowed anywhere in the file.

Two control entries are defined: $ORIGIN and $INCLUDE. $ORIGIN is followed by a domain name and resets the current origin for relative domain names to the stated name. $INCLUDE inserts the named file into the current file and may optionally specify a domain name that sets the relative domain name origin for the included file. $INCLUDE may also have a comment. Note that an $INCLUDE entry never changes the relative origin of the parent file, regardless of changes to the relative origin made within the included file.

The last two forms represent RRs. If an entry for an RR begins with a blank, the RR is assumed to be owned by the last stated owner. If an RR entry begins with a *domain-name*, the owner name is reset.

rr contents take one of the following forms:

```
[TTL] [class] type RDATA
[class] [TTL] type RDATA
```

The RR begins with optional TTL and class fields, followed by a type and RDATA field appropriate to the type and class. Class and type use the standard mnemonics; TTL is a decimal integer. Omitted class and TTL values default to the last explicitly stated values. Since type and class mnemonics are disjoint, the parse is unique.

*domain-name*s make up a large share of the data in the master file. The labels in the domain name are expressed as character strings and separated by dots. Quoting conventions allow arbitrary characters to be stored in domain names. Domain names that end in a dot are called absolute, and are taken as complete. Domain names that do not end in a dot are called relative; the actual domain name is the concatenation of the relative part with an origin specified in an $ORIGIN, $INCLUDE, or argument to the master file-loading routine. A relative name is an error when no origin is available.

character-string is expressed in one of two ways: as a contiguous set of characters without interior spaces, or as a string beginning with " and ending with ". Inside a "-delimited string any character can occur, except for " itself, which must be quoted using a backslash (\).

Because these files are text files, several special encodings are necessary to allow arbitrary data to be loaded. In particular:

.

 Of the root.

@

 A free-standing @ denotes the current origin.

\X

 Where X is any character other than a digit (0–9), \ is used to quote that character so that its special meaning does not apply. For example, \. can place a dot character in a label.

\DDD

> Where each D is a digit in the octet corresponding to the decimal number described by DDD. The resulting octet is assumed to be text and is not checked for special meaning.

( )

> Parentheses are used to group data that crosses a line boundary. In effect, line terminations are not recognized within parentheses.

;

> A semicolon is used to start a comment; the remainder of the line is ignored.

Character Case

(From RFC 1035, page 9)

For all parts of the DNS that are part of the official protocol, all comparisons between character strings (e.g., labels, domain names, etc.) are done in a case-insensitive manner. At present, this rule is in force throughout the domain system without exception. However, future additions beyond current usage may need to use the full binary octet capabilities in names, so attempts to store domain names in seven-bit ASCII or use of special bytes to terminate labels, etc., should be avoided.

Types

Here is a complete list of resource record types. The textual representation is used in master files. The binary representation is used in DNS queries and responses. These resource records are described on pages 13–21 of RFC 1035.

A address

(From RFC 1035, page 20)

Textual Representation

```
owner ttl class A address
```

Example

```
localhost.movie.edu.    IN A 127.0.0.1
```

Binary Representation

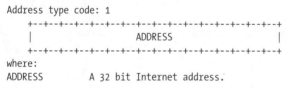

```
Address type code: 1
    +--+--+--+--+--+--+--+--+--+--+--+--+--+--+--+--+
    |                    ADDRESS                    |
    +--+--+--+--+--+--+--+--+--+--+--+--+--+--+--+--+
where:
ADDRESS         A 32 bit Internet address.
```

CNAME canonical name

(From RFC 1035, page 14)

Textual Representation

owner ttl class CNAME *canonical-dname*

Example

wh.movie.edu.   IN   CNAME   wormhole.movie.edu.

Binary Representation

CNAME type code: 5

```
+--+--+--+--+--+--+--+--+--+--+--+--+--+--+--+--+
/                     CNAME                     /
/                                               /
+--+--+--+--+--+--+--+--+--+--+--+--+--+--+--+--+
```

where:

CNAME   A *domain-name* which specifies the canonical
                  or primary name for the owner. The owner name is
                  an alias.

HINFO host information

(From RFC 1035, page 14)

Textual Representation

owner ttl class HINFO *cpu os*

Example

grizzly.movie.edu.   IN   HINFO   VAX-11/780 UNIX

Binary Representation

HINFO type code: 13

```
+--+--+--+--+--+--+--+--+--+--+--+--+--+--+--+--+
/                      CPU                      /
+--+--+--+--+--+--+--+--+--+--+--+--+--+--+--+--+
/                      OS                       /
+--+--+--+--+--+--+--+--+--+--+--+--+--+--+--+--+
```

where:

CPU   A *character-string* which specifies the CPU type.
OS   A *character-string* which specifies the
                  operating system type.

MX mail exchanger

(From RFC 1035, page 17)

Textual Representation

owner ttl class MX *preference exchange-dname*

Example

```
ora.com.  IN  MX  0   ora.ora.com.
          IN  MX  10  ruby.ora.com.
          IN  MX  10  opal.ora.com.
```

Binary Representation

MX type code: 15

```
    +--+--+--+--+--+--+--+--+--+--+--+--+--+--+--+--+
    |                  PREFERENCE                   |
    +--+--+--+--+--+--+--+--+--+--+--+--+--+--+--+--+
    /                  EXCHANGE                     /
    /                                               /
    +--+--+--+--+--+--+--+--+--+--+--+--+--+--+--+--+
```

where:

PREFERENCE   A 16 bit integer which specifies the preference
              given to this RR among others at the same owner.
              Lower values are preferred.

EXCHANGE   A *domain-name* which specifies a host willing
              to act as a mail exchange for the owner name.

NS name server

(From RFC 1035, page 18)

Textual Representation

owner ttl class NS *name-server-dname*

Example

```
movie.edu.  IN   NS   terminator.movie.edu.
```

Binary Representation

NS type code: 2

```
    +--+--+--+--+--+--+--+--+--+--+--+--+--+--+--+--+
    /                   NSDNAME                     /
    /                                               /
    +--+--+--+--+--+--+--+--+--+--+--+--+--+--+--+--+
```

where:

NSDNAME   A *domain-name* which specifies a host which
              should be authoritative for the specified
              class and domain.

PTR pointer

(From RFC 1035, page 18)

Textual Representation

owner ttl class PTR *dname*

Example

```
1.249.249.192.in-addr.arpa.  IN PTR wormhole.movie.edu.
```

Binary Representation

```
PTR type code: 12
    +--+--+--+--+--+--+--+--+--+--+--+--+--+--+--+--+
    /                     PTRDNAME                  /
    +--+--+--+--+--+--+--+--+--+--+--+--+--+--+--+--+
where:
PTRDNAME        A domain-name which points to some location in
                the domain name space.
```

SOA start of authority

(From RFC 1035, pages 19–20)

Textual Representation

owner ttl class SOA *source-dname mbox* (*serial refresh retry expire minimum*)

Example

```
movie.edu. IN SOA terminator.movie.edu. al.robocop.movie.edu. (
                    1        ; Serial
                    10800    ; Refresh after 3 hours
                    3600     ; Retry after 1 hour
                    604800   ; Expire after 1 week
                    86400 )  ; Minimum TTL of 1 day
```

Binary Representation

```
SOA type code: 6
    +--+--+--+--+--+--+--+--+--+--+--+--+--+--+--+--+
    /                      MNAME                    /
    /                                               /
    +--+--+--+--+--+--+--+--+--+--+--+--+--+--+--+--+
    /                      RNAME                    /
    +--+--+--+--+--+--+--+--+--+--+--+--+--+--+--+--+
    |                      SERIAL                   |
    |                                               |
    +--+--+--+--+--+--+--+--+--+--+--+--+--+--+--+--+
    |                      REFRESH                  |
    |                                               |
    +--+--+--+--+--+--+--+--+--+--+--+--+--+--+--+--+
    |                      RETRY                    |
    |                                               |
    +--+--+--+--+--+--+--+--+--+--+--+--+--+--+--+--+
    |                      EXPIRE                   |
    |                                               |
```

```
    +--+--+--+--+--+--+--+--+--+--+--+--+--+--+--+--+
    |                    MINIMUM                    |
    |                                               |
    +--+--+--+--+--+--+--+--+--+--+--+--+--+--+--+--+
```
where:

MNAME   The *domain-name* of the name server that was the
            original or primary source of data for this zone.
RNAME   A *domain-name* which specifies the mailbox of the
            person responsible for this zone.
SERIAL   The unsigned 32 bit version number of the original
            copy of the zone. Zone transfers preserve this
            value. This value wraps and should be compared
            using sequence space arithmetic.
REFRESH   A 32 bit time interval before the zone should be
            refreshed.
RETRY   A 32 bit time interval that should elapse before
            a failed refresh should be retried.
EXPIRE   A 32 bit time value that specifies the upper limit
            on the time interval that can elapse before the
            zone is no longer authoritative.
MINIMUM   The unsigned 32 bit minimum TTL field that should
            be exported with any RR from this zone.

TXT text

(From RFC 1035, page 20)

Textual Representation

owner ttl class TXT *txt-strings*

Example

cujo.movie.edu. IN TXT "Location: machine room dog house"

Binary Representation

TXT type code: 16

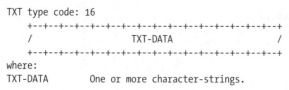

```
    +--+--+--+--+--+--+--+--+--+--+--+--+--+--+--+--+
    /                    TXT-DATA                   /
    +--+--+--+--+--+--+--+--+--+--+--+--+--+--+--+--+
```
where:

TXT-DATA   One or more character-strings.

WKS well-known services

(From RFC 1035, page 21)

Textual Representation

owner ttl class WKS *address protocol service-list*

Example

```
terminator.movie.edu.  IN  WKS 192.249.249.3  TCP ( telnet smtp
                                               ftp shell domain )
```

Binary Representation

```
WKS type code: 11
    +--+--+--+--+--+--+--+--+--+--+--+--+--+--+--+--+
    |                    ADDRESS                    |
    +--+--+--+--+--+--+--+--+--+--+--+--+--+--+--+--+
    |      PROTOCOL      |                           |
    +--+--+--+--+--+--+--+                           |
    |                                               |
    /                    BIT MAP                    /
    /                                               /
    +--+--+--+--+--+--+--+--+--+--+--+--+--+--+--+--+
```

```
where:
ADDRESS        An 32 bit Internet address.
PROTOCOL       An 8 bit IP protocol number.
BIT MAP        A variable length bit map.  The bit map must
               be a multiple of 8 bits long.
```

New Types from RFC 1183

AFSDB Andrew File System Data Base (experimental)

Textual Representation

owner ttl class AFSDB *subtype hostname*

Example

```
fx.movie.edu.  IN  AFSDB  1 bladerunner.fx.movie.edu.
               IN  AFSDB  2 bladerunner.fx.movie.edu.
               IN  AFSDB  1 empire.fx.movie.edu.
               IN  AFSDB  2 aliens.fx.movie.edu.
```

Binary Representation

```
AFSDB type code: 18
    +--+--+--+--+--+--+--+--+--+--+--+--+--+--+--+--+
    |                    SUBTYPE                    |
    +--+--+--+--+--+--+--+--+--+--+--+--+--+--+--+--+.
    /                    HOSTNAME                   /
    /                                               /
    +--+--+--+--+--+--+--+--+--+--+--+--+--+--+--+--+
```

```
where:
SUBTYPE        Subtype 1 is an AFS cell database server. Subtype 2
               is a DCE authenticated name server.
HOSTNAME       A domain-name which specifies a host that has a
               server for the cell named by the owner of the RR.
```

ISDN Integrated Services Digital Network address (experimental)

Textual Representation

owner ttl class ISDN *ISDN-address sa*

Example

```
delay.hp.com.    IN   ISDN  141555514539488
hep.hp.com.      IN   ISDN  141555514539488 004
```

Binary Representation

```
ISDN type code: 20
    +--+--+--+--+--+--+--+--+--+--+--+--+--+--+--+--+
    /                 ISDN ADDRESS                  /
    +--+--+--+--+--+--+--+--+--+--+--+--+--+--+--+--+
    /                  SUBADDRESS                   /
    +--+--+--+--+--+--+--+--+--+--+--+--+--+--+--+--+
where:
ISDN ADDRESS    A character-string which identifies the ISDN number
                of owner and DDI (Direct Dial In) if any.
SUBADDRESS      An optional character-string specifying the
                subaddress.
```

RP Responsible Person (experimental)

Textual Representation

owner ttl class RP *mbox-dname txt-dname*

Example

```
; The current origin is fx.movie.edu
@            IN  RP   ajs.fx.movie.edu.    ajs.fx.movie.edu.
bladerunner  IN  RP   root.fx.movie.edu.   hotline.fx.movie.edu.
             IN  RP   richard.fx.movie.edu.   rb.fx.movie.edu.
ajs          IN  TXT  "Arty Segue, (415) 555-3610"
hotline      IN  TXT  "Movie U. Network Hotline, (415) 555-4111"
rb           IN  TXT  "Richard Boisclair, (415) 555-9612"
```

Binary Representation

```
RP type code: 17
    +--+--+--+--+--+--+--+--+--+--+--+--+--+--+--+--+
    /                   MAILBOX                     /
    /                                               /
    +--+--+--+--+--+--+--+--+--+--+--+--+--+--+--+--+
    /                   TXTDNAME                    /
    /                                               /
    +--+--+--+--+--+--+--+--+--+--+--+--+--+--+--+--+
where:
MAILBOX         A domain-name that specifies the mailbox for
                the responsible person.
```

```
TXTDNAME            A domain-name for which TXT RR's exist.  A
                    subsequent query can be performed to retrieve
                    the associated TXT resource records at
                    txt-dname.
```

RT Route Through (experimental)

Textual Representation

owner ttl class RT *preference intermediate-host*

Example

```
sh.prime.com.  IN  RT  2    Relay.Prime.COM.
               IN  RT  10   NET.Prime.COM.
```

Binary Representation

```
RT type code: 21
    +--+--+--+--+--+--+--+--+--+--+--+--+--+--+--+--+
    |                    PREFERENCE                 |
    +--+--+--+--+--+--+--+--+--+--+--+--+--+--+--+--+
    /                   INTERMEDIATE                /
    /                                               /
    +--+--+--+--+--+--+--+--+--+--+--+--+--+--+--+--+
where:
PREFERENCE          A 16 bit integer which specifies the preference
                    given to this RR among others at the same owner.
                    Lower values are preferred.
EXCHANGE            A domain-name which specifies a host which will
                    serve as an intermediate in reaching the host
                    specified by owner.
```

X25 X.25 address (experimental)

Textual Representation

owner ttl class X25 *PSDN-address*

Example

```
relay.pink.com.  IN  X25   31105060845
```

Binary Representation

```
X25 type code: 19
    +--+--+--+--+--+--+--+--+--+--+--+--+--+--+--+--+
    /                 PSDN ADDRESS                  /
    +--+--+--+--+--+--+--+--+--+--+--+--+--+--+--+--+
```

```
where:
PSDN ADDRESS    A character-string which identifies the PSDN
                (Public Switched Data Network) address in the
                X.121 numbering plan associated with owner.
```

New Types from RFC 1664

PX pointer to X.400/RFC 822 mapping information

Textual Representation

owner ttl class PX *preference RFC822 address X.400 address*

Example

```
ab.net2.it.  IN  PX  10   ab.net2.it.  O-ab.PRMD-net2.ADMDb.C-it.
```

Binary Representation

```
PX type code: 26
      +--+--+--+--+--+--+--+--+--+--+--+--+--+--+--+--+
      |                  PREFERENCE                   |
      +--+--+--+--+--+--+--+--+--+--+--+--+--+--+--+--+
      /                    MAP822                     /
      /                                               /
      +--+--+--+--+--+--+--+--+--+--+--+--+--+--+--+--+
      /                    MAPX400                    /
      /                                               /
      +--+--+--+--+--+--+--+--+--+--+--+--+--+--+--+--+
where:
PREFERENCE   A 16 bit integer which specifies the preference given to
             this RR among others at the same owner.  Lower values
             are preferred.
MAP822       A domain-name element containing rfc822-domain, the
             RFC 822 part of the RFC 1327 mapping information.
MAPX400      A domain-name element containing the value of
             x400-in-domain-syntax derived from the X.400 part of
             the RFC 1327 mapping information.
```

New Types from RFC 3596

AAAA IPv6 Address

Textual Representation

owner ttl class AAAA *IPv6-address*

Example

```
ipv6-host    IN    AAAA    4321:0:1:2:3:4:567:89ab
```

Binary Representation

```
AAAA type code: 28
    +--+--+--+--+--+--+--+--+--+--+--+--+--+--+--+--+
    |                      ADDRESS                  |
    +--+--+--+--+--+--+--+--+--+--+--+--+--+--+--+--+
where:
ADDRESS         A 128 bit Internet address.
```

New Types from RFC 2782

SRV Locate Services

Textual Representation

owner ttl class SRV *Priority Weight Port Target*

Example

```
_http._tcp.www.movie.edu.   IN  SRV  0  2  80   www.movie.edu.
```

Binary Representation

```
SRV type code: 33
```

The RFC does not contain a diagram of the binary representation. The *priority*, *weight*, and *port* are unsigned 16 bit integers. The *target* is a domain name.

New Types from RFC 2915

NAPTR Naming Authority Pointer

Textual Representation

owner ttl class NAPTR *Order Preference Flags Service RegExp Replacement*

Example

gatech.edu IN NAPTR 100   50   "s"   "http+I2L+I2C+I2R"   ""   _http._tcp.gatech.edu.

Binary Representation

SRV type code: 35

```
+--+--+--+--+--+--+--+--+--+--+--+--+--+--+--+--+
|                    ORDER                      |
+--+--+--+--+--+--+--+--+--+--+--+--+--+--+--+--+
|                  PREFERENCE                   |
+--+--+--+--+--+--+--+--+--+--+--+--+--+--+--+--+
/                    FLAGS                      /
+--+--+--+--+--+--+--+--+--+--+--+--+--+--+--+--+
/                   SERVICES                    /
+--+--+--+--+--+--+--+--+--+--+--+--+--+--+--+--+
/                    REGEXP                     /
+--+--+--+--+--+--+--+--+--+--+--+--+--+--+--+--+
/                  REPLACEMENT                  /
/                                               /
+--+--+--+--+--+--+--+--+--+--+--+--+--+--+--+--+
```

where:

ORDER   A 16-bit unsigned integer specifying the order in which
            the NAPTR records MUST be processed to ensure the correct
            ordering of rules.

PREFERENCE A 16-bit unsigned integer that specifies the order in
            which NAPTR records with equal "order" values SHOULD be processed,
            low numbers being processed before high numbers.

FLAGS   A *<character-string>* which contains various flags.

SERVICES   A *<character-string>* which contains protocol and service
            identifiers.

REGEXP   A *<character-string>* which contains a regular expression.

REPLACEMENT A *<domain-name>* which specifies the new value in the
            case where the regular expression is a simple replacement
            operation.

Classes

(From RFC 1035, page 13)

CLASS fields appear in resource records. The following CLASS mnemonics and values are defined:

IN 1: the Internet

CS 2: the CSNET class (obsolete—used only for examples in some obsolete RFCs)

CH 3: the CHAOS class

HS 4: the Hesiod class

DNS Messages

In order to write programs that parse DNS messages, you need to understand the message format. DNS queries and responses are most often contained within UDP datagrams. Each message is fully contained within a UDP datagram. If the query and response are sent over TCP, they are prefixed with a two-byte value indicating the length of the query or response, excluding the two-byte length. The following sections detail the format and content of the DNS message.

Message Format

(From RFC 1035, page 25)

All communications inside the domain protocol are carried in a single format called a *message*. The top-level format of the message is divided into five sections (some may be empty in certain cases), shown here:

```
+--------------------+
|      Header        |
+--------------------+
|     Question       |  the question for the name server
+--------------------+
|      Answer        |  RRs answering the question
+--------------------+
|     Authority      |  RRs pointing toward an authority
+--------------------+
|     Additional     |  RRs holding additional information
+--------------------+
```

The header section is always present. The header includes fields that specify which remaining sections are present and specifies whether the message is a query or a response, a standard query or some other opcode, etc.

The names of the sections after the header are derived from their use in standard queries. The question section contains fields that describe a question to a nameserver. These fields are a query type (QTYPE), a query class (QCLASS), and a query domain name (QNAME). The last three sections have the same format: a possibly empty list of concatenated *resource records* (RRs). The answer section contains RRs that answer the question, the authority section contains RRs that point toward an authoritative nameserver, and the additional records section contains RRs that relate to the query but are not strictly answers for the question.

Header Section Format

(From RFC 1035, pages 26–28)

```
                                  1  1  1  1  1  1
    0  1  2  3  4  5  6  7  8  9  0  1  2  3  4  5
  +--+--+--+--+--+--+--+--+--+--+--+--+--+--+--+--+
  |                      ID                       |
  +--+--+--+--+--+--+--+--+--+--+--+--+--+--+--+--+
  |QR|   Opcode  |AA|TC|RD|RA|   Z    |   RCODE   |
  +--+--+--+--+--+--+--+--+--+--+--+--+--+--+--+--+
  |                    QDCOUNT                    |
  +--+--+--+--+--+--+--+--+--+--+--+--+--+--+--+--+
  |                    ANCOUNT                    |
  +--+--+--+--+--+--+--+--+--+--+--+--+--+--+--+--+
  |                    NSCOUNT                    |
  +--+--+--+--+--+--+--+--+--+--+--+--+--+--+--+--+
  |                    ARCOUNT                    |
  +--+--+--+--+--+--+--+--+--+--+--+--+--+--+--+--+
```

where:

ID
A 16 bit identifier assigned by the program that generates any kind of query. This identifier is copied the corresponding reply and can be used by the requester to match up replies to outstanding queries.

QR
A one bit field that specifies whether this message is a query (0), or a response (1).

OPCODE
A four bit field that specifies kind of query in this message. This value is set by the originator of a query and copied into the response. The values are:

0   a standard query (QUERY)
1   an inverse query (IQUERY)
2   a server status request (STATUS)
3-15   reserved for future use

AA
Authoritative Answer - this bit is valid in responses, and specifies that the responding name server is an authority for the domain name in question section.
Note that the contents of the answer section may have multiple owner names because of aliases. The AA bit corresponds to the name which matches the query name, or the first owner name in the answer section.

TC
TrunCation - specifies that this message was truncated due to length greater than that permitted on the transmission channel.

RD
Recursion Desired - this bit may be set in a query and is copied into the response. If RD is set, it directs the name server to pursue the query recursively. Recursive query support is optional.

RA	Recursion Available - this bit is set or cleared in a response, and denotes whether recursive query support is available in the name server.
Z	Reserved for future use. Must be zero in all queries and responses.
RCODE	Response code - this 4 bit field is set as part of responses. The values have the following interpretation:

	0	No error condition
	1	Format error - The name server was unable to interpret the query.
	2	Server failure - The name server was unable to process this query due to a problem with the name server.
	3	Name Error - Meaningful only for responses from an authoritative name server, this code signifies that the domain name referenced in the query does not exist.
	4	Not Implemented - The name server does not support the requested kind of query.
	5	Refused - The name server refuses to perform the specified operation for policy reasons. For example, a name server may not wish to provide the information to the particular requester, or a name server may not wish to perform a particular operation (e.g., zone transfer) for particular data.
	6-15	Reserved for future use.

QDCOUNT	An unsigned 16 bit integer specifying the number of entries in the question section.
ANCOUNT	An unsigned 16 bit integer specifying the number of resource records in the answer section.
NSCOUNT	An unsigned 16 bit integer specifying the number of name server resource records in the authority records section.
ARCOUNT	An unsigned 16 bit integer specifying the number of resource records in the additional records section.

Question Section Format

(From RFC 1035, pages 28–29)

The question section is used to carry the "question" in most queries, i.e., the parameters that define what is being asked. The section contains QDCOUNT (usually one) entries, each of the following format:

```
                       1 1 1 1 1 1
 0 1 2 3 4 5 6 7 8 9 0 1 2 3 4 5
```

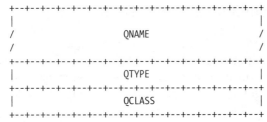

```
+--+--+--+--+--+--+--+--+--+--+--+--+--+--+--+--+
|                                               |
/                     QNAME                     /
/                                               /
+--+--+--+--+--+--+--+--+--+--+--+--+--+--+--+--+
|                     QTYPE                     |
+--+--+--+--+--+--+--+--+--+--+--+--+--+--+--+--+
|                     QCLASS                    |
+--+--+--+--+--+--+--+--+--+--+--+--+--+--+--+--+
```

```
where:
QNAME         A domain name represented as a sequence of labels, where
              each label consists of a length octet followed by that
              number of octets.  The domain name terminates with the
              zero length octet for the null label of the root.  Note
              that this field may be an odd number of octets; no
              padding is used.
QTYPE         A two octet code which specifies the type of the query.
              The values for this field include all codes valid for a
              TYPE field, together with some more general codes which
              can match more than one type of RR.
QCLASS        A two octet code that specifies the class of the query.
              For example, the QCLASS field is IN for the Internet.
```

QCLASS values

(From RFC 1035, page 13)

QCLASS fields appear in the question section of a query. QCLASS values are a superset of CLASS values; every CLASS is a valid QCLASS. In addition to CLASS values, the following QCLASS is defined:

*   255 Any class

QTYPE values

(From RFC 1035, pages 12–13)

QTYPE fields appear in the question part of a query. QTYPES are a superset of TYPEs; hence, all TYPEs are valid QTYPEs. Also, the following QTYPEs are defined:

AXFR
> 252 A request for a transfer of an entire zone

MAILB
> 253 A request for mailbox-related records (MB, MG, or MR)

MAILA
> 254 A request for mail agent RRs (obsolete—see MX)

*

> 255 A request for all records

Answer, Authority, and Additional Section Format

(From RFC 1035, pages 29–30)

The answer, authority, and additional sections all share the same format: a variable number of resource records, in which the number of records is specified in the corresponding count field in the header. Each resource record has the following format:

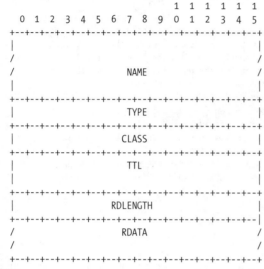

```
                                  1  1  1  1  1  1
    0  1  2  3  4  5  6  7  8  9  0  1  2  3  4  5
  +--+--+--+--+--+--+--+--+--+--+--+--+--+--+--+--+
  |                                               |
  /                                               /
  /                     NAME                      /
  |                                               |
  +--+--+--+--+--+--+--+--+--+--+--+--+--+--+--+--+
  |                     TYPE                      |
  +--+--+--+--+--+--+--+--+--+--+--+--+--+--+--+--+
  |                     CLASS                     |
  +--+--+--+--+--+--+--+--+--+--+--+--+--+--+--+--+
  |                     TTL                       |
  |                                               |
  +--+--+--+--+--+--+--+--+--+--+--+--+--+--+--+--+
  |                    RDLENGTH                   |
  +--+--+--+--+--+--+--+--+--+--+--+--+--+--+--+--|
  /                     RDATA                     /
  /                                               /
  +--+--+--+--+--+--+--+--+--+--+--+--+--+--+--+--+
```

where:

NAME   A domain name to which this resource record pertains.

TYPE   Two octets containing one of the RR type codes. This
            field specifies the meaning of the data in the RDATA
            field.

CLASS   Two octets which specify the class of the data in the
            RDATA field.

TTL   A 32 bit unsigned integer that specifies the time
            interval (in seconds) that the resource record may be
            cached before it should be discarded. Zero values are
            interpreted to mean that the RR can only be used for the
            transaction in progress, and should not be cached.

RDLENGTH   An unsigned 16 bit integer that specifies the length in
            octets of the RDATA field.

RDATA   A variable length string of octets that describes the
            resource. The format of this information varies
            according to the TYPE and CLASS of the resource record.
            For example, if the TYPE is A and the CLASS is IN,
            the RDATA field is a 4 octet ARPA Internet address.

Data Transmission Order

(From RFC 1035, pages 8–9)

The order of transmission of the header and data described in this document is resolved to the octet level. Whenever a diagram shows a group of octets, the order of transmission of those octets is the normal order in which they are read in English. For example, in the following diagram, the octets are transmitted in the order they are numbered:

```
 0                   1
 0 1 2 3 4 5 6 7 8 9 0 1 2 3 4 5
+-+-+-+-+-+-+-+-+-+-+-+-+-+-+-+-+
|       1       |       2       |
+-+-+-+-+-+-+-+-+-+-+-+-+-+-+-+-+
|       3       |       4       |
+-+-+-+-+-+-+-+-+-+-+-+-+-+-+-+-+
|       5       |       6       |
+-+-+-+-+-+-+-+-+-+-+-+-+-+-+-+-+
```

Whenever an octet represents a numeric quantity, the leftmost bit in the diagram is the high order, or most significant, bit. That is, the bit labeled 0 is the most significant bit. For example, the following diagram represents the value 170 (decimal):

```
 0 1 2 3 4 5 6 7
+-+-+-+-+-+-+-+-+
|1 0 1 0 1 0 1 0|
+-+-+-+-+-+-+-+-+
```

Similarly, whenever a multioctet field represents a numeric quantity, the leftmost bit of the whole field is the most significant bit. When a multioctet quantity is transmitted, the most significant octet is transmitted first.

Resource Record Data

Data Format

In addition to two- and four-octet integer values, resource record data can contain *domain names* or *character strings*.

Character string

(From RFC 1035, page 13)

A character string is a single length octet followed by that number of characters. A character string is treated as binary information, and can be up to 256 characters in length (including the length octet).

Domain name

(From RFC 1035, page 10)

Domain names in messages are expressed in terms of a sequence of labels. Each label is represented as a one-octet length field followed by that number of octets. Since every domain name ends with the null label of the root, a domain name is terminated by a length byte of 0. The high order two bits of every length octet must be 0, and the remaining 6 bits of the length field limit the label to 63 octets or less.

Message compression

(From RFC 1035, page 30)

In order to reduce the size of messages, the domain system uses a compression scheme that eliminates the repetition of domain names in a message. In this scheme, an entire domain name or a list of labels at the end of a domain name is replaced with a pointer to a prior occurrence of the same name.

The pointer takes the form of a two-octet sequence:

```
+--+--+--+--+--+--+--+--+--+--+--+--+--+--+--+--+
| 1  1|                OFFSET                   |
+--+--+--+--+--+--+--+--+--+--+--+--+--+--+--+--+
```

The first two bits are ones. This allows a pointer to be distinguished from a label, since the label must begin with 2 zero bits because labels are restricted to 63 octets or less. (The 10 and 01 combinations are reserved for future use.) The OFFSET field specifies an offset from the start of the message (i.e., the first octet of the ID field in the domain header). A zero offset specifies the first byte of the ID field, etc.

BIND Compatibility Matrix

Table B-1 shows you which versions of BIND support various features.

Table B-1. BIND compatibility matrix

Feature	BIND version			
	8.2.3	8.4.7	9.1.0	9.3.2
Multiprocessor support			X	X
Dynamic update	X	X	X	X
TSIG-signed dynamic update	X	X	X	X
TSIG-based update policy			X	X
NOTIFY	X	X	X	X
Incremental zone transfer	X	X	X	
Incremental zone transfers with manual zone editing				X
Forwarding	X	X	X	X
Forward zones	X	X	X	X
Use of RTT for forwarders	X	X		X
Views			X	X
Round robin	X	X	X	X
Configurable RRset order	X	X		
Configurable sort list	X	X	X	X
Disabling recursion	X	X	X	X
Recursion access list	X	X	X	X
Query access lists	X	X	X	X
Zone transfer access lists	X	X	X	X
EDNS0		X	X	X
IPv6 transport		X	X	X
AAAA records	X	X	X	X
DNSSECbis				X

Compiling and Installing BIND on Linux

The versions of BIND shipped with most versions of Linux are fairly recent. Still, BIND 8.4.7 is the most current BIND release (at the time of this writing), and the ISC recommends that you upgrade to BIND 9. For those of you who can't wait until your version of Linux updates to the latest version of BIND 8 or 9, this appendix will show you how to do it yourself.

Instructions for BIND 8

Compiling and installing the latest version of BIND 8 is easy. (Because the path to BIND 8 includes following the link *bind-8*, you will always get the latest version.) The following sections provide detailed instructions.

Get the Source Code

First, you must get the source code. There's a copy on *ftp.isc.org*, available for anonymous FTP:

```
% cd /tmp
% ftp ftp.isc.org.
Connected to isrv4.pa.vix.com.
220 ProFTPD 1.2.0 Server (ISC FTP Server) [ftp.isc.org]
Name (ftp.isc.org.:user): ftp
331 Anonymous login ok, send your complete e-mail address as password.
Password:
230 Anonymous access granted, restrictions apply.
Remote system type is UNIX.
Using binary mode to transfer files.
ftp>
```

Now you need to find the right file:

```
ftp > cd /isc/bind/src/cur/bind-8
250 CWD command successful.
ftp > binary
200 Type set to I.
```

```
ftp > get bind-src.tar.gz
local: bind-src.tar.gz remote: bind-src.tar.gz
200 PORT command successful.
150 Opening BINARY mode data connection for bind-src.tar.gz (1600504 bytes).
226 Transfer complete.
1600504 bytes received in 23 seconds (56 Kbytes/s)
ftp > quit
221 Goodbye.
```

Unpack the Source Code

Now you have the compressed *tar* file that contains the BIND source. Just use the *tar* command to uncompress and un*tar* it:

```
% tar -zxvf bind-src.tar.gz
```

(This assumes you have a version of *tar* that can handle compressed *gzip*'ed files; if you don't, you can get a new copy of *tar* via anonymous FTP from *ftp.gnu.org* in */gnu/ tar/tar-1.15.tar*.) This creates a *src* directory with several subdirectories, including *bin*, *include*, *lib*, and *port*. Here are the contents of these subdirectories:

bin

> Source code for all BIND binaries, including *named*.

include

> Copies of include files referenced by the BIND code. You should use these to build your nameserver instead of using those shipped with your system because they have been updated.

lib

> Source code for libraries used by BIND.

port

> Information BIND uses to customize compilation settings and compile-time options for various operating systems.

Use the Proper Compiler Settings

Before you can build everything, you need a C compiler. Nearly every version of Linux comes with *gcc*, the GNU C compiler, which works fine. If you need to get *gcc*, you can find information at *http://www.gnu.org/software/gcc/gcc.html*.

By default, BIND assumes that you're using the GNU C compiler and various other GNUish utilities, such as *flex* and *byacc*. These are a standard part of most Linux development environments. If your version of Linux uses different programs, though, you'll need to modify *port/linux/Makefile.set*. This file lets BIND know which programs to use.

Build Everything

Next, you compile everything from the top-level directory. First, run:

```
% make stdlinks
```

Then, run:

```
% make clean
% make depend
```

This removes any old object files you might have sitting around from previous compilation attempts and updates the *Makefile* dependencies. Then, compile the source code by running:

```
% make all
```

The source code should compile without any errors. Next, install the new *named* and *named-xfer* programs into */usr/sbin*. You'll need to become root to do this. Use the command:

```
# make install
```

Instructions for BIND 9

Here's how to compile and install BIND 9 on your Linux host. (At the time of this writing, 9.3.2 is the latest version.)

Get the Source Code

As with BIND 8, you must get the source code first. And again, this requires FTP'ing to *ftp.isc.org*:

```
% cd /tmp
% ftp ftp.isc.org.
Connected to isrv4.pa.vix.com.
220 ProFTPD 1.2.1 Server (ISC FTP Server) [ftp.isc.org]
Name (ftp.isc.org.:user): ftp
331 Anonymous login ok, send your complete email address as your password.
Password:
230 Anonymous access granted, restrictions apply.
Remote system type is UNIX.
Using binary mode to transfer files.
ftp>
```

Change to the right directory and get the file you need:

```
ftp> cd /isc/bind9
250 CWD command successful.
```

At this point, you should check to see what is the latest version available by doing a *dir* command. At the time of this writing, 9.3.2 is the latest version.

```
ftp> cd 9.3.2
250 CWD command successful.
ftp> get bind-9.3.2.tar.gz
local: bind-9.3.2.tar.gz remote: bind-9.3.2.tar.gz
200 PORT command successful.
150 Opening BINARY mode data connection for bind-9.3.2.tar.gz (4673603 bytes).
226 Transfer complete.
4673603 bytes received in 92.4 secs (35 Kbytes/sec)
ftp> quit
221 Goodbye.
```

Unpack the Source Code

Use the *tar* command to uncompress and un*tar* the compressed *tar* file:

```
% tar zxvf bind-9.3.2.tar.gz
```

Unlike the BIND 8 distribution, this creates a *bind-9.3.2* subdirectory in your working directory for all the BIND source code. (BIND 8 distributions always unpacked everything into the working directory.) The *bind-9.3.2* subdirectory will have subdirectories called:

bin
> Source code for all BIND binaries, including *named*

contrib
> Contributed tools

doc
> Documentation for BIND, including the invaluable Administrator Resource Manual

lib
> Source code for libraries used by BIND

make
> Makefiles

Run configure, and Build Everything

Also unlike BIND 8, BIND 9 uses the near-miraculous *configure* script to determine the appropriate includes and compiler settings. Read through the *README* file to determine whether you need any special settings. *configure* supports command-line options that allow you to build without threads, use a different installation directory, and much more. To run *configure*:

```
% ./configure
```

Or, if you need to disable threads, for example, run:

```
% ./configure --disable-threads
```

To build BIND, type:

```
% make all
```

The source code should compile without errors. To install BIND, type this as root:

```
# make install
```

That's all there is!

Top-Level Domains

This table lists all the two-letter country codes and all the top-level domains that aren't countries. Not all the countries are registered in the Internet's namespace at the time of this writing, but there aren't many missing.

Domain	Country or organization	Domain	Country or organization
AC	Ascension Island	BE	Belgium
AD	Andorra	BF	Burkina Faso
AE	United Arab Emirates	BG	Bulgaria
AERO	Aeronautical Industry	BH	Bahrain
AF	Afghanistan	BI	Burundi
AG	Antigua and Barbuda	BIZ	Generic
AI	Anguilla	BJ	Benin
AL	Albania	BM	Bermuda
AM	Armenia	BN	Brunei Darussalam
AN	Netherlands Antilles	BO	Bolivia
AO	Angola	BR	Brazil
AQ	Antarctica	BS	Bahamas
AR	Argentina	BT	Bhutan
ARPA	ARPA Internet	BV	Bouvet Island
AS	American Samoa	BW	Botswana
AT	Austria	BY	Belarus
AU	Australia	BZ	Belize
AW	Aruba	CA	Canada
AZ	Azerbaijan	CC	Cocos (Keeling) Islands
BA	Bosnia and Herzegovina	CD	Congo, Democratic Republic of the
BB	Barbados	CF	Central African Republic
BD	Bangladesh	CG	Congo

Domain	Country or organization	Domain	Country or organization
CH	Switzerland	FX	France, metropolitan
CI	Cote d'Ivoire	GA	Gabon
CK	Cook Islands	GB	United Kingdom[a]
CL	Chile	GD	Grenada
CM	Cameroon	GE	Georgia
CN	China	GF	French Guiana
CO	Colombia	GG	Guernsey, Alderney, and Sark (British Channel Islands)
COM	Generic (formerly commercial)	GH	Ghana
COOP	Cooperatives	GI	Gibraltar
CR	Costa Rica	GL	Greenland
CU	Cuba	GM	Gambia
CV	Cape Verde	GN	Guinea
CX	Christmas Island	GOV	U.S. Federal Government
CY	Cyprus	GP	Guadeloupe
CZ	Czech Republic	GQ	Equatorial Guinea
DE	Germany	GR	Greece
DJ	Djibouti	GS	South Georgia and the South Sandwich Islands
DK	Denmark	GT	Guatemala
DM	Dominica	GU	Guam
DO	Dominican Republic	GW	Guinea-Bissau
DZ	Algeria	GY	Guyana
EC	Ecuador	HK	Hong Kong
EDU	Education	HM	Heard and McDonald Islands
EE	Estonia	HN	Honduras
EG	Egypt	HR	Croatia
EH	Western Sahara	HT	Haiti
ER	Eritrea	HU	Hungary
ES	Spain	ID	Indonesia
ET	Ethiopia	IE	Ireland
EU	European Union	IL	Israel
FI	Finland	IM	Isle of Man
FJ	Fiji	IN	India
FK	Falkland Islands (Malvinas)	INFO	Generic
FM	Micronesia, Federated States of	INT	International entities
FO	Faroe Islands	IO	British Indian Ocean Territory
FR	France	IQ	Iraq

Domain	Country or organization	Domain	Country or organization
IR	Iran	MK	Macedonia, the Former Yugoslav Republic of
IS	Iceland	ML	Mali
IT	Italy	MM	Myanmar
JE	Jersey (British Channel Island)	MN	Mongolia
JM	Jamaica	MO	Macau
JO	Jordan	MOBI	Mobile devices
JOBS	Jobs	MP	Northern Mariana Islands
JP	Japan	MQ	Martinique
KE	Kenya	MR	Mauritania
KG	Kyrgyzstan	MS	Montserrat
KH	Cambodia	MT	Malta
KI	Kiribati	MU	Mauritius
KM	Comoros	MUSEUM	Museums
KN	Saint Kitts and Nevis	MV	Maldives
KP	Korea, Democratic People's Republic of	MW	Malawi
KR	Korea, Republic of	MX	Mexico
KW	Kuwait	MY	Malaysia
KY	Cayman Islands	MZ	Mozambique
KZ	Kazakhstan	NA	Namibia
LA	Lao People's Democratic Republic	NAME	Names
LB	Lebanon	NATO	North Atlantic Treaty Organization
LC	Saint Lucia	NC	New Caledonia
LI	Liechtenstein	NE	Niger
LK	Sri Lanka	NET	Generic (formerly networking organizations)
LR	Liberia	NF	Norfolk Island
LS	Lesotho	NG	Nigeria
LT	Lithuania	NI	Nicaragua
LU	Luxembourg	NL	Netherlands
LV	Latvia	NO	Norway
LY	Libyan Arab Jamahiriya	NP	Nepal
MA	Morocco	NR	Nauru
MC	Monaco	NU	Niue
MD	Moldova, Republic of	NZ	New Zealand
MG	Madagascar	OM	Oman
MH	Marshall Islands	ORG	Generic (formerly organizations)
MIL	U.S. military	PA	Panama

Domain	Country or organization	Domain	Country or organization
PE	Peru	SY	Syrian Arab Republic
PF	French Polynesia	SZ	Swaziland
PG	Papua New Guinea	TC	Turks and Caicos Islands
PH	Philippines	TD	Chad
PK	Pakistan	TF	French Southern Territories
PL	Poland	TG	Togo
PM	St. Pierre and Miquelon	TH	Thailand
PN	Pitcairn	TJ	Tajikistan
PR	Puerto Rico	TK	Tokelau
PRO	Professionals	TL	Timor-Leste
PS	Palestinian Authority	TM	Turkmenistan
PT	Portugal	TN	Tunisia
PW	Palau	TO	Tonga
PY	Paraguay	TP	East Timor
QA	Qatar	TR	Turkey
RE	Reunion	TRAVEL	Travel
RO	Romania	TT	Trinidad and Tobago
RU	Russian Federation	TV	Tuvalu
RW	Rwanda	TW	Taiwan, Province of China
SA	Saudi Arabia	TZ	Tanzania, United Republic of
SB	Solomon Islands	UA	Ukraine
SC	Seychelles	UG	Uganda
SD	Sudan	UK	United Kingdom
SE	Sweden	UM	United States Minor Outlying Islands
SG	Singapore	US	United States
SH	St. Helena	UY	Uruguay
SI	Slovenia	UZ	Uzbekistan
SJ	Svalbard and Jan Mayen Islands	VA	Holy See (Vatican City State)
SK	Slovakia	VC	Saint Vincent and The Grenadines
SL	Sierra Leone	VE	Venezuela
SM	San Marino	VG	Virgin Islands (British)
SN	Senegal	VI	Virgin Islands (U.S.)
SO	Somalia	VN	Vietnam
SR	Suriname	VU	Vanuatu
ST	Sao Tome and Principe	WF	Wallis and Futuna Islands
SU	Union of Soviet Socialist Republics	WS	Samoa
SV	El Salvador	YE	Yemen

Domain	Country or organization	Domain	Country or organization
YT	Mayotte	ZM	Zambia
YU	Yugoslavia	ZR	Republic of Zaire
ZA	South Africa	ZW	Zimbabwe

[a] In practice, the United Kingdom uses "UK" for its top-level domain.

BIND Nameserver and Resolver Configuration

BIND Nameserver Boot File Directives and Configuration File Statements

Here's a handy list of all the boot file directives and configuration file statements for the BIND nameserver, as well as configuration directives for the BIND resolver. Some of the directives and statements exist only in later versions, so your nameserver may not support them yet. Most of this information is based on the *named.conf* manual page, so you can check your manual page if your version of BIND is a newer than 8.4.7or 9.3.2.

The *options* statement has become quite extensive. At the end of this appendix, we have included the description of each configuration option from the *BIND 9 Administrator Reference Manual*, in case you don't have easy access to the manual page. For BIND 8, this information is on the *named.conf* manual page.

BIND 8 Configuration File Statements

acl

Function
Creates a named IP address matching list, for access control and other uses.

Syntax
```
acl name {
    address_match_list;
};
```
Covered in Chapters 10 and 11.

controls (8.2+)

Function

Configures a channel used by *ndc* to control the nameserver.

Syntax

```
controls {
    [ inet ( ip_addr | * ) port ip_port allow address_match_list; ]
    [ unix path_name perm number owner number group number; ]
};
```

Covered in Chapter 7.

include

Function

Inserts the specified file at the point the *include* statement is encountered.

Syntax

```
include path_name;
```

Covered in Chapter 7.

key (8.2+)

Function

Defines a key ID that can be used in a *server* statement or an address match list to associate a TSIG key with a particular nameserver.

Syntax

```
key key_id {
    algorithm algorithm_id;
    secret secret_string;
};
```

Covered in Chapters 10 and 11.

logging

Function

Configures the nameserver's logging behavior.

Syntax

```
logging {
  [ channel channel_name {
    ( file path_name
        [ versions ( number | unlimited ) ]
        [ size size_spec ]
      | syslog ( kern | user | mail | daemon | auth | syslog | lpr |
                   news | uucp | cron | authpriv | ftp |
                   local0 | local1 | local2 | local3 |
                   local4 | local5 | local6 | local7 )
      | null );

    [ severity ( critical | error | warning | notice |
                  info  | debug [ level ] | dynamic ); ]
    [ print-category yes_or_no; ]
    [ print-severity yes_or_no; ]
    [ print-time yes_or_no; ]
  }; ]

  [ category category_name {
    channel_name; [ channel_name; ... ]
  }; ]
  ...
};
```

Covered in Chapter 7.

options

Function

Configures global options.

Syntax

```
options {
  [ allow-query { address_match_list }; ]
  [ allow-recursion { address_match_list }; ]
  [ allow-transfer { address_match_list }; ]
  [ also-notify { ip_addr; [ ip_addr; ... ] }; ]
  [ auth-nxdomain yes_or_no; ]
  [ blackhole { address_match_list }; ]
  [ check-names ( master | slave | response ) ( warn | fail | ignore ); ]
  [ cleaning-interval number; ]
  [ coresize size_spec; ]
  [ datasize size_spec; ]
  [ deallocate-on-exit yes_or_no; ]
  [ dialup yes_or_no; ]
  [ directory path_name; ]
  [ dump-file path_name; ]
  [ edns-udp-size number; ]
  [ fake-iquery yes_or_no; ]
```

```
    [ fetch-glue yes_or_no; ]
    [ files size_spec; ]
    [ forward ( only | first ); ]
    [ forwarders { [ ip_addr ; [ ip_addr ; ... ] ] }; ]
    [ has-old-clients yes_or_no; ]
    [ heartbeat-interval number; ]
    [ hostname hostname_string; ]
    [ host-statistics yes_or_no; ]
    [ host-statistics-max number; ]
    [ interface-interval number; ]
    [ lame-ttl number; ]
    [ listen-on [ port ip_port ] { address_match_list }; ]
    [ listen-on-v6 [ port ip_port ] { address_match_list }; ]
    [ maintain-ixfr-base yes_or_no; ]
    [ max-ixfr-log-size number; ]
    [ max-ncache-ttl number; ]
    [ max-transfer-time-in number; ]
    [ memstatistics-file path_name; ]
    [ min-roots number; ]
    [ multiple-cnames yes_or_no; ]
    [ named-xfer path_name; ]
    [ notify yes_or_no; ]
    [ pid-file path_name; ]
    [ preferred-glue ( A | AAAA ); ]
    [ query-source [ address ( ip_addr | * ) ] [ port ( ip_port | * ) ]; ]
    [ query-source-v6 [ address ( ipv6_addr | * ) ]
                      [ port ( ip_port | * ) ] ; ]
    [ recursion yes_or_no; ]
    [ rfc2308-type1 yes_or_no; ]
    [ rrset-order { order_spec; [ order_spec; ... ] }; ]
    [ serial-queries number; ]
    [ sortlist { address_match_list }; ]
    [ stacksize size_spec; ]
    [ statistics-file path_name; ]
    [ statistics-interval number; ]
    [ suppress-initial-notify yes_or_no; ]
    [ topology { address_match_list }; ]
    [ transfer-format ( one-answer | many-answers ); ]
    [ transfer-source ( ip_addr | * ); ]
    [ transfer-source-v6 ipv6_addr; ]
    [ transfers-in  number; ]
    [ transfers-out number; ]
    [ transfers-per-ns number; ]
    [ treat-cr-as-space yes_or_no; ]
    [ use-id-pool yes_or_no; ]
    [ use-ixfr yes_or_no; ]
    [ version version_string; ]
};
```

Covered in Chapters 4, 10, 11, and 16.

server

Function

Defines the characteristics to be associated with a remote nameserver.

Syntax

```
server ip_addr {
  [ bogus yes_or_no; ]
  [ edns yes_or_no; ]
  [ keys { key_id [ key_id ... ] }; ]
  [ support-ixfr yes_or_no; ]
  [ transfers number; ]
  [ transfer-format ( one-answer | many-answers ); ]
};
```

Covered in Chapters 10 and 11.

trusted-keys (8.2+)

Function

Configures the public keys of security roots for use in DNSSEC.

Syntax

```
trusted-keys {
  domain-name flags protocol_id algorithm_id public_key_string;
  [ domain-name flags protocol_id algorithm_id public_key_string; [ ... ] ]
};
```

Covered in Chapter 11.

zone

Function

Configures the zones maintained by the nameserver.

Syntax

```
zone "domain_name" [ ( in | hs | hesiod | chaos ) ] {
  type master;
  file path_name;
  [ allow-query { address_match_list }; ]
  [ allow-transfer { address_match_list }; ]
  [ allow-update { address_match_list }; ]
  [ also-notify { ip_addr; [ ip_addr; ... ] }
  [ check-names ( warn | fail | ignore ); ]
  [ dialup yes_or_no | notify; ]
  [ forward ( only | first ); ]
```

```
    [ forwarders { [ ip_addr; [ ip_addr; ... ] ] }; ]
    [ notify yes_or_no; ]
    [ pubkey flags protocol_id algorithm_id public_key_string; ]
};

zone "domain_name" [ ( in | hs | hesiod | chaos ) ] {
    type (slave | stub);
    masters [ port ip_port ] { ip_addr; [ ip_addr; ... ] };
    [ allow-query { address_match_list }; ]
    [ allow-transfer { address_match_list }; ]
    [ allow-update { address_match_list }; ]
    [ also-notify { ip_addr; [ ip_addr; ... ] }; ]
    [ check-names ( warn | fail | ignore ); ]
    [ dialup yes_or_no; ]
    [ file path_name; ]
    [ forward ( only | first ); ]
    [ forwarders { [ ip_addr; [ ip_addr; ... ] ] }; ]
    [ max-transfer-time-in number; ]
    [ notify yes_or_no; ]
    [ pubkey flags protocol_id algorithm_id public_key_string; ]
    [ transfer-source ipv4_addr; ]
    [ transfer-source-v6 ipv6_addr; ]
};

zone "domain_name" [ ( in | hs | hesiod | chaos ) ] {
    type forward;
    [ forward ( only | first ); ]
    [ forwarders { [ ip_addr ; [ ip_addr ; ... ] ] }; ]
    [ check-names ( warn | fail | ignore ); ]
};

zone "." [ ( in | hs | hesiod | chaos ) ] {
    type hint;
    file path_name;
    [ check-names ( warn | fail | ignore ); ]
};
```
Covered in Chapters 4 and 10.

BIND 9 Configuration File Statements

Comments

- C style: /* */
- C++ style: // to end of line
- Unix style: # to end of line

acl

Function

Creates a named IP address matching list, for access control and other uses.

Syntax

```
acl string { address_match_element; ... };
```

Covered in Chapters 10 and 11.

controls

Function

Configures a channel used by *rndc* to control the nameserver.

Syntax

```
controls {
  inet ( ipv4_address | ipv6_address | * )
       [ port ( integer | * ) ]
       allow { address_match_element; ... }
       [ keys { string; ... } ];
  unix unsupported; // not implemented
};
```

Covered in Chapter 7.

include

Function

Inserts the specified file at the point where the *include* statement is encountered.

Syntax

```
include path_name;
```

Covered in Chapter 7.

key

Function

Defines a key ID that can be used in a *server* statement or an address match list to associate a TSIG key with a particular nameserver.

Syntax

```
key domain_name {
  algorithm string;
  secret string;
};
```

Covered in Chapters 10 and 11.

logging

Function

Configures the nameserver's logging behavior.

Syntax

```
logging {
  channel string {
      file log_file
          [ versions ( number | unlimited ) ]
          [ size size_spec ];
      syslog optional_facility;
      null;
      stderr;
      severity log_severity;
      print-time boolean;
      print-severity boolean;
      print-category boolean;
  };
  category string { string; ... };
};
```

Covered in Chapter 7.

lwres

Function

Configures the light-weight resolver daemon.

Syntax

```
lwres {
  listen-on [ port integer ] {
      ( ipv4_address | ipv6_address ) [ port integer ]; ...
  };
  view string optional_class;
  search { string; ... };
  ndots integer;
};
```

The light-weight resolver daemon is not covered in this book.

masters

Function

Defines the masters for a zone. You can define the masters for a zone directly inside the zone statement, or you can define the masters in one place (using this statement), give the list a name, and refer to the list name inside the zone statement.

Syntax

```
masters string [ port integer ] {
  ( masters | ipv4_address [port integer] |
  ipv6_address [port integer] ) [ key string ]; ...
};
```

Covered in Chapters 4 and 10 as part of the zone statement.

options

Function

Configures global options.

Syntax

```
options {
  avoid-v4-udp-ports { port; ... };
  avoid-v6-udp-ports { port; ... };
  blackhole { address_match_element; ... };
  coresize size;
  datasize size;
  directory quoted_string;
  dump-file quoted_string;
  files size;
  heartbeat-interval integer;
  host-statistics boolean; // not implemented
  host-statistics-max number; // not implemented
  hostname ( quoted_string | none );
  interface-interval integer;
  listen-on [ port integer ] { address_match_element; ... };
  listen-on-v6 [ port integer ] { address_match_element; ... };
  match-mapped-addresses boolean;
  memstatistics-file quoted_string;
  pid-file ( quoted_string | none );
  port integer;
  querylog boolean;
  recursing-file quoted_string;
  random-device quoted_string;
  recursive-clients integer;
  serial-query-rate integer;
  server-id ( quoted_string | none |;
  stacksize size;
```

```
statistics-file quoted_string;
statistics-interval integer; // not yet implemented
tcp-clients integer;
tcp-listen-queue integer;
tkey-dhkey quoted_string integer;
tkey-gssapi-credential quoted_string;
tkey-domain quoted_string;
transfers-per-ns integer;
transfers-in integer;
transfers-out integer;
use-ixfr boolean;
version ( quoted_string | none );
allow-recursion { address_match_element; ... };
sortlist { address_match_element; ... };
topology { address_match_element; ... }; // not implemented
auth-nxdomain boolean; // default changed
minimal-responses boolean;
recursion boolean;
rrset-order {
    [ class string ] [ type string ]
    [ name quoted_string ] string string; ...
};
provide-ixfr boolean;
request-ixfr boolean;
rfc2308-type1 boolean; // not yet implemented
additional-from-auth boolean;
additional-from-cache boolean;
query-source querysource4;
query-source-v6 querysource6;
cleaning-interval integer;
min-roots integer; // not implemented
lame-ttl integer;
max-ncache-ttl integer;
max-cache-ttl integer;
transfer-format ( many-answers | one-answer );
max-cache-size size_no_default;
check-names ( master | slave | response )
    ( fail | warn | ignore );
cache-file quoted_string;
suppress-initial-notify boolean; // not yet implemented
preferred-glue string;
dual-stack-servers [ port integer ] {
    ( quoted_string [port integer] |
    ipv4_address [port integer] |
    ipv6_address [port integer] ); ...
}
edns-udp-size integer;
root-delegation-only [ exclude { quoted_string; ... } ];
disable-algorithms string { string; ... };
dnssec-enable boolean;
dnssec-lookaside string trust-anchor string;
dnssec-must-be-secure string boolean;
```

```
dialup dialuptype;
ixfr-from-differences ixfrdiff;


allow-query { address_match_element; ... };
allow-transfer { address_match_element; ... };
allow-update-forwarding { address_match_element; ... };

notify notifytype;
notify-source ( ipv4_address | * ) [ port ( integer | * ) ];
notify-source-v6 ( ipv6_address | * ) [ port ( integer | * ) ];
also-notify [ port integer ] { ( ipv4_address | ipv6_address )
    [ port integer ]; ... };
allow-notify { address_match_element; ... };

forward ( first | only );
forwarders [ port integer ] {
    ( ipv4_address | ipv6_address ) [ port integer ]; ...
};

max-journal-size size_no_default;
max-transfer-time-in integer;
max-transfer-time-out integer;
max-transfer-idle-in integer;
max-transfer-idle-out integer;
max-retry-time integer;
min-retry-time integer;
max-refresh-time integer;
min-refresh-time integer;
multi-master boolean;
sig-validity-interval integer;

transfer-source ( ipv4_address | * )
    [ port ( integer | * ) ];
transfer-source-v6 ( ipv6_address | * )
    [ port ( integer | * ) ];

alt-transfer-source ( ipv4_address | * )
    [ port ( integer | * ) ];
alt-transfer-source-v6 ( ipv6_address | * )
    [ port ( integer | * ) ];
use-alt-transfer-source boolean;

zone-statistics boolean;
key-directory quoted_string;

allow-v6-synthesis { address_match_element; ... }; // obsolete
deallocate-on-exit boolean; // obsolete
fake-iquery boolean; // obsolete
fetch-glue boolean; // obsolete
has-old-clients boolean; // obsolete
maintain-ixfr-base boolean; // obsolete
max-ixfr-log-size size; // obsolete
multiple-cnames boolean; // obsolete
named-xfer quoted_string; // obsolete
```

```
      serial-queries integer; // obsolete
      treat-cr-as-space boolean; // obsolete
      use-id-pool boolean; // obsolete
   };
```
Covered in Chapters 4, 10, 11, and 16.

server

Function

Defines the characteristics to be associated with a remote nameserver.

Syntax

```
server ( ipv4_address | ipv6_address ) {
   bogus boolean;
   edns boolean;
   provide-ixfr boolean;
   request-ixfr boolean;
   keys server_key;
   transfers integer;
   transfer-format ( many-answers | one-answer );
   transfer-source ( ipv4_address | * )
        [ port ( integer | * ) ];
   transfer-source-v6 ( ipv6_address | * )
        [ port ( integer | * ) ];

   support-ixfr boolean; // obsolete
};
```
Covered in Chapters 10 and 11.

trusted-keys

Function

Configures the public keys of security roots for use in DNSSEC.

Syntax

```
trusted-keys {
   domain_name flags protocol algorithm key; ...
};
```
Covered in Chapter 11.

view

Function

Creates and configures a view.

Syntax

```
view string optional_class {
  match-clients { address_match_element; ... };
  match-destinations { address_match_element; ... };
  match-recursive-only boolean;

  key string {
      algorithm string;
      secret string;
  };

  zone string optional_class {
      ...
  };

  server ( ipv4_address | ipv6_address ) {
      ...
  };

  trusted-keys {
      string integer integer integer quoted_string; ...
  };

  allow-recursion { address_match_element; ... };
  sortlist { address_match_element; ... };
  topology { address_match_element; ... }; // not implemented
  auth-nxdomain boolean; // default changed
  minimal-responses boolean;
  recursion boolean;
  rrset-order {
      [ class string ] [ type string ]
      [ name quoted_string ] string string; ...
  };
  provide-ixfr boolean;
  request-ixfr boolean;
  rfc2308-type1 boolean; // not yet implemented
  additional-from-auth boolean;
  additional-from-cache boolean;
  query-source querysource4;
  query-source-v6 querysource6;
  cleaning-interval integer;
  min-roots integer; // not implemented
  lame-ttl integer;
  max-ncache-ttl integer;
  max-cache-ttl integer;
  transfer-format ( many-answers | one-answer );
```

```
max-cache-size size_no_default;
check-names ( master | slave | response )
    ( fail | warn | ignore );
cache-file quoted_string;
suppress-initial-notify boolean; // not yet implemented
preferred-glue string;
dual-stack-servers [ port integer ] {
    ( quoted_string [port integer] |
    ipv4_address [port integer] |
    ipv6_address [port integer] ); ...
};
edns-udp-size integer;
root-delegation-only [ exclude { quoted_string; ... } ];
disable-algorithms string { string; ... };
dnssec-enable boolean;
dnssec-lookaside string trust-anchor string;

dnssec-must-be-secure string boolean;
dialup dialuptype;
ixfr-from-differences ixfrdiff;

allow-query { address_match_element; ... };
allow-transfer { address_match_element; ... };
allow-update-forwarding { address_match_element; ... };

notify notifytype;
notify-source ( ipv4_address | * ) [ port ( integer | * ) ];
notify-source-v6 ( ipv6_address | * ) [ port ( integer | * ) ];
also-notify [ port integer ] { ( ipv4_address | ipv6_address )
    [ port integer ]; ... };
allow-notify { address_match_element; ... };

forward ( first | only );
forwarders [ port integer ] {
    ( ipv4_address | ipv6_address ) [ port integer ]; ...
};

max-journal-size size_no_default;
max-transfer-time-in integer;
max-transfer-time-out integer;
max-transfer-idle-in integer;
max-transfer-idle-out integer;
max-retry-time integer;
min-retry-time integer;
max-refresh-time integer;
min-refresh-time integer;
multi-master boolean;
sig-validity-interval integer;

transfer-source ( ipv4_address | * )
    [ port ( integer | * ) ];
transfer-source-v6 ( ipv6_address | * )
    [ port ( integer | * ) ];
```

```
    alt-transfer-source ( ipv4_address | * )
        [ port ( integer | * ) ];
    alt-transfer-source-v6 ( ipv6_address | * )
        [ port ( integer | * ) ];
    use-alt-transfer-source boolean;

    zone-statistics boolean;
    key-directory quoted_string;

    allow-v6-synthesis { address_match_element; ... }; // obsolete
    fetch-glue boolean; // obsolete
    maintain-ixfr-base boolean; // obsolete
    max-ixfr-log-size size; // obsolete
};
```

Covered in Chapters 10 and 11.

zone

Function

Configures the zones maintained by the nameserver.

Syntax

```
zone string optional_class {
    type ( master | slave | stub | hint |
        forward | delegation-only );
    file quoted_string;

    masters [ port integer ] {
        ( masters |
        ipv4_address [port integer] |
        ipv6_address [ port integer ] ) [ key string ]; ...
        };

    database string;
    delegation-only boolean;
    check-names ( fail | warn | ignore );
    dialup dialuptype;
    ixfr-from-differences boolean;

    allow-query { address_match_element; ... };
    allow-transfer { address_match_element; ... };
    allow-update { address_match_element; ... };
    allow-update-forwarding { address_match_element; ... };
    update-policy {
        ( grant | deny ) string
        ( name | subdomain | wildcard | self ) string
        rrtypelist; ...
    };
```

```
notify notifytype;
notify-source ( ipv4_address | * ) [ port ( integer | * ) ];
notify-source-v6 ( ipv6_address | * ) [ port ( integer | * ) ];
also-notify [ port integer ] { ( ipv4_address | ipv6_address )
    [ port integer ]; ... };
allow-notify { address_match_element; ... };

forward ( first | only );
forwarders [ port integer ] {
    ( ipv4_address | ipv6_address ) [ port integer ]; ...
};

max-journal-size size_no_default;
max-transfer-time-in integer;
max-transfer-time-out integer;
max-transfer-idle-in integer;
max-transfer-idle-out integer;
max-retry-time integer;
min-retry-time integer;
max-refresh-time integer;
min-refresh-time integer;
multi-master boolean;
sig-validity-interval integer;

transfer-source ( ipv4_address | * )
    [ port ( integer | * ) ];
transfer-source-v6 ( ipv6_address | * )
    [ port ( integer | * ) ];

alt-transfer-source ( ipv4_address | * )
    [ port ( integer | * ) ];
alt-transfer-source-v6 ( ipv6_address | * )
    [ port ( integer | * ) ];
use-alt-transfer-source boolean;

zone-statistics boolean;
key-directory quoted_string;

ixfr-base quoted_string; // obsolete
ixfr-tmp-file quoted_string; // obsolete
maintain-ixfr-base boolean; // obsolete
max-ixfr-log-size size; // obsolete
pubkey integer integer integer quoted_string; // obsolete
};
```

Covered in Chapters 4 and 10.

BIND Resolver Statements

The following statements are for the resolver configuration file, */etc/resolv.conf*.

; and

Function
Adds a comment to the resolver configuration file.

Syntax
```
; free-format-comment
```
or:
```
# free-format-comment
```

Example
```
# Added parent domain to search list for compatibility with 4.8.3
```
Covered in Chapter 6.

domain

Function
Defines your resolver's local domain name.

Syntax
```
domain domain-name
```

Example
```
domain corp.hp.com
```
Covered in Chapter 6.

nameserver

Function
Tells your resolver to query a particular nameserver.

Syntax
```
nameserver IP-address
```

Example
```
nameserver 15.255.152.4
```
Covered in Chapter 6.

options attempts (8.2+)

Function

Specifies the number of times the resolver should query each nameserver.

Syntax

```
options attempts:number-of-attempts
```

Example

```
options attempts:2
```

Covered in Chapter 6.

options debug

Function

Turns on debugging output in the resolver.

Syntax

```
options debug
```

Example

```
options debug
```

Covered in Chapter 6.

options ndots

Function

Specifies the number of dots an argument must have in it so that the resolver will look it up before applying the search list.

Syntax

```
options ndots:number-of-dots
```

Example

```
options ndots:1
```

Covered in Chapter 6.

options no-check-names (8.2+)

Function

Turns off name checking in the resolver.

Syntax

```
options no-check-names
```

Example

```
options no-check-names
```

Covered in Chapter 6.

options timeout (8.2+)

Function

Specifies the resolver's per-nameserver timeout.

Syntax

```
options timeout:timeout-in-seconds
```

Example

```
options timeout:1
```

Covered in Chapter 6.

options rotate (8.2+)

Function

Rotates the order in which the resolver queries nameservers.

Syntax

```
options rotate
```

Example

```
options rotate
```

Covered in Chapter 6.

search

Function

Defines your resolver's local domain name and search list.

Syntax

```
search local-domain-name next-domain-name-in-search-list
... last-domain-name-in-search-list
```

Example

```
search corp.hp.com pa.itc.hp.com hp.com
```

Covered in Chapter 6.

sortlist

Function

Specifies networks for your resolver to prefer.

Syntax

```
sortlist network-list
```

Example

```
sortlist 128.32.4.0/255.255.255.0 15.0.0.0
```

Covered in Chapter 6.

BIND 9 Options Statement

Remember that statement that had way too many choices for you to consider?

```
options {
  avoid-v4-udp-ports { port; ... };
  avoid-v6-udp-ports { port; ... };
  blackhole { address_match_element; ... };
    ...
}
```

This section explains each choice.

This text came from the *BIND 9 Administrator Reference Manual* (created by Nominum). If you are running BIND 8, look for similar information in the *named.conf* manual page.

Definition and Usage

The *options* statement sets up global options to be used by BIND. This statement may appear only once in a configuration file. If there is no *options* statement, an options block with each option set to its default is used.

directory

> The working directory of the server. Any nonabsolute pathnames in the configuration file will be taken as relative to this directory. The default location for most server output files (e.g., *named.run*) is this directory. If a directory is not specified, the working directory defaults to ., the directory from which the server was started. The directory specified should be an absolute path.

key-directory

> When performing dynamic update of secure zones, the directory where the public- and private-key files should be found, if different than the current working directory. The directory specified must be an absolute path.

named-xfer

> This option is obsolete. It was used in BIND 8 to specify the pathname to the *named-xfer* program. In BIND 9, no separate *named-xfer* program is needed; its functionality is built into the nameserver.

tkey-domain

> The domain appended to the names of all shared keys generated with *TKEY*. When a client requests a *TKEY* exchange, it may or may not specify the desired name for the key. If present, the name of the shared key will be "*client-specified part*" + "*tkey-domain.*" Otherwise, the name of the shared key will be "*random hex digits*" + "*tkey-domain.*" In most cases, the *domainname* should be the server's domain name.

tkey-dhkey

> The Diffie-Hellman key used by the server to generate shared keys with clients using the Diffie-Hellman mode of *TKEY*. The server must be able to load the public and private keys from files in the working directory. In most cases, the *keyname* should be the server's hostname.

dump-file

> The pathname of the file the server dumps the database to when instructed to do so with *rndc dumpdb*. If not specified, the default is *named_dump.db*.

memstatistics-file

> The pathname of the file the server writes memory usage statistics to on exit. If not specified, the default is *named.memstats*.

pid-file

The pathname of the file the server writes its process ID in. If not specified, the default is */var/run/named.pid*. The *pid-file* is used by programs that want to send signals to the running nameserver. Specifying *pid-file none* disables the use of a PID file: no file will be written and all existing files are removed. Note that *none* is a keyword, not a filename, and therefore is not enclosed in double quotes.

statistics-file

The pathname of the file the server appends statistics to when instructed to do so using *rndc stats*. If not specified, the default is *named.stats* in the server's current directory.

port

The UDP/TCP port number the server uses for receiving and sending DNS protocol traffic. The default is 53. This option is mainly intended for server testing; a server using a port other than 53 can't communicate with the global DNS.

random-device

The source of entropy to be used by the server. Entropy is primarily needed for DNSSEC operations, such as *TKEY* transactions and dynamic update of signed zones. This option specifies the device (or file) from which to read entropy. If this is a file, operations requiring entropy will fail when the file has been exhausted. If not specified, the default value is */dev/random* (or equivalent) when present, and none otherwise. The *random-device* option takes effect during the initial configuration load at server startup time and is ignored on subsequent reloads.

preferred-glue

If specified, the listed type (A or AAAA) is emitted before other glue in the additional section of a query response. The default is not to preference any type (NONE).

root-delegation-only

Turns on enforcement of delegation-only in TLDs and root zones with an optional exclude list.

Note that some TLDs are not delegation-only (e.g., "DE," "LV," "US," and "MUSEUM").

```
options {
    root-delegation-only exclude { "de"; "lv"; "us"; "museum"; };
};
```

disable-algorithms

Disables the specified DNSSEC algorithms at and below the specified name. Multiple *disable-algorithms* statements are allowed. Only the most specific will be applied.

dnssec-lookaside

> When set, *dnssec-lookaside* provides the validator with an alternate method to validate DNSKEY records at the top of a zone. When a DNSKEY is at or below a domain specified by the deepest *dnssec-lookaside*, and the normal *dnssec* validation has left the key untrusted, the *trust-anchor* is appended to the key name, and a DLV record is looked up to see if it can validate the key. If the DLV record validates a DNSKEY (similarly to the way a DS record does), the DNSKEY RRset is deemed to be trusted.

dnssec-must-be-secure

> Specifies hierarchies that must/may not be secure (signed and validated). If *yes*, then *named* accepts answers only if they are secure. If *no*, normal *dnssec* validation applies, allowing for insecure answers to be accepted. The specified domain must be under a *trusted-key*, or *dnssec-lookaside* must be active.

Boolean Options

auth-nxdomain

> If *yes*, the AA bit is always set on NXDOMAIN responses, even if the server is not actually authoritative. The default is *no*; this is a change from BIND 8. If you are using very old DNS software, you may need to set it to *yes*.

deallocate-on-exit

> This option was used in BIND 8 to enable checking for memory leaks on exit. BIND 9 ignores the option and always performs the checks.

dialup

> If *yes*, the server treats all zones as if they are doing zone transfers across a dial-on-demand dialup link, which can be brought up by traffic originating from this server. This has different effects according to zone type and concentrates the zone maintenance so that it all happens in a short interval, once every *heartbeat-interval* and hopefully during the one call. It also suppresses some of the normal zone maintenance traffic. The default is *no*.

> The *dialup* option may also be specified in the *view* and *zone* statements, in which case it overrides the global *dialup* option.

> If the zone is a master zone, the server sends out a NOTIFY request to all the slaves (default). This should trigger the zone serial number check in the slave (providing it supports NOTIFY), allowing the slave to verify the zone while the connection is active. The set of servers to which NOTIFY is sent can be controlled by *notify* and *also-notify*.

> If the zone is a slave or stub zone, the server suppresses the regular "zone up to date" (refresh) queries and performs them only when the *heartbeat-interval* expires in addition to sending NOTIFY requests.

Finer control can be achieved using *notify*, which sends only NOTIFY messages; *notify-passive*, which sends NOTIFY messages and suppresses the normal refresh queries; *refresh*, which suppresses normal refresh processing and sends refresh queries when the *heartbeat-interval* expires; and *passive*, which just disables normal refresh processing.

Dialup mode	Normal refresh	heartbeat refresh	heartbeat notify
no (default)	Yes	No	No
yes	No	Yes	Yes
notify	Yes	No	Yes
refresh	No	Yes	No
passive	No	No	No
notify-passive	No	No	Yes

Note that normal NOTIFY processing is not affected by *dialup*.

fake-iquery

In BIND 8, if this option is enabled, it simulates the obsolete DNS query type IQUERY. BIND 9 never does IQUERY simulation.

fetch-glue

This option is obsolete. In BIND 8, *fetch-glue yes* caused the server to attempt to fetch-glue resource records it didn't have when constructing the additional data section of a response. This is now considered a bad idea, and BIND 9 never does it.

flush-zones-on-shutdown

When the nameserver exits due receiving SIGTERM, flush/do not flush any pending zone writes. The default is *flush-zones-on-shutdown no*.

has-old-clients

This option was incorrectly implemented in BIND 8 and is ignored by BIND 9. To achieve the intended effect of *has-old-clients yes*, specify the two separate options *auth-nxdomain yes* and *rfc2308-type1 no* instead.

host-statistics

In BIND 8, this option enables statistics to be kept for every host the nameserver interacts with. Not implemented in BIND 9.

maintain-ixfr-base

This option is obsolete. It was used in BIND 8 to determine whether a transaction log was kept for incremental zone transfer. BIND 9 maintains a transaction log whenever possible. If you need to disable outgoing incremental zone transfers, use *provide-ixfr no*.

minimal-responses

If *yes*, then when generating responses, the server adds records to the authority and additional data sections only when they are required (e.g., delegations, negative responses). This may improve the performance of the server. The default is *no*.

multiple-cnames

This option is used in BIND 8 to allow a domain name to have multiple CNAME records in violation of the DNS standards. BIND 9.2 always strictly enforces the CNAME rules both in master files and dynamic updates.

notify

If *yes* (the default), DNS NOTIFY messages are sent when a zone the server is in is authoritative for changes. The messages are sent to the servers listed in the zone's NS records (except the master server identified in the SOA MNAME field) and to any servers listed in the *also-notify* option.

If *explicit*, notifies are sent only to servers explicitly listed using *also-notify*. If *no*, no notifies are sent.

The *notify* option may also be specified in the *zone* statement, in which case it overrides the *options notify* statement. It is necessary to turn off this option only if it causes slaves to crash.

recursion

If *yes*, and a DNS query requests recursion, the server attempts to do all the work required to answer the query. If recursion is off, and the server does not already know the answer, it returns a referral response. The default is *yes*. Note that setting *recursion no* does not prevent clients from getting data from the server's cache; it only prevents new data from being cached as an effect of client queries. Caching may still occur due to the server's internal operation, such as NOTIFY address lookups. See also *fetch-glue*.

rfc2308-type1

Setting this to *yes* causes the server to send NS records along with the SOA record for negative answers. The default is *no*. Not yet implemented in BIND 9.

use-id-pool

This option is obsolete. BIND 9 always allocates query IDs from a pool.

zone-statistics

If *yes*, the server collects statistical data on all zones (unless specifically turned off on a per-zone basis by specifying *zone-statistics no* in the *zone* statement). These statistics may be accessed using *rndc stats*, which dumps them to the file listed in the *statistics-file*.

use-ixfr

This option is obsolete. If you need to disable IXFR to a particular server or servers, see the information on the *provide-ixfr* option.

provide-ixfr

This clause determines whether the local server, acting as master, will respond with an incremental zone transfer when the given remote server, a slave, requests it. If set to *yes*, incremental transfer is provided whenever possible. If set to *no*, all transfers to the remote server are nonincremental.

request-ixfr

The *request-ixfr* clause determines whether the local server, acting as a slave, will request incremental zone transfers from the given remote server, a master.

treat-cr-as-space

This option was used in BIND 8 to make the server treat carriage return ("\r") characters the same way as a space or tab character, in order to facilitate loading of zone files on a Unix system that were generated on an NT or DOS machine. In BIND 9, both Unix "\n" and NT/DOS "\r\n" newlines are always accepted, and the option is ignored.

additional-from-auth
additional-from-cache

These options control the behavior of an authoritative server when answering queries that have additional data, or when following CNAME and DNAME chains.

When both options are set to *yes* (the default), and a query is being answered from authoritative data (a zone configured into the server), the additional data section of the reply is filled in using data from other authoritative zones and from the cache. In some situations, this is undesirable, such as when there is concern about the correctness of the cache, or when servers have slave zones that may be added and modified by untrusted third parties. Also, avoiding the search for this additional data speeds up server operations at the possible expense of additional queries to resolve what would otherwise be provided in the additional section.

For example, if a query asks for an MX record for host *foo.example.com*, and the record found is "*MX 10 mail.example.net*," normally the address records (A and AAAA) for *mail.example.net* are provided as well, if known, even though they are not in the *example.com* zone. Setting these options to *no* disables this behavior and makes the server search for additional data only in the zone it answers from.

These options are intended for use in authoritative-only servers or in authoritative-only views. Attempts to set them to *no* without also specifying *recursion no* causes the server to ignore the options and logs a warning message.

Specifying *additional-from-cache no* actually disables the use of the cache not only for additional data lookups but also when looking up the answer. This is usually the desired behavior in an authoritative-only server when the correctness of the cached data is an issue.

When a nameserver is nonrecursively queried for a name that is not below the apex of any served zone, it normally answers with an "upwards referral" to the root servers or the servers of some other known parent of the query name. Since the data in an upwards referral comes from the cache, the server can't provide upwards referrals when *additional-from-cache no* has been specified. Instead, it responds to such queries with REFUSED. This should not cause any problems because upwards referrals are not required for the resolution process.

match-mapped-addresses

If *yes*, an IPv4-mapped IPv6 address matches any address match list entries that match the corresponding IPv4 address. Enabling this option is sometimes useful on IPv6-enabled Linux systems. It works around a kernel quirk that causes IPv4 TCP connections such as zone transfers to be accepted on an IPv6 socket that uses mapped addresses. As a result, address match lists designed for IPv4 fail to match. The use of this option for any other purpose is discouraged.

ixfr-from-differences

When *yes*, and when the server loads a new version of a master zone from its zone file or receives a new version of a slave file via a nonincremental zone transfer, it compares the new version to the previous one and calculates a set of differences. The differences are then logged in the zone's journal file such that the changes can be transmitted to downstream slaves as an incremental zone transfer.

By allowing incremental zone transfers to be used for nondynamic zones, this option saves bandwidth at the expense of increased CPU and memory consumption at the master. In particular, if the new version of a zone is completely different from the previous one, the set of differences are comparable in size to the combined size of the old and new zone version. The server then needs to temporarily allocate memory to hold this complete difference set.

multi-master

This should be set when you have multiple masters for a zone and the addresses refer to different machines. If *yes*, *named* will not log when the serial number on the master is less than what named currently has. The default is *no*.

dnssec-enable

Enables DNSSEC support in named. Unless set to *yes*, *named* behaves as if it does not support DNSSEC. The default is *no*.

querylog

Specifies whether query logging should be started when *named* starts. If *querylog* is not specified, the query logging is determined by the presence of the logging category *queries*.

check-names

Restricts the character set and syntax of certain domain names in master files and/or DNS responses received from the network. The default varies according to usage area. For *master* zones, the default is *fail*. For *slave* zones, the default is *warn*. For answer, received from the network (*response*), the default is *ignore*.

The rules for legal hostnames/mail domains are derived from RFC 952 and RFC 821 as modified by RFC 1123.

check-names applies to the owner names of A, AAA, and MX records. It also applies to the domain names in the RDATA of NS, SOA, and MX records, and to the RDATA of PTR records when the owner name indicates when it is a reverse lookup of a hostname (the owner name ends in IN-ADDR.ARPA, IP6.ARPA, IP6.INT).

Forwarding

The forwarding facility can create a large site-wide cache on a few servers, reducing traffic over links to external nameservers. It can also allow queries by servers that do not have direct access to the Internet but wish to look up exterior names anyway. Forwarding occurs only on those queries for which the server is not authoritative and does not have the answer in its cache.

forward
> This option is meaningful only if the forwarders list is not empty. A value of *first*, the default, causes the server to query the forwarders first, and if that doesn't answer the question, the server then looks for the answer itself. If *only* is specified, the server queries only the forwarders.

forwarders
> Specifies the IP addresses to be used for forwarding. The default is the empty list (no forwarding).

Forwarding can also be configured on a per-domain basis, which allows global forwarding options to be overridden in a variety of ways. You can set particular domains to use different forwarders, have a different *forward only/first* behavior, or not forward at all.

Dual-Stack Servers

Dual-stack servers are used as servers of last resort to work around problems in reachability due the lack of support for either IPv4 or IPv6 on the host machine.

dual-stack-servers
> Specifies hostnames/addresses of machines with access to both IPv4 and IPv6 transports. If a hostname is used, the server must be able to resolve the name using only the transport it has. If the machine is dual-stacked, the *dual-stack-servers* have no effect unless access to a transport has been disabled on the command line (e.g., *named –4*).

Access Control

Access to the server can be restricted based on the IP address of the requesting system.

allow-notify

Specifies which hosts are allowed to notify this server—a slave—of zone changes in addition to the zone masters. *allow-notify* may also be specified in the *zone* statement, in which case it overrides the *options allow-notify* statement. It is only meaningful for a slave zone. If not specified, the default is to process notify messages only from a zone's master.

allow-query

Specifies which hosts are allowed to ask ordinary DNS questions. *allow-query* may also be specified in the *zone* statement, in which case it overrides the *options allow-query* statement. If not specified, the default is to allow queries from all hosts.

allow-recursion

Specifies which hosts are allowed to make recursive queries through this server. If not specified, the default is to allow recursive queries from all hosts. Note that disallowing recursive queries for a host does not prevent the host from retrieving data that is already in the server's cache.

allow-update-forwarding

Specifies which hosts are allowed to submit dynamic DNS updates to slave zones that are forwarded to the master. The default is *none*, which means that no update forwarding is performed. To enable update forwarding, specify *allow-update-forwarding any*. Specifying values other than *none* or *any* is usually counterproductive because the responsibility for update access control should rest with the master server, not the slaves.

Note that enabling the update-forwarding feature on a slave server may expose to attacks those master servers that rely on insecure IP address–based access control.

allow-v6-synthesis

This option was introduced for the smooth transition from AAAA to A6 and from "nibble labels" to binary labels. However, since both A6 and binary labels were then deprecated, this option was also deprecated. It is now ignored with some warning messages.

allow-transfer

Specifies which hosts are allowed to receive zone transfers from the server. *allow-transfer* may also be specified in the *zone* statement, in which case it overrides the *options allow-transfer* statement. If not specified, the default allows transfers to all hosts.

blackhole

Specifies a list of addresses the server doesn't accept queries from or use to resolve a query. Queries from these addresses aren't responded to. The default is *none*.

Interfaces

The interfaces and ports that the server answers queries from may be specified using the *listen-on* option. *listen-on* takes an optional port, and an *address_match_list*. The server listens on all interfaces allowed by the address match list. If a port is not specified, port 53 is used.

Multiple *listen-on* statements are allowed. For example:

```
listen-on { 5.6.7.8; };
listen-on port 1234 { !1.2.3.4; 1.2/16; };
```

enables the nameserver on port 53 for the IP address 5.6.7.8, and on port 1234 of an address on the machine in net 1.2 that is not 1.2.3.4.

If no *listen-on* is specified, the server listens on port 53 on all interfaces.

The *listen-on-v6* option specifies the interfaces and the ports on which the server listens for incoming queries sent using IPv6.

When:

```
{ any; }
```

is specified as the *address_match_list* for the *listen-on-v6* option, the server does not bind a separate socket to each IPv6 interface address as it does for IPv4 if the operating system has enough API support for IPv6 (specifically if it conforms to RFC 3493 and RFC 3542). Instead, it listens on the IPv6 wildcard address. If the system has incomplete API support for IPv6, however, the behavior is the same as that for IPv4.

A list of particular IPv6 addresses can also be specified, in which case the server listens on a separate socket for each specified address, regardless of whether the desired API is supported by the system.

Multiple *listen-on-v6* options can be used. For example:

```
listen-on-v6 { any; };
listen-on-v6 port 1234 { !2001:db8::/32; any; };
```

enables the nameserver on port 53 for any IPv6 addresses (with a single wildcard socket) and on port 1234 of IPv6 addresses that is not in the prefix 2001:db8::/32 (with separate sockets for each matched address).

To make the server not listen on any IPv6 address, use:

```
listen-on-v6 { none; };
```

If no *listen-on-v6* option is specified, the server doesn't listen on any IPv6 address.

Query Address

If the server doesn't know the answer to a question, it queries other nameservers. *query-source* specifies the address and port used for such queries. For queries sent over IPv6, there is a separate *query-source-v6* option. If *address* is * or is omitted, a wildcard IP address (*INADDR_ANY*) is used. If *port* is * or is omitted, a random unprivileged port is used; *avoid-v4-udp-ports* and *avoid-v6-udp-ports* can prevent *named* from selecting certain ports. The defaults are:

```
query-source address * port *;
query-source-v6 address * port *;
```

Note that the address specified in the *query-source* option is used for both UDP and TCP queries, but the port applies only to UDP queries. TCP queries always use a random unprivileged port.

See also *transfer-source* and *notify-source*.

Zone Transfers

BIND has mechanisms in place to facilitate zone transfers and set limits on the amount of load transfers place on the system. The following options apply to zone transfers:

also-notify

Defines a global list of IP addresses of nameservers that are also sent NOTIFY messages whenever a fresh copy of the zone is loaded, in addition to the servers listed in the zone's NS records. This helps to ensure that copies of the zones will quickly converge on stealth servers. If an *also-notify* list is given in a *zone* statement, it overrides the *options also-notify* statement. When a *zone notify* statement is set to *no*, the IP addresses in the global *also-notify* list are not sent NOTIFY messages for that zone. The default is the empty list (no global notification list).

max-transfer-time-in

Inbound zone transfers running longer than this many minutes are terminated. The default is 120 minutes (2 hours). The maximum value is 28 days (40,320 minutes).

max-transfer-idle-in

Inbound zone transfers making no progress in this many minutes are terminated. The default is 60 minutes (1 hour). The maximum value is 28 days (40,320 minutes).

max-transfer-time-out

Outbound zone transfers running longer than this many minutes are terminated. The default is 120 minutes (2 hours). The maximum value is 28 days (40,320 minutes).

max-transfer-idle-out

Outbound zone transfers making no progress in this many minutes are terminated. The default is 60 minutes (1 hour). The maximum value is 28 days (40,320 minutes).

serial-query-rate

Slave servers periodically query master servers to find out if zone serial numbers have changed. Each such query uses a minute amount of the slave server's network bandwidth. To limit the amount of bandwidth used, BIND 9 limits the rate at which queries are sent. The value of the *serial-query-rate* option, an integer, is the maximum number of queries sent per second. The default is 20.

serial-queries

In BIND 8, the *serial-queries* option sets the maximum number of concurrent serial number queries allowed to be outstanding at any given time. BIND 9 does not limit the number of outstanding serial queries and ignores the *serial-queries* option. Instead, it limits the rate at which the queries are sent as defined using the *serial-query-rate* option.

transfer-format

Zone transfers can be sent using two different formats, *one-answer* and *many-answers*. The *transfer-format* option is used on the master server to determine which format it sends. *one-answer* uses one DNS message per resource record transferred. *many-answers* packs as many resource records as possible into a message. *many-answers* is more efficient, but is only supported by relatively new slave servers, such as BIND 9, BIND 8.x, and patched versions of BIND 4.9.5. The default is *many-answers*. *transfer-format* may be overridden on a per-server basis using the *server* statement.

transfers-in

The maximum number of inbound zone transfers that can be running concurrently. The default value is 10. Increasing *transfers-in* may speed up the convergence of slave zones, but it also may increase the load on the local system.

transfers-out

The maximum number of outbound zone transfers that can be running concurrently. Zone transfer requests in excess of the limit are refused. The default value is 10.

transfers-per-ns

The maximum number of inbound zone transfers that can be concurrently transferring from a given remote nameserver. The default value is 2. Increasing *transfers-per-ns* may speed up the convergence of slave zones, but it also may increase the load on the remote nameserver. *transfers-per-ns* may be overridden on a per-server basis by using the *transfers* phrase of the *server* statement.

transfer-source

transfer-source determines which local addresses are bound to IPv4 TCP connections that fetch zones transferred inbound by the server. It also determines the source IPv4 address, and optionally the UDP port, used for the refresh queries and forwarded dynamic updates. If not set, it defaults to a system controlled value that is usually the address of the interface closest to the remote end. This address must appear in the remote end's *allow-transfer* option for the zone being transferred, if one is specified. This statement sets the *transfer-source* for all zones but can be overridden on a per-view or per-zone basis by including a *transfer-source* statement within the *view* or *zone* block in the configuration file.

transfer-source-v6

> The same as *transfer-source*, except zone transfers are performed using IPv6.

alt-transfer-source

> An alternate transfer source if the one listed in *transfer-source* fails, and *use-alt-transfer-source* is set.

alt-transfer-source-v6

> An alternate transfer source if the one listed in *transfer-source-v6* fails, and *use-alt-transfer-source* is set.

use-alt-transfer-source

> Use the alternate transfer sources or not. If views are specified, this defaults to *no*; otherwise, it defaults to *yes* (for BIND 8 compatibility).

notify-source

> *notify-source* determines which local source address—and, optionally, UDP port—is used to send NOTIFY messages. This address must appear in the slave server's *masters* zone clause or in an *allow-notify* clause. This statement sets the *notify-source* for all zones but can be overridden on a per-zone/per-view basis by including a *notify-source* statement within the *zone* or *view* block in the configuration file.

notify-source-v6

> Like *notify-source*, but applies to notify messages sent to IPv6 addresses.

Bad UDP Port Lists

avoid-v4-udp-ports and *avoid-v6-udp-ports* specify a list of IPv4 and IPv6 UDP ports that aren't used as system-assigned source ports for UDP sockets. These lists prevent *named* from choosing as its random source port a port that is blocked by your firewall. If a query is sent with such a source port, the answer doesn't get by the firewall, and the nameserver has to query again.

Operating System Resource Limits

The server's usage of many system resources can be limited. Scaled values are allowed when specifying resource limits. For example, 1G can be used instead of 1073741824 to specify a limit of one gigabyte. *unlimited* requests unlimited use, or the maximum available amount. *default* uses the limit that was in force when the server was started.

The following options set operating system resource limits for the nameserver process. Some operating systems don't support some or any of the limits. On such systems, a warning is issued if the unsupported limit is used.

coresize
> The maximum size of a core dump. The default is *default*.

datasize
> The maximum amount of data memory the server may use. The default is *default*. This is a hard limit on server memory usage. If the server attempts to allocate memory in excess of this limit, the allocation will fail, which may, in turn, leave the server unable to perform DNS service. Therefore, this option is rarely useful as a way to limit the amount of memory used by the server, but it can be used to raise an operating system data size limit that is too small by default. If you wish to limit the amount of memory used by the server, use the *max-cache-size* and *recursive-clients* options instead.

files
> The maximum number of files the server may have open concurrently. The default is *unlimited*.

stacksize
> The maximum amount of stack memory the server may use. The default is *default*.

Server Resource Limits

The following options set limits on the server's resource consumption that are enforced internally by the server rather than the operating system:

max-ixfr-log-size
> This option is obsolete; it is accepted and ignored for BIND 8 compatibility. The option *max-journal-size* performs a similar function in BIND 8.

max-journal-size
> Sets a maximum size for each journal file. When the journal file approaches the specified size, some of the oldest transactions in the journal are automatically removed. The default is *unlimited*.

host-statistics-max
> In BIND 8, specifies the maximum number of host statistic entries to be kept. Not implemented in BIND 9.

recursive-clients
> The maximum number of simultaneous recursive lookups the server will perform on behalf of clients. The default is 1000. Because each recursing client uses a fair bit of memory, on the order of 20 kilobytes, the value of the *recursive-clients* option may have to be decreased on hosts with limited memory.

tcp-clients

The maximum number of simultaneous client TCP connections the server will accept. The default is 100.

max-cache-size

The maximum amount of memory to use for the server's cache, in bytes. When the amount of data in the cache reaches this limit, the server causes records to expire prematurely so that the limit is not exceeded. In a server with multiple views, the limit applies separately to the cache of each view. The default is *unlimited*, meaning that records are purged from the cache only when their TTLs expire.

tcp-listen-queue

The listen queue depth. The default and minimum is 3. If the kernel supports the accept filter "dataready," this also controls how many TCP connections are queued in kernel space waiting for some data before being passed to accept. Values less than 3 are silently raised.

Periodic Task Intervals

cleaning-interval

The server removes expired resource records from the cache every *cleaning-interval* minutes. The default is 60 minutes. The maximum value is 28 days (40,320 minutes). If set to 0, no periodic cleaning occurs.

heartbeat-interval

The server performs zone maintenance tasks for all zones marked as *dialup* whenever this interval expires. The default is 60 minutes. Reasonable values are up to 1 day (1,440 minutes). The maximum value is 28 days (40,320 minutes). If set to 0, no zone maintenance for these zones occurs.

interface-interval

The server scans the network interface list every *interface-interval* minutes. The default is 60 minutes. The maximum value is 28 days (40,320 minutes). If set to 0, interface scanning occurs only when the configuration file is loaded. After the scan, the server begins listening for queries on any newly discovered interfaces (provided they are allowed by the *listen-on* configuration), and stops listening on interfaces that have gone away.

statistics-interval

Nameserver statistics are logged every *statistics-interval* minutes. The default is 60. The maximum value is 28 days (40,320 minutes). If set to 0, no statistics are logged.

statistics-interval is not yet implemented in BIND 9.

Topology

All other things being equal, when the server chooses a nameserver to query from a list of nameservers, it prefers the one that is topologically closest to itself. The *topology* statement takes an *address_match_list* and interprets it in a special way. Each top-level list element is assigned a distance. Nonnegated elements get a distance based on their position in the list, in which the closer the match is to the start of the list, the shorter the distance between it and the server. A negated match is assigned the maximum distance from the server. If there is no match, the address gets a distance that is further than any nonnegated list element and closer than any negated element. For example:

```
topology {
    10/8;
    !1.2.3/24;
    { 1.2/16; 3/8; };
};
```

prefers servers on network 10 the most, followed by hosts on network 1.2.0.0 (netmask 255.255.0.0) and network 3, with the exception of hosts on network 1.2.3 (netmask 255.255.255.0), which is preferred least of all.

The default topology is:

```
topology { localhost; localnets; };
```

The *topology* option is not yet implemented in BIND 9.

The sortlist Statement

The response to a DNS query may consist of multiple resource records (RRs) forming a resource records set (RRset). The nameserver will normally return the RRs within the RRset in an indeterminate order. The client resolver code should rearrange the RRs as appropriate, that is, using any addresses on the local net in preference to other addresses. However, not all resolvers can do this or are correctly configured. When a client is using a local server, the sorting can be performed in the server, based on the client's address. This requires configuring only the nameservers, not all the clients.

The *sortlist* statement (see below) takes an *address_match_list* and interprets it even more specifically than the *topology* statement does. Each top-level statement in the *sortlist* must itself be an explicit *address_match_list* with one or two elements. The first element (which may be an IP address, an IP prefix, an ACL name, or a nested *address_match_list*) of each top-level list is checked against the source address of the query until a match is found.

Once the source address of the query has been matched, if the top-level statement contains only one element, the actual primitive element that matched the source address selects the address in the response to move to the beginning of the response. If the statement is a list of two elements, the second element is treated the same as the *address_match_list* in a *topology* statement. Each top-level element is assigned a distance, and the address in the response with the minimum distance is moved to the beginning of the response.

In the following example, any queries received from any of the addresses of the host itself will get responses preferring addresses on any of the locally connected networks. The next most preferred are addresses on the 192.168.1/24 network, and after that, either the 192.168.2/24 or 192.168.3/24 network; no preference is shown between these two networks. Queries received from a host on the 192.168.1/24 network prefer other addresses on that network to the 192.168.2/24 and 192.168.3/24 networks. Queries received from a host on the 192.168.4/24 or 192.168.5/24 network prefer only other addresses on their directly connected networks.

```
sortlist {
    { localhost;                                    // IF   the local host
        { localnets;                                // THEN first fit on the
            192.168.1/24;                           //   following nets
            { 192.168.2/24; 192.168.3/24; }; }; };
    { 192.168.1/24;                                 // IF   on class C 192.168.1
        { 192.168.1/24;                             // THEN use .1, or .2 or .3
            { 192.168.2/24; 192.168.3/24; }; }; };
    { 192.168.2/24;                                 // IF   on class C 192.168.2
        { 192.168.2/24;                             // THEN use .2, or .1 or .3
            { 192.168.1/24; 192.168.3/24; }; }; };
    { 192.168.3/24;                                 // IF   on class C 192.168.3
        { 192.168.3/24;                             // THEN use .3, or .1 or .2
            { 192.168.1/24; 192.168.2/24; }; }; };
    { { 192.168.4/24; 192.168.5/24; };              // if .4 or .5, prefer that net
    };
};
```

The following example gives reasonable behavior for the local host and hosts on directly connected networks. It is similar to the behavior of the address sort in BIND 4.9.x. Responses sent to queries from the local host will favor any of the directly connected networks. Responses sent to queries from any other hosts on a directly connected network will prefer addresses on that same network. Responses to other queries will not be sorted.

```
sortlist {
            { localhost; localnets; };
            { localnets; };
};
```

RRset Ordering

When multiple records are returned in an answer, it may be useful to configure the order of the records placed into the response. The *rrset-order* statement permits configuration of the ordering of the records in a multiple-record response.

An *order_spec* is defined as follows:

```
[ class class_name ][ type type_name ][ name "domain_name"]
    order ordering
```

If no class is specified, the default is ANY. If no type is specified, the default is ANY. If no name is specified, the default is "*".

Here are the legal values for *ordering*:

fixed
> Records are returned in the order they are defined in the zone file.

random
> Records are returned in a random order.

cyclic
> Records are returned in a round-robin order.

For example:

```
rrset-order {
    class IN type A name "host.example.com" order random;
    order cyclic;
};
```

causes any responses for type A records in class IN that have *host.example.com* as a suffix to always be returned in random order. All other records are returned in cyclic order.

If multiple *rrset-order* statements appear, they are not combined: the last one applies.

 The *rrset-order* statement is not yet fully implemented in BIND 9. BIND 9 currently does not support fixed ordering.

Tuning

lame-ttl
> Sets the number of seconds to cache a lame server indication. 0 disables caching; this is *not* recommended. Default is 600 (10 minutes). Maximum value is 1800 (30 minutes).

max-ncache-ttl
> To reduce network traffic and increase performance, the server stores negative answers. *max-ncache-ttl* sets a maximum retention time for these answers in the

server in seconds. The default *max-ncache-ttl* is 10,800 seconds (3 hours). *max-ncache-ttl* cannot exceed seven days and is silently truncated to seven days if set to a greater value.

max-cache-ttl

> *max-cache-ttl* sets the maximum time for which the server caches ordinary (positive) answers. The default is one week (seven days).

min-roots

> The minimum number of root servers that is required for a request for the root servers to be accepted. Default is 2. Not yet implemented in BIND 9.

sig-validity-interval

> Specifies the number of days in the future when DNSSEC signatures automatically generated as a result of dynamic updates will expire. The default is 30 days. The maximum value is 10 years (3,660 days). The signature inception time is unconditionally set to one hour before the current time to allow for a limited amount of clock skew.

min-refresh-time
max-refresh-time
min-retry-time
max-retry-time

> These options control the server's behavior on refreshing a zone (querying for SOA changes) or retrying failed transfers. Usually the SOA values for the zone are used, but these values are set by the master, giving slave server administrators little control over their contents.

> These options allow the administrator to set a minimum and maximum refresh and retry time per-zone, per-view, or globally. These options are valid for slave and stub zones, and clamp the SOA refresh and retry times to the specified values.

edns-udp-size

> *edns-udp-size* sets the advertised EDNS UDP buffer size. Valid values are 512 to 4096 (values outside this range are silently adjusted). The default value is 4096. The usual reason for setting *edns-udp-size* to a nondefault value is to get UDP answers to pass through broken firewalls that block fragmented packets and/or block UDP packets that are greater than 512 bytes.

Built-in Server Information Zones

The server provides some helpful diagnostic information through a number of built-in zones under the pseudo-top-level-domain *bind* in the *CHAOS* class. These zones are part of a built-in view of class *CHAOS*, which is separate from the default view of class *IN*; therefore, any global server options such as *allow-query* do not apply to these zones. If you feel the need to disable these zones, use the following options, or hide the built-in *CHAOS* view by defining an explicit view of class *CHAOS* that matches all clients.

version

> The version the server should report via a query of the name *version.bind* with type *TXT*, class *CHAOS*. The default is the real version number of this server. Specifying *version none* disables processing of the queries.

hostname

> The hostname the server should report via a query of the name *hostname.bind* with type *TXT*, class *CHAOS*. This defaults to the hostname of the machine hosting the nameserver as found by *gethostname()*. The primary purpose of such queries is to identify which of a group of anycast servers is actually answering your queries. Specifying *hostname none;* disables processing of the queries.

server-id

> The ID of the server should report via a query of the name *ID.SERVER* with type *TXT*, class *CHAOS*. The primary purpose of such queries is to identify which of a group of anycast servers is actually answering your queries. Specifying *server-id none;* disables processing of the queries. Specifying *server-id hostname;* causes *named* to use the hostname as found by *gethostname()*. The default *server-id* is *none*.

Index

We'd like to hear your suggestions for improving our indexes. Send email to *index@oreilly.com*.

cannot set resource limits on this system
(syslog message), 159
canonical names
domain names in NS records, 211
mailers looking for, 95
PTR records and, 60
(see also CNAME records)
canonical, domain names, 6
canonical name records (see CNAME
records)
canonicalization (sendmail), 116
aliases in sendmail features, 60
canonicalization filter, disambiguating
hostnames, 118
carriage return and a newline
(Windows), 268
Carroll, Lewis, xx
categories (logging), 148, 154–158
BIND 8, 154
BIND 9, 156
config, 154
default, 150
syslog and, 151
logging to channels, 148
specifying in channel logging
statement, 150
viewing all category messages, 157
CD (Checking Disabled) flag, 333
chain of trust, 330–333
chaining fowarders, avoiding, 245
channels (logging), 148, 152–154
configuring, 149
data formatting, 154
discarding default category messages, 150
file, 153
logging categories to, 148
null, 154
severity levels of messages, 149
stderr, 154
syslog, 153
CHAOS class, 530
Checking Disabled (CD) flag, 333
checksums, UDP checksums disabled, 430
chmod(1) manual page, 128
chroot( ), 292
chrooted environment, setting up, 293
CIDR (Classless Inter-Domain Routing), 49
class $=w names (sendmail), 116

Class A, Class B, and Class C networks, 49
subnetted Class A and B networks on
nonoctet boundaries, 216
subnetted Class C networks on nonoctet
boundaries, 216
CLASS fields in resource records, 530
classes
error in, 164
for internets, 16
of networks, 49
record types defined by, 17
Classless Inter-Domain Routing (CIDR), 49
cleaning-interval substatement, 265
client/server architecture of DNS, 4
clients, limiting number served by
nameserver concurrently, 264
CNAME (canonical name) records, 59,
483–488
attached to interior nodes, 483
in data portion of resource record, 163
finding out host aliases, 486
hosts moving into subdomain from
parent, 212
looking up, 486
mailers and, 95
multiple
attached to a domain name, 485
used to set up round robin, 251
network or subnet hosts moved to new
subdomain, 223
pointing to CNAMEs, 484
query statistics on BIND 8
nameserver, 170
resolver getting instead of PTR, 429
sendmail and, 116
in resource record data, 485
updating for hosts in zone datafiles, 137
using address records instead of, 60
com domain, 17, 46
interpreting domain names (example), 20
command (ndc program), 130
command line, changing nslookup options
from, 352
command-line option (BIND
debugging), 380
comments, 553
BIND resolvers, version 4.9, 111
in zone datafiles, 56

hosts *(continued)*
  domain names, 6
  per-host statistics, BIND 8, 171–175, 183
  represented by domain names, 14
hosts database, 119
  listing with ypcat, 397
hosts.equiv file, adding domain names to
        hostnames, 117
HOSTS.TXT file, 3
host-statistics substatement, 169, 183
human resources management industry (jobs)
        domain, 19
HUP signal, 136

I

ICANN (Internet Corporation for Assigned
        Names and Numbers), 19
ICMP (Internet Control Message Protocol)
  port unreachable message, 196
  port unreachable, host unreachable, or
        network unreachable, 107
identity (update-policy statement), 233
idle time, limiting for zone transfers, 261
IDN (Internationalized Domain Names), xiv,
        48, 504–506
ifconfig command, 196
in-addr.arpa domains
  subdomains of, 214–220
    subnetting on nonoctet
        boundary, 215–220
    subnetting on octet boundary, 215
in-addr.arpa zones, 51
  delegating, 212
  delegation by internal roots, 310
  registering nameservers, 191
$INCLUDE statement, 144, 147
include mechanism (SPF TXT records), 98
include statement, 144, 554
  reading key statement from another
        file, 285
incremental zone transfer (IXFR), xiii,
        39, 240–244
  calculating from differences in zone
        datafile versions, 241
  configuring in BIND 8, 242
  configuring in BIND 9, 243
  files, 242
  limitations of, 241
inet substatement (controls), 131
info domain, 19, 46

info severity, 149
  messages sent to syslog and debug
        file, 152
int (international organizations) domain, 18
interface ID (IPv6 addresses), 269
interface interval, 266
internal view, 249
  recursion turned on, 300
Internationalized Domain Names (see IDN)
international organizations (int) domain, 18
Internet
  history of, 1
  necessity of DNS, 10
  versus internets, 2
Internet access, types of, 53
Internet class, 530
Internet connections
  dial-up, 489–494
    authoritative nameservers over
        dial-on-demand, 493
    dial-on-demand with multiple
        hosts, 492
    dial-on-demand with one host, 492
    dialouts, avoiding, 490
    dialouts, causes of, 490
    manual dial-up, with multiple
        hosts, 492
    manual dial-up, with one host, 491
Internet Control Message (see ICMP)
Internet Corporation for Assigned Names
        and Numbers (ICANN), 19
Internet domain namespace, 17–21
  reading domain names, 20
  top-level domains, 17–19
Internet firewalls
  DNS and, proxies, 302
  types of software, 301
Internet forwarders, 304–309
Internet root nameservers, 27
Internet service providers (see ISPs)
Internet Software Consortium (see ISC)
Internet Systems Consortium, 9
internets
  TCP/IP-based, deciding on use of
        DNS, 10
  versus the Internet, 2
InterNIC
  Network Modification form, 191
  site, 47
intranets, 2

---

namespaces
  shadow, 315
  split, 315–322
name-to-address lookup, 54
name-to-address mappings, 58
  WIndows XP clients, 124
nametype (update-policy statement), 233
naming, views, 248
naming services, hosts database, 119
NAPTR records, 502–504
  spoofing, 504
ndc program, 128–131
  –c option, 128, 294
  changing debugging level with control
      messages, 380
  getting statistics from BIND 8
      nameserver, 168
  help, 129
  interactive and noninteractive modes, 129
  signals, equivalent to commands, 135
  start and restart commands, 130
  support for commands by rndc
      program, 134
  toggling query logging, 136
negative caching, 34
  BIND 8, 393
  BIND 9, 394
  max-ncache-ttl options
      substatement, 266
  nameserver inability to, 430
  TTL, 56, 194
  Windows XP resolver, 125
negative responses
  authenticated (NSEC record), 328–330
  format of, 267
net domain, 18
Net::DNS module, 470–473
Net::DNS Perl module, 287
NetBIOS names, 506
NetBIOS naming service (WINS), 124
netgroup, filesystems for NFS-mount, 115
network identifiers, 49
Network Information Service (see NIS)
network infrastructure, organizatins
      providing, 18
network interface IP address, advertising
      nameserver listening on, 298
network interfaces, scanning for nameserver
      host, 266
Network Modification form, 191
network resources, mirrored, 250

Network Solutions, Inc., 47
network time protocol (NTP), 286
networks
  checking registration, 48–50
  classes of, 49
  deciding number of nameservers, 177
  failures, coping with, 198–200
    long outages (days), 198
    really long outages (weeks), 199
  failures, planning for, 195–198
  loss of connectivity to Internet, 417–419
  names and numbers, 494–496
  specifying for preference by the
      resolver, 109
newlines, 268
newsgroups, BIND, 39
NFS service, 115
NIS (Network Information Service), 10
  deciding if problem is caused by, 396
  domains, DNS domains versus, 15
  nslookup and, 351
"no" preceding nslookup option's name, 352
no response from server error, 367
no-check-names (resolver option), 111
nodes, DNS database, 4
nonauthoritative answers, 356
noncommercial organizations, 18
none (address match list), 227
nonexistent domain message, 368
nonrecursive queries
  sent between nameservers, 244
  (see also iterative queries)
NOTFOUND condition, 119
notice severity, 149
NOTIFY, xiii, 186, 235–240
  adding nameservers besides those in zone
      NS records to list, 239
  announcement identification, 236
  announcements sent by slave after zone
      transfer, 236
  BIND slave nameservers not supporting
      (NOTIMP error), 239
  response by slave to NOTIFY
      announcement, 236
  sending messages to alternate ports, 271
  turning off, 239
  zone transfer scheme, complex, 238
notify substatement (zone), explicit
      argument, 239
notify-source substatement, 272
notify-source-v6 substatement, 273

severities
    debug level 1, 154
    logging messages, 149
    specifying for file channel, 153
shadow namespace, 315
    zone datafile, 316
shell scripts, programming with nslookup or
        dig, 438–444
shuffle address records, 250
signals, controlling the nameserver, 135
signature expiration field (RRSIG
            records), 344
        signature inception field (RRSIG
            records), 327
signature field (RRSIG records), 328
signature inception field (RRSIG
            records), 344
signatures, cryptographic (TSIG), 232
signer's name field (RRSIG records), 328
signing, 324
    zones, 336–342
        generating key pairs, 336
        parent zone, 341
        sending keys to be signed, 340
sig-validity-interval substatement, 344
Simple Mail Transfer Protocol (SMTP), 90
size substatement (file channel), 153
slash (see /)
slave nameservers, 25
    AXFR queries to initiate zone
            transfers, 171
    caching-only server lookups in zone, 187
    changes to zone datafiles, 137
    checking zone (BIND 8, Debug Level
            1), 389–391
    checking zone (BIND 9, Debug Level
            1), 392
    configured to use forwarder, 244
    datafiles, 26
    inbound zone transfers (named-xfer), 147
    loading zone data from other slaves, 186
    network traffic between hidden primary
            and, 477
    NOTIFY announcements, sending after
            zone transfer, 236
    NOTIFY announcment response to
            master, 236
    polling mechanism to determine need for
            zone transfer, 235
    preventing zone transfers from, 291
    putting on delegated subdomain, 213

reconfiguring as primary during
        outages, 198
    registering, 189
    setting up for new, delegated
            subdomain, 210
    signing zone transfer requests, 291
    TTL, 193
    unable to load zone data, 411–413
    unable to reach master for zone
            transfer, 161
    zone transfer requests, matching to
            primary's IXFR capabilities, 243
slave zones, storing datafiles in separate
            directory, 144
SMTP (Simple Mail Transfer Protocol), 90
snapshot of current statistics (syslog
            message), 160
SOA (start of authority) records
    adding to zone datafiles, 57
    changing values, 194
        refresh value, 194
    check_soa example program
        C version, 459–469
        Perl version, 472
    checking for delegated subdomain, 221
    email address of zone technical
            contact, 42
    in-addr.arpa zone corresponding to your
            ISP's network, 51
    limiting number of queries on
            nameserver, 265
    MNAME field, listing primary nameserver
            for a zone, 228
    no NS RR for SOA MNAME, 428
    query statistics on BIND 8
            nameserver, 170
    serial numbers, 137
    slave nameserver queries, source address
            for, 271
    subdomain created in parent's zone, 205
sockets, Unix domain, 128, 131
software, nameserver host, 179
sortlist directive (BIND resolvers), 109
sortlist substatement, 254
spcl.DOMAIN file, 143
SPF (Sender Policy Framework), xiii, 97
split namespaces, 315–322
    configuring the bastion host, 317–319
    protecting zone data on bastion host, 319
    security precautions on bastion host
            nameserver, 319
    views, using on bastion host, 321

About the Authors

Cricket Liu graduated from the University of California at Berkeley, that great bastion of free speech, unencumbered Unix, and cheap pizza. He joined Hewlett-Packard after graduation and worked there for nine years.

Cricket began managing the hp.com zone after the Loma Prieta earthquake forcibly transferred the zone's management from HP Labs to HP's Corporate Offices (by cracking a sprinkler main and flooding a Labs computer room). Cricket was host-master@hp.com for over three years and then joined HP's Professional Services Organization to co-found HP's Internet Consulting Program.

He left HP in 1997 to form Acme Byte & Wire, a DNS consulting and training company, with his friend (and now coauthor) Matt Larson. Network Solutions acquired Acme in June 2000 and, later the same day, merged with VeriSign. Cricket worked for a year as Director of DNS Product Management for VeriSign Global Registry Services.

He joined Infoblox, a company that develops DNS and DHCP appliances, in March 2003, and is currently its Vice President of Architecture.

Cricket, his wife Paige, their son Walt, and daughter Greta live in California with their two Siberian Huskies, Annie and Dakota.

Paul Albitz is a software engineer at Hewlett-Packard. He earned a Bachelor of Science degree from the University of Wisconsin, LaCrosse, and a Master of Science degree from Purdue University.

Paul worked on BIND for the HP-UX 7.0 and 8.0 releases. During this time, he developed the tools used to run the hp.com domain. Since then, he has worked on various HP products during his 19-year career: HP JetDirect software, HP OfficeJet fax firmware, the HPPhoto web site, and HP Photosmart Premier software.

Paul and his wife Katherine live in San Diego, California with their two cats, Gracie and Tiffany.

Colophon

The animals on the cover of *DNS and BIND*, Fifth Edition, are grasshoppers. Grasshoppers are found all over the globe. Of over 5,000 species, 100 different grasshopper species are found in North America. Grasshoppers are greenish-brown, and range in length from a half inch to four inches, with wingspans of up to six inches. Their bodies are divided into three sections: the head, thorax, and abdomen, with three pairs of legs and two pairs of wings.

Male grasshoppers use their hind legs and forewings to produce a "chirping" sound. Their hind legs have a ridge of small pegs that are rubbed across a hardened vein in the forewing, causing an audible vibration much like a bow being drawn across a string.

Grasshoppers are major crop pests, particularly when they collect in swarms. A single grasshopper can consume 30 mg of food a day. In collections of 50 or more grasshoppers per square yard—a density often reached during grasshopper outbreaks—grasshoppers consume as much as a cow would per acre. In addition to consuming foliage, grasshoppers damage plants by attacking them at vulnerable points and causing the stems to break off.

The cover image is from the *Dover Pictorial Archive*. The cover font is Adobe ITC Garamond. The text font is Linotype Birka; the heading font is Adobe Myriad Condensed; and the code font is LucasFont's TheSans Mono Condensed.

Better than e-books

Buy *DNS and BIND*, 5th Edition, and access
the digital edition FREE on Safari for 45 days.

Go to www.oreilly.com/go/safarienabled
and type in coupon code CGBF-PCSB-IXEA-BDBK-ZM3G

Search
thousands of
top tech books

Download
whole chapters

Cut and Paste
code examples

Find
answers fast

Search Safari! The premier electronic reference
library for programmers and IT professionals.

Related Titles from O'Reilly

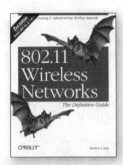

Networking

802.11 Wireless Networks: The Definitive Guide, *2nd Edition*

Asterisk: The Future of Telephony

Cisco Cookbook

Cisco IOS Access Lists

Cisco IOS in a Nutshell, *2nd Edition*

DNS & BIND Cookbook

DNS & BIND, 4th Edition

Essential SNMP, *2nd Edition*

Exchange Server Cookbook

IP Routing

IPv6 Essentials

IPv6 Network Administration

LDAP System Administration

Managing NFS and NIS, *2nd Edition*

Network Troubleshooting Tools

RADIUS

sendmail, *3rd Edition*

sendmail Cookbook

SpamAssassin

Switching to VoIP

TCP/IP Network Administration, *3rd Edition*

Unix Backup and Recovery

Using Samba, *2nd Edition*

Using SANs and NAS

VoIP Hacks

Time Management for System Administrators

Windows Server 2003 Network Administration

Wireless Hacks, *2nd Edition*

Zero Configuration Networking: The Definitive Guide

The O'Reilly Advantage

Stay Current and Save Money